If Mama Ain't Happy, Ain't Nobody Happy!

Lindsey O'Connor

HARVEST HOUSE PUBLISHERS
Eugene, Oregon 97402

Cover by Terry Dugan Design, Minneapolis, Minnesota

IF MAMA AIN'T HAPPY, AIN'T NOBODY HAPPY

Copyright © 1996 by Lindsey O'Connor
Published by Harvest House Publishers
Eugene, Oregon 97402

Library of Congress Cataloging-in-Publication Data

O'Connor, Lindsey, 1961–
  If mama ain't happy, ain't nobody happy / Lindsey O'Connor.
      p.   cm.
  ISBN 1-56507-488-2 (alk. paper)
  1. Mothers—Psychology. 2. Mothers—Religious life. 3. Contentment
  4. Optimism. 5. Family I. Title.

HQ759.03234 1996   96-10715
248.8'431—dc20   CIP

Printed in the United States of America.

For my mom
Judy Earlene Britton
who now truly lives in the fullness of joy

❧ Acknowledgments ❧
My heartfelt thanks to...

My wonderful children: Jacquelyn, Claire, Collin, and Allison. Thank you for loving me even when Mama ain't happy and for making it easy for me to make the choice to rejoice. And my soul-mate Tim: You are my sparkle.

Susan Gragg, my creative consultant, manuscript reader, and research assistant—not to mention my cohort in joyful living! Thanks for always knowing which hat I needed you to wear, for cheering me on at all the right places, and for making your feet like wings, Sahib. I'm looking forward to "winging it" for you over your manuscript!

Lois Ash, the personification of a soul who serves with joy. Thank you for serving me and my loving children. I am blessed to have you as a friend.

Susan Weisiger (child nurturer), Marguarite Mutchler (meals on wheels), Robin Murray, and Lisa Rutledge. Thank you for your help and, most of all, your prayers.

Dad and Barbara, who bonded with the grandkids when I needed to bond with my manuscript. Thanks for the gifts of time and love.

Brenda Koinis and Posy Lough: You two have added to this manuscript and to my life.

Lael Arrington and the Tomball Christian Writers' Group: "As iron sharpens iron," you have sharpened me.

Lisa Guest, for your enthusiasm for this project, prayers, and skillful editing. The Process has been . . . a joy.

And a special thanks to all of you who filled out my survey. Your input was invaluable.

∽⋞ Contents ⋞∽

Part Three
Practicing Joy and Contentment in Our Homes
What We Do

A Bit About
Being Joyful

You've probably seen the T-shirt that proclaims, "I am woman. I am invincible. I am tired!" Is it too much to ask to also be joyful? To maybe find a sparkle here and there in life?

That's what I wondered years ago when, on top of trying to be a good wife and mother, I was juggling my work, church activities, home, and to-do list—and looking for a little bit of joy at the same time. I thought, "What's the point of going through the motions of life—what's the point of the accomplishments or the struggles—if there's no joy along the way? And what does God's Word say about joy anyway?" Besides, if I wanted to teach my children how to be joyful and content, I'd better figure it out myself. And so began my joy journey—a journey I'm still on and the journey I share with you in these pages. But a funny thing happened on the way to the word processor . . . I discovered a bit about "being."

Now, any one of us can learn how to do something, but learning how to be something—ah, that's harder. I had "doing" down pretty well, but "being"? Well, that transformation (and I'm still in process!) has been one aspect of the journey that led to this book. A book about being. About being joyful. About being content. It's about using our heads, hearts, and homes to know and share joy where we are. And, although it's primarily about being, I do offer you a few how-to's to make it practical. (If I just said, "Be joyful" but didn't help show you how, you could just listen to Bobby McFerrin's song "Don't Worry, Be Happy" and be done in three minutes!)

So why the title? Well, apparently lots of women can relate to the idea that "if Mama ain't happy, ain't nobody happy." When people heard the title while I was writing the book, most smiled or laughed or thoughtfully murmured, "Oh, yes"—perhaps picturing themselves as that mama. I asked 50 of these people to fill out a survey about their own journey toward joy, and I will share with you what they told me.

But before I begin telling my story and theirs, let me be quick to say that this book is not about making Mama happy. I am simply using a tongue-in-cheek colloquialism to point to the influence of the woman in the home and the important role she plays in the well-being of her family. I am not suggesting that our happiness is paramount or more important than our family's needs. In her book *Choices*, Mary Farrar has some strong words about that false premise, and I couldn't agree more:

> I am deluded if I think that what my child and husband need most is for me to be "happy." What a can of worms this opens up! What about a man who decides to leave his wife and children for the sake of personal happiness? Men have tried to argue the same point—that everyone will be much better off in the long run. Not so, life tells us. My personal happiness simply cannot be the plumb line for family decisions. Personal responsibility always precedes personal happiness if a family is to survive and thrive.[1]

Mary Farrar is so right. I've seen families torn apart as husband and children drown in the wake of Mama's pursuit of happiness. Besides, being happy isn't necessary for us to experience joy. And every Mama can use a little more joy than what's in her dishwater!

You may be up to your neck in more than dishwater. We women are busy, sometimes stressed, sometimes hurting, often tired. Can we possibly get through today's list and find a little sparkle along the way? Can we learn to be content where we are even when we don't like where we are?

Yes, we can! My Father told me so. In fact, He told me that savoring the sparkle was quite all right—and I always trust my Father. He says, "These things I have spoken to you, that My joy may be in you, and that your joy may be made full" (John 15:11). Our heavenly Father wants us to be joyful!

So if you're overwhelmed, tired, hurting, or maybe just missing the sparkle in your life, get cozy as I take you on a joy journey. And by the way—loosen up a bit and find your smile, maybe even a chuckle or two. This trip should be fun!

❧ 1 ❧

Sparkles in the Rocks—
Life Is Hard;
We Need a Little Sparkle!

Stress can make you stupid. I know. My trip to Canada proved it.

It started even before I left. The stupidity, that is—the stress had been present for a while. The night before I left, I stayed up until 2:30 A.M. trying to find the bottom of my desk. (I was sure all those papers were busy multiplying in the dark while I slept.) There had been so much to do before leaving. Find this...call so and so...pack tickets...get cash. Finally I was ready. I said goodbye to my family and drove to the airport for the brief trip.

Juggling my luggage, I glanced at my watch. *Oh, no! Only 27 minutes! I hope I'm at the right terminal,* I thought. I knew I didn't have time to catch a shuttle to the other terminal, so I bypassed the line and quickly asked the nearest agent if I was at the right place. She curtly asked me if I'd checked the departure monitors. *Whoops! Didn't even think of those! I've practically grown up in an airport. What am I thinking?*

I quickly scanned the screen and was surprised to find that I was indeed at the right terminal and even at the right gate—to no credit of my own. I waited in line and guess which ticket

11

agent I got? Of course the one who'd reminded me about the invention of departure monitors. *Great.* She processed my ticket and said, "May I have your passport, please?" *My WHAT?*

"Umm, I don't have it," I told her.

"You don't have your passport with you?" she asked.

"No," I replied. *And I'm not about to tell her I don't have one at all.*

"How about your birth certificate?" she continued.

"No, I don't have that either," I said, starting to feel quite foolish. *I think my parents still have it.*

"OK. Just give me your voter registration card," she persisted. *I wonder if mine is current.*

Not finding it, I said, "You're not going to believe this, but I don't have that either."

"Well," she said, a bit irritated, "you can enter Canada, but you may have trouble leaving."

"Fine!" I responded. "I just have to get to Canada and I can't miss this flight!" Desperate women are capable of desperate moves.

However, I came to my senses long enough to hear her say something about calling the customs office downstairs. I suddenly considered being stranded, alone, in Canada, in self-imposed exile. "Yes, please call," I said.

She did and then told me to go ahead to my gate. I smiled and said, "Thank you. I'm really not this stupid—really!" She sort of smiled back, probably thinking, *Sure you're not! Would you like some crayons for the flight?*

I walked up to the flight attendant at the gate and asked where the nearest restroom was. "On the plane," she said, "but you only have six minutes and you still need to check in at the desk." *Oh, yeah. How could I have forgotten?*

I checked in with the gate agent. "May I have your documents, please?" she asked. *Same song, second verse.* I explained my dilemma and told her the other agent had approved it. She skeptically pulled my ticket and gave me a boarding pass. Then I went to the jetway to board the plane. The flight attendant there asked, "May I have your boarding pass and travel documents, please?" *Again? Maybe I should wear a sign saying, "YES, I'M TRYING TO GO TO CANADA WITHOUT ANY TRAVEL DOCUMENTS."*

"I don't have any," I replied.

"And they let you through?" he asked in disbelief. "Let's see if they wrote that little love note anywhere on here." At this point, I think even a note from my mother would have helped.

While he looked, I asked him if I could just have my documents faxed to me there.

"Let's see. Do they have faxes in Canada?" he quipped. *OK. I deserved that.* I told him I would have my documents sent to me, and he stamped the magic words, "Documents OK" on my ticket. Then he added, "Be a good girl and be sure to do that, honey."

"Be a good girl"? I was a grown woman. I had a family. I had a business. But I also had to admit that my daughter could have done a better job getting to Canada than I was doing so far. How could I have considered leaving for a foreign country without any travel documents? What was worse, the thought of getting documents hadn't even crossed my mind. I had navigated flights many times before, but this time I had acted like a freshman flier.

I boarded the plane and slumped in my seat with a sigh of relief. *I made it. Now, if I can just regain my brain before we land....*A little later, during the meal service, I managed to get salad dressing in my lap and up my sleeve. How I did that I'll never know. The man next to me was somewhat amused and, no doubt marveling at my grace, offered me napkins. Then, to top it off, I didn't even have a pen in my purse to fill out the customs form before landing. *Maybe I should have asked that first agent for a crayon after all!* I borrowed a pen from the napkin man.

After we landed, Canadian airport personnel said, "May I see your passport, please?" *Oh, no. Here we go again!* I reiterated my situation (quite succinctly by now), and they let me through, muttering, "Where'd you think you were going, lady? Idaho?"

As I walked through the airport toward a taxi with everything intact but my dignity, I noticed that most people had coats with them. *Terrific. I just flew north and didn't even think to bring a coat. That confirms it. I'm an idiot!* Disgusted with being fuzzy-headed, I thought of all the people who had witnessed my "untogetherness." I imagined them all—the ticket agent, the flight attendant at the gate, the second ticket agent, the boarding pass collector, the man next to me on the plane, and the Canadian official—standing together shaking their fingers at me and saying in unison, "Get your act together, woman!"

I was in Canada to be interviewed on TV about my book *Working at Home*. I was supposed to have my act together. At least when the interviewer asked about the pitfalls of combining family life and a home business, I could share from personal experience that sometimes the combination is stressful—and I could warn with first-hand knowledge that stress can cause stupidity. Then I prayed, *Thank You, Lord, that I'm here in spite of myself—and please don't let any of those people see me on TV!*

Walking outside, I realized that for the first time in a long time I was walking slower than everyone else. *This feels pretty good!* As the stress began to loosen its vise-grip on me, I began to relax. Then I saw something that I hadn't noticed since I was a little girl. The sidewalk sparkled!

Immediately I was taken back to when I was about seven years old and I paid attention to things like sidewalks and sparkling pavement and shiny rocks. I remember walking down the sidewalk on a hot summer day (stepping over the cracks of course) and marveling at all the sparkles in that concrete. With the sun shining on it, the sidewalk shimmered. It had little diamonds stuck in it! I was amazed. "How wonderful! Has everyone noticed this incredible thing?" I wondered. The sidewalk was actually a pretty boring shade of gray, but at the right angle and in the right light, it sparkled!

Most of us adults never pay much attention to sidewalks. We just keep our eyes straight ahead and rely on our peripheral vision to help us stay on track. But stepping across that sidewalk and back in time that day made me think about that sparkle. Those glimmering diamonds in the sidewalks of my childhood—and in the sidewalks of my city today—really are diamonds. Actually,

I try to look on the bright side of life and ignore the dull.

~Beulah G.

they're diamond dust. It's added to the concrete of some sidewalks to increase their hardness and durability in high traffic. So as a kid I was right all along. Those really are diamonds glistening in the gray!

That got me thinking during my trip. *That's what's been missing from my life lately—the sparkle! I've been working so hard to balance all my responsibilities and be the kind of woman, wife, and mother that I should that I've slipped into the rut of a life without sparkle. Or maybe, just like the sidewalk, the sparkle is there and I just haven't noticed.*

Then it hit me. *The sparkle in life is the glimmer of joy! That's what I need.* A life of disciplines and duties and dailyness without joy is a life without sparkle. I'd been so busy *doing* for so long that I'd forgotten the value of *being*. And what I desperately wanted was to be...joyful. I wanted a life with a little sparkle.

Sparkles in the Rocks

Perhaps you've seen the bumper sticker/T-shirt slogan: "Life is hard—and then you die." For many people, that has the same effect of fingernails scraping on a chalkboard. While certainly factual, it's a grating statement because it leaves out all the hope and joy and points only to life's hardship and death. It misses all the beauty in the journey. It skips all the flowers and refers only to the rocks. The dull, gray rocks—not even the kind with sparkles.

Sometimes life is as hard as the hardest rock and as colorless as the dull, gray ones. Sometimes there just aren't any flowers growing in the crevices. We find only rocks—the rocks of pain, disappointment, or difficult circumstances; the rocks of busyness, tedium, or stress—littering or even blocking our path. Perhaps right now you find some of these rocks looming between where you are and a point of joy and contentment. Sometimes the rocks of life can form a huge mountain, blocking our path to joy. Or maybe the rocks are just pebbles of irritation that get in the way. We will always find rocks of some type along our journey. But instead of letting them hit us on the head or push us six feet under, we can learn to navigate our way around them and—just as important—to notice the ones with sparkles.

Sometimes rocks sparkle only because they are polished. When I was about eight, my parents gave me a rock tumbler for Christmas. It came with some dull, ugly rocks. I put them in the tumbler and plugged it in, and the slow polishing process began. When the tumbler finally stopped, those ugly rocks had been beautifully transformed into shiny stones. Their streaks of color made them suitable for hanging on chains and wearing around my neck, which I did. In fact, not long ago, my daughter found such a piece of jewelry in my things. "Mom, *what* is this?" she asked as she pulled out my creation.

"Oh, that's a work of art!" I replied. When she looked dumbfounded, I explained, "I used an ugly rock and a rock tumbler to make that necklace."

When I explained how it worked, Jacquelyn was truly amazed. She asked, "Oh, may I have this necklace? I won't lose it! I'll take good care of it so I can pass it down to my children!" (Oh, those lucky future grandchildren of mine!)

What intrigued me about that rock tumbler when I was a child—and what intrigued my child—is the fact that something pretty, colorful, and sparkling can come from something as ugly as a gray or brown rock. None of us would ever hang a plain, dull rock around our neck, but a polished gem—now that's another story. With a little friction and a little time, something hard and lackluster comes to reveal the sparkle that was there all along. And so it is with us.

There are several ways to think of the rocks in the tumbler. Sometimes the rocks are the hurts and trying circumstances that litter our life. When we look at these rocks of pain or unpleasantness, we don't see anything beautiful in them; we don't see any sparkle. But God can smooth things out so that at some point we will be able to see the beauty. He can also polish the rough edges off someone who's causing us pain. Sometimes He simply changes a situation and brings beauty out of ugliness.

Another way to think of the rocks and the tumbler is that sometimes we ourselves need to undergo the polishing process. We must get in the tumbler and allow God to polish us. Time and friction have to do their job on us before the sparkle in us is revealed. This refining work has to be done before the dull rock can shine. And, just as rocks are polished by time and friction, God can use both the passage of time and the friction of difficult circumstances or challenging people in our life to smooth our rough edges. When we submit ourselves to His polishing process, He can produce a beautiful shine in us, a reflection of the joy of the Lord. We can be joyful knowing that, even though the process may not necessarily change the circumstances in our life, God is changing us. As He refines us, we gain His perspective. As we are polished, others see the sparkle of His joy as it is reflected in our life.

What are the rocks in your life? And how's the tumbling process going? Perhaps the tumbling seems to be taking much too long or you're a little tired of the friction. Maybe you feel like nothing beautiful can be made of the ugly rocks in your life. But, friend, with just the right amount of friction and His perfect timing, God can make something beautiful out of even the ugliest rocks. He can polish them so that you can see the sparkle, and He can also polish you and produce His shine in your life.

There's still another way to see sparkles in the rocks. While some rocks sparkle on the outside because they are polished, others sparkle because of what's inside. Have you ever seen a geode? The outside can be very rough, with no shimmer at all no matter what angle or in what light we look at it. We can throw the geode in the tumbler for a spin, and we'll get a pretty, polished rock. If we stop there, we may be pleased with the shine, but we'll miss something much greater—the real beauty within. The inside of a geode is far more beautiful than a polished crust can ever be. Geodes contain gorgeous crystals in beautiful and varied shapes, sizes, and colors. Even in the shadows, these crystals are lovely. When they're held up to the light at just the right angle, they are exquisite. Before this beauty can be revealed, however, the rock must be cracked open. Only with enough pressure to fracture the rock do the sparkles become visible. Without that breaking, we have only a rock—rough or polished—and we miss the real beauty within. The treasure remains hidden.

We are like the geode. Sometimes the sparkle is within us. Just as the treasure of a geode's crystals lies hidden inside the rock, such a treasure can be inside us, too. Even if life is dull or hard and completely without sparkle you can know that the sparkle lies within you if you are a child of the King, having named Jesus as your Savior and Lord. Scripture teaches that the

Holy Spirit lives in those of us who put our faith in Jesus: "the Spirit of Him who raised Jesus from the dead dwells in you" (Romans 8:11a). And one of the ministries of the Holy Spirit in the life of the believer is giving joy: "The kingdom of God is not eating and drinking, but righteousness and peace and *joy in the Holy Spirit*" (Romans 14:17, emphasis added). The Holy Spirit also produces fruit in believers who are the likeness of Christ—and one characteristic is joy (Galatians 5:22). The sparkle of joy can be found within believers because the Holy Spirit dwells there.

Sidewalks, rock tumblers, and breaking open geodes aren't the only way to see sparkles in the rocks. Just imagine the sparkle in the eyes of the early gold prospectors who said, "There's gold in them thar hills!" Gold rushes began and entire towns were established practically overnight because men hoped to find the glimmer of gold and claim it for themselves. Even today, in a privately-owned gold mine in Colorado, tourists can see shiny gold veins embedded in the rock. As you walk down the tunnel, you see how a narrow vein gradually widens until it reaches the mother lode where the vein of visible gold is about as wide as a car. The parking lot even sparkles with flecks of gold dust. But gaining the glitter isn't easy. About three million pounds of ore must be processed to produce a single approximately-30-pound brick of gold. That's a lot of sifting!

Although I'm no geologist or rock hound, I've seen quite a bit of gleam in rocks. I've seen sparkles in sidewalks, admired the shine after a rock has been tumbled, collected a few geodes, and panned for gold dust. Why? Because seeing the sparkle in the rocks is fun and often valuable. So is seeing the sparkle in the rocks of life. And joy is that sparkle in the rocks of life.

Seeing the joy in life is fun because it makes the dull places shine. Joy adds a touch of beauty to life. Seeing the joy is also valuable. It gets us through some rocky places on our journey when happiness can't be found. But the value of joy doesn't lie in the fact that it makes us feel good. It lies in the fact that it enables us to live a life that gives. Joy is the fuel for a life of service. To live life fully and richly—to live in service to God and others—is a wonderful thing. Joy helps us do just that.

Besides being a fruit of the Spirit, joy is also a gift from God. Jesus Himself said, "These things I have spoken to you, that My joy may be in you, and that your joy may be made full" (John 15:11). What a precious gift Jesus wants to give us! At times we simply stumble across joy. Sometimes joy is an attitude we deliberately choose. Often, joy is a gift freely given. That's why this book isn't about searching for joy. (If we do that, we may never find it.) This book is about living a life that yields joy and seeing joy in everyday miracles. It's about external joys like a beautiful sunset and internal joys like a sweet spiritual discovery at just the right time. Throughout this book, I will refer to all of these things, different ways of looking at the joy we have in Jesus and different ways of receiving His touch of joy.

After all, it seems to me that experiencing joy and contentment is a lot like seeing sparkles in pavement and rocks. The sparkles we see in sidewalks are like the external joys scattered across our path. The road may still be hard and gray, but when we look from the right angle (God's perspective) and in the right light (the light of God's love), we can see the sparkle. Sometimes we miss it simply because we're not paying attention. Stopping to take in a beautiful example of God's handiwork in nature, holding hands with someone you love as you walk along together, or looking into the eyes of a child saying, "I love you"—these are sparkles in life. So are good books, intellectual stimulation, heart-to-heart conversations, and ice cream. Joy can be found all around us when we pay attention. In fact, often it's the small things in life that add joy. Look for them and be thankful, for thankfulness is the heart of joy.

But maybe everything around you right now seems colorless and drab. Like the gray sidewalks, dull rocks, and rough geodes, your life may not have a lot of sparkle either. After all, sometimes we're like sidewalks on a cloudy day. People have walked all over us all day long and, since the sun is hidden, no sparkle is visible. On other days, we're like rocks—cold, hard, rough, and dull to the bone. (Sounds like a PMS day!) But every day we really are geodes: the outside can be polished, but the real sparkle is within. So, when all we see and feel is the hardness of life's rocks, we must remember that joy can be found sparkling, precious, and beautiful like gold. But getting to that golden joy isn't always easy.

The Struggle to Know Joy

Have you ever wondered why it's sometimes so hard to be joyful? We all want to be happy. None of us deliberately sets out to be miserable, discontent, or bored. Even when we desperately want to know joy, it can prove frustratingly elusive. Since life is hard and we need a little sparkle, why is finding it sometimes such a struggle? Because . . .

- Life can be so . . . **overwhelming**—as in *"Joy is probably here somewhere if I can just find her under this pile before she smothers. But where do I start?"*

To overwhelm means "to submerge" or "to cover over completely." Do you ever feel submerged in a pile of things to do that require far more time than you have available? No matter how progressive our society seems, most women still meet the majority of the family's needs whether we work for pay or not. We usually do the majority of the housework, meal planning, shopping, cooking, gift buying, card giving, and boo-boo kissing.

Then there are the holidays, another responsibility that falls mostly on our shoulders. And, frankly, those special times probably wouldn't have quite the pizzazz if we left the planning to the men. What man would sit down with the kids to watch a Martha Stewart TV special, and then actually try making wreaths and gingerbread houses? (I do draw the line at gilding and drilling nuts with a dremmel drill [whatever that is] for stringing on garlands. My house looks just fine with the nuts we already have.)

Often the many balls women struggle to keep up in the air simultaneously require us to be both juggler and magician. The act is stressful and exhausting, and all that effort can really get to

> *When I find it difficult to remember my last experience of pure joy, it sets me back.*
>
> ~Carla F.

us. As Barbara M. says, "I feel overwhelmed at times, trying to balance household chores, bills, our children's activities, and my drama and church work, all the while trying to be a supportive wife to my husband."[1]

Single moms and moms working outside the home or at an in-home business know a lot about juggling many balls and a very full plate. Lisa V. describes this struggle quite well:

I Am Overwhelmed!

I have three young children—
   And I'm working full-time.
I have two bathrooms to clean and no time for one—
   And I'm working full-time.
I have eight loads of laundry (not including the pile on
my husband's side of the bedroom) —
   And I'm working full-time.
I'm late for work, the kids won't cooperate, the
lunches aren't made, and I just put a run in my last
pair of pantyhose—
   And I'm working full-time.
All I want to do is go to the movies with my friends
for the first time in a year—but the groceries aren't
bought, dinner's not planned, laundry isn't done, the
house isn't clean, the kids have Girl Scout cookies to
sell, and my husband "just wants to be able to watch
football."

Even when fatigue—whether physical, emotional, or spiritual—and the pressure of balancing our many roles make life overwhelming, we can choose to find joy in the Lord.

- Life can be so . . . **daily**—as in *"What's so joyful about the 367th load of laundry?"*

We plan, buy, prepare, and serve a meal—only to find that the people we fed have the nerve to get hungry again within four hours or so! We finally get the last of the laundry gathered, sorted, washed, dried, folded, and put away—and then discover three days' worth of our son's dirty laundry stuffed in the toy box and moldy socks next to the wet towel under the bed. And, of course, more dirty clothes will be in the hamper again tonight. We get the whole house de-cluttered, organized, dusted, mopped, and swept—and in one short weekend the whole thing looks completely undone.

Iva H. expresses the feelings that go along with this cycle: "I believe the thing that keeps me from being joyful is getting bogged down with everyday things. I know if I could be a little more organized, I'd be happier." Robin M. struggles with "the fact that I would like to spend most of my time creating (writing, decorating, teaching my children arts and crafts), but I feel obli-gated to spend it maintaining my homelife (cleaning, cooking, disciplining the kids)." Betty M. adds, "The dailyness gets to me when I am physically exhausted and overwhelmed with house-hold chores." Haven't we all been there?

Life happens daily. Monotony and tedium can be huge rocks in our path—but I maintain that we can see the sparkle even in those rocks if we look from the right angle.

> • Life can be so . . . **busy**—as in *"A joyful life? I can't think about that today. I'm too busy. I'll think about finding joy tomorrow. Gotta run."*

America does busy quite well. Perhaps you've asked friends over to dinner only to hear, "Oh, we'd love to get together, but we're so busy right now." Or maybe someone has invited you somewhere and that's been your reply. And why is it that our immediate response to "How've you been?" seems to be "Re-ally busy"? We have our Daytimers, our schedules, our commit-ments. We coordinate car pools, sports, church events. We rarely sit down to take a deep breath. Is this how God intended us to live?

Microwaves, minivans, modems, and miscellaneous ma-chines are supposed to make life easier. They do—and I'm not ready to give them up—but these timesavers also make our lives busier. We don't use these tools to do our work more quickly and gain more leisure time. Instead, too often, we fill the time saved with yet another item on our to-do list.

Do you find yourself busy but barren? Are you filling your days with countless activities but finding yourself not really fulfilled by those things? Barren busyness can stifle joy and contentment, but having the Lord's perspective on what we do can bring real joy. Keep reading!

- Life can be so . . . **disappointing**—as in *"I never thought life would be like this."*

Are you looking back at unfulfilled dreams or unmet expectations, wishing things had turned out differently? Are your current circumstances discouraging? Have people let you down? One woman writes, "I thought my life would turn out like I pictured when I was young. I had such high hopes. I just never counted on my husband having an affair and my son turning out like he did. I still love them, but the disappointment is huge."

What disappointments are keeping you from joy?

One of my favorite lines from the movie *Steel Magnolias* comes when Julia Roberts tells her mother (Sally Field) that she doesn't want to go through life always playing it safe and missing out on really great moments, like having children. She says, "I'd rather have 30 minutes of wonderful, than a lifetime of nothin' special." She doesn't want to get to the end of the road and, looking back, see only the gray disappointment of "nothin' special." I don't want a lifetime of nothin' special either, and neither do you. The good news is that we are not destined to "nothin' special." Despite the inevitable disappointments, we can live life joyously!

- Life can be so . . . **painful**—as in, *"How can I be joyful when all I feel is pain?"*

Different people can tolerate different levels of pain. Some of us can handle a great amount of pain and still function, but others of us are more sensitive and react at a much lower pain threshold. Whenever we reach our threshold, however, our main focus is usually the relief of that pain. When it's unrelenting or unmanageable, when we can't make it stop or get it under control, joy can become a mere memory.

Former flight attendant Janetlee H. knows about pain, both physical and otherwise. Since 1985, when she was hurt in an accident, she has been in chronic pain. I asked her if her pain makes finding joy and contentment a struggle. Her reply was:

It totally does. My pain brings migraines, and sometimes my thought processes aren't as clear as I'd like. I feel like my pain robs me. Pain is the enemy trying to take over and keep me from a joyful life, and it's just as subtle as Satan, creeping up on me without me realizing it until suddenly I'm not in control anymore. Sometimes I get weak, shaky, and extremely stressed because of pain that gets out of control. Sometimes the little things snowball and I just explode. Then I have to go back to the people in my life and apologize for reacting like that instead of simply responding.

Maybe you, too, know the rocky path of physical pain, or maybe you know the rough road of emotional pain.

Pam R. knew about emotional pain. It seemed to dominate her life. You see, she lost a child. Her precious two-year-old daughter was killed in an accident. Ever since then, Pam has struggled with the pain caused by a gaping hole in her heart, a hole created when her child was taken from her. Whenever she saw a child of the same age happily playing or holding a parent's hand, she felt as if her heart would break. Pam still thinks of her child every day, and every day her heart aches. For a long time, Pam thought she would never know happiness again, but over time it's returning. More importantly, she has learned that even in the most painful moments of her heartbreak—when the joy of life is missing—the joy of the Lord is still present.

Whether your pain is a hurt in your body or an ache in your heart, you know how it can mask much that is good and happy and joyful in life. But let me hold out to you the hope that God's joy can penetrate that pain.

The Storms of Life

Life is indeed hard, and sometimes seeing the sparkle in the rocks is difficult because we're engulfed in a storm, and when that happens joy can seem to be in the clutches of the undertow or dashed on the rocks. And, like you, perhaps I know such storms. I don't write to you from the mountaintop shouting down, "Be joyful, O ye women!" I'm not sitting above the hubbub of life, having never been touched by high waters or rough winds. No. I write to you as a fellow sojourner whose lived in the valley and on the mountaintop and along the somewhat rocky path between the two. Like you, I know from experience the overwhelming, busy, disappointing, and painful days of life—especially the painful ones . . .

Six years ago, when the seeds for this book were first sown, I began to study what God's Word said about joy. I started thinking about, praying over, and writing down what God was teaching me about being a joyful woman, about being a mama who was happy. Not too long after that, the storms began, and I desperately wanted to keep from losing all my joy in the gale. That turbulence tested everything I had learned about joy, and it tested my faith as well.

The first storm broke when my husband's company downsized and Tim was laid off. Needless to say, finances got tight. When he found another job, he began traveling Monday through Friday. We were only together as a family on the weekends. Then one Wednesday afternoon I got a call from my dad and the second storm was unleashed. I knew my mother had been feeling bad for some time and had gone in for some testing, but I wasn't at all aware there was anything seriously wrong. Dad called from her hospital room, and I'll never forget his words: "Honey . . . well . . . we've got a little problem with your mother."

My insides began to quiver. "What kind of problem?" I was afraid to hear his answer.

"We've got a little cancer."

A little cancer! Is that like a little pregnant or a little dead? A little cancer? Oh, Lord, please! Not my mom!

As my father described the recent events and explained the diagnosis, I struggled to keep my composure. The word "lymphoma" hung in the air, a dark cloud that had just descended over our lives. Little did I know how familiar I would become with that word. Dad, Mom, and I were quite strong until he asked, "Do you want to talk to your mom?"

"Yes, please."

As soon as I heard her familiar, "Hi, honey," the shock of the news gave way to grief. Neither of us could say anything for some time. I had been all right until I heard her voice, and she had been strong until she heard mine. Mom and I were very close. She was my cheerleader, my advisor, and my best friend in a different way than Tim is. Mom met needs in my life that only a mother can. The news that she had cancer was devastating.

While I was on the phone, my good friend Jill dropped by. Seeing that something was dreadfully wrong, she took care of my children while I talked. After I hung up, I had in Jill the shoulder, the hug, the helping hand, and the prayer warrior I desperately needed. How sweet of the Lord to send my unexpected visitor. With Tim gone, I needed Jill's support. I had just had my first taste of grief.

Within days, we made the decision to put our things in storage and move to Houston where Tim was working and my parents were living. (We were homeschooling at the time, so the quick move was possible.) Tim was still employed out of his Dallas office, so we weren't moving to Houston permanently. We were just going to live with him in his corporate apartment for about six weeks until we knew where his job would take him— or so we thought.

The next few years brought pain into my life like I'd never before experienced. I came to understand the meaning of what some people call the tear in life's membrane—the point where the protective envelope around you breaks and life's hardness comes crashing into your world. It had come into mine. I was dealing with two separate struggles simultaneously: my mom's health and my immediate family's uprootedness. I felt so misplaced.

The corporate apartment was just down the street from my parents' home. Although the apartment was very convenient, it was very small—and some of the walls were painted red. I would come home from consultations, scans, tests, and hospital visits with my mom to a very tiny and dark apartment with red walls. They weren't a beautiful, bold cranberry color. They were fire-engine red walls that represented to me the harsh, jarring intrusions in my life.

After one month there, we moved to another small but brighter corporate apartment nearby. We kept thinking that we would be permanently moved to Houston or relocated back to Dallas at any time. Then we'd get our things out of storage in Dallas; I had only packed for six weeks, but we stayed away for well over six months.

That period of time was a roller coaster of emotions for me. Not only was I struggling to cope with the harsh reality of my mother's cancer, but I was also struggling with our less-than-ideal and very uncertain living situation. And, to top it off, I was pregnant with our fourth child—a blessed event, but it was wreaking havoc with my hormones. I call those days our Nomadic Period. Boy, could I relate to those Israelites!

Every Friday, Tim came home with some tidbit of news, but the situation changed almost weekly. For seven months we lived from day to day, not knowing where home would be. I'd like to say I trusted in the Lord and never worried, but I can't. Oh, there were days when I rested in Him, but there were also days when, taking Scripture literally, I entered my "prayer closet." (The only way I could get away from everyone was to go into my bedroom closet. I'd shut the door, turn off the light, pray . . . and cry.)

My maternal nesting instinct had also kicked in by now. There I was, in an apartment with none of our things and nothing we needed for the baby. So we made an overnight trip to Dallas to get the crib and the rocking chair out of storage. As we started getting ready to check out of the motel and head back to Houston, I realized that our daughter Claire, five years old at the time, was having a hard time figuring out where home was, too. When we began packing our suitcases, baby things in tow, Claire said in a forlorn little voice, "We're moving again? I thought we were going to live here!"

I started to laugh, but suddenly I felt like crying! My child thought we were changing our address to the Motel 6! She had no idea where home was. Of course, the children didn't understand. *I* was struggling to understand. Much that was stable in our lives—our home, our church, our friends, and the health of loved ones—had been stripped away. I didn't know if my mother was going to live or die or where home was going to be. For most of my fourth pregnancy I didn't even know in which city the baby would be born. Our insurance company kept me guessing about whether I'd go into labor and have to make the four-hour drive to Dallas, hoping Baby Number Four didn't debut in the parking lot of the Corsicana Dairy Queen along the way! (She didn't—much to the relief of the Dairy Queen manager and me!)

But our tiny apartment got even smaller when we brought our fourth child home. "Cozy" took on new meaning as the six of us shared two tiny bedrooms. Knowing others have much worse living conditions did nothing for my post-partum days of "displacement." With Tim working a lot of overtime, I had many hours alone (as alone as one can be with four children) during which I pondered all the uncertainties of my life while the noise of the neighbors' quarrels and bathroom habits wafted through our thin walls. (I got to know those people quite well, although they never knew it.)

That period of my life would have been hard even without the pain of my mother's battle against cancer. My lifeline during that time was the quiet moments I had with the Lord before the children awoke. I would read my Bible and pour out my heart to God: "Lord, how can you possibly have me writing about joy? I'm not joyful! In fact, I'm miserable. I hate my circumstances, and I'm certainly not content. I want my mom whole, I want my husband to be here with us, I want to know where home is. I want my old life back!"

I kept waiting for God to say, "OK, Lindsey. Here's your old life—or at least part of it—back" or, "This is hard, but here's My joy on a silver platter." He didn't. Instead, everything I ever knew, or thought, or thought I knew about joy was put to the test. Before this, I knew about joy on the mountaintop, joy in the mundane, and joy in unpleasant circumstances. This experience, however, taught me about joy in the valley—and this valley was littered with more rocks than I'd ever had to face at one time. Although I didn't know it then, bigger and heavier rocks lay ahead. But during my struggle in that valley, God began to show me the sparkles.

Finding Joy in the Journey

Perhaps you're facing struggles that make my story seem like a walk in the park. I know many of you are. However, as a friend of mine who has lived through more tragedies than any woman should have to endure, once told me, "It's not always the traumas in life that are difficult to get through. God's grace is very encompassing. Sometimes the everyday stuff is a challenge." Even the everyday struggles and less-than-traumatic events can rob us of our joy when we try to operate in our own strength and when we forget to look for the sparkles in the midst of trouble. Instead of trying to climb over the rocks or haul them off ourselves, let's learn to navigate among them, guided by the One who can move the whole mountain. It's only in Him that we find joy that lasts—joy that weathers life's storms and shines like the sparkle in the rocks.

As you've probably sensed, this isn't a five-steps-to-joy book. Instead, it presents a lifestyle and perspective in which joy is the result, not the goal. It's a look at life where joy—the attitude, gift, and fruit—is possible, both internally and externally. We can make choices that cultivate joy in our heads, hearts, and homes.

It is my prayer that as you read these pages you will discover new truths about the joyful, abundant life God offers us and, in turn, learn to cultivate contentment and find joy in your journey, whether the path takes you up to the mountaintop, down through the valley, or somewhere between the two. In the triumphs, tragedies, and dailyness of our lives, each of us can find a sparkle in the rocks. It might be shining right in front of us in simple external joys like the glitter in the sidewalk. The sparkle might be the reflection of the joy of the Lord in our lives when we allow Him to polish us like a rock in a tumbler to produce that shine. And, as Christians, the sparkle—the Holy Spirit's capacity for the fruit of joy in our lives whether we feel it or not—is always within.

So where are you in your journey? Are you enjoying the sparkles along your path? Or are you staring at immovable rocks in a valley? Are you longing for a deeper joy and greater understanding and experience of the God-given sparkle that lies within? Are you struggling with

The fruit of the Spirit is love, joy, peace, patience, goodness, faithfulness, gentleness, self-control.

~Galatians 5:22,23

some of the things that keep us from seeing the sparkle in life? Are you overwhelmed? Stuck in the dailyness of life? Or are you so busy that you're missing the joy in the moment? Are past disappointments keeping you from experiencing joy today? Or are you simply looking for relief from your pain?

Life is hard. There's no denying that, but there's a way, my friend, to find joy in the journey. You can experience joy in the moment, regardless of the circumstances of your life. You can know a deep and abiding sense of fulfillment and purpose, whatever the unsettledness, struggle, or discouragement you are dealing with. Making the choice to rejoice, connecting with the Giver of joy, and being attentive to the sparkles in the moment are worth every ounce of effort involved. When we cultivate a lifestyle conducive to joy, this attitude and fruit is ours! And sometimes our heavenly Father surprises us with a sparkle in the rocks when we least expect it—a glimmering, shimmering gift—simply because we are His children.

❦ 2 ❧

If Mama Ain't Happy,
Ain't Nobody Happy
So Maybe I'd Better Smile

I t had not been a good day. I woke up late, spilled coffee grounds on the clean floor, and burned the toast all within minutes of my reluctant entry into the morning. I had a headache and felt like everything needed to be done at once. My toddler had an accident just as we were walking out the door (naturally), and Pearl, our new kitty, had an accident on my white comforter. To make my already partly cloudy day worse, I began to detect a storm of PMS hovering on the horizon. If only I could find that number and call in sick as a mom!

That afternoon I raced home from the grocery store (shopping is such fun with four children) and pulled into the driveway to find that the overnight company I was expecting later that evening had just arrived! And there I was with dinner in grocery bags! So I did what any savvy, together woman does. I pretended I'd planned it this way and, through clenched teeth, feverishly directed the children when the guests weren't looking. "Pssst! Jacquelyn, quick! Could you make the salad? . . . Claire, run upstairs to see if anybody pottied on the bed in the guest room . . . Collin, quit thumping Allison . . . Allison, quit eating the butter!"

No, it had not been a good day. Later that evening my third-grade daughter, Claire, slumped down on her chair to write about her day in her journal. "Mom," she said, "how do you spell 'horrible'?"

If Mama ain't happy, ain't nobody happy! Male or female, most people agree with that statement. Women usually smile a knowing grin, saying, "Oh, have I been there!" Men usually chuckle and add a bit too loudly, "Boy, isn't that the truth!" When people hear this statement, they think of themselves, their mate, their mother, or someone they know. It's widely recognized that Mama's happiness is important to the happiness of the rest of the family.

Have you ever heard the expression, "If Daddy ain't happy, ain't nobody happy"? I used to say, "Never!" until I read Colleen A.'s comment: "The phrase that would more accurately describe our family experience would be, 'If Daddy ain't happy with his job, ain't nobody happy.' I've been surprised to discover how much I am a reflector of my husband's happiness. I've found that I can be happy anywhere and in most situations if my husband is content and happy, especially in his career." Hear! Hear! Daddy happy on the job and Mama happy in general—we may be on to something!

Although the father profoundly influences the family, Mama gets the credit (or, in this case, the rap). Besides, when Daddy loses his...uh...happiness, Mama is often there to smooth things over. Made by God to be relationally oriented, we women tend to be the peacemakers and nurturers in the family. Here's a case in point.

One morning, after I'd worked on this manuscript long into the night, our entire family woke up late. I hadn't gotten

___

*I*f Mama ain't happy, ain't nobody happy.

It is better to live in a corner of the roof, than in a house shared with a contentious woman.

~Proverbs 25:24

___

enough sleep—and apparently neither had anyone else. It was a look-at-me-wrong-and-I-might-box-your-ears kind of morning. I commented (politely, I thought) that Tim needed to hang his bath towel (the size of Rhode Island) on the towel bar or shower door to dry. (After all, I knew *he* wasn't going to be the one scrubbing mildew off the bathroom door!) Well, his three hours of sleep sharply responded to my five hours of sleep, and my claws came out. Then, hearing myself, I thought, *Oh my! Who is this person—and why is she screaming at my husband like this?*

Tim went back to shaving and commented to his shaving buddy, three-year-old Allison, "Boy, if Mama ain't happy, ain't nobody happy, Alli. Somebody ought to write a book about that!"

I put on my shoes while the darts of conviction fully lodged in my heart. I thought, *I am pond scum. And he has the wherewithal to humor this old amoeba, swimming in sometimes murky waters!*

Our Circle of Influence

You and I influence—for better or worse—the people we are close to whether or not we intend to. When we recognize the incredible influence we have and direct it in a healthy, nonmanipulative, encouraging way, we can change a person's life. And that person may be someone we love.

• *We influence our husbands.*

Encouraging words and loving support can enable a man to go farther than he could go alone. Likewise, a critical, judgmental spirit can tear a man down. The truism "behind every great man is a great woman" is often just that—true! We can help our mate become the person God intends him to be by being a wife who builds up, comforts, loves unconditionally, and cherishes her husband. We are in a unique position to encourage our mate in ways that no one else can or would. Our respect and support can have a profound and positive impact on his self-image and, in turn, on who he is, what he does, and what he accomplishes. The book *Building Your Mate's Self-Esteem* points out how vital we are in this process: "Your mate's self-esteem will either hinder or enhance his ability to learn, make decisions, take risks and resolve conflicts with you and others. It will either restrain him or refuel him."[1] Our mate needs us.

• *We influence our children.*

Nineteenth-century English writer John Ruskin was well aware of this. He said, "My mother's influence in molding my character was conspicuous. She forced me to learn daily long chapters of the Bible by heart. To that discipline and patient, accurate resolve, I owe not only much of my general power of taking pains, but the best part of my taste for literature." Some have called Ruskin the most influential English writer of the 1800s. His art, literature, and writing on social issues helped form the tastes of Victorian England and influenced many people. That mother influenced a son who then influenced a nation.

The children you and I have a chance to influence come into this world moldable, malleable, and ready to be gently shaped into the kind of person God created them to be—and we are the dominant force in that molding. What an amazing privilege! And, as moms know, the wonderful bond between mother and child begins at (and even before) the moment of birth. Some psychologists call this early interaction "the dance." Dr. Brenda Hunter describes it: "Through her voice pitch, tempo, [and] facial expressions, a mother communicates her emotional state to her baby, and he dances synchronously in response to the messages he receives."[2] Other child development experts have called the mother/baby attachment the foundation stone of personality with the mother being the touchstone in a child's life.

Children need their mother's love as much as they need food. They learn they are loved and develop their self-concept from attachments to their parents, significantly their mother. "Simply put," says Dr. Hunter, "if a child's parents are consistently loving and sensitive to his needs, the child incorporates the message: 'I am loved, I am worthy, others will love me just as my parents love me.' If, on the other hand, the child's parents are rejecting, emotionally inaccessible, or absent, then a child may come to feel: 'I am unloved. Therefore, I am unworthy. How can I expect others to love me if my parents don't?'"[3]

Tell a child that he is special and watch him blossom. Treat a child as if she is special and watch her flourish. We influence children by the things we tell them, by the lessons we teach them, and, most powerfully, by how we live. Children learn what is modeled before them (more on that later). We profoundly influence the children God has entrusted to us. What an awesome responsibility and tremendous privilege.

• *We influence people in our circle.*

Whether we are married or single, mothers or not, we influence our extended family, our friends, our neighbors, and our coworkers. We can be the light that draws a family member back into the fold or a friend back to faith in God. We can be the person who makes a difference in the life of a neighbor. We can be salt and light to coworkers. We can show "random acts of kindness" in a world where kindness is much too rare.

In *Disciplines of the Home,* Anne Ortlund describes the influence we women can have on others as she gives three cheers for Mother:

> Over the centuries she's worked as hard as father, and for very different reasons.
> He has built the houses; she's added the colors, the smells, the music.
> He has shaped constitutions to make citizens protected; she has sewn flags to make them weep and cheer.
> He has mustered armies and police forces to put down oppression; she has prayed for them and patted them on the back and sent them off with their heads up.
> He has shaped decisions; she has added morale.[4]

The fact is that we women greatly influence our mate, our children, and the people whose paths we cross each day, and we do so through our personality, worldview, degree of optimism (or pessimism), character, and faith. Created by God distinct and very different from men, we women view life and people through a very different filter than men do. We often approach life focused more on relationships. We tend to be more intuitive and emotional. We exercise our influence on others differently than men do. It's no surprise that Mama's happiness (or lack thereof) affects the people in her circle of influence; it does so because we women function as thermostat, chief operating officer, and heart of the home.

Living Thermostats

Think about what a thermostat does. It regulates the temperature, controls the atmosphere, and can be adjusted to meet the need of the moment. If things need warming up, we raise the setting of the thermostat. If they need cooling off, we adjust the thermostat and lower the temperature.

Now the *World Book Encyclopedia* has a great description of a thermostat, which I will share with you (embellishments, no extra charge).

> A thermostat [us] is a device that helps control the temperature of an indoor area or an appliance [like a home or a husband]. A thermostat is set to keep an area or an appliance [the home/or husband] at a certain temperature [cool on the outside and hot on the inside—the husband that is]. It measures temperature changes [like when your husband wrecks his car] and automatically controls the heating or cooling [we instinctively and immediately soften our voices and cook his favorite dinner].[5]

Then *World Book* gets into some boring stuff about coils, uncoils, and bimetallic strips. The really interesting part (although that last bit would certainly interest *my* husband) is this: "Most thermostats turn heating or cooling equipment completely on [with the kids at Grandma's, we greet hubby at the door wearing !!!] or completely off [we suggest he might be more comfortable under Rover's roof tonight]."[6]

Some thermostats, however, use a method called proportional control. These "measure the difference between the actual temperature and the desired temperature and then adjust the amount of heating or cooling according to this temperature difference. Proportional control thermostats [our goal] can provide an extremely even temperature [and more consistent comfort]."[7]

Clearly, you and I are the thermostats in the home. By our very presence, we regulate the temperature of our family and therefore control the atmosphere in our homes. Properly set, we can—by our attitude and actions—meet the specific need of a given moment. (Have you ever noticed, for instance, that if you raise your voice, your children raise theirs? If we talk softly, our children talk softly. Whisper to a toddler and that little person will often whisper back.) Furthermore, we are able to read family members to determine the proper setting. When things get too heated, we can lower our setting and cool things off. If things are a bit too cool, we can take action to warm the place up. Our very presence can be the thermostat that keeps the family from sweltering in the jungle of life or freezing in the coldness of an uncaring world.

Chief Operating Officers

While fathers may be the chief executive officers in the home, mothers are the chief operating officers. (I wonder if COOs are paid the same as CEOs? Of course, any pay at all for COOs would be a step up!) We are the managers who usually run this enterprise known as "family." Often single-handedly, we oversee the day-to-day operations of the family unit—although I don't know a woman alive who wouldn't like an extra hand or two (either to grab an extra dishtowel or applaud her amazing juggling act—probably the former the most!). We are chef, chauffeur, chief bottle

We need to take [family management] as seriously as career success, because home is where success really matters.... Whether we're changing a diaper or closing a deal, our work has dignity, honor, and value.

~Kathy Peel,
The Family Manager

washer, social director, and, often, maid. We plan, prepare, and perform everything from cleaning clothes to remembering to buy food and toilet paper so that daily life is doable.

As chief operating officers of the family, we also know who is supposed to go where, at what time, with what, and with whom. We often schedule the family activities, and, as the members grow (in number and age), managing that schedule can feel like we're directing fast-moving freeway traffic with mere hand signals. We try not to schedule Aunt Rose's visit when the house has just been fumigated or little brother's birthday party when older sister has the debate team over. Simple stuff like that. Someday when we're old ladies, I just know our kids will come back and thank us for that. Until then, we can take pride in knowing that being the family's chief operating officer is a just, noble, and very important endeavor, if not a little arduous and sometimes downright exhausting.

Heart of the Home

Often nobody's happy if Mama ain't happy because we are the heart of the home. Dad may be the backbone, but we are the heart, the feeling center. Mother tends to be the one person in the family who is in touch with every other member of the family. We usually know where each family member is emotionally, physically, and, hopefully, geographically—although that's not always the case. Once when I was quite busy with my many COO duties, I took a minute to visit with a friend who stopped by. When she left, I went back to what I had been doing, thankful that the children were all playing so quietly. About ten minutes later the phone rang.

"Lindsey? This is Susan. Are you missing anybody?" she asked.

I thought for a second. Then, thankfully, before I could answer, she added, "Are you missing Collin?"

"Do you know where he is?" I asked, too embarrassed to admit that I didn't. (Oh, I would have missed him...eventually.)

"Yes. I got all the way home and when I pulled into the driveway, Collin jumped up from behind the backseat with his hands high in the air and yelled, 'Ta-da! I'm here, Mrs. Weisiger!' He nearly scared me to death! Since he was so proud of himself, I just told him it was very nice of him to pay me a visit and next time we might even let Mom know. I'll have Dirk bring him home."

Yes, it does pay to know where everyone is—geographically and otherwise. I feel somewhat comforted knowing that I am not the only parent to ever temporarily misplace a child. Another mother once called me after a birthday party to make sure her daughter had been picked up by her husband. She said, "I'm just checking. I told him her schedule, but he gets confused. Once when I had to be gone, I told him where and when to pick her up, but he forgot and had no idea where she was. If I hadn't come home, she could have stayed there for days!"

. Besides keeping track of where everyone is geographically (usually), we also keep up with the condition of their lives. We intuitively know when our child is upset or when our husband has had a bad day. We can read a face, a voice, even a walk because we are students of those we love. God gave us mothers a heart for our family members that is very different from the loving and caring heart He gave fathers.

Now, like most generalities, this statement doesn't hold true across the board. In some families, the husband is the nurturer, and in other families both the man and woman are equally nurturing. And, sadly, we've also heard tragic stories of child abuse or even murder by the hand of a mother, but most mothers cannot even fathom such acts. Most mothers intuitively put the needs of their children first and love their children so completely they would give their lives to save them. That's one reason why we're the heart of the home.

And, in this role, we women meet most of the emotional needs of the family. We don't just see that Janie has her homework and her lunch in her backpack, clean clothes for tomorrow, and cookies for the class party. We are also there to scrape her up off the floor after school because of another child's cruel and hurtful words. We provide that important hug and listening ear.

God has designed us to be able to keep up with where each of our family members is emotionally, academically, physically, and spiritually. The knowledge is intuitive. I can tell, for instance, when my husband needs my full attention at the end of the day and when he needs to unwind by himself. I know when Jacquelyn needs a little extra love after a hard day, when Claire needs extra snuggles more than extra sleep, when Collin needs time to talk and pray just with Mom, and when Allison is ready to learn a new Bible story and song.

Instinctively we women put our arms around a crying child, whether it be our daughter whose friends ignored her at school or the little lost boy at the department store who needs us to help him find his mom. We know which child needs an extra hug and who needs a little space. We can tell the difference between a baby's cry of boredom and his cry of pain. We usually know where our children are spiritually, delighting in their every move closer to our heavenly Father. We can also spot when a child is really praying in church and when she's sleeping! We can keep up with all these people at the same time and on many different levels because God gave women hearts and minds that reflect our amazing ability to do, think about, and keep track of many things all at once. Another reason we women can keep track of the condition of everyone's heart as well as their spiritual walk and geographical location is that our hearts are linked to theirs just as strongly as their body was linked to ours in the womb. We are the heart of the home because God designed us that way. He gave us a soft spot in our souls that yearns for the closeness and well-being of our family.

As the thermostat, the chief operating officer, and the heart of the home, we women influence the people in our family by adding warmth, managing the home and schedules, and nurturing each individual. Since we function in these vital roles, it's no surprise that our joy and contentment—or their absence— directly impact our family and, often, our friends, neighbors, co-workers, and acquaintances. Within our circle of influence, each of us has a tremendous opportunity to touch people with the love and joy of the Lord. What a privilege to impact another person's life through our friendship! How precious to be able to teach a child about Jesus and make a difference for eternity! And what joy to be the soulmate our spouse needs!

But Who's Happy—and Why?

Since Mama's happiness affects the people around her, let's consider for a moment who is happy and what makes them so. Are members of the opposite sex, younger or older folks, or people of a different nationality happier than you are? Psychology has long studied the darker side of humanity, but researchers in what's sometimes called "the science of well-being" are providing new information about the subjective mindset of happy people. In an attempt to determine who is happy and why, these "happyologists" have randomly surveyed people and asked them to report their level of happiness or unhappiness and how satisfied they are with life.

What did these researchers discover? In his book *The Pursuit of Happiness,* David Meyers reports that no particular age, race, gender, or nationality inherently enjoys more happiness in life. This finding dispels many common assumptions. So who is happy—and why? According to some studies, happy people tend to have several characteristics in common. Meyers says the most important traits of happy people are: optimism, extroversion, self-esteem, and personal control.

They also tend to have good health and a supportive network of family and friends; and enjoy productive work and an active faith.

This secular look at faith and its connection to happiness intrigued me. The study defined "active faith" as one which meets people's deep needs—our needs for a greater joy, for strength during a crisis, for a support system, for an eternal perspective of life and death, and as something for which to live and die. Science is verifying what many of us have known for a long time!

As you look at the study's findings, however, you may be saying, "I want to be happy and I want my family to be happy, but that list of characteristics doesn't exactly describe me." Many of us are naturally introverted, some of us struggle with self-esteem, and others tend to be rather pessimistic. If we're not outgoing, confident, or optimistic, are we destined to less happiness? Statistically speaking, it seems so. The science of well-being suggests we're not in the running for high levels of happiness without those traits, but studies also indicate that those traits are hardly genetically encoded. The researchers used random surveys and merely noted these common threads in people's answers. These traits are quite logical contributors to happiness, and they serve as a wonderful springboard for identifying areas we might work on if we aren't as happy as we wish.

The real question for us, however, is, "Can I have joy with-out these traits?" Yes, yes, yes! And you can because the joy God gives is far different than the happiness the world offers. You and I may have less happiness in life than someone with all these "happiness qualities," but the only way we are sentenced to less joy is if we are missing the last characteristic listed above—an active faith in God.

Happiness vs Joy

Many people use the words "happiness" and "joy" inter-changeably, but I don't. The two words mean far different things. Oh, if Mama isn't happy, everyone can feel the effects, but this book talks about joy which is something far deeper than happiness. Although happiness is wonderful and greatly enhances family life, being a woman of joy is far more important. And each of us can be a woman who chooses to be joyful, who radiates the joy of the Lord, who experiences joy in this journey, and who lives out and gives out joy to our families.

Perhaps contrary to popular opinion, happiness is not a pre-requisite for joy. The two are quite different in nature: happi-ness is external, joy is internal. Happiness is based on circum-stances; joy isn't. Happiness is defined as a "state of well-being and contentment or pleasurable satisfaction." Joy is defined as "a feeling of great pleasure or hap-piness that comes from success, good fortune, or a sense of well-being; something that gives great pleasure or happiness." Clearly, joy looks like the better pursuit, but the meanings are still

> *I* doubt whether anyone who has tasted [joy] would ever, if both were in his power, exchange it for all the pleasures in the world. But then joy is never in our power and plea-sure often is.
>
> ~C. S. Lewis, *Surprised By Joy*

quite similar. Webster is saying, essentially, that happiness is well-being and joy is just a little bit more well-being.

But that's not exactly what the epistle-writer James had in mind when he wrote, "Consider it all joy, my brethren, when you encounter various trials" (James 1:2). Consider trials "great well-being"? I don't think so. James is referring to the kind of joy Jesus spoke of when He told us that His joy would be in us and it would be full (John 15:11). In these words of promise, Jesus is surely not describing something as ordinary as mere or even great pleasure (flowers give me great pleasure) or telling us that His well-being would be in us (eating my vegetables gives me a sense of well-being). I want something better than pleasure and well-being, something better than flowers and vegetables. I want the joy Jesus offers!

Joy is a special gift from the Creator—a fruit of the Spirit, an attitude of the heart, an element of the very nature of God—and that joy is available to us. Happiness is the result of things; joy can be in spite of things. Happiness responds to circumstances; joy is possible even when the circumstances are difficult. Barbara B. put it simply for her children when they were young: "Happiness is based on happenings and joy is based on Jesus." This difference between happiness and joy is the reason James can write, "Consider it all joy, my brethren, when you encounter various trials, knowing that the testing of your faith produces endurance. And let endurance have its perfect result, that you may be perfect and complete, lacking in nothing" (James 1:2-4). Encountering trials in my life certainly doesn't give me pleasure or a sense of well-being, but knowing what God can do as a result of that work in me—the work that James is talking about—enables me to "consider it all joy." So don't think you need to wait for happiness before you can know joy. It's not a prerequisite!

Our Female Makeup

When I glance in the mirror in the morning, I am so glad to know that my makeup is in my drawer waiting to help me put my best face forward. But that's not the kind of makeup I'm talking about here. Instead, I'm referring to that inner makeup we have that is unique to us as women and which affects how we feel and respond. Several aspects of who we are as women warrant special attention because they can rob us of joy. Oh, sometimes Mama isn't happy because she really isn't happy or the joy robbers have attacked (we'll talk about them in a later chapter), but sometimes what's affecting Mama is simply fatigue, hormones, or emotions. Recognizing the role this threesome plays in our lives and, yes, explaining it to our families can mean the difference between "ain't nobody happy" and "let's ride this one out together."

Fatigue

We women work at our jobs or in our home businesses or homeschooling our children or volunteering at church and in the community—and then we pick up our COO responsibilities. Most women, including those working outside the home, do at least twice as much housework and childcare as men. With what's left of us, we try to be the loving wife and mother that everyone—including us—is expecting. (No pressure there, ladies!) In light of that job description, it's no wonder that we fight fatigue—and I won't even mention the fatigue that comes from...shhhhhhhh...aging.

Remember when you had a little more energy, like, say, when you were three years old? I've often dreamed of the rich and energetic woman I'd be if only I could figure out a way to siphon off some of the energy from my preschooler, infuse it into my tired body, and sell the surplus. (I'd be happy if anybody could figure out how to do that. Forget the rich part. I'd pay for more energy—and I'd pay a lot!) Many of us women fight fatigue—particularly mothers of preschoolers, working moms, and single moms. So often when we blow it—when we lose our temper and our tongue with our families—what was really talking was our fatigue.

Sleep experts say that nearly every American adult is sleep deprived. The rate of illnesses, accidents, and ulcers is up because our sleeping time is down. The Better Sleep Council says we are the "walking weary as a society," getting an average of 7½ hours of sleep a night, but really needing an extra hour. And to some bleary-eyed souls, 7½ hours would be a dream! Could you use an extra hour—or two or three? (Personally, I could go for an extra week right about now!)

So many times I try to be the wonderful, fun, energetic mom with lots of patience and tenderness for my children—only to get to the end of the day with an empty tank. Even if it's been a good day and I've been that kind of mom, I'm running on fumes by the children's bedtime. I'm sure you know the feeling: *If we do the 30-second teeth routine, leave baths for the morning, and read the abridged version of the story (one or two lines per page), I may be able to keep from collapsing until I'm near the sofa.*

Then there are those days when I totally lose the battle against fatigue, and, once again, my children pay the price. Although I start out trying to be Wondermom, I decide that simply being very patient and a little bit of fun is a more realistic goal and shoot for that. But before I get to "Goldilocks walked into the three bears' house, broke some stuff, got scared, and never went back again," my energy is gone. It's then that things like toothpaste on the toilet seat and wet clothes on the bathroom floor after bath time really take their toll on me. When I recently got to that place, I noticed that my voice started rising. Every word was clipped and terse, building to a full-fledged, *"HOW MANY TIMES HAVE I TOLD YOU?"* routine, followed by the "NOW, GO TO SLEEP AND I DON'T WANT TO HEAR A PEEP!" line. Nobody peeped. Yes, I know the saying well. Mama wasn't happy—nobody was.

I went downstairs and flopped on the couch, in tears for reducing my children to tears (again) all because I was tired. *I don't want to be this way. I want to be that patient-loving-kind-fun-wonderful mother. Where does she go at the end of the day?* I'm learning that on nights like I just described, I am not really an ogre. I'm just completely exhausted, and in my tiredness that ogre-like behavior emerges. So I'm trying to take precautions during the day to prevent that total drop-dead feeling. I'm even learning to nap. Since I get up early with my children and frequently stay up late with my husband, I often take a catnap during the day. When I do, it's amazing how much happier I am during the arsenic hour.

I have also stopped feeling guilty about those naps. One day, when I told Tim I was really tired, he said, "You should take a nap tomorrow. I'd take one every day if I worked from home."

"You would?" I said, in shock that my hard-working husband had spoken those words.

"Yeah. They ought to build that into the corporate structure like some cultures do. The break makes you much more productive." (Viva, Mexico! Everything there shuts down for a nap after lunch. I wonder if we can lobby for internationalizing the siesta? It would no doubt make the world a kinder, gentler place!)

"They" also ought to write that bit of wisdom in an instruction manual for all: Naps make Mama happier! In fact, I'm about ready to lobby for an addition to all birth certificates in bold type: **Naps required for all babies, toddlers, and mothers of such.**

It really is OK to sit down. I don't know why I (and you, too?) keep forgetting that! If you work outside the home, a short rest after work and before entering the "wild zone" can help. Don't feel guilty about plopping down on the sofa for a few minutes after you get home. "Taking ten" like that will help you get through the end of the day. Or you could do what a friend of mine does. Most days, during her lunch hour, she takes a 15-minute nap. She says it makes a huge difference in her energy level later that evening when she's with her family.

Yes, fatigue is an enemy we all know, but it's an enemy we shouldn't try to fight standing up. Let me say it again: It really is OK to sit down! Rest is rejuvenating.

Hormones

Another aspect of our makeup that influences whether or not Mama is happy is our fluctuating hormone level. Just consider this entry from one of my journals:

> What an emotional week for me! Hormones. YEEEEK! I began to sense my patience waning and my tension rising, and for three days I turned into this barely recognizable crazy person. I screamed and cried and asked myself, "Who is this woman? I don't know her and I wish she'd leave." Then, three days later, the hormone rage died down, and she left as suddenly as she had come. Was I ever glad to see her go!

The medical profession continues to document that hormone-driven premenstrual syndrome affects our personality and feelings. Those hormonal shifts in our bodies make a Dr. Jekyll/Mr. Hyde transformation seem tame. Our Mrs. Hyde routine can really make us wonder who is living in this body of ours! Being aware of our hormonal patterns and learning how to navigate the rough seas they stir up is crucial to our well-being and our family's! A friend of mine is ready to rent a garage apartment from her mother-in-law just for "those days"—and she's thinking of opening it up to women everywhere. She'd call it "The PMS Hospice: An Escape for Hormonally-Harried Women." Imagine the marketing possibilities! It would be a nice break for us and a great relief for the family as well. After all, as far as I'm concerned, Kathy Peel's description of PMS in her book *Do Plastic Surgeons Take Visa?* is right on target. Surely those letters stand for "Psychotic Mood Swings"!

But hormonal shifts in a woman's body are not a laughing matter, as Janetlee H. knows. Battling with major hormonal fluctuations was a way of life for her, but it wasn't until her hormonal imbalance got to dangerous levels and nearly immobilized her that she saw the problem for what it was. She says, "I didn't realize the effect my hormones were having on me. At first I thought I was going crazy. Then I thought it must be a spiritual attack or there was something wrong with me as a person, wife, mother, or friend. I tried to make changes on my own, but nothing worked."

Janetlee didn't realize there was anything wrong for a long time because she was so busy taking care of her family, her job, and other people. She had stopped looking out for herself. She says, "I had gotten caught up in the world telling me I could do it all—but I couldn't. I looked at others who appeared to be doing it all and wondered why I couldn't. Women 20 years older than me and single mothers with kids and without household help were functioning. I couldn't make myself do it all any longer, and I wondered, 'What's wrong with me?'"

What was drastically wrong, Janetlee discovered, was a major hormone imbalance which led to a hysterectomy. As Janetlee's case illustrates, sometimes hormones cause problems much more severe than your average PMS. Listen to your body. Physical problems need to be found and treated. With the right help, we can manage hormonal fluctuations. We can even learn to manage garden-variety PMS.

A friend of mine, for instance, has learned to read the warning signs in her body and anticipate her moods. "I note on my calendar when I am most likely to suffer from hormonal shifts, and I plan my schedule accordingly," she explains. "I try to never make major decisions during that time because my perspective isn't quite right and my thinking isn't quite as clear as normal. I also make sure that I get lots of extra rest on those days."

That kind of planning ahead is a great idea. However, I'm usually not that together, nor can I always predict those days. Too often I find myself short-tempered, emotional, or being a screamin' meanie, and wonder, *What is wrong with me?* Then the light will go on. *Oh, yeah.* Maybe you can relate? Some women don't know they are dealing with PMS because of an irregular monthly cycle. As one woman said, "It was hard to ever blame PMS for how I felt or acted because I never knew when it was my hormones and when it was just me."

Once some health concerns prompted my doctor to, in her words, "play around" with my hormonal balance. "Great! I'll be sure to warn my family to batten down the hatches," I said—and I did. I find it helps to explain to family members that there is a physical reason why Mom is being less than her wonderful self. Women can use a little extra support and nurturing during that time, but we won't get it if we don't ask for it. We also need to quit beating ourselves up when we blow it and remember that sometimes Mama is simply experiencing the physical effects of hormonal shifts—a victim of her own physiology.

Emotions

Sometimes women are emotional because of fatigue or hormones, but other times we're emotional because we are uniquely female. Perhaps this fact about us is what gave rise to the "If Mama ain't happy" saying in the first place. We've gotten a bad rap by bewildered men and perplexed children. "Women are too emotional" is a common response to us. Some women, perhaps. At times, perhaps. But just as disturbing is the woman who has too little emotion. What is called for, but difficult to achieve, is a beautiful balance of emotion and control so that emotions are shared in just the right amount at just the right time. And—may I put your mind to rest?—the only person who was ever capable of that perfect balance was Jesus. His emotions were always appropriate to the given situation, and He is a model for you and me. But sometimes we need more than His example alone.

Dee D. is a woman who knows all too well the power that our emotions can have over us. She struggled with hormonal problems, extremely fluctuating emotions, and a difficult marriage. One day while she and her husband Brynn were arguing, her emotions and hormones were raging out of control. Naturally quiet, Dee found herself standing at the top of the stairs yelling down at Brynn. Without thinking, she picked up a huge plant and hurled it down the stairs as easily as if it had been a baseball, narrowly missing her shocked husband. Realizing that she was out of control, he simply began to clean up. Soon after that event, Dee found medical help for her hormone problems.

She and Brynn became Christians soon after that, but her fragile emotions and difficult marriage were still realities. One day she completely shut down emotionally. She explains:

> Brynn and I were in the car, and I began thinking how I was so tired of feeling this way and fighting. I thought, "I'm not going to take this anymore." So I just started staring out the window. It was like I had turned off my emotional switch and took myself out of myself. For three days I was in a daze, not uttering a word or leaving the house. Some men from the church prayed with me, and I just watched them, thinking, "It's nice that they're doing this," but there was no feeling whatsoever. My body was there, but my emotions were someplace else. My husband then admitted me to a psychiatric hospital.
>
> I struggled because I knew that, as a Christian, I wasn't "supposed" to be this way. I got on my knees and cried out to God, "Lord, what am I doing in here? You've got to give me something to hang on to." Then I read Psalm 31—"Because Thou has seen my affliction, Thou hast known the troubles of my

soul....I am forgotten as a dead man, out of mind, I am like a broken vessel....But as for me, I trust in Thee, O Lord, I say, 'Thou art my God.'" I read that psalm for the six weeks I was there and kept getting different things from it. That was the beginning of my healing. For the first time I began to know God and know that I could trust Him.

When Dee was released from the hospital, the Lord led her through a slow, gentle time of recovery, marital counseling, spiritual growth, and healing. Today she is active in her church, a testimony to the healing that God can do with even the most fragile and damaged of emotions.

Emotions—Can You Trust Them?" asks the title of one of Dr. James Dobson's bestselling books. I think the resounding answer would be "Not usually!" We aren't to live in the emotions, letting them wildly rule us. We're to live in the will, allowing our emotions to reveal what's inside. That's a big difference. Oh, I praise God that we are emotional creatures, for this God-given attribute helps us be nurturers. Our emotions allow us to feel happiness and joy, to cry with someone who's hurting, to be compassionate, to laugh, to mourn, to smile, to love. Even as we strive for balance, we can still cherish this aspect of our femininity. It truly is a gift. After all, without our emotions, we'd be nothing more than Mr. Spock in heels—efficient but as cold as ice.

Now, the next time you slip into your "Mama ain't happy" scenario, remember that fatigue, hormones, and emotions may be at work in you. Recognize when fatigue is reaching a toxic level and rest before you lose your cool. Understand how hormonal shifts affect your body and figure out what you can do to stay on an even keel. Strive for that healthy

> $\mathcal{W}$e have no more right to consume happiness without producing it than to consume wealth without producing it.
>
> ~George Bernard Shaw, "Candida"

balance between emotions and control. Accepting these aspects of our female makeup can help us take precautions before we, in our "unhappiness," make "nobody happy."

Trickle-Down Joy

Finding joy and contentment in life is the driving force behind most of what many people do. That inner satisfaction affects our thoughts, our attitudes, and our actions which, in turn, affect other people. This is trickle-down joy, and that's what the rest of this book is about. We'll examine this trickle-down effect and see how we can choose joy and contentment with our head, cultivate joy and contentment in our heart, and practice joy and contentment in our home. We can indeed be women who choose to be joyful, who radiate the joy of the Lord, who experience joy in this journey, and who live out and give out joy to those in our circle of influence. We don't have to wait for happiness based on happenings. We can make the choice to rejoice!

~≫Part One≪~

Choosing Joy and Contentment in Our Heads
What We Think

❦ 3 ❧

It's All in Our Heads
Making the Choice to Rejoice

I f your mother ever told you "that's all in your head," she may have been right! Oh, I'm not suggesting that you make things up. I am suggesting, however, that feeling good about who we are and where we are in life often starts in our heads. It starts with what we think—in a word: *attitude*.

Attitude is a state of mind and heart. It colors how we respond to all that happens in our lives. Our attitude is the filter through which we view the world and the perspective from which we interact with it. Some people perceive and approach life through a beautiful rosy filter (most of the time). Others have a filter that could use a little cleaning. And some folks (and we all know at least one person like this!) have a filter that's so damaged they ought to pitch it and get a brand-new one. (If only changing attitudes were that simple!) Through what kind of filter do you see life? With what kind of attitude do you approach each day?

It's in Our Heads

Old Webster was a funny guy. He first defines "attitude" as "the arrangement of the body or figure (posture)." That sort of gives new meaning to having a bad attitude, doesn't it? Then he snaps out of it and explains that attitude is "a mental position or feeling regarding a fact or state." I would add that it's an outward expression of our inward feelings. Again, it's in our heads. And Scripture supports that fact: "As a man thinks within himself, so he is" (Proverbs 23:7). What we think determines who we are and how we act.

Now we may be able to hide how we feel for a time, but sooner or later our behavior and demeanor will be affected by how we feel. When we least expect it, our attitude sneaks out and gives us away. Sometimes our attitude makes its appearance rather subtly at first. We may think we're doing and saying things ever so pleasantly, but then our attitude slips out, revealed by our words or actions, and we're discovered. Attitude reflects what's really going on in our hearts. Let me give you an example.

I have served on a number of committees in the past and have found that, while often effective and occasionally fun, they accomplish things in a rather...umm...interesting way. (Just ask the folks who think that camels are really horses put together by committee!) At one such meeting, I had some definite and rather strong ideas about one of the issues we were going to discuss, but I went to the meeting fully intending to just listen. Well, my brain forgot to remind my mouth of that great plan, and before I knew it I was expressing myself.

At first I thought, "This is good. These things need to be said." Perhaps, but the problem was that my words, body language, and facial expressions were dripping with attitude—and it soon became quite apparent that it wasn't good. I proceeded to offend some, make others defensive, and I ushered in a big chill—all in one liberated moment of self-expression. *Boy, it's getting a little tense in here,* I thought. Then I realized that I was a chief contributor to the mood. When all was said and done, God used that meeting—as is His custom—to draw us together and teach me that my attitude sometimes peeks out of my actions just as easily as my slip peeks out from under my dress. Neither one makes us look very good.

At other times our attitude is about as subtle as a 400-pound monster wearing gold lamé. There's no missing it for the world! You can see it coming a mile away! One unnamed daughter of mine occasionally battles that kind of attitude, although without most of those pounds or the gold lamé. (What kind of mother do you think I am?)

"So, honey, how was your day?" I asked cheerfully one day when she got home.

"Fine," she said with the same tone of voice I'd use to exclaim, "The neighbors' dog pooped in our yard again!"

"Oh, that good," I replied, while stirring the night's dinner.

She slammed her books on the table as she walked by. One of them fell on the floor. She ignored it and bumped into her brother on her way to the fridge.

"'Scuse me. You're in my way," she barked at him. "What's for dinner?" she asked me.

"The world's best vegetable soup. How 'bout that?"

"Again? I'd rather eat cat food!" she complained as she rifled through the refrigerator.

"No problem—that can be arranged."

"What's for snack?" she asked, first searching a cabinet unsuccessfully and then slamming the door.

"Popcorn."

"Again? How come we *never* have anything good to eat?" She checked the fridge one more time to be sure something good hadn't appeared in the 20 seconds since she last looked.

"Honey, would you take this laundry upstairs, please?"

"OK. But why is *she* getting to watch Reading Rainbow? She *never* has to do any work," this daughter said of her sister.

She grabbed the basket and headed upstairs, each footstep proclaiming her attitude.

"Did anything happen at school today?" I probed when she returned to the kitchen.

"No!" she said sharply—and then she screamed, "Mom, look! Allison just spit on my math homework. Scat, you!"

As I removed Allison from the scene of the crime, Collin entered and helped himself to the hot popcorn sitting on the table next to the unnamed and clearly unhappy daughter's backpack. It spilled—into the backpack, of course. When my daughter with an attitude returned from cleaning her homework, she shrieked, "Mom, get them outta here!"

Whether our attitude is camouflaged and subtle or screaming out at the world in no uncertain terms, three things are certain: our attitude helps shape who we are, it affects other people, and its appearance—what it looks like when it does appear—is completely our choice.

The Power of Our Attitude

The attitude with which we approach life determines the kind of woman we are, the kind of wife we are, and the kind of mother we are. It shapes the kind of friend we are and the kind of servant we are. It affects how we view our circumstances, our world, and our future. To a great extent, our attitude also influences our goals and the enjoyment we find in reaching them.

In the words of Christian writer and pastor John Maxwell, our attitude rather than our aptitude determines our altitude. Our attitude, not our ability or knowledge, determines how high we can soar. In his book *The Winning Attitude,* Maxwell gives several reasons why our attitude is so very important:

1. Our attitude determines our approach to life.
2. It determines our relationships with people.
3. Often our attitude is the only difference between success and failure.
4. Our attitude at the beginning of a task will affect its outcome more than anything else.
5. It can turn our problems into blessings.
6. It can give us an uncommonly positive perspective.
7. It is not automatically good just because we are Christians.[1]

How good is man's life, the mere living! how fit to employ All the heart and the soul and the senses forever in joy!

~Robert Browning, *"Saul"*

Let me say it again: Our attitude shapes who we are and what we are able to accomplish.

Abraham Lincoln is a great historical example of a man with a wonderful attitude in spite of tremendous adversity and a teacher's disparaging remarks: "When you consider that Abe has had only four months of school, he is very good with his studies, but he is a daydreamer and asks foolish questions." Woodrow Wilson and Albert Einstein encountered similar teachers during their school years. One of Wilson's teachers said, "Woodrow is a unique member of the class. He is ten years old and is only just beginning to read and write. He shows signs of improving, but you must not set your sights too high for him." And one of Einstein's teachers said, "Albert is a very poor student. He is mentally slow, unsociable, and always daydreaming. He is spoiling it for the rest of the class. It would be in the best interest of all if he were removed from school at once."[2] Without a positive attitude, these men might have believed their teachers! Thankfully, they didn't listen. They kept on going.

And that ability to keep on going when the going gets tough is part of the good attitude that employers look for in employees. Hiring managers have reported that, when choosing between two equally qualified job applicants, they would pick the one with the better attitude—the one who values and enjoys working—over any other quality. Over half of the managers surveyed care more about a potential employee's *attitude* than their *aptitude*.[3]

Read what Charles Swindoll says about the importance of attitude:

> The longer I live, the more I realize the impact of attitude on life. Attitude, to me, is more important than facts. It is more important than the past, than education, than money, than circumstances, than failures, than successes, than what other people think or say or do. It is more important than appearance, gifting, or skill. It will make or break a person, a school, a church, a company. The remarkable thing is we have a choice every day regarding the attitude we will embrace for that day. We cannot change our past.... We cannot change the fact that people will act in a certain way. We cannot change the inevitable. The only thing we can do is play on the one thing we have, and this is our attitude....I am convinced that

life is 10 percent what happens to me and 90 percent how I react to it. And so it is with you.... We are in charge of our attitudes.[4]

What kind of shape is the attitude that you're in charge of?

A Positive Look at Life

Would you say that your attitude is basically positive or basically negative? Are you a natural optimist or a die-hard pessimist? Is your water glass half-full or half-empty? Or maybe you're like Ziggy, who said, "My glass may be half-empty, but there will be less to clean up when I spill it!" He gives his pessimistic outlook a positive twist—which is better than being positively negative! Or—yet another possibility—maybe you're like my husband. When I asked Tim if he considered himself an optimist or pessimist, he replied, "Neither. I'm a pragmatist." And he is, always choosing the practical approach to life's problems and situations. But I contend that even a pragmatist can choose to be optimistic.

An optimist is someone who naturally sees the brighter side of things and hopes you do, too. I think of a waiter I had recently. After I finished a mediocre Mexican food lunch, he came to my table and said with a Texas-size smile and south-of-the-border accent, "Everything was just about perfect?" I didn't know if that was a question or a statement, but he seemed so cheerful and confident that it had been good, that I just agreed with him. "Yes, it was," I replied. I could have mentioned that the enchiladas were lukewarm and a little dry, but I didn't want to spoil his impressive optimism.

Another impressive thing about optimists is their ability to see problems as challenges. Optimism turns roadblocks into bridges. Whether we choose to be stopped or to travel to the other side depends on our attitude. And hundreds of studies and thousands of anecdotes support the fact that people with a positive attitude excel in college, on the job, in sports, in politics, and in most other fields, often despite some really tough circumstances.

While working on this book, I met two folks who know the importance of this kind of positive attitude in their employees and who view problems as opportunities for blessings. Jim and

Joycelyn McLachlan Clairmonte are the hosts of the beautiful McLachlan Farm Bed and Breakfast in Spring, Texas, where I spent several days alone to write this book. (Most of these pages, however, were written with a child nearby or occasionally on my lap.) The Clairmontes greeted me warmly and immediately made me feel like family. (I knew when I first heard her name— *Joycelyn*—that I'd like the hostess!)

One night I took a break from my self-induced sequestering when they invited me to join them for dinner. As we visited (and they didn't even know I was working on this chapter!), Joycelyn and Jim told me stories about some of the many weddings they have hosted—like the one where the groom showed up for an abbreviated service so he could get back to the hospital from which he'd been given a three-hour leave. Then there was the rainy-day wedding when the entire set-up—from the chairs to the arches—had to be moved three times and the bride (choosing to keep the wedding outside) had to wade through ankle-deep water in her wedding gown in a pouring rainstorm to get to the outdoor pavilion. But then there was an indoor evening wedding when a storm blew out the electricity, but a multitude of candles set in beautiful porcelain teacups around the room turned what could have been a disaster into one of the most beautiful weddings they'd hosted.

Clearly, Joycelyn and Jim's quick thinking and great attitude have made special memories out of potential chaos, but as I heard these stories, I wondered how the brides handled these emergencies as the most special event of their lives was about to take place. Joycelyn said, "There's one thing I tell all of my brides when they consider having their wedding here: 'Honey, don't get your heart set on things. Lots of things can happen at an outdoor wedding,' and you have to approach this with the right attitude. With the right attitude, we can handle anything that comes up.'"

"You talk about attitude with all the brides that come here for their weddings?" I asked.

"Absolutely," she said. "I can handle about any situation— except a hysterical bride. I also make sure that the employees I hire have a good attitude. I won't hire them if they don't. Hard work is just hard work, so it helps to tackle it with a good attitude. A bad one affects everyone, and we try to have fun while we work." By George, I think she's got it! And this woman, with her great attitude toward life, is influencing countless brides and employees! Way to go, Joycelyn!

Optimism Is Good for Your Health

A positive attitude does more than help success come your way and make life more fun. At the same time that medical science continues to point to chronic stress, anger, and depression as leading causes of a host of diseases and even death, doctors are finding that a positive attitude is good for our health and our life expectancy. One article reported: "Scientists suspect that sensations like optimism, curiosity, rapture—the giddy, goofy desire to throw wide your arms and serenade the sweetness of spring—not only make life worth living, but also make life last longer. They think that euphoria...is good for the body, that laughter is protective against the corrosive impact of stress, and that joyful people outlive their bilious counterparts."[5]

A *Good Housekeeping* article entitled "The Secrets of People Who Never Get Sick" also reported that optimism is key to good health. Optimists have fewer sick days and doctor visits. They are also more inclined to take care of themselves by exercising and taking medications as prescribed. The author wrote, "Optimism strengthens the immune system...and optimists are also healthier because they encounter fewer bad life events [such as divorce or job loss]; they anticipate problems and do something before disaster strikes, and they have more social support."[6] Bring on that optimism and joy!

Our Attitude Affects Others

Our attitude affects not only us, but everyone with whom we come in contact. Unless we live in Siberia, we will rub elbows with other people, so a good attitude is helpful. (Of course, Siberia is so cold, I don't think anyone's expected to have a good attitude there!) It's a simple fact of life that people who have pleasant attitudes are pleasant to be around. Those who don't, aren't.

Whatever our attitude, we carry it with us everywhere we go, and people form opinions about us based on that attitude.

When we happen to share our bad attitude with the butcher, baker, or candlestick maker, you can bet that's who we'll run into the next time we go shopping. When we're irritated with the cashier at the checkout line and let her know it, we can rest assured she'll be the visitor sitting in the next pew on Sunday morning. More important than saving face after our bad attitude slips out is realizing what that bad attitude communicates to those who don't know us or the Savior we represent. If our attitude stinks, so does our influence for Christ.

Our Children

Artist Mary Engelbreit has a wonderful print depicting a young child looking up at her mother from the threshold of their door, facing the world beyond. A book and world globe sit on the floor, and a picture on the wall reads "Dare to Dream." The mother is looking at the outstretched world before them, gesturing toward it with one arm and holding her child with her other arm, as if to say, "This, my child, awaits you. Go! Do! I am behind you!" At the top, the artist has written, "All that I am or hope to be, I owe to my mother"—the words of Abraham Lincoln.

We mothers do indeed have an amazing opportunity and responsibility when it comes to shaping the attitude of our children. After all, each of us picks up much of our outlook toward life when we are young and carries it with us into adulthood. (At that point, change is difficult but not impossible—which we'll get to in a minute.) When we are young, we take on the traits we see modeled, and they become very much a part of us. Child development experts say that future success has its roots in a positive environment in the early years. Our children, therefore, deserve to have a mom who lives out before them a positive perspective and attitude. What we teach them with our words and, more importantly, with our lifestyle can affect who they become and what they try to accomplish.

If you and I constantly complain, so will our children. If we see the negative in life before we see the positive, our children will learn to do so, too. If you feel you're a pessimist by nature ("That's just how I'm wired") and are content to remain a pessimist forever, your children will probably be destined to the same gloomy perspective. If we are optimistic, our children have a better chance of learning to be that way, too—as Colleen A. knows. Saying that her attitude affects her ability to be joyful and content, she explains that she had a great teacher: "In situations where I've decided to be content, I have been. I credit a wonderful mother with a very positive attitude about most things as a significant role model for me." Of course many a positive mom has negative children. After all, each child comes into this world with his or her own unique temperament, but a child has a much greater chance of becoming optimistic about life if mom is.

Now having a bad attitude from time to time is human nature. It's the habitual bad attitude that becomes a problem. In fact, I doubt that I could find a mother alive who hasn't had an occasional bad attitude. (I think it goes with the territory.) But moms are usually very aware of the fact that, when it surfaces, that bad attitude affects our children. Just ask Pam H. She had just come home from running errands with her young sons, Caleb and Clay. She was tense and tired and furious with Caleb for disobeying her. As they walked through the living room, she began to read him the riot act. When she got to the bedroom, three-year-old Clay was talking on his toy phone, but she was in no mood to pretend with him now.

He looked at her and said, "Mama, you have a phone call. It's God."

That took her aback. Curious, she looked at him and asked, "Oh really? What does He want?"

"He said He's not very happy with the way you're treating Caleb," Clay said. "He wants to talk to you."

Pam stopped short and took a deep breath, surprised by her

> *The greater part of our happiness or misery depends on our dispositions, and not on our circumstances. We carry the seeds of the one or the other about with us...wherever we go.*
>
> ~Martha Washington

young child's words. She took the phone and said, "Hello...!
Yes, God...You're right.... I am angry and I am out of control....
You're right...I have been a little bit rough on my children today.
I know it's partly my fault because they're tired and hungry and
I should have fed them and put them to bed sooner.... Yes, God,
I'm sorry. I'll try to do better, and I will apologize to my kids."

Pam handed the toy phone back to Clay, knelt down so she
could look her boys in the eyes, and said she was sorry. Then
she prayed with them and asked God to forgive her for her bad
attitude. She told me, "I have learned to take time out to learn
from my kids and to let them learn from me by asking for forgiveness and an improved attitude." Pam could have snapped at
Clay to put the phone down and be quiet but, instead, she made
the choice to change her attitude.

Our Attitude Is Our Choice

Choice is key to attitude. We alone are responsible for our
attitude. We can choose it, and we can change it. "We are either the masters or the victims of our attitudes," says John
Maxwell in *The Winning Attitude.* "It is a matter of personal
choice. Who we are today is the result of choices made yesterday. Tomorrow we will become what we choose today. To
change means to choose to change."[7] Put simply, we can make
a choice to rejoice.

And whether we are wealthy or poor, filled or hungry,
healthy or ill, intelligent or simple, we all have an equal opportunity to choose the kind of attitude we will have. We all possess
that freedom. Mary H. has learned to choose wisely and well:
"I've learned that I have control over my attitude. I choose to be
joyful the same way that I choose to be in a funk. I refuse to be
a victim, and I choose joyfulness as often as possible."

I'm trying to consistently make the same choice that
Mary has learned to make. Some years back, when I was
struggling to complete a Bible study on prayer, I realized how
important that choice is. The study part wasn't the problem;
the rising-early-and-praying part was. One day I didn't wake
up until almost 8:00, my alone time gone and my morning
routine shot. I was frustrated with myself for my lack of commitment and inconsistency, and that frustration soured my

whole attitude. All morning I felt apathetic and couldn't seem to shake it. About midday, I wondered what was robbing me of my joy, and it suddenly struck me: My enemy was my attitude! Simply pinpointing that I wasn't very joyful because of what was going on in my head helped a little. I tried to change my course for the rest of the day. I changed scenery, too. I took the kids out for lunch, we went home for their nap, and then I enjoyed a visit with a friend. The change in my head and in my location helped me change my attitude, and my joy began to reappear.

It helped to realize that only I could change the way I was outwardly expressing my inward feelings and that it was my responsibility to do so, and I did change my attitude that day. If only I could say that it's been in perfect shape ever since! But, alas, sometimes it slips back into the mucketymuck, and I have to drag it out, wipe it off, and try again. Sometimes others in my family (and occasionally people outside that circle) gently remind me to do just that.

Tim and I try to teach our children that an upbeat, positive attitude is right up there with cleanliness and godliness. After all, nothing can ruin a family outing, a family dinner, or any other kind of family time more completely or more quickly than for one person (or more!) to have a bad attitude. When trying to explain the importance of a good attitude, I have found myself telling my children things like "That kind of an attitude, young lady, will not be tolerated!" Tim would often add, "You change your attitude right now!" You know how it goes.

Well, one day I hadn't yet made my choice to rejoice. I didn't have a good attitude at all, and I knew it. It was one of those days when I felt like running into the street in my pajamas yelling, "Yeah, I'm in a bad mood. Wanna make something of it?" The thought of doing that sort of tickled me. I pictured my oldest daughter shaking her finger at me for going outside in my pj's and screaming in the street and then telling *me* that my attitude just would not be tolerated so I'd better change it right now. (After all, I tell her to do that.)

And that's when the light bulb went on. At that instant, I could no more change—or be forced to change—my attitude than I could fly to the moon. Why did I think my children could do so ? First of all, I didn't feel like changing my attitude. Second, if I were told to perform such an instantaneous attitude transformation, my ol' human nature just might kick in with, "Oh, yeah?

Let me see ya make me!" (Now I would never actually say that, but those hidden little thoughts sometimes creep up.) Issuing a "change now" demand to my children was unfair, and that realization has helped me try to replace the demand with gentle reminders that only they can improve their attitude. I can't change their attitude for them, nor can I make them do it. They are in control, and, for children, that's a very big deal since there's not a whole lot that young ones are in total control of.

Back to that bad-attitude day. I want you to know that I resisted the urge to run outside in my pj's and scream in the street. Far more importantly, I was reminded that I cannot make my children change their attitudes just as no one can make me change mine. Choosing our attitude—making the choice to rejoice—is an individual freedom and responsibility.

Changing an Attitude

Knowing that we can choose to develop and maintain a positive and joyful attitude leads to the question, "How?" And the answer is "by remembering that your desire, decision, direction, and deep roots in Christ enable you to make and live out the choice to rejoice." One very important note: I am not offering these four ideas as the "be-ye-joyful-plan." Being joyful is much too complex to be reduced to four (or even 14) easy steps. But these four points may help you begin—or begin again—to choose a joyful attitude and maintain it.

Desire

Before we can ever change anything about ourselves, we must have the desire to change, and that desire often comes once we realize that we need to change. Some of us, however, walk around with an attitude that could use some adjusting, but we don't see that there's a problem. So take a moment to evaluate your attitude. Is your attitude in good shape? When is it—and when isn't it? Does your attitude need to be adjusted very often? Are you as positive as you'd like to be? Write down your answers and then ask someone who knows you well and loves you to assess your attitude. After evaluating your attitude and considering the reasons for developing a positive one, you may find the desire to improve yours. You may realize you want to change. That's the first step.

Decision

Once you realize that you want to change, your next step is deciding to do something about making that change. Confirm that decision by saying to yourself or writing in your journal, "I hereby make the choice to rejoice!" Such a decision is required, a deliberate act of the will to make the choice to rejoice. Paul made the decision when he said, "I will rejoice" (Philippians 1:18), and we can, too!

But sometimes making that decision isn't as simple as it sounds. Sometimes our mind is willing ("Yes, that sounds like a great idea"), but our will is not ("but I can't possibly do that!"). That is when we have to be willing to be made willing. We have to be willing to let God change our heart or mindset so that we can be willing to choose a joyful attitude over a negative one. If you aren't yet at the place where you have decided to make the choice to rejoice or you don't know how to actually make that decision, you can start with a simple prayer: "Lord, please make me want to choose to incorporate Your joy into my attitude. I am willing for You to make me willing to do Your will. I'm willing for You to make me willing to rejoice." Imagine the possibilities of God at work in a willing heart and mind "for His good pleasure" (Philippians 2:13)!

Direction

When we desire to change our attitude and we've decided to make that change, we must then have a sense of direction before we can change our location on the attitude spectrum. We must know where we're going and have a plan to get there. As you make a plan to alter your attitude, consider the following:

1. Know that attitudes follow actions.

We don't have to wait until we feel good to start living out a good attitude. If we did, we could be waiting a long time! Besides, attitudes have a funny way of following actions and feelings often follow behavior. When we begin to act in a certain way, our feelings often catch up. So, if you and I want to have a good attitude, we must start acting as if we have a good attitude. If you want to be more joyful, start acting more joyful. If you want to be more patient, start acting that way. The feelings often follow the actions—as I tried to help my two older daughters learn this concept recently.

One thing I can't stand is their bickering, and one day they were really going at it. Since there was no end to it in sight, I took each one of them aside, separately, and said, "I know you don't feel like being kind to your sister right now, but you may not continue to act this way. Even if you don't feel like being kind to her on the inside, please show her kindness on the outside—and then watch what happens." And I stopped there. I didn't offer any further explanations, and each daughter thought the talk was for her ears only.

Well, their curiosity piqued, my girls weren't about to miss seeing what would happen, and I quietly observed them the rest of the day. I could tell they were still mad at each other, but each took on the newly-assigned role with great gusto. *"You* go first," one said. "No, after *you,"* the other responded, both of them speaking with saccharine sweetness. They practically knocked themselves out being kind to each other as they waited to see what would happen.

And you know what happened? Although initially they may have been expecting candy to fall from heaven because they were being pleasant, the phoniness gave way to the real thing, and they didn't even notice. Their attitudes began to follow their actions. And so can ours. When we make the choice to rejoice, the feelings can follow. But I must mention here that lasting change comes only with a changed heart, not merely with changed actions (that's the topic of chapter five). Right now changing your actions is a good first step toward a better attitude.

2. Replace bad thought habits with good ones.

The only way to replace bad thoughts is to work at developing good thought habits. (Replace "I always do things wrong" with "I'm just having a bad day," for instance.) Our thoughts influence our actions which affect our attitude which, in turn, affects our thoughts, and so the cycle goes. We start with a thought, we dwell on that thought, and then we make a decision and act based on that thought. This action reinforces the thought, leading to a habit. That habit influences our future thoughts, and the cycle starts again.

For example, we start with the thought, "I'm down today . . . again." Then we dwell on that negative thought: "I feel so crummy. I think I'll help myself to some comfort food." Then comes the decision: "Yes, that's just what I need! There's a whole bag of Oreos in the pantry"—and off we go for the cookies. Next comes the negative action and negative attitude: We eat half the bag and think, "I'll never feel good or be thin." And the cycle continues.

Replacing those bad thought habits with good ones might look something like this: "I feel down today, but I don't want to stay like this." Then we dwell on this positive thought: "Hmmm, what I need is some fresh air and exercise." Then the decision and action: "I think I'll change into walking shoes right now"—and out the door we go. Good habits yield good attitudes: "I feel better already." Our habits affect our attitudes and our attitudes affect our habits. Although our thought habits are often deeply ingrained, we can train them to be positive.

3. Change what you can.

If you can change something that is causing your bad attitude, do so. If, for instance, you are frequently late (a bad habit) and the frustration makes you cranky (a bad attitude), you can change your habit and thereby positively affect your attitude. You can learn to become punctual (by setting the alarm a little earlier, minimizing what you try to get done before you leave the house, and so on), which will limit and maybe even eliminate your reason to be cranky—and your attitude will be better. So look for what is causing your bad attitude and do what you can to change those contributing factors when you can.

4. Commit to work on improving your attitude daily.

Change isn't easy; change takes work. To successfully change your attitude, commit to work on it daily. The fruit of your efforts will definitely be worth the energy you spend cultivating a good attitude.

5. Find someone to hold you accountable for your attitude.

Ask that person to remind you (gently and lovingly, of course!) when your attitude needs adjusting. Too often it's hard to recognize when our own attitude is in need of adjustment, and that's where a friend or loved one's constructive comment can open our eyes. If I'm exuding negativity, sometimes a lighthearted, "What are you so cheerful about?" delivered with a wink can be just what I need to realize that my attitude could use a tune-up.

6. Look for mentors and models.

If you want to be more positive, try to surround yourself with positive people. Nothing can drag you down more quickly than negative folks.

7. Press on when you slip up.

You will slip. We all do. I haven't heard of anyone in the last 2000 years or so who had the right attitude all the time. When you mess up, forget what lies behind and reach forward to what lies ahead. Press on just as Paul did: One thing I do: forgetting what lies behind and reaching forward to what lies ahead, I press on toward the goal for the prize of the upward call of God in Christ Jesus (Philippians 3:13,14).

You now have a sense of direction and some ideas about how to get going that way. There's one more point to consider as you undertake permanent attitude adjustment.

Deep Roots

If we stop with the above suggestions for improving our attitude, we are limited to a self-help fix. While that superficial effort may do the job for some, we don't want to be the only help we have in this major reconstruction job. And, as a Christian, we are not in this alone. God's Word tells us that we have a helper in the Holy Spirit who enables us to accomplish God's will when our strength isn't enough. To develop the kind of attitude that is pleasing to God, pleasant for others, and a worthy model for our children, we need to turn to our heavenly Father, His written Word, and His Holy Spirit. Making the choice to rejoice a decision that will last requires us to dig our roots deep into God and His Word, relying on His Spirit to transform our heart as we do so. (There's more on this in chapter five.)

Choosing Joy

If joy is an attitude of the heart (as we saw earlier) and we can choose our attitudes, then I can choose joy—and you can choose joy! Each of us can choose to live a joyful life. Being joyful begins in the head, with our choice to have a good attitude, be positive, learn optimism, and model these things for our children. Taking that first step—choosing to think this way—is a deliberate act of the will. Other factors are involved—as we'll see—but an attitude of joy begins with our thinking. We can indeed make a choice to rejoice!

That fact is the basis of *Happiness Is a Choice,* by Doctors Frank Minirth and Paul Meier, in which they write, "Both of us can say with a deep inner conviction that a majority of human beings do *not* have the inner peace and joy about which I am thinking. We are also convinced that all human beings are capable of having this inner joy and peace if only they will choose it and follow the right path to obtain it."[8]

Making the choice and following the path won't always be easy, though. Sometimes we can simply say, "I choose joy!" as Christian singer Larnelle Harris does in his song by that title, and that's all there is to it. More often than not, however, making the choice to rejoice is only the beginning of our journey.

Even when we're in pain, we have that choice to rejoice. Perhaps you've heard of Lucy Mabery, the wife of Trevor Mabery who was one of the Focus on the Family board members killed in a plane crash. Lucy knew tremendous pain and grief at her husband's tragic death, but she learned from that experience that we have to work through our pain and that we can find joy again. She told me, "When Trevor was killed, I could have chosen to crawl into a hole, but instead I chose to allow others to watch me walk through the process. You can choose happiness. You can change your mindset. You can say, 'These are bad circumstances, but I'm not going to let them overwhelm me, so I won't drown.' I also decided not to be stoic. I allowed people to see me being real. The more I did that, the stronger I got."

Like Lucy, the apostle Paul knew about choosing the right attitude. Despite all his sufferings for the Lord (2 Corinthians 11:23-27), he stands out as one of the most joyful people in the Bible. In the first chapter of Philippians, for instance, Paul describes some of his afflictions and then says, "... and in this I rejoice, yes, and I will rejoice" (verse 18). He decided to rejoice today ("in this I rejoice") and he decided to rejoice in the future ("I will rejoice"). You and I can do the same.

Choosing Is Not Creating

Let me add that choosing joy does not mean trying to conjure up joy by your own power. You and I can never create joy, but we can make the choice to develop joy as an attitude of the heart. Joy is much more than just an attitude. It is also a gift from the heavenly Father and a fruit of His Spirit, and those things can never be created. We can choose joy in the sense that we can choose our attitude. We can choose how we look at life, express ourselves, relate to people, and relate to God. We can choose to look at life through a rosy filter of a joyful attitude or one that is gray or cracked. Choosing to have a joyous attitude can help make a ho-hum, lackluster life one that sparkles. Which do you choose?

Different Temperaments, Same Joy

The various ways people approach life and express their joy is fascinating. We are all so different. My husband and I have completely different personalities, as this simple story illustrates.

One day I went to a new salon. I was ready for a transformation from my "college hair," a style I had worn for too many years, to a totally new "do." My friend Robin went along to offer moral support—and to make sure

We can live as though Christ died yesterday, rose today, and is coming tomorrow, or we can live as though Christ died, period. We can count blessings, or we can count calamities.... It's our choice.

~Barbara Johnson,
Splashes of Joy in the Cesspools of Life

that I didn't chicken out. When Sal got done, I was (to my surprise) quite pleased and decided I just had to stop by Tim's office and show him the new me immediately. (Temperament clue here.) Tim casually walked out (another temperament clue), surveyed the big change, and calmly said, "That's nice."

"But do you like it?" I asked.

"Yes, it's nice," he replied. I could tell he liked it, but I continued.

"'Nice' is boring. I want you to be gaga!" I said.

"OK, consider me gaga," he said flatly, but with a smile.

I have learned that, for Tim, he was being gaga! I would have been thrilled if he'd exclaimed, "*WOW*! Honey, you look incredible! How about a night on the town?" I knew that's what he meant, but he would never think of saying it quite like that. After all, his temperament is different than mine.

We all express ourselves differently, and our display of joy is no exception. All of us can make the choice to rejoice, but our approach to that decision can vary widely. Here's a fun look at how four different personality types might handle that choice:

• *Fun-loving Sally Sanguine,* looking for an exuberant approach, might make the choice to rejoice by bouncing across the room in her bright red outfit, laughing just for the fun of it, and loudly exclaiming, with her arms open wide, "Hello, world! It's gonna be a great day!"

• *Controlling Carol Choleric,* looking for her own approach, might make her choice to rejoice very decisively. Deliberately and confidently, she might stride across the room, get everyone's attention, and say, "I have decided to rejoice for the rest of my life. I'll begin with this big grin. [Smile.] Now here's the rest of the plan, so all of you get out something to take notes on. You can be joyful, too."

• *Perfectionist Milly Melancholy,* looking for the proper approach to joyfulness, might straighten her skirt, carefully gather her data on the subject, and say, "I will make the choice to rejoice after I've analyzed this book and completed my attitude graphs. I certainly can't jump into this joyfulness thing without first giving it careful and thorough consideration. Can I get back to you next week?"

• *Laid-back Felicia Phlegmatic*, looking for the simple approach, might say, "This is no big deal. It's certainly nothing to get excited about. I made the choice to rejoice years ago. I'm just smiling on the inside!"

Each person—depending on his or her temperament—is going to approach joy and express it a little differently. (In some cases, a lot differently!) You may laugh uproariously, you may flash a big toothy grin, you may smile only when you deem it appropriate, or you may laugh on the inside. You may be exuberant in your expression of joy or you may have a quiet sense of contentment, a calm sense that life is good. Whatever your expression of joy, whichever your approach, you can make the choice to rejoice. It's up to you—and don't worry if your joy looks different than someone else's joy.

❧ 4 ❧

Taming the Monster of Discontent

Wanting What We Have

Have you ever thought, "I'll be happier when..."? Perhaps you're thinking, "I'll be happier when I have more money" or "I'll be happier when I have a better job." Maybe it's, "I'll be happier when I feel good again," or even "I'll be happier when I get all my children potty trained!" Have you ever muttered, "I'd rather be anywhere but here?" I have. I know all too well that menacing monster of discontent and how difficult a monster it is to battle. The problem is that just when we think we're the conqueror, it's breathing down our necks again. Since it keeps rearing its ugly head, I've decided to try to tame it.

Why a chapter on contentment in a book about joy? Because the monster of discontent has a way of pushing aside joy. It's very difficult to be joyful and discontent at the same time. But the opposite is true as well. The more joy I have, the less room I have for discontentment. And part of being joyful is learning to be content.

What does it mean to be content? Contentment is not so much having what we want as it is wanting what we have. (Go ahead and read that sentence again!) "Content" is defined as "happy enough with what one has or is; not desiring something

77

more or different; satisfied." Now there's a concept that's foreign to lots of people! Some of us have fought off the ugly monster and can say that we're genuinely happy with what we have. (But maybe you struggle with this.) Many of us can say we are happy with who we are. (But too many people don't like themselves.) The part of the definition that sounds so foreign is the phrase "not desiring anything more or different." That almost sounds downright unAmerican. I can just hear that monster asking, "How can you be happy with what you have when so much more is available? How can you be happy with who you are? Don't you desire personal growth? And how could you possibly not desire anything more or different? Don't you ever go to the mall?"

Contentment—not desiring anything more or different—is a rare trait today. Mention it and you could get lambasted for discouraging others from bettering themselves and improving their lives. After all, isn't wanting more and better the American way? And there are times when there's nothing wrong with that. Bettering ourselves with an education, improving our life with tools we need, or buying a better house *is* the pursuit of the American dream. These are good things in themselves. But there's a fine line between obtaining from need and obtaining from greed. Contentment falls somewhere on the line between want and excess—a line that's in a different place for different individuals and that shifts during one's own life. The question that occurs to me, then, is: "Where is my heart? When do my wants take me over the line of contentment and into the monster's territory?"

Being Happy Where We Are

Learning to be happy where we are is one of the more difficult lessons in life. One reason is that "where we are" is always changing. Just about the time we get used to one place—be it an address, an age, a job, a season of life—we have to move to a whole new place and get used to it. After all, first apartments make way for starter homes, and fall precedes winter. Babies stop being newborns and learn to sit up and crawl away. The twenties always lead to the thirties and then to the forties (which hopefully doesn't lead to midlife crisis!). Even "aging gracefully" can't go on forever, for physical life must eventually end, allowing our spirit to go home to a new address. Nothing stays the same forever, so throughout our lives we always have an opportunity to learn to be content in whatever place or season we find ourselves.

Greg P., a man who filled out one of my surveys, has learned the value of contentment. He said, "Meeting, dating, and marrying my wife, Donna, taught me that God's will is perfect and sovereign. I learned to be content in His will as a single, even though I sometimes doubted God would ever send me the soulmate I desired. That was important because being content where I was helped me establish who I was as a man in Christ prior to meeting my wife."

But sometimes we are too busy looking ahead to the perfect moment when contentment will be easy. Aware of this fact, a mother wrote these words to her college-age daughter:

> Don't you get the feeling that nearly everyone you meet has the same ideal—to be about 30 years old, at the peak of their powers, healthy, and in control of their life? It's as if there is one ideal moment in life and all would be well if we could just freeze the action right at that point.[1]

We delude ourselves—whatever our age—if we think there is one ideal moment in life when all will be well and contentment will become as natural as breathing. That's not how life works, and an ideal world is not the best breeding ground for real contentment.

True contentment is being able to say, "I am happy right here where I am"—and mean it *regardless of the circumstances*. Getting to that place isn't easy, but that's the point to which God calls us: "Godliness with contentment is great gain" (1 Timothy 6:6 NKJV). Thankfully, I know what it feels like to live in that place—but I have struggled to

Joy is peace dancing.

~Tim Hansel,
Holy Sweat

get there. I also know what it feels like to be scared away from that place by the monster of discontent—but I know it can be tamed. Contentment is a virtue worth pursuing for it brings great joy and incredible freedom. Continuing her letter, that mother writing to her daughter wisely added that we must "learn to cultivate the virtue of contentment—which frees us from forever wanting to exist in just one stage of life."[2] Contentment also frees us to savor the gift of the present and to know the joy God wants us to experience today.

The Seeds of Discontentment

We can better pursue contentment when we understand the strategy of the monster of discontent. We can strengthen our stand against that monster when we realize that it rears its ugly head through comparisons, commercialism, and circumstances.

Comparisons

One of the quickest ways to breed discontentment in your life is to make comparisons. Comparing yourself, your possessions, and anything else connected to you with someone else can lead to only two things: pride or discontentment. Let's first consider pride.

If we compare ourselves to people who have less than we do, pride can take root. We can become smug about the things we have and begin to lose sight of the fact that everything we have and everything we are is a blessing from God. The self-made man or woman is a myth. He or she has simply been blessed by God. Wise and wealthy King Solomon knew that "it is the blessing of the LORD that makes [one] rich" (Proverbs 10:22).

The kind of comparing which leads to pride might begin with, "Look, Bill! The Smiths' car is broken down in front of their house. I think it's the third time this month." There's no problem with this simple observation, especially if it leads you to see if the Smiths need your help. But the path can get treacherous. *Hmmm. It sure looks bad sitting there jacked up. I wonder how long they're going to leave it there. I hope it's gone before our company comes. I am so glad we got our new car before they got here.* Ah, the seeds of pride have been sown before we realized what was happening.

Pride is like that. It can start small, taking root as a tiny seed in our hearts but growing into one of those seven deadly sins. Comparing what we have can lead to pride in our possessions. Comparing who we are or where we are can lead to self-pride. Both are sins and contrary to the self*less* attitude of Christ, which should be our goal.

Again, if we compare ourselves with those who have less than we have, we risk becoming proud. But if we compare ourselves with those who have more than we do, we risk becoming dissatisfied with what we have, where we are, and even who we are. We find ourselves becoming discontent.

Comparing ourselves with others can begin so subtly: "Look, Bill! The Smiths got a brand new car. It sure is pretty." This simple observation seems safe enough. "I'm so happy for them. They really needed one. She was telling me just the other day how she was stranded three times last month." This time the observation includes some rejoicing in the blessing another has received. But at this point, if we don't watch it, we can find ourselves walking the dangerous path of making comparisons. *Hmmm. I hadn't noticed our car looking quite this ratty.... The paint sure is faded. The upholstery is even torn. The car runs, but it sure looks bad. In fact, I don't think I want to be seen driving it.* Before we know it, the monster of discontent is behind the wheel and has taken control, driving away the awareness of our blessings. We find ourselves wanting more than what we have, and we lose sight of the fact that we are very blessed to have a vehicle that runs well and is dependable.

"Well, that's rather simplistic," you may be thinking. "Besides, I would never do that." Maybe not—maybe not with a car, or at least not in one sitting and not intentionally. To better understand the destructive power of making comparisons, maybe you need to consider something other than a car. What if the object of comparison was a house or new furniture or your children's accomplishments or...? You plug in the thing that lights your fire. Satan knows our vulnerabilities, and he will find ways to tempt us. Comparing what we have with others seems so harmless—and it is when we stay within the confines of noticing their blessings and sharing in their joy. But when we take the next step (and this move can be subtle) and start making comparisons between us and them, Satan can use it as a tool to scatter seeds of discontent. The rate of their growth can be quick if they were sown in fertile ground (if we're focusing on something we value) and if we water them with continued comparison. The seeds germinate with that kind of nourishment and grow into a field of weeds that chokes out our ability to enjoy the blessings we've received.

I learned early on that my parents wouldn't tolerate the complaining that comes with being discontent, and my father shared a lesson he learned in junior high to explain why. He had a teacher who hung a sign at the front of the classroom. It said, "I complained because I had no shoes—until I met a man who had no feet." No matter what our situation, there's usually someone worse off than we are. My dad never forgot this message and, subsequently, neither have I.

Again, maybe you're not real picky about what kind of car you drive. I'm not. Satan has never brought me pride or discontentment because of someone else's car. (If you could see my car, you'd know pride in that area is no problem!) However, plug in something that touches me a little more personally—like, say, a house or decorating or achievements—and that's where I need to guard my heart. After all, the effects of pride and discontent can be devastating and far-reaching. Ministries have toppled because of pride, and marriages have been ruined by discontentment. It's no simple thing, and Satan knows it. He will sow seeds using things that tempt us, so protect your soil.

One way we can protect our soil and stop making comparisons is by realizing that comparisons aren't always what they seem. What we see in other people doesn't always tell the whole story. The grass isn't always greener in someone else's life—as a friend of mine learned at the beauty shop.

When Posy was getting her hair done one day, she saw this beautiful girl with gorgeous hair. "Wow," she thought. "Why can't I have hair like that?" At first she wasn't going to say anything since she figured the girl was probably tired of hearing everyone tell her how beautiful her hair was, but she changed her mind.

"You have beautiful hair!" Posy exclaimed.

"Thank you. I kind of like it, too," she said. "It's what came in after the chemotherapy."

No, the grass isn't always greener, as my friend saw. But it often looks greener when we don't see the big picture—and that's a lesson Maria can teach us. You undoubtedly have a Maria in your life. She has a clean and well-organized home; she feeds her family wonderful, nutritious meals; her children seem well-mannered; and you just can't imagine her ever running out of groceries or clean clothes. She even finds time to serve at church, take part in a Bible study, and entertain. She makes us feel rather inadequate.

To counter such feelings, read what Carol Mader wrote in an article entitled "Dare to Not Compare" from the newsletter "The Proverbs 31 Homemaker."

> Many women compare themselves to others, whether consciously or otherwise. We use yardsticks such as the neatness of a house or how many extra activities a woman appears to be handling. We contrast and compare only to feel that we never measure up. Judging by externals, we fail to look beyond the facade. So it occurred to me, if I were going to compare my household with Maria's, I needed to compare every aspect.
>
> Maria's son, Shawn, and my son, Ivan, were close in age. While Shawn nursed three times a day, my son nursed every two hours even with solids. Shawn would play happily with his toys for hours, but my son screamed if I got more than two feet away. Shawn took two long naps each day and slept twelve hours at night. My baby napped once a day for 45 minutes and never more than nine hours at night. While Maria changed eight diapers a day, I was changing a whopping 22 diapers a day! Maria's husband happily assumed child care duties every evening, yet my husband was busy fourteen hours a day, seven days a week, with graduate school. No wonder I was exhausted.[3]

Carol found that Maria had 35 hours free of child care that she didn't have—and that didn't count the help from her husband and the fact that she had a happier baby. With 35 extra hours a week, Carol could get her act together like Maria. Carol adds:

> Maria's life and my own, I realized, were simply very different although on the surface they appeared similar. I found that comparisons were really an exercise in futility. Each family and their priorities are unique.[4]

Think again about the Maria you know. If you're discouraged by the comparison, stop comparing. Dare to not compare! After all, you can't have a clear picture of that other person's life. You're only dealing with what you see on the outside from a distance, and that's hardly an accurate picture.

Like Carol's Maria, your Maria is a real threat to your level of contentment. But maybe the Maria in your life is a little different from Carol's Maria. She always looks great, does the appropriate thing at the appropriate time, and meets her family's every need, in a gorgeous and orderly home, with gentle, lovingkindness. This woman is impeccable, unflappable, punctual, and—more importantly—impossible! This Maria lives only in your imagination, and Satan can use her to destroy your self-esteem and rob you of the contentment God wants you to have.

We must not allow that old monster to put this fictitious woman on a pedestal before us. Take in a big breath of reality and blow her off. Stop looking around and comparing yourself to other people (real and fictitious). Instead, look up to God and realize that He calls you to be a Proverbs 31 woman, "an excellent wife...[whose] worth is far above jewels...a woman who fears the LORD...[whose] children rise up and bless her; her husband also, and he praises her saying: 'Many daughters have done nobly, but you excel them all'" (Proverbs 31:10, 30, 28). Don't be seduced by the charms you see, whether in a real-life Maria or the Maria of your imagination. Comparisons lead to pride or discontentment. Comparisons cripple contentment.

Commercialism

We are a people who want more, and our society breeds that desire. Everywhere we turn, we are offered something newer, bigger, or better. Advertisers threaten our contentment with what we have by trying to sell us what they have. Our clock radios wake us up with a call to buy. During breakfast, interruptions to the morning television show invite us to purchase. Then, as we drive around running errands, billboards remind us of what we could acquire. Our culture is saturated with advertising—and the pace picks up during December!

Advertisers put a lot of money into this call to consume. Some reports say that every year the industry spends almost $500 per American. Advertisers are banking on the fact that they can make us discontent with what we have, help us discover needs that we weren't aware of, and compel us to spend our money. In the bestselling book *Your Money or Your Life* , authors Joe Dominguez and Vicki Robin say, "Advertising technology, armed with market research and sophisticated psychology, aims to throw us off balance emotionally—and then promises to resolve our discomfort with a product. Fifty to 100 times before 9 A.M. every day."[5] (I don't know about you, but I don't like being thrown off balance emotionally by 9 A.M. With that much of the day left, I need every emotion I've got! Who knows which one will come in handy later? Besides, sometimes I can lose my balance all by myself.)

Advertising exacerbates our perceived needs and can, in turn, steal our contentment. You know how it works. You go to the mall to get that gift you have to buy, and on your way out you spot this cute outfit in the window. You stop. *Now that's a great outfit.* You leave. You turn around and glance one more time. *I bet that would look great on me.* You go back and try it on. *I was right! But I really can't afford this now.* You leave—for real this time—but you take a bit of the mall with you mentally. During the week, you think about how much you'd love that outfit, even though it wasn't on your list when you entered the mall. Later, when you're trying to decide what to wear, nothing quite holds a candle to that outfit at the mall. Your wardrobe is fine, but you left your satisfaction with what's in your closet at the store window. As you think about the outfit some more, you begin to see your want as a need, even though it isn't. And that's the goal of advertising.

The situation is different if we need the clothing and have the money. Then we can make the purchase and enjoy the new outfit. But when we allow our "needs" to be determined by what we see in the mall and hear in the ads, we are letting our commercial culture influence what we buy as well as how we feel about what we already own. We are letting the demon of commercialism define our needs and rob us of our contentment.

Now I'm not knocking the advertising industry. First, I've worked in the business and, second, I'm always grateful when advertising alerts me to products, prices, and services that are useful. However, we all need to be aware that repeated exposure to ads can make us think that we need things we really only want. There's nothing inherently wrong with wanting things—as long as that wanting doesn't interfere with our contentment. Most people want things occasionally (some of us want more frequently than others!). The danger comes—and it often comes subtly—when our wanting blurs our thinking about what we really need and makes us unable to see the blessings of what we already have. Maybe that's why we're told in a famous top-ten list not to covet—and that's a word you don't hear much today. You never hear someone say, "I'm sure coveting that outfit which I don't need and can't afford." After all, can it really be coveting when there were three others on the rack? You don't want what someone else has. You simply want one just like it! Fine line, isn't it?

How can you protect yourself from the appeal of commercialism? Here are some basic ideas. If you're struggling to be content with your wardrobe, for instance, don't go window shopping. If you're becoming discontent with your home decor, slack off on those magazines that feature decorating ideas. If frequenting the mall makes you want stuff, try frequenting some place else. Often window shopping, women's magazines, the mall, and other exposure to material goods and services are wonderful, but if you begin to find commercialism turning your contentment to discontentment, do your best to disconnect.

Circumstances

A young man runs into his professor one day. The professor asks, "How are you doing?" The young man replies, "Okay, I guess, under the circumstances." The wise professor quickly responds, "Under the circumstances? How did you ever get under those?"

It's all too easy to get under the circumstances of our life, isn't it? Well, when I feel that circumstances have piled up and piled up, I sometimes imagine God holding that pile in the palm of His hand and watching me squirm and sweat under there. He's lifting the edges so I can breathe, but I've been so busy screaming about the hugeness of the pile that I haven't heard Him say, "Hel-LO in there! Have you forgotten that you're still in My hands?" I need that reminder that "Thou hast enclosed me behind and before, and laid Thy hand upon me" (Psalm 139:5). Don't we all?

We humans certainly tend to let our circumstances affect whether we are content or discontent. When things are going well, we are content. Mama is happy. But when the tide turns and our circumstances change, discontentment creeps back into our lives and tries to edge out our joy. It is so easy to adopt straightjacket thinking about this pattern: *If things are as I wish, I am content. If things are not as I wish, I am discontent.* With this very human and very binding line of thinking, we let bad circumstances restrict our contentment, holding us hostage until more favorable circumstances come along and, Houdini-like, free us from the straightjacket. Rick, an attorney friend of ours, experienced this recently.

Rick had been working on an extremely difficult case. Preparing to bring it to trial had been exhausting, both physically and emotionally. So when he went home, he decided to unwind with some channel surfing. He, the remote, and the sofa became one! He sat there, blindly flipping through the channels, a victim of the bleary-eyed blahs. The next day, he won the case and was thrilled. That night when he went home, he noticed the drastic difference between how he felt then and how he had felt the

> *My* content-ment comes from knowing that I rest in God's will and that He has protection and provision should I ever need it.
>
> ~Nancy N.

night before and started thinking about how the circumstances had affected him. If he'd lost the case, he knew he would have been more down than the night before even though losing the case wouldn't have meant losing his job or personally paying the settlement. The Lord turned on the light for him, and Rick realized how closely his contentment was tied to his circumstances.

Now there are some circumstances in life where we cannot be content, nor should we be (an abusive situation or a situation that is painful beyond description, for instance). I'm not saying we should accept such circumstances and endure them. Sometimes we must take bold actions and do what we can to change those circumstances that are damaging and clearly out of God's plan for us. But most of the time, when we're under the pile of life, we can learn to cultivate contentment despite our crummy circumstances. After all, those circumstances don't come to stay. They "come to pass," and our heavenly Father is holding us—and the pile—in the palm of His hand. And God has taught me that that fact is key to our contentment.

A Lesson in Contentment

When we moved into the house we are currently living in, I was very grateful to be out of those dinky corporate apartments and into a place that would allow us to get our things out of storage. After living in a motel-like setting for seven months, we had great fun watching our belongings come off the truck. "Oh, look, honey! There's the table....And here come the kids' toys....Yea! *our bed!*"

"Settle down," said my calm, cool, and usually collected husband, but even he was thrilled at the prospect of once again sleeping in the comfort of our own familiar bed.

Unpacking was actually fun, and I was content...for a while. The house was (and is) a real blessing, but as soon as the boxes began disappearing from the living room, we began to notice just how much work the place needed. I kept repairmen coming and going for the first three weeks. The house is not just older, it's brittle. Quite often when we would open a cabinet or drawer, part of it would come off in our hands. I've got pieces of woodwork all over the place begging to be glued together.

Does the scene in *It's a Wonderful Life*, where the banister knob keeps coming off in George's hand ring a bell? That's us.

In fact, one day as I looked out the back window, I noticed something lying in the yard and saw a big board hanging down from the top of the house. I went outside to find the siding coming off and some boards near the roof hanging on by a nail or two. Realizing that the house was literally falling apart, I yelled, "Kids! Whatever you do, don't play outside. You might get hit in the head by the house!"

There are days when the torn vinyl, rotting wood, and the carpet which is 15 years past its prime all get to me. And since the house is a rental property, we aren't able to personalize it at all. If we paint, the color must first be approved by the management company, and then, when we move out, we must repaint it with their lovely beige. If I want to plant flowers, I must first ask ("Excuse me. Do you mind if I beautify your property with a pansy?"). Needless to say, I have been discouraged from doing much to this place.

Why am I telling you all this? Because God has taught me a lesson here. Let me back up. We all know that Satan attacks us where we live, and that's where he has attacked me—literally. Women tend to be more emotionally tied to our homes than men, and I am no exception. I don't like living in a place that's falling apart, and I don't like being unable to spruce it up without running my idea by Congress. But those haven't been the hard things. For me, the hard thing has to do with light. You see, I love sunshine and want as much of it flooding into my home—and my life—as possible. I like my home, as they say in real estate ads, "light and bright." That's good for me, as studies confirm. Researchers have discovered, for instance, that extended darkness can alter people's moods. Locales with long, gray rainy seasons and little sunshine tend to have higher depression and suicide rates than other places. People who work night shifts and see little sunshine over long periods of time can also succumb to a downward slump in attitude and depression. I can personally attest to the accuracy of these findings.

Yet right now I am living in what I call "my cave"—unless it's cold outside, and then I call it "our sieve." This house is so dark that we have to turn on the lights in the den at midday even in the summer. For three years, I've been "in the dark," struggling to keep a good attitude. "No big deal," you may say, and it's certainly not. I've faced *much* greater darkness in my life. However, often it's little irritants in life—like dark homes—that can steal our joy, rob us of contentment, and keep us from living the abundant life that God has promised us and wants to give us.

And this promise-making, promise-keeping God is using this house, as He uses everything in each of our lives, to teach me. For a long time, the struggle to be content in a dark, dingy abode was intense, especially since we're living near a very materially blessed area. I have to continually guard against falling into the comparison trap. At first I focused on how much I disliked the house, the repairs, and especially the dark. I began to ask God for a different house.

> Lord, You've called me to be in the home as a homemaker and full-time mom first and as a home-based worker second, and I thank You for that, but does it have to be in such an ugly place? Please, Lord, will You *GET ME OUTTA HERE?*"

I struggled with feeling unspiritual as I prayed that request. Then I decided it was OK to ask God for anything if the requests were made for the right reasons and with pure motives and a right heart. Then I found myself praying a bit more contritely. *Lord, please, if it be Your will, can we move?* Not yet. God wasn't finished teaching me. At that point my prayer became, *Yes, Lord, I'm beginning to see. Thank You for this house....* *Are we done yet?* Nope. Not yet. Try again—and I did after a little more time, a few more broken fixtures, and a little more darkness. *But, Lord, I want to be in the light. Please, will You take me to the light?* And then the light began to shine—not in my house (it's still as dark ever), but in my heart. The light began as a pen light, but then it grew to a night light, then to a flashlight, and pretty soon to a floodlight which illuminated my lack of contentment. I couldn't leave this dear old (emphasis on "old") house until God taught me true contentment. I began to feel and not just say prayers of thanks for where we lived. *Oh, Lord, thank You that this house is so big. Thank You for enough bedrooms, the big yard, a large kitchen, plenty of*

storage. And in Your will, I'll take that new address any time.
But I still had more to learn.

Sometimes we don't realize we're in a bubble until we get outside of it. That was my experience as I continued to learn the lesson God had for me. I began to realize that while I had been busy comparing what I didn't have with what my upwardly mobile friends did have, much of America didn't live the way they do or even the way we do. As I traveled, I saw how really blessed my family and I are. And, as I thought about other countries, I remembered that most of the world lives far below our standards. At that point, I began to appreciate a fact I'd known for ages: The blessings we enjoy as Americans are bounteous. As my genuine thankfulness increased, so did my contentment.

Now some of you might visit our house and say, "No wonder you prayed so hard!" (Some people have actually said this!) When I once told someone that I could stay in this house for another year or so, she replied, "I don't think it will last that long!" Yet another visitor even said, "It's nice things are sort of…like this, with your children and everything." (I loved that one!) Other people, however, might come and say, "Oh, how truly blessed you are! It would be so nice to live in a house like this." And people have said this, too. Your perception depends on your perspective; what you see depends on where you have come from.

Only now does my perspective agree with those who say, "Oh, how truly blessed you are!" God humbled me greatly by showing me how sinful my discontentment was. I have learned to be thankful for what I have right now. I now see that I have much. Oh, I don't *like* the house any better—it's as dark and drafty as ever—but I am quite thankful to be here. I am quite content. At first I was surprised I could actually say that. I am also very glad that God didn't remove His blessing of this invaluable lesson in contentment by giving me the blessing I had asked of Him.

At this point you need to know that I've lived in an apartment, a trailer, and an old school—where I slept on a cot—and I was content in each place. Then God blessed me with the biggest (albeit ugliest!) house of all to let me learn that we can be discontent anywhere no matter how much we have and that we can be content no matter how little we have. After all, contentment isn't based on the things around us. It's not based on our possessions or our position. Our contentment is based on the attitude we choose to have toward these things. Contentment comes when we hold loosely all that we are stewards of, for nothing is really our own. Everything is a gift from God. When we are grateful for these gifts—be they many or few—then we can know contentment.

And, as surprising as it may sound, knowing contentment can sometimes be a struggle even in a beautiful setting. Joycelyn Clairmonte knows this. The bed-and-breakfast inn she and her husband run is picture perfect. Standing in the middle of 40 acres, it has wood floors, rambling porches, rocking chairs, quilts, and a barn, and every impeccably decorated room looks as if it were taken straight out of a magazine. Even with all this, Joycelyn still sometimes wrestles with the monster of discontent:

> I love to decorate. When a place gets finished, I start feeling like it's time to move on so I can do another one....I'm certainly not unhappy, because we absolutely love to share our home with guests, but sometimes it's hard not having a place of our own to go home to at night....We share our home so much that we have to keep it as close to perfect as possible. I love things neat, but sometimes I just want to leave my shoes in the middle of the floor and be able to wear my pajamas around....We even have to move out sometimes when we rent all the rooms....This business is our gift, our calling, and our ministry, and we love it. But sometimes it's hard not living like real people, and I find myself getting discontent.
>
> Sometimes I want to put my head in a vise and yell, "Joycelyn, get your head together." I have to remember to take every thought captive and deliberately praise God for the blessings of this beautiful home, the property, my husband, the country, and so many other things. When I focus on my one lack and let that override all that's good, I feel discontent and ungrateful. I even feel self-pity.

As Joycelyn's words suggest, it doesn't matter how much we have. Satan can find a way to shift our focus from our blessings to our "one lack" and, in so doing, undermine our contentment. A grateful spirit and the expression of that gratefulness in thanksgiving to the Lord will help us tame that ornery and persistent monster of discontent.

We Have So Much—But Do We Want What We Have?

You and I, living in this country at this time, have more possessions, more conveniences, and more luxuries than any other place and time in history. We have some of the highest household incomes in the world. Two-thirds of us Americans own homes, six out of ten young people receive a college education, medical and health care advances are increasing our lifespans, and we have more luxury and leisure items than we have time for.

Technological advancements have turned backbreaking, daylong labor for necessities into simple and convenient acts. Instead of grinding the grain for home-baked bread, waiting months for a letter, and driving a day or more to the general store in a horse-drawn wagon, as the American pioneers did, you and I can heat a frozen entree in the microwave to eat in the minivan while we talk on our cellular phone on the way to the mall. I don't know about you, but I'll take a minivan over a buckboard any day! We are truly blessed.

You'd think that all this affluence and increased leisure have made us happier, right? They haven't. In fact, some experts say that only between 10 to 33 percent of Americans consider themselves very happy. Some psychologists say one-third of Americans are depressed, with more people suffering from this emotional problem than from all others put together. Furthermore, depression is the leading cause of suicide. Self-help books are hot sellers, psychologists' offices are full, and "personality-altering" drugs are at the center of a new controversy. A Christian counselor recently told me, "Every couple I counsel is unhappy. That's why they are coming. They want to be happy, to be transformed by their marriage partners, their jobs, their money. In short, their circumstances." It's no wonder America is singing the pop song, "All I Wanna Do Is Have Some Fun!"

Many people are even asking the very question researcher and author George Barna used to title his book: *If Things Are So Good, Why Do I Feel So Bad?* Despite our plethora of toys, tools, and trinkets, when we are asked if life gets any better than this, many of us are saying yes, explaining that we would like to know personal peace and fulfillment. Barna states, "Far from crowing about the supremacy of America and the joys of modern living, Americans are entangled in a battle for survival, striving to get through today, somehow, so they can take another crack at making things more fulfilling tomorrow. The sad truth, for most people, is that we are committed to minimizing our pain rather than maximizing our joy."[6]

We are a nation of people who have so much, yet we aren't very happy. We are richly blessed, but often we're not content. Is it because we forget to ask ourselves, "How much is enough?" When do we think we'll have *enough* money and *enough* things? When is our car, our house, or our job nice enough? Susan Gregory, author of *Out of the Rat Race*, recommends that we ask ourselves these questions and explains why answering them is important:

> We will not find satisfaction until we identify what is *enough*. Without *enough* we will continue to spend beyond our means. Without *enough* we will diminish our ability to realize our dreams and to fulfill our purpose in life....Just to remind you, the definition of *enough: adequate for the want or need; sufficient for the purpose or to satisfy desire.*[7]

Defining "enough"—with guidance from the Lord—is indeed key to contentment.

The acquisition of new, trendy, and better things without knowing how much is enough can obscure the joy that God provides when we live within His will and within our means. Sometimes we even forget to determine what enough is in our activities, filling a busy schedule with traveling or just go-go-going. Perhaps we need to teach our children to discover the line of enough as they juggle school responsibilities, clubs, sports, lessons, friends, church, and family. And we can all benefit from doing what Greg P. does: "I try to seek God's will for my contentment as I plan a budget and schedule." That poses a question we should all ask ourselves: "With what does God want me to be content?"

One woman learned a real lesson in contentment and enough when she flew from her home to another state to spend a few final days with her father. In her letter printed in *Focus on the Family* magazine, she described the last lesson he taught her:

> As I entered his room at the nursing home, he gestured with his arm to his half of the area and said with wonderment, "Just think... *all* this...is *mine!*"
>
> Startled, I looked around and saw a few pictures, his writing materials, a few clothes and toiletries. In that moment, I took an important mental snapshot of what genuine contentment and gratefulness is. He and Mom had made the climb from small living quarters to lovely parsonages and cozy homes—then back to an apartment, followed by an "assisted living" room, and finally, half of a room. Never had there been any complaint. Even at the end, there was still an amazement for God's goodness and provision.[8]

That reminds me of something someone else once wrote about enough and sufficiency. Two thousand years ago, the apostle Paul wrote, "My God shall supply all your needs according to His riches in glory in Christ Jesus" (Philippians 4:19).

I spent a summer in India and that taught me to be very thankful for our big, beautiful houses, clean water, hot showers, food without bugs and plenty of it.

~Colleen A.

In light of that truth, we need not continue our search for enough. It is being taken care of by our loving and generous heavenly Father. Our circumstances are in His hands.

When comparisons, commercialism, or circumstances threaten to move us from being content to discontent, stay in the first "tent." Don't even think about packing your bags. Instead, stay where you are by choosing a life of contentment and remember that "godliness with contentment is great gain" (1 Timothy 6:6 NKJV). When we stop comparing ourselves with others, when we reject commercialism's influence on our desires, and when we strive to live above our circumstances rather than under them—then we can begin to want what we have. When we view what we have as a blessing instead of comparing our possessions to what we don't have or considering what else we could obtain, we begin to be content. Getting to that point is not always easy, but then most worthwhile pursuits aren't. Being content with what we have and where we are calls for discipline of the mind. It demands changing how we think, which was not a lesson I learned easily, as you'll see next.

The Secret of Contentment

What I've Learned Thus Far

Meanwhile, back at the ranch....Or I should say that I wished I were living on a ranch instead of where I was.

In the last chapter, I told you how I came to learn contentment. You may be thinking, *Yeah, but you didn't really tell us how.* Quite right. The "how" actually began long before I finally learned the lesson. And maybe the learning process has already begun for you. Perhaps, for instance, you agree with chapter three that your attitude is "all in your head," and you want to do more of chapter four and "tame the monster of discontent," but you're wondering, *How can I have the right attitude, choose joy, and be truly content?* I wondered the same thing.

Joy and Contentment in the Pits

Before I left the dinky corporate apartments that held none of my stuff to become discontent in a big house with all of my stuff, God started working in me. I told you how I would go into my closet to cry and pray. I'd try to distance myself from the children long enough to heave up a prayer and then listen for His voice, but I often just heard the neighbors in their bathroom.

When I couldn't hear His word, I went to see His Word. I took to reading my Bible in the morning right when the birds announced they were up, which was, thankfully, before my children did the same. I began to study Philippians because I'd always been taught that it was the joy book of the Bible and boy did I need some of that!

I loved the first few verses where Paul thanks God when he remembers his friends. I could relate to that. I missed my friends back home, so I joined Paul in thanking God for them. Paul prays joyfully for them and says he has them in his heart. *Yeah, Paul, me too. They brought me great joy, and missing them makes my heart kind of hurt.* He goes on about love abounding. *Good stuff, Paul. I miss my mother being healthy, my husband being home, and my friends being here. I need lots of love. Let's get on to the joy part.* He does, but first I had to learn more about his circumstances or—should I say, his afflictions.

This changed man—forgiven, cleansed, and living beyond the chains of his past when he persecuted Christians—was now preaching the gospel. Yet his ministry wasn't reaping him accolades, standing ovations, and appreciation dinners. Instead, he was beaten and jailed, thrown into a cold, dark, damp cell and bound with shackles and chains. There were probably bugs, rodents, and a minimal amount of food—not a pretty picture. Outside the prison people were trying to discredit him (Philippians 1:15-17). As he sat in prison, Paul was evidently waiting on the court's verdict—his very life was at stake!

If there were ever a situation where a complaint or two and a grumble here and there might be expected, this would be it. I doubt that Paul would have gotten much criticism if he'd expressed his discontentment and said something like, "The food here sure isn't homecooking" or "How come some of my converts are preaching from motives of envy and strife, but I'm the one in jail?" Instead, Paul says, "And in this I rejoice, yes, and I will rejoice" (Philippians 1:18). He was *in* prison urging those *outside of* prison to rejoice! He wrote the book of Philippians to tell the saints about having joy and contentment *during* adversity—and he practiced what he preached. *How could he do that? More importantly, how could I?*

I looked around my apartment and thought of Paul. Here I was with a clean place to sleep, freedom to come and go, plenty of food, and numerous other blessings—and I was complaining! I was discontent! I was struck by the sharp contrast between Paul's crummy circumstances yet incredible attitude and my don't-hold-a-candle circumstances and lousy attitude. What a dichotomy! I'd wallow in discontentment for a while and then follow it up with a dip into the guilt pool. *I'm so miserable.... I have no right to be.... I would make Paul sick! What does he say about that joy in adversity again?* and I went on to chapter two of his letter, trying to make what I knew of Paul real in my own life.

Have the Attitude of Christ

I call Philippians 2 the attitude chapter. The man who lived in the pits with joy did so, in part, because he had the proper attitude, and he tells us what that should be. In Philippians 2:5 Paul says, "Have this attitude in yourselves which was also in Christ Jesus." We are to be Christlike. We are to have the same attitude that Christ had—and His was one of selflessness and humility:

Although He existed in the form of God, [Jesus] did not regard equality with God a thing to be grasped, but emptied Himself, taking the form of a bond-servant, and being made in the likeness of men. And being found in appearance as a man, He humbled Himself by becoming obedient to the point of death, even death on a cross (Philippians 2:6-8).

There is no greater example of selfless living, no greater sacrifice. It is the sacrifice on which I base my faith, indeed the sacrifice on which I stake my very life. Christ was God, but He laid aside His privileges as God to become

I must not let earthly things distract me from my goal.

~Terri F.

a servant on this earth, humbly submitting to His Father's plan to the point of death—and He did this because He loves us. *And I feel like I'm sacrificing these days in my life—but nothing compares with that!* I thought long and hard about the issue of self-sacrifice.

In Philippians 2:3,4 (I love these verses), Paul tells us to have a selfless attitude:

> Do nothing from selfishness or empty conceit, but with humility of mind let each of you regard one another as more important than himself; do not merely look out for your own personal interests, but also for the interests of others.

This was Christ's attitude and it can be ours, too. In fact, after I studied them, Tim and I adopted them as the O'Connor Creed and Motto. I want to teach the children that we are to avoid selfishness, look out for others first, and do so for the right reasons and that, in so doing, we become more like Christ—and His is the attitude for which we strive. We added verse two to our creed because it describes the wonderful joy of unity: "Make my joy complete by being of the same mind, maintaining the same love, united in spirit, intent on one purpose" (Philippians 2:2). What a great goal for the family—the one under our roof as well as the one who shares our faith. Then I really got on a roll and, for obvious reasons, added verse 14: "Do all things without grumbling or disputing." As a mother, that one's my favorite!

Continuing my study of Philippians, I moved on to chapter three and began to learn more about attitude and perspective. Paul starts off boldly: "Finally, my brethren, rejoice in the Lord. To write the same things again is no trouble to me, and it is a safeguard for you" (Philippians 3:1). *Again, he's telling me to rejoice, but my joy's pretty thin. I could use a safeguard.*

I kept on reading and realized that I'm not just to take on Christ's attitude. I'm also to *know* Him. Paul tells us to "put no confidence in the flesh" (verse 3), to "know [Jesus], and the power of His resurrection" (verse 10). You and I are encouraged to fully seek to know Christ instead of having confidence in the flesh. When we have confidence in our own accomplishments, we have an attitude of arrogance, but when we "count them but rubbish in order [to] gain Christ" (verse 8), we begin to have an attitude of humility.

Paul tells us to forget what lies behind and reach forward to what lies ahead (verse 13) and to press on (verse 14)! *This is another aspect of the attitude he encourages me to have.* Don't put confidence in yourself, but strive to know Christ. Forget your past and press on to reach the prize of eternal life. Paul then says, "Let us therefore, as many as are perfect, *have this attitude*; and if in anything you have a different attitude, God will reveal that also to you" (Philippians 3:15, emphasis added). *Hmmm. Selfless, humble, knowing God, pressing on....Great attitude!*

But wait a minute, I thought. *There's no way I can have that kind of attitude. The verse even says "as many as are perfect," so that leaves me out.* Only one Person has ever been perfect—Jesus—but that doesn't mean you and I are off the hook. In the original Greek language, this word "perfect" means "mature." Paul is basically saying, "For those of you mature enough, this is the attitude to have, and when you mess up, God will let you know." So many times I am convicted about my lack of a selfless attitude. When my attitude stinks, it invariably has its roots in my selfishness: I'm thinking more of me and my situation than anything or anyone else. And when I have a bad attitude, I am never truly humble. Despite our humanness, you and I must not look at the attitude described in these verses as an impossibility. God did not give these words to Paul to pass on to us for our self-condemnation. (No guilt trips, please! Everyone has a bad attitude now and then.) Instead, we are to look on these verses as a goal to attain. And Jesus is our ultimate model!

From the Head to the Heart

I'd read Paul's letter to the Philippians many times before, but not until I got disgusted with my own bad attitude and my own lack of joy and contentment in my circumstances did my understanding of what he says change from head knowledge to heart knowledge. That change began with my study of Philippians 4. There I read a very familiar passage:

Not that I speak from want; for I have *learned to be content* in whatever circumstances I am. I know how to get along with humble means, and I also know how to live in prosperity; in any and every circumstance I have learned the secret of being filled and going hungry, both of having abundance and suffering need (Philippians 4:11,12, emphasis added).

"For I have *learned* to be content." I latched onto that phrase. If Paul said he learned, then maybe I could, too. He didn't say he *was* content in his circumstances; he said he *learned* to be content in them. During the rest of our stay in the dinky corporate domiciles and during the first few years of living in my "cave," this teaching began to really cook for me. These thoughts were percolating in my head and stewing in my heart. I'd love to be able to tell you that I simply read all these verses and then, just like Jiffypop, I was done. I was content. I was "perfect attitude" personified. Sometimes God works that way, but not this time. He let me sit on the back burner awhile, His precious lesson simmering in my life until it was ready to be tasted. And how rich the flavor that comes with such simmering! If I may be so bold, let me share what I have learned thus far from the Master Chef.

The secret of having a great attitude and being content while we're in the pits involves three things:

- Renewing our thought life.

- Remembering the Source of our strength.

- Resting in that Source's sovereignty.

Let's look at each of these now.

> *There is no joy in the soul that has forgotten what God prizes.*
>
> ~Oswald Chambers,
> *My Utmost For His Highest*

1. Renew Your Thought Life: Know on What to Dwell

You and I need to choose joy and contentment in our heads by adjusting what we think. Attitude is purely a mental process—a head-thing—so to change it we must change how we think. We must *renew* our thinking. Adopting an "out with the bad, in with the good" approach, we must stop thinking one way and start thinking another way. Paul encourages us to renew our thinking when he says:

> Finally, brethren, whatever is true, whatever is honorable, whatever is right, whatever is pure, whatever is lovely, whatever is of good repute, if there is any excellence and if anything worthy of praise, let your mind dwell on these things (Philippians 4:8).

Sometimes instead of dwelling on what is true, however, we look at what we lack—which isn't a true picture. Instead of thinking on things that are honorable, our thoughts honor no one. Instead of pondering the lovely, we look at the unloveliness of our situation and surroundings. Sometimes we don't find anything excellent about things because we don't look for it, and when we can't think of anything worthy of praise, it's often because we aren't focusing on the One who is always worthy of praise.

But Paul knew on what to dwell! When we harness our thought life, choose (in our head) to think about things that are true, lovely, worthy of praise, and so on, and consciously choose to let our mind dwell on these things, we begin to train our attitude and tame the monster of discontent. When we think about the kind of things God calls us to think about in Philippians 4:8, our mind begins to be renewed. Our attitude begins to change. Contentment becomes attainable regardless of our circumstances! And there are two reasons why.

Our thought life determines our attitude. As we've seen, what we think determines how we feel which, in turn, affects our attitude. I love what John Maxwell says in *The Winning Attitude*. "Two things must be stated to emphasize the power of our thought life. Major premise: We can control our thoughts. Minor premise: Our feelings come from our thoughts. Conclusion? We can control our feelings by learning to change one thing: the way we think....Our thought life, not our circumstances, determines our happiness.[1] That's pretty straightforward.

Our thought life determines our contentment. Being content is not based on what happens to us (our circumstances) or how we feel about what happens to us (our emotional response to our circumstances). Being content is based on our thoughts. Contentment begins with what we think about ourselves and our situation. It's not based on what happens to us, but instead on how we think about and emotionally respond to what happens to us. If we can control what we think, we can better control how we feel, and our feelings determine our ability to be content ... or not be content. Renewing our thinking is renewing our mind, and Scripture says that doing so can transform us:

> Do not be conformed to this world, but be *transformed* by the *renewing of your mind*, that you may prove what the will of God is, that which is good and acceptable and perfect (Romans 12:2, emphasis added).

Instead of moaning about his circumstances, Paul knew on what he was to dwell. Instead of focusing on what was happening to him (which is so easy to do), he began to look at the bigger picture and was lifted above his circumstances. Then he found joy.

Renewing our mind involves "taking every thought captive" (2 Corinthians 10:5) and learning to think God's thoughts. It is a lifelong process, something that we must pursue daily. Renewing our minds sounds like work, but "along life's way...it brings a peace and delight that can only come from having embraced the mind of Christ."[2] It brings true joy.

2. *Remember the Source of Our Strength: Know Who Is Empowering Us*

Adopting the right attitude and changing our thinking will not make us content when we try to do it in our own power. That would be nothing more than simply practicing positive thinking, which can be good but which only goes so far. Our ability to harness what we think is limited, but there is a Source that knows no limits and is available to us as believers. The second part of the secret of contentment, then, is to remember that *God is the source of our strength.*

We need to ask ourselves, "In whose strength are we operating? Who is controlling my life? Is it me and my circumstances—or is it God?" Paul knew that he was not in control and that he was not operating on his own strength, but that it was Christ in him. He knew who was in control and providing the power when he wrote: "I can do all things through Him who strengthens me" (Philippians 4:13).

When we rely on our own strength, our ability to change is limited. Our strength is finite; God's strength is not. In our own might, our determination to be content is undermined by the limits of our willpower and our ability to accept our circumstances. To make the choice to rejoice and tame that monster of discontent, we must recognize the Source of our strength: God is at work in us. As Paul might say, I have "a confidence that I measure up to any situation I am facing because of the resources of strength that God has made available to me."[3]

Knowing the Source of our strength and His unending, omnipotent nature can give us the confidence we need to choose and live a life of contentment. To make sure you are accessing His strength and not just relying on your own, remember the source of your strength—dwell on it and keep it in the forefront of your mind. Do what Paul did and acknowledge that it is Christ in you who provides the power to change your thinking and, therefore, your attitude. Remind yourself of this and thank God that the things you do are really done through Him who strengthens you.

3. *Rest in the Sovereignty of That Source: Know That God Is in Control and That God Is Good*

God is sovereign. He is in control over each and every circumstance of our life. Here we just have to take God at His word—the Word.

God created everything and controls even the weather: "It is He who made the earth by His power, who established the world by His wisdom; and by His understanding He has stretched out the heavens. When He utters His voice, there is a tumult of waters in the heavens, and He causes the clouds to ascend from the end of the earth; he makes lightning for the rain, and brings out the wind from His storehouses" (Jeremiah 10:12,13).

God can do anything He wants to do: "Whatever the LORD pleases, He does, in heaven and in earth, in the seas and in all deeps" (Psalm 135:6).

God knows everything that happens to us and He cares: "Are not two sparrows sold for a cent? And yet not one of them will fall to the ground apart from your Father....Therefore do not fear; you are of more value than many sparrows" (Matthew 10:29,31).

Sometimes our circumstances appear completely out of control, and we feel tossed about by life. When that's the case, we must remember that God has the power to control anything and everything (even these circumstances in our lives) and that He can do so in an infinite number of ways (He can do as He pleases), and that—most importantly—He cares about what happens to us (remember the sparrow?). The God who sent His only Son to die for us and bothers to know the very number of hairs on our heads (see Matthew 10:30) also knows what is going on in our lives, and He cares greatly.

Many times we know that God cares about the big picture, but we need to be reminded that He is also always aware of what's in our little bitty viewfinder of life. I think of what God did for the Koinis family, my longtime friends. After much detailed planning and great anticipation, Steve and Brenda took their two children to Disneyland for a vacation. They had planned and prayed for this trip, and the kids were about to burst with excitement—when raindrops started hitting the windshield on the drive from their hotel to the

> *I* have to continually remind myself of who is in control. God knows all things and loves me more than anyone else.
>
> ~Vicki K.

theme park. Brenda said, "OK, we know that 'God causes all things to work together for good to those who love God, to those who are called according to His purpose,' and that's us, so let's pray." (See Romans 8:28.)

They did, and the children fully expected the raindrops to cease and the clouds to part. They didn't. When they got to the park, the drops had become full-fledged rain. By the time they got to the ticket gate wearing their yellow ponchos, rain was coming down in buckets. They got their tickets and went in even though it was raining so hard that Brenda thought her contacts were going to float away. She and Steve told the children that God could use this for their good—to help them learn to trust God as completely as Jesus did—even though He didn't answer their prayer for dry skies as they had asked.

Other good soon became apparent: They practically had Disneyland to themselves. Wearing their bright yellow slickers, they went from one attraction to another...without having to stand in long lines. They were having the time of their lives, and seeing everything in one day instead of the two they had planned. The next day they were able to visit a waterpark—a vacation bonus not on their itinerary, but on their Father's. It was a memorable trip for the fun as well as the spiritual truth the Lord had demonstrated. Now, years later, when the children wonder how good might come from bad circumstances, their parents remind them that God used a pouring rain at Disneyland for their good and that He can use this (whatever the situation at the moment) for their good, too.

I believe that God cares deeply about the little things in our lives as much as He cares about the big things when we allow Him to use them to reveal something about Himself. Sometimes we pray for the biggies because we desperately want an answer. But I think, somehow, God must be especially pleased when we pray even for small things because it shows that we care about His involvement in our daily lives. My friend, Betty, prays before she goes shopping and even before she chooses her clothes for the day, saying, "Father, You know what You have planned for me today. How can I best represent You?" Once she needed a safety pin to keep her dress intact, but she doesn't sew and knew she didn't have a pin. She prayed for a pin, and when she opened her eyes, there right at her feet was a safety pin. A coincidence or an answered prayer? Betty believes God answers even prayers about small things.

God recently showed me in a very personal way that He cares about the small things. I just got back from a wonderful women's ministry retreat which, for several years, has been held in a beautiful country setting. A shop in the nearby town sells prints of the big country house where we stayed, with an excerpt from the Psalms written on it in calligraphy. Last year I decided that I would get one the next time I was there. I told no one that I wanted this print, and this year, I was working on this manuscript during our free time and didn't have a chance to go shopping with everyone else. My little want would have to wait. However, when we were leaving the retreat, a friend handed me a simply wrapped gift. You guessed it. It was the print I had wanted for a year. I was touched by her thoughtfulness and awed once again that God even cares about the little insignificant desires that we have and loves to prove that to us! A coincidence? I think not. I agree with the little sign on my bulletin board that says, "A coincidence is when God does a miracle and chooses to remain anonymous." God cares about all the details—from life and death to pins and prints. Nothing escapes the notice or reach of our sovereign God.

In order to rest in God's sovereignty, however, we must know that He is completely good—good in character and good to us. His Word teaches that "the LORD is good, for His lovingkindness is everlasting" (Jeremiah 33:11), that He is "the good shepherd" (John 10:11), and that we are to "give thanks to the LORD, for He is good" (Psalm 106:1). We must simply

> *A*s a single person, I want a husband and family like the picture in my mind I grew up with. However, only God knows what I need—my wants are not necessarily my needs.
>
> ~Tamhra L.

take God at His word. The Scriptures state definitively that goodness is part of God's character, and we must choose to believe that. The Bible also gives a clear picture of God's goodness from the beginning of creation, through His provision for and involvement with the people who have served Him through the ages, through His redemptive plan for us in Christ, and, ultimately, in His promise of what awaits us in the kingdom to come. Every page of Scripture points to a God who is indeed good despite what we see and experience in our fallen world.

Now, look for a moment at your own life. Recall the times that God has provided for you and consider all the things He has done for you. Reflect on His blessings—both material and spiritual. Remember the big things and the small. Don't forget His provision for the "pins and prints" in your life. Ponder what God has done for you and how He has demonstrated His goodness to you in both the big ways and the little ways. Reflecting on these things and becoming fully convinced that God is indeed good can mean the difference between choosing faith and choosing doubt when dark days come. We'll talk about this more in chapter eight, "Joy in the Dark." But right now determine in your heart to believe that God Himself is good no matter what your circumstances suggest. Goodness is part of God's character and He never changes.

When we choose to believe that God is in control and that He is good, we can rest in His sovereignty. We can relax knowing that because He loves us dearly, He is always at work to make us more like Christ in our faith and ability to trust Him.

Seeing God's Perspective

The apostle Paul knew joy and contentment because he saw all of life from God's perspective. Paul knew what to think about, he knew that God was his strength, and he rested in the fact that God was in control. His one objective was to know Christ as he continued the race for his prize in heaven, taking as many people with him as he could. His body was here on earth, but his heart was in heaven. His body was in prison, but his mind was not. This focus on what was unseen—this hope in the Lord—allowed Paul to continue to be used by God even when he was in jail. He just watched God alter the way in which he was used.

No longer able to minister in freedom, Paul began his letter-writing ministry behind bars, something for which Christians through the centuries can thank him. He surrendered his vision, his dreams, and his plans for ministry to God and allowed God to alter them. His imprisoned body but free mind truly knew God and saw God's perspective. Paul had been privileged to get a glimpse of heaven, and he knew what was waiting after this life. This understanding of God's plan for eternity dominated Paul's life and ministry and enabled him to have a heavenly perspective on his own sufferings. When we, like Paul, begin to live for the world to come instead of just living for this world, we begin to see everything from God's perspective. As we mature in our faith and choose to believe in His goodness and sovereignty regardless of what we're experiencing now, we grow in our ability to see those circumstances as God sees them.

Trusting to Joy

I would like to point you to something that I find very pivotal in the life of a joyful Christian. On the surface, it's a simple thing. It is also something quite rich, to be cultivated throughout one's life. It is this: "When we *trust* God and exercise our *faith*, then we can *yield* ourselves completely and experience the byproduct of joy." Let's look at those key words.

Trust

When we trust God. Many Christians are joyful because they are saved, but that is where joy begins and ends. Joy was meant to be much more than gratitude to God that He has made a way for us to escape hell. He also intends for us to live in joy in the present—no matter what that present is. But we can't do that unless we trust Him.

If we know that God has saved us (from eternal death, the penalty for our sins), is sovereign (in control over any and all circumstances that come into our life), and is completely good (in character and to us), then we can know that we are safe no matter what. Knowing that enables us to trust Him completely, which brings great joy. We trust God with what happens after death (because He has saved us from hell), and we trust Him with our life before death (because we have determined that He is sovereign and good).

Trusting God with all of our life like this is possible when we truly become intimate with Him. The better we know Him, the more we can trust Him. (We'll look closely at this in chapter seven.) When we trust God, we allow Him to work in us. We trust; God "does." So don't get caught up in trying to do joy. Just trust God first. The Lord will take care of what you entrust to Him. There is great joy in total trust.

Faith

When we trust God and *exercise our faith*. My intent here is not to dive into the deep theological waters of faith, but to look at it as it applies to joy. When we trust someone, we can have faith in him or her. When we trust God, we can exercise our faith in Him. Put simply, faith is absolute and complete belief regardless of proof. Being able to exercise such childlike faith is both the first step of our spiritual life and fundamental to our spiritual growth (see Matthew 18:3,4). Exercising faith as an act of our will is the beginning of our life as Christians. It is what takes us from death to eternal life. Continuing to live and exercise that faith is what growing and maturing is all about. As Hannah Whitall Smith wrote over 100 years ago in *The Christian's Secret of a Happy Life*, "The soul that has discovered this secret of simple faith has found the key that will unlock the whole treasure-house of God."[4] Without faith, there is no lasting joy.

We can learn about faith and trust when we look at our children. My four children have faith in their father and me because they trust us. They know we take care of them and that we are good to them. They also blindly trust us with their future because they know our character and they know we love them. They trust, and we take care of them. They are secure and carefree. My children play freely in my house, not fretting about their next meal or next week's schedule, and I want to be just as carefree and trusting in my heavenly Father's care. You and I can begin to know a life of joy when, like children, we put our total faith in Him because we trust Him with our present and our future.

Indiana Jones shows us how this works in one of his movie adventures. To reach the treasure he's seeking, he must get from one precipice to another but there appears to be no way to cross. Only a steep cliff and imminent death lie between him and the treasure. Yet, mustering up all the faith he has, Indiana attempts the crossing anyway and steps out into the open air. Wondrously, a bridge appears with each step he takes. He looks down, amazed that he's seeing something where there was nothing before his leap of faith. Step by step he makes his way safely across.

That scene is a vivid picture of what the Christian life is all about. And this scene is a call to trust. If you desperately long for a life of joy—the full and abundant life that Christ talked about—go ahead and make the leap of faith into total surrender even if you can't see the path beneath you. It is there.

Yield

When we trust God and exercise our faith, then we can yield ourselves completely. When we yield to oncoming traffic, we give up the right to go where we want to go. We either stay right where we are or we get out of the way to make way for what's coming. We can do the same thing with our life when we yield ourselves—body, soul, and spirit—to God. We can also think of yielding as consecration, complete obedience, and (my favorite) utter abandonment. These words and phrases all mean an entire surrender of our whole self to God. When we do this, we make it possible for God to bless us with His joy.

Why is this sometimes so scary? Many of us are afraid that the minute we say, "OK, God, I'm Yours. I completely surrender to You and Your will," God is going to look down on us and reply, "Aha! Now I've got you where I want you! With which misery shall I start? A mission trip to Africa?" But the truth is that God desires to give us good gifts just as we desire the best for our children. If our children were to tell us that they want to do exactly as we wish, we would not respond, "Great! Now, how hard can I make things for you?" What mother's heart doesn't soar when she sees her child trying exceptionally hard to be obedient? What mother isn't touched when her child shows sweet and complete obedience? I think the heart of God soars with compassion and love for us when we demonstrate that we want to be in total submission to Him. When we surrender ourselves with utter abandonment, we can trust Him. We can know that if He wants us in Africa, He will make Africa our heart's desire.

Furthermore, when we surrender ourselves to God, we are like clay in the hands of a skilled potter. A potter is able to make something beautiful of the clay when the clay is pliable, yielding to his hands, submitting to his touch. He shapes it, scrapes it, turns it, molds it, lets it dry, and puts it in the fire. The clay doesn't try to jump off the potter's wheel or run from the fire. The clay submits. It isn't expected to help the potter in any way; it is merely to remain workable in his hands. As a result, the potter is able to produce something beautiful.

But living in a culture that values doing, we find it a real challenge to merely *be* in God's presence—to *be* the clay in His hands. When we yield to the Master Potter's skillful and loving shaping of us as well as to the firing, the results are a beautiful vessel fit for use in His service. (By the way, whether we are an earthen crock, an everyday mug, or fine bone china depends on how long we are in the fire!)

When we offer our bodies and our minds to God (Romans 12:1,2) without thinking of the cost and we commit ourselves to do whatever God wants, we are yielding ourselves to Him. When we are consecrated (fully obeying Him) and abandoned (completely surrendering our whole being to Him), we are yielded. And when we are yielded to God, we can accept life with its rocks and mountains and shadows and, in the process, experience the beautiful by-product of joy.

But how do we do that? By whatever means we can—and I don't mean that flippantly. Scripture doesn't outline three easy steps for yielding yourself to God. But know that God can use anything in your life to bring you to this place and that He will take you however you come. In her books, Barbara Johnson describes this yielding point in her life as the time she told God, "Whatever, Lord!" Hannah Whitall Smith speaks of "utter abandon" as a means of yielding. Devotional writer Oswald Chambers puts it this way:

> It is a transaction of will, not of sentiment. Tell God you are ready to be offered; then let the consequences

be what they may, there is no strand of complaint, now, no matter what God chooses....Go through the crisis in will, then when it comes externally there will be no thought of the cost....Tell God you are ready to be offered, and God will prove Himself to be all you ever dreamed He would be.[5]

Chambers also explains that to be truly abandoned to God also requires that we not consider the cost beforehand:

Beware of talking about abandonment if you know nothing about it, and you will never know anything about it until you have realized that John 3:16 means that God gave Himself absolutely. In our abandonment we give ourselves over to God just as God gave Himself for us, without any calculation. The consequence of abandonment never enters into our outlook because our life is taken up with Him.

The call to yield to God truly is an invitation to joy. Have you accepted?

For some people who have, yielding to God may happen with a simple prayer in the quiet of life. For others, it may come during a period of pain and darkness. It may happen on the occasion of a life-changing event that you will always remember, or it may result from a prayerful lifestyle. The odd thing about giving everything to God, though, is that we humans have the tendency to keep snatching it back even when we don't want it! We play "hot potato" with our problems and areas of self that we want God to control. But whenever we realize that we're carrying all that around again, we can empty our arms as fast as we can. We must fling it all back to God as often as necessary.

However you want to describe your submission before God—surrender, yielding, consecration, abandonment, or "whatever, Lord"—consider this description from *The Christian's Secret of a Happy Life*:

...an entire surrender of the whole being to God—spirit, soul, and body placed under His absolute control, for

Him to do with us just what He pleases. We mean that the language of our hearts, under all circumstances and in view of every act, is to be "Thy will be done." To a soul ignorant of God, this may look hard, but to those who know Him it is the happiest and most restful of lives.[6]

When we trust God and exercise our faith, then we can yield ourselves completely and experience the by-product of joy. The ability to surrender our whole selves to God with complete trust and childlike faith is the key to possessing the abundant life filled with the fruit and gift of the joy of the Lord.

As we learn to renew our thought life, remember who is the Source of our strength, and rest in God's sovereignty, we begin to see all of life from God's perspective and therefore truly learn the secret of contentment. Gaining this perspective and learning this lesson, however, isn't a one-time event; it's more of a process. It isn't a quick course to be gobbled up and never tasted again. New struggles and temptations will be put on our plates, allowing us to exercise what we've learned. I pray that my responses—and yours—will be savory to the Father as we continue to be nourished at the bounteous table of His Word and teaching, be life bitter or sweet.

The bottom line is, "Do I trust Him?" I think the longer we walk with the Lord, the truer, deeper our joy and contentment become because we are so acquainted with His faithfulness.

~Kellie M.

~❧ Part Two ❧~

Cultivating Joy and Contentment in Our Hearts
What We Feel

~❧ 6 ❧~

How Can I Be Joyful When I Feel Like a Grump?

Where We Start When the Feelings Won't

Well, that's just great," you may be thinking. "I've made the choice to rejoice. I'm taming that monster of discontent, and I've chosen joy. But I still feel like an irritated junkyard dog—cranky and at the end of her rope." Maybe a birthday card a friend of mine received would be appropriate for you. It said, "I searched all day to find a birthday gift that matches your personality...but nobody carried a pit bull in high heels![1] Maybe you're a pit bull, or maybe you're a teddy bear that's happened to dehibernate. Some days, even the most gentle of us are cross. Sometimes we just don't feel joy in our heart.

Unfortunately, even if we choose joy and contentment in our heads, feeling it in our hearts isn't automatic. Although feelings often do follow actions (as we've talked about), they don't necessarily follow our thoughts. Just because we decide to choose joy—to change what we think, to see life from God's perspective, and to learn to think God's thoughts—doesn't mean we will immediately feel joyful, and that can be so frustrating. That is why many of us when we hear "happiness is a choice" advice and songs like "I Choose Joy" on the radio scoff, "Oh, yeah? I did, too, but it doesn't work!" Sometimes it doesn't work because we stop at the point of making a choice. We say, "OK, I choose." Period. Then we wait for some kind of magic to work in us—an instantaneous transformation from pit bull to pleasant puppy. But joy is not the result of magic. Besides, we must not expect that our choice to rejoice will make us laughing hyenas or playful otters if that is not our nature. Instead, we need to say, "I choose joy. Now what's next?" Don't stop with the choice; proceed from choosing joy in the mind to cultivating joy in the heart!

If you expect change to come simply because you've made the choice to rejoice, if you expect your behavior and your feelings to immediately follow suit, you will probably be disappointed. Often we can act our way into a feeling (and we can usually do that more easily than we can feel our way into an action), but we should not depend on this method for attaining real joy. We can't assume that once we begin to act as if we're joyful, joy will follow and will last over the long haul. Oh, we may know joy for a time with that "act first" method, but the charade will wear thin, then so will our disposition, and, if we're not careful, even our faith. To say that if we just change our behavior we will grow spiritually and emotionally is really a false assumption, as Doctors Henry Cloud and John Townsend say in their book *False Assumptions: Twelve "Christian" Beliefs That Can Drive You Crazy*. What, then, are we to do? They say this:

> The Bible presents an answer. Instead of attempting to fix our symptoms, we can actively take ourselves to good nutrients. Just as a tree planted in rich soil can flourish, so can we expose ourselves to God's healing resources.
>
> The only behavior we can practice that will move us to emotional and spiritual adulthood is picking ourselves up and taking ourselves to good nutrients— that is, to God and his people.[2]

In other words, we can't know lasting joy by finding an action that produces that feeling and trying to continue that action. We can only truly know joy by accessing the real Source of joy—which is God Himself.

"But didn't you just say, not too many pages back, that I'm supposed to *choose* joy?" you might ask. Yes, yes, yes—and then go straight to the heart. A person can't become joyful by an act of will alone any more than an alcoholic can simply stop drinking or a depressed person can cheer up just by deciding to do so. You and I must first choose joy in our head and then cultivate it in our heart. Although the will is quite powerful, real change must occur within the heart. Ultimately living a life of joy will be the result of inward change, not the other way around. Inward change does not come simply with new behaviors. Sustaining power to change is based on God above and not merely on our will within.

I've realized that from being in that certain spot between pit bull and otter, wanting desperately to splash in the joy instead of growling in the pit, yet realizing that the metamorphosis wasn't happening. I was trying to jump into the joy with my pit bull self and ended up all wet and a little bit mad. No, a pit bull can't swim like an otter (although I bet that would be quite interesting to watch, as perhaps I was). Nor can a pitbull change itself into an otter. But, unlike that pit bull, you and I are not destined to remain in the doghouse growling at the world and chewing on bones. We can live in peace and feast on the fruit of the joy of the Lord, but first we must let Him transform our heart.

I remember all too well what it feels like to be in that place of wanting to be the otter, of longing to feel "splashes of joy in the cesspools of life," as Barbara Johnson puts it in the title of her book. Sometimes we want more than anything else to know joy, but wanting it and finding it can seem worlds apart. But the goal is not light-years away; the distance between wanting and finding joy is

Fixing our eyes on Jesus, the author and perfecter of faith, who for the joy set before Him endured the cross,...

~Hebrews 12:2a

Imagine the joy that's awaiting us!

actually a little journey—a journey of the heart in our walk of faith. How can we be joyful when we feel grumpy, and where do we start when the feelings won't? Start with seeking the Source.

Seeking the Source

A young child stood close to his mother, clinging to her skirt as he watched a group of children tearing into beautifully wrapped presents. They were squealing with delight as they each opened their package. The little child, obviously not part of the celebration, looked longingly at the joyful children. Then he looked around to see where these lucky children had gotten their presents. He left his mother's side and wandered for quite some time around the room, hoping that the person who had blessed these children would think he was part of the party and bless him with a package. Finally he spotted the giver and ran to tell his mother. "Mother, look at all those presents! It looks like such fun! I'm going to go get one, too," he said expectantly. "No, child, you aren't," replied his mother. "Although you've found the giver, you may not get a gift from him. You don't know him."

And so it is with us sometimes. We desperately want the gift of joy, but we look in the wrong places. Like the child searching the room to find out where the children got their gifts, we search for joy by filling our schedules and lives and minds with things that we hope will lead us to that gift. We pursue this job and that hobby or sport and crowd our lives with various activities in an attempt to find joy. We think that marrying this guy, having this child, taking this job, pursuing this ministry, or buying this thing will finally bring us joy, and when we miss the sparkle we are dumbfounded. We are like that child searching for the source of the gift and, initially, coming up short.

Oh, many of our pursuits are wonderful, and they bring us great happiness and, yes, even some joy. But when we look to them as the source of our joy, we will eventually be disappointed. Our mate will let us down, our child will make a wrong choice, the job will not work out, the ministry will become difficult, the thing we bought will lose its luster. Then we will see only the rocks in life and none of the sparkle. The things that fill our lives certainly can and do add sparkle, but we must know that they are not the true source. The only real source of our joy is Jesus Christ. When we have trusted Him for our salvation and are in relationship with Him as our Lord, we have access to the wellspring of joy. We aren't limited to playing in the spring; we can drink from its very source! Jesus said, "If any man is thirsty, let him come to Me and drink. He who believes in Me, as the Scripture said, 'From his innermost being shall flow rivers of living water'" (John 7:37,38). He also said, "I am the bread of life; he who comes to Me shall not hunger, and he who believes in Me shall never thirst" (John 6:35). Not only will we not thirst, but the water that Jesus offers us "shall become in [us] a well of water springing up to eternal life" (John 4:14).

Just as the mother might ask the child who wants a present, "Do you know the giver?" I need to ask you if you know the Giver. Some of you may have never made the choice to get to know the Giver of eternal life and joy and to trust Him as your Savior and Lord. If you want assurance of eternal life and the incredible joy that comes from knowing Jesus Christ, put your faith in Him. Simply acknowledge that He is the Son of God, that He died on the cross as payment for your sins, and that He rose again, defeating death and the power of Satan. Then, having made that basic confession of faith— having chosen by an act of will to believe this wondrous truth—choose to pursue a relationship with Him. In other words, act on the promise we find in the gospel of John: "As many as received Him, to them He gave the right to become children of God, even to those who believe in His name" (John 1:12). And, as His child, you will spend eternity with God. Knowing that your eternal destiny is taken care of is a source of great joy, as the apostle Peter explains:

> Though you have not seen Him, you love Him, and though you do not see Him now, but believe in Him, you greatly rejoice with joy inexpressible and full of glory, obtaining as the outcome of your faith the salvation of your souls (1 Peter 1:8,9).

Or, perhaps you made the faith decision years ago, but you've never developed much of a relationship *with* God. Please know that it's never too late to start. God desires a relationship with you! Do you know Him, friend?

Now, you may have made these choices and have been a Christian for many years, but perhaps your joy stops with the knowledge that you are saved. Maybe you've thought, "Yes, I have joy knowing that God has saved me, but my problems far outweigh my joy." Oh, listen, dear reader. Joy is meant to be so much more than gratitude to God for making a way for us to escape hell. He also wants us—through His joy—to be free of the things of this earth that bind us up, whatever they are. We miss this joy and its accompanying freedom because we, like the little child, search for the Giver of the gifts and, not finding Him, look to external things to provide our joy. We miss that joy for another reason, too.

Sometimes we are like the child after he has found the giver. We ask for the gift, but we are asking someone we don't know. We know who the Source is, but we don't know Him well. And we don't receive gifts from strangers any more than the child receives a gift at the party where he doesn't know the host. Instead, gifts come from those people whom we know well. The gifts that mean the most to us are from those whom we know and love. How well do you know the Giver of Joy? How much do you love Him? *To receive the gift of joy, become intimate with the Giver.*

Enter His Presence

The only way to become intimate with someone is to spend time with that person, and this principle is true for God. Not only can we become more intimately acquainted with God when we spend time with Him, but we will also find joy when we are in His presence. "Splendor and majesty are before Him, strength and joy are in His place" (1 Chronicles 16:27).

Other versions of the Bible say instead that there is "joy in his dwelling place" (NIV). Would you like more than just your everyday joy? Would you like your joy cup full? Then enter into the presence of God, for, as David proclaimed in a song, "In [God's] presence is fulness of joy; in [His] right hand there are pleasures forever" (Psalm 16:11). There is indeed great joy in dwelling with God, as the psalmist knew when he wrote, "How lovely are Thy dwelling places, O LORD of hosts! My soul longed and even yearned for the courts of the LORD; my heart and my flesh sing for joy to the living God" (Psalm 84:1,2).

Are you there, dear reader? Does your heart sing for joy to God? Does your soul long for His courts? If so, then you know the joy of which I speak. You can join the psalmist in exulting, "How lovely are Thy dwelling places!" But what if you can't say that? What if all your heart and flesh long for right now is a little more sleep or freedom from pain or an end to the quarrels? In times like these, the dwelling place of God seems far off and very much out of reach. How can we possibly enter His presence when just getting through each day is a struggle?

And then, making the experience of joy seem even more unreachable, we are often victims of our culture: We are a people more interested in "seven steps to joy" than in learning how to live in the presence of God. Too often we want quick applications and simple how-to's rather than learning gradually how to truly experience all that God has for us. Titles like *Quick Tips for...*, *Secrets of Success in...*, and *Ten Ways to Instantly...* jump from the covers of magazines and books and fill the broadcast airwaves, offering ideas for how to solve our problems and satisfy our society that wants instant everything. We want a fulfilling marriage—tonight. We want to end our depression—today. We want and need answers to our troubles, but those answers won't always come with a ten-easy-steps approach. When we go for the quick fix, we often wind up with less depth. Finding true joy is no exception. Happi-

By your own deliberate choice, by an act of your will, develop the holy habit of being consciously aware of Him and drawing on Him.

~Ray and Anne Ortlund,
In His Presence

ness is a quick fix—nice, but temporary and undependable. Joy is different.

So I offer you no simple, quick steps to joy. Instead, I offer you my hand (in my heart, I can hold yours if you are hurting and longing for the joy of the Lord), and I say to you, "Yes, the joy is there and it is available to you! The Father longs for you to enter His presence and to bless you with His joy!" I also stretch out my hand to point you to the Way, to Jesus Christ Himself. I am pointing to His presence: "Jesus said to him, 'I am the way, and the truth, and the life; no one comes to the Father, but through Me'"(John 14:6).

Entering that presence, that dwelling place of the Lord, is not a specific, isolated experience. We don't, for instance, enter His presence only when we enter and worship in a church. Furthermore, we don't learn to enter His presence just during our quiet time. We need not be at a certain place, at a certain age, or in just the right circumstances to be in His presence. Through His blood shed on the cross, Jesus made a way for us to continually enter His presence (Hebrews 10:19), to learn to live in His presence—something Old Testament saints couldn't do (Leviticus 1:3; 1 Samuel 6:19,20). We are the dwelling place of God; we are the temple (1 Corinthians 6:19). Unfortunately, sick children, financial pressures, quibbling family members, scary medical test results, and a multitude of other problems and everyday circumstances can keep us from being in and sensing His presence.

"Yes, that's me," you may say. "How do I live in His presence when my life is so demanding. And just what in the world does 'living in His presence' mean anyway? How can I do that when I feel so unspiritual?"

I'm continually learning more and more about what "living in His presence" means in my life (and I don't mean theological learning). For me, living in God's presence is having a constant awareness of His love and presence in my daily life—in the sick kids, work pressures, dirty dishes, and everything else. He cares about it all, and He is in it all. I have learned, for instance, that I can enter into the presence of God while washing dishes or rocking a child in the night just as easily as I can when I'm worshiping in a cathedral. If I wait until I feel particularly "spiritual" to enter His presence, I may never even bother! But when I acknowledge His presence with me while I'm scrubbing the tub or buying broccoli or writing a book or doing whatever, I am practicing His presence in every part of my life, something Brother Lawrence describes in *The Practice of the Presence of God*:

> Attention to God was to be not just a slot of time every day, but all day long, every day. His presence was to permeate everything. We would commit ourselves to do everything for the love of God, in simple rest and without fear.
>
> We would seek to live as if absolutely nothing mattered except loving God, pleasing God, trusting God....
>
> The psalmists had sung to God, and so would we, "I am always with you; you hold me by my right hand" (Psalm 73:23).[3]

Read those words again and consider how close God is to you. These simple statements of Brother Lawrence changed Ray and Anne Ortlund, as they explain in their wonderful book *In His Presence*. When they were first learning this truth and making it a habit in their lives, they held each other accountable for practicing the presence of God, and they worked on it in very practical ways. Ray, for instance, set his wristwatch alarm to go off every 15 minutes as a reminder to think of God. He also put self-stick notes on his desk, mirror, and car with the letters "PTP" for "Practice the Presence." Anne put a paper with the word "JESUS" written on it on the floor beside her bed to remind her to begin her day by worshiping Him. The Ortlunds write that "the most important thing one person (or couple) can do for another is to bring him (or her) into the presence of God, and leave him there!...Living in His presence is the secret to living."[4]

Truly, I am just beginning to learn this secret and live this wonderful, life-changing truth. I am not writing to you as one who has reached that goal, but as one who struggles (as you may) but who is beginning to see how exciting it is to live in God's presence. I remember the day, before I had even thought about the phrase "practice His presence," that this principle first became real to me. I was at a time-management seminar led by a woman who explained that she had gotten very little sleep the night before due to a sick child. I was about to feel sorry for her *(That poor woman only got a few hours sleep and has to get up and speak all day),* but that thought went no further. She continued: "But I don't mind. In fact, I count it a privilege to have the pleasure of rocking a child in the wee hours of the morning, holding him, singing to him, wrapped in the presence of the Lord." I scarcely remember anything else she said that day because God spoke so clearly to my heart through those few, simple words and her attitude. I thought about what my attitude might have been: *Can you believe it? That child threw up all night and insisted on me rocking him. I only got a few hours of sleep and look at all I've got to do today!* Instead, this gracious woman pointed out that our difficulties can in fact be blessings because God is present in them. Even in the simple and not especially "spiritual" act of rocking a child we can be in His presence!

The seed the woman planted that day is continuing to grow deep roots. I am learning to choose to remember God in the routine and mundane moments of my day. I am learning that the phrase "abide in Christ" is much more than Christianese, that it is relevant to me in the car pool line and in traffic as well as in church. Abiding in Christ is a lifestyle that grows out of my growth in Him and my realization of His great love for me. It is a way of life that can be chosen and practiced. It is a way of life that brings great joy.

I have so much to learn about this way of thinking and living. It sounds simple, but its impact on us can be profound, as the Ortlunds describe in their book. They talk about how the great love the Father has for us can draw us into a life lived in the love of the One who loves us completely. They also caution:

> Please hear us carefully! "Practicing God's presence," unless it flows out of the nourishing, deep-rooted truths of our Christian faith, becomes purely experiential, shallow, and eventually silly.
>
> What you believe about God—your theology—is what shapes and defines the real you. More than what how-to seminars teach you (although they can be helpful), how you behave in marriage, raise children, and generally function as a person *will flow out of your knowledge of God and your life with Him.*[5]

We behave how we behave because we believe how we believe. It is that knowledge of God and our life with Him that I want to turn to next—our life as part of the vine.

The Vine Life

I remember the first time Tim and I ever experimented with gardening. We lived in a suburban neighborhood with a postage-sized backyard, but we wanted to do our share of tilling the earth. The first garden was actually his; I just got to help. And I'm glad he gets the credit because, in spite of his efforts, about the only thing that little plot produced was okra trees. We didn't just grow your average suburban tomato. We grew giant foliage, elephant ear-sized plants peering over our fence. My friend Donna commented, "I've seen a lot of gardens, but I've never seen okra trees." It was rather fun, if not a little humiliating. We got exactly half a bowl of okra from those enormous plants—enough for everyone in the family to have three fried okras. But that garden bore more than those okra. You see, I learned much from that little plot. Things I'd read and heard about vine-life living took root in my heart more deeply as I watched actual vine life unfold before me.

As I watched that garden grow, so did my fondness for John 15, that "vine life" chapter which describes so plainly our relationship to Christ. Those familiar words came to life as I watched our garden. I saw why Christ referred to growing things to teach so many lessons. Jesus says, for instance, "I am the true vine, and My Father is the vinedresser" (John 15:1). As I looked at our okra trees and the other more normal vegetation, I thought of God as my Master Gardener—and kept reading. Jesus continues, "Every branch in Me that does not bear fruit, He takes away; and every branch that bears fruit, He prunes it, that it may bear more fruit" (verse 2). I looked at the pile of recently pruned foliage that had been keeping the plant from producing more okra. "Abide in Me, and I in you. As the branch cannot bear fruit of itself, unless it abides in the vine, so neither can you, unless you abide in Me," Jesus teaches in verse 4. I got up close and personal with the vines in our garden. The branches were not merely attached or temporarily connected to that vine—they were part of the vine; they were grafted to it. I began to wonder,

Am I merely attached or am I grafted to Him? Abiding began to take on new meaning for me.

My favorite part of that passage of Scripture—and the basis of this book—is verse 11 when Jesus says, "These things I have spoken to you, that My joy may be in you, and that your joy may be made full." That's the reason Christ tells us about the vine life. He wants us to have His joy, and He wants that joy to be full! We are to live the vine life abiding in Christ so that we can yield the fruit of His joy! He doesn't tell us to abide in Christ so that we will be good Christians. He doesn't tell us to be part of the vine, willing to be pruned and abiding in His love, just because He says so. He lovingly tells us the reason for His call to abide in Him ("these things I have spoken to you") because He desires that we have incredible joy, His joy ("that My joy may be in you"). He doesn't stop at telling us we can have His joy (what a gift in itself!), but He tells us we can have gobs of it ("that your joy may be made full").

Vine life is about abiding in God's love, keeping His commandments, allowing Him to prune us, and bearing fruit for the kingdom. Joy is some of that fruit. Living the vine life is the foundation for joy. So often I had read that section of Scripture and focused only on the abiding, pruning, and bearing fruit. It hadn't sunk in that the reason Jesus tells us about the vine life in the first place is so that we can live with His abundant joy within us. Lots of joy! A fullness of joy! Knowing His joy is important to Jesus, as you can see from John 15. Never doubt that He wants you to have His joy. Never side with the philosophers and nay-sayers who suggest that joyful living is selfish. Read Christ's words for yourself. He wants you to live a life of joy, and you can do that by abiding in Him!

> *It is impossible for us really to live in Jesus, as a branch in a vine, and not have His joy flowing into us.*
>
> ~Colleen Townsend Evans,
> *The Vine Life*

～7～

Three Powerful P's

Becoming Intimate with the Gift-Giver

T he most formidable task of relocating is not unpacking a household of belongings; it's reconnecting. After we moved back to this part of Texas, my family and I faced that task again. Although I'm no stranger to moving (I've moved 24 times since birth), putting down new roots and developing friendships still takes time.

One month after we moved here, Tim and I were in a hotel lobby and I noticed a group of women with cute name tags who looked like they were really enjoying themselves. "I'll bet they're a church group," I told Tim. "In fact, they look like a group I could fit in with." But I never found out who they were. Later, we joined a church in our area, and a year-and-a-half after that I made plans to go on their women's retreat. One woman said to me, "This year we're going to the country."

"Where have you usually met?" I asked.

"At a hotel," she replied.

"At the same time of year?" I asked.

She nodded.

"Which hotel?" I continued.

She told me and, amazingly, my new church friends were the

131

same joyful women I'd observed in that hotel lobby a year-and-a-half before.

By now, my roots are deeper. God has blessed me with friendships and the joy of a couple of kindred spirits. Moving from observation...to acquaintance...to friendship...to kindred spirit—these are heartwarming moves. When we leave the casual, superficial realms of a relationship and begin to enter into intimate soul territory, the bond takes on a new value, for these relationships are rare. It is sweet when an acquaintance becomes a friend and a friend becomes a kindred spirit. When someone we love becomes our soulmate rather than just the object of our love, we have a precious treasure indeed, for soul-territory is where we are touched at our deepest level—the fiber of our being. Likewise, when we leave behind a casual, superficial, "religious" relationship with God and enter into soul-territory, we become intimate with the Giver of joy.

In the last two chapters, we've looked at the importance of knowing God's thoughts, renewing our mind, seeing His perspective, and abiding in and yielding to Him. *The extent to which we can do these things is a significant indicator of the extent of the joy we will know, for at this soul-spot the truest, deepest, most pervasive joy occurs.* The only way to know such profound joy is to get to know God in a deep and intimate way. As I point to three powerful P's for becoming intimate with the Gift-Giver, let me encourage you to read with your heart. Although these activities are probably familiar to you, ask God to show you the unfamiliar in them—the place where you may perhaps move from the casual to the intimate, from the surface to the soul.

The three P's for becoming intimate with God are:

1. Poring over His Word
2. Praising Him
3. Praying to Him

Doing these three P's will enable us to abide more deeply in Him, enhance the ease and frequency with which we enter His presence, and increase our ability to think His thoughts. The time we spend with God in these ways does indeed bear the fruit of His joy in our lives.

1. *Poring Over God's Word*

If you want to hear from someone who truly loves God's Word, read Psalm 119. The longest chapter in the Bible, this acrostic psalm (the writer devotes eight lines to each letter of the Hebrew alphabet) praises the Scriptures; and all but four of its 176 verses mention the Word of God (law, testimonies, statutes, and so on). If we are to live a life of joy, we cannot neglect the Scripture. As we see in this psalm, God's Word not only brings us joy, but it is to *be* our joy. As the psalmist says, "I have inherited Thy testimonies forever, for they are the joy of my heart" (Psalm 119:111) and "I rejoice at Thy word" (verse 162).

Besides bringing joy, God's Word is able to convict, correct, confirm, and train in righteousness (2 Timothy 3:16). Through His Word, we come to know Him as well as His will for us (Psalm 40:8); the Creator of the universe reveals Himself to us through His Word. If we don't read it, we can't really know Him. If we read it a little, we will only know Him a little. If we want to renew our minds—if we want to change our perspective, our thinking, and our attitude—we must learn to think God's thoughts and apply them to our lives. The only way to do that is to read in His Word what His thoughts are, meditate on them, and let His Spirit make them a part of us. As Bible commentator Henry H. Halley says,

> We read the Bible frequently and regularly, so that God's thoughts may be frequently and regularly in our minds; that His thoughts may become our thoughts; that our ideas may become conformed to God's ideas. To run God's thoughts through our mind often will make our mind grow like God's mind; and as our mind grows like God's mind, our whole life will be transformed into His image. It is one of the very best spiritual helps we can have.[1]

And that help is available to each one of us.

Our fountain of joy, the foundation of an abundant life, a handbook for living, our refreshment when we need to be revived, the hope of victory over sin, a source of wisdom, an avenue of fellowship with Christ, nourishment for our spirit—the

Bible is all this and more. So why is it that, all too often, we let this food get a little dusty until it is no longer appetizing? We know we should be reading His Word, but we don't. Or we don't read it consistently. We just nibble here and there, never fully tasting its flavor or truly getting nourished as He intends. This is probably one of the biggest guilt trips that we Christians take: "I know I should, but I'm not reading the Bible regularly. When will I ever get consistent?"

How do we stir our heart to hunger for God's Word? By feeding it! You know how it works in your physical body. You develop an appetite by exercising and eating regularly. Exercise strengthens our muscles (if we don't use a muscle it can atrophy) and makes us hungry. Eating fills us for a time, but then we get hungry again. In fact, we train our body to want food when we feed it regularly. I know because I've frequently been a breakfast skipper. I could go until early afternoon without eating when I was busy because my body was used to going that long without food. But when I began to eat breakfast regularly, I began to get hungry in the morning. I was amazed when, after a short time of making myself eat in the morning, I began to wake up hungry (a new experience for me). Just as we can train our bodies to be hungry, we can also turn off that hunger. As odd as it sounds, if we fast, we begin to lose our hunger pangs after an initial time of hunger.

And so it is in our spiritual body. When we regularly feed it the nourishing food of God's Word and exercise our spiritual muscles, we train our spiritual body to want more food. We develop in our spirit a craving for God's Word, and we learn to depend on it for sustenance. The opposite is true as well. We can lose our hunger for God's Word. If we fast too long—if we don't

> *If God's Word in your life is limited to a weekly 30-minute sermon, you won't have joy in the Christian life.*
>
> ~Dave Anderson,
> *Pastor,*
> *Faith Community Church,*
> *The Woodlands, TX*

open up that cover and spend time with the Lord—we won't feel hunger for that time with Him.

But regular nibbling doesn't make a dry meal a banquet, and maybe you're not finding Scripture a feast right now. That was the case for my friend Martha. She called me one day and began to tell me how she had little joy in her life. She said, "Don't try to tell me to just read my Bible. I do that almost every day and I still don't have joy. It's just so...dry." Being too busy to consistently read God's Word makes for spiritual dryness. We can't strengthen our spiritual bodies or develop a hunger for God's Word with a hit-and-miss approach of just a few minutes a day. Reading with no purpose further contributes to the feeling that this holy food has lost its flavor. Nibbling here and there without any direction in our reading deadens our taste buds for this spiritual nourishment.

For real spiritual growth to occur and our hunger for the Scriptures to be stoked, we must read consistently and with a plan. Any plan will do. Choose whatever suits you. Many Bible scholars recommend reading the Bible through in a year, and many churches and devotionals have suggestions for a reading schedule to accomplish this. Others suggest reading a book at a time or reading chronologically. It doesn't matter what your plan is—just have one! And trust the Holy Spirit to be your teacher, for "His anointing teaches you about all things" (1 John 2:27).

Also, try reading with a pen and notebook in hand to record your thoughts, insights, and questions for God, as well as your impressions of what He is saying to you. Add study materials (a concordance, Bible dictionary, or commentary) to this time of reading, take notes on what you read, and the material begins to become yours. It doesn't go just into your head; it has a chance to stay in your heart. When you go a step further and keep your notebooks or—for you more organized women—file your notes by Bible book or subject, you can go back and review what you learn. You can see where you were spiritually at a given time, and you may even be ready to teach others what God has taught you. In fact, when we study anything under the premise that we are sometime going to teach it (whether to a Sunday school class or our own kids), we retain much more. So try that approach in your study.

"Wait just a minute! How do you possibly expect me to do that?" some of you may be asking. "I have a young family, and

I scarcely find the time to get dressed every day!" Keep in mind that there are seasons of our lives. If you are in a "baby season," you may not be able to sit down every day for in-depth study. But even in the read-whenever-you-can times we can still read with a purpose. Try grabbing a few verses while you dry your hair (as a friend of mine did when her children were young), catch a few more verses during nap time, listen to Bible tapes in the car, or carry a pocket Bible in your purse for unexpected quiet moments. You and I can make time for what is important to us. Reading God's Word as purposefully and as regularly as possible—and applying what you find there—can change your life.

Yet there are times when Bible study feels more like just another "should" on the to-do list. Sometimes, and for some people (maybe you right now), reading God's Word is done merely out of a sense of duty, a sense of discipline rather than desire. If that's where you are right now, that's okay. At least start there. But if you find you don't move beyond duty to desire—to the point where you want to read God's Word—perhaps you're just reading it instead of studying it. The deeper you dig into the Word, the deeper you find yourself in soul-territory and the more compelled you are to return there. So, again, begin with prayer every time you read the Bible; ask the Holy Spirit to teach you as you try to get beyond the surface to the substance. If the desire is still lacking, you need to take this matter to the Lord in prayer and, perhaps, repentance. Sometimes we need to say, "Lord, my heart's not in it. Forgive me—and please develop in me a heart that hungers for You and Your Word." God wants our devotion, not just our discipline; He wants a heart that hungers for Him. Spending time in God's Word—starting, perhaps, as a mere discipline and moving to times of deep study—and going before Him with an open heart will help develop within you that hunger and devotion.

Consider the devotion of George Muller, the man of faith who founded many orphanages in England: "I believe that the one chief reason that I have been kept in happy useful service is that I have been a lover of Holy Scripture. It has been my habit to read the Bible through four times a year; in a prayerful spirit, to apply it to my heart, and practice what I find there. I have been for sixty-nine years a happy man."[2] Whether you read through the Bible four times a year (!), once a year, or once every 20 years, just read it! God's Word—read and obeyed—is the fountain of joy and the path to knowing Him.

2. *Praising God*

When we study God's Word and begin to get a glimpse of who He is and what He has done for us, we cannot help but praise Him. He has given us the ability to praise, and His Word is full of commands to do just that. (The call to praise God appears more than any other command in the Old Testament.) The more we know God, the more we will want to praise Him— and I'm not talking praise in a "religious" way, that semiautomatic, robotic uttering of "Praise the Lord" in response to a sermon or testimony. Praise is not something we do just in church when we are feeling particularly spiritual. We need not be able to play an instrument, have a great voice, or be a spiritual giant. We can praise God whoever and wherever we are simply because of who God is and His great love for us.

Furthermore, praise is one thing we can do that will shift our focus from ourselves and our problems to God. Have you ever been in a situation that is overwhelming? The daily grind, the busy but barren, the painful, or the disappointing days have you focused on your problems. You try to focus on the Lord, but your attitude and perspective don't change. Scripture gives us an antidote. It's praise. When we praise God, we turn our focus to who He is and what He has done for us ("He is your praise and He is your God, who has done these great and awesome things for you which your eyes have seen" [Deuteronomy 10:21]). The psalmist models when we are to praise God: "I will bless the LORD at all times; His praise shall continually be in my mouth. My soul shall make its boast in the LORD" (Psalm 34:1,2). When we look to God like this, our attitude can't help but improve. As Myrna Alexander says in *Behold Your God*,

> Praise keeps the character of God before our minds. The practice of praise forces us to relate God's character to the issues of life. The effect of praising God on our mental attitude is liberating, for praise focuses our attention on the person and work of God....Praise leads you to behold your God![3]

So what does praising God look like?

Myrna Alexander says we can praise God by describing His character and attributes and by declaring what He has done for us or in a particular situation. We can tell Him or others how awesome we think He is because of His many attributes (descriptive praise), and we can tell Him or others how blessed we are because of something He has done (declarative praise).[4] We can also praise God descriptively and declaratively with our songs. Singing alone for His ears (and our edification), we can praise Him for His character and His deeds, or we can bless others with our praise in song. (In my case, that wouldn't be much of a blessing so be glad I'm writing this and not trying to express myself on a CD!) Whether your praise is descriptive or declarative, to God alone or to others, follow the example of the psalmist who wrote, "I will give thanks to the LORD with all my heart; I will tell of all Thy wonders. I will be glad and exult in Thee; I will sing praise to Thy name, O Most High" (Psalm 9:1,2).

The psalms are an excellent place to go to learn how to praise God. Called in Hebrew the "Book of Praise," Psalms is filled with expressions of praise and commands to praise. Intended to be set to music and sung in worship, these poems were written as songs of devotion and trust in God. We see in some psalms that David could not be stopped from praising God whether his circumstances were causing him joy or anguish. One commentary describes David's attitude:

> David literally LIVED IN GOD. "Praise" was always on his lips. David was always asking God for something, and always thanking Him with his whole soul for the answers to his prayers.
>
> "Rejoice" is another favorite word. David's unceasing troubles could never dim his joy in God. Over and over he cried, "Sing," "Shout for Joy."[5]

The ultimate psalm of praise is the last one, Psalm 150. Here we are called to praise God for "His mighty deeds" (what He's done for us) and "excellent greatness" (His character). We can praise with trumpet, harp, lyre, tambourine, dancing, stringed instruments, pipe, and loud, resounding cymbals. In case that list leaves anyone out, the psalmist adds, "Let every-thing that has breath praise the LORD. Praise the LORD!" (verse 6). That pretty much covers it!

David knew the importance of music in praising God. He wrote, "Stringed instruments have made Thee glad" (Psalm 45:8) and, my favorite, "Sing for joy in the LORD, O you righteous ones; praise is becoming to the upright" (Psalm 33:1). If your joy is wan-ing, take the advice of David and follow the many admonitions in Scripture and sing! Praise and singing lead to joy—even when we don't feel at all joyful. I know from experience.

When I was in college, I worked with a campus ministry in Hawaii for a summer. Friends and family had fun giving me grief about suffering for Jesus in that land of sunshine, beaches, and pineapples. To some, my assignment looked like Utopia, but in many ways it was a very difficult summer. To earn my keep, I opened oysters for tourists looking for pearls and cleaned houses before landing an office job as a receptionist. My em-ployers were seldom there, so I was alone much of the time in that cold, dark, windowless office. (There's that "cave" scenario again. I think God's been trying to teach me something about my source of light for a long time!) I hated what I was doing as well as my work-week environment, so I had to seek my joy to-tally in the Lord. I always went to work early and sat in an outer office that had a wall of windows facing a beautiful mountain. There I would have my quiet time with God.

One morning the sunrise was particularly spectacular, and I began to sing, "[Lord,] in the morning will I direct my prayer unto thee, and will look up" (Psalm 5:3 KJV). Do you know what that did for me? Suddenly I was filled with joy! Indescribable joy! Tears came to my eyes as I watched the beauty God unfolded before me that morning and felt His joy descend on me as a gift. I sang my psalm of thanksgiving (as Psalms 81 and 95 describe) and became, just as His word promises, joyous! That time of praising God carried me through the long, lonely workday. Throughout the day, I hummed just a bit of that song in my mind, and the Lord comforted me with the remembrance of that special time with Him. Even now, the memory of that morning and the words of that song bring me great joy. When we praise God, we are transported from our circumstances, from our thought life with its limitations and burdens, to the very presence of God. Our focus shifts to His greatness. The praise corrects our perspective and the singing bypasses our minds, cutting straight to our heart and producing wonderful joy! Praise truly is a gift from the Father!

God knew, however, that mountaintop experiences like that would not be the norm for us. We are told to praise Him continually, but sometimes our spirits will not soar. We may try our best to get above our circumstances, but all we can think about is our problems. We don't feel like praising the Lord, let alone singing to Him. It is for moments like those that God gives us this instruction: "Through Him then, let us continually offer up a sacrifice of praise to God, that is, the fruit of lips that give thanks to His name" (Hebrews 13:15). When we don't feel like praising God, we are to offer it up anyway, in spite of our feelings, as our sacrifice of praise to Him.

A few years ago I was doing dishes and, for no particular reason, I was feeling down. My heart was heavy, and I didn't feel joy. I knew in my head that I should probably praise God, but I didn't feel like doing it. I wiped the bubbles off my hands and turned on a tape of praise music. *There. Praise.* But I immediately knew in my heart that the sounds filling my kitchen were someone else's expression of praise. It wasn't my own. I knew *I* had to praise. *But, Lord, I don't feel like it.* The sense I should be praising Him wouldn't go away. *Okay, Lord, but it's certainly going to fall into the "sacrifice" category.* Softly and without feeling, I began to sing with the tape. Then, still singing, I got involved with my dishes and by the time I had finished the last dirty plate, my sacrifice of praise had yielded the fruit of joy! *What a great trick I just played on my emotions. God's Word is so true!* And I went to my Bible and turned to this passage:

> O come, let us sing for joy to the LORD;
> Let us shout joyfully to the rock of our salvation.
> Let us come before His presence with thanksgiving;
> Let us shout joyfully to Him with psalms
>
> — (Psalm 95:1,2).

I highlighted these words in pink and circled the one *joy* and two *joyfully's.* What a simple act my praise had been! My singing was just an everyday occurrence in my kitchen, but our faithful God is always so sweet to meet us right where we are. He met me with my hands in dishwater and my spirits in the dumps, and He showed me that He is pleased even when praise is a sacrifice.

You and I can praise God anytime, anywhere, and in many ways. Our praise can come in a quiet moment of intimate adoration, a silent offering to God in church. It can be in a fun song with our children as we dance around the living room. We can praise God as we sing in the shower or with a tape in the car. We can occasionally even cut loose as David did (2 Samuel 6)! (Just watch out for your Michal, the person who—like David's wife—might be embarrassed by demonstrative expressions of praise!) You and I can cut loose to yell, cheer, scream, and express our enthusiasm at sporting events, parades, concerts, and the like, so why don't we do so in our personal praise to God?

My favorite time to cut loose is in the morning. Sometimes, before anyone's up, I put on my headphones and a praise tape while I exercise. For me, that's a wonderful way to praise the Lord with all my heart and all my body! I remember the first time I really "got into it" as I exercised. Before I knew it, my exercise was simply an expression of my praise for God as I abandoned my self-consciousness. (No one was even looking!) If we can go to jazzercise, why don't we dance before the Lord, as Scripture says, in our private moments? God's Word also tells us to "clap your hands, all peoples; shout to God with the voice of joy!" (Psalm 47:1). We are to "sing for joy" and "shout joyfully to the God of Jacob" (Psalm 81:1). Like the children's song goes, "If you want joy you must sing for it...clap for it..." Even the most timid Christian can find a way to privately sing, shout, or even dance(!) before the Lord in praise. Whether you praise with hair-flying, limb-moving exuberance or with a soft stanza of "This Is the Day That the Lord Hath Made," just do it! Praise God in the privacy of your home, car, shower, or wherever—and, oh yes, you and I are also to lift our voices in praise at church. Wherever you praise God and whether you do so with gusto or quietly, praise Him with all your heart! After all, when we know God, we can't help but praise Him. And since the Lord inhabits the praises of His people, we can enter His presence when we praise Him and find there "fullness of joy" (Psalm 16:11)!

3. *Praying to God*

If we want to get to know people, not only do we spend time in their presence, but we talk with and listen to them. And that is exactly what prayer is: two-way conversation with God. Prayer is the opportunity to approach God directly. The God who created the universe and us loves us enough to allow direct communication and, even more amazing, He deeply desires it. When we find ourselves feeling cavalier about prayer (and that's sometimes easy to do), we should remember that it is indeed a privilege. Do you exercise that privilege as often as the Father desires you to?

The ability to have direct access to God by simply lifting our voice or heart to Him in prayer is a gift, and it is one we can approach with childlike faith. When I was eight years old, I had plenty of that kind of faith. At Easter, which fell in April that year, I visited my grandparents in Oklahoma. Since they were already enjoying nice spring weather, Grandma took me downtown to buy me a new short-sleeved Easter dress. One night Grandma came to tuck me in and say my prayers with me.

"Grandma," I said, "I want to ask God for snow." I lived in a warm climate, but I knew that Grandma and Grandpa got snow in the winter.

"This year?" she asked.

"Yes. I want it to snow so I'm going to ask God. It never snows where we live."

"Well, honey, you can if you want to, but it's just the wrong time of year for that now. I don't want you to be disappointed."

Grandma said I could pray that prayer, and that was all I heard. She probably said a few more things about the impossibility of

> *My own plan (for praying), when hard pressed, is to seize any time, and place, however unsuitable, in preference to the last waking moment.*
>
> ~C.S. Lewis,
> *Letters to Malcolm:*
> *Chiefly on Prayer*

snow in April at her house, but all I remember is the asking—and, of course, the answer. The next morning Grandma came rushing into my room and very excitedly said, "Honey, have you looked outside yet?" Immediately remembering my prayer, I threw open the curtains to a very cold window and a white winter wonderland beyond—in April! I'll never forget the smile on Grandma's face and the excitement in her voice when she said, "From now on, when I need serious praying done I know who to call! God sure did answer your prayer!"

The physical reality of snow then and there, with or without my prayer, is not the issue. Would it have snowed even if I hadn't prayed? I don't care. I was eight years old and all I knew was that it was warm when I went to bed and there was snow when I awoke because I had prayed. At least that is what God allowed me to see. At that tender age, I experienced a God who was very real, a God who heard and answered my prayer, and that moment greatly influenced my faith.

But even when we experience God's dramatic intervention in our life, our prayers can still grow stale and seem quite ineffective. At those times, we can put off praying for a variety of reasons. Years ago when I was having one of those times, I thought a personal Bible study on prayer might help. The accompanying workbook was filled with wonderful information, but the study didn't really do much to change my prayer life—at first. I kept looking forward to being finished with the book. I wanted to get it all down so I could really get into prayer. Then it hit me. *How ridiculous! No wonder praying has become a burden. I'm spending more time learning about prayer than doing it!* I stopped focusing on the study and my approach to prayer and, instead, began to focus on the One to whom I was praying. I was soon filled with the desire to pray. My morning times of talking with God became much more important than my first cup of coffee. Those mornings became sweet moments of building a relationship with my Savior and Lord.

One frustration still remained, however. I wanted huge chunks of time when I could get out my prayer notecards and notebook and enter my prayer closet for some serious communication—no small feat for a busy mother of little ones. I eventually realized that my abiding in the Lord was going to be different during this season of my life. Oh, I still scheduled a morning appointment time with God, but when sleepless nights with babies prevented me from being there, I learned to have an attitude of prayer even though my body was in motion; I learned to fit in talk time with my Father wherever I could instead of berating myself for missing it. I found great delight in doing so, and this lifestyle approach to prayer became a real pleasure and a real necessity instead of another "ought to" in my life. I invite you to make that discovery, too.

I also invite you to heed the command we find in 1 Thessalonians:

> Rejoice always; pray without ceasing; in everything give thanks; for this is God's will for you in Christ Jesus (5:16-18).

Paul's simple language indicates a direct connection between the three commands God gives here: The reason we can rejoice always is because we are praying without ceasing and giving thanks in everything (*in* everything, not *for* everything). There was a time when that thought just overwhelmed me. *Yeah, right. I'm learning a lot about prayer, but "pray without ceasing"? Easy for Paul to say! He was in full-time ministry. How can I do that with all of my work and daily duties?* Then I learned the secret.

God isn't calling us to be on our knees in prayer all the day long. We couldn't do that even if He were, but we can learn to live in an attitude of prayer as we go about our daily activities. We can have an attitude of prayer as we work and play, drive and rest. We can have an ongoing dialogue with the Lord in our hearts while we attend to our business. "OK, kids! Get in the car and put on your seatbelts." *Lord, thank You that we've never had to test those.* "Does everyone have their homework? Love you, guys! Bye!" *Father, please bless their day and help Jacquelyn on her test.* "Oh, it's a gorgeous day." *Thank You, Lord, for Your handiwork.* You see how it works. This kind of praying (while it may look a little silly in print) is abiding in God; it's being connected with the heavenly Father in the dailyness of life. In addition to our "appointments" to pray, we can integrate prayer into our daily life with an ongoing heart-cry to God.

A Life-Changing Source of Joy

When we discover the power of prayer and see it bear fruit in our life, we can't help but be changed. Recognizing answers to our prayers can give us the assurance that God is holding everything together and remind us that we have access to a very powerful Source of help. Seeing God's power made manifest in answered prayer is exciting, faith building, and even life-changing. Seeing God answer prayer also brings great joy—even if His answers don't come in the timeframe we request—as my Aunt Glenna learned.

Glenna married a former Navy man who was tough both inside and out. She prayed that God would make her husband's heart soft toward Him and toward their marriage, but God didn't answer her prayers in her timing. "God has shown me His love, care, and direction so many times," Glenna now says. "Especially at a time when my marriage was very unstable, He showed me that He was all I needed. Not only did my communication with God see me through lonely days, but God honored my faithfulness, and I am so thankful."

Glenna prayed for her husband for 20 years, and in 1987 he committed his life to Christ. "God has given me the godly husband I always desired and healed my marriage," she says. "To see Him work through Duwayne has made all my heartaches and frustrations worthwhile." Today Duwayne is active in a prison ministry. God answered the persistent prayers of a faithful wife in His time and for His glory. And such answered prayer brings great joy, no matter what the timing.

Intercession—praying for other people—is another source of joy and another opportunity to see power and fruit. The apostle Paul knew that joy and wrote of it in Philippians: "I thank my God in all my remembrance of you, always offering prayer with joy in my every prayer for you all" (1:3,4). When we get outside of ourselves and beyond our own needs and lay other people's needs before God, we can experience great joy. It really is wonderful to be part of the miracle of answered prayer in another person's life—no matter how large or small the concern.

One day while working on this book, I called my editor. As a mom who works at home, she was having an unusually difficult day. Her seven-month-old baby wasn't feeling well and hadn't nursed in 24 hours. Those of you who have nursed a child know that's far too long a hunger strike for both baby and mother! I hung up and immediately prayed for them. Now there are times when you know in your spirit that God has heard your prayers, and this was one of those precious times. I decided to call her back in an hour to see if little Sarah had eaten. Thirty minutes later, Lisa called me. "Guess what?" she said. "Sarah nursed and is now fast asleep." Lisa and I both built a touchstone for our faith that day as we saw God immediately answer our prayer.

One of the most life-changing things about prayer—whether the answer is long-awaited or immediate—is the growth in our relationship with God that accompanies an active prayer life. And that greater degree of intimacy is a fundamental source of joy. I can share "grown-up" examples of incredible answered prayer (answers far more wonderful than the snow that April morning), and I can also tell you of desperate prayers that God did not answer according to my requests. Although God has the power and ability to answer any request we bring before Him, His answer is not the most important thing. The action of praying and the relationship that results from doing so is. As Oswald Chambers says, "Whenever the insistence is on the point that God answers prayer, we are off the track. The meaning of prayer is that we get hold of God, not of the answer."[6] We "get hold of God" when we spend time talking to Him. Our relationship with Him grows when we want to commune with Him, not just receive the object of our requests. If we only want our answer, we'll find it difficult to know God and His joy. But when we are able to accept His "yes," His "wait," and even His "no" and continue in our dialogue with Him, we can find great joy.

We can learn much about prayer, and the joy which results from prayer, in Scripture. God's Word teaches what to pray for, how to pray, when to pray, and it offers us models—great men and women of prayer—and stories of the results of their prayers (like Hannah who diligently prayed for a child and was so blessed [1 Samuel 1]). When we pray through ACTS (prayers of Adoration, Confession, Thanksgiving, Supplication, and then add intercession)—and when we do so with a pure heart (Psalm 66:18,19), in faith (Matthew 17:20), and in Christ's name (John 14:13), praying according to God's will, not our own (1 John

5:14)—we are approaching God as Scripture teaches. So learn what Scripture and study tools teach about prayer; let the Holy Spirit teach you, too.

Learn, too, from the methods which have helped other believers be more faithful in prayer. Some people, for instance, find it helpful to write out their prayers. When author Becky Tirabassi first committed to pray for one hour every day, she discovered that writing down her prayers helped her stay focused. She organized a notebook into different sections for different parts of her prayers (Praise, Admit [confess], Request, and Thanks) as well as a section for what God says to her in Scripture and sermons. She said, "After 12 years and more than 4,000 one-hour appointments with God, I understand firsthand that sometimes God says yes and sometimes He says no, but no matter the outcome, He still loves me."[7]

Some people's prayer notebooks serve as a pictorial reminder about what to pray for. They use pictures (and words) to remind them of specific prayer requests to pray for on specific days. Other people like to record their prayers and God's answers in a daily journal. When I began to do that—a simple act requiring only the purchase of a spiral notebook to get me going—my prayer time and spiritual life became much richer. I am now able to keep track of what I am praying for, and my record of God's answers are a written reminder of His work in my life. Also, remember that prayer and God's Word are virtually inseparable. As Andrew Murray said, "Power in the use of either depends on the presence of the other!"[8] So I write down all that's on my heart and then record what He seems to be saying to me through His Word and the impressions He lays on my heart during those silent moments I spend with Him. Prayer *and* Bible study make for a meaningful dialogue with the Lord.

Whatever approach to prayer you take, remember that the most important thing is this: Just do it! Don't wait to ascend to your ivory tower and don robes of righteousness to begin praying. Pray today, wherever you are, in whatever condition you find yourself. If you are hurting, tell God. If your life is full of pain, pour it out in words to God. If you are mad at God for something, tell Him. It's OK! Psalm 55:17 tells us, "Evening and morning and at noon, I will complain and murmur, and He will hear my voice." So open up the lines of communication. We get to know God better when we talk with Him often, and talking with Him often—walking through each day with Him—is one way of abiding in Him. Jesus Himself said, "If you abide in Me, and My words abide in you, ask whatever you wish, and it shall be done for you" (John 15:7). Abiding and prayer are closely related: Prayer is both a result of and a way to abide in our Lord and Savior.

Joy in Worship

One cannot talk about poring over God's Word, praising Him, and praying without mentioning worship. Whenever and wherever we read the Bible, praise God, and pray with (as Webster puts it) "an extravagant respect, honor, or devotion," we are indeed worshiping. We can read the Bible...and find it flat. We can praise...with lip service only. We can pray...like a robot. But when we add that "extravagant respect, honor, and devotion" of our heart and do these things as an expression of our love for God, we turn our "three P's" into acts of worship!

Each one of us was created to worship God, something my friend Kellie understands well. As our women's ministry worship leader, she is passionate about worshiping God. For her, worship is more than a religious activity or occasional experience; worship is the God-given purpose of her life on this earth. She first began to understand that one day while she was mopping the floor and listening to a man on the radio describe how God showed him that he was to be a preacher. Kellie leaned on her mop and said out loud, "Lord, what am I about? Who am I for You?" It was as if lightning pierced her heart. She knew instantly that God was speaking to her. She recalls:

> He said to me, "You're a worshiper!" I grabbed that mop, stood up straight, and said, "Yes, Lord! I am! That's it!" As I was mopping that floor, the Lord revealed my identity as a worshiper and a worship leader in spite of my inadequacies. That moment has impacted my life daily since then. I worship the Father every day. It's my passion and bliss! It's who I am!

Kellie likes to worship with her family, in the car, and when she runs in the morning, but her favorite way is in her clothes closet:

> Without any music and where no one can hear, I worship God alone. His Spirit touches my spirit and His presence comes down and envelops me. It changes me, renews my mind, and adjusts my focus back to Him and who He is. Worship fills my soul with such joy!

And that joy Kellie refers to is the joy of the Lord—a joy far deeper than external joys the world offers.

The joy of the Lord is joy straight from the Source, poured out on those who bother to sit at His feet and enter His presence. In the Bible, Jesus' friend Mary knew how to do just that, but her sister Martha was busy "doing" for Jesus. Do you remember which action He valued? "Martha, Martha, you are worried and bothered about so many things; but only a few things are necessary, really only one, for Mary has chosen the good part, which shall not be taken away from her" (Luke 10:41,42). Jesus wants us to be with Him, not just "do" for Him. When we make worship the top priority that God desires it to be, we take part in an activity that "shall not be taken away." The worship of God has eternal value.

So be careful not to relegate worship to only a Sunday church service. Instead, learn to experience His presence in times of Bible study, praise, prayer, giving, and daily living. That is what worship really is. When we do even the little things in our life out of our love for God, then all of our life becomes worship of Him. In fact, some of our most powerful

We must take time to get to know Him in the quiet times of our life to be able to trust Him in the crisis.

~Lucy Mabery

times of worship can be when we do those "hidden things" for God, when we do what He has called us to do. With the right heart—with a heart tuned to God—we can be worshiping God whether we're leading a Bible study at church or sweeping the floor at home.

And that perspective on what we do—that attempt to make all that we do worship—is key to knowing joy day to day. Instead of knowing that joy right now, are you worried and bothered about many things? Perhaps you're feeling like Martha was because you're not sitting at Jesus' feet, in His presence, as Mary did. If your worship is weak, Bible reading boring, praise scant, or prayers lifeless, you are missing out on the rich, full, joy that is found by being in the presence of the Lord. Begin to discover—or rediscover—that joy by being honest with God. Acknowledge that you are feeling empty and admit that you haven't spent the time with Him that you and He both want. You may need to say, "Lord, I am so dry, but I don't know how to worship You with my whole heart. Please come and fill me up and teach me through Your Holy Spirit." Having named Jesus our Savior and Lord, we have received "the Spirit who is from God, that we might know the things freely given to us by God" (1 Corinthians 2:12). The Spirit will teach us to worship when we ask Him to. He will meet us where we are!

Poring over His word, praising Him, and praying to Him can be lackluster duties, but done with a spirit of worship, they become sparkles in the rocks of life. Has God touched your heart with a desire to know soul intimacy with Him? It is there we are able to taste the joy of the Lord. I encourage you to step up to the table today. Become intimate with the Gift-Giver, the One who gives joy.

Joy in the Dark
And Other Tales of Hope

Were you ever afraid of the dark? Perhaps you remember what it felt like to be about six years old, lying in your bed at night, surrounded by darkness. The room was pitch black, and that blackness seemed to creep up on you, ready to deliver danger at any minute. You couldn't get up and run to the light for safety. Doing so would have put your ankles perilously close to whatever was under your bed. You clutched your teddy bear and tried to be calm as you strained your eyes in the inky darkness, but still your heart beat faster and faster. Suddenly fear overtook you, and you dove under the covers, leaving no part of you exposed to the monsters. Then, finally, you gathered the courage to peer out from beneath the blanket. You weren't sure about anything in that room because it was so hard to see, but gradually the total blackness gave way to shadows. Then you saw that the imminent danger was nothing more than a few scattered toys on the floor. Things that in the light are familiar and comforting become unrecognizable and frightening in the dark.

But do you know how dark, dark can be? You do if you've ever visited a cave and had the tour guide turn out the lights. When you put your hand in front of your face and move your fingers, you see only blackness. To literally not be able to see your hand in front of your face—that is *really* dark. The cold, damp air of the cave and that utter blackness make the dark almost tangible.

When circumstances begin to chill the air and dim the light, the darkness of life can also be almost tangible. And all we need to do to get a glimpse of this darkness is turn on the radio or television news or pick up the newspaper. A man takes the stand in a spouse abuse trial, a 15-year-old commits suicide, cancer takes a young husband and father of three, a heart attack claims another life, a sexual abuse case rocks a small town, and a couple files for bankruptcy. That's just a sampling of the darkness from this morning's paper. There's no mistaking that we live in a fallen world; we see the evidence all around us.

Have you ever known a more personal darkness? A time when difficult circumstances surrounded you, threatening danger and causing you to strain to see things clearly? Things that in bright circumstances are familiar and comfortable can become strange and even frightening in such dark times. Sometimes monstrous circumstances make you want to dive under the covers rather than face a darkness you can almost feel. Your darkness may be so black that you can't see your hand in front of your face, or your darkness may be more shadowy, making familiar things unrecognizable. Or perhaps your days have been pretty sunny, but you know that sometime you may be called on to face the darkness. Wherever you are today, know that sparkles of joy shine in even the blackest darkness.

God Is Sovereign; God Is Good

Whether we drown in the darkness or are able to see a glimmer of joy often depends on the condition of our head and our heart *before* the light fades. Our ability to find joy depends on whether we have settled several issues before the tough times come. Have we mastered those three actions which are key to developing a great attitude and practicing contentment? Specifically, do we know how to renew our thought life? Are we remembering the Source of our strength? And are we resting in that Source's sovereignty? If we are to know joy in our dark days, we must focus especially on God's sovereignty. Knowing that God is in control and that He is good, we will be able to withstand the dark when it comes. As discussued earlier, if God is sovereign (in control of everything, capable of anything, and knowledgeable of all things) and good (in character and in His plans for us), then we can rest assured that His sovereignty and goodness will sustain us and that His intentions for us are not just for our good, but for our best even when that possibility is inconceivable.

When the darkness overtakes us, we have to believe that God in His goodness will redeem the events of our lives. In Romans 8:28, the apostle Paul tells us so: "We know that God causes all things to work together for good to those who love God, to those who are called according to His purpose." When Christians go through difficult times, this is one of the most quoted (and perhaps most misunderstood) Scriptures passed along by well-meaning family, friends, and clergy. The promise rings hollow when the fires rage, when all we see around us is evidence of pain. We want to yell, "Don't tell me that when I'm hurting ! How can any good come from this?" That's when we must read the next verse—and choose to believe it. Verse 29 explains God's "purpose" for us is that we "become conformed to the image of His Son." Sometimes we're allowed to see and understand how God brings this ultimate good out of evil, but at other times, when life seems unfair and suffering unjust, we must believe by faith that "all things" are working together to make us more like Christ. Deciding that this truth applies to our life *before* the crisis hits makes believing it *in* the crisis easier.

> *Never let anything so fill you with pain or sorrow, so as to make you forget the joy of Christ risen.*
>
> ~Mother Teresa,
> *Suffering into Joy*

Crisis of Faith

When we struggle with circumstances that don't make sense and when we can see no point in the pain, we are in dangerous waters. Unwanted divorce, sudden illness, early death, and countless other tragedies in the lives of people who have loved God and served Him bring many of us to a crisis point in our faith. We become frustrated or even angry with God, and we question the very foundation of our beliefs. In *When God Doesn't Make Sense*, Dr. James Dobson writes:

> This [progression from frustration to questioning our faith] is particularly true when things happen that seem illogical and inconsistent with what had been taught or understood. Then if the Lord does not rescue [them] from the circumstances in which they are embroiled, their frustration quickly deteriorates into anger and a sense of abandonment. Finally, disillusionment sets in and the spirit begins to wither.[1]

But the spirit does not have to wither!

When we settle the faith issues of God's sovereignty and goodness before the storms hit and get to know Him deeply, we can avoid a crisis of faith when circumstances don't make sense and aren't fair. We can survive the adversity and even find joy in the dark. Scripture shows us that even when we are shaken we can make the choice to rejoice if foundational truths about God have been firmly established in our heart and mind. Hear what David says in this psalm:

> I have set the Lord continually before me;
> Because He is at my right hand, I will not be shaken.
> *Therefore my heart is glad, and my glory rejoices;*
> My flesh also will dwell securely
>
>   (Psalm 16:8,9, emphasis added).

Suffering and pain bring no joy in themselves, and this passage is not saying we should be glad and rejoice in painful times simply because it is the proper thing to do as a Christian. That very presumption causes many Christians to reach the crisis point. They can't reconcile what they actually feel about their circumstances with how they think they should feel because they are serving Christ. This verse suggests—and it's true—that we can rejoice even when we are in trouble. That gladness of heart and rejoicing can come because we know that the Lord is "continually before me" and "is at my right hand." The psalmist knew that, even when his flesh was threatened, God was able, God was before him, and God was beside him. We can know that same truth today.

Nineteenth-century writer Hannah Whitall Smith knew that truth. She says this: "Better and sweeter than health, or friends, or money, or fame, or ease, or prosperity, is the adorable will of our God. It gilds the darkest hours with a divine halo, and sheds brightest sunshine on the gloomiest paths."[2] When we know that the will of God is for our good, when we rest in that fact when life doesn't make sense, then even darkness can have some sparkle to it. We must, however, choose to trust in His goodness and sovereignty—no matter what comes our way. After all, God's goodness is better than health, friends, money, fame, or prosperity—some of the many things we pray for. In His sovereignty He makes that goodness happen.

Fruit in Due Season

And that goodness will come in His perfect time or, to use the image of Psalm 1, "in its season." Psalm 1:3 says that the person who delights and meditates on God's Word "will be like a tree firmly planted by streams of water, which yields its fruit in its season." Every fruit has its season. If the season isn't right, the fruit doesn't come forth. As a fruit of the Spirit, joy will be yielded when the season is right. And, as surprising as it may be, I have found three seasons which are right for harvesting joy when dark days descend; I have found joy sprinkled through the dark, revealed after the dark, and even in the dark.

Joy Sprinkled Through the Darkness

Is your life full of rocks rather than manicured grass and beautiful flowers? Are hard, dark circumstances making your path rough? When those rocky circumstances become a mountain which towers between you and the sun, the shadow can be quite dark—as you know if you've ever stood in the shadow of a real mountain. If right now you're standing in a shadow caused by a mountain of hard circumstances, seeing no way out of the dark, look around you. Some of the rocks sparkle. Even on dark days, God sprinkles little sparkles of joy in the most unexpected places among our shadows.

I entered a shadowland when my mother's cancer was diagnosed. Suddenly our family faced imposing rocks of survival statistics, doctors' visits, therapy options, and disease management. Simple Saturday morning phone chats, frequent weekend visits, and ideas about family reunions and spring break with her grandkids suddenly became things of the past instead of pleasures of today and plans for the future. When the kids and I left our home, our belongings, and our friends to join Tim and be near my mom and dad, we also left behind a life of security—and that move cast another dark shadow. Other shadows came as my family and I learned about the mindset and strategy necessary in a battle against cancer; about adjusting to life when one's normal routine and dreams for the future are sidelined; and about trauma. In my valley, these shadows loomed large.

As my mother fought her battle, my husband's mother, Mary O'Connor, fought one of her own. She was rushed to the emergency room one Friday afternoon, and that night we watched helplessly as they loaded her into a waiting helicopter to take her to another hospital. One doctor said, "It doesn't look good" as they wheeled her past us. The strong wind from the helicopter's propeller and its lights in the night sky as it whisked off a woman we loved made the event quite surreal. That moment felt more like a scene from a movie than a scene from our life.

For a week we spent long hours at the hospital. My heart was heavy with the pain of watching her suffer and the pain of my own mother's increasingly intense battle for life. I was hurting for my mother-in-law, hurting for Tim, his sister, and his brothers, and hurting simply because I loved her. Carrying this double burden made my chest ache with real, physical pain.

At the end of that week, Mom O'Connor died. Then, three short weeks later, my mother died, too. My grief for both my mother and my mother-in-law intertwined, and the emotional and physical pain created a darkness that was almost tangible. I had read that there can be great joy in suffering, but at that time I vehemently disagreed. I was being choked by a darkness that was foreign to me. I desperately wanted to call for my mother to come turn on the light, just as she had done when I was six years old and alone in the dark.

Besides trying to offer one another comfort, Tim and I tried to be there for our children who had their own pain and their own questions after losing both of their grandmothers in the same month. And, sitting together at the kitchen table, we wrote thank-you notes after the funerals—Tim to his mother's friends and me to my mother's. We were together, yet alone, sharing the same yet separate griefs.

Now I told you earlier that God gives sparkles in the dark. Having never lived for so long in a shadow that was so dark, I didn't know that there could be sparkles in the dark. But one day during that time of intense grief, I was aching; I was physically and emotionally exhausted. As Tim and I pulled into the driveway, my toddler ran toward me for a hug, but then broke loose to grab a dandelion. Her older sister said, "Look, Mama! Flowers!"

"Honey, those aren't flowers. Those are weeds," I impulsively responded. But immediately I thought, "No, she's right. Those are flowers. They're only weeds because of my perspective." I knelt on the sidewalk and scooped up my little one, her flower firmly in her hand. Then I really looked at her and what she held. *Lord, You're right. She's right. It really is a flower and it's beautiful.* As I studied the beauty of both that flower and my daughter's sweet, innocent eyes which saw beauty in something I considered a problem, God suddenly gave me a great gift. I felt His joy! Instantly, my heart lightened and I delighted in the precious face of my child and the sweet aroma of a weed-turned-flower. Then I felt greater joy simply because I had heard God speak to my heart. My heavenly Father loved me enough to help me see beauty in ugliness and discover His perspective through my child's eyes. And—*for a moment*—the pain in my chest was replaced by a warmth in my heart. God had given me a sprinkling of His joy—a sparkle right there on the sidewalk—in the midst of my darkness.

That was not the only time He let me see the sparkle. Oh, I never felt a great fullness of joy while I was making my way through the dark, but God did open my eyes to the sparkles of joy sprinkled here and there. At that time, I didn't know great joy in the dark; I didn't have a full-fledged "go to the fountain and drink fully" experience. The joy I knew at the time was, instead, an occasional bubbling up from the wellspring of the Lord's joy, an occasional sparkle of His light. It was a comforting undercurrent, usually invisible, but strong—mostly undetected, but somehow very present. The joy of the Lord came as glimmers in the rocks when I wasn't expecting it—a shimmer of His love sprinkled throughout the pain. These sparkles were just enough to get me through and remind me that joy was not gone completely or gone forever.

Joy *After* the Dark

Not all fruit matures at the same rate. For some people and in some difficult seasons of life, the fruit of joy needs a little more time on the vine before it's ready for harvest. In some cases, therefore, the reaping of God's joy comes *after* the dark. That was the case for Dianne G.

Dianne has known more than one season of darkness. Even her childhood days were lived in a shadowland since she was abused, eventually abandoned, and placed in a children's home at age 14. After marrying later and having four of her six children, Dianne descended into despair when her 15-year-old daughter was killed in a car accident. The avalanche of pain didn't end there, however. Over the years, her husband was diagnosed with brain cancer, she discovered she was diabetic, and she was given the dismal news that she had breast cancer—twice. Despite all this pain and suffering, this woman knows and feels the joy of the Lord. She has learned much through her difficulties, some faced without God and the rest bearable because of His presence in her life.

When her daughter died, Dianne was devastated. She turned her back on God and spent years in despair. To outsiders, she appeared to be coping well, but on the inside, she suffered a faith crisis that kept her away from God for 11 years. Then she was told her husband had brain cancer. Michael's surgery revealed that the "cancer" was actually only an infection, but the surgery left him weak on one side with impaired speech, seizures, and permanent neurological damage and depression. For many months, she grieved deeply for the "old Michael," the active father of their two sons, the successful businessman. Fear and anger invaded her life and took away her joy. Believing that God didn't care, Dianne was truly suffocated by her sadness. But God had plans for her beyond the pain.

Desperate for answers, Dianne accepted a friend's invitation and began to attend Community Bible Study. Her 11-year anger with God gave way to a new relationship. She says:

> When my daughter died, I didn't ask God for His strength, but now I knew I had to turn back to Him. I couldn't change what had happened; I had to change how I was dealing with it. So I cried out to God, "Please hear me. I'm here and I need You now!"He heard and He responded. Reestablishing my relationship with God brought me out of my despair and helped me cope. God helped me understand the blessings I still had—Michael was alive, he could walk, and eventually he could even talk clearly. I began to thank God for letting him live. With this gratefulness and hope, I was more joyful. I also realized I had to stay close to God. With the peace He placed in my heart, I was able to fight my battles with breast cancer and diabetes with more joy and less fear than I had during any of my other trials. I know that to have joy anywhere in or near the darkness, you have to have God. I've tried it both ways and I won't ever leave Him again!

When Dianne turned back to God, she found peace in the midst of her darkness, and joy soon followed as the light of His presence and the passage of time brought her out of some of her darkest days.

Outside of testimonies like Dianne's, how do we know that there is joy *after* the darkness? We have God's Word on it. The psalmist says, "Weeping may last for the night, but a shout of joy comes in the morning" (Psalm 30:5b). He goes on: "Thou hast turned for me my mourning into dancing; thou hast loosed my sackcloth and girded me with gladness" (verse 11). The loss of a child or a spouse, a job or a dream can feel like a life sentence, but it isn't. Oh, we may hurt every single day, but God is able to shake loose the sackcloth of pain that suffocates us and replace it with gladness. Who else but God could turn our mourning into dancing? God does this so that our "soul may sing praise to Thee, and not be silent" (verse 12). We were created with a soul that yearns for something beyond ourselves, that needs communion with God. A silent soul is therefore perhaps more suffocating than sackcloth. When our soul is silent, how can there be joy? Wanting our souls to praise Him, God turns our mourning into dancing. He allows weeping for the night, but He doesn't leave us there. So if there is no joy in your darkness, take heart. The light of morning always follows the dark, and you have His Word that a song of joy will come.

Joy *in* the Dark

To people deeply wounded by the events of life or working through profound grief, the thought of experiencing joy while they are in the dark may be inconceivable. Please don't shake your head in disbelief and label me a Pollyanna. I'm not talking about feeling happy when you hurt. I'm talking about having hope if you're struggling through painful circumstances, straining to see in the shadows, or groping along the dark days of grief. I want you to have hope—to know that even if you feel you'll never be happy again, a measure of joy in your darkness is possible. The joy that our heavenly Father gives is available regardless of our circumstances. Know, too, that even if you have matters to work through or need time to pass before you know happiness again, the Giver of joy can bless you now. Wherever you are in the dark, He can find you. You may not be able to see your hand in front of your face, but He has no trouble. He is light (John 8:12), and when you seek Him in your darkness—when you choose to shift your focus from your pain to His presence even if only for a moment—He will bless you with a bit of joy, a tiny sparkle to keep you going.

If, however, you are angry with God and caught in a crisis of your faith, if you haven't predetermined that God is good and sovereign, you may have to wait for another season to harvest the fruit of joy. The only way I know to taste that fruit in the midst of the dark is to both know in your mind and believe in your heart—no matter what happens—that God is good and still in control even if your world is out of control. Settling this truth before a crisis comes is so important. When we do, a taste of joy is still possible even in the deepest darkness.

My good friend Susan knows this well. She and her family were just beginning to recover from dire financial circumstances when she learned that an aunt she was close to was diagnosed with breast cancer. Before her aunt was out of the hospital, Susan fell and injured her back, resulting in two months of almost total disability followed by back surgery. Three weeks later came the devastating news that her mother had incurable lung cancer, and one month later she learned that her husband, Marty, had advanced malignant melanoma. Those days were dim and difficult for Susan as she recovered physically and walked her husband and mother through illnesses that God chose not to heal. Susan was not only devastated for herself, but she also hurt deeply for her children, especially as she watched them say goodbye to their earthly father. Marty and her mother died five weeks apart. Susan's grief was intense; happiness was just a memory—but joy was not.

Well-grounded in God's Word after six years of intensive Bible study, Susan had learned that, no matter what, God is sovereign and God is good. When her crisis hit, she didn't question God's power or goodness because she had already settled those issues in her heart. The facts of His goodness and sovereignty were a part of her belief system, a part that sustained her in the darkness.

In July, a month before Marty's death, Susan once again made the hour-long drive to the hospital to visit him in intensive care. Like most other days, she was playing Christian music in her car, singing with the radio

*G*ive unto them beauty for ashes, the oil of joy for mourning, the garment of praise for the spirit of heaviness.

~Isaiah 61:3

and praising God with genuine gladness. That day, however, she was suddenly aware of the unlikelihood of someone praising God and smiling while on her way to visit her terminally ill husband. She wondered, "How can I feel this joy? Am I in denial?" No. She knew that barring a miracle her husband was about to die and she had begun to plan his funeral. So why was she able to energetically sing God's praises? As she wondered where this joy came from, God spoke to her heart. She describes what He said:

> It was then that I realized that I was praising God because I knew He could be trusted. Even in this, my husband, our children, and I were safe with the Lord. I had studied God's Word enough to know this truth deep in my heart. I was overwhelmed with gratitude that God had seen fit to reveal His goodness to me and that He had made even the discovery of Him a joyful experience. I realized that it had been in the joy of discovery that the discovery of joy had come.

When we discover something new about God, when we gain new spiritual awareness as Susan did, we discover joy. And that joy sustained Susan during her dark days. She had predetermined that God is sovereign and good regardless of what the circumstances of her life suggest. Susan reflects, "There's no way I could have disciplined my mind to dwell on a truth that wasn't settled in my heart. If the truth of God's sovereignty and goodness hadn't already been settled in my mind, it would have been a very different and joyless two years." Many times throughout this season in her life, Susan was asked why she was able to show such incredible strength. Her reply came straight from Nehemiah 8:10: "The joy of the Lord is [my] strength." Susan's joy during this time was literally translated into strength.

Is it odd to pour out our heart to God in gratitude, praise, and joy during our darkest of days? Certainly, when that darkness is all we are able to focus on. But in those moments when we can truly enter into His presence, find something (even a little something) for which to be grateful, and reflect on His goodness despite the bad, and His control amid the uncontrollable, joy is possible—even in the blackest darkness.

"Count It All Joy"

On the survey I did for this book, I asked women to "describe a time when you felt joy in an unpleasant or painful situation." Liz H. answered for mothers everywhere when she said, "Childbirth!" No other situation in life more vividly illustrates the possibility of feeling joy even as you feel pain. As difficult as the process is, the birth of a child is indeed one of life's greatest joys. (For good reason, too. If joy were absent in the birth, people would become absent on earth!) The joy of holding your newborn in your arms for the first time makes the pain of childbirth worth it. Even when we are in labor, we know that the pain will yield something wonderful.

And so can other pain in our lives. In fact, the pain and problems of life can be looked at as gifts. Paul even says that we can "exult" and find joy in our tribulations because they produce in us perseverance, character, and hope—the hope in Christ which does not disappoint (Romans 5:3-5). James writes these words: "Consider it all joy, my brethren, when you encounter various trials, knowing that the testing of your faith produces endurance. And let endurance have its perfect result, that you may be perfect and complete, lacking in nothing" (James 1:2-4). Notice that James doesn't say *if* we encounter trials; he says *when* we encounter them. Peter also reminds us that tough times are inevitable and, like James, calls us to rejoice in them: "Beloved, do not be surprised at the fiery ordeal among you, which comes upon you for your testing, as though some strange thing were happening to you; but to the degree that you share the sufferings of Christ, keep on rejoicing; so that also at the revelation of His glory, you may rejoice with exultation" (1 Peter 4:12,13).

In the Scriptures we are not told to count it all joy because our life is carefree. Instead, we are told to expect trials and to respond to that adversity with joy! This command flies in the face of our natural instincts and the world's understanding, yet we can obey it and respond with joy when we are aware that God is maturing and refining us through our trials and that our rewards are not in this life, but in His kingdom to come.

I once heard a pastor say this about darkness: "A plant always grows toward the light. Therefore the side in the darkness grows twice as fast as that in the light. Even in adversity, we grow toward the Light—God Himself—twice as fast as when we are in the light. Thank God, then, for adversity!" God doesn't waste pain or darkness in our lives. We can indeed experience great spiritual growth during those difficult times.

Still, perhaps one of the great mysteries of life is that the followers of Christ suffer. Over 800 years ago, St. Francis of Assisi addressed that issue when he said, "This is perfect joy—to share in the sufferings of the world as Christ did." And "sharing in the sufferings of the world" is exactly what Mother Teresa is doing. She has dedicated her life to serving the downcast and dying in India. Speaking about the slums where this modern-day saint serves, Eileen and Kathleen Egan write in *Suffering into Joy,* "How is it possible to emerge from such human squalor with such a message of joy? That is Mother Teresa's gift. To her, the pain and agony she relieves are that of the Savior himself. Therefore, each person she serves has an inviolable dignity and sacredness.[3] Mother Teresa ministers with joy and teaches by her life that suffering can produce joy in believers' hearts. She says this about our personal suffering: "You have suffered the passion of the cross. There is a purpose in this. Because of your suffering and pain, you will now understand the suffering and pain of the world."[4]

Another benefit of our dark times Paul identifies is that because of our suffering and pain we can indeed better understand the suffering and pain of the people around us. He writes that God "comforts us in all our affliction so that we may be able to comfort those who are in any affliction with the comfort with which we ourselves are comforted by God" (2 Corinthians 1:4). God comforts us in our pain in a way that transcends human explanation, and when we have received His comfort, we are then able to share it with others.

That's something my mother's good friend Jackie did so well. Jackie had fought off breast cancer, but two years later it was back. Within weeks of that news, her husband suffered a fatal heart attack. One would think that learning cancer had returned and losing your husband shortly thereafter would be enough to snuff out all joy. Those events were indeed devastating, but Jackie found joy again and shared it with my family.

What was one source of joy in her life after these events? First, she knew that James's desire was to be with the Lord and that he was at last with Jesus. Jackie also says this: "I woke up one day and realized that, with James gone, my pipeline to heaven had been taken away because he had discipled me. I decided that I was going to have to put into action on my own everything he had taught me. Doing that gave me great joy."

Although Jackie had many tough days, she still often served my mom with joy as they battled the same disease. She wanted to drive our family to the large cancer center—so familiar to her—the first time we had to go, and she often stopped by to visit with my Aunt Linda, who cared for my mom while Dad worked. Smiling, Jackie once asked Linda, "Do you think it would be too presumptuous for me to ask God, when I get to heaven, if I can be an angel? I really, really want to help others." My aunt smiled and said, "Jackie, you already are!"

Jackie told me, "I cling to my faith and family and friends. That's where your joy comes from." She indeed comforted others with the comfort she had received.

Degrees of Darkness

The dark which each of us encounters—brought on by the pain and problems of life—has numerous hues and intensities ranging from pale gray to pitch black. The shadows cast by looming mountains can, for instance, be as dark as a cave with the lights turned out. Sometimes the mountain is a little smaller and the shadows a little lighter, and sometimes the dark isn't a shadow as much as it is just the slight gray of an overcast day. If you've lost someone or something dear to you, you've faced a dark shadow. If painful circumstances trouble you, perhaps your mountain is a little smaller. But maybe it's not searing pain or soul-wrenching loss as much as the stuff of life clouding your day and making you wish you stood under brighter skies.

Whatever the shade of darkness, how do we find joy in the dark? What do we do to see that sparkle of joy when life has lost its luster? Remember the sidewalk, the tumbled rock, and the geode from chapter one? They—like joy in our darkness—all sparkle, but in different ways and at different times.

The Sidewalk:
The Sparkles Sprinkled Throughout

The surface of the sidewalk sparkles in the sunlight, but sometimes we miss those sparkles because we're focusing on our darkness. When we're sandwiched between dark skies above and the dim hardness of our gray path, we need to remember that—even in that gray—Sonlight is always present ["He Himself has said, 'I will never leave you nor forsake you'" (Hebrews 13:5 NKJV; Deuteronomy 31:6)]. To see sparkles on a sidewalk, we find the right angle and the right light. Likewise, to see sparkles sprinkled throughout our darkness, we must look from the angle of God's perspective (an eternal viewpoint) and in the light of the Son—Jesus Christ. The skies may still be dark and our path may still be gray, but when we adjust our perspective to match that of the Son (what would Jesus think, do, say?) and look for the sparkles (the little joys He scatters along our way), we can indeed find sprinkles of joy brightening our walk even when we tread in hard places.

We can miss sidewalk sparkles when we don't take the time to look for them. Likewise, during our dark days, we must take the time to look out across the sidewalk in the Son's light and notice the sparkle. When we take the time to notice them, we can find sparkles of joy in the external things in our life. We see sparkles when we notice the beauty of a child's face and her weedy flowers (or is it flowery weeds?), when we do something for someone we love, and when we spend two minutes watching the sunset. Look for the shimmers on the water as you drive by a pond, lake, or ocean and relish that sparkle. Look at the things of life that are all around you and notice them if only for an instant. Also, recognize the gleam of joy when you become aware of God's voice in the dark. Impressions and directions from God can illuminate our path or simply glow in our darkness. You may find sparkles of joy sprinkled through the grayness of life just like sparkles that are scattered across the sidewalk. Pay attention. These sparkles of joy really can lift your heart.

The Rock Tumbler: A Shine after a Tumble

Now consider the rock in the tumbler. Hard and sometimes ugly, it is tossed upside down and scraped and thrown against other rocks—and the end result is a beautiful shine. As I said in chapter one, the rock in the tumbler can be two different things. Sometimes the rock is a hurt or difficult circumstance that litters our life. God can smooth those circumstances and polish those rocks that lie before us—or even remove the rocky road to show us the sparkle. But at other times we ourselves are the rocks which must yield to the tumbler and allow God to polish us.

Maybe you're familiar with the rock tumbler of life. We get tossed upside down, unable to figure out which way to turn. We get in all kinds of scrapes, and we bump into all kinds of people. God can use the hard things in our life as well as the daily friction to polish us so that we may shine forth His light and reflect Jesus who lives within us. In this case, the sparkle comes *after* the tumbling, but the beauty is worth the wait. We must allow God to use those things that make us tumble (that job loss, prickly relationship, deep grief, or long-held pain) to polish us. When we allow Him to polish us, we know the fruit of joy. The process itself isn't joyful, but the fruit we taste *after* the tumbling stops is. Oh, it might be easier to watch the rock before us being polished, but I'd much rather go through the refining process myself so that afterwards I can be a reflection of Christ, polished with His touch. That's definitely a sparkle worth waiting for. Having Jesus shine from within us, reflected in our life, is a sparkle that others can see. That truly is a source of joy—and it comes after the tumbling.

For I will turn their mourning into joy, and will comfort them, and give them joy for their sorrow.

~Jeremiah 31:13

The Geode: The Sparkle from Within

Finally there is the sparkle within the geode, those beautiful crystals hidden beneath a rough exterior waiting to be revealed. If that geode's sparkle is to become visible, the crust must be broken. Pressure must be applied to shatter the hard outer shell. Likewise, if life is hard and rough and unpleasant for you right now, know that the capacity for sparkles of joy lies within you. After all, if you are a believer of Christ, you have His Holy Spirit dwelling inside you. Where His Spirit is, there is joy—although we cannot always see it or feel it in the darkness.

You might be content just knowing that joy lies within you because of Who resides within. But to fully enjoy the beauty of that joy, you must allow God to use the pressures of life to bring you to the breaking point and reveal the radiance of His light shining in you. If our hard outer crust is never penetrated—if the geode is never broken—the beauty within will never shine forth. The breaking of our crust of "self" allows God to penetrate our heart and shine in our brokenness. That is when His joy can truly sparkle from within us.

I must mention, though, that sometimes the sparkle within a geode is visible in its natural formation if we know how to look. Picture the hollow sphere of a geode having a portion of its crust missing. When we look at this geode with the crust facing us, we might think we're looking at an ordinary rock. But if we were to look at the other side, we would see the beautiful crystals exposed. Looking at that one side doesn't tell the whole story. We must change our perspective to get a complete and accurate picture of the geode. And so it is with life.

Sometimes we get so focused on the hard exterior of our life that we think that's all there is. We forget that there might be something beyond the pain and hurt and grief. Those of us who can find joy in the darkness are people who remember that the Source of that sparkle lies within us. We change our perspective and, for a time, focus on the sparkle. The rock remains as hard as ever, but it's more pleasant to look at. Seeing the joy does not make the hardness of the days disappear; it just makes that hardness easier to bear. Again, we can see that sparkle of joy in the dark because of the Light that resides *within us*.

Joy in the Dark

Joy in the dark—it really is possible. But don't expect joy to come cascading into your life abundantly in the midst of your darkness (although it can). Instead, look for the glimmers sprinkled *through* the hard circumstances like the diamond dust in the sidewalk. Choose peace while you're in the tumbler and look forward to the shine that you'll see *afterwards*. And along the way take a moment to change perspectives and enjoy the sparkles that shine forth from *within* even in the dark, hard places of life.

A few more suggestions for seeing joy in the dark.

• *Cling to the Vine*—Live as a branch grafted to the vine of Jesus Christ and remember that God is the Master Gardener. Let Him illuminate your way through the darkness as you stay close to Him by poring over His word, praising Him, and praying.

• *Be alert to the sparkles*—Sometimes we just don't notice them because we're going so fast or are too focused on the dark. Keep your eyes open to the sparkles God can bring in the little things. They can do much to lift your spirits and light your way.

• *Think on reasons to be thankful*—Even in the deepest darkness, there is always something to be thankful for. *Always.* So renew your mind by dwelling on those things for which you can give thanks (see Philippians 4:8). Look for the truth even when you're surrounded by lies. Search for the honorable even when you have been dishonored. Look for at least one thing that is right, not for all that is wrong. Focus on something that is pure when life seems tainted. Find one lovely thing outside of your unlovely situation. Think on things with a good reputation and turn away from those that are bad. Focus your mind on something that is excellent even when you're dwelling in imperfection. And find something to praise even if you'd rather curse.

• *Keep an eternal perspective*—Such a perspective is sometimes the only way to know joy in the pitch-black darkness. That was the perspective that fueled the apostle Paul's fire and gave him joy in the dark: He lived for the world to come—not this one. Follow his example and don't look for justice, fairness, and equity here. Those are waiting in the kingdom beyond this life, and they are real and more wonderful than our earthly minds can imagine. Also waiting for us is freedom from tears and pain (Revelation 21:4). Remember, too, that although this earth holds some rewards, our real rewards are in heaven. So if you are groping in the dark because of pain or grief, hold on to this eternal perspective.

I needed these tips last night as I pondered the shade of gray that had descended on my day. It certainly wasn't a dark gray, just a little cloudy. My heart was heavy and my body tired. I was a bit overwhelmed. *I'll be glad when I can see my way clear again. It's hard to write about joy when things are a little overcast.* Then, right in the middle of my thoughts about that gloom, God shined His flashlight on the "true and lovely" of my situation. Right then, I saw a sparkle in the gray of my sidewalk! A flicker of light was shining on something good, so I began to dwell on that and I found myself feeling truly thankful. Then I felt a tiny leap in my heart. (A subtle hop, actually, but nonetheless there!) That made me praise God. *Lord, You are awesome to point to the good in my clouds with the mag-light of your finger.* (So what if it doesn't sound like King David's praise? We can be creative!) As I talked with God and praised Him—an act important to life on the Vine—the clouds began to part some and the dark was a little lighter. For a millisecond, I got a glimpse of my place in these clouds and remembered God's eternal perspective. The sparkle sprinkled on my rock helped me get in touch with the sparkle within. Nothing in my circumstances had changed. I was still tired and rather overwhelmed, but I had found sparkles of joy in the gray.

Looking, Listening, and Learning in the Dark

When the darkness comes, it can seriously interrupt our daily life. Calling such a time "a disruptive moment," author Gordon MacDonald writes, "Where a disruptive moment leads is anyone's guess. But it is nevertheless a time, perhaps unlike any other, when one is more apt to move into communion with God and be receptive to the most searing truths about self and the world. When this happens, it has usually occurred at what I call the soul-level."[5]

Russian writer Alexander Solzhenitsyn experienced an eight-year "disruptive moment" when he served in labor camps, after which he was exiled for so-called "political treason." When he wrote of those experiences and the good he saw in them, he was able to say, "So bless you, prison, for having been in my life." Would that be your response or mine? Can we say "bless you" to the dark prisons that bar us from an easy, affliction-free life? Gordon MacDonald has come to agree with Mr. Solzhenitsyn: "Like [him], I have gradually become thankful for my disruptive moments. They have forced me inward and downward into soul territory. My journals suggest that almost every useful encounter I have had with God has occurred in the wake of a disruptive moment. And as a result, I have not since been the same."[6]

Nor have I. I would never choose to relive my darkest days, and I wish desperately that my mother and mother-in-law were still alive. I miss them every day. Yet, even so I am grateful for what I have learned in the tumbling process. I am realistic enough to know that darkness can be darker and come more frequently with age, but even so I am able to smile at the future.

"At times God puts us through the discipline of darkness to teach us to heed Him..." writes Oswald Chambers. "Song birds are taught to sing in the dark, and we are put into the shadow of God's hand until we learn to hear Him. When you are in the dark, listen, and God will give you a very precious message for someone else when you get into the light."[7] The dark is a time to listen. It is also a time to look. Even in our pain, we must listen to what God is wanting to teach us and look for the sparkles of joy He sprinkles throughout the dark, reveals after the tumbling, and plants within us.

God whispers in our pleasures, but shouts in our pain.

~C.S. Lewis

I Didn't Lose My Joy— It's Been Stolen

Catching the Joy Thieves

I t was Tim's first year as a post-collegiate working man, and one night after work he drove his shiny new Mazda RX-7 into his driveway. He locked it and went inside. Apparently, he wasn't the only one who admired that car. The next morning it was gone!

When we have something valuable, we must be alert. When we possess something beautiful, we are at risk of having it stolen. And joy, with its ability to brighten our life, is something valuable indeed. It shines like a precious gem and must be guarded as such, for thieves lurk who wish to steal it.

A ring of bandits worse than Bonnie and Clyde or the Dalton Gang and led by an insidious mastermind is desperate to steal our joy. That mastermind—known as Satan—is a thief and a murderer, the biggest killjoy around. Interested in more than simple petty theft, Satan knows the true value of joy and he is intent on taking it from us. He knows that it is more than just a beautiful blessing. Satan knows that "the joy of the LORD is your strength" (Nehemiah 8:10b).

This prowling devil absolutely delights in weak Christians because, first, when our joy is gone, so is our witness. If we are pickle-faced, joyless Christians we can't expect the world to come clamoring to find out how they can be just like us. Second, when our joy is gone, so is our delight in Christ and in His salvation, and Jesus paid a high price for that salvation—His very life. "What was the purpose of our Lord's atonement on the cross," writes Sherwood Wirt in *The Book of Joy*, "what is the whole point of salvation from sin if there is no ultimate fulfillment and delight in the Lord?"[1] Third, when our joy is gone, we lose our ability to model it before our children. Children learn what they live and what is lived out before them. Fourth and finally, when our joy is gone so is the soaring spirit that God gives to His children and our pleasure in His gift of life. Clearly, as Nehemiah knew, when we lose our joy, we lose our strength—the strength we need to witness, to delight in the Lord, to model joy to our children, and to savor the blessing of life itself. So protect that gift of joy, dear reader, from the wiles of Satan and his den of thieves by knowing who the robbers are, how they attack, and what security systems we can install.

The Thieves

While there may be more, the primary ringleaders in the great joy heist are stress, fear, anger, sin, adversity, and depression. Although they sometimes team up to ambush the unaware, their individual attacks are quite effective. We must be on our guard against these thieves.

Stress

We are a culture that knows much about stress. These days, all of us, including children, can suffer from tension, pressure, or emotional strain—in a word, stress. Webster defines "stress" as "a factor that induces bodily or mental tension and may be a factor in disease causation; a force that tends to distort a body." Have you ever been so stressed that you knew the addition of one more stressor would "distort" you for sure? I have! And it's not a pretty picture.

And neither is the "disease causation" mentioned in the dictionary definition. Even those Webster word people know what many medical studies have found: Too much stress triggers chemical reactions in our body that are harmful to our health. When we're under great stress, these chemical reactions suppress the immune system and, according to one report, "increase our odds of contracting everything from colds to strokes to heart disease and even cancer."[2] Some researchers say that illnesses and accidents directly linked to stress comprise three-fourths of all lost work time. Author and physician Peter Hanson writes the following in *The Joy of Stress*:

> Stress is also implicated in the majority of cases seen in the doctor's office, hospital beds, and ultimately the graveyard. In spite of all the media attention to health, stress-related problems take the vast majority of people by *surprise*. They might have known that stress can harm others, but never fully realized what it could do to *them*.[3]

(Are those words a wake-up call to you?)

Yet, seemingly contrary to these statistics, all stress is not bad. Some stress is good for us; its mismanagement is what does us harm. Manageable levels of stress can, for instance, cause us to accomplish more than we would without the incentive that's causing stress. The stress of a deadline, say, can cause our productivity to increase and our mental acuity to sharpen. The stress of competition causes athletes to excel. The rush of adrenaline that comes with stress enables us to accomplish more than we would otherwise. But when additional factors enter in, causing too much stress, or when we lose our ability to control the stresses in our life, we begin to suffer from its bad effects. That's when stress can harm us physically and steal our joy.

Stress robs us in several ways. Stress can cause us to neglect certain disciplines—physical and spiritual—that help us lead balanced lives and feel good (see chapter ten). Too much stress can make us forget to take proper care of our body, and then our own biology can keep us from feeling joyful. Also, consider that stress management requires a great deal of energy. In times of stress overload, energy we would use to engage in activities that bring us joy is diverted to stress management. Stress can also rob us of joy because it tends to shift our focus to surviving and coping, rather than enjoying. Coping with life is good, but enjoying it is better. Finally, stress also causes us to focus on the things we cannot control instead of on the Source of control and of joy.

In fact, having a sense of control seems to be the biggest factor in effective stress management. One researcher had two groups of workers concentrate on a given task. Both groups were subjected to irritating background noises, but only one group was given an out. Workers in that group had a panic button in front of them that they could push at will to stop the noise. Which group do you think was more productive? Of course the group with the button—but, interestingly, not one person in that group ever pressed the button. The fact that they had control (not that they exercised it) accounted for their higher productivity.[4] When we lose control or the sense of control, our stress level increases. As we focus on the stressors that we can't control, we lose sight of the big picture: that God is in control even when our circumstances are out of control. And, as I've said before, when we focus on our seemingly out-of-control circumstances rather than on the steady and omnipotent Source of our joy, a loss of joy is inevitable. The apostle Paul—a man who knew a lot about stress—used the Greek word *thlipsis,* meaning "pressure" and translated "tribulation," when he talked about difficult times of stress. And Paul calls us to face that tribulation with joy!

Fear

Fear is one of the sneakiest robbers, creeping up on us when we least expect it and attacking despite our best defensive weapons—our reason, our intellect, and our logic. Whether or not it is based in reality, fear can prompt a full-blown battle and completely wipe out our joy. In many cases, if the thief attacks hard, joy completely retreats.

Fear can turn a strong, joyful woman into a wreck, trembling and terrified. Donna D. knows about that. Fear used to be the driving force in her life despite her head knowledge about the joy of Christ. She just couldn't seem to get that knowledge—that joy—into her heart or emotions. Consequently her fears—and they were many—were all consuming. A confrontation with a Peeping Tom when she was young led to a nearly paralyzing fear that someone was going to lift her garage door and break into her house. She sometimes stood at the top of her stairs, shaking, because she was convinced that someone was downstairs. Then one night it happened. She heard the garage door go up, but no one answered when she called downstairs. Then, while she called 911, she heard someone come in the door—only to discover moments later that the intruder was her son.

She was also fearful that her only son would be in a car accident. At one point, Donna even slept in her makeup because she "knew" she was going to be called to the hospital in the middle of the night. But that wasn't her worst fear. What terrified her most was being alone. Whenever her husband Bob had to travel, they would argue before he left because Donna could not bear to stay by herself. She was so bound up with fear that she would pin her drapes closed in the daylight and then go outside to see if you could see in. But her heavenly Father wanted to free this hostage from her fear.

After their children were out of the nest and two days after Donna and Bob moved into a new house, he had to leave the country for six weeks on a work assignment. Donna was terrified of being completely alone in a new place for that much time, but God used those six weeks to deliver her from her fear. She describes what happened:

> I began to again ask God to take away this awful fear, and I said, "There's no way that I'll feel safe with Bob gone, Lord. I can't be by myself!" As I kept asking Him to remove the fear and buried myself in my Bible, God began to show me that I wasn't alone. He was with me. I got to a place where I let go of much that kept me bound because I wanted so badly to be free.

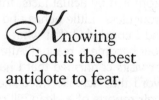

Knowing God is the best antidote to fear.

~Cheri Fuller

As I clung to God's Word and talked with Him constantly, He carried me until I was ready to step into the waters of healing and face my fears. He wonderfully healed me of my fear of being alone. Before, I couldn't say that I was a woman who could smile at the future, but now I can. Fear is gone.

Is your fear gone? Or is it robbing you of joy?

Before you answer those questions, consider the different degrees and sources of fear we can encounter. A novice skydiver standing at the plane's open door ready to jump knows fear about the impending jump. The keynote speaker soon to address an unfriendly crowd feels fear before the event. These are real fears, yet some of our fears are only played out in the arena of our mind. We fear, for instance, things in the future, things that may never happen: We fear the unknown.

I faced that kind of fear of the unknown when I was told that my ovarian cysts were probably malignant. For one week (that felt like one month) I battled fear, playing out the various scenarios of the cancer diagnosis which the doctors had suggested. That battle went fairly well for even though I tearfully poured out my heart to God and openly expressed my fears to Him, I prayed that He would make me able to bear the news— even if it were bad. Of course I knew great joy when the test results were negative.

After I lost my mother, however, I didn't do as well in another battle against fear. While my first scrimmage had been prompted by actual facts, this second bout with fear was totally groundless. Little aches and pains got my imagination stirring, and I concluded that what I was spared of the first time would now become a reality ("After all, just look at my mom."). Doctor visits confirmed that I had nothing to fear, but it was God's Word that actually freed me from fear and helped me rest in their reports of a clean bill of health. I had fought quite a battle against fear in my mind, and my joy had been stolen. It was only restored when I once again turned my trust to the Lord.

As my friend Cheri Fuller, author and speaker, teaches in her public speaking and her book *Trading Your Worry for Wonder*—and as I know from experience—fear takes a high toll: It causes us to miss the present; paralyzes our faith; zaps our physical, emotional, and spiritual energy; causes burnout; harms our relationships; confuses our thinking; and greatly limits our potential. No wonder we lose our joy when we operate in fear! So what can we do to safeguard ourselves? What battle plan can we adopt?

Cheri says, "The best weapon for fear is to refocus on God's character and His name. As we meditate on who He is, by praising Him through His many names and attributes, our joy and trust and gratefulness go up."[5] How, for instance, can we fear when we are spending time with the Alpha and the Omega (the Beginning and the End), Elohim ("the God who is my Source"), and Jehova-shammah ("the Lord who is present")? Fear recedes when we focus on our all-powerful, all-loving God.

We can also fight fear by remembering what God has done for us. The Old Testament tells that the Israelites erected stone altars as monuments of God's provision, and we need the same kind of reminders. We need to look back on what God has done in our life as a steppingstone to praise (even when we don't feel like it) and greater faith (even when we're feeling hopeless).

Finally, the greatest weapon of all for fighting fear is knowing that God's Word says "perfect love casts out all fear" (1 John 4:18). We know that perfect love through Jesus Christ and His death on the cross for us. Because God is perfect love, we can abide in Him and take Him at His word: "Fear not, for I am with you" (Isaiah 41:10 RSVB).

Focusing on who God is, remembering what He has done for us, and drawing close to Jesus—these are key elements of our strategy against fear, an effective thief of joy.

Anger

Fear can issue a sneak attack and steal our joy from behind the scenes, but its cohort in crime—anger—tends to be a bit more demonstrative. Anger usually makes its presence known, sometimes quite loudly and dramatically. Anger itself is not a sin (what we do with our anger can be sinful—which is why Paul wrote, "Be angry but do not sin" [Ephesians 4:26a RSVB]), but it's almost impossible to feel joyful when we are angry. Joy doesn't necessarily leave us completely when we are angry, but it certainly goes underground. When we express our anger, we can still have the joy of the Lord within us, but the *feeling* of joy is definitely incompatible with the feeling of anger.

I know, for instance, that I would lose my feelings of joy if I burned dinner and stubbed my toe and then found out that the children had jumped on the bed where the folded laundry lay and, in the process, broke my favorite vase. I would definitely feel like expressing anger—and I wouldn't feel particularly joyful in the process. Yet if I'd had a full measure of joy before expressing my anger and I expressed my anger in a healthy way rather than letting it linger, then I could soon return to a joyful state. That return to joy comes more easily when we are truly angry but we sin not, following Jesus' example when He overturned the tables of those selling in the temple (Mark 11:15-17). Our Lord fully expressed His anger. Turning over chairs and tables is quite demonstrative, yet He did not sin. At other times, Jesus expressed His anger quietly. When the Pharisees were watching Him in the temple to see if He would heal on the Sabbath so they could accuse Him, Jesus looked "at them with anger, grieved at their hardness of heart," and healed the man's withered hand (Mark 3:5).

Although anger can definitely steal our joy, I'm not suggesting that we squash it. Instead, we are to control it in a healthy way as Jesus modeled. After all, anger is a natural reaction to grief and pain; it's how we deal with our anger that makes it right or wrong. In *Splashes of Joy in the Cesspools of Life*, Barbara Johnson tells about driving to a dump late at night to grieve over her "second deposit in Heaven," the loss of a second son. She would rant and rave at God in private, this outpouring of anger an expression of her grief. Today, in her ministry to hurting parents, she tells them that "it is okay to express these emotions and it is okay to be mad at God. When we scream in agony and rage at Him through our grief, He doesn't say, 'Off to hell with you, Sister!' Instead, He patiently loves us...carries us...wraps His blanket of tenderness around us while we are balking, hissing, and rebelling in every way."[6] God made us creatures capable of emotion, so He's not offended when we share our feelings. In fact, we're not telling Him anything He doesn't already know! That's one reason why venting is okay.

Releasing the anger that naturally arises from grief and pain is not only okay, it is important to our emotional health and healing. If we stuff our pain, thinking it wrong to express our anger, we are like a pressure cooker with a missing vent. We're building up steam and the pressure increases, but there is no release. Once my mother made rice in a pressure cooker and didn't know that the vent was clogged—until it exploded. Rice went everywhere, practically coating the kitchen. Luckily she wasn't in the room then. Can you imagine calling 911? "Please come quickly. I've been hit with a blast of exploding rice." That unvented pressure cooker could have been embarrassing, if not downright dangerous. And it is, in fact, dangerous for us if we fail to vent the pain and anger in our life.

In her book *Women and Stress,* Jean Lush teaches that when we are frustrated or angry high amounts of tension and emotional energy swirl around inside us, and energy always seeks to be discharged. How we discharge that energy varies depending on how we manage the "storage pots" which we use to contain this energy. Some people's pots are small and can't hold very much tension. These people rarely close the lid: "Whenever they are tense, they immediately unload their tension, regardless of the cost." Others have a larger capacity for this emotional energy. Since they rarely open their lids to release the tension, it gets discharged inwardly and manifests itself in psychosomatic illnesses, depression, avoidance, and procrastination.[7] Even my doctor's office distributed pamphlets describing the danger of "stuffing" anger, cautioning that it can lead to a host of physical problems.

If we rarely close the lid we will act out all of our emotions—which is not always appropriate and certainly hinders a joyful life. If we rarely open the lid we build up pressure until we explode—which is not healthy and which can also hinder a joyful life. Perhaps the balance lies in the image of a properly functioning pressure cooker with a clear and open escape vent. The lid fits properly to process what's inside, but the vent is open so pressure doesn't build to the point of explosion.

When anger does explode or when we allow it to linger, become a habit, or rage out of control, it begins to steal our joy. I have experienced the kind of lingering anger that crosses the boundary of healthy expression, and it robbed me of my joy. I felt that anger shortly after my mother died. I wasn't exactly mad at God, but I did find myself struggling with a great deal of anger. When I'd see a mother and daughter together having a good time, I'd get angry about my loss. In a movie I saw, the look a mother and daughter exchanged spoke volumes about how well they understood each other and what a unique bond they shared. My loss of that kind of relationship at a young age made me angry. I should have taken Barbara Johnson's advice and regularly vented. Instead, my "pot"—as Jean Lush describes—leaked, and I found myself expressing my anger in ways and at times that were not always in the best interest of my family. I became entangled in my anger even though in my heart I longed for joy. Sometimes little things set me off and my un-released anger exploded. (I have a chip in my stove today that's a testimony to that explosion!) Walking around with an under-current of anger is a big joy robber. A friend of mine knows about that, too.

Aware I was writing this book about when Mama ain't happy, this friend said, "You may not understand, but I struggle with anger and often feel like screaming." It's because I understand that struggle with anger that I venture to tell you that a life of joy is possible. That thief quit stealing my joy when I learned about the importance of releasing my anger privately (instead of in front of my children) and when I took my anger (and its some-times uncontrollable and lingering presence) to the cross. I had told God many times that I was angry and that I didn't like living in its shadow, and I'd asked Him to help me deal with it, yet I still struggled. But one day He did more than just help me control it. He freed me from this joy robber.

That day, I expressed to the Lord how I felt and confessed my occasional but sinful outbursts that affected my family—something I'd done before. But then I asked a close friend to pray for me. It was during that prayer time with her that God gave me a mental image of just how free I could be. While we prayed, I pictured myself bound up, a thick rope wrapped tightly around my body (which is how the anger made me feel). As my friend asked God to untangle that rope of anger, I pictured myself standing before Jesus at the foot of the cross. As I placed one end of my tangle of rope into His pierced hand, the entire thing began to loosen until it fell from my body in a heap...at the foot of the cross. He still held in His hand the end I'd given Him, but I was free to walk away—which I did.

Do I still get angry? Of course, but not in an out-of-control, misdirected way, and my anger no longer steals my joy. The vivid picture that the Lord gave me that day was freeing. Now, every time I'm tempted to grab that rope of anger again, I remember that Jesus took it from me. I can express my anger, but I don't have to let it bind me and cut off my joy because I left that rope with Jesus at the cross.

I use other safeguards against anger, too, and you might try them as well. First, to protect our joy, we are to be slow to anger since anger doesn't "achieve the righteousness of God" (James 1:19,20) or "make us good" (TLB). Second, remember the storage pots and the pressure cooker and be sure you have proper vents when you're under pressure so you don't explode. Third, we must acknowledge our anger and try to resolve the matter before the sun goes down (Ephesians 4:26b) so that it doesn't linger or become uncontrolled wrath. Fourth and finally, the prophet Nehemiah offers this model: "When I was angry...I consulted with myself" (Nehemiah 5:6,7). What a great thing to remember to do! Many times we would be much better off if we would "consult with ourselves" (that's akin to counting to ten!) before we react. When we contemplate our anger, we might ask ourselves, "Is the blocked goal worth the anger? Is the anger appropriate (is it righteous indignation or a response to someone who has sinned against me?) or inappropriate (is it based on selfishness or perfectionism?)? Is my expression of anger going to hurt someone else? What am I doing to resolve the issue?" If we act out our anger inappropriately or allow our anger to linger and become bitterness, it will indeed steal our joy. After all, wrongly expressing anger and harboring bitterness in our heart are sins—which moves us to the next joy robber.

Sin

"Sin" is as distasteful a word as "joy" is delightful. The word "sin" is also quite rare outside of the church. You never hear newscasters report, "There was great sin in our city today." No. They simply describe the results of our sin without any comment on the root cause. And, like the newscasters, we don't usually walk around saying, "I'm really struggling with my sin today." No, "sin" just isn't a frequently used word in our culture. For the most part, no one likes to be reminded of their sin, and many of the people doing the reminding these days don't seem to like their job either. More and more churches are getting away from talking about sin, opting instead for more ear-tickling, pew-filling, positive messages.

Webster defines "sin" as "an offense against God," and the Bible calls it unrighteousness (1 John 5:17), adding that it's something we all do (Romans 3:23). Defined as a "weakened state of human nature in which the self is estranged from God," sin is a powerful member of the joy heist gang. The estrangement that results from unconfessed or habitual sin prevents us from knowing joy in the Lord. Our sin separates us from God and damages our relationship with Him—as sinners, we cannot draw close to the true Source of joy.

Oh, we may feel a joyful thrill for a time since sin can be fun, but that momentary thrill is not true joy. If we are engaged in habitual sin—if we're doing that which we know is wrong yet we willfully continue—we are further cutting ourselves off from the joy of the Lord. The prophet Isaiah describes that cold, joyless place: "Your iniquities have made a separation between you and your God, and your sins have hidden His face from you, so that He does not hear" (Isaiah 59:2). Sin is a joy robber since it causes God to hide His face from us.

King David knew about God hiding His face after he and Bathsheba had quite the little affair. He must have thought he was pretty powerful and crafty, what with arranging to have her husband killed in battle and all, but he ultimately saw that the "joy" of their moments together was nothing compared to the joy in the Lord he had known before. When he was confronted by Nathan, David fully confessed his sin, acknowledging that his actions were sinful and asking God to "blot out my transgressions" (Psalm 51:1). He also asked God to "make me to hear joy and gladness" (verse 8) and "restore in me the joy of Thy salvation" (verse 12). And as Sherwood Wirt points out in *The Book of Joy*, "It was not God's salvation that David wanted restored; it was the joy of it. The salvation may hold, but if the joy of it slips away, something very precious is lost."[8] God heard David's confession, forgave his sin, and, as the psalms David later wrote reveal, restored his joy.

And God can do that for you and me regardless of the nature of our sin. I once saw a woman publicly confess before her church just what David did. The pain in her face and the remorse with which she asked forgiveness testified to the empty "joy" and passing thrill of sin compared to the true joy of an unbroken relationship with God. We can all know God's forgiveness and restoration, but what can we do to better maintain that unbroken relationship with Him? The safeguard God gives us human beings, who are sinners by nature, is explained in the promise of 1 John 1:9. There we learn that, "If we confess our sins, [God] is faithful and righteous to forgive us our sins and to cleanse us from all unrighteousness." Honesty in our confession is essential. We must be as real with God about our sin as we are when we tell Him we're afraid or angry. God doesn't expect us to change—He knows we need Him to accomplish that. But He does expect us to be honest, for then we demonstrate that we are willing to be molded and shaped by Him. Furthermore, God loves us so much that He doesn't reward us according to our sins, but instead, "as far as the east is from the west, so far has He removed our transgressions from us" (Psalm 103:12). Amazing grace! Confession and forgiveness are key to keeping sin from robbing us of our joy.

Adversity

One last member of the thieving joy heist gang is adversity—those unpleasant circumstances, accidents, mistakes, and misfortunes that are a part of life, that range from the minor to the catastrophic, from light afflictions to life-and-death matters. Adversity is often a very dark place that leaves us longing for the light of God's joy. You read more about that in the previous chapter, but here I'll offer the most important safeguard against allowing adverse situations to rob us of joy. We simply need to remember that adversity is merely a set of circumstances, albeit bad ones, and that our joy is not contingent on our circumstances. Then, when adversity does come, we need to remember that God's grace sustains us in seemingly hopeless situations. As Christ said, "My grace is sufficient for you, for [My] power is perfected in weakness" (2 Corinthians 12:9). That promise falls into "the peace that passes all understanding" category: We cannot fathom God's grace being all that we need in times of adversity until we experience it for ourselves.

Right after my mother-in-law died, I vacillated between hope and despair—hope that my mother might rally and win her fight for life and despair because Tim's mother hadn't, and I was afraid mine wouldn't either. I didn't see how I could possibly bear the loss of both of them at the same time. Then my dear friend reminded me of a statement by Corrie ten Boom: "You don't need the ticket until you get on the train." I struggled most to find joy in my darkness when I was living out in my mind that which had not yet happened. Picturing the worst case scenario before it even happened, I found myself unable to comprehend how God's grace would be sufficient. My friend's words reminded me that I wasn't on that train yet so I didn't need the ticket, and that God would provide it when I did. And that's exactly how it happened. God's grace was indeed sufficient as I dealt with the pain of two goodbyes.

We can safeguard ourselves and keep adversity from stealing our joy by remembering that God can use tough times to refine our faith, produce in us proven character, and show Himself strong (see 1 Peter 1:6-9). Without such testing, how will we ever know if our faith is really real? If we have a car that's supposed to be really fast but we never really open it up, opting instead for a safe 30-miles-per-hour pace, how will we know if it's as fast as the owner's manual says? God's Word tells me that He is capable of great performance at fierce speeds, on rough terrain, and in the worst of conditions. I've been in those places. I know the rough terrain of heavy afflictions (losing both my mother and mother-in-law in three short weeks) as well as the wear and tear of each day's trying circumstances, and I know how great God's faithfulness is.

> *Therefore you too now have sorrow; but I will see you again, and your heart will rejoice, and no one takes your joy away from you.*
>
> ~John 16:22

Daniel and his friends also knew how faithful God is. As they stood before a raging Nebuchadnezzar who had just threatened to throw them in a fiery furnace, they showed incredible faith, saying, "Our God whom we serve is able to deliver us...but even if He does not [we won't worship your gods]" (Daniel 3:17,18). These young men knew that God was able to deliver them from their adversity and that sometimes He chooses not to. Likewise, as he underwent severe trials at the hand of Satan, Job was able to say, "The LORD gave and the LORD has taken away. Blessed be the name of the LORD" (Job 1:21). Faith that is tested shows its true value.

When our faith is tested, the experience can alleviate any doubts that it is real. In fact, many followers of Christ throughout history—from the first-century apostles to contemporary believers like Corrie ten Boom and Mother Teresa—have undergone great adversity, resulting in powerful testimonies and vibrant faith. If we want such a testimony, we shouldn't run from the test. Besides, it is more important to know who God is and the reality of His power than to live a life of continual comfort!

Although some believers have a strong faith despite having never been called to face much adversity, I think they are the exception. Trials tend to be the forge of unshakable and contagious faith. Then there are those believers who have never faced great adversity but who live fearful that the ax will fall at any moment. If you fall into this category, consider that God may be calling you to a life of faith characterized by a calm staying power over the long haul. But if testing does come your way, don't be fearful. God enables us to respond to adversity—great or small—with joy! That thief may enter our house, but it doesn't have to take our prize!

Depression

One major joy robber for many women (and men) is depression. "Depression...black as a thousand midnights in a cypress swamp. Loneliness that is indescribable. Confusion regarding God. Frustration with life and circumstances. The feeling that you have been abandoned, that you are worthless. Unlovable. The pain is excruciating"[9]—that's how Cynthia Swindoll, executive director of Insight for Living, describes this dark thief of joy in the foreword of the book *Depression*. In *Surviving the Darkness*, Dr. Grace Ketterman says that depression is a complex mixture of "varying proportions of fear, anger, sadness, helplessness, guilt, remorse, and sometimes hopelessness" and lists the causes of depression: inherited genetic factors; family influences (learned behavior, reactions, and feelings taught within families); the impact of our environment (the coldness or warmth of our climate and of the people in our life); and the stress factor.[10] Dr. James Dobson says that low self-esteem as well as fatigue and time pressure are two of the top sources of depression in women.[11]

Depression is not only a joy robber in our life, but—as the title of this book suggests—it robs our family of joy, too, because our emotional state affects our children. Dr. Ketterman writes, "Family influences, I believe, create the core of beliefs, emotions, and self-concept that predispose individuals to depression or health."[12] It's my opinion that this influence is not license to blame our parents (or for our children to blame us) for the way we (or they) turn out, for we all make choices that affect us throughout our life. Yet the influence of the family in which we were raised (or are raising our children) cannot be overlooked as a contributor to depression.

A friend of mine has battled depression for two years. She has experienced a lack of joy during this time and told me, "I've been asking myself, 'What can I do to make myself happier?' I've decided there were some faith issues and hurts from my past and my family of origin that I have to deal with before I can experience joy." Indeed, working through such issues, often with the help of a qualified Christian counselor, is important to our healing and recovery from depression.

Geri R. suffered from depression, too. For her, it began during adolescence and reached its peak in her early forties. She shares her struggle and ultimate return to a life of joy:

> I was full of bitterness from my failed first marriage, afraid of rejection, locked in an unhappy second marriage, forced to suppress my true self at work, and overwhelmed by guilt from an abortion. I saw no hope for my future and felt no worth for my life. I wanted to die. Through the help of a Christian

counselor and over time, the Lord healed me and restored my marriage. Through the Scriptures, prayer,
and close fellowship with caring Christian friends, the
Lord freed me from strongholds of bitterness, rejection, and quiet. He demonstrated Psalm 30:11,12
(NIV) in my life: "You turned my wailing into dancing,
you removed my sackcloth and clothed me with joy,
that my heart may sing to you and not be silent."
Now, I gratefully receive His daily gift of joy and His
promise of hope.

If depression in any of its complex forms is stealing your joy,
know that there is indeed hope. Depression is not a place where
you have to stay. As Dr. Ketterman concludes in her book,
"With expert help, personal honesty, great patience, and persistence, you can win the battle against depression. I wish for
you the courage to work and the steadfastness to endure until
you know the joy that the Creator wants you to know!"[13]

The Thief Within

Finally, the wisdom of the cartoon character Pogo applies
here: "I have seen the enemy and he is us!" Sometimes we ourselves are the thief that is robbing us of our joy. Oh, I know
some folks would say that "other people" should be included in
my band of joy robbers, but I contend that very few people actually intend to take away another person's joy (although there
are those whom we could swear that is their sole mission in
life!). When people rob us of our joy, we are usually allowing
them to do so. People may treat us badly, sin against us, and
make life miserable for us, but we choose how we respond to
them. We can let them rain on our parade and wash away our
joy, or we can choose to remain joyful in spite of them, even
hoping that some of it will rub off on them!

I'm sure you know people whose cup of joy in life isn't exactly half-full or even close to bubbling over. I challenge you to
consider these folks your "joy project." (I've had one of my
own!) Those potential robbers may, of course, look at you
funny, but keep on offering them lemonade when they hand you
lemons. On those occasions when you could let those folks zap

some of your joy, act as your own sentry. Guard against allowing them to take that which you have—joy in the Lord despite the circumstances of your life and despite the robbers who are attempting to take it away.

This was something that, as a new bride, I didn't know how to do. I prepared one of my best recipes from home for our first dinner together in our new apartment after our honeymoon. It was ready when Tim walked in, and I was ready for his praise. Instead, he said it was "interesting" and that it would be OK if I lost that recipe. My high hopes for domestic kudos that night were crushed, and I let him steal my joy. Today, if people at my dinner table complain about a meal, I simply tell them the short-order cook has the night off so they'd better eat—and I enjoy my dinner. While I love to please my family, I consider comments like "this looks like dog food" their problem—and I tell them they may not bless the neighbor's dog with it. They can't touch my joy with something that is their problem.

For a more recent example, I went to a gathering and greeted several women as I walked by. One of them looked at me as I called her by name, said nothing, and then quickly looked away. *I've been snubbed! How rude. What did I do to her?* I wondered. Then I decided that I didn't want to let her steal my joy. In fact, she wouldn't have been stealing anything. If I mulled over all the possible reasons why I'd been snubbed and then got angry about her rudeness, I would be *allowing* my joy to be stolen. My choice would be the thief. So, instead, I decided to enjoy my evening. As Linda T. points out, "Most things [like that snubbing] that happen have very little—if anything—to do with me. If someone fails to speak to me, then I just assume they are having a bad day. I don't think it's

> *I* learned early in life that I'm a child of the King—that makes me a princess! So why should I be discontented or ever lack self-esteem?
>
> ~Norma M.

about me." People are probably thinking about us much less than we presume.

But bigger issues make that choice to not let someone steal our joy more difficult. One person I know was the victim of a business deal gone awry—she'd been "taken" by someone she cared about. Although deeply hurt by the incident, this person chose to embrace forgiveness and release bitterness—a key to guarding our joy. She chose not to allow the other person's actions to steal her joy. That choice can be tough to live out, but we can become a guard of our joy instead of a target of robbery. It's a choice we can learn to make when we practice letting other people's problems remain their problems and when, instead of trying so hard to be a people-pleaser, we seek approval from God and find self-esteem in knowing who we are in Christ. The job of the sentry may get tough, but we don't have to let people steal our joy. Instead, we can offer to share it.

As we've seen, choices we make about our attitude and our level of contentment can make us either sentries of our joy or thieves. Many daily decisions also either contribute to our level of joy or rob us of it. The presence or lack of disciplines to help us in these decisions is the subject of the next chapter. Read on.

❧ Part Three ❧

Practicing Joy and Contentment in Our Homes
What We Do

✣ 10 ✣

Disciplines of a Joyful Person
Practical Tips for Practicing Joy

D iscipline and joy? What does discipline have to do with joy?" you may be thinking. Quite a lot actually! The phrase "disciplines of a joyful person" really isn't an oxymoron. Although a life of discipline certainly doesn't sound like the goal of Jovial Jane, she—and we—can pursue certain disciplines which are conducive to joy. We can make choices that will help us live more joyfully.

Still, "discipline" can be such a painful word—perhaps because it evokes images of feet hitting the floor at 5 A.M., sweat pouring off a body doing its 500th push-up, or a person sitting at the computer while her friends go to the movies. The word "discipline" also brings to mind images of the "board of education" (the kind that meets the seat!). After all, "If you disobey, you will be disciplined!" is a comment many of us have both made and experienced.

So how can the words "discipline" and "joyful" appear in the same sentence? Let me explain. Although the gift and fruit of joy is certainly from God and not something we create, we can choose to engage in certain disciplines which contribute to an attitude and feeling of joy. When these disciplines are combined with the heart issues of joy stemming from our faith (issues which we've already discussed), the result is a life conducive to genuine joy and not mere happiness. When we adopt these practical disciplines of lifestyle, labor, and love, we are able to practice joyful living.

1. *The Disciplines of Lifestyle*

The choices we make and the disciplines we adopt shape our lifestyle, which in turn either helps or hinders our joyfulness. A simplified lifestyle that includes disciplines of the mind, body, and spirit can make joyful living possible.

The Discipline of Simplicity

Have you noticed that many Americans are reevaluating their lifestyle? We've been hearing much this decade about Americans who have traded fast-paced, whirlwind, lots-of-overtime lives for more family time and a simpler, more relaxed lifestyle often characterized by less purchasing power and less purchasing. In its January 2, 1996 edition, The *Houston Chronicle* reported the Trends Research Institute finding that this movement toward a simpler life is one of the top trends of the '90s and "probably the most fundamental shift in lifestyle changes since the depression." A *Time* cover story on "the simple life" said this about Americans: "They've been thinking hard about what really matters in their lives, and they've decided to make some changes. What matters is having time for family and friends, rest and recreation, good deeds and spirituality."[1] Sometimes simplicity can bring felicity—and increased joy in life!

Like many of those searching for a better lifestyle, I have struggled with barren busyness, being over-committed, and living a life that was anything but simple. In my quest for a joyful, contented, simplified life, I have lived the words of Erma Bombeck: "Do I have it all yet? I hope so. I'm half-dead."[2] And half-dead is a terrible way to live. I have since discovered and, as most women today know, that "having it all" (or even some of it) is a bunch of hooey. But the myth is a powerful one—which is why I totally related to Erma when she said the modern woman may have it all, but she doesn't want it anymore. She wrote:

It sounded so great when I heard there wasn't anything as a woman I couldn't do. "All" sounded so all-encompassing. Now it's turned out to be the same "all" as in one-size-fits-all. All of what?...I began hearing about what a great source of untapped energy and talent I was and that I should volunteer it for the community. I did that. Then someone suggested that I should be paid for all this expertise and get a job. I did that. The slick magazines came along and said, "Why work for someone else? You should be running the company." Running for Congress. Running for your health. Running for the bus. Running...running...running. I've been doing it ever since.[3]

Been there; done that. I know what it is to try to balance husband, children, church, home, career, social life, etc. Sometimes it's the "etcetera" that gets us—that and all that running! I know. Years ago I lived life at quite a rapid pace (some might have called it a sprint), which was manageable...for a while. Tim had a busy job, and I was running my own part-time business at home, speaking, writing, occasionally broadcasting, and volunteering at church. And I was doing all that in addition to my primary priority of raising our children and trying to be a good wife and homemaker. I never did all of these things on any given day or even in any given month, but—as crowded as it sounds—all of them were in my life. (Remember, I told you I was better at doing than being. I have lots of practice "doing"!) Every activity seemed important, and I wanted to be doing all of them. But just like the frog in the kettle that doesn't realize when his tepid bath becomes a boiling broth (and that he's dinner!), I failed to see the overall effect of all these activities—the too many etceteras—on my schedule and my life.

Ringing phones, crowded schedules, frequent deadlines, less frequent sleep, dirty laundry, and dinner-from-a-box became much too common. Too much to do in too little time had become a normal way of life for me and, although I enjoyed what I was doing, I often felt overwhelmed. But I was the frog unaware that my broth was about to boil. Oh, I knew I was in the kettle surrounded by hot water, but I didn't quite know how to get out. Besides, where I was, wasn't entirely unpleasant. So it is for the frog—right up to the point when he becomes dinner.

The first time I ever gave any serious consideration to the depth of the water and the rising temperature of my swirling lifestyle was several years before my mother became ill. I didn't really know there was a particular problem with how I was living until she came for a week's visit. She graciously helped out around the house and with the children while I worked at home. One morning, though, I walked through the kitchen and stared at the refrigerator, which she had just given the cleaning of its life. I looked at it, standing there shining in my kitchen. *Hmm. I hadn't even noticed it was that dirty.* There was also something else I hadn't noticed.

"Did you know, my dear, that you are a pack rat?" my mother asked.

"Me? A pack rat? Do you mean you think I keep too much stuff?"

"Honey, you have so much stuff you don't even know what you have. Let's clear out and clean out. Do you mind?" *Did I mind? Would you mind if I gave you a million dollars?*

"Of course not!" She began to clean out cupboards, organizing as she went. I walked back into my office, musing over this new thought. *Me a pack rat? Interesting.*

What made this possibility interesting was that I had to maintain a certain level of efficiency to keep all the balls I was juggling in the air. I found running a home business and managing a busy family a real blessing in my life, and I'd had some degree of success in that. I knew what was where in my business. I had a filing system and I kept up with my organizing notebook. I even knew where the kids' shoes were (most of the time). But I was also aware that, although things were running pretty well, there were pockets of chaos in my life that ran very deep. That awareness came into clear focus during my mother's visit.

When Tim came home from work that night, he walked through the kitchen and then stopped. "What happened to the refrigerator?" he asked.

"Mother cleaned it," I replied.

"Wow!"

The funny thing was that he had not even opened it! He just

noticed from across the room that the door was shining. A new concept!

One day, my mother asked, "Does the phone always ring this much?"

"Yes," I said. "This is the usual pace around here." She just breathed a bit deeply and gave me one of those motherly glances; she didn't say anything. *Hmmm. It does ring a lot....*

As simple as that sounds, a clean refrigerator (and a husband who noticed), the realization that I was a pack rat, and a ringing (and ringing and ringing) phone marked the beginning of a turning point in my life. The following conversation clinched it.

"So, you say things are always this busy for you?" Mother asked.

"Well, not always, but it's not unusual," I answered.

"And are you happy?"

"Yes, well...I'm glad I get to be home with the children and I like what I do. Is that what you mean?"

"No. I know you're happy about that. Are you happy with your lifestyle? Are you happy with who you are as a person?" she asked.

"Ummm..." I had to think.

"You're living at such a fast pace that you can't even enjoy the fruits of your labor." Then she told me about a letter from my aunt, who agreed with her.

We sat down and talked for a long time.

Later that afternoon while running an errand (there I was running again), I did something I hadn't done in ages. I drove slowly. I drove under the speed limit and let everyone else be the first to take off after the light turned green. *So this is how it feels.* Then I stopped and bought a key chain proclaiming my new goal: *"Slow Down."*

For me, the unwinding process after years of very tightly-wound wires was not an overnight accomplishment. Here's a case in point. About this same time I found out that I needed minor surgery (minor only if you're not the one on the operating table). My doctor told me he wanted to schedule the surgery within a few days.

"I can't, Doctor, because I'm scheduled to go to Canada for a Christian television interview." (And I already told you about *that* trip!) He suggested the next week.

"Oh, I can't then because I have a speaking engagement," I continued.

"And," he replied in a fatherly fashion, "I'm sure you've got something scheduled after that. We need to do the operation next week." As I obligingly consented, he added, "There comes a point when you must slow down and take care of yourself first!"

There it was again—"slow down." The message was crystallizing for me, but it took the insight of others to help me see that my lifestyle needed to change. The physical, emotional, and work pressures were taking their toll, and the words of my mother and my doctor got me doing some soul-searching. *Is this joyful living?* I had thought so. I enjoyed being home with my children. I enjoyed my homemaking and my work. But I did not enjoy them all at once and at the speed I was doing them. There were too many etceteras, and there was too much running. My complicated lifestyle had made me settle for far less joy than I knew was possible. I'd said yes too many times and had lost sight of a simpler lifestyle and its rich joys.

Immediately I took a few steps toward simplicity. I had a big garage sale and sold or gave away more junk than I'd realized we'd collected. I reorganized my home—with Mom's help. I dropped some of the responsibilities that I could drop and put many of the things that crowded my life on hold. I began moving toward a simpler life.

I also began to change my thinking, for the discipline of a lifestyle of simplicity starts there. From my journal:

> Lord, show me how to open up blocks of time for my family to find each other again and for me to find joy.

Another entry:

> It's taking me quite some time to slow down. I'm so used to being in a hurry everywhere I go because I was packing so much into such a short time. Even when I shouldn't have been in a rush, I usually ended up that way. But worse than that—I had that attitude.

The hurried mentality.

I drove in a hurry—I always had a knot in my stomach trying to get some place.

I ate in a hurry—often fast food.

I talked in a hurry—Why not if the brain can listen eight times faster than I can speak?

I even hurried at home—"Hurry up, kids!"

Now I'm making better choices. I find myself realizing when there's not enough time to fit "this" in before "that." I'm hurrying less and relaxing more. After a few months of this, I'm beginning to notice changes. I don't always search for that maximum speed in a minimum of time. I walk slower. I lingered at a neighbor's house yesterday. But the best thing was when I realized that I was beginning to slow down in my lifestyle and in my mind. While driving, I hit the brakes slightly in order to be sure to catch the approaching yellow-then-stop light. I smiled at my progress. However, I really don't talk any slower. I guess some things never change.

Later, I was on a radio broadcast with Dr. James Dobson discussing my book *Working at Home*. As Brenda Koinis, Posy Lough, and I talked about some of the pitfalls of working at home, Dr. Dobson said something that I had lived: "The subtleties of overcommitment never cease to amaze me. Just when you think you've gotten your time schedule under control, you say yes three times when you should have said no—and the next thing you know your own successes become a trap!" Boy, did I know that!

When we say yes too many times, we get away from a life of simplicity. Know the value of a "yes," but remember there is also value in a "no." And evaluate the timing of an opportunity. As Anne Ortlund puts it in *Disciplines of a Beautiful Woman*, one of the best ways to seriously simplify one's lifestyle is to learn to "eliminate and concentrate."[4] That's how I began my simplifying process: I eliminated the unimportant so I could concentrate on present priorities. As we simplify, we can also ask ourselves, "When do we have enough?" As we saw in Chapter 4, more is not always better; sometimes "more" just complicates life. Determining what is enough—in our home, our activities, our income—can be a starting step toward simplicity.

Disciplines of the Whole Person

Once we're taking steps toward a simpler life, we will be better able to work on the next lifestyle discipline—which I call "disciplines of the whole person." We can live a life of joy when we feed, exercise, and rest our mind, body, and spirit.

• Disciplines of the Mind

As we've already discussed, the mind is directly linked to the emotions. If we want to feel joyful, we must discipline our mind by carefully controlling what we put into it. We've heard it before: garbage in, garbage out. If we input trash—things that are disturbing or fruitless, sinful or negative—we will dwell on that trash. That's why Paul tells us to dwell on whatever is true, honorable, right, pure, lovely, of good repute, excellent, and worthy of praise (Philippians 4:8). That clearly limits what we should allow ourselves to see and hear.

For instance, I abhor the murder-and-mayhem portion of the local news, in spite of the fact that I have worked in that profession. I like keeping up with current events, but I really don't need to know the gory details of all the horrors that occur in my city each day. Television images take you to the scene and, frankly, I'd rather be just about anywhere than at some of the scenes that are piped into my living room every night in vivid color.

Years ago, when I worked in television news, I happened on a terrible head-on car accident that had just occurred. I saw a colleague's van and camera lights and I stopped. When I got to the scene, there were three injuries. When I left the scene, there were three fatalities. About to do an on-camera report, I thought, "I can't stand being here. Does anybody at home really need to be here either?" I didn't think so.

Today I carefully guard what I put into my mind and the minds of my children. Like the psalmist, my prayer is, "Turn my eyes away from worthless things" (Psalm 119:37 NIV). So, when I do choose to get my news from television, I keep the remote nearby and my younger children out of the room. One family I know guards the input in their home, particularly the movies they see, by asking, "Would I want Jesus to see this with me?" When they began asking this question, their viewing habits changed, making it easier for them to dwell on the honorable and excellent. And hear what the prophet Isaiah promises when we think on those things and limit the negative: "He who stops his ears from hearing about bloodshed, and shuts his eyes from looking upon evil; he will dwell on the heights" (Isaiah 33:15b,16a).

Some women, however, get caught up in the addictive time-waster and killjoy of daytime television. What good comes from the provocative revolving-bed soap operas and talk-show trash that fill the airwaves? These programs hardly add joy to our lives. While television offers many redeeming and informative programs, much of what is on the air simply robs us of joy. Why let input on topics like "mothers who date their daughter's boyfriends" steal your joy? I know people addicted to these shows; I've heard them hashing over these worthless subjects. When we watch these things, we can't help but dwell on them. It's human nature, but to think about them for longer than one second after the program's off is a second too long. Our lives— our thought lives—can be much richer than that.

Of course, many people aren't particularly sensitive to what is portrayed in the media, but perhaps as a nation we should be. We who are parents can shape the sensitivities of our children and we should. So guard the input carefully—be it from television, radio, movies, music, or the printed page. Trash abounds. Help your children learn the discipline of the mind by carefully selecting the input.

We mustn't merely limit the negative input. We must also supply positive input. If we want a healthy, active mind, we must feed it nourishing food, exercise it, and give it rest. We exercise as well as feed our mind when we read good books which stimulate our mind or entertain us with positive messages, listen to beautiful and edifying music, engage in thoughtful conversation, and learn something new. Learning a new task or skill actually does exercise our brain. In fact, some researchers have found that the people who live long lives and remain mentally alert are those who continue to engage their minds with challenging stimuli. Just ask Audrey Stubbart. She works a 40-hour week as a proofreader and columnist with *The Examiner* in Independence, Missouri. Audrey's smiling face was recently on the cover of *Parade* magazine—Audrey is 100 years old.[5]

As important as feeding and exercising your mind is giving it rest. We need to stop worrying and stewing about things we can't help or change (Matthew 6:25-34). At the close of each day, when it's time for our body to rest, we need to turn to God with our worries and cares, trust them all to Him, and let our mind rest, too. Besides being an act of obedience, this step of trust is an act of mental rest, a move toward freedom from burdens, and, therefore, a step toward knowing joy.

• *Disciplines of the Body*

Sometimes we struggle with feeling joyful simply because we don't feel well physically, and that can be directly related to some of our lifestyle choices. When we discipline our bodies by getting the proper amount of rest, exercise, and good food, we feel better physically as well as emotionally. Research reveals that people who get close to eight hours of sleep a night, engage in some type of regular physical exercise, and eat a reasonably healthy diet are happier than those who do not do these things.

Now before you happy, sedentary, junk-food-junkie nightowls ask what all this has to do with Mama's happiness, I must tell you that I have science on my side—but one foot in your camp! I like to stay up late, sleep in, and eat nachos *occasionally*, and that doesn't mean I'm living less joyfully. In fact, sometimes those things add a sparkle to my day. But in terms of my lifestyle I strive to sleep as much as I need, eat my veggies and grains, and get the ol' heart pumping as often as I can. Remember, we are talking about lifestyle disciplines here—choices that we live out habitually.

> *O*bedience is the seed of joy.
>
> ~Gloria Gaither

To begin you need to ask some questions. How much sleep do you routinely get? How many hours does your usual night's sleep last? Some people can function well on about five hours of sleep a night while others need nine or ten, but the average amount needed is eight hours per night. Some sources suggest that if we consistently need an alarm clock to wake up, we are somewhat sleep deprived—which is no shock to the millions of busy women who burn the candle on both ends in order to meet all the demands of their day. As most of us know, "A bad night [of sleep] leaves you with slower reaction times, poorer concentration, and a smaller pool of energy from which to draw the next day."[6] According to some researchers, sleep allows our body tissues a chance to rest after a day's use; others say it restores brain function. Whatever is happening while we snooze, a good night's sleep is the difference between awakening ready to seize the day or ready to seize the innocent bystander who gets between you and the coffeepot. To seize the day, seize enough sleep.

And once you're up, make time for exercise—that wonderful activity that we love to hate. Although some people simply love it and others just hate it, exercise has the ability to keep us feeling well, functioning well, and looking well. If we could ingest exercise in pill form, people would probably stand in line for hours and pay big bucks to buy the benefits contained in the bottle. The bad news is that there is no pill, but the good news is that the benefits of exercise are available to anyone willing and able to do it.

As those of us who have overcome inertia know, regular and moderate exercise increases energy; improves overall health; reduces stress, the "blues," and the risk of some diseases; boosts our immune system; increases resistance to some infection; revs up our metabolism; helps us sleep better; and elevates our mood. Studies have shown that people who exercise have improved moods and higher scores on the "happiness tests" (those tests which measure psychological well-being). All that from exercise—when we "just do it."

And did you know that we can turn an energy deficit into a surplus when we exercise? Paradoxically, using energy increases energy. That's especially true for aerobic exercise because it wakes up the nervous system and boosts our metabolism, giving us a good supply of energy and reducing our fatigue. This increased metabolism helps us burn more fat and calories, and these effects continue for hours after we exercise. The more consistent and long-term our exercising is, the greater our overall physical fitness level, which further increases our stamina and improves our health.

But knowing the benefits of exercise doesn't necessarily make it easy to start exercising. Many of us start exercise programs so we'll have better health and greater energy—only to throw the running shoes under the bed and use our cycling machine as an expensive clothes hanger. In fact, just 40 percent of Americans exercise regularly and only half of them do so vigorously enough to benefit aerobically.[7] What can you and I do personally to improve these statistics? The most important thing is finding an activity we like that fits our style, schedule, and needs. Choosing an exercise that we enjoy and can do regularly determines whether we will stick with it or not. Now, let's consider how we'll fuel that exercise.

We want to feel good. We want boundless energy. We want health. And we want it from the drive-through window when we grab a quick bite as we zip down the fast lane. Our love for the "typical American diet" coupled with our busy lives keeps many of us from fueling our bodies for optimum health and energy with that simple thing called...good food. It's not so much what we're eating that's so terrible. It's what we're *not* eating. As a nation, we opt for fast foods over good foods, get caught in the diet trap (lose weight, gain it back, lose weight, gain it back), and eat sporadically until our growling tummies and low blood sugar make us choose food that's less than the best.

I'm no nutritionist, but I know someone who is and, despite my share of driving through for Jack's "two tacos for a buck," even I can be taught. In *Food for Life*, nutritionist and author Pam Smith says, "The key to healthy eating is having the right perspective. You have to defeat the lie that says [healthy] food is boring and tasteless. Eating well is not denying yourself. It's giving yourself a precious gift. Eating well is not focusing on foods to avoid; rather it is focusing on the fresh, flavorful and fun foods that give the body energy and health—and give you better moods!"[8]

Pam encourages us to eat the right foods in the right balance and at the right time so we can have energy, think clearly, and manage the stress of our life—in her phrase, "walk in well-ness." As she says in some of her "Secrets for Staying Fit, Fu-eled and Free," "Eating is better than starving—eat early, often, balanced, and lean. Water is the beverage of champions—drink eight to ten glasses a day. Variety is the spice of life—a healthy variety includes good food choices over time, including whole grain, low-fat meals full of a mix of brightly colored fruits and veggies."[9]

Remember it's not the single meal that counts or even that week of meals. It's the lifestyle that counts. A lifestyle of junk food makes us feel like junk, and that inevitably leads to a Mama who ain't happy!

• Disciplines of the Spirit

Just as we must feed, exercise, and rest our bodies for op-timum efficiency, we must feed, exercise, and rest our spirit. A regular and healthy diet for our spirit gives us the solid nour-ishment we need to be God's people. We need both the milk of the Word and, as we mature, solid food (Hebrews 5:12-14). Without such nutrition, we would dry up and blow away; an anorexic spirit destroyed from malnutrition.

Poring over God's Word, praising Him, and praying to Him (the three P's for becoming intimate with God discussed in chapter 7) feed our spirit and keep it healthy. When we do these things as a discipline in our life, we are ensuring long-term growth and developing a heart of devotion as well as an appetite for being with the Lord. (After all, we usually don't need to be reminded to feed our bodies when we're hun-gry!) Adopting the three P's as a discipline will help keep us from neglecting our spiritual food by whetting our appetite for time with our heavenly Father.

Regularly reading God's Word and hearing it taught feeds our spirit and is vital to our growth. Involvement in a church that teaches the Bible, participation in group Bible studies, and lis-tening to Christian radio, television, books, tapes, music, and videos can nourish our spirit and feed our soul. Once, shortly af-ter we moved to a new city and before we became active in a church, a friend knew that I was rather lonely and could use some supplemental feedings. For a time, she sent me tapes of some sermons and guest speakers at her church with the note, "Thought you might like some extra nourishment." Another friend and I frequently trade cassettes of Christian radio programs or speakers.

Now, I'm not suggesting that we immerse ourselves in Christian culture and it alone. Much in the world that isn't necessarily labeled "Christian" is worth our attention. The Academy Award-winning film *Chariots of Fire* isn't a "Christian" movie, but it has a great message and is extremely well done. Wonderful music, literature, and art exist beyond the realm of what's labeled "Christian." After all, God is the Author of *all* creativity, and He certainly doesn't need a label. However, we shouldn't be surprised if we find ourselves feeling a little distant from God when we don't go to church, listen only to secular music, limit our reading to trashy bestsellers, and are undiscriminating about our entertainment. In that case, it's no wonder our spirit becomes anemic. Enjoy life—but watch the diet!

At the same time we're feeding our spirit God's Word, we can exercise our spirit through the discipline of thankfulness. Each of us can discipline ourselves to be grateful to God and to express that gratitude with thanksgiving. Developing this discipline will do more for increasing your joyfulness than any of the other disciplines combined, and it starts with a grateful attitude. I first learned that when I was a young teenager standing in line for an amusement ride at Astroworld with my best friend Teresa and her older sister Diana. While we stood in the hot sun complaining about some adolescent catastrophe, Diana reminded us that the apostle Paul was able to rejoice because he had a thankful attitude. She encouraged us to memorize this passage:

> Rejoice in the Lord always; again I will say, rejoice! Let your forbearing spirit be known to all men. The Lord is near. Be anxious for nothing, but in everything by prayer and supplication with *thanksgiving* let your requests be made known to God (Philippians 4:4-6, emphasis added).

Note that Paul doesn't say rejoice *for* everything, but *in* everything.

I never forgot that verse or lesson. Both are permanently seared in my mind—a video snippet of two teenagers standing in the middle of an amusement park and making up a song to memorize that bit of Scripture. Two lives were influenced that day because of one young woman's willingness to teach the value of a thankful heart.

LaJewyl S. is a Bible-study leader prone to depression and the blues. She used to wake up with a sense of foreboding, but became aware of the value of gratitude in fighting that feeling. What began as an antidote for her struggle has become a discipline of thankfulness. Every morning before her feet hit the floor, LaJewyl thanks God for seven things. Initially her thankfulness centered on material things, but as she grew in this discipline, she moved on to express gratitude for spiritual blessings. "This is the way," says LaJewyl, "that I make sure I begin the day with a grateful heart and practice the presence of the Lord the first thing in the morning." Thankfulness moves us beyond ourselves and into the place of joy and contentment.

Expressing thankfulness as LaJewyl did is a spiritual exercise. So is walking in obedience to what we learn in God's Word. Although that obedience doesn't always come easily, it can bear wonderful fruit of joy. Julie M. writes, "When the Lord directed me to stay home with the children, I felt a joyfulness that I cannot describe. I walked around for many weeks smiling all the time. I know my obedience (doing what I knew the Lord wanted me to do) played a large part in the joy I felt." Some of our deepest joys are in simple, hidden places of obedience. Maybe you know that truth from your own experience. If so, keep exercising—if not, start!

Obedience is indeed a spiritual discipline, but so is rest. We let our spirit rest when we are quiet with the Lord. God calls us to such quiet and promises to meet us there: "Be still, and know that I am God" (Psalm 46:10 NIV). He also tells of the rest we can find in the shadow of His wings (Psalm 91:1). What a precious invitation to those of us (to all of us) who are too busy, too frazzled, too burdened, too joyless.

Feeding, exercising, and resting the mind, body, and spirit—these are the disciplines of lifestyle. These are disciplines which lead to joy.

2. The Disciplines of Labor

People who greatly enjoy life tend to be those who are involved in the disciplines of labor—service and meaningful work—and balance those with fun.

Meaningful Work

Have you ever known the drudgery of having to pry yourself out of bed in the morning to face another day of doing work that you hate? Perhaps once in their lifetime everyone should have (briefly) at least one job like that in order to fully appreciate a more satisfying job and to better understand the many people who hate what they do. Feeling good about the work you do every day is certainly a big joy booster (more on this in chapter 13), but even more important to our level of joy than enjoyable work is meaningful work. Studies have shown that people who engage in interesting, challenging work that has meaning for them are happier—even if that choice of occupation means making less money. Work that is at times hard and unpleasant but valuable to the individual worker can be a great source of happiness.

Now it's been said that some people play at their work and work at their play. Although "playing at work" suggests a poor work ethic and a poor way to live, the idea is not all bad. When we find a way to work that has elements of play in it for us, we get caught in that wonderful state that some psychologists call "flow"—that marvelous spot of being challenged enough to fully captivate our mind but not enough to become frustrated. It's when we get so caught up in what we're doing that we lose track of time.

People who flow in their work as well as in their play are among the happiest, according to some reports. So consider what Herb Kelleher, chairman and CEO of Southwest Airlines, says about work in a *Fortune* magazine cover story entitled "America's Best CEO?" This hard-working man, much loved by his employees, thinks critics who accuse him of being a workaholic miss the point. He doesn't consider his job work. "I used to tell them if your vocation is your avocation as well—it's what you enjoy—it's not stress. It's not work. It's fun."[10] Happy people pursue work that has meaning, engages them, and is challenging without being overwhelming. What do you see when you look in that mirror?

Service

To give away some of our self in an act of service is another source of joy and another discipline of labor. When we serve others, we lose sight of ourselves for a moment and contribute to the good of someone or something else. The wonderful by-product of serving with a proper motive and pure heart is that helping others feels good. A life of great service is indeed a life of great joy.

And there are countless ways to serve. Several people I know spent their Thanksgiving working together at a local soup kitchen, and one of them just beamed as she told of the blessing it was to serve those appreciative people. My friend Sharon opened her home for over a year to a young woman in a crisis pregnancy. While sharing her faith with others wasn't difficult for Sharon, living out that faith on a daily basis in front of a stranger presented its challenges, but she says she wouldn't trade that experience for the world. "Even though it was hard, uncomfortable, and stretching at times, there was a deep measure of joy as only God can give because there was visible fruit. I got to see a young woman's new faith in Christ grow, and there was great joy in the baby's birth. The real joy I felt through that ministry, though, was God working in me."

I could offer countless other stories of service, ministry, and altruism from all over the world, examples of people serving where they can and in whatever ways they can—from building churches in Mexico to working in their own church nursery.

Like these people, you and I can serve our fellow human beings, the body of Christ, and Christ Himself when we keep our eyes and heart open to others and allow God to use us right where we are. Both joy and contentment come when we serve where God has us, as Sue J.'s life testifies. She and her husband,

The truest joy is in obedience. To feel His smile and to know that He is pleased—ahh, this is real joy.

~Kellie M.

Max, had moved from California to Tennessee in hopes of finding better work in the car business. Unfortunately, it took Max a while to learn he wasn't cut out to sell cars. He'd tell people, "This is a lovely car, but you can't afford it." Since that sales approach didn't help pay their bills, Sue and Max moved in with family and later into a beat-up, bug-infested trailer—the only place they could afford.

The night they moved in, as Sue sat in the middle of the clutter rocking her five-month-old baby, she saw a roach scurry across her pillow on the mattress. Rocking back and forth, she repeated over and over, "Please, God, don't make me live here. Please, God, don't make me live here." The next day she got busy deinfesting and scouring the little place, trying to make it as nice as possible. As she sought the Lord, she knew that God wanted her to live there until it was okay with her if she never left. And that is exactly how long she stayed there.

What made it okay was the purposeful work she found in serving *right where she was*. When Sue began to look for why God had put her where she was and what she could do there, she saw her neighbors, some of whom were far below the poverty level:

> I started reaching out, looking for meaningful service right there. Whatever I could do, I did. I used my cake decorating skills to bake for them. I listened to their stories, taught them God's Word, and befriended and counseled them. I jumped whole-hog into service and learned that God can use me where I am and can take all of my circumstances and shape and mold me into a unique servant. He said, "Sue, stop worrying about ministering to the hurting women around the world. Go next door!" So I did. In the process I found joy and contentment.

Where does God have you? What can you do for Him, His people, His kingdom right from where you are? That kind of service brings unbelievable joy.

Fun

It's important to work hard and to serve others, but it's also important to remember to have fun. For the sanguine socialites among us, this is among their life's mission, but many melancholy types wouldn't know fun if it came up, painted their face, and gave them a balloon. Of course, a balance between the two is the goal. Is your life in balance? Do you make time for active leisure? So-called happiness studies say that people who enjoy life make time for active forms of leisure that engage their skills. Sometimes all we seem to have the energy for is zoning out in front of the TV, but much more pleasurable is leisure that's somewhat active, that engages us or our skills in some way instead of just happening to us or in front of us. So turn off the tube and take a dance class, read a classic, rollerblade, plant some flowers, or play a game. More on this in the next chapter. Right now, just remember that the disciplines of labor are fulfilling work, service for the Lord, and time for fun.

3. The Disciplines of Love

If "the disciplines of a joyful person" sounded like an oxymoron, "disciplines of love" sounds even more like one. By the phrase "disciplines of love" I simply mean the disciplines of nurturing those whom we love, and those disciplines do make for joy.

Social psychologists have found that people who are truly fulfilled and happy in life are actively involved in loving relationships. As Ann H. says, "I lack joy when I lack intimacy." An intimate relationship with those we feel close to greatly increases joy in this life. (As we know if we've ever been in love!) One article reported, "Sadly, our increasingly individualistic society suffers from impoverished social connections, which some psychologists believe is a cause of today's epidemic levels of depression....In contrast to the interdependence valued in Asian societies, Americans celebrate independence."[11] While Hillary Clinton highlights that kind of interdependence in her book *It Takes a Village,* and "family values" are now politically correct, there is still some truth to Ronald Reagan's words that we live in "the age of the individual." This individualism makes being closely connected to people we love and nurturing those relationships so important.

Among those relationships which need our nurturing and which contribute to our joy is a lasting, loving marriage. Research shows that "married people are happier and live longer than those who are single, widowed, divorced, or who never married."[12] Reports also reveal that people who have several close, supportive friends with whom to share their lives are healthier and happier than those who don't.

Practicing the disciplines of love requires that we give priority to those whom we love and take time to nurture our relationship with them. We can do that by spending time with them, looking for ways to do things for them, not taking them for granted, letting them know we appreciate them, being kind, and sharing with them our thoughts and dreams, our hurts and hopes, to name just a few possibilities. Nurturing a relationship doesn't always come naturally, and that's where the discipline comes in.

Our Spouse: Work schedules of late have meant a season of too little "together time" in my marriage, and I have felt its withering effects. But Tim and I are dedicated to the discipline of nurturing our relationship, even when it's hard. Recently, my comment of "I feel like we don't know each other very well lately" was met by his "We don't. How could we?" That lonely moment led to a wonderful weekend together. But it might not have without the discipline of commitment and time.

Make time for your husband. Schedule a regular date night or just be at home together with the children in bed and the newspaper and bills out of sight. One woman I know couldn't afford a night out with her husband, so she put a lace tablecloth on a card table in their bedroom for a romantic, candlelight dinner. They followed that with a walk in the woods, holding hands and discussing their dreams. We can and must make time to nurture our relationship with our husband even if our days are long. Once after the children were in bed, for instance, Tim set up a tape player on the patio, and we enjoyed soft music, hot coffee, and a few minutes of time alone under the stars. Moments like that are free, don't take long, and can be fit into the busiest of schedules—and they nurture a marriage.

Our Children: We nurture our relationship with our children by regularly spending time really connecting with each child. We need to talk *with* them, not just *to* them. We need to know what they're doing as well as what's going on in their heads and hearts. Robin M. says, "One of the principles I live by in practicing joy is to be sure I spend one-on-one time with each family member throughout the week." More on children to come.

Our Friends: Years ago, a close friend and I were discussing our priorities, noting how women's priorities can differ. We went down the list.

"Let's see. God, husband, children, and so on....Wait a minute. I forgot friends. I've got to fit that in," she said.

"Well, that's not on my list. Who has time for shopping and lunch out with friends when I have a baby and all my other responsibilities?" I replied.

Yet "friends" was (and is) on my list. As a mother of young children, I didn't do many of the daytime activities that some of my friends enjoyed together, or spend hours on the phone, or go places with them in the evenings, but I did make time for that one special friend, and my life has been richer for it. We all need someone who is our "kindred spirit," a soul who knows us well, loves us still, and connects with those things dear to our heart. Nurturing such a close friendship and finding fellowship with other believers adds immeasurable joy to life.

If right now you are more familiar with loneliness than the joy of close connections, reach out! Don't sit around waiting for someone else to do the reaching. Instead of wondering why no one brings us cookies when we move into a new neighborhood or invites us to do anything when we visit a new church, we can do the cookie baking and the inviting. In fact, one of the biggest reasons we stay lonely and miss this joy is that we don't reach out—even if no one is reaching out to us. Tim Hansel puts it well in his book *Through the Wilderness of Loneliness:*

> Waiting for the world to come to you is a lonely place. I admit that it takes a lot of courage sometimes to reach out to others, but it is critical that we do so. Reaching out to others is the greatest evidence of the Power that lives within us. Joy is doubled when it's

divided. It is a great maxim that if you can't find joy, then the best thing to do is to give it away to someone else who is more in need than you are. The joy will then double back to you in ways that you never expected.[13]

You don't believe Tim's words? Try it out! Take the risk and reach out to a new or old friend—and take the time to nurture your relationship with your husband and your children as well. These disciplines of love bring love to us as well as joy.

Practice Makes Perfect (At least it helps!)

Joy itself is never something we can practice, but we can practice living a lifestyle that includes disciplines conducive to joyfulness. And like many things, when we practice we improve. So let me introduce you to Jovial Jane and the Fruitful Five. No, that's not a new rock group. It's my practical "joy barometer." If you're lacking joy in your life, try quizzing yourself on the Jovial Jane Fruitful Five to see if you're living the FINER life. Ask yourself: "Am I getting enough fun, intimacy, nutrition, exercise, and rest?" (That's not necessarily the order of importance, but the initials spell a good word that way!) Being out of balance in any of those areas can explain why Mama ain't happy.

The disciplines of the mind, body, and spirit could be interpreted as a call to "live perfectly and know joy." But I'm not saying, "Watch a *Pollyanna* video, train for a marathon, eat rice cakes, go to church, and live a careful, safe life—and you'll find joy." We all know better than that. We can be joyful if we eat chocolate every day. We can even be joyful if we never go to bed before 1 A.M. But if Jovial Jane watches trash-TV, gets four hours of sleep a night but never any exercise, and habitually feeds her body and spirit junk food, it's no wonder she struggles to be joyful.

And sometimes I struggle, too. I told you earlier that this isn't an "I have arrived" book; it's an "I'm on the path too" book. Even as I wrote this chapter, I was struggling with some of these disciplines. (Old habits die hard.) The coffeepot brewed gallons

Jovial Jane's Fruitful Five
The FINER Life
Five Questions to Ask If Your Joy Has Fizzled

1. **F**un

   Am I making time for things that are enjoyable in my life? Am I balancing meaningful work and service with fun?

2. **I**ntimacy

   Am I nurturing my intimate relationships? Am I making time for God, making my spouse a priority (making time for talking and for sex), communicating with my children, and enjoying fellowship with a kindred spirit?

3. **N**utrition

   Am I eating enough good food to fuel my body? Am I getting my five-plus-eight a day? (That's five fruits and vegetables plus eight glasses of water!) Am I feeding my mind a healthy diet of books, movies, television, and music? Am I feeding my spirit with time with the Lord? Am I poring over His Word, praising Him, and praying to Him?

4. **E**xercise

   Am I recharging my energy, fitness, health, and moods with regular exercise four to six times a week? Am I exercising my mind by learning one thing new each day? Am I exercising my spirit by being thankful and walking in obedience?

5. **R**est

   Am I getting enough sleep? Do I awake rested and refreshed—or could I use an extra hour or two of sleep? Am I trusting God with my cares and concerns so that my mind can rest? Am I resting my spirit by regularly sitting quietly with God?

of caffeine, the midnight oil flowed, and, as I wrote about eating good food, I was struck with the sharp desire to jump in the car for those two tacos for a buck.

Despite the struggle to maintain these lifestyle disciplines, I am more convinced than ever that practicing them contributes to a life of joy. After years of keeping a very simple schedule, I found last fall to be quite busy. It would have been easy to get right back into the harried, hurried, joy-challenged life that I described earlier, but I worked very hard at these disciplines. Among other things, I ran or walked consistently, and each day I nourished my spirit with God's Word and my body with a good diet. And guess what? Instead of overwhelming stress and a Mama who wasn't happy, I was filled with joy! Even when life gets busy, I keep simplicity the goal— and you can, too. And during those busy times, don't neglect these disciplines. They really do add joy!

> *I* find joy in being able to rest in the Lord without worry in spite of difficult circumstances.
>
> ~Nancy K.

So what's the first step you can take to begin practicing disciplines that encourage joy? Where can you start? Perhaps with the issue that most strongly touched your heart as you read this chapter. When we simplify our life; when we feed, exercise, and rest our mind, body, and spirit; when we live with a balance of meaningful work, service, and fun; and when we nurture our intimate relationships, we are taking practical steps toward a more joyful life. Join me in the journey!

❦ 11 ❧

Laugh and Lollygag
It Lightens the Load

I grabbed my keys and headed out the door to pick up my children from school. I was thankful for a break in my difficult day. *I'll enjoy the drive,* I thought. But then I discovered that my car was so dead that the starter didn't even click, let alone turn over. One of my four "meddlers" had left a light on in the car overnight. I called a friend to help me jump it, but it still wouldn't start so she loaned me her car. No problem. I knew I could zip over and get the kids and zip right back. She asked me to drop off Teresa, her cleaning lady, at the bus stop on the way back. No problem.

I picked up my three school-aged children who crowded into the hot car along with Teresa and her baby. The car trouble had made me late to get my children, and Teresa asked me in broken English if we were going to be late for her bus. It was almost 90 degrees outside, and there were four children and two adults in a tiny car with no air conditioning and 260,000 miles of wear and tear. I could sense a problem heading my way.

As I was about to peak the hill of the freeway overpass, the car's get-up-and-go got up and went. I was stranded on an incline in the middle lane. Since the car wouldn't go forward, I had only one option—backwards. I made sure everyone had fastened their seatbelts and then eyed my goal: the gas station at the bottom of the hill behind me. I explained my plan and my passengers said, "You're going to do WHAT?" I assured them it would be "no problem" as long as everyone driving forward in the lane behind me got out of the way.

With sweaty palms and a racing heart, I rolled down my window and, like a crazy woman, made wild arm circles, sign language for "Everybody get out of the way!" Miraculously, they did until one car pulled up behind me while I was still coasting towards the station, forcing me to brake short of my goal. *What is she doing?...Oh, helping me.*

She offered me a quarter, and I called my friend to tell her the great news about her car. She said, "No problem. I'll borrow Kay's car and be right there." When she got to Kay's house, she was red-faced and breathing hard. Kay said, "Lois, did you run all the way here?"

"No," Lois gasped. "I rode my bike. but both the tires were flat."

We were certainly having our problems.

When Lois got within a block of us, she started honking the horn in "here I am to save the day" fashion and, for some reason, that struck Teresa funny and she started to laugh (which was amazing considering she'd just missed her bus). Laughing knows no language barrier, and she got me tickled. One of the children said, "Why are you laughing? I don't see a thing funny about this!" Then Lois told us about the flat tires and that did it—we all roared!

Two broken cars and two flat bike tires, hot children, frustrated women, and a missed bus—we had definite reasons to lose our cool, but we didn't. While teetering between the "I'm going to be joyful" and "I'm gonna lose it!" options, we decided to jump on the joy side and see the humor in the situation. Laughter softened our tough afternoon and made a great memory for my kids. It also gave our friends in our small Bible study an opportunity—at my expense—for a good howl. Somehow they found great humor in picturing me (and, I might add, imitating me) waving like mad while I coasted backwards downhill with sweaty, squished, scared passengers. But three cheers for laughter! It certainly helps lighten our load!

What Is Laughter?

Laughter is a "diaphragmatic, epiglottal spasm,"[1] of course! Can you imagine whispering that to your children the next time they start giggling in church: "Psssst...kids! Quit those di aphragmatic, epiglottal spasms right now!" They'd either stop immediately, wondering what language you were speaking, or they'd roll under their pew in greater hysterics. You might want to try that line at home to be on the safe side.

If you're joyful, you will laugh (at some point!) because laughter is an expression of joy. And it's also a whole lot of fun! *The Women's Study Bible* says, "Laughter is one way that the Creator gives us to switch gears and punctuate the monotony with joy....Humor is an exit from the mundane road of life...a simple, reasonable prescription for some of life's problems and most of its tedium."[2] After we've washed our fifteenth load of laundry in a week, it helps to laugh when we discover we've accidentally turned all of our husband's underwear pink and the children just dressed the dog in some of the finally clean, momentarily folded clothes.

Laughter acts as a much-needed diversion amid life's trials. When life is hard, laughter helps us cope with the pain and gives us a break from it—if only for a few seconds. When we let go to laugh, we release tension and momentarily lose ourselves in the thing that tickled us. Our moments of laughter give us a mini-vacation from the problems at hand. And laughing at our own mistakes and actions keeps us from taking ourselves too seriously. These are just a few of the reasons laughter has great value.

The Value of Laughter

Read what Scripture says about laughter and the joyful heart it springs from:

A joyful heart is good medicine, but a broken spirit dries up the bones (Proverbs 17:22).

A joyful heart makes a cheerful face, but when the heart is sad, the spirit is broken (Proverbs 15:13).

He who is of a merry heart has a continual feast
(Proverbs 15:15b NKJV).

She shall rejoice in time to come (Proverbs 31:25
NKJV. That literally means she laughs at the
future, confident in God and free of worry.)

How wonderful! Life without laughter dries up our bones, so
life with laughter must be good for our body. Life with laughter
lifts our spirit (that's a plus) and makes our face cheerful (another
plus). And how wonderful that a heart which can laugh sits at a
never-ending and (yea!) calorie-free feast of the spirit. Furthermore, God created us with the ability to laugh. Why wouldn't He
enjoy hearing us laugh? Clearly, laughter is good for the body,
spirit, and face! And there's more!

If you hate to jog, try laughing. It will give you a workout without all the sweat, which may be why Norman Cousins calls it
"internal jogging." Sustained hilarity has great aerobic benefits.
One hundred laughs are equivalent to 10 minutes of rowing, according to one article. Neck, shoulder, and abdominal muscles
quickly contract and release, heart rate and blood pressure go up,
and breathing quickens. When the laughter stops, the blood pressure and pulse can fall to levels lower than before the glee began.
When you laugh, you use the large muscle groups in your body—
making it, by the way, very difficult to pick up anything very
heavy. (Just try to rearrange your sofa the next time you are con-
vulsed with hilarity!) Laughter also combats stress and is a physical release for tension. Some even say that laughter contributes to
a longer life. It also increases our ability to withstand pain, thanks
to the increase in endorphins (the body's natural feel-good chemical and painkiller) that comes when we laugh.[3]

Science is also seeing that laughter is healing. A hospital in
Georgia designated a "laughing room" where patients could go
to watch funny movies and read funny books. The hospital staff,
trying to help people get well through laughter, reports that "the
laughing room decreases people's need for pain medication and
serves as an antidepressant."[4]

These benefits of laughter aren't news to Norman Cousins, author of *An Anatomy of an Illness*. When he was told that he had

an incurable disease of the connective tissue in his body (he describes it as "becoming unstuck), he got involved with his doctor in determining his treatment. He reasoned that if negative emotions could harm our health, why couldn't positive emotions help it? He decided to laugh as much as possible every day, and he read funny books and watched Laurel and Hardy movies and "Candid Camera" reruns to get started. A year later he was well. Whether he would have been cured anyway is unknown, but his doctors hadn't suggested that possibility when they told him his dismal prognosis.[5]

One more note from the scientific community. Those wacky scientists have a bit of difficulty studying joy (how can you duplicate it in a lab?), but they have been able to study its expression—laughter. And they have reported on its downside—if you can imagine a downside to laughter! *The Good Health Magazine* reported:

> One paper describes a man who arrived at an emergency room in Ohio after having accidentally inhaled a mild insecticide. The patient had no symptoms beyond slight numbness, tremors and uncontrollable laughter. Doctors could find no physical or neurological damage, but the man continued to laugh for 55 minutes, to the point where he complained his abdominal muscles were killing him. He was given a tranquilizer intravenously, his laughter ceased, and the doctors sent him home—no doubt with frowns of triumph plastered firmly on their faces.[6]

I am all in favor of laughing.... It unfreezes pride and unwinds secrecy; it makes men forget themselves in the presence of something greater than themselves....

~G.K. Chesterton,
The Common Man

Perhaps these scientists are related to *Star Trek's* Data, the character who's always searching for the reason why people laugh at jokes. I say stop analyzing and simply enjoy!

Filling the Home with Laughter

In a *Christian Parenting Today* article, John Trent says, "It's a sign of wisdom to add laughter to your home. Joyful behavior actually strengthens you and your children—physically and spiritually."[7] He also suggests that it's a mainstay in close-knit homes, as a survey of teenagers and adults supports. The survey gave 20 answers to choose from in response to the question, "In addition to growing closer to Christ, what would make your family even closer than it is today?" Spending more time together was first, but second on the list was: "Adding more laughter to our home."[8] What's the laughter level in your home?

If you want to strengthen your family's health, spirit, and closeness, simply cultivate laughter in your home. Even if laughter is scarce right now, know that this joyous gift can be developed. Here are five suggestions.

1. Cultivate friends who make you laugh.

The easiest way to start laughing more is to be around people who laugh easily. Cultivate friendships with those merry souls, those folks with a great sense of humor and a ready laugh. Their laughter can be very encouraging and quite contagious. Two of my closest friends have the gift of laughter, which I greatly enjoy whenever I'm with them. They give truth to these lines from *The Book of Joy*, "Keep company with the more cheerful sort of the godly; there is no mirth like the mirth of believers.'"[9]

2. Look for the humor in life.

It's everywhere. When we're open to and looking for the humor all around us, everyday life can be very funny. But sometimes we're just too busy or too grumpy to notice. It helps to have the attitude of Linda T. who said, "A lot of things strike me funny, so I laugh easily. A good laugh can make my day—or someone else's."

Kids are often a source of a good laugh. When asked what God does all day, for instance, one child answered, "Most days he builds boats. All kinds of boats. Nobody knows why."[10] Liz H. says, "We definitely laugh in our home—my kids provide all the material!" When one of my daughters was little, she watched me applying makeup and said, "Mom, I bet it's hard to do that and stay in the lines. Try real hard, though, and do your face like you did on the back of your book—it was santational!" I laughed—and then worked very hard at staying in the lines.

I once heard a story which my friend insists is true. He once saw a lady at a gas station who was pumping gas in front of him. When she was finished she went in to pay—with the nozzle still in her gas tank. After she paid, she walked to her car and drove off. Immediately the hose broke loose from the pump and flew around in the air spraying gasoline everywhere. The woman stopped, backed up, got out of her car, and casually remarked, "I hate when that happens." As if it happened often! Be alert. Life can be funny.

3. **Learn to laugh at yourself.**

In the words of Ethel Barrymore, "You grow up the day you have the first real laugh at yourself."[11] In the midst of the car catastrophe I described earlier, I laughed at the situation, but later that evening when I told Tim the story, I really laughed—that time at myself. I imagined how funny we must have looked stranded in the middle of traffic with me doing my best windmill imitation out the car window. Being able to laugh at myself enabled me to join in when my friends found my adventure quite amusing. So, again, be alert! You may give yourself many reasons for a good laugh!

4. **Lighten up! Life can be heavy, but we don't have to be!**

Sometimes we take ourselves so seriously, but getting stuck in traffic or catching your toddler smearing the last few drops of your new makeup all over her face and the floor really isn't a big deal. Just smile—and hand her a big sponge! Yet sometimes we blow such incidents all out of proportion. While we should be "of sober spirit" about our earthly and spiritual responsibilities (1 Peter 5:8), the Bible says a lot more about being joyful than it does about being sober. After all, Christ came that we might know fullness of joy. In light of that fact, I think God must sometimes sit in the heavens and laugh (or cry!) at our mixed-up priorities and our concern about things which are unimportant in the big picture. That project or deadline that's weighing us down seems so all-important, but is it in God's scheme of things? He may be looking down on us, saying, "Lighten up, my dear child. Remember that my burden is light" (Matthew 11:30). *Translation:* Don't sweat the small stuff.

5. Foster an atmosphere of laughter in your home.

Create opportunities to laugh as Mary H. does. "I try to leave decks of cards around, puzzles in process, cartoon books, and other things out to encourage laughter and play. I let myself laugh. I howl over 'I Love Lucy' reruns, and I post cartoons and David Letterman's Top Ten lists on the refrigerator." Encourage laughter by having funny books and articles, videos, tapes, and cartoons in your home. The more we read, see, and hear funny things, the easier it is to laugh.

I know what a gift laughter is because I grew up in a home where corny jokes were standard fare, and my dad is keeping that tradition alive with his grandchildren. Iva H. also fosters humor in her home. She says:

> In our family, we laugh and play a lot. One time the children were all home for Christmas and the grandchildren were all in bed. All eight of the children plus Bob and I had been playing a game. It was late and everything got funnier and funnier. We were laughing at everything and getting sorer by the minute. Pretty soon Rob, our eldest, said, "I can remember when I was little and our aunts and uncles would be here. We'd be in bed trying to sleep and you all would be laughing and carrying on so loudly that I would wonder what you could possibly be doing to be laughing and having so much fun. Now I'm part of it, and I know you really don't have to be 'doing' anything. It's just the joy of being together and letting our

spirits interact." Of course, we all had to laugh again
at his "sage" thoughts.

What are you doing to foster laughter in your home?

Let me add my ideas to my dad's and Iva's. In our home, we
love to share cartoons with one another. Every year I buy a "Far
Side" daily calendar for Tim, who frequently calls me from work
to share that day's cartoon. Our children get in on the act, too.
Claire recently taped a cartoon to the fridge that depicted the difference between how men and women grocery shop. The woman
compares the price per unit for the best value, factoring in store
brands, generics, and triple coupons. The man tastes the free
sample and says, "Mmmm. Gimme eight boxes." My daughters
and I chuckled and thought about putting Tim's picture over the
cartoon face. As Carl Reiner said, "The absolute truth is the thing
that makes people laugh."[12]

If you're struggling with being able to laugh and feel the
lightness of life, remember Job 8:21: "He will fill your mouth
with laughter and your lips with joyful shouting." Write this
verse on an index card and stick it to your refrigerator or bathroom mirror. God filling us with laughter—isn't that a wonderful thought? So be creative, have fun, and sow seeds for
laughter in your home. The harvest will be worth the effort because laughter is indeed good for the body, the spirit, and the
face!

The Gift of Play

Another way to lighten life's load is to make time to play.
Lollygag! If you think of lollygagging negatively (as in "wasting
time"), I invite you to change your perspective. To lollygag—to
enjoy the gift of play—can do much to lighten the cares of life.
(Incidentally, you might want to avoid saying, "I feel like lollygagging." If you say that, people might only hear the "gagging"
part and hand you an airsickness bag!)

One thing many of us can learn from children is the value
of play. They don't need to be reminded to play—it's part of
their nature. Often they even approach their household chores
playfully. Not that most children always work cheerfully, but
often without thinking they intersperse play into their work. The

broom becomes a partner as they dance to a song. The dish-soap bubbles make a great beard until they decide to fling the suds into the air for the sheer pleasure of watching them "almost float." Riding down the banister is always more fun than walking down the stairs. And throwing the laundry down the stairs so they can ride the basket down is much more fun than carrying a full basket to the laundry room.

And what do we adults so often do in response to this very healthy attitude of play? "Stop, stop!" we say. "Pick up that broom and finish sweeping....Stop throwing bubbles....Walk down the stairs—don't slide...Get out of that laundry basket." Then we add our famous last words: "Right now!" These words and the attitude they reflect can teach our children that play is of little value and work is paramount. Instead, some of us would do well to learn from our kids, for not all of us know how to play like a child, completely absorbed in the fun and free to enjoy it.

In *Play: It's Not Just for Kids*, the authors describe just such a mother and child arriving at a quiet, calm beach for a weekday visit.

> I watched the boy as he shed the tightness and duty and rigid living rules that so wrap up the life of a child today. His eyes blinked and took on the loose, mind-wandering gaze that carried him everywhere at once. I watched in delight as his whole body gave over to soaking up moments of awareness with stones, shells, and water-hardened sand ridges.[13]

Carried away in the delights of the beach, the child walked and wiggled in the sand, digging in his fingers and toes. He was lost in a world of wonder, completely content—until...

> Rasping, breaking the air like a rusty knife, came his mother's irritating voice commanding him to go into the water and not to play along the beach. That's what they came for. That's what they had sacrificed money, time, and duties for. Startled, he tried to obey, but each time the hold of imaginative minutiae halted his mind and eyes and he'd slip into the world of peace.

Again and again came the rusty knife. Finally, in disgust, the mother gathered up their belongings and hauling him by one wrist, she hurried him off to the too hot, too metallic car. Under her breath she muttered about his ungratefulness and foolish response to opportunity. He followed obediently, and they drove off.

And a strange grief welled in my throat. I had seen the death of peace—the gift of peace—rejected. And I prayed for the boy, and I wept for the boy, and I heard God murmur, "I know, I know."[14]

I, too, murmur, "I know, I know" until God reminds me that I have wielded my own rusty knife. Mine may be a different style from the mom at the beach, but it's piercing just the same. Calls of "Quit dancing and pick up that broom!" or "Stop sliding down the stairs!" have the same sharp way of cutting into the beautiful spirit of play, naturally abundant in children.

Instead of cutting their play short, let's learn from our children the beauty of getting lost in the wonderment of the world. The pleasures of splashing in a puddle and picking up leaves. Lying on our backs and watching the clouds move until we're sure we can feel the earth spinning. Clinging to a merry-go-round horse and watching the world whiz by. And throwing rocks in the water for no other reason than watching them splash. We know with our head that the world is wonderful and intriguing, but too often we wait for the big, scheduled moments—that drive to the Grand Canyon or the next ski trip—to enjoy the beauty of God's creation. Instead, let's try to rediscover the child within and recapture that child's heart, a heart that's intrigued by a rain-swollen ditch or the mound of dirt in the backyard. Let's rediscover play and once again wonder at the world we live in, once again find play a way to express our joy at being alive.

The Value of Play

Some people are good at playing when the play will accomplish a purpose. Sometimes, for instance, we sit down with a child to play Monopoly because we think it's a good thing to do (which it is) and we want to spend quality time with

230 • Lindsey O'Connor

that child (another good thing). Sometimes I play because I know that I should as a mom. I'll even get out (gag) Candy Land because I know it's fun for my child. But how long has it been since you and I played simply because *we* thought it was fun? If your assignment right now were to go play for 30 minutes, do you know what you'd do? (If I said, "Go rest," you'd have no trouble there!) Many of us need to learn that play recharges us, is part of a balanced life, is an expression and cause of joy, promotes a childlike spirit, and strengthens families.

Play recharges us. Like laughter, play has the ability to take us away from our problems and give us a momentary vacation. When we allow ourselves to be totally engaged—mind, body, and emotions—in the moment of our play, we exchange our problems for a taste of joy. Becoming absorbed in an enjoyable activity is key to preventing burnout in our less-enjoyable activities—that sense of being overwhelmed and wanting all the people in our life to take a slow boat to China. When we are frustrated to the point of burnout, we need to reconnect with our playful spirit. Doing so will help us both shift our focus from ourselves or our situation and find new energy for the challenges we face.

$\mathcal{W}$e play games with our kids and grandkids, have water fights, and try new things. We know we're making [good] memories!

~Loretta K.

Play is part of a balanced life. All work and no play makes each of us dull. Play, like laughter, helps us keep a healthier perspective on the work and service we're doing and makes us quit taking ourselves so seriously. It helps us step out of the rat race long enough to realize that, as Lily Tomlin says, "we're still a rat." But even rats play, don't they?

Play is both an expression and a cause of joy. When we are absorbed in our play as opposed to playing out of a sense of duty, our play can be an expression of the joy that's in our heart. When we're in touch with that joy, we just might roll around in the leaves with our children on a crisp autumn day. Play can also contribute to our joy; it can cause us to feel joyful. Playing a hearty game of tennis or chasing the kids or the dog can increase our feeling of joy. Play is a way of expressing and fueling our joy at the same time.

Play promotes a childlike spirit. A childlike spirit is dear to the Father's heart. As Jesus Himself said, "Whoever does not receive the kingdom of God like a child shall not enter it at all" (Mark 10:15). Childlikeness is the state of simple trust, innocence, and sense of wonder in which our spirit is open to God. It's not to be confused with a childish spirit—an immature state which we are to avoid ("Brethren, do not be children in your thinking; yet in evil be babes, but in your thinking be mature" [1 Corinthians 14:20]). On "Insight for Living," Chuck Swindoll shared how a friend of his carries around a toy car in his pocket to remind him that he's not that far away from the child within. Play can help you stay close to your child and be childlike, not childish.

Play strengthens the family. If the family that prays together stays together, then the family that prays and plays together must not only be close, but have a great time in the process. When families take the time to enjoy one another as they play together, they strengthen their bonds in a way that nothing else can. Parents who play with their children are telling them with their actions, "I love you. I want to spend time with you. You are important"—messages which children desperately need to hear. Families that play together also create fond memories which, over the years, weave a tapestry of time and togetherness that hangs in the hearts and minds of each family member throughout their lives. To be wrapped up in the huddle of a family hug or buried in the tangle of arms and legs of a "roughhouse pile" on the floor is to be part of something greater than the fun of the moment. It is a time of bonding, another thread woven into the tapestry of the close-knit family.

Years ago, a young mother told me, "I don't have time to play with my children." She didn't say it with regret. Sadly, she made the statement in a rather factual way, reflecting her priorities. Unfortunately, even when we want to play, the true busyness that causes us to neglect playing together as a family can easily become habitual. It's all too easy to get so completely caught up in our work and grown-up life that we forget how important a mud pie and cup of pretend tea is to a child. Besides leading our children to Christ, is there anything more important than making them feel loved and special?

Recently, I walked into my six-year-old son's room. "Hi, Collin," I said.

"I need somebody to play with," he responded. Now there were three other siblings in the house. What he really meant was, "Mom, I need you to play with me."

"Sure," I said. *The laundry and other chores can wait a bit longer, I guess.* "How about building a Lincoln Log fort?" I suggested. His eyes lit up.

"A whole fort? Not just one cabin?" he asked.

"Yes," I said. We studied the picture on the box and made a less-than-perfect copy. As we balanced an Indian on Fort Smith and placed the sign on the OK Corral, I looked at my son. He was totally engrossed. I smiled. It was a moment of joy. When we finished, I asked him if he wanted to leave it up to show his dad.

"Oh yeah! He'll think it's great!" he said.

Fort Smith took center stage on his floor for several days—a testimony to play shared by a mother and her son. When I passed it, I smiled and thought, *Why don't I do that more often?* Then I silently thanked God for the blessing of play. If you don't know it already, I hope you get to know the blessings—and the benefits—of play.

Learning to Play

Some people don't take the time to play, but others genuinely don't know how to play. Unfortunately these people work at their play, and they lose its real benefits without even realizing it. These people approach their play with the same seriousness with which they approach life. To plan a picnic with the family, for instance, they make their list, check it twice, get several weather reports, inspect the location prior to the big event, and pack all the gear two days prior to leaving. Upon arriving at the predetermined spot, they check wind direction, calculate the sun's movement, note its effect on the availability of shade, and—analysis complete—determine the *perfect* site. "From 11:00 to 11:30 we'll unpack and set the picnic table. At 11:30 we can eat. At 12:00 I will set up the badminton net, Junior's field hockey set, and Susie's sand toys. Then we'll have a water and bathroom break. If we stay on schedule, we can leave right at 2:30." Is it any wonder these folks need to rest and recover from their play?

While there's great value in preparation and organization, we must not lose sight of the purpose of play—which is to have fun. Prior planning certainly helps vacations and outings run smoothly, so by all means plan, but don't be afraid to grab some fruit and cheese and jump in the car just in time to catch a magnificent sunset over the lake. Spontaneous play renews our childlike spirit. Become absorbed in the play, not in the planning and procedures.

The book *Play: It's Not Just for Kids* describes renewing play. It's when we get lost in the activity, forget any criteria for success, freely choose what we do, allow spontaneity, and feel a deep joy.[15] So let yourself be absorbed. Ignore thoughts of *I feel foolish. I must look ridiculous. Someone my age shouldn't be doing this.* You've got nothing to lose and a lot to gain! I know because I come from a family that knows how to play.

When I was little, my family gathered at Grandma and Grandpa Britton's house along with many of my dad's six brothers and sisters and their families. One summer afternoon, when they were looking for something fun to do while everyone was together, they hit on the perfect idea—grass sledding. After gathering and flattening large appliance boxes, they found a perfect long, sloping hill by the railroad trestle and began to sail down it. Never mind that sometimes the box went sideways and they continued downward! Rolling down the hill was just as much fun as sliding down it! While the little folks (including me) were home with Grandma, the big folks sledded for about two hours until everyone was worn out from the activity and laughter. Even the more reserved members of the family, not used to such frivolity, enjoyed the fun. Just hearing about that event over the years made an impact on me. *Wow. My parents and aunts and uncles sure know how to have fun. I guess you don't have to stop playing just because you grow up.*

By all means, our play needs to remain within the limits of good taste and the law, but forget about what others think is appropriate. Author and pastor Charles Swindoll finds great pleasure in riding his Harley motorcycle. He apparently doesn't worry whether people think it is appropriate for a man of his age and pastoral stature. Ride on, Reverend Swindoll! And have fun!

And you do the same! Jump on your motorcycle, make a grass sled, or find something else that floats your boat! Rejuvenating, bonding fun is to be had when we shed our self-consciousness, give ourselves wholeheartedly to our play, and find joy in the process.

Lessons for the Recreationally Challenged

1. *Pick something you enjoy that suits your needs and personality.* If you have a high-stress job, you might want to listen to music while you sit on your deck. If your job is boring or mundane, you might find play in listening to music while you *build* a deck. My point is that one person's work is another's play. Obviously different people enjoy doing different things. My husband and I are a case in point. I once asked Tim why he doesn't like amusement parks. He replied, "What's fun about standing in line with hordes of people for a ride that makes you sick?" Fun for one isn't necessarily fun for all. Find the thing that makes you smile and then...

2. *Do it!* Don't wait for chunks of leisure time. They may never come. Even if we "don't have time to play" (to picnic, garden, paint, and so on), we can still drop the broom and dance for a minute.

3. *Develop a childlike heart.* Practice having a playful spirit as you deal with everyday life. Lose yourself in the wonder. Let a child lead you—as Julie M. did one special afternoon: "I have a hard time being silly, but one time during the early fall, I went outside with my son and we jumped on the trampoline and really played. When we tired of this, we lay down on it and closed our eyes, listening to the sounds and trying to identify them. Then we played 'I Spy' with colors. It was truly a joyful moment because I allowed myself to see things through my child's eyes."

Those eyes can indeed lead to a childlike and more playful heart.

4. *Enjoy playing.* Don't fret over what you're not doing while you're playing. Freely enjoy what you are doing *right then!* As Robin M. says, "I learned from my mom that I can sit around and read with no guilt. From my dad, I learned the knack of ignoring the small stuff." Have you learned those lessons? They can help you play more freely!

5. *Plan to do it again!* Once you play, plan another session. Play can be habit forming—so let it be. Incorporate it into a balanced work/play/rest cycle in your life. You'll be glad you did—and so will your family!

Whatever play you choose, enjoy it with a childlike heart. Ride your bike, play tennis, get out the cards, plant a garden, play a game, dance, swim, paint, sew, tickle the kids, have a pillow fight...or ride a carousel. Lose yourself in the fun and watch what that does to your joy quotient!

At this point, I'm ready to follow my own advice. I just unearthed my rollerblades from the closet! And, although finishing this book has been wonderful play as well as hard work, it has edged out much of my leisure time but certainly not my playful spirit. I still managed to see a movie. I had dinner out with my husband. I laid on the floor with my eyes closed and listened to music during a few minutes of peaceful solitude. I had Claire drop her broom and we two-stepped across the kitchen, music blaring, dish-bubbles sailing, and dishes waiting (as

One of the best things about having kids is sometimes getting away with acting like one. If I take my kids to the park and go down the slide with them, we all have a great time.

~ Pat K.

they always do). I even emptied the laundry basket at the top of the stairs so the kids could slide down, but we discovered that a plastic mat is much faster and less bumpy. (Besides, it fits me better!) No rusty knife to be found here!

❧ 12 ❧

Candles
and Confetti
Creating an Atmosphere of Joy

W hen I was a little girl, one of my favorite places to visit
was Grandma and Grandpa Britton's house. It was a
place of hugs and kisses, good smells (like Grandma's
biscuits) coming from the kitchen, happy family gatherings, and always much laughter. Simply decorated, their house was always
clean and neat with pictures of their large brood everywhere. It was
indeed a place of joy, for it was a home that reflected the joy of its
inhabitants who found their joy in Christ. Grandma and Grandpa
Britton are both in heaven now, but my memories of being in their
home taught me that we can create an atmosphere of joy. That's
what we'll look at in this chapter as we consider the ministry of joy
our homes can have.

Did you even know that your home can have a ministry? In *A
Place Called Simplicity,* Claire Cloninger writes that homes can
and should have a ministry, a way to be used for God's kingdom:
"Simple homes are gracious places that have a ministry of their
own in much the same way that people do."[1] She and her husband, Spike, have a remote log cabin in Alabama, and its ministry
is one of rest and refreshment. The home of a friend of hers has
a wonderful ministry of prayer, but of course I especially liked another home she described:

The home of our friend Annie Hunt has a distinct ministry of joy. The wonderful, eclectic blend of furnishings, the colorful artwork, the framed photographs of Annie's children and grandchildren on every tabletop combine with the radiant personality of the hostess to present each guest with the gift of joy.[2]

Isn't that a wonderful thought—to be able to present each guest who enters your home with the gift of joy? As Marguarite M. said, "My home is my best witness of a joyful life." And wouldn't it be wonderful to live in a home which has that ministry? Well, we can! All it takes is a heart that knows joy, the willingness to put forth a little effort, and the desire to make our home reflect our heart.

Candles: The Spirit of Warmth

Picture your living room...and now imagine several lighted candles placed on the tables and a pair burning on the mantle. Besides generating a bit of light and a soft scent, the burning candles create a lovely atmosphere of warmth with their soft glow.

Candles are more than just my metaphor for a home's warm atmosphere. They really do add a charming, cozy, homey ambiance to a room. Candles gently but effectively say, "Welcome! We were expecting you!" So don't save candles just for a formal meal or a romantic evening. They can make any time more special. My children know that, and they love to light our candles— from the Yankee candle that scents a room to the tapers on the mantle—whenever company comes to visit.

At Christmastime, we were having some friends over, and Jacquelyn was helping me get ready. I decorate our home with a lot of Christmas candles during that wonderful season, and she asked to light some of them. I let her while I finished in the kitchen. About that time, the guests started arriving, so I began greeting them. At one point our friend Kirk said, "Lindsey, you've got quite a few candles going. In fact, I've never seen so many lit in one room!" Then I noticed that my daughter had lit about 40 candles. The place was aglow! She must have thought that if a few candles were good, then 40 must be hostessing brilliance in every sense of the word.

Since things were heating up quite a bit (candles add warmth both literally and figuratively!), we blew out some candles and shared a chuckle. What I remember most about that time was the joy that Jacquelyn, Claire, and I shared as we prepared our home to welcome our guests and to celebrate the season of Christ's birth. We had cooked, put a wreath on the door, and set up the nativity scene, and Jacquelyn had hung garlands that, with their little stars and circles, looked like confetti. After our guests had left, I went to blow out the candles but stopped for a moment. I looked at that "confetti" and the candles and thought what perfect symbols they were of a joyful home. Not only did they make the rooms look nice, but they represented the warmth and spirit of celebration present year-round in homes filled with the joy of the Lord.

What can we do to have our home be inviting, to have it generate a spirit of warmth and coziness whether or not candles are burning? Let me offer some basic guidelines:

Clean Up. The best first step toward creating a joyful home that has a warm, inviting spirit is to clean it well. A decorator once told me, "It doesn't matter what's in your home, expensive or not. Unless you start with a clean home, don't bother spending any money or time decorating" or—I would add, trying to create an atmosphere of joy and hospitality. A dirty house doesn't welcome people even if it's been filled with fine furnishings or elaborately decorated. Although the spirit of the people who live there is far more important than what's inside, we must begin with clean if we want our home to be inviting. Besides, clean is something that any of us can do, regardless of our budget.

But let me add that there's clean—and then there's pristine! I have known people who have been such perfectionists in this department that their houses were more like museums than homes. Every room was perfectly arranged, nothing was allowed to be out of place, and these dear people continually straightened up while you visited. That's not warmth! It may be clean—but it's cold. Then there's the other extreme. I've been greeted with great warmth and welcome and given wonderful refreshment, but struggled to find a place to sit! It was apparent that little attention or priority had been given to cleaning the house. A really dirty home is anything but warm and inviting.

The obvious goal is a balance between these two extremes. Begin with a thorough cleaning, but allow loved ones to "live" there. Then, when company comes, concentrate more on the people than on the fact that things might not be perfect (which, if you have children, is usually the case). We can strive for regular maintenance to keep our home clean, but we shouldn't always insist on "company perfection" before having people over. The folks I know never come to my house and do the white-glove test before they sit down, but I'm sure they feel more welcome in a clean house than they would in a dirty one.

Get Rid of the Clutter. If you're like most women I surveyed (and like me!), order is very important to you—and to your sense of joy. For many women, a home that's out of order is a huge negative; it detracts from their joy. Others said the same thing more positively, stating that order adds to their joy. One woman, for instance, said, "If the laundry is done and the kitchen is tidy, everything runs more smoothly. Then it's easier for me to be joyful."

The lack of order, commonly called clutter, can indeed steal a bit of our joy. In her book *Get More Done in Less Time,* Donna Otto says this about organization:

> We all have a basic need to be orderly. Every woman—those who are involved primarily in their homes as wives, mothers, and full-time household managers and those who work outside the home—will be able to benefit from bringing her life under control. The woman herself will be the one who will reap the rewards of being organized. She will feel better, have more energy, reach goals, and be relieved of many of the pressures she has always had to cope with. She will discover a freedom she has never had before: the freedom to use her mental energies to be creative and to have fun.[3]

And that freedom certainly adds to our joy in life.

Donna also points out that it's the things we don't do that make us tired, not the things we do.[4] I agree. Procrastination is more tiring than work because we spend so much energy worrying about and dreading the task we're avoiding (like regaining order in our home). In fact, we often spend far more energy thinking about the project than we would if we just went ahead and did whatever we're stewing over. Great freedom comes when we finally tackle that project and do something to declutter and gain order in our home.

Take the family's socks, for example. You know the routine. Everyone takes their socks off at the end of the day, three-fourths of them make it into the hamper (if you're lucky), and a third of those disappear somewhere between the washer and the dryer—and that's even when you use those plastic doodads to keep them together in the wash! For months I fought the sock war in my house, trying unsuccessfully to match scores of strays. Then one day, in utter frustration, I said, "Kids, this is it! I'll pay you for every pair you match." We gathered all the socks in the whole house and ended up matching 47 pairs—and finding 101 extra singles! They half-filled a garbage bag! When I pitched that bag, I also pitched a major source of clutter, both in the dresser drawers and in my mind. Regaining order is truly liberating.

Regaining order also contributes to a feeling of joy in a home. Have you noticed that it's often hard to feel joyful and offer this ministry of joy to others if your home is out of control? One friend of mine has a particularly peaceful, orderly home. She says the key is avoiding clutter. She throws a lot away and uses her storage space to get things out of sight. Some cupboards are very full, and a few are sometimes very messy, but the "junk" is out of sight until it's needed. She also picks up each morning and evening and always opts for very neat over very clean. She says, "When your home is neat, your spouse and your guests will assume it's clean and not notice the dusty corners. When it's messy, though, everyone will assume it's dirty and not notice the sparkling bathtub."

Standards for neatness and cleanliness differ, however. My books, scattered all over the house, would bother some people, but I love them. They add to my sense of joy. Likewise, you may love lots of antique kitchenware decorating your counters, but someone else might call that clutter. Once again, balance is key. Peace and joy come with the right balance for you. What degree of cleanliness and order is right for you? My mom knew how to achieve balance in this area. She truly lived out the adage "cleanliness is next to godliness," yet she was also extremely hospitable. Tim keeps coaxing me toward the godliness side of cleaning, and I keep coaxing him to pick up his clutter. In the meantime, he keeps the top of the fridge dust-free, and I declutter some of his junk. This teamwork brings both of us joy.

You can get organized—and when you have an organized life...you get done what you want to do. You save energy, money, and time...On an everyday basis you live the life that goes where you want it to.

~Sunny Schlenger and Roberta Roesch, *How to Be Organized in Spite of Yourself*

Decorate from Your Heart. Have you ever noticed that when you walk into an art gallery you enter an atmosphere of calm and quiet? That's no accident; that's the goal. Like the curators of a museum, we can create the atmosphere we want in our home. We can help our home have an atmosphere of joy, for instance, by the way we decorate and the things we display. Hiring an expensive decorator isn't necessary; decorating from the heart is. Our homes can be a reflection of our joy in the Lord as well as our personality.

Color is a great mood-setter. We can use color to change moods or encourage a certain state of mind. For a home of joy, decorate with the colors that make you happy and match your personality. Used harmoniously, colors can produce a feeling of peacefulness and well-being. Believe me, living in a home without much color has often been a challenge to my moods! Color—as Martha Stewart might say—it's a *good* thing!

When we accent our home with family mementos and things that are significant to us, our home reflects who we are. Paintings, china, and crystal are beautiful, but they aren't necessarily joyful. If a decorator fills our home with sparkling new things but we fail to add items that express what is in our heart, our home will be a reflection of fine taste but not necessarily joy.

In our home, one item that expresses my heart is a beautiful stoneware crock, with handpainted ivy and the words, "In thy presence is fullness of joy." This jar reminds me of my vine life in Christ and daily speaks to my heart. You undoubtedly have certain things in your home that express something about you or have special meaning to you. Pull them out of storage and use them as accents—and be creative. My mother-in-law gave me three beaded evening bags which I wasn't able to use very often. One day I got them out of my closet and hung them on a wall. Now I enjoy them every day. I have also framed old family photographs of several generations of my family and Tim's, and I'm making a shadow box of special family heirlooms.

I can't encourage you strongly enough to liberally display in your home photographs of your family and friends or other mementos that are meaningful to you. It's one of the best ways to create an ambiance that says, "This is a joyful home!" Many people have their hallway portrait galleries, but my friend Kim goes beyond that. Using one full wall and inexpensive frames, she hangs pictures practically from floor to ceiling. Guests are always drawn to these pictures of their life—fun, candid shots of everything from college days to a chronicle of their children growing up. That wall reflects the joy of the people who live there.

People who took my "joy survey" offer other ideas. Pam P. has hung a brightly-colored flier from somewhere they vacationed to remind them of the wonderful time they had. Shirley T. shows her taste for fun by displaying a bright metal chicken, while Beth A. hangs gold-framed paintings of tea cups. The things we display reflect our personality and say something about who we are. But these displays don't necessarily require much money—just some thought. What hobbies, interests, people, or family heirlooms bring you joy? Find a way to display them in your home! Frances L. does this and explains, "My home is my canvas, and everything I did, I did with the grocery money!" Money can make a home beautiful, but creativity can make it reflect joy.

And my friend Claudia—whom I have dubbed the Americana Queen—has all kinds of creative ideas for making her home a joyful place. Her home is filled with red, white, and blue Americana, from flags to crocks to checkerboard sets. Claudia's home is beautiful, orderly, and immaculate, but what makes it *joyful* is that it is a *celebration of family*. On a table near her entryway, she displays seasonal photographs of her children, both current and from days gone by. At Christmas, she sets a family photo alongside old pictures of her children on Santa's knee. In the summer she sets out their vacation shots, and on each child's birthday, she puts their pictures in this place of honor. Her friends love to see who's being featured when they visit. To keep this special display going, Claudia simply stores various pictures in envelopes labeled with the season or person. She keeps these—along with some different sized, inexpensive frames—in the table drawer on which she displays them, so it takes her just a moment to change her tabletop gallery.

Other sentimental items in Claudia's home are a reflection of her love for her family. She keeps, for instance, a big wooden bowl on her kitchen table filled with folded papers with questions on them like "What's your favorite food?" and "Share a favorite memory." She initially used these as conversation starters to get to know her children's friends better after they first moved here. Not surprisingly, her home is a frequent gathering place for many of their friends because Claudia's a fun mom who makes everyone feel welcome. Her hospitality truly focuses on people, not on entertaining, which draws attention to the event or the hostess. We can make our home a place of welcome and a reflection of our joy within when we decorate from our heart.

Don't Forget the Touches of Beauty. Some people may think that spending money or time beautifying one's surroundings is worldly and pointless. While good stewardship of our time and our finances is important, I couldn't disagree more with that viewpoint. Beauty is important to us as women. Besides enhancing our life, touches of beauty add to our sense of peace and that of our children's as well. In *Women and Stress,* Jean Lush agrees. She writes:

> Beauty and a sense of order in your home are functional. They have a purpose and are not unnecessary luxuries. Creating beauty around us gives us a sense of accomplishment, charges us with energy, and reduces tension. Beauty is not just for the rich and famous. It is right for everyone and fundamental to emotional health. You see, beauty creates energy.[5]

She also relates that American architect Frank Lloyd Wright taught his students that beauty dissolves conflicts, quiets, refreshes, consoles, and inspires us as well as creates a sense of happiness and serenity. Beauty, his lesson continued, is neither unnecessary nor impractical.[6]

A final word of caution about beauty. At the same time that we value beauty and benefit from it, we must never place too much value on our beautiful or special things. They are just *things* even though they are things that God allows us to enjoy. Years ago I gave my mother a red plate that said, "You Are Special." She used it on special occasions and inscribed on the back each guest or event for which it was used. Before she died, she gave it back to me. Now Mother was very practical, and I knew she wanted me to use the plate—which I did. Consequently, one day one of the children dropped it. Shattered glass went everywhere. Not a single word from the back of the plate was left intact. I fought back tears, but then thought, *What would my mother say right now? She'd say, "Remember, it's just stuff, honey!"* Then I cleaned up the mess and reassured my child as I knew my mother would have. As special and important as the beautiful things in our homes may be, they're just stuff!

Make Things Special. Bed-and-breakfast hostess Joycelyn Clairmonte has a knack—no, the gift—of making things beautiful or special with little money and little time. She told me, "I didn't grow up with a lot of things, but when I was young, I visited a woman who often served everyday meals on china plates and regularly used cloth napkins. If she used paper plates, she set them out in their wicker holder. And she didn't serve chips in the bag; she put them in a napkin-lined basket. She made a huge impression on me. I decided I wanted to be like that when I grew up." And she is.

When I visited their inn, Joycelyn and her husband left for church one night. She had told me she'd left me some soup on the stove and to help myself. But when I went downstairs, I found a china bowl sitting on a china plate, a cloth napkin in a napkin ring, and a matching glass. What I thought was going to be just a quick bite of soup had become a meal that nourished my spirit as well as my body. She had shown me love by making my solitary meal very special.

It really does take so little to make things special. Use the china instead of keeping it in the cabinet. Get out the table-cloth—it won't add much to your laundry. Pull things out of your kitchen cabinets and closets and use the things that have meaning and add beauty to your life. If you drink tea, use your pretty china cups. Look for ways to carve out a moment of serenity, beauty, and calm in your busy life. It brings a sparkle of joy.

Set the Mood. With just a few simple touches, we can create a definite mood in our homes. And one of the quickest ways to create a joyful mood is to be sure to fill it often with beautiful *music.* In the Bible, David gave specific instructions to God's people to "raise sounds of joy" using their voices as well as harps, lyres, and loud-sounding cymbals (1 Chronicles 15:16). We can raise sounds of joy in our homes as well.

Norma M. says, "Beautiful music wakes joy in my soul." And Posy L. adds, "Music above all else brings me great joy. Classical music and particularly great anthems of the church, like Handel and Bach, make me feel full of joy and often move me to tears." Another woman said that her family has soft Irish folk music or classical music on much of the time. In our home, we play a lot of classical and contemporary Christian music, not to mention lots of children's tapes. And on the weekends, Tim will sometimes get out his Irish CD reminiscent of his childhood or tune in a Cajun station for some lively tunes, and we have a great time. My friend Nancy has a family that enjoys music, too. She says, "Many Saturday mornings, Ron wakes up ready to *party* with the family. He's got the whole day to get stuff done, and he wants to jam while he works. So he cranks up some fun contemporary Christian music, and he and the kids dance around all day!"

As I've mentioned before, *light* can affect our moods just as music can. So, whenever possible, let the sunshine in! Open the blinds, clean the windows, add additional indoor lighting to dark rooms, and even paint the walls for a lighter environment. Colleen A. did some of those things and more. She says, "I try to let in as much light as possible. In St. Louis, we moved into a house that was very dark, and it affected my mood for the worse. So I took off the curtains and the ugly wallpaper, and I painted the walls white. Then it seemed more like a happy home than a cave. I think a woman's home environment has a big impact on her joy and contentment."

Another thing we can add to our home environment are great smells. Everyone knows that fragrances are pleasant, but did you know that certain aromas may be able to influence how we feel, settle our nerves, and enhance our concentration? That's what some researchers are discovering. The article "Probing the Power of Common Scents" in *Prevention* magazine (October 1991) reported that "fragrance affects us more than previously thought. New research indicates that smells may influence our minds, our moods and our bodies." So get out the potpourri, light a candle, bake something that smells delicious, and create a welcoming atmosphere through scent. Some gift shops even sell home fragrance sprays, a big step up in quality (and price) from the grocery store air fresheners, but worth it to some people.

I remember some advice I heard years ago. This wise woman said, "You know it really doesn't take that much effort to bake a loaf of bread and put some flowers on the table. You just have to want to do it. The results are worth the effort." We can't always make time for these things, but when we do— when we add the little touches discussed in this chapter—we add to the spirit of warmth in our home, and that nourishes our soul and blesses our family.

Confetti: The Spirit of Celebration

When you hear the word "confetti," what do you think of? The pessimists among us might say, "What a mess! It's sure hard to clean up." But most people think of one thing—a celebration!

And that's something almost everyone loves. A home whose inhabitants live with a spirit of celebration is a happy home. A home that celebrates is a home where love reigns, people are important, and family is center stage. A home with celebrations builds strong families. No matter what the occasion, celebrations say, "You are important! You are special! You are loved!"

Celebrations are a part of our nation's traditions—but in too many homes there isn't enough celebrating. A 1992 family behavior study by the Barna Research Group uncovered some sad statistics: "One of the most significant transitions has been the abandonment of family traditions. Those repetitive, predictable activities between parent and child that served as a mechanism allowing kids to ease into adulthood and maximize the enjoyment of youth have been lost."[7] The report also showed that simple traditions like eating together, playing games, praying and attending church as a family, and family vacations are not as common as they have been in years gone by. Some estimates, in fact, show that the typical parent only spends somewhere between 6 and 90 minutes with their child each day. With either estimate, George Barna says, "The bottom line is that children these days get cheated out of the time they need if they are to absorb the sense of personal value and societal responsibility that is viewed as healthy and beneficial."[8] Far too many children are learning that they are not as important as other people and activities in their parents' life.

But that doesn't have to be the case in your home or mine. We can make family traditions and celebrations a high priority. Our children will benefit greatly, and our family unit will be stronger. Read what Cheri Fuller writes in *Christmas Treasures of the Heart:*

> *I* received a telegram one day. It said simply: Until Further Notice— Celebrate Everything.
>
> ~Tim Hansel,
> *Holy Sweat*

Traditions say, "This is who we are and what we hold dear as a family." They help make up the glue that holds families together...."How do we keep our balance?" asks Tevye, the Jewish dairyman in the beloved musical play *Fiddler on the Roof*. "Tradition!" he rightly concludes. "Without tradition, our lives would be as shaky as a fiddler on a roof."[9]

Traditions can be as simple as a nightly butterfly or Eskimo kiss, but these celebrations are major memory-makers. And they'll definitely add joy to your home!

Celebrate often. Look for reasons to celebrate! Make up excuses! We don't have to limit our celebrations to major holidays and family birthdays. Reasons to throw a party are all around us. Here's a list for starters:

Minor holidays (President's Day, St. Patrick's Day, Flag Day, Arbor Day, etc.)

Baptism

Salvation: welcoming Jesus into your heart

Spiritual birthdays ("Amy became a Christian two years ago today!")

A new birth

An adoption

Half-birthdays

A new job

A good report card

An improved report card

The first lost tooth

Learning to ride a bike or tie shoes

Learning anything new

A new season

A new year in school

A new home (dedicate it to God!)

Grandparents Day

Anniversaries (of marriages, moving to a new house, etc.)

A goal met

An appreciation celebration

Just because! No Reason at All!

Whatever reason you choose, remember that the celebration doesn't need to be elaborate. To mark her child's half-birthday, for instance, a friend came to our house with her children, some frozen pizza, a simple dessert, and some paper cups and napkins she had on hand. That turned a plain Tuesday into a special day and made her child feel special. So be creative and have fun!

Lots of money and lots of planning are not required. A woman I know wanted to give an engagement party for her friends, but she didn't have time to cook. So she bought fried chicken and two side orders, quickly put a lace tablecloth on her table, lighted a few candles, and served the food in pretty bowls. She gave them something she had sitting around to remind them of the little impromptu party, and it became a great memory for them.

When we put a decorative paper cup and napkin into our child's lunch sack along with a piece of candy and a "Way to go!" or "To remind you I love you!" note, we are sending them to school with a celebration in a sack. Throw in a sprinkle of confetti for that party feel, and your child will feel a touch of your love at school. (This same thoughtfulness works for husbands, too!)

You can get ideas from a party one woman gave which took very little planning but was a lot of fun. Her husband was turning 50 years old and three of their friends had turned 40, so she had a big celebration. She made a simple sign for the porch that greeted each guest with, "Welcome to the Home for the Aged." Each chair had a blanket on it. She set several fans around the room for the women "with mid-life crisis hot flashes," and her husband's place of honor was a rocking chair. One man had made a point of telling everyone he was only 38, so the hostess set his place setting with a rattle and a baby cup and told her guests that there was a child in their midst! Skipping the black, over-the-hill theme, they poked fun at the birthday folks and had a great time. This woman didn't have much money to spend on the party and gave only an hour or two to the preparations (including fixing the dinner). We can celebrate without spending a lot of time or money.

Anita K. often hosts simple tea parties for her granddaughter. She says, "Some of the deepest talks we've had were over cookies and tea, served in a pretty china cup. I want her to look back and remember the fun we had together." In her beautiful book *If Teacups Could Talk*, Emilie Barnes describes how she does the same thing.[10] She also gives great ideas for other tea parties, one of which I borrowed for a close friend's birthday. I got a picnic basket and filled it with some cookies, a thermos of hot water, tea bags, a candle and matches, a pretty teapot, and two china cups, saucers, and small plates. I wrapped the china in a towel, placed a folded lace tablecloth over the top of the basket, and surprised my friend at her home. I knew her children were going to be with their grandmother that day (her husband was in on the surprise), so we enjoyed a quiet tea party and made a fun memory. It really takes such little effort to make a memory.

Many of us, myself included, need ideas to draw on whether we want to do the simple or the elaborate. Don't let those "entertaining" books make you think, "I could never pull that off!" Instead, get ideas from those resources to use in your own way rather than trying to duplicate a book or magazine layout. Remember, you aren't trying to entertain anyway. You're celebrating, and that always puts the emphasis on the person or event you're honoring! Also, keep in mind how and when creativity tends to work. It's once we decide to make something special that our creative juices start flowing. We start thinking, "What have I got? What can I use? Won't it be fun to...? I might try...!" Until we make the decision to do it, the creativity doesn't start! When we do, then it comes. Choose something to celebrate and you'll see!

Remember to stay flexible. When Jim and Joycelyn Clairmonte were remodeling their family farmhouse into a bed and breakfast, they had lots of help from friends. To thank the six couples and say, "We couldn't have done this without you!" Joycelyn planned a nice dinner party—and she put a lot of planning into that celebration! She wrapped a little gift and put it on each person's plate along with a thank-you poem tied with a ribbon. Then she added those special touches to her table—candles and confetti! (When she told me this story, I smiled. She didn't even know about this chapter!) Everything was perfect—until the church flooded. The dinner had to be postponed for an hour and a half. Then, when it could finally begin, some people came dressed up, and those who had been cleaning up at the church came in work clothes. The food was warmed, and the party went on as planned. The evening was still a great success largely because the hostess stayed flexible.

Hanging on to your sense of humor and remembering why you're celebrating can help you be flexible when the best-laid plans are foiled again!

Keep it simple. Keeping celebrations simple will encourage us to look for reasons to celebrate and to celebrate often. Although we can have great fun planning and giving elaborate parties, we won't find ourselves doing these big productions very often. Besides, what we want in our home is the spirit of celebration; what we want in ourselves is a heart that's quick to look for ways to celebrate people. Here are some hints for simplifying the "confetti" part of a "candles and confetti" spirit:

• Have candles and confetti on hand—literally! Buy them on sale and keep them in the ready position. Lighting some candles and sprinkling confetti on the table turns an ordinary dinner into an instant celebration.

• Stock up on paper goods during after-season sales. My friend Lois is always buying items at 75 percent off after the event they celebrate has passed. A supply of plain red cups and napkins can be used for Christmas, Valentine's Day, and—throw in something blue—Memorial Day, the Fourth of July, or any other national holiday.

• Think ahead. Don't wait until the morning of February 14 to see if you have any valentines or pink food!

• Don't be afraid of the hassle. A celebration usually takes much less effort than we anticipate.

• Finally—and this is the most important ingredient—bring a *joyful attitude* to your celebration. Your enthusiasm and sense of fun can set the tone for family fun.

Again, simple works! In fact, the simpler we keep our celebrations, the more often we'll look for reasons to celebrate. I have tons of great ideas, but if it's elaborate or time intensive, it'll be ready about three seasons from now. Simplicity makes celebrations happen at our house, and it can help them happen at yours too.

Involve the children. Children love planning parties as well as attending them. So let your kids be involved however they can—even if that means the quality's not quite what you would do. My children love to help set the table and make placecards for our family and guests whenever they can. Involving the children in the preparations promotes family unity and self-esteem. Their willingness to be involved is far more important than perfect presentation. Barbara M. agrees. She says, "The boys help me decorate for all the seasons. They love helping, and I've found that they're both very creative."

Sometimes we don't know our children's talents (and neither do they) because we always do it ourselves! My older children are getting to the point that I can say, "Sure, go ahead and do the whole table," and they love it. They're even coming up with their own spur-of-the-moment celebrations. On a hot August night last summer, for instance, my girls decided to surprise us and set the patio table for dinner. They added a fan to keep us from melting and they hung sheets to hide the garden tools and the neighbors' view. And, of course, they put candles on the table. Then they dragged us outside with our eyes closed to see their surprise. My husband looked at me with big eyes and whispered, "We can't eat out here. It's 98 degrees and humid enough to shower on the patio!" But we braved the heat, read a portion of a funny book aloud, and together made a great memory. After all, kids can have great ideas and a wonderful sense of fun. They seem to have a spirit of confetti quite naturally. So tap into these resources! I bet you'll be glad you did!

The celebrating spirit need not limit itself to party time. This means that celebration shows itself in little moments of grace as well as in rambunctious revelry.

~Emilie Barnes,
The Spirit of Loveliness

❦

Connection: The Spirit of Love

A home needs not only candles and confetti to make it joyful—a home also needs connection. Candles offer the spirit of warmth. Confetti adds the spirit of celebration. And connections tie warmth and celebration together with those we love. Connections which happen through *relationships* and *activities* give our homes a spirit of togetherness. We connect through our relationships when we do the following:

Minimize strife. A joyful home is one in which such signs of strife like fighting and arguing are minimal. Achieving that goal isn't easy when we have more than one child living under our roof. Most of us with more than one child experience that challenge of parenthood known as sibling rivalry. If only we could inoculate against that right along with the DPT shot! Then, when the squabble heated up, we could simply cool everyone off with, "You know, it's about time for your anti-strife booster!" Imagine the peace!

Instead, peace and joy come to a home when parents keep their disagreements private, teach children how to solve their differences quickly, and encourage them to coexist peacefully. Such training isn't easy, but our efforts will contribute greatly to the amount of joy in our home. A home with a lot of fighting is no joy to live in or visit, no matter how many candles we light or how much confetti we sprinkle.

Maximize time together. We connect with the people in our home when we spend time with one another. Sometimes we are so busy with living—with earning a paycheck, paying bills, cleaning, and cooking, not to mention kid activities and church commitments—that our time together as a family is limited to leftovers. A joyful home, however, is one in which relationships between family members are nurtured by spending time together.

Enjoy one another. We connect through relationships when we spend time together and—just as important—when we enjoy that time. So, when you sit down on the floor to play a game with the kids, don't review your to-do list or let your frustration about unfinished work simmer on the back burner. Get into that game. Take the time and make the effort to engage your mind and your heart. Really enjoy your kids! Sometimes all that requires is a simple attitude adjustment.

Respect one another. A home where family members feel respected and respect one another is a home where joy can blossom. Without respect, it's hard for anyone to feel very secure, content, or joyful. Disrespect is a weed that chokes out the fruit of joy.

Share a loving touch. Touch is a balm that soothes souls, reinforces love, and communicates care. It is as important as nourishment to babies, children need large doses of it, teenagers want us to think they are "too old" for such things (but don't let them fool you!), and every vibrant marriage needs it. So kiss your spouse and children every day. Give lots of hugs. Pat a hand. Touch an arm while you talk. Greet visitors with an outstretched hand or open arms. Rub a family member's shoulders just because. And follow your children's lead when they initiate family hugs and then join in the laughter when the child in the middle squeals with delight.

We also connect through our activities. Here are some ideas:

Make memories from mishaps. With a little creativity and an attitude of joy, we can often turn problems into memories. When my washing machine broke this week, flooding my utility room, I mopped up the mess and loaded 12 loads of laundry and four kids into the van. A quick stop en route to the laundromat for canned Juice Fizz—and boxed Lunchables—turned a headache into a highlight. The kids thought that eating dinner at the Wash-O-Rama was one of the best things they'd done in ages. They helped me wash, dry, and fold all 12 loads and, amazingly, when we left to go home, they all shouted, "Thank you, Mother! That was fun!" A joyful attitude (and a little Juice Fizz) can go a long way!

Occasionally do the unexpected. Routine can be the framework for a life that runs smoothly, and children need the stability and predictability which it provides. But everyone needs a break from it occasionally. A joyful home is one in which routine is occasionally sidelined for something unexpected and fun. Take the kids to a dollar movie in the middle of the week. Or one day after school, instead of doing chores or homework, surprise them with an ice cream cone or a stop at the park. Do something your family would never expect you to do and watch the joy flow!

Practice J.O.Y. Joyful homes teach and practice the tried-and-true saying: joy comes by putting **J**esus first, **o**thers second, and **y**ourself third. Our children need to know that Jesus is the whole reason we can have joy in spite of circumstances and that "self" is not the number one priority in life. (Come to think of it, we adults could use a reminder from time to time!)

Connect with nature. Sometimes making the choice to rejoice is easier if we get out of the confines of our four walls and into the beauty of God's creation. So go outside! It's too easy to limit our experience in the great outdoors to the time we walk between the house and the car, the car and our destination. Sometimes making "outside" our destination results in a huge and wonderful attitude adjustment. We won't always be able to look around at a beautiful, inspiring vista to connect with God's handiwork, but we can always look straight up even if we're surrounded by skyscrapers. Just noticing the huge sky, the moving clouds, or the twinkling stars can remind us of the vastness of God—and the relative size of our problems.

Incorporate each individual's ideas of what makes a joyful home. What do your family members think makes a home joyful? I didn't know my own family's answers to that question until I asked recently. My thoughtful child said, "A clean house, good attitudes, and no fighting." My fun-loving daughter said, "Where the parents play with the children once a day." My husband smiled and made reference to the "loving touch" category. Since external sources of joy differ for individuals, we need to know what it is that makes the hearts of those we love sing.

So how connected are you with those you share your home with? I hope these ideas help you improve your relationships and reenergize your activities and, consequently, help everyone experience more joy.

Your Personal Presence

Candles, confetti, and connection—creating a warm feeling, looking for ways to celebrate, and bringing people together by nurturing relationships and sharing activities—can go far in helping us create a joyful home, but they're not the most important factors. The most important ingredient is you!

Haven't you noticed how a person's presence can create a certain atmosphere? Our attitude, countenance, words, voice, and demeanor create an environment around us, and it affects the people who come in contact with us and live with us. If we are anxious or hurried, that is the ambiance around us. But if we are calm and lighthearted, that can be the mood we set. If we know the Lord and His joy, we can create an atmosphere of joy wherever we are—in our home and elsewhere.

And, as this book teaches, we know God's joy when we dwell in Him. When we live connected to Jesus—the vine life—He can grow in us those qualities He adores, qualities that can contribute to an atmosphere of joy around us. God calls us, for instance, to focus on our inner person, "the hidden person of the heart," and to cultivate "the imperishable quality of a gentle and quiet spirit, which is precious in the sight of God" (1 Peter 3:4). We are also told to "pursue righteousness, godliness, faith, love, perseverance and gentleness" (1 Timothy 6:11). And then we are told that "the fruit of the spirit is love, joy, peace, patience, kindness, goodness, faithfulness, gentleness, self-control" (Galatians 5:22-23). As we grow in Christ and yield to Him, we see this fruit—the very likeness of Him—take shape in us. And that fruit makes for a personal presence and therefore a home characterized by love and peace with joy sandwiched right between the two, just as it is in the Galatians 5 list.

So, while it's fun to decorate our home and celebrate every occasion and non-occasion we can think of, we need to pay attention to the atmosphere we ourselves create. If our home is to welcome guests and bless its inhabitants with the gift of joy, we need to stay close to God so that we can know His joy and its presence in our life. No matter how much we decorate our homes or how many celebrations we have, no matter how much effort we put into relationships or how creatively we plan togetherness activities, we are the main ingredient in the recipe for a joy-filled home.

The danger is that we begin to simply endure our seasons rather than celebrate them, and we let life slip away imperceptibly. . . .

~Tim Hansel,
*When I Relax
I Feel Guilty*

A Quick Inventory

As we cultivate joy in both our person and our home, we do well to consider the five senses. Are we appealing to each of them—touch, hearing, sight, smell, and taste? After all, God provided our senses for more than our protection; He provided them for our pleasure.

We can greet guests with the gift of joy, by welcoming them with a gentle touch, be it a hug or a pat on the arm, and offer them a soft chair. We can let them hear a voice that is gentle as they enter a home filled with music and void of strife. We can let them see us looking our best—neat and smiling—as we try to reflect our Savior. And perhaps let's treat them to the beauty of a lighted candle that says, "I was expecting you." We can be something of the "fragrance of Christ" as we usher them into a room that comforts with its pleasant aroma, be it from a candle, potpourri, flowers, or freshly baked anything. And why not tickle their tastebuds with good things from the kitchen—and let those things remind them that we are all to "taste and see that the Lord is good" (Psalm 34:8). Our presence can be warm and welcoming to those who visit and those who abide, and our homes truly can bless all with the gift of joy.

~❧ 13 ❧~

Living and Giving Joy and Contentment
Modeling These Gifts for Our Families

One day my friend was busy loading the dishwasher when her three-year-old daughter Erica looked up at her and said, "Mommy, are you happy?" Her mom replied, "Why, yes, honey, I'm happy." To which Erica replied, "Then why are your eyebrows always down?"

Happy on the inside doesn't automatically translate into joy on the outside. As Erica reminds us, "down eyebrows" speak loudly to a three-year-old, even when we're unaware they're down. Erica also reminds us that we are influencing the people in our life, either positively or negatively, whether we're aware of it or not. That truth got me wondering about the kind of influence I've had in my home.

So I recently asked my two older daughters if they could think of anything they do because of my influence—and I explained I wasn't asking about their regular responsibilities like taking a bath and making the bed, but about things not necessarily expected of them. Jacquelyn quickly said, "Oh, yes, I read all the time and drink lots of water like you. And you know how you're always trying to be happy when things aren't going so good? I try to do that, too." *Hmm. Not bad. She didn't mention a single negative.*

Claire then added, "I like to write in my journal and make notes on my calendar of what I have to do and what I did, and I like to read my Bible." Then she giggled and added, "I think I got that from you." *Oh, how sweet. I never realized she thought that.*

Then they decided to speak for their younger brother and sister. Jacquelyn said, "Yeah—and remember that time when Collin picked up a newspaper and pretended to read it? Then he put his feet up on the kitchen table and crossed his ankles. He was doing exactly what Daddy does." Then Claire jumped in, "And Allison, Mom—she's all the time shaving with her plastic razor like Dad and putting makeup on her face and her dolls and holding her little pink Bible upside down pretending to read to be like you." Then they were off to play. (By the way, I read my Bible right side up!)

If only that were the complete picture....I was touched that my girls could even articulate a way that they have been influenced by Tim and me. And I was thrilled that they immediately thought of the positive, as children often do. But I know all too well that we parents can also have a negative effect on our kids. I know because I have lived the "if Mama ain't happy, ain't nobody happy!" routine. I have seen what happens when I revert to communicating vocally with great expression. (Tim calls it yelling.) And I've noticed the dramatic change in the atmosphere of my home when I'm not living the FINER life (see chapter 10). How about you? What stands out most to you and your family? The times when you model joy or the times when you don't? And which times are more prevalent? The answer to those questions are a good indication of what you're modeling and how effective (for good or bad) your modeling skills are.

The Art of Modeling

We influence the people around us and especially members of our family in so many ways, but none is more powerful than the life we live before them. That's the essence of modeling—influencing those around us by the way we live. Our flesh-and-blood example impacts the people close to us far more than any words we could ever say or write. They may hear what we say, but they will do what they see. As St. Francis of Assisi said, "In all you do, be a witness. If necessary use words." Our actions speak and teach more than words ever could, so we need to be sure we're teaching joy and contentment with our actions using words only when absolutely necessary.

Learning to be a more joyful and content person is important simply because we are individuals made in the image of God. But the importance of our joy and contentment doesn't stop with us. We want to be women who model these traits before others, especially our children. In order to give joy, we have to live it. When Brenda K. was asked on her survey if she was content, she responded, "Yes! Partly because I was raised to be." Our influence carries over into our children's adult years. So let's not stop with learning to be joyful and content for our own fulfillment. Let's also learn to model these traits for our children, who then can influence others. Granted, the level of our kids' joy and contentment isn't solely our responsibility, but our example certainly helps. Living in a home with a mama (and/or daddy) who's joyful and content—and learning from her what joy is all about—is far better than living with a mama who ain't happy and learning those lessons.

So how can you and I model joy and contentment for our family and other people in our life? Here are ten ideas.

The Top Ten Ways to Model Joy and Contentment

1. Express Joy through Your Words
2. Express Joy with Your Voice
3. Sing Often
4. Smile More Often
5. Have Fun
6. Live Out a Joyful Faith
7. Share Your Joys with Others
8. Nurture a Spirit of Giving
9. Focus on the Blessings
10. Express Joy and Contentment Any Way You Can

---

1. Express Joy through Your Words

As the old song says, we can use words to "eliminate the negative, accentuate the positive." When we do this with the words we say and the tone of voice we use, we allow our joy in the Lord to shine through. In fact, it's very difficult for us Mamas to model joy before our child when we're not using words or a tone of voice that reflects joy. Our children need to hear us and see us being joyful. We can learn to express the joy in our heart and demonstrate our contentment by limiting the negative words we say, accentuating the positive words, and tempering our negative responses.

First, we need to limit—if not completely eliminate—the hurtful, negative words we speak. Both a complaining spirit which focuses on the negative aspects of a situation and a critical spirit which reveals our negative view of a person certainly hinder our joy and the joy of those around us, so we must be careful to watch our words. Having "roast pastor" on the way home from church, for instance, will leave a bad taste in the mouth of a child because it models a critical spirit—hardly our goal as parents. One woman wrote me and said, "We are building a new church and there have been power struggles and discontentment within the church family. God gave me this verse, 'Set a guard, O Lord, over my mouth; keep watch over the door of my lips' (Psalm 141:3). To me, that means keeping the things that come out of our mouth joyful and unto the Lord." Doing so will keep us more joyful and make us a better example for our children.

It will also keep us from presenting a double standard to our children, a risk we very human moms run. That double standard happens when, for example, we tell our children, "Be joyful!" and yet we fly off the handle when things don't go our way. Our message about joy also becomes skewed when we fall apart after leaving the beauty salon looking like we're wearing a hair hat. In that case, we may end up modeling "Mama is joyful when things go her way." We can certainly express our frustration, but we should stop short of wailing and gnashing teeth. The better option is to look at our disastrous "do" (or whatever crisis, big or small) as an opportunity to model Philippians 4:4: "Rejoice in the Lord always; again I will say, rejoice!" Besides, why not laugh? A hair hat could be quite amusing (and certainly fixable)!

At the same time that we temper our negative responses, we can model proper responses to negative things for our children. Our friends Ron and Nancy use two simple words to remind their children to go with the flow even when things aren't going well: "We teach our kids to say, 'Oh, well.' That phrase sums up the attitude I'd like them to develop!" And that attitude—that simple phrase "Oh, well"—can head off a critical, complaining spirit.

Second, we can accentuate the positive by the words we say, both to those in our home and to others. We can use words like "You're terrific," "Good job," "I knew you could do it," "I'm so proud of you," and "You're a lot of fun" to build up a child's self-esteem. And we can say those things no matter how old our children are. Lydia G. does: "I am an 85-year-old widow, mother, and grandmother living alone, but in my letters and telephone calls, I tell all [my children and grandchildren] that I love them and how special they are in God's sight as well as mine, and I encourage them in their achievements." Way to go, Lydia! Words are powerful, and we can use them either to build up or to destroy. Tamara L. agrees: "I think we have the power to make another person happy or we can crush their spirit with what we say. I try to encourage, not discourage." Amen! Let's be builders, not wreckers, in the lives of the ones we love.

2. Express Joy with Your Voice

Our tone of voice can be loud and clear in its expression of joy as well as the lack of it. I was reminded of that fact in a rather unusual way once. I was talking with a salesperson on the telephone when a child came in, got a snack out of the refrigerator, and walked

> *K*ids won't buy a double standard. When you give them permission to call you on the carpet for a violation, they will feel ownership of the rules.
>
> ~Kathy Peel,
> *The Family Manager*

off leaving the door wide open. I was on hold so I told my child (a bit sharply), "Close that door."

"But I want a snack," she responded (also a bit sharply).

"You may have one, but you forgot to say 'please,'" I replied.

Suddenly to my surprise, the voice on the other end of the phone said, "But you didn't say please to her."

"Excuse me?" I said.

"You told her to close the door, and you didn't say 'please.' She was just responding to you in the way and with the tone of voice you used with her," she replied. At first I was taken aback that she heard me (hold can be tricky, you know) and that I had been rebuked through fiber optics by a stranger. But I realized that she was exactly right. My child was only living out what was being modeled before her. Now I'd like to say there's never been a problem since that phone call ten years ago, but you know better. So I try to watch my words and tone of voice...even when I'm not on hold.

Another woman I met told me about a time she was having words with her teenager. Apparently, the words weren't good, and neither was the tone of her voice. The daughter stomped off and ran up the stairs towards her room, leaving behind her a trail of less-than-respectful words. The mother yelled up the stairs, "Don't you talk to me like that! Did you forget that I'm your mother?" The daughter replied, "No—but please don't talk to me like that either. Did you forget that I'm your daughter?"

Our children really do follow the model that they see and hear as they grow up. It takes just a little thought and effort to speak gently and sweetly to the people in our lives, but the rewards are worth it. After all, the tone of voice we use can make or break someone's day and, in the long run, someone's spirit.

One day when I wasn't feeling very good, I certainly wasn't doing much on this "Top Ten" list, but I did make the effort in one area. I didn't feel like singing or having fun or smiling, but I made a conscious effort to speak with a sweet voice even though I didn't feel at all sweet inside. Later that day, Claire said, "Mom, you sure were nice today!" All I had done was weigh my words and deliver them sweetly. I had followed the advice of a sign on my friend's refrigerator: "Oh, Lord, may my words be sweet and tender, for tomorrow I may have to eat them!" We must dish nothing from the menu of our mouth that we do not wish to have served back to us!

3. Sing Often

When I asked a friend of mine if she grew up in a happy home, she said, "Oh, yes! My mother sang all the time." Funny. One of the first things we lose when we're angry or down is our song. So perhaps the first thing we should do when we're in such a state is try to find it! Besides, Scripture is full of exhortations to sing for joy :

> O come, let us sing for joy to the LORD;
> Let us shout joyfully to the rock of our salvation.
> Let us come before His presence with thanksgiving;
> Let us shout joyfully to Him with psalms (Psalm 95:1,2).

> O satisfy us in the morning with Thy lovingkindness,
> That we may sing for joy and be glad all our days
> (Psalm 90:14).

In fact, the Hebrew word for "rejoice" means "to sing for joy." But which comes first—the singing or the joy? Neither and both! The circle is continuous. If you are joyful, you will sing. If you need joy, you must sing for it! God commands us to sing, promises joy when we obey that command, and gives reasons for constant rejoicing and continuing song. Many times when we are exhorted to sing, we are given a reason why we can sing with joy, as in this passage:

> It is good to give thanks to the LORD,
> And to sing praises to Thy name, O Most High...
> For Thou, O LORD, has made me glad by what Thou
> hast done,
> I will sing for joy at the works of Thy hands
> (Psalm 92:1,4).

James wrote, "Is anyone cheerful? Let him sing praises" (James 5:13b). Indeed, that's the key to truly joyful singing—letting it become praise to God. And did you know that your joy can be offered as a sacrifice to God even as it lifts your spirits?

> And now my head shall be lifted up above my en-
> emies all around me;
> Therefore I will offer sacrifices of joy in His taber-
> nacle;
> I will sing, yes, I will sing praises to the LORD
> (Psalm 27:6 NKJV).

Praise through song lifts our spirits to a place of joy like nothing else can.

Singing is not only good for us; it's also great for our kids. Most children love to sing and will do so with exuberance. Young children are especially enthusiastic because they have yet to become self-conscious. They couldn't care less how they sound to others. They just sing because it's fun. It's a natural expression of their joy. When our kids grow up, they may not remember the words we sang or how good (or bad) we sounded, but they will remember that we did it. So sing even if you can't carry a tune in a bucket. Joy comes whether or not we're right on key!

And that joy is something we model every time our children see and hear us singing, but we model much more when our singing is praise. When our songs are praise, we teach our children about God, about being in relationship with Him, as well as Scripture verses, great hymns of the church, and truths of our faith. For reasons such as these, our children need see us praising God at church and at home, and we can teach them to join in our song. Lydia G. knows about the joyful fruit from singing. She says, "I was glad to make a joyful noise to God by singing in the choir for 70 years." No wonder she says she's joyful most of the time!

4. Smile More Often

Even if we feel as if we're usually a happy Mama, we can benefit from an occasional quick glance in the mirror. Are our eyebrows up or down? Sometimes we need to remind our face to reflect the joy in our heart. And that's what a smile is.

A smile is a wonderful way to model joy! It's free, immediate, painless, and practically effortless. (It takes far fewer muscles to smile than to frown.) And just in case you thought almost everyone in old photographs was completely joyless, here's some smile trivia. Even though early American life was hard, those folks did smile—but not for pictures. The early daguerreotypes (also known as tintypes) sometimes had exposure times of up to ten minutes. Facial muscles can ache from holding a grin for that long, so be grateful for modern photography. It allows us to leave our children with a visual record of our joyful expressions, also known as "the family photo album."

And of course smiles shouldn't be reserved for pictures or "reasons" to smile—as Liz G. learned. When her son was six years old, he was sitting at the table waiting patiently for his lunch. She noticed he looked sad and somewhat fretful. When she asked him what was wrong, his response hit her like a ton of bricks. "Nothing," he said. "I was just wondering why your face had no smile on it." Liz said, "I found him feeling sad because ᴉe presumed I was sad. All the joy that had been on his face a few minutes before had faded, and what was left was the tone I had set unintentionally. I wasn't even sad that day. I just had nothing to smile about!"

My own son reminded me of the value of a mom's smile one night after I tucked him in. I was about to walk out the door, and he said, "Mom?"

"Yes, son," I said.

"Where's your smile?" I had to think about that a second. I hadn't noticed it was missing.

"Is my smile gone?" I asked him.

"Yeah—and I think mine is, too." Then I scooped him up in the biggest bear-hug-for-locating-lost-smiles possible.

"Oh, no, it's not! I see your smile!" I teased.

"And I see yours! Mom, I like it when you smile!" he said, and melted my heart. Then we made a pact. Whenever we notice the other one walking around without a smile, we inquire of its whereabouts. "Where's your smile?" is now our special game, and so far it's the best lost-smile-finder around. Works every time!

5. Have Fun

If you want a reading on your success as a family merry-maker, simply ask your children if they think your home is a fun place. What do you think your frivolity rating would be? If we're completely in the dark about what their answer might be, chances are we need to learn to have a little more fun. In the survey I did for this book, only two people said they thought they might have too much fun. Most people agreed that fun was important, and many thought they could add a bit more fun to their life. As we saw in chapter 11, there is great value in laughter and play, but I mention it again here because the ability to have fun is a great way to model joy for our children. Our children love it when we're spontaneous and silly with them. Liz H. said, "I 'play' when I read to my kids with *much* dramatics." When you read a story to your child, get into it! Don't just read a story about a bear—become the bear!

Another important source of fun is fellowship with other believers as well as those we love. Such times are not just for our own benefit (although, as we saw in chapter 10, nurturing friendship is key to a happy Mama); our children benefit, too. When they see us inviting friends over for dinner or meeting another family at a park for a picnic, they learn that there is value and enjoyment in Christian fellowship. I learned that as a very young child. I have memories from way back of my parents having people over to visit. I still remember my dad throwing his head back in laughter, and my mom making everything just perfect, even if she served hot dogs. What impressed me most was how our family and our guests would hold hands in a circle and pray before they left. I remember the warm feeling in my heart as I looked up at them as they prayed, glad to be included in this special circle of love. I learned early that there is great value in fellowship with other believers.

The apostle Paul thought so, too. He thanked God for his brothers in Christ and prayed for them with joy (Philippians 1:3,4). Fellow believers were a great joy to Paul, and he loved them deeply. He wrote, "Therefore, my beloved brethren whom I long to see, my joy and crown, so stand firm in the Lord, my beloved" (Philippians 4:1). We model the joy that comes with Christian fellowship when we take time to include it even in a busy life.

And, of course, we mustn't forget to have a sense of humor! In fact, it should be standard equipment and firmly installed before we bring a baby home from the hospital. It comes in handy over the 18 years or so that follow! Wouldn't it be nice to walk the aisles of Super Baby World and see diapers, strollers, humidifiers, and Sense-o-Humor in a box? How great it would be to run to the store to stock up when our supply runs low! And we'd never be at a loss for what to buy for a baby gift again!

Besides, a sense of humor and the ability to laugh at ourselves make for a great model of joyfulness—and my father, Paul Britton, is a great example. Many years ago, he was attending a sales convention at a prominent downtown Houston hotel. Nature called, so he went to the restroom. While in the stall, an unexpected sneeze came upon him, apparently with the force of a strong gale, and blew his denture right out of his mouth! Unfortunately, it didn't land at his feet. Instead it flew right *under* the stall door, slid across the floor, and stopped near the center drain in the middle of the bathroom.

He peeked under the door, hoping to find an empty bathroom, but to his dismay, a man stood at the sink washing his hands—steps away from the misplaced teeth. Not knowing if the man had noticed, he quietly opened the stall door. Without looking up, lest he lock eyes with someone in his Moment of Great Embarrassment, and with his trousers still at his knees, he quickly waddled the few steps to the center drain, grabbed the denture, and backed up into the blessed privacy of the stall. To this day, he doesn't know if that man ever noticed, and he's been careful ever since to keep a good supply of denture adhesive around. He never leaves home without it!

When I asked his permission to tell this story, he said, "Sure, isn't that the point you're making—that it's important to be able to laugh at yourself?" And that's something he's done often over the years. He laughs easily at himself (and his Moment of Great Embarrassment)—and we would do well to follow his example. Having fun with our kids, enjoying fellowship and fun with other believers, and laughing at ourselves—these are three ways we can model joy to those around us.

6. Live Out a Joyful Faith

Another great way to model joy is through our faith. While it's important to teach reverence, respect, and fear of the Lord, it's also important for our children (and other people in our life) to see that we find great joy in our faith. We need to show them that the Christian life is a life of joy! What better way to do that than by displaying a faith that knows how to laugh? If all our kids ever see is a solemn, grim-faced approach to Christianity, they may not stay in its ranks when they get older.

Of course we must teach our children reverence for their Creator, devotion to Christ, and the sobering, awesome truth of what Jesus did for them on the cross. We must know exactly what we believe and why so that we can teach these fundamentals to our children. But, in addition, we must also show them by our example that those beliefs do not relegate us to a life in Boresville. There's nothing ho-hum about a vibrant faith! Because of our faith, we have hope and joy today as well as the knowledge that today's joy will be overshadowed by the joy to come in His kingdom. What a wonderful privilege to be able to show our children that faith in Jesus Christ is indeed joyful!

As a child, I noticed the absence of such joy after a certain part of the worship service, so I asked my mother one Sunday why everyone in church was always so sad after the sermon. They sang joyfully at the beginning of the service, but after the preacher preached, they sang "Just As I Am" with soft, sad voices. I kept hoping that—just once—the preacher would forget to talk so everyone could stay happy. Then my mother explained to me some deeper aspects of faith, like conviction of sin and the call to discipleship.

Childhood is an adventure to be joined by parents whenever possible. By grabbing pockets of time together... you create pleasant memories for both you and your child.

~Susan Newman,
*Little Things
Long Remembered*

But because my family lived out a joyful faith, I was not left with a downhearted view of the Christian life. To the contrary!

In fact, Tim and I try to offer our kids the same kind of joyful faith I grew up with. We love to have what we call "family praise and worship time." Tim will play praise songs on his guitar, sometimes accompanied by the children with their toy instruments, and we all offer up a joyful noise to the Lord. (It's a good thing it's joyful because the Von Trapp Family Singers we aren't!) We have a great deal of fun, and the children love to dance around the room to the fast songs—and we let them. Then, at one point, the mood changes, and Tim has them sit still as we focus on other aspects of our God. We're not really regular with our family praise, but we sure have a good time when we get together.

And, of course, family fun in worship can also happen with the extended church family. In our former city we were in a fellowship group that met once a month for fellowship, food, and prayer—but we also liked to have fun. For one evening meeting, we were told to bring our favorite breakfast food and come in our pajamas—and almost everyone did. (One or two folks decided to partake of our fun with their dignity untarnished. Bah humbug!) So there we were praying and praising God in our bathrobes and fuzzy slippers! We had a beautiful time sharing our needs and answered prayers, and we also had a lot of fun. As we laughed together, I thought about how God must be smiling, since He delights in our fellowship and He wants us to know His joy! I especially loved that our children saw us going to a Christian meeting and enjoying a touch of silliness. They see plenty of reverent worship done in Sunday clothes. This kind of fun showed them that we find great joy in our faith—an important thing to model.

7. Share Your Joys with Others

The expression "a joy divided is a joy multiplied" is so true. When we share our joy with others, our joy increases. And we can share our joy two ways: by telling people about it and by involving them in it. So, instead of being quick to share our complaints, let's be quicker sharing our joys. When something good happens to us, let's tell someone. When something brings you joy, share that with another person. When you find joy in learning something new about God or in reading His Word, share it with someone who encourages your faith walk. In a world filled with depressing news, sharing joy with another person is good for both the sharer and the "sharee." While it's nice to tell someone about our joys, hearing someone else tell us about their joy can be just as uplifting. Comments like, "I'm feeling so good today," "The best thing just happened..." or "Guess what the Lord just showed me?" really can make someone's day, whether that person is the speaker or the hearer. Try it. See for yourself that joy is twice as sweet when we have someone to share it with.

And there are as many ways to share our joy as there are sources of joy. A great meal at a beautiful table can be a sparkle of joy in our day, and the joy increases when that meal is shared. For me, a visit to a good bookstore is a sparkle of joy, and I often include my children on those trips. Now going to a bookstore is a joy for them as well. During my mother's illness, I wanted to give her a little sprinkle of joy, so I made her a joy basket. I bought a heart-shaped basket and filled it with things I thought would bring her joy: some books, a card, a few trinkets, an inexpensive Walkman with headphones, and a tape with Scripture set to music—and all the songs were about joy. She filled her mind with God's words about joy, and those words were a real comfort to her. In her books, Barbara Johnson suggests making such joy baskets for yourself to make you smile when the "gloomees" attack, and that can be a great way to spark some joy that you can, in turn, share with others.

We can literally give someone a basket of joy, or we can share our joy simply by telling them about the good God is doing in our life. Either way, sharing our joy offers those we know and love a sweet respite in an often gloomy world.

8. Nurture a Spirit of Giving

To nurture a generous spirit is to cultivate the gift of joy. My friend Posy learned this as a young girl. She said, "My mother taught me that it is always better to give than to receive. We didn't have much money growing up, so if we wanted to give gifts, they had to be homemade. Through her teaching and example, I learned that giving brings me great joy." No matter what we give to another—an actual gift, time, a deed—we are usually more than repaid by the joy we feel in our heart. Posy adds, "If I do something for someone else when I'm feeling down, I almost always feel better. Because my mother taught me to focus on doing for others first, I rarely feel I need to focus on myself or enter into self-pity."

Liz G. also finds great joy in doing for others, and she models this virtue for her family. She has a real soft spot for elderly people who need help with transportation. Liz will closely watch someone walking along and, after seeing that the person seems safe (for example, she isn't carrying any large bags or wearing heavy garments that could conceal something dangerous), she often pulls over and offers them a ride. "I'll never forget the day," Liz says, "when I was taking my son to afternoon kindergarten and there was the sweetest little 'bag lady' walking across the busy intersection. I quickly observed the situation, prayed for God's safety, and offered this lady a ride. She was a sweet lady who had not eaten that day and was hungry. I looked down and saw I still had half of a hamburger. I offered it to her and she gladly ate it. My son learned how to help people that day and since then we've helped others, prompted by the compassion of my little ones. It gives them—and me—great joy to help those in need."

What are you doing to model the joy of giving and to share that joy with your children?

9. Focus on the Blessings

One of the best ways to teach joy and contentment in—or in spite of—present circumstances is to focus on our blessings and to teach our children to do the same. When we point out our blessings and express our gratitude for them, we teach gratefulness, and a grateful heart is usually a joyful heart! Besides, it's hard to express gratitude and be discontent at the same time. When we express our gratefulness to God and to others, our children learn to do the same. And we can show our gratitude verbally, in writing, and by our attitude.

Verbally—The more we talk about our blessings, the more we teach our children to do the same. Kathy P. tries to do this with her family: "Daily, Troy and I talk with our children about all of the blessings God has blessed us with instead of dwelling on the things that are negative and not uplifting. The more good that goes into our hearts and minds, the more good comes out."

The words we speak really can affect our level of contentment as well as that of our children. If we are constantly putting things down and griping, so will our children. When we first moved into our cavelike house, I realized I'd been too verbal about my frustration when I heard my young son say, "Man, this house is the pits!" I quickly began to point out its blessings to him. As I did, he began to mirror my thankfulness with his words, reflecting a more positive outlook. Mary H. has also learned to watch what she says: "I try not to verbalize dissatisfaction with the house or our things (even when I'm thinking the sofa is looking pretty tacky). I also attempt to constantly affirm the value of things like the fact that we love each other and are so blessed."

One family I know teaches their children to be content with a simple family phrase: Be happy for what you've got! When cries of "That's not fair" or "That one's bigger" surface, they counter with "Be happy for what you've got!" Sometimes they shorten it to "BHFWYG," a fun and immediate call to contentment.

In writing—Blessings and answered prayer are always causes of great joy. Writing them down ensures that we don't find joy in them only when they happen. A written record of God's goodness to us and His activity in our life gives us the chance to go back and review the blessings. Julie C. keeps a journal to record her thoughts of thanksgiving as well as her requests. Then, when she has a bad day or life seems too much to handle, she looks back in her journal two years ago and reads about how she was feeling then. Using the beautiful gift of hindsight, she sees that what seemed so overwhelming then turned out okay and that God takes care of things. She adds that both writing and later reading her words of thanksgiving are "calming and comforting [activities], like dipping your hands in reality. I read it and realize that my problems aren't insurmountable." Julie uses pretty cloth journals and stores them on a bookshelf. As she lines them up, they add a touch of beauty to her home, but more importantly they serve as a visual reminder of the many reasons to give thanks for God's faithfulness.

In the Old Testament, God's people did the same thing, but their visual reminders of God's faithfulness and their tangible expressions of gratitude and thanksgiving to God took the shape of stone altars (Genesis 8:20) and monuments (Joshua 4:1-7). God wanted His people to remember His work in their life and to tell future generations about His faithfulness. God wanted these monuments to "be a sign among you when your children ask in time to come, saying, 'What do these stones mean to you?' Then you shall answer them" (Joshua 4:6,7a NKJV). How often we forget what God does in our life. Sometimes it's hard to remember what God did last month, let alone what He did years ago. A thanksgiving journal can be our monument to God's faithfulness and a reminder to tell our children about His goodness.

I like keeping my own personal chronological journal, and the children recently made a family thanksgiving journal. We put Joshua 4:6,7 on the front, and they decorated a page for various categories, which include family, friends, church, activities, feelings, blessings given, and blessings received. Anyone of us is free to write in our thanksgiving journal at any time, and we date each entry. We hope this book will become a permanent record of the faithfulness of God in our family—a monument of our thankfulness.

In attitude—Once, before we started our thanksgiving journal, I noticed that my older girls were beginning to compare our home and possessions with those of their friends. A red light flashed in my head, "Danger zone! Danger zone!" I know how perilous the comparison trap is for adults and our attitude, and I certainly didn't want my children to get caught up in that. So, instead of going straight home from our friend's house, I made a quick turn, crossed the tracks—literally, and drove toward a very poor part of our area. Without driving slowly enough to invade anyone's privacy, I gave my children a quick glimpse of something they'd never seen before: shacks that served as people's homes, lean-tos on shanties with broken windows, yards littered with junk, a man asleep in a broken-down pickup truck in his yard. I don't remember seeing a single flower. "Do people actually live here?" Jacquelyn asked in astonishment. "Yes, honey, they do." We rode in silence as they tried to imagine such a life.

As we got closer to home, we broke the silence and discussed what Jesus said about the poor and ways we might be able to help some of those people. As we drove into our driveway, our old house suddenly looked like a mansion. The hanging baskets of ferns and the geraniums by the front door were a glorious welcome to a home where blessings flowed. "Mom," Jacquelyn said. "We are so blessed!" My children were deeply moved. New perspective firmly in place, they talked about their blessings all afternoon, and I watched their level of joy and contentment take a big leap.

All of us get blind to God's goodness to us. When we take time to remember His faithfulness, look around at the countless ways He cares for us, and build an altar with paper and pen, we will have a wonderful source of joy. Focusing on the blessings can't help but make us joyful in our Lord.

10. Express Joy and Contentment Any Way You Can

If we are joyful and content in the deepest place of our being but never outwardly express those feelings, we aren't modeling these virtues for our children. By its very nature, joy needs to be expressed. Contentment may be a quieter feeling of calm satisfaction, yet it also needs to be shown if we are to help our children learn what it is to be content. If we want to teach them to our children, our joy and contentment are not to be secrets hidden in our heart.

Fortunately there are many ways to express our joy. The Bible describes several expressions of joy: singing, the use of musical instruments, praise, shouting, and even just having a joyful heart. Nancy K. expresses her joy with quite a repertoire: "I sing, yell, stomp, and clap." Katie R. says, "I always start my day with Psalm 118:24, 'This is the day which the LORD has made; We will rejoice and be glad in it' (NKJV)."

Spunky morning talk show host Kathie Lee Gifford often does the same thing when her two-year-old daughter comes to her requesting, "Hosanna, Mommy! Hosanna!" That's when she and Cassidy and five-year-old Cody march around their deck, singing, "This is the day the Lord has made. We will rejoice and be glad in it! Hosanna! Hosanna!" She's sure the people in her neighboring state hear her, but she says this:

> I don't care what they think. I believe worship should be fun and exciting so children can embrace it.

After all, David leaped and danced before the Lord with all his might, and sang out with joy.

We Christians don't do that enough. Often we're all so terrified of what somebody's going to say. But if you love the Lord, you should *show* it. *The joy of the Lord is your strength.*[1]

People often ask Kathie Lee where she gets her energy, and she says that what most people perceive as her energy (and she's *very* energetic) is really her strength of spirit. "It comes from the joy of knowing God, loving Him, and being loved by Him," she explains. "It's so simple we sometimes stumble past it."[2] She goes on:

That's why I jump in wholeheartedly to join Cassidy and her five-year-old brother, Cody, when we march around the deck doing our hosannas. They are learning from their earliest days that God loves them and has a plan for their lives. The joy of the Lord is *their* strength too.[3]

Is the joy of the Lord your strength as well? It can be. He wants it to be!

Maybe you're like Cindy G., who "seems to always have a little laugh right under her breath ready to come out." Or maybe your temperament is more subdued, like my mother who preferred to laugh on the inside but was quick with a quiet smile. No matter what your temperament, no matter how you express your joy and contentment, just be sure you do. After all, you are modeling these qualities—or the lack of them—for the people you love. Besides, joy shared really is joy increased—and none of us can ever have too much joy!

To show a child what once delighted you, to find the child's delight added to your own—this is happiness.

~J.B. Priestley,
Reader's Digest

❧ Epilogue ❧
Finding Purpose and
Joy in the Moment

Have you ever asked yourself why you're here? More importantly, have you come to any conclusions? Also, how long has it been since you've lived? And I don't mean just breathing and having your heart beat, but really living with all your senses fully engaged, totally aware of the moment at hand? Knowing who we are and why we're here and finding joy in the moment are key to really living joyfully and with purpose—and that's an incredible way to live. It's the difference between being a "mama who ain't happy" and a mama who's making the choice to rejoice.

Knowing Who We Are and Why We're Here

Most of us know who we are unless, of course, mothering has taken its toll and Mama's desperate enough to claim amnesia if only to get a brief vacation at The Home for Misplaced Persons. Although we probably still have a handle on our name and address, most of us need to guard against spiritual amnesia—that condition where we forget who we are in Christ and the reason we can be joyful always.

Know who you are in Christ. Because I have been adopted as a child of God through Jesus' death on the cross for my sins, I have an inheritance more precious than any of earth's joys (Ephesians 1:5). As one of the women I surveyed said, "Because I am a child of the King, that makes me a princess!" True enough! I also know this about our identity in Christ: "Having also believed [in the gospel of salvation], you were sealed in Him with the Holy Spirit of promise, who is given as a pledge of our inheritance" (Ephesians 1:13,14a). And that inheritance is eternal life (John 3:16). So I'm a daughter of the King who has the Holy Spirit to guarantee that I will live forever with Jesus. God's Word also tells me that one of the fruits of the Holy Spirit is joy (Galatians 5:22). How wonderful! So, as believers in Christ, we are princesses who have an eternal future with Him and the ability to live joyfully today because of the Holy Spirit and God's grace! We need never doubt our worth to God or our ability to know joy. You and I must choose joy, but God's grace makes it possible for us to experience it.

Know who you are as an individual and why you're here. Besides knowing who we are in Christ, we need to know within that framework and on a more personal basis who we are and why we're here. Some of us learn in an instant who we are: a sudden spiritual discovery, experience, or happening shines a light on that spot in our soul that yearns to know who we are and why we're here. For others, that discovery may seem to take a lifetime. And, sadly, I'm afraid, many people just exist. They do their job, clean their house, and go to church without any real sense of their God-given mission in this world. They are missing the great joy that comes from knowing their unique purpose in life—why God made them. When we know that, we know our mission. And that mission can involve just about anything because—and it's essential to know this—no matter who we are or where we are, God wants to use us for His glory. We just have to be willing to be used. And no matter where you are in life, it's never too late to discover your mission.

I remember the first time I began to sense my purpose. I was 17 and had enjoyed writing since I was 9 years old. I was contemplating my future in communications as I prepared for college, and I learned that I could have a mission in life unrelated to "missions" in the evangelistic sense. My pastor told me, "God can certainly use Christians in secular work, especially the media. You can be called to that just as easily as someone can be called to the mission field overseas." I had begun to discover part of my individual purpose in life, and God has continued to reveal and reaffirm my calling and purpose over the years as my life has changed.

God places gifts and desires within us that we can use to serve Him, and that's key to knowing joy in this life. Sometimes people miss out on joy because they think that if they enjoy doing a certain work, then it must not be God's will for them. But it is God who gives us our gifts and works through our minds and desires to accomplish His will: "For it is God who is at work in you, both to will and to work for His good pleasure" (Philippians 2:13,14).

Acknowledging our gifts and identifying our desires are important steps toward knowing who we are, what we're here for, and how God can use us. God can accomplish His purposes through us because He uniquely created us to be used by Him in a role that only we can fill. No one else can evangelize just like Billy Graham does, no one can minister to the poor exactly as Mother Teresa does, and no one can do your job or raise your children like you can. We are uniquely qualified to influence the children God gave us. We are uniquely able to make a difference in whatever we do when we recognize that God can use us *where we are!*

Accepting this truth gives us vision and a mission for living. In *Holy Sweat,* author Tim Hansel writes about the importance of a vision for our life:

> In fact, to have an inner vision is critical if we're going to live our lives to the fullest. The good news is that you have the answer with you all the time. Where? God's imprinted it, stamped it on your being. Elizabeth O'Connor, in her book, *Eighth Day of Creation*, explains: "We ask to know the will of God without guessing that his will is written into our very beings. We perceive that will when we discern our gifts. Our obedience and surrender to God is in large part our obedience and surrender to our gifts."[1]

Having this "inner vision," this mission in life, however lofty or simple it is, makes getting up in the morning worth it. It gives reason to the mundane. No matter how simple our mission is or how ordinary we feel our specific purpose in life is, we must remember that God can use us where we are for His purposes. That truth gives meaning to whatever we do—from cleaning house and cooking meals to running a corporation. When we know God has a purpose for us and believe He wants to use us right where we are and when we follow the exhortation of Colossians 3:17 ("Whatever you do in word or deed, do all in the name of the Lord Jesus"), we can clean and cook or run a business with joy! Those acts can become our service and even worship offered up to Him, and we really can find great joy in it!

I love a story Gordon MacDonald tells in *The Life God Blesses* of having breakfast with some bus driver friends who were complaining about their job. What, if any, significance can come from driving a bus? Pastor MacDonald explained that God can make any job interesting when we believe He wants to use us in it. This is what he told his friends: "Tomorrow morning before anyone gets on your bus, close the door, face all the empty seats, and say loudly, 'In the name of Jesus, I declare this bus a sanctuary for the next eight hours. And I declare that all the people who enter this sanctuary will experience the love of Christ through me whether they realize it or not.[2] A few months later, one of the drivers told Gordon that following this suggestion had changed his life. He said:

> Each day I've been turning my bus into a sanctuary, and it's made all the difference in the way I do my job. Why, the other day a guy got on my bus, and he was so mad at me because I wouldn't let him off at a stop that was illegal. He cussed me out something awful. And you know? There was a day when I think I would have gotten up and let him have it. But not in a sanctuary. I let him off at the next stop and said, "Hope you have a good day, sir. Nice having you aboard." And a lady behind me said, "Charlie, how can you be so nice to a jerk like that?" I just muttered to myself that it wasn't hard if you were driving a sanctuary and not a bus.[3]

After I read that, I started making my minivan a sanctuary for afternoon car pool!

One of the greatest joys that we can experience is knowing and doing what God made us to do. We may have many roles and they may change over time as we grow, but discovering what they are and how they work together to fulfill our ultimate mission in life is a very joyful thing. My favorite movie line of all time is from *Chariots of Fire* when Olympic runner Eric Liddel says, "When I run, I feel His pleasure." I feel God's pleasure when I use my gifts to serve Him. Once, while taping a radio broadcast, I stopped and prayed, *Thank You, Lord. I feel You smiling. This work I do as worship to You.* I also feel God's pleasure in my primary role as a wife and mother. When I'm able to express joy instead of impatience with my children or view yet another load of laundry as an act of worship to God, I know He is pleased.

Let me direct you to a place that I think is one of the most joyful places on earth. It is the convergence point of who we are and who we are in Christ. It's that point on the line when the knowledge of our mission in life intersects with the realization that we can reflect who we are in Christ as we do that work. At that point of convergence, God can use us and we can know great joy. That convergence impacts how we live, the choices we make on this journey, and the amount of joy we find along the way.

Joy in the Moment

The other day I passed a man at the post office who stood out like a sore thumb. Everyone was hurrying about, but he stood perfectly still on the edge of the sidewalk, with his eyes closed and his face turned up towards the sun. He was drinking in the moment, and he looked so content. People probably thought he looked strange, but as I passed I smiled. *He's got it!* I thought. *He's enjoying the moment!*

How easily we forget to find joy in the moment. We work hard, endure difficulty, and wait for the biggies in life to bring the feeling of joy: a new baby, a new house, a vacation. We get so busy trying to live our life that sometimes in the process we forget what it means to really live.

We miss the joy in the moment when we look for joy in the future. Do these poignant words by an anonymous writer strike a little too close to home?

> First I was dying to finish high school and start college.
> And then I was dying to finish college and start working.
> And then I was dying to marry and have children.
> And then I was dying for my children to grow old enough for school so I could return to work.
> And then I was dying to retire.
> And now I am dying...and suddenly I realize I forgot to live.

As these words remind us, if we wait until tomorrow to enjoy life, we may miss out. It's so easy to get caught up in our daily schedules that we leave little room for things that can bring us joy. We must learn how to really live today. We can do simple things that give us gladness of heart. What things make your heart sing? I love to write, visit bookstores, go "antiquing," read to my children, and go on family outings, to name a few things. Making time in my life for these things brings me great joy.

For Posy L., it's working in the yard. "With a name like Posy," she says, "it comes naturally. I love learning about and growing flowers. Having a beautiful yard thrills me—it's my way of glorifying and affirming God's presence in my life." One day she noticed that her then-eight-year-old son was watching her work in the yard.

"Mom, I was watching you because you are so happy when

> *If you let yourself be absorbed completely, if you surrender completely to the moments as they pass, you live more richly those moments.*
>
> ~Anne Morrow Lindbergh

you work with your flowers. And I think I know why."

Wondering what was coming, she asked, "Why?"

"Because you don't have a sandbox. The yard is your sand-box, Mom!" he replied. And it is. It's the place for her that each of us needs. "A place to go," Posy says, "to just mess around, where there are no right or wrong answers, where one can relax and open the soul to God." A place or thing that gives us gladness of heart. What or where is it for you?

We miss the joy in the moment when we look for it in the past. I was tempted to hang on to joys from the past when my mom died, and maybe you're there right now. But if we live in the past, we won't find joy today. We must live in the moment and be alert to the joys of those moments, no matter what the past was like. And, as Nicole Niederer's lyrics point out, the call of the past can be powerful.

This Is Now

Familiar feelings creeping inside of me,
Amazing how a simple conversation,
Things I thought I'd buried way back when;
Fear and insecurity, I thought that I had victory,
But tonight I face the battlefield again.
Amazing how a simple conversation
Can cause the loss of so much ground I've gained.
A long-forgotten memory, invading my stability;
At times like this, it helps for me to say,
"I'm here, this is now; I'm exactly where God wants me.
I'm here, this is now, and the past no longer taunts me."
It's really very clear, all that matters is I'm here.
I'm here and this is now.[4]

You and I are here and this is now—and the now really can have its own sparkle. We must get beyond the past and keep a vision for the future and, as we do so, find our joy in the moment that is now! The present is not just what we pass through on the way to the future. It is filled with what one writer calls "real moments." She says, "What was missing from my life were more 'real moments,' moments when I was not trying to get somewhere or be something, moments when I was fully experiencing and enjoying where I was, now.[5] To find such "real moments" and enjoy the present, we must slow down and be aware of what we're doing.

Slow Down and Pay Attention

We probably miss many moments of joy because we're too busy and inattentive. We must pay attention to what is going on at any given moment. When we can put our problems, our tasks, and our disruptive thoughts out of our mind long enough to totally focus on the moment at hand, we have a chance to experience joy. I remember doing that one night when my son was an infant. From my journal:

> Last night I was tired, it was late, and I just wanted to finish the dishes. But Collin screamed out and I went to get him. He wasn't feeling well, so I just sat and rocked him. I sat and stroked his velvety soft cheek and tiny jaw and felt his little hand touching my face, and I was overcome with unexpected joy. His head leaned against me, and he looked up into my eyes with total peace, contentment, and love. What a moment. I think I'll forever have that picture in my mind. Lord, show me more moments like these. Let me not be too busy to seize such moments.

Lately, I've really been practicing paying attention. The other night on my way to the store, I drove with the windows down, a 70-degree wind blowing my hair, and the radio playing—loudly. *At this very instant, I feel joy*, I thought. On another evening, I stepped outside and was still for a minute. I looked up at the sky, noticed the North Star, and for just a moment the sky was that gorgeous deep blue color that it gets right before nightfall. *Mmmm. Another bit of joy. Glad I paid attention.*

Of course some joyful moments just can't be missed. Like the other day when my son and I were driving along and he said, "Mom, I know what I'm going to be when I grow up."

"What, honey?" I asked, waiting to hear him announce his future career.

"A shepherd," he said with all the seriousness in the world.

"You mean, like...with sheep?" I stammered.

"Yep. A shepherd, " he said. Then he changed the subject as if that were all the discussion necessary, and he began telling a new story. I choked back a laugh. I didn't have the heart to tell him there really wasn't much of a job market for that these days. There was joy in that moment from both the humor of Collin's career choice as well as the pleasure of a shared connection with my very self-absorbed young son!

Even now as I write these words, I'm finding great joy in the moment. Normally I write at my computer, but to close this book I wanted to fully experience my life as a writer. I wanted to feel the pen in my hand scratching out words on paper, my heart to yours, with the sun on my face and God's beauty around me. So here I sit on a park bench at the edge of a lake. I have slowed my body and mind, wanting to be alert to the things around me. My five senses are engaged in lifting my spirits. I see the beauty of a tree-lined lake, and I feel the warmth of the sun. I hear the sounds of life in the birds, the children playing, and the snippets of conversations from people walking by. I smell pine trees and fresh air, and I just tasted a nice lunch and a little bit of life. It is just an ordinary day, but today I'm paying attention. I've been to this park before and seen all these same things, but I didn't take them in as I'm doing today.

So, to find joy in the moment, we must know our purpose in Christ and we must seize the day (although sometimes we just want to *cease* the day!). In *Carpe Diem* (Latin for "seize the day"), Tony Campolo writes: "This book is meant for us regular people who still believe that the miraculous is a hidden dimension of the mundane and would like to figure out how to touch and taste it."[6] We can see the miraculous and taste the joy when we're paying attention. But we must not make joy our goal. If that is our goal, we will never find it. It's like that butterfly that we can't force to land on our shoulder. We can enjoy its beauty whenever it happens to alight if we're paying attention, but—like knowing joy—we can't make it happen. Sometimes we are seeking so intently, we are "so conscious of the goal," as Tim Hansel writes, "[that we miss] the miracles along the way."[7] So don't seek after joy, but do be alert for its sparkle. Sometimes we find the sparkle of joy in the mundane when we're paying attention and have relaxed our striving a bit. Remember—don't focus on the joy; focus on the journey and the joy will come.

Be a gardener. A good gardener doesn't just plant to reap the fruit. She can go buy fruit if that's all she's after. She prepares the soil, plants, cultivates, nourishes, prunes, and—all along the way—enjoys every aspect of the process. The fruit is a beautiful by-product. And so it is in our life of joy. Don't seek the fruit itself. Moments of pleasure and mere happiness can be had almost any day. But when we set out to live life to its fullest, aware of our purpose and yielding to God, and when we are alert to the extraordinary in the ordinary moments, we find the by-product of joy.

Happiness Is Overrated—Go for Joy Instead!

So what about Mama? Can we really make the choice to rejoice? Picture this: It's a "Mama ain't happy" day. She's doing her very best "state of distemper." She's grumping and doing her pit-bull-in-high-heels impression. Her eyebrows are most definitely down. Now, mentally, send her to her room to get a grip.

Next, think about the Mama we'd all like to be. She's made the choice to rejoice. She's tamed that monster of discontent, she's learned to become intimate with the Giver of Joy and how to be joyful even when she feels like a grump. She's installed her security system to protect against the joy robbers, and she's practicing Jovial Jane's FINER life. She's learned to laugh and lollygag more. She's even been trying her hand at candles and confetti. Sometimes she faces the dark, but she's learned to look for the sparkle even there. By learning and practicing these things and, more importantly, turning to God's Word to help her vine life, she's become a Mama capable of modeling joy and contentment for her family.

Which Mama do we want to be? Which Mama do we want our children to see? Not a hard choice, is it? Oh, we'll never fully achieve all of these traits, but this isn't a book about perfection. This book is about process and the fruit available along the way. We will never arrive once and for all at unshakable joy—that is, until our final, heavenly destination. Then we will be greeted by the Fullness of Joy Himself who will look at us and smile and say, "Well done, good and faithful servant....Enter into the joy of your master" (Matthew 25:21).

But, until that time, we must remember that although joy awaits us at the end of our trip, there's also joy in the journey. Since Jesus wants us to have that fullness of joy, let's take Him up on it. We can be women, wives, and mothers who have the joy of the Lord and know true contentment—visible fruit of the abundant life in Christ. But that's not all. As the Talmud says, "When you teach your son, you teach your son's son." We can make the choice to rejoice to influence our family as well as future generations. Even if Mama ain't happy, she can make the choice to rejoice—it's possible, it's worth it, and it's up to us.

If you desire this gift from the Father, ask Him for it.

Until now you have asked for nothing in My name; ask and you will receive, that your joy may be made full
~(John 16:24).

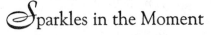

Sparkles in the Moment

What Brings You Joy?
Answers from my Joy Survey

Relishing God's beautiful handiwork.

Beautiful music.

Wisdom, as in skillful living and making choices that honor God.

Friends, cards, a hug from a child, a bright smile from someone whom I haven't seen in a while.

Seeing God's hand in my life; having fun with my family.

Delivering meals on wheels; taking the elderly to the doctor when necessary.

My husband who is also my best friend. My only prayer was for God to give me a husband who loved the Lord as much as me and to bless us with years to serve Him together. How can I not feel joyous having had that prayer answered?

The birth of my children.

The birth of my grandchildren.

Kisses from my children.

A hug from a grandchild.

Hearing grandchildren laughing.

I feel joy when I'm doing things well, so I find ways to constantly improve what I do but that are suited to my abilities and schedule. For example, I will never commit to cooking on Saturday, cleaning on Monday, ironing on Tuesday...I would fail if I set goals like that. Flexibility is important.

Smiling; dancing; playing.

Good smells; dancing uninhibited.

Looking at the countryside from my house.

Seeing our house clean; having friends in our home; and hosting family gatherings and special celebrations.

Walking on crisp new-fallen snow; the beauty of autumn.

Knowing I'm in God's perfect will for my life.

Reading; friends; nice perfumes; hot showers.

Fulfilling my mission statement: to help others; to strive to be the unique individual God made me; to live ecstatically and die gratefully.

Life itself.

~❧ Notes ❧~

A Bit About Being Joyful

1. Mary Farrar, *Choices* (Sisters, OR: Multnomah Press, 1994), p. 87.

Chapter 1—Sparkles in the Rocks

1. Barbara M. is one of the 50 people—mostly women—who completed a survey on joy for me while I was working on this book.
   You'll meet many of the others on a first-name/last-initial basis throughout these pages.

Chapter 2—If Mama Ain't Happy, Ain't Nobody Happy

1. Dennis and Barbara Rainey, *Building Your Mate's Self-Esteem* (San Bernardino, CA: Here's Life Publishers, 1986), p. 38.
2. Dr. Brenda Hunter, *Home by Choice* (Portland, OR: Multnomah Press, 1991), p. 38.
3. Ibid., p. 27.
4. Anne Ortlund, *Disciplines of the Home* (Dallas: Word Publishing, 1990), p. 76.
5. World Book Encyclopedia, 1976, volume 19, s.v. thermostat.
6. Ibid.
7. Ibid.
8. Leslie Barker, "No Snooze, You Lose," in *The Dallas Morning News,* September 2, 1991, p. 3c.

Chapter 3—It's All in Our Heads

1. John Maxwell, *The Winning Attitude* (Nashville: Thomas Nelson Publishers, 1993), pp. 26, 29, 33, 36, 38, 41, 44.
2. Transcript of "Attitude, Not Aptitude, Determines Altitude," a speech by Richard L. Weaver II, at Bowling Green University, April 3, 1993, in *Vital Speeches of the Day,* p. 478.
3. Gillian Flynn, "Attitude More Valued Than Ability," in *Personnel Journal,* September 1994, p. 16.
4. Charles Swindoll, *Strenghening Your Grip* (Dallas: Word, 1982), p. 207.
5. Natalie Angier, "The Anatomy of Joy," in *New York Times Magazine,* April 26, 1992, p. 50.
6. David Levine, "The Secrets of People Who Never Get Sick," in *Good Housekeeping,* December 1995, p. 73.
7. Maxwell, *The Winning Attitude,* p. 145.

8. Dr. Frank Minirth and Dr. Paul Meier, *Happiness Is a Choice* (Grand Rapids: Baker Book House, 1978), pp. 12-13.

Chapter 4—Taming the Monster of Discontent

1. "Letter to a Daughter: Being Contented," in *Christian Century*, March 16, 1994, pp. 270-71.
2. Ibid.
3. Carol Mader, "Dare to Not Compare," in "The Proverbs 31 Homemaker" newsletter (P.O. Box 17155, Charlotte, NC, 28270), January 1996), p. 3.
4. Ibid.
5. Joe Dominguez and Vicki Robin, *Your Money or Your Life* (New York: Penguin Books, 1993), pp. 18-19.
6. George Barna, *If Things Are So Good, Why Do I Feel So Bad?* (Chicago: Moody Press, 1994), pp. 12-14.
7. Susan Gregory, *Out of the Rat Race* (Ann Arbor, MI: Vine Books, 1994), pp. 83-84.
8. Grace Merrill, "Lessons in Contentment" in *Focus on the Family* magazine, November 1995, p. 16.

Chapter 5—The Secret of Contentment

1. John Maxwell, *The Winning Attitude* (Nashville: Thomas Nelson Publishers, 1993), pp. 159-60.
2. Study notes in *The Open Bible (expanded edition), New American Standard Version* (Nashville: Thomas Nelson Publishers, 1985), p. 1141.
3. John Maxwell, Injoy Life Club tape study notes: "Content or Discontent— Which Tent Do You Live In?," p. 1.
4. Hannah Whitall Smith, *The Christian's Secret of a Happy Life* (Uhrichsville, OH: Barbour and Company, 1870, 1985), p. 29.
5. Oswald Chambers, *My Utmost for His Highest* (Uhrichsville, OH: Barbour and Company, 1935, 1963), pp. 26-27, 52-53.
6. Smith, *Christian's Secret,* p. 48.

Chapter 6—How Can I Be Joyful...

1. Innovisions (Chicago, IL), Card #986.
2. Dr. Henry Cloud and Dr. John Townsend, *False Assumptions: Twelve "Christian" Beliefs That Can Drive You Crazy* (Grand Rapids: Zondervan Publishing House, 1995), p. 59.
3. Brother Lawrence, *The Practice of the Presence of God*, quoted in Ray and Anne Ortlund, *In His Presence*, pp. 3-4.
4. Ray and Anne Ortlund, *In His Presence*, p. 5.
5. Ibid., p. 28.

Chapter 7—Three Powerful P's

1. Henry H. Halley, *Halley's Bible Handbook* (Grand Rapids: Zondervan Publishing House, 1927,1965), pp. 807, 809.
2. Ibid. p. 807.

3. Myrna Alexander, *Behold Your God* (Grand Rapids: Zondervan Publishing House, 1978), pp. 115, 122.
4. Ibid., pp. 119-20.
5. Halley, *Halley's Bible Handbook,* p. 250.
6. Oswald Chambers, *My Utmost for His Highest* (Uhrichsville, OH: Barbour and Co., 1935, 1963), p. 32.
7. Becky Tirabassi, "Let Prayer Change Your Life," in *Focus on the Family* magazine, February 1996, p. 12.
8. Andrew Murray, *The Inner Life*, quoted by Tirabassi, "Let Prayer Change Your Life," p. 12.

Chapter 8—Joy in the Dark

1. James Dobson, *When God Doesn't Make Sense* (Wheaton, IL: Tyndale House Publishers, 1993), p. 12.
2. Hannah Whitall Smith, The Christian's Secret of a Happy Life (Uhrichsville, OH: Barbour and Co., 1870, 1985), p. 29.
3. Eileen Egan and Kathleen Egan, *Suffering into Joy* (Ann Arbor, MI: Servant Publishers, 1994), p. 21.
4. Ibid., p. 19.
5. Gordon MacDonald, *The Life God Blesses* (Nashville: Thomas Nelson Publishers, 1994), pp. 26-27.
6. Ibid., p. 28.
7. Oswald Chambers, *My Utmost for His Highest* (Uhrichsville, OH: Barbour and Co., 1935, 1963), p. 32.

Chapter 9—I Didn't Lose My Joy—It's Been Stolen

1. Sherwood Eliot Wirt, *The Book of Joy* (New York: McCracken Press, 1994), pp. 23-24.
2. Bill Hendricks, "Studies Suggest That Stress Is Weakening Americans' Health," in *The Houston Chronicle*, June 4, 1995, p. 12A.
3. Peter Hanson, *The Joy of Stress* (New York: Andrews, McMeel & Parker, 1986), pp. 11-12.
4. Ibid.
5. Cheri Fuller, *Trading Your Worry for Wonder: A Woman's Guide to Overcoming Anxiety* (Nashville: Broadman & Holman), chapter 1.
6. Barbara Johnson, *Splashes of Joy in the Cesspools of Life* (Dallas: Word, 1992), pp. 40-41.
7. Jean Lush, *Women and Stress* (Grand Rapids: Fleming H. Revell, 1992), p. 18.
8. *Wirt, The Book of Joy,* p. 26.
9. Don Baker and Emery Nester, *Depression: Finding Hope and Meaning in Life's Darkest Shadow* (Portland, OR: Multnomah Press, 1983), p. 7.
10. Grace Ketterman, M.D., *Surviving the Darkness* (Nashville: Thomas Nelson Publishers, 1988, 1993), p. 1.
11. Dr. James Dobson, "Focus on the Family" radio broadcast, December 12, 1995, discussing "What Wives Wish Their Husbands Knew About Women."
12. Ketterman, *Surviving the Darkness,* p. xvii.
13. Ibid., p. 230.

Chapter 10—Disciplines of a Joyful Person

1. *Time* magazine, "The Simple Life," April 8, 1991, p. 58.
2. Erma Bombeck, "The Modern Woman: She's Tired of Having It All," Universal Press Syndicate, 1991.
3. Ibid.
4. Anne Ortlund, *Disciplines of a Beautiful Woman* (Dallas: Word, 1977), p. 69.
5. Caryl Stern, "Who Is Old," in *Parade*, January 21, 1996, p. 45.
6. "Ten Ways to Take Charge of Your Health," in *Good Housekeeping*, March 1995, pp. 194-95.
7. Pam Smith, *Food for Life* (Lake Mary, FL: Creation House, 1994), p. 137.
8. Ibid., p. 24.
9. Ibid., see page 36 and related chapters.
10. Quoted in Charles Boisseau, "Southwest's Pilot," in *The Houston Chronicle*, March 10, 1996, pp. 1-2D.
11. David G. Meyers, "Pursuing Happiness," in *Psychology Today*, July/August 1993, p. 66.
12. David Levine, "The Secrets of People Who Never Get Sick," in *Good Housekeeping*, December 1995, p. 72.
13. Tim Hansel, *Through the Wilderness of Loneliness* (Elgin, IL: David C. Cook Publishing, 1991), p. 134.

Chapter 11—Laugh and Lollygag

1. That's how John Trent describes laughter in his article "Strength Training" in *Christian Parenting Today*, July/August 1995, p. 64.
2. *The Woman's Study Bible* (Nashville: Thomas Nelson, 1995), p. 1051.
3. The following sources provided information for this chapter: Pam Smith, *Food for Life* (Lake Mary, FL: Creation House, 1994); Natalie Angier, "The Anatomy of Joy," in *New York Times Magazine,* April 26, 1992, p. 50; John Trent, "Strength Training" in *Christian Patenting Today,* July/August 1995, p. 64; Carole Mayhall, "A Laugh a Day," in *Today's Christian Woman,* January/February 1995, pp. 35-37.
4. Catherine and Loren Broadus, *Play: It's Not Just for Kids!* (Dallas: Word, 1987), p. 106.
5. Norman Cousins, *Anatomy of an Illness As Perceived by the Patient* (New York: W.W. Noton Company, 1979), pp. 39-40.
6. Natalie Angier, "The Anatomy of Joy," in *New York Times Magazine*, April 26, 1992, p. 50.
7. Trent, p. 64.
8. Ibid., p. 65.
9. Sherwood Eliot Wirt, *The Book of Joy* (New York: McCracken Press, 1994), p. 1.
10. Dandi Daley Mackall, "What Does God Do All Day?" *Kids Say the Greatest Things About God* (Wheaton, IL: Tyndale House, 1995).
11. Source unknown.

12. *Webster's 21st Century Book of Quotations* (Nashville: Thomas Nelson, 1992), p. 127.
13. Broadus and Broadus, *Play: It's Not Just for Kids*, p. 13.
14. Ibid., p. 14.
15. Ibid., pp. 99-100.

Chapter 12—Candles and Confetti

1. Claire Cloninger, *A Place Called Simplicity* (Eugene, OR: Harvest House Publishers, 1993), p. 93.
2. Ibid.
3. Donna Otto, *Get More Done in Less Time* (Eugene, OR: Harvest House Publishers, 1993), pp. 22-23.
4. Ibid.
5. Jean Lush, *Women and Stress* (Grand Rapids: Fleming H. Revell, 1992), pp. 199-200.
6. Ibid.
7. Barna, pp. 160-61.
8. Ibid.
9. Cheri Fuller, *Christmas Treasures of the Heart* (Tulsa: Honor Books, 1995), pp. v, vi.
10. Emilie Barnes, *If Teacups Could Talk* (Eugene, OR: Harvest House Publishers, 1994), p. 46.

Chapter 13—Living and Giving Joy and Contentment

1. Kathie Lee Gifford, "Where Do You Get Your Energy?" *Guideposts*, January 1990, p. 6.
2. Ibid.
3. Ibid., p. 8.

Epilogue—Finding Purpose and Joy in the Moment

1. Tim Hansel, *Holy Sweat* (Dallas: Word, 1987), p. 80.
2. MacDonald, *The Life God Blesses* (Nashville: Thomas Nelson Publishers, 1994), p. 125.
3. Ibid., pp. 125-26.
4. "This Is Now" words and music by Nicole Niederer, copyright 1991. Used by permission.
5. Barbara De Angelis, Ph.D., *Real Moments* (New York: Delacorte Press, 1994), p. xi. Note: This book is very interesting, but it has a "mother earth" flavor rather than a Christian worldview.
6. Tony Campolo, *Carpe Diem* (Dallas: Word, 1994), p. 233.
7. Tim Hansel, *When I Relax, I Feel Guilty* (Elgin, IL: David C. Cook Publishing Co., 1979), p. 105.

Other Good Harvest House Reading

MOMS MAKE A DIFFERENCE
by *Lindsey O'Connor*

Celebrating motherhood, Lindsey delves into the lives of biblical prophet Daniel's mother, Susannah Wesley, George Washington's mother; pioneer mothers; and contemporary moms to showcase the far-reaching effects of a mother's love, guidance, and godly values.

LOVING GOD WITH ALL YOUR MIND
by *Elizabeth George*

Making every thought pleasing to God can be a challenge when you're drained by fear, worry, or sadness. Elizabeth shows women how to enjoy a more vibrant love relationship with God.

THE CONFIDENT WOMAN
by *Anabel Gillham*

The author spent her life trying to be the perfect wife, mother, and Christian. But her life was light-years away from her dream. A passionate look at the transforming power of surrender to God.

THE STAY-AT-HOME MOM
by *Donna Otto*

The stay-at-home mom deserves a book that applauds her choice. Donna's contagious warmth and boundless enthusiasm for home and personal organization overflow in this practical guide to living out the magic moments of motherhood.

15 MINUTES ALONE WITH GOD
by *Emilie Barnes*

A devotional for every busy woman who finds it hard to squeeze in a consistent "quiet time" and Bible reading. Each devotion takes 15 minutes or less and contains a key verse, an uplifting meditation, and several "Thoughts for Action."

MINUTE MEDITATIONS FOR WOMEN
by *Emilie Barnes*

Encouraging readers to seek the Lord in every circumstance, these 5-minute readings offer gentle insights and Scripture to highlight the joys of sharing Jesus; encouraging husbands; becoming children of God; and more.

MOM MATTERS
by *Jane Jarrell*

Bursting with ideas, *Mom Matters* shows readers quick and easy ways to create an inviting atmosphere. Emphasizing God as a foundation for peace, Jane encourages women to make their homes a place of rejuvenation.

The Rising Tide

BY ANN CLEEVES

THE VERA STANHOPE SERIES

The Crow Trap

Telling Tales

Hidden Depths

Silent Voices

The Glass Room

Harbour Street

The Moth Catcher

The Seagull

The Darkest Evening

The Rising Tide

THE SHETLAND SERIES

Raven Black

White Nights

Red Bones

Blue Lightning

Dead Water

Thin Air

Cold Earth

Wild Fire

THE TWO RIVERS SERIES

The Long Call

The Heron's Cry

ANN CLEEVES

The Rising Tide

MINOTAUR BOOKS
NEW YORK

To Orla Wren. And her father.
New members of the clan.

Published in the United States by Minotaur Books, an imprint of
St. Martin's Publishing Group

THE RISING TIDE. Copyright © 2022 by Ann Cleeves. All rights reserved. Printed in the United States of America. For information, address St. Martin's Publishing Group, 120 Broadway, New York, NY 10271.

www.minotaurbooks.com

Our books may be purchased in bulk for promotional, educational, or business use. Please contact your local bookseller or the Macmillan Corporate and Premium Sales Department at 1-800-221-7945, extension 5442, or by email at MacmillanSpecialMarkets@macmillan.com.

ISBN 978-1-250-20453-0 (hardcover)
ISBN 978-1-250-20455-4 (ebook)
ISBN 978-1-250-20454-7 (trade paperback)

Originally published in Great Britain by Macmillan, an imprint of Pan Macmillan

First Minotaur Books Trade Paperback Edition: 2023

10 9 8 7 6 5 4 3 2 1

Acknowledgments

This is my thirtieth year of being published by Pan Macmillan and I'm so lucky to still be working with this team. There are too many people to mention individually, and everyone has played an important part in supporting me throughout my career, so this is a big shout-out to them all. I couldn't have been with a more enthusiastic and skilful bunch.

My agent and friend, Sara Menguc, has been with me almost from the beginning of this terrific journey. Huge thanks to her and to all her wonderful co-agents.

Minotaur in the US has become a big part of my life in recent years and they now feel like part of the extended family too. I can't wait to get back to the US to meet them all in person again.

Emma Harrow is a fabulous publicist: wise and full of the best advice.

My assistant, Jill Heslop, besides keeping me on track and taking on much of the admin load, has headed up the Reading for Wellbeing project – while allowing me to take much of the credit.

ACKNOWLEDGMENTS

Thanks to Helen Pepper, friend and advisor, for all her help with forensic details in *The Rising Tide*. Of course, any errors are mine. Sue Beardshall is the kindest person I know. Thanks to her for my base in North Devon, for fun and the Cava Sundays.

Charlotte Thomas donated to the Tarset Village Hall Fund, and so became a character in the book. As did Skip the dog.

For more than twenty years I've had the support of Murder Squad, my writing friends in the North. Writing can be a lonely business and we need the company of people who understand us.

Finally, and most importantly, thanks to readers. Readers who buy and borrow our books and keep us in business, readers who are writers too and who have provided an escape and a challenge with their work, and readers who are booksellers that share their passion and spread the joy.

Author's Note

Whilst the Holy Island background for this latest Vera novel is real, any specific settings, on the island or the coast nearby, are the product of my imagination and in no way are intended to resemble or reference any that already exist.

Chapter One

PHILIP WAS FIRST OF THE GROUP to the island. He'd had to drive overnight but it was worth the effort to get here before the morning high water, before the day trippers crossed from the mainland in their cars and coaches to buy ice cream and chips. He tried not to resent the squabbling children and the wealthy elderly, but he was always pleased when the island was quiet. As he did at every reunion, he wanted to sit in the chapel and reflect for some time in peace. This year would mark fifty years of friendship and he needed to offer a prayer of thanks and to remember.

The most vivid memory was of the weekend when they'd first come together on the island. Only Connect, the teacher had called it. Part outward bound course, part encounter group, part team-building session. And there *had* been a connection, so strong and fierce that after fifty years the tie was still there, unbroken and still worth celebrating. This was where it had all started.

The next memory was of death and a life cut short.

Philip had no fear of dying. Sometimes, he thought he would

welcome death, as an insomniac longs for sleep. It was as inevitable as the water, which twice a day slid across the sand and mud of the shore until the causeway was covered. Eventually, he would drown. His faith provided no extra comfort, only a vague curiosity. Almost, he hoped that there would be no afterlife; surely that would take energy and there were days now when he felt that he had no energy left. It had seeped away in his service to his parish and the people who needed him.

He did regret the deaths of others. His working life moved to the beat of funeral services, the tolling of the church bell, the march of pall-bearers. He remembered the babies, who'd had no experience of life at all, the young who'd had no opportunity to change and grow. He'd been allowed that chance and he offered up another prayer of gratitude.

An image of Isobel, so young, so bonny, so reckless in her desires and her thoughtlessness, intruded into his meditation and he allowed his mind to wander.

Was it Isobel who kept the group returning to the Holy Island of Lindisfarne every five years? Had her death at the first reunion bonded them together so tightly that, despite their differences, they were as close as family? Perhaps that deserved gratitude too, because these people were the only family he had left.

In the tiny chapel, with its smell of damp and wood polish, he closed his eyes and he pictured her. Blonde and shapely and sparking with life. A wide smile and energy enough for them all.

From the first floor of the Pilgrims' House, he'd seen her driving away to her death. He'd watched the argument that had led to her sudden departure. Forty-five years ago, Isobel had drowned literally. No metaphor had been needed for her. Her body had been pulled out of her car, once the waters had retreated. Her vehicle had been swept from the causeway in the high tide of the equinox, tossed from the road like a toy by the wind and the waves. Once she'd set out on her way to the mainland, there had been no chance to save her.

Had that been the moment when he'd changed from a selfish, self-opinionated, edgy young man to a person of faith? Perhaps the conversion had begun a little later, the evening of the same day, when he'd sat in this chapel in the candlelight with his friends and they'd cried together, trying to make sense of Isobel's passing. Annie and Daniel, Lou and Ken, Rick and Philip. The mourning had been complicated because none of them had liked Isobel very much. The men had all fancied her. Oh yes, certainly that. She'd featured in Philip's erotic dreams throughout his undergraduate years. But she'd been too demanding and too entitled for them to *like* her.

Philip opened his eyes for a moment. The low sunlight of autumn was flooding through the plain glass windows into the building, but he knew he had time for more reflection – more guilt? – before the others arrived. He closed his eyes again to remember Isobel and that argument which must surely have led to her death. He hadn't heard the words. He'd been in his first-floor room in the Pilgrims' House looking down, an observer, not a participant. Isobel and Rick had been fighting in the lane below him. There'd been no physical contact – it hadn't come to that – but Philip had sensed the tension, which was so different from the weekend's general mood of easy companionship.

The fight had seemed important. Almost intimate. Not a row between casual friends or strangers. Even if Philip had been closer, he might not have made out what was being said, because there was a storm blowing and the wind would have carried the words away. He'd relished the drama of the scene, looking on with a voyeur's excitement, as he'd watched the row play out beneath him.

Then, from where he'd stood, he'd seen Annie rounding the bend in the lane, a woven shopping bag in one hand. She must have been into the village for provisions. No longer a mother, she'd mothered them all that weekend, and now, all these years later, she was still the person who shopped and cooked.

Rick and Isobel hadn't noticed her, because they were so focused on each other, spitting out insults. Rick had hurled one more comment and suddenly Isobel had been flouncing away, her long hair blown over her face, feeling in the pockets of her flowery Laura Ashley dress for her car keys. At that point Philip could have changed history. If he'd rushed downstairs and outside, he might have stood in front of the car and stopped her driving away. He'd known after all that the tide was rushing in and it would be foolhardy to attempt the crossing.

But Philip hadn't moved. He'd stayed where he was, staring out of the window like a nebby old woman, waiting to see what would happen next. And Isobel had started her car and driven to her death.

So, here Philip was, a priest on the verge of retirement, an old believer, yet with no great desire to meet his maker. Here he sat, hands clasped and eyes shut, waiting for his friends, longing again for the connection and the ease that only they could give, pondering the moment of Isobel's death. It seemed to him now that he'd spent the rest of his life trying to find relationships that were as intense and fulfilling as those developed here. Nothing had lived up to expectation. Not even, if he was honest, his trust in Christ.

Perhaps that was why he'd never married. Later, there'd been women he'd fancied himself in love with, but there'd never been the same depth of understanding, and in the end, he'd refused to compromise. If one of the women who'd shared that first weekend of connection had been free, perhaps that would have worked. Now, it crossed his mind again that Judith, the teacher who'd brought them together, might make a suitable partner, that he might find company and intimacy in old age. They were both alone after all. But Philip knew that he was probably too cowardly and too lazy to make a move. He smiled to himself; he wasn't sure he wanted to share his life after all this time. He was too comfortable, and too set in his ways.

He got to his feet, walked down the narrow aisle and out into the sunshine. He could smell seaweed and salt. He felt at home.

Chapter Two

Annie Laidler shut the deli door and locked it. A regular customer turned up two minutes late and looked through the window. Usually, Annie would have let her in, all smiles and welcome – but today she pretended not to see. Jax had already left and this was October, a reunion year. Annie had been planning the moment for weeks.

She began to pack the two wicker hampers with jars and dried goods. They'd already been pulled from the shelves and were standing in a line on the counter. Then she turned her attention to the fresh items. There were green and black olives, all scooped into separate tubs. Slices of charcuterie glistening with fat. Cheese: Doddington, with its black rind and hard, sharp taste, Northumberland nettle, oozing brie and crumbling Wensleydale. Squat loaves of ciabatta and sourdough baked by Jax early that morning. Local butter, wrapped in greaseproof paper. A taste of home for her friends who'd moved away. A reminder to them that she and the region had moved on.

Still, at the last moment she added stotties – the flat-bread cakes that they'd filled with chips when they'd all been kids – then home-baked ham and pease pudding. Traditional Geordie fare. A kind of irony, a joke that they'd all appreciate. Through this food, memories would be triggered, and anecdotes would follow. Images clicked into her head like slides dropping into an old-fashioned projector carousel. A school play dress rehearsal. Rick in full costume as Claudius, collapsing suddenly in giggles and the rest of them losing it. Except Philip, who was Hamlet, furious that his long speech had been interrupted. And Miss Marshall, their English teacher, almost in tears because she thought the performance itself would be a disaster.

More slides. More images of Only Connect – the event originally organized by the school, or at least by Miss Marshall, as an attempt to bring together some of the new lower sixth. She wanted to challenge their preconceptions, she'd said; to open their minds to possibilities beyond Kimmerston Grammar. That initial weekend gathering – a kind of secular retreat – had turned them into this tight group. Still friends fifty years on; still meeting in the same place every five years. This time the recollection was of teenagers, talking endlessly, sitting at the long tables in the kitchen at the Pilgrims' House, dipping stotties into the veggie soup, hardly pausing the conversation long enough to eat.

After the first reunion, and Isobel's death, Annie had wondered if the reunions would continue, but they had. Rick had said to meet up would be an act of remembrance, but after all this time, the mentions of Isobel had become a ritual, no more meaningful than the Friday night drinking, or the Saturday afternoon walk.

The hampers were almost too heavy for Annie to carry to the car. Five years ago, she must have been fitter, stronger.

She'd get someone to help her at the other end. One of the men. Rick was always keen to prove how macho he was, with his tales of marathons run, and trips to the gym.

Outside the sun was low. They'd stuck with October for the reunions, and there was always this sense of the year coming to an end. That first meeting of Only Connect had been a time of transition. They all agreed on that. So the date seemed appropriate.

Later kids had come along. Annie had swallowed her envy and her hurt and pretended to enjoy them. The reunion weekends had grown then; sometimes the place had the vibe of a chaotic playgroup, and later of a youth club for moody teens. They'd only come together for evening chapel at dusk. Now, the adults were alone again, and oddly it was as if they'd gone full circle. They had the same freedom and lack of responsibility as they'd had when they'd first come together as sixteen-year-olds. Tonight, she felt suddenly wild, ready for an adventure.

Some of their children had become friends and they met up too, independently in smart London wine bars. Not in an austere former convent on Holy Island, which had been refurbished now, but still smelled a little of mould and elderly women. As if the ghosts of the original occupants still lingered.

It was early evening when she arrived at the Pilgrims' House. She'd crossed the Lindisfarne causeway over the sand and the mud from the mainland just before the evening tide, and the road was empty. There'd be no day trippers to the island now. The setting sun behind her threw long shadows from the rescue towers and set the shore on fire. Although she lived closest, Annie was always the last to arrive. She drove through the village and on towards the house, isolated in the centre of the island, surrounded by scrubby, windblown trees. From here, it felt like a real island. There was no view of the causeway, only of the castle, towering above them. The others' cars were parked in the lane. She sat in the van for a minute, with a sudden moment of shyness, even foreboding. The usual sense of awkwardness, as if she didn't quite belong.

It had been different when she and Dan had still been married. He'd been at the original conference and she'd fallen in love with him then, deeply, dangerously, self-destructively, as only a teenager can. It hadn't been his scene, and she'd sensed his discomfort throughout, but he'd come back with her to the first reunion. Then there'd been the tragedy of Isobel's death. She couldn't blame him for staying away after that. She couldn't blame him for anything. Not the guilt nor the divorce. Nor her loneliness.

It was almost dark and she could see a soft light of candles in the clear glass windows of the tiny chapel. There was no fancy stained-glass here. She supposed the others were already inside and realized she must be even later than she'd antici-pated. Perhaps they were waiting for her before they started their time of silence and meditation. She left the hampers in the van and hurried into the building. The candles had been lit on the table that served as an altar. There was that smell of old stone and incense. The roof was hardly bigger than one of the upturned cobles, the small boats pulled onto the beach during bad weather, and she thought she could smell the wood it was made from too.

Her friends were sitting on the wooden benches, taking the same seats as they always did. Habit now. They turned and smiled at her but nobody spoke. That was the deal for evening chapel. Twenty minutes of silence and private meditation. Prayer for those who believed in it. It had seemed alien to them as teenagers, but now, Annie thought, they welcomed the peace, the ritual.

Annie took a seat near the back, and Phil stood up and gave the welcome, and started them off. 'Take this time to be grateful.' But left to her own thoughts, here in the chapel, Annie found gratitude hard to conjure. She sat with her eyes closed and remembered a baby lying in a cot with blue covers – because Annie had decided she never wanted pink for her little girl – and saw the white cold skin. When Philip brought them all back to the present, Annie found that her cheeks were wet with tears. She was pleased she was sitting at the back and that the light was so poor, because she would have hated the others to see and to ask what the matter was.

Chapter Three

RICK KELSALL SAT IN THE CHAPEL and let his mind wander. He'd never been very good at sitting still, and he struggled to stop his foot tapping on the stone floor. Also, it was bloody cold. His head was full of plans and ideas, all jostling for priority. It had been an interesting day, and he still wasn't quite sure what he'd do with the information he'd gained. Then there was the book, which might redeem him, or at least bring him back into the public eye. He'd complained about the attention when he'd been on the telly every week, but now he missed his public: the smiles, the waves, the recognition. He'd only been gone for a few months, but it was as if he'd disappeared into a black hole. When people did know who he was, there was more likely to be abuse than admiration. He shifted in his seat and wished he'd worn a scarf.

The door opened and he turned to see Annie hurry into the building. She still looked good for her age. She'd never been a beauty like Charlotte, but she was interesting without trying, without realizing. He'd never fancied her, not really. Not like he'd fancied Louisa. He'd always felt close to Annie though. Friendship was too bland a word to describe it. He wriggled again and tried to find a better way to express how he felt about her.

Philip stood up to call them to order. When they'd first come here as teenagers, nobody would have bet on Philip becoming a priest. Not in a million years. He'd been Rick's most exciting friend, full of anger and rebellion and wild, impossible plans. Now he seemed to live his life in a state of complacency and contentment. Philip had achieved, Rick supposed, a kind of wisdom. He no longer battled the inevitable. He knew he was getting old but didn't seem to care. Soon, he'd retire from his parish and his life would become even more boring. He might well move north again – so predictable – and he'd live out his smug, boring life until he died.

Perhaps Philip didn't even miss the adventures of their youth. Rick missed them all the time. He longed for them with a desperation that sometimes overwhelmed him. He would give anything to be seventeen again and sitting in this chapel for the first time. He would sell his soul for it. He wouldn't even mind being twenty-two and fighting with Isobel, then watching her drive away to her death. Then, at least he'd felt alive.

He realized that Philip had sat down once more. Rick hadn't heard anything he'd said, hadn't made the effort to listen; it would, no doubt, be much the same as at every reunion. Every introduction. These days, Philip provided comfort not originality.

The chapel was quieter than any other place Rick knew. He'd lived in the city since he'd left home for university and there was always that background hum. Traffic. The rumble of a train. People shouting in the street, even in the early hours. Rick disliked silence. He wondered why they had to go through this ritual every time they came back to the island, though part of him knew that he'd be the first to complain if one of the others suggested ditching it. Partly to be awkward, but also, he supposed, because this quiet time in the chapel was part of the whole experience. It reminded him again of his youth. For one weekend, he felt as if he was starting out again, at the beginning. Not approaching the end.

Almost before he'd settled into it, the twenty minutes was over. Philip was on his feet again, and they were making their way out. Rick waited for a moment, letting the others go ahead of him, gearing up for the evening ahead. He felt like an actor preparing for another performance, and wondered briefly what it would be like for once in his life to go on stage unscripted and unrehearsed.

Chapter Four

OUTSIDE THE CHAPEL THEY STOOD, CHATTING awkwardly. It was always a little awkward for the first few minutes. But it was cold and quite dark so they quickly moved into the house. Annie asked Rick and Phil to help her carry the food from her van into the kitchen. Afterwards she stood there, unpacking the hampers, stocking the fridge, glimpsing her friends at a distance through the open door in the hall, which led into the common room. The fire was already lit. She couldn't see them all, but did catch Rick parading in, with a bottle of wine in each hand. He set them on the table, then pulled a corkscrew from his jacket pocket, like a conjuror performing some amazing trick, playing as always as if to an audience. The light in the room was dim, and Annie thought his silhouette was strange, almost demonic, with the flames dancing behind him.

The others started on the booze then, but that was traditional too. They'd always drunk far too much on Friday nights, even when they'd had kids with them. There'd been times, she thought, when social services could legitimately have expressed concern about the children's safety, though they'd had two teachers in their number, and really, they should have known better. Annie had stumbled to bed on a couple of occasions in the early hours, aware of children running through the corridors, whooping and laughing in some game of their own.

As they'd all grown older, she'd come across pale-faced teenagers sitting on the floor in corners, with tears rolling down their cheeks. It had only occurred to her later that they'd probably been drinking too, or taken some form of drug. Her child had never been old enough to be troublesome and she'd been naive about such things. She knew Rick and Philip had smoked cannabis when they'd been younger, but in spite of her hippy clothes, the flowers in her hair and the bare feet, she'd always been wary. Not worried about any potential danger to her health, but about making a fool of herself.

She went back outside to the van to fetch a last tray of baking, and the air smelled not of weed, but of woodsmoke and ice. She hadn't bothered putting on a coat and the sudden cold chilled her bones. There was a frost forecast, the first of the year. There would be a dark sky full of stars, when the light eventually seeped away, a sliver of moon. She shut the van again and stepped back into the house.

The door to the common room was still propped open and Annie could look in without being seen. They'd switched on the lights and she had a better view of them. Her first full view after the candlelight in the chapel and the clumsy greeting in the dusk. They'd offered to help when they'd all come inside, but that had been routine politeness. Annie always prepared the Friday night meal and they knew she'd catch up with them once supper was under way. She stood for a moment observing them.

Her first response was shock that they'd aged so much in

the past five years. Perhaps it was Ken, sitting with Lou, attentive by his side, and Skip his dog at his feet, that prompted the thought. Ken looked misty-eyed, seemingly struggling to appear aware of what was going on, and horribly frail. Lou had phoned them all in advance to warn them.

I've been worried about him for a while, but we only got a diagnosis a few months ago. Alzheimer's.

'But he's so young!' Annie had said. Meaning: *He's the same age as me.*

'He's sixty-six,' Lou had said. 'Not so young.' Had there been an edge of smugness in her voice? Because Lou was three years younger than the rest of them. She'd been a fourth year when the rest of them had been in the lower sixth, that year they'd first come here, and stayed up all night, intense, talking until the first rays of the sun had caught the room's mess of discarded crisp packets and overflowing ashtrays. Lou hadn't been here. Perhaps that had always made her something of an outsider. Not quite part of the group.

Ken had very much been seen as a baby-snatcher then, and Annie had resented the arrival of Lou into the mix, her presence at parties, the shows of affection, even in school. Annie had rather fancied the solid, reliable Ken herself. They'd kissed a few times. After lock-ins in the Stanhope Arms, the pub they'd adopted in Kimmerston Front Street. Drunken fumbles when they were walking home. Because they'd lived in the same village a couple of miles out of town. Their dads had both worked in the pit.

Then Ken had shyly announced that Lou had agreed to go out with him. Annie remembered the moment. The start of double French one spring morning. Daffodils in the school garden on the edge of the tennis courts. And of course, she shouldn't have been surprised. She'd had no claim on Ken, and, after all, *she'd* snogged most of the lads in the group at one time or another. Certainly Rick. Nothing Rick liked more than a commitment-free grope. And more, given the chance.

When #MeToo had been all over the news Annie had felt a moment of guilt. Sometimes Rick's approaches had been so bloody forceful that it had felt almost like assault. Not that he'd raped her, nothing like that, but he'd come pretty close. Made her uncomfortable. And she'd gone along with it, hadn't she? Now, she thought she should have been more confident, told him to stop. Then he would have got the message earlier that he couldn't behave like that. He wouldn't have tried it on with his young colleagues. He might still have his show on the BBC.

Now, in the fading light of the Pilgrims' House common room, Louisa was still attractive, but even she was showing her age. The hair was beautifully cut and dyed, but there were lines around her eyes, and horizontal wrinkles between her nose and her mouth.

We're all old! Of course we are. What was I expecting? That by meeting up with my old school friends, I'd magically become the girl that I was when we first came together? We're lucky that we've all survived. All, except Isobel.

Annie switched on the oven and put the pie she'd made inside. She put plates to warm and laid the big kitchen table, with the mismatched cutlery from the dresser drawer. Then she went back to the hall, watching again from the shadows, plucking up courage to interrupt Rick, who was in full flow, when Philip stood up.

'Annie Laidler, what are you waiting for?' The voice loud and rich, and honed in the pulpits of large draughty churches. 'You need some wine, of course you do. You're the one who's been slaving over a hot stove, while we indulge ourselves.' He laughed as he poured a giant glass of red and wrapped his arms around her in a hug. Suddenly all the nervousness disappeared. She was here with her best friends in the world and it would be a fabulous weekend.

And so, the evening rolled on, much as the reunions always did. Friday night supper supplied by Annie, salad brought by the others. Philip always made and brought the puddings. The others made a fuss of his creations, though in Annie's opinion, they never tasted quite as good as they looked. Jax would very definitely have turned up her nose. Later though, when Philip was at the sink in the kitchen, an apron tied round his ample waist, doing the washing-up, Annie felt a moment of overwhelming affection for him. How kind he was! And how much he'd changed since she'd first got to know him.

That first weekend, Philip had been angry, argumentative, arrogant. He'd mellowed a little as Only Connect had progressed, but to the end he'd chafed at the restrictions, the silence of evening chapel. He'd been a swearer in the group sessions and he'd led a break-away group to the pub on one of the evenings. Annie still couldn't quite understand how Philip, the rule-breaker, the non-conformist, the awkward sod, had become an Anglican priest.

Perhaps he was still all those things. Certainly, he stood out in this company of liberal, lefty, angst-ridden individuals. As the rest of them aged and raged against the good night to come, he faced it with equanimity, even with amusement. Death, he said, was the last big adventure. He didn't know with any certainty what lay beyond the grave, but he was curious to find out.

Inevitably, after the meal, they carried on drinking, even

Louisa, who was usually the most sober of them all. Annie had to survive the photos of a new grandchild, the stories of hip and kitchen replacements, of holiday plans and care home choices for very elderly relatives. Things changed in five years. So, Annie brought out the photo she'd found while she'd been sorting through a few boxes at home. The photo of them on that first weekend, standing in front of the Pilgrims' House. All flared jeans and cheesecloth. Her and Dan, Isobel and Philip, Rick and Charlotte. It must have been taken on the first evening because Charlotte was still there. Ken was standing to one side, looking in at them. Judy Marshall standing in the middle, a bit aloof. A bit uncomfortable. Trying to pretend that, as the teacher, she was entirely in control.

As the evening wore on, they regressed back to the age they'd been in that photograph. Back in the common room, when the meal was over, and the plates washed and cleared away, they played sixties music. They danced. How embarrassing it would be if someone walked past and saw them through the uncurtained window! The old anecdotes were dragged out and, as always, there were new revelations, memories that only one of them held deep in their unconscious, and which had never previously been shared. The pile of logs in the basket on the grate shrank and the bottles emptied, and they became less rowdy and more reflective. A silence fell and even a set of footsteps in the lane – probably some islander on his way home from the Seahorse – startled them.

This year, the previously untold story came from Rick. He was sitting on the floor close to the fire, still wearing the leather jacket he always turned up in. Annie thought he must be sweating. But then he'd moved south straight after school, so perhaps he'd become soft.

He turned away from the fire and grinned a wolfish smile. 'Did I ever tell you that I had sex with Miss Marshall?'

The first few words held no surprise. Many of his stories began with: *Did I ever tell you I had sex with . . .*

But Miss Marshall had been a teacher. Young, just out of college. Short skirts and tight, wet-look boots. Straight black hair and a fringe almost into her heavily made-up eyes. She'd taught them English and drama and had been passionate about Dylan Thomas. And Dylan. Serious, intense and rather unworldly. Only Connect had been her idea and she'd been here with them on that first occasion.

Annie still saw Judith around in Kimmerston. Her name wasn't Marshall anymore – she'd married. Annie couldn't remember what she was called these days. Her husband had died. Jax knew her because she did charitable work for the church and the deli donated any stuff approaching its best before date to the food bank there. So, she was someone else who'd changed dramatically if Rick's story was to be believed.

Annie remembered Judy Marshall greeting them at the door of the Pilgrims' House that first time. The pupils had arrived together in one of the school minibuses, but Miss Marshall had driven up herself. She had a little Citroën. Bright yellow. She must have heard the bus on the lane, because she'd been there in the doorway as they'd climbed out of the vehicle. They'd been stretching and groaning because it hadn't been the most comfortable ride.

Back in the present, Rick was telling the story of how he'd screwed Judy Marshall at the post-school play party, but Annie was lost in a different past. She remembered the teacher's words as she'd welcomed them inside.

'Come along,' she'd said. 'You're in for a great adventure.'

Which were almost exactly the same words Philip used now when he was speaking of death.

Annie thought it a little strange that she found this coincidence more interesting than yet another of Rick's tales about his conquests.

Chapter Five

EVEN AS HE WAS TELLING THE story about Judy Marshall, Rick was wondering how much of it was true. It was quite possible that he'd elaborated details in his head over the years. He'd had fantasies about the encounter in the empty periods between wives and girlfriends, before the wonders of Internet dating had filled those times of boredom and misery. It had happened after the school play. His parents had been away – his dad had been a GP and his mother an anaesthetist and there'd been a medical conference somewhere – so of course he'd decided he'd have the post-performance party at his house. He might not have been chosen to be the star of the show – and that still rankled – but he could throw a party that people would remember long after some dreary school play. His folks wouldn't be happy when they found out, but he was an only child, spoiled rotten, and they'd get over it.

He'd snogged the teacher. No doubt about that. He remembered an intense conversation about Russian literature, just the two of them in the kitchen after most of his friends had left. She'd fixed him with those stary, intense eyes, and his attention had wandered when she started talking about authors he'd never heard of, never mind read. He'd reached out and kissed her. And she'd responded, hadn't she? Of course she had. He'd been pissed, naturally, but then so had she.

'After you lot all buggered off,' he said now, 'I took her upstairs. We had sex in my parents' bed, if you really want to know.'

Of course they wanted to know. Even Phil, who pretended to disapprove, was hanging on his every word. This was what he'd missed since the BBC had axed his show. The audience. Rick needed immediate feedback, a live response. A pre-record was never the same. He always said that he was a serious journalist and he *was*. But he was a serious journalist who needed to interact with his readers and viewers.

Trouble was, he couldn't remember being with the teacher in his parents' room. He knew he'd woken up there, alone the next morning, the sheets crumpled and the room smelling of fags and stale beer, but the rest was just a blur, a blank.

'So,' Lou asked, 'what was she like?'

He was tempted to continue the tale. The words were already in his head: Judy Marshall saying how brilliant it was. He was. That she'd had the best time in her life. But in the end, he looked at Annie, who seemed miles away, hardly interested. And he remembered that he was supposed to be careful now about what he said. These were all close friends, but even close friends leaked to the press. He couldn't afford any more lurid stories.

'Honestly, Lou?' Rick smiled. 'I really can't remember.' A pause. 'You'll have to read all about it when my book comes out. It's fiction naturally, but very definitely based on fact.

You'll find our pasts very much brought back to life. *All* our secrets, actually, finally seeing the light of day.'

Of course, they all demanded more details. He could tell they were intrigued. Some of them a little anxious, which they deserved to be. *Just you wait*, he thought. *Just you wait.*

They drifted off to bed soon after that. The rest of them had become elderly, not just in their bodies, but in their minds. Phil asked if anyone wanted a herbal tea before they turned in. Rick thought that summed him up. Phil might live in London, but he was hardly cosmopolitan.

Although his parish was officially Central London, in reality it felt suburban, a bit left-behind. Rick had been to the red-brick rectory for supper a few times. Philip had invited him after both his divorces, offering sympathy and Christian comfort. He'd gone because anything was better than staying in his flat. He hated being on his own. They'd been best friends at school, even before Only Connect, and Rick had seen more of him than anyone else over the years. He still couldn't quite get used to Philip at work though, dressed up in a black dress with the clergyman's collar. As if he was still performing in a weird school play. Or a pantomime.

Rick's room felt chilly after the warmth of the common room. He supposed the heating was on a timer and had been switched off. The place had stopped being a convent even before Only Connect, but there was still an air of the frugal. Hardship was something to be embraced, not avoided. Before the convent, it had been two farmworkers' cottages, and Rick supposed that they must have been pretty primitive too.

A religious order had taken the place over after the war. Three nuns had lived in one of the cottages. He'd researched their history and they'd been attached to the island's priory, spreading the word about St Cuthbert, following in the footsteps of the monks who'd lived in the monastery in the Middle Ages. They hadn't been part of an enclosed order – there were no cells or cloisters – and only the little chapel, which the islanders had built for them in the field next door, had any sense of the religious. Rick thought the place must almost have been like a student house-share. Three women, working during the day and coming back to the cottage to eat and sleep together. And, he supposed, to pray.

Then the adjoining cottage had come up for sale and the sisters obtained funding to knock through and extend, to form a place of retreat. Not just for religious groups who came from all over the country to experience the island and its history, but for educational and cultural purposes. The only stipulation had been the dusk time of silence in the tiny chapel. That had been written into the contract signed by everyone who came to stay.

The nuns had moved on. The accommodation had been upgraded a little since the group's first visit as teenagers. He always bagged the downstairs bedroom, the only single large enough to swing a cat. It was part of the more modern extension, created from an attached outbuilding. It had a long window with a view out to the fairy tale castle on its hill, a vaulted ceiling crossed by sturdy beams. He looked out of the window now and looked up at a sky full of stars, the space dizzying, terrifying.

He hadn't slept here on that first weekend. It must have been used by Judy Marshall or the fierce older woman who'd run the place. His room had contained two sets of bunks, metal-framed with stained mattresses thin as cardboard, which had since been replaced. He'd shared with Philip and two boys whose names he'd forgotten and who'd not really participated in any of the sessions. All he could remember was their acne and the gruesome snoring. Yet he'd been able to go straight to sleep and hadn't woken until Philip had shouted that breakfast was ready the next morning.

These days, it seemed, he hardly slept at all. He'd been obsessed with dying when he was a small boy. He'd banged his head against the pillow in an attempt to drive away the thoughts. How was it possible not to exist? How could *he* not exist? As a teenager, the preoccupation was still there, but he'd hidden it more skilfully, turning the obsession into an intellectual pose, a cloak to hide his real terror. Charlotte, his first serious girlfriend and his first wife, had mocked his nightmares.

'Why do you always talk about dying?'

He'd laughed off the question, made more pretentious noises, thrown in a reference to Sartre. She'd ignored the response and returned to painting her toenails with a focus that made that act the most important thing in the universe. More important, certainly, than any abstract notion of life and death.

As an adult he'd always been a bad sleeper. Things had got worse after the last divorce. Now he was getting older and there was the real possibility of death. Rick could cope with the prospect of illness and pain, but a world existing without him terrified and haunted him, especially at night. Even if he dropped off to sleep soon after going to bed, he woke several times, his heart racing, his muscles tense. Astonished, it seemed, to find himself still alive. He thought that was how he would die in the end: a sudden, violent jerk to consciousness would trigger a heart attack. He'd been prescribed blood pressure tablets but had stopped taking them because they had unpleasant side effects – they stopped him making love effectively – and he was as obsessed with sex as he was with death.

Rick supposed there were worse ways to go than a fatal heart attack. Anything, surely, would be better than descending into dementia like Ken. The cloudy eyes and unfocused thoughts, the restless twitching of the hands. That was surely a kind of death. It was as if Ken was disappearing almost before their eyes but becoming at the same time deeper and more nuanced. In health, Ken had been an uncomplicated soul, a husband, a primary school head teacher, a good dad. He'd loved his football and his music, been steady in his happiness. Almost complacent. Now hidden anxieties were emerging and Rick wondered if they'd always been there.

He left the curtains open. He felt close to the landscape outside and even this far from the sea, he fancied he could hear the suck of water on shingle. He undressed. It was a matter of pride that he hadn't worn pyjamas since the age of six and he pulled the duvet round him to keep out the chill. It was still so cold that he worried sleep would be impossible, so he went into the shower room and put on the dressing gown, which had been hanging on a hook behind the door. From his bed, he could see the black, starless shape of the hill and the light-spangled sky behind it. A tawny owl was calling in the woodland at the other side of the house.

His phone rang. He looked at the number, but didn't recognize it. Usually, he didn't bother answering calls like that, but so late at night? It might be an emergency.

'Hello.' He realized that he was quite drunk now and his speech was slurred.

There was a rush of angry words at the other end. A voice he thought he almost recognized.

'I'm sorry,' he said. 'I don't know what you're talking about.'

He switched off his phone and shook his head to clear the memory of the bitterness at the other end of the line. Some mad person. Since the allegations had been made, he'd had a few of those calls. They weren't worth bothering with. It was the price of fame. Soon, the bastards would realize he was more of a victim than his accusers.

As he drifted off, it occurred to him that he could come home now that his show had been pulled. He could work on his book anywhere, and he'd already planned that most of the action would take place in the North-East. Phil might soon retire north. He'd spoken of it. Annie was here so he'd have a friend. Here, in the end, he might sleep.

Chapter Six

On Saturday morning, Annie woke early, so she could get to shower first in one of the communal bathrooms – only Rick had his own – then she made her way to the kitchen. It looked out from the back of the house over the ill-kept garden. There'd been a frost, and each blade of the long grass which made up the lawn was white, separate. It was only just dawn and there was something other-worldly about the scene, the white ground and the pale light.

She checked her phone. There was broadband now at the Pilgrims' House and she messaged Jax about an order for the deli that had slipped her mind before. Jax was her business partner and co-owner of the deli. Jax had founded the place and Annie had started working for her after she and Dan had separated. Later, when Annie's parents had died, leaving her a bit of money, she'd bought into the business.

Jax had become her friend. The woman's parents had come to England with the *Windrush* and arranged for her to be sent from Barbados to join them as a teenager. In the eighties, she'd moved north to Newcastle, following a musician boyfriend, and had stayed in the North-East once the relationship had ended. She'd somehow put up with the confusion and rudeness of locals in a region where there were few people of colour, and racism was as ingrained as support for the Toon, and she'd laughed off the petty aggressions and fought back with humour and style.

Who else would think to open a classy deli in a county where the pits had recently closed, money was scarce and unemployment the highest in the UK? But that had been more than twenty years ago, and here Jax still was. Bread and Olives was an institution. The wealthy would drive miles from the city for the 'artisan' bread or the local cheese.

To be recognized by name by Jax was an accolade. Annie had seen at least one regional celebrity slink out of the shop because Jax had shouted over their head to a customer behind them. She smiled at the thought and turned back to her phone.

When they'd come to Holy Island that first time, there'd been no screens in the house, not even a television. There'd been one pay phone but she couldn't remember anyone using it, except Charlotte summoning her father to take her home. She was sorry for kids now; Annie and her friends had had so much more freedom when they were teenagers. Many nights she'd walked home from Kimmerston after under-age drinking sessions in the Stannie Arms. The roads had been narrow, the street lights few and far between, but nobody had thought it might be dangerous or even unwise. Now, parents seemed to track their kids' every move, and they flew into panic if a text or a phone call was left unanswered.

Annie made coffee. Soon the others would appear. She'd put Jax's freshly baked croissants into the freezer the night before and retrieved them now and put them in the bottom of the oven to warm and crisp. She laid the long table, with the jumble-sale plates, with dishes of jam and honey and her own Seville marmalade. The sun rose slowly, an orange semi-circle on the flat land that ran north-east towards Emmanuel Head, the shape spiked by branches which were already losing their leaves.

Phil popped his head round the door.

'I'm just going out for a wander to clear my head. Start breakfast without me. I won't be long.'

'No worries.'

Almost immediately afterwards, Louisa and Ken came in, the dog at his heels. Ken gave a lovely smile. 'Good morning, Annie!' At least today he remembered her name.

Louisa had said the night before, that sometimes he forgot *her* name. 'Sometimes,' she'd said, 'he thinks I'm his mother.'

Usually, Annie felt a little intimidated by Louisa, who hadn't been one of the core friendship group. She'd only joined them because of her attachment to Ken. Louisa was beautifully groomed, with clear, unchipped varnish on her nails. She'd worked as a head teacher and had been parachuted in to failing schools, to bring them up to scratch. Annie had always felt a failure in comparison, but now, she felt sorry for Louisa and admired her easy care of her husband. There was no sense that she was embarrassed by him. Annie felt a little guilty that she hadn't been a better friend.

'We'll wait, shall we? Philip said not to, but I'm sure he won't be long. He's just gone out for a walk. And Rick will turn up soon.'

'I was talking to Phil last night.' Louisa poured coffee for herself and for Ken. She added sugar and milk to Ken's and set it in front of him. 'He was telling me how special these weekends are for him. At work, it's hard for him to be himself. I suppose it must feel like a kind of performance, being a vicar. So often, you're officiating at ceremonies, and even at a normal service, you're up there at the front with everybody staring.'

'Philip was always an actor,' Annie said. 'I think he rather enjoys it. At school, we knew he'd get the lead role every time. We believed he was destined to be a star. He had the good looks, the attitude.'

'I'd have thought Rick would be the one to take centre stage.'

Annie thought about that. 'Well, Rick wasn't such a good actor and he never had Philip's looks.' This was a stalling tactic while she took herself back all those years. It was true though. Rick had been too short to be traditionally handsome, but he'd made up for that with energy, a charisma that could light up a room. And confidence. He'd had that in abundance. Confidence and charm.

'He hasn't changed, has he?' Louisa broke into Annie's thoughts. 'After all those dreadful rumours and accusations, you'd have thought he'd be quieter, a bit subdued.'

'I can't imagine Rick ever being subdued.'

'Well, that's true.' Louisa turned her attention to her coffee. 'I saw an article by one of his daughters in the *Observer*. Rather cruel, I thought, to go public.'

'I didn't see it.' That was true. They opened Olives and Bread as a cafe as well as a deli at the weekends and she never had time to read the Sunday papers. She'd heard about it though. Rick was a local boy. Some of her older customers had been patients of his father. There'd been gossip over the coffee and the pastries. Annie had wanted to defend Rick, but after all his attitude to younger women was indefensible these days, and she'd remained silent.

'I wasn't even sure that he'd be here this weekend,' Louisa said. 'It showed a certain courage coming to face us all.'

'Rick's always been pretty fearless.' *And we're his friends. He knows we'd accept him. Love him, despite his faults and his ridiculous ego. I can't believe he actually did all the things he's been accused of. Besides, we owe him. He's been there for us through the bad times.*

When Dan had walked away, leaving Annie penniless, Rick had been there, offering a loan, which they'd both realized would be a gift. It had helped pay off a few of her more vocal creditors. It had given her a little dignity, bought her time to think about the future. And before that, when Freya had died, and Dan had been useless, lost in a world of his own, it had been Rick Annie had phoned, sobbing down the line. Rick, who'd jumped on a plane from London to be with her, holding her, sharing her grief. Then when Dan had left the scene entirely, Rick had been back again with the money, helping her to find a place to live.

'Do you really think so?' Louisa set down her empty mug. 'I've always thought he was scared of the world, that all that running after women and stories, the endless travelling, was a kind of distraction.'

Louisa occasionally came out with phrases like that, but Annie remembered what Charlotte, Rick's girlfriend, had said during that first weekend, halfway through Only Connect, just before she'd phoned her rich father and summoned him to take her away. *Rick Kelsall is obsessed with dying.* Perhaps that was a better explanation.

But she just nodded. 'You're probably right.' There was no point, Annie thought, arguing with Louisa. She was one of those women protected by certainty.

There was the sound of a door opening and closing and Philip stood in the doorway. He still had on his outdoor clothes and a strange purple hat with a bobble on a plaited woollen string, knitted, Annie remembered now, by one of his elderly parishioners. He'd mentioned that the night before. Phil leaned against the wall, one foot raised, so he could take off his boots.

'I smell coffee,' he said. 'Wonderful coffee.'

He was still good-looking in a grandfatherly, silver-haired sort of way, though he'd put on a lot of weight. He padded into the kitchen in his thick woolly socks, and Annie wondered, not for the first time, how he'd changed from the edgy, tense boy to this relaxed and generous man. Perhaps that was what faith did for you. He was a walking advertisement for Christianity.

At that point, Annie expected Rick to make an entrance. He'd have been out running, of course, and would put them all to shame. He'd wait until they were all gathered then come in glowing, mud on his trainers. *Only 5K today but I'll go out later, run a bit further.* Though she thought he too had put on a bit of weight round the belly since she'd last seen him. Perhaps he hadn't been getting so much exercise lately.

The others were laying the table and making plans for the day. There was a decision to make. Should they stay on the island or explore a bit further afield? A yomp up Simonsides, or a leisurely day in Berwick.

'Where's Rick?' Louisa asked. 'If we don't get a move on, it'll be lunchtime before we're ready to leave. There's so little light now and we don't have so long because of the tide.'

'I'll give him a shout.' Annie was glad of the excuse to be on her own, even for the few minutes it would take to get to Rick's bedroom. She was so used to living alone that gatherings of people, even people she cared about, freaked her out a bit. It was a sort of claustrophobia and occasionally she felt close to a panic attack. She walked along the corridor to Rick's room and knocked on the door. When there was no answer, she opened it and looked in.

Rick was hanging from a white plaited cord from the beam that crossed the vaulted ceiling. He was wearing a striped woollen dressing gown that had flapped open to reveal a body otherwise naked. Everything about him looked different. It took her a while to believe that this *was* Rick, that it wasn't a stranger who'd taken up residence. There were red pinpricks around his eyes and eyelids. He looked very old, his chest wrinkled and sprouting grey hair. There was nothing attractive about this body. Rick would hate anyone to see him like this.

She reached out and touched his wrist. It was icy, and when she felt for a pulse, there was nothing. Rick had killed himself. There was an overturned chair on the floor beneath him. He'd stood on the chair, strung the dressing-gown cord around the beam, and kicked it away. Charlotte had said all those years ago that he was obsessed with dying and Annie could understand that he might want to choose his own time to let go. This must be suicide. He'd had so much pressure. The accusations of bullying by his young colleagues. The dreadful stories in the press. His former wives selling their tales of his misdeeds. Then the fact that his show had been axed. He'd always liked a dramatic gesture and suicide was certainly that.

What did surprise her was the fact that, under the dressing gown, he was naked. Rick loved clothes and he loved dressing up. He would have prepared his departure from this life with care. He must have been desperate to leave like this, with so little dignity, so little thought for the picture he'd leave behind.

There was something ridiculous, almost clownish, in the figure before her.

The shock hit her then and she opened her mouth. What came out was a scream, but it almost sounded like hysterical laughter. She cupped her hand around her mouth to stop the noise, because, more than anything in the world Rick hated to be laughed at.

Chapter Seven

IT WAS SATURDAY MORNING, AND VERA actually had plans
for the weekend that didn't involve work. Joanna, her neighbour,
was taking part in a book festival in North Yorkshire. Joanna
wrote crime fiction and sometimes she picked Vera's brains,
though when the books appeared they had nothing to do with
reality. Vera enjoyed reading them for the escape they provided,
the joy of loose ends tied up.

Joanna had asked if Vera might like to go along to the festival.
For company and reassurance, and at least to get a change of
scene because Vera rarely left Northumberland. Though obviously there were worse places to be.

'It's a huge thing for me,' Joanna had said. 'A proper literature festival in a marquee in the grounds of a grand country
pile. They'll put us up in the main house. And they've promised that they'll feed us very well.' Joanna had named a few
other writers who'd be there: a politician, a TV chef, a forensic
pathologist who'd recently written an account of his work
investigating the massed graves of the former Yugoslavia.

'I thought you might be interested,' she'd said. 'And of

course, they'll be fascinated to meet you. A real detective, with so many stories to tell.'

Vera had agreed because it had been kind of Joanna to think of her. Kindness had often been in short supply in her life. She was keen to meet the pathologist, who had been a hero for years. Not for his work in the Balkans, but because he'd been involved in one of her cases and he'd had a mind of his own, refusing to be bullied by lawyers or the police. It would be good to meet him again. He'd liked a drink as she remembered, and was especially fond of a good island malt. She was curious too to see Joanna at work, talking about her stories, in front of an audience. Here in the hills, she was very much a farmer. Her life was sleepless nights lambing, struggling to make ends meet.

The phone call came when Vera was packing her overnight bag and was already having second thoughts about the trip. She wasn't good at small talk, unless it was about murder. What if she was put next to the politician at dinner? She'd end up drinking too much and making a tit of herself. The call was from Joe Ashworth, her second in command. Her surrogate son, and her conscience.

'What is it? It's my weekend off.' None of her team thought she had any sort of life away from work and it did no harm to put them right. 'I'm on my way out.'

'We've got an unexplained death.' A pause. 'Well, not so unexplained. Probable suicide. A hanging.'

'They don't need me then. Or you.'

'The boss wants us to take charge.' The boss, Watkins, was Welsh. Vera didn't hold that against him, but she did hate his obsession with rules, forms, emails, Teams talks and webinars. And his youth.

She was going to say that she didn't care what the boss wanted. It was still her weekend off – she wasn't even on call – but Joe had continued talking. 'The dead man is in the news a lot. Local boy made good. Until the rumours and accusations started and he lost his gloss.' A pause. 'It's Rick Kelsall.'

'That irritating little journo?' Despite herself, Vera's interest was piqued. 'The one who's on the telly on a Saturday morning?'

'The one who *used* to be on the telly on a Saturday morning.' Another pause. 'Until he resigned. Or was pushed.'

'That would explain the suicide then.' Her voice was still cheery, dismissive, but she was wavering. Definitely wavering. 'If he'd lost the limelight, he might not have been able to face life. Some people just need the world to revolve around them.'

There was a moment of silence and Vera wondered, just for a second, if there might be an impertinent response: *Not like you then, Vera.* But Joe had worked for her for so long that he knew better than to try a clever remark like that. She never found such banter amusing. She'd been teased at school about her weight and her clothes and her weird father. It had felt a lot like bullying and the jibes still lingered in her brain, even when she was most in charge.

'There are a couple of odd circumstances. There'll be a post-mortem of course. We'll know more then.'

'What kind of odd?'

'It doesn't matter if you're on your way out. I can deal with it.' Joe was calling her bluff.

'Come on, Joe! Don't piss me about.'

'He wasn't wearing any clothes. Only a dressing gown, and as he'd used the cord to string himself up, that didn't cover him up much. The woman who found him thought that was strange. He cared about his appearance. She said he might have wanted to kill himself, but he wouldn't have wanted to look ridiculous while he was doing it.' A pause. 'They didn't find a note. He was a writer. You'd think he'd want to leave a few words for his friends.'

'A bit tenuous, that.' But, thinking about it, Vera could see how it would make you wonder. Especially if you were getting on a bit – and despite his defiantly brown hair, this man was certainly older than her – you wouldn't want the world to see all your bumps and wrinkles. And she'd seen this guy on the television. He'd liked the sound of his own voice. He wasn't the sort to go out quietly, without any sort of explanation. Joe was right about that.

'Anything else to suggest murder?'

'Nothing on the body apparently, but we've only got the evidence of the people he was staying with. They describe marks around the eyes which could be petechial haemorrhaging.' Joe paused. 'But until the tide goes out nobody can get in to check. That's the other complication. The death took place on Holy Island, in somewhere called the Pilgrims' House.'

Holy Island. Known to southerners as Lindisfarne. Vera had been there many times with Hector, her father. She'd acted as lookout while he raided the nests of wading birds, then she'd been forced to wait in the Land Rover while he had a celebratory pint in one of the pubs. Until she'd got older and rebellious and had told him to do his own dirty work.

'When can we get over?' Because Vera had decided she *would* be there. The decision made, she felt lighter. There was a release of tension. She would be happier, and a lot more comfortable, at a potential murder scene than with a handful of famous writers. Very much happier.

'It'll be safe to cross in an hour, apparently, so not worth getting the helicopter in the air.'

'We treat it as unexplained until we know any different. Get Paul Keating there. And have Billy Cartwright on standby. Depending on what the doc says, we'll call in the CSIs.' Her mind was racing now. 'If the death turns out to be suspicious, we might have to stay over. Book us somewhere. Provisionally. You, me and Hol. The doc and Billy can look after themselves and they might even be finished in time to get back before high water. Some of the pubs do rooms.' She'd been working non-stop all summer. Boring, routine shouts. Brawls in bars that had got out of hand. Pathetic little men killing their wives for taunting them about their inadequacies. It felt like years since she'd had a full evening in a pub. She thought wistfully of the smell, the taste of that first, hand-pulled pint. 'It'll save us traipsing back and forth, and we won't be dependent on low water.'

'Okay.' He sounded dubious. Sal would give him bother about an overnight trip. Vera found herself grinning.

She'd just finished the call when there was a tap on the door and Joanna opened it without waiting to be asked. She stood on the doorstep and looked in.

'Just checking everything's okay. I was thinking we should leave about ten. That'll give us plenty of time.' Joanna had kept the voice of her privileged childhood. It was as rich as the family she'd left behind, mellowed by good red wine.

'Eh, sorry, pet. Something's turned up at work. A suspicious death. I won't be able to make it after all. That was Joe Ashworth on the phone.' Vera was already planning the first steps of the investigation. She thought it was just as well she'd already packed an overnight bag. It would come in useful if they *did* have to stay. If this turned out to be murder.

'Oh Vera, that's such a shame.' But something in Joanna's face suggested a fleeting moment of relief. Perhaps she'd been anxious that Vera would make a tit of herself too, in front of her new, influential friends. 'Another time, then.'

'Of course.' As Joanna turned to go, Vera added: 'And thanks for asking me. It was kind. Very kind.'

A brief, almost conspiratorial smile, passed between them. They both knew this was for the best.

It took Vera less than an hour to drive to the coast, and she began to catch glimpses of the sea from the road over the tops soon after leaving home. It gleamed, a line of light on the distant horizon. This was the very north of her patch. She crossed the A1, the main road leading to Scotland, then she drove through farmland, the grass still frosty in the shade, even here, so close to the shore. Through a gap in the hedge and across the wide curve of the bay, she saw Rede's Tower, an ancient pele tower which had been almost derelict when she was a lass and was now the hub of a grand holiday park, with lodges and a spa and a fine-dining restaurant.

Minutes later she'd arrived at the causeway and the wedge shape of Holy Island was ahead of her. She didn't have a spiritual bone in her body, but there was something about this place that moved her. It was history – St Cuthbert, St Bede and the dawn of British Christianity – and it seemed to sum up the importance of Northumberland in the world. Her county. Her home.

Next to the causeway, a line of poles across the sand marked the Pilgrims' Way, where the faithful sometimes crossed by foot, paddling, trousers rolled to their knees, packed lunches in small rucksacks. Ahead of her was the island, the highest point furthest away from her, and perched there on the top of the cliff, the sandstone castle, majestic, looking out towards Scandinavia.

A couple of incomers had pulled their cars into the parking spot to study the crossing times, but she drove on, through the water left by the retreating tide, until she reached the other side. When the water returned, it would be an island proper again, cut off from the mainland, but the boundary between sea and land was shifting, uncertain, made up of sand and mud and dune.

This was a real community, however, once the road rose from the shore, and it attracted the curious tripper as well as the faithful. The car park on the edge of the settlement was already busy. It might be October, but it was half-term, and the morning tide made it possible for families to visit for the day. She drove on slowly through the village, past the guest houses, pubs and gift shops. A stream of walkers flowed towards the slope to the castle. Vera moved slowly, unsure now where she was going, but just beyond the houses, there was a wooden sign marked 'The Pilgrims' House', pointing towards a narrow lane, a lonnen, leading east. The retreat house was halfway along the track, close to the centre of the island. The building was unassuming, not quite what Vera had been expecting. One door had been bricked in, and it was clear these had once been two attached cottages, tied homes probably, belonging to the castle. She'd thought a celebrity like Rick Kelsall would holiday somewhere grander.

She climbed out of the Land Rover and paused for a moment to take note of her surroundings. To one side of the house was a small chapel, stone-built and squat. A skein of geese flew over as she stood there. Their calls made her think again of

Hector and other wild places he'd dragged her to. The far boundary of the house was marked by a hedge, heavy with sloes, and for a moment she was distracted. She wished she had a bag with her. This was just the time to pick them, after the first frost took the edge off the tannin. She was still thinking of sloe gin for Christmas, and that she might make some for Jack and Joanna, save her buying a daft present the couple probably wouldn't need, as she made her way into the building.

As Vera had thought, she was the first of her team to arrive. The residents were waiting for her in the common room. The heating was on, but they'd lit a fire anyway and the room smelled of logs and coffee. There were four of them, all of an age. The fit elderly. Because sixty was the new forty, wasn't it? That, at least, was what Holly, one of her younger colleagues, had told Vera when she'd once complained of aches and pains.

'What are you implying?' Vera had never thought of herself as vain, but Holly's comment had hurt. 'I'm nowhere near sixty!' Which wasn't entirely true. Another few years and she'd be there and HR would be pestering her to discuss the possibilities of retirement.

A black and white springer spaniel was lying on the rug in front of the fire. It looked up and wandered slowly over to Vera. That too was elderly, then. Spaniels didn't usually wander. She stroked its head and neck, looked up at the group and introduced herself.

'Which of you found Mr Kelsall?'

A woman in jeans and a black sweatshirt, with the image of a white dolphin embroidered on the front, stuck up her hand, and triggered a memory of the best bread Vera had ever tasted. Her hair was undyed, pulled back into a clip at the back of her head. Vera thought she'd probably worn it like that since she was a teenager. She still had the build of a young woman, great cheekbones, grey eyes. Still attractive without realizing it. Vera had a moment of envy.

'I know you, don't I? You run that deli in Kimmerston.'

The woman nodded. She'd been crying. 'Annie Laidler.'

'You okay to show me the room, pet? You don't have to go in.'

'Yeah, all right.'

They walked together down the corridor that linked the two former cottages. Annie stopped outside a door. 'He's in there.'

'On the ground floor then?'

'Yes, he liked this room. He said it brought him closer to nature and he needed that because he spent so long in the city.' A pause. 'The real reason was that it's a single, with its own bathroom, the most expensive in the place. Rick wasn't used to slumming it anymore and I suppose he could afford it.'

'You've all been here before?'

'We come every five years. Have done since we were teen-agers. There've been a few changes over the years. Wives and girlfriends have come and gone, and the kids have all grown up, but the core group is the same.'

'A school reunion?'

'Yes. Rick, Philip, Ken, Lou and I were at Kimmerston Grammar together.' A pause. 'The reunion is to mark a weekend course the school ran. Only Connect. It brought us together. That was exactly fifty years ago.'

Vera thought about that and had another stab of envy. She hadn't really made many friends at school and she'd left as soon as she could to become a police cadet. That was when she'd found her tribe. In the police service she'd made friends and found a substitute family, still keeping her distance, but at last feeling she belonged.

'I can take it from here, pet.' She pulled on a scene suit with its hood, mask and bootees, making her look like a nurse out of ICU. At the end of the corridor, Annie Laidler turned back and looked at her. She stopped for a moment, shocked by the transformation. Vera gave a little wave. 'Don't mind me! Just a precaution.' She put on the blue gloves and waited until Annie had disappeared from view.

Vera opened the door and stood for a moment, looking in. She could see why Rick Kelsall had liked the room. The ceiling was vaulted – the room as high as it was wide – but a horizontal beam stretched across the empty roof space. The dead man was hanging from this. Vera ignored him for the moment and looked at the rest of the space. It was compact, with a single bed and a small chest of drawers doubling as a bedside cabinet, a narrow white wood wardrobe in one corner. If this was the best room in the place, the others must be pretty basic. The bed had been slept in, the duvet rumpled, still a dent in the pillow where his head had been. There was a long sash window with a view south-east towards the castle.

A bentwood chair had been placed next to the window, and there'd been a bright yellow hand-woven cushion to make it more comfortable. It would be pleasant to sit there and to look out over the island. But now the chair was overturned, lying on one side, and the cushion was on the floor beside it. Perhaps Kelsall had stood on the chair and thrown the rope over the beam to form a noose and then kicked it away so he was hanging unsupported. Perhaps. Vera felt the flutter of excitement that came at the beginning of an interesting case. It was shameful to want this to be murder, but all the same.

Still, she kept her attention away from the body. Gratification delayed. Through an open door she saw the shower room, which was small too, hardly more than a cupboard in one corner. A towel had been folded on a heated rail but seemed not to have been used.

A small cabin bag was open on the floor next to the bed. Inside, a pair of jeans, spare socks and underwear. The clothes Kelsall had been wearing the day before – trousers, shirt, sweater and socks – had been placed on the chest of drawers. Not folded, but then how many people did fold their clothes when they took them off, especially after a few drinks. Because they would have had a few drinks, surely. A bunch of mates getting together for the first time in five years. Vera couldn't imagine that would be a sober affair.

She spent some time searching for a note. Kelsall had made his living through words. She thought again that surely the man wouldn't have killed himself without leaving a message for the people close to him. His friends. His children. This silent slipping away seemed out of character. But there was no note to be found.

At last, she turned her attention to the dead man. Or rather, first to the rope. This was very obviously the cord which would have held his dressing gown together. Kelsall was a small man, but even so, there'd be no guarantee that it would hold his weight. If this was suicide, surely it must have been impulsive, unplanned. If he'd organized this suicide in advance – recognizing the importance of the place to his life, wanting to be among friends at the end – surely Rick Kelsall would have brought rope with him. Vera had a hazy memory of seeing the journalist on television, halfway up some cliff in the Lake District, presenting a feature about the anniversary of the National Parks. Showing off his athletic prowess. He'd seemed at home there, and might well have access to a strong, light rope, which would do the job well. But he hadn't brought it. If this was suicide, it had been an impulsive decision. What had happened during the evening to provoke Kelsall to kill himself?

Now, Vera did look at the body. He was a small man, wizened, almost monkey-like. The hair on his head was quite a different colour from the hair on his chest, and that gave him an odd manufactured appearance, as if he'd been put together using a number of alien body parts. A mini creation of Frankenstein. Another reason, surely, why he would have worn clothes for his final curtain call. Certainly, he looked nothing as he had on the screen. Make-up could do that, she supposed, but as a performer he'd been very alive, always moving, almost manic. It was the energy that had held the viewers' attention; that was why she remembered having seen his programme.

Vera pondered the possibilities. Kelsall might have been small, but a deadweight was tricky to handle. Could one person have strung him up? A fit man could certainly have done it alone. But a woman? Vera went through the motions in her head. You'd make the noose first, then drag Kelsall's body so he'd be almost sitting on the chair. Put the noose over his head and throw the other end of the cord over the beam. Easy enough then to pull him into position. Harder to maintain that tension while you climbed onto the chair to tie the cord in place. Vera thought a strong young woman might do it. But one of these residents, who were in their sixties? It seemed unlikely.

She was still working through the possibilities when there was a tap on the door, and Paul Keating came in. Despite the scene suit she recognized him. He was the forensic pathologist and they'd worked together many times before. He still had the Northern Irish accent of his birth, and he still, despite his work, had his faith.

'Well,' he said. 'What have we got? Murder or suicide?' Asking as a kind of courtesy, not because he needed Vera's opinion. He'd make up his own mind.

She didn't answer directly. 'What do you think?'

He approached the body. 'Everything would indicate suicide,' he said. 'The petechial haemorrhaging certainly. No sign of manual strangulation. And there are faint ligature marks around his neck.'

'I saw those. But that might happen, wouldn't it, if he was strung up soon after death?'

'It would, yes.' He paused and turned to her. She saw serious grey eyes above his mask. 'Do you have any reason to think this was murder?'

'Nothing concrete.'

'But?'

'Ah, Dr Keating, you know me so well.' Vera paused. 'Our victim was a celebrity, a vain man. He was with friends last night and there was nothing to suggest that he was depressed or unstable. He'd been drinking all evening, but he wasn't so drunk that he'd do something completely out of character. I can buy him killing himself. But not like this. Not in a shabby dressing gown, showing an ageing body to the world. And not without leaving a note.'

'I take it you'd like a speedy post-mortem?'

Vera could feel herself grinning and was pleased Keating couldn't see her face behind the mask. He wasn't a man who liked shows of emotion.

'The boss would certainly like it. This man is a celebrity. There'll be a lot of press speculation until we can find out for certain how he died.'

'I could do it today. There's something distasteful, a little humiliating, about the media hovering over a dead body. And you know, Inspector, that I dislike working on a Sunday.'

'I'd like to stay here overnight,' Vera said, 'just in case we have a murder investigation.'

And because I've been dreaming all day about drinking a pint in a real pub.

'But I'll send one of my team to join you at the post-mortem,' she went on. 'Let's get this sorted, shall we? Let's give his friends and relatives some sort of answer as quickly as we can.'

Chapter Eight

PHILIP HAD GONE TO LOOK AT Rick's body before the police arrived. He'd wanted to make sure that the man was dead. Annie had walked into the kitchen, white and trembling, saying what she'd seen, but Philip had struggled to believe it. He hadn't gone right into the room. He'd watched enough cop shows – his way of relaxing after stressful days of parish politics – to know that would be a mistake. Instead, he'd stood at the doorway and looked in. Back in the common room he'd nodded to the others.

'Suicide,' he'd said. 'Poor, poor Rick. Why couldn't he tell us that he was feeling so desperate?'

Annie had stared at him as if she was about to challenge the statement, but she'd just said, 'I've called the police. An inspector is on her way.'

He hadn't known how to answer that, but perhaps a police presence was necessary even for suicide. 'Rick was always obsessed with death,' he said.

Suddenly he was sixteen again, sat in this room, the first morning of Only Connect. It was the first time he'd heard about Rick's fixation with dying. They were sitting in two circles, sprawled on the floor, on cushions or leaning against chairs. A dozen of them split into two groups. Philip had been with Rick, Annie, Daniel Rede, Ken and Charlotte. Two marriages had come out of that weekend. Annie had ended up with Daniel, outsider, rough country lad, not an intellectual bone in his body, and Rick of course had married the beautiful Charlotte. Isobel had been in the room too, but in the other group. Miss Marshall was in charge, though after the first hour they didn't call her that.

The teacher was dressed in purple loons that morning and a skimpy long-sleeved T-shirt. He and Rick would argue later about whether she was wearing a bra. 'I think for this weekend you should call me Judy,' she said, very earnest.

They sniggered a bit, because she was still a teacher, wasn't she? Not one of them. But in the end, they went along with it.

'Introduce yourself to the person sitting next to you,' she went on. 'Tell them something intimate, something you've shared with no other person.'

Philip was sitting next to Charlotte, whom he fancied like hell, but claimed to despise. Charlotte was long-legged and blonde, and going out with Rick. Her father owned a string of nightclubs in Newcastle, and had the reputation of being a gangster, but Charlotte spoke with a cut-glass accent. You'd have thought, from the perfectly formed southern vowels, that her family were aristocrats. She couldn't help it, she said, when they teased her about her voice. She'd had elocution lessons. If she hadn't passed the eleven-plus, she'd have gone to a boarding school. Her parents had wanted that for her anyway, but she preferred to stay at home and go to the local school.

After A levels, which she'd just scraped through, she'd gone to London to be a model and none of them had seen her again until they'd been invited to her wedding. She'd become Mrs Charlotte Kelsall, first wife to Rick, and for a while the couple had been celebrities of a sort, their pictures in the papers. When their daughter had been born there'd been four colour pages in *Hello!* magazine. Rick had sent him a cutting.

Since then, of course, Charlotte had changed career again, reinventing herself, and now she was telling other people the best way to live their lives. She'd never come to the reunions, even when she was still married to Rick, even that first time, when she'd been his fiancée and Isobel had died.

Philip didn't want to think about that now. Another death. Instead, he took himself back to Only Connect and to Charlotte, sitting cross-legged, looking bored. At first, he thought she wouldn't even bother to engage with the bonding exercise, but she spoke in the end.

'I'll tell you something *nobody* knows.' She turned to Philip and gave a languid smile. They'd moved away from the others to share their confidences and now they were sitting together on the floor in a corner. 'Rick Kelsall is terrified of dying.'

'But that's about him. Not you.' Philip thought this was cheating. If you were going to play these ridiculous games, surely you should play by the rules. Charlotte was giving nothing of herself away.

'This is just a game,' Charlotte said, almost echoing his thoughts, 'and I don't want to play.'

She hadn't played. She'd phoned her father halfway through the weekend and he'd come in a very flash car and driven her away. Philip had been on a solitary walk to the Snook, and had seen the giant vehicle travelling very fast, splashing through the water that was already starting to cover the causeway. It had been reckless, too close to high tide, and had the sense of a desperate escape.

Five years later, when Isobel had died in similar circumstances, Philip had thought of Charlotte running away from them all. But her father's car had been solid and grand, and he'd been an experienced driver. Isobel's had been a flimsy tin box and she hadn't stood a chance.

Chapter Nine

HOLLY GOT THE MESSAGE FROM JOE ASHWORTH while she was running. Running had become part of her life. The last thing in the world she wanted was to end up like the boss. Vera was bloated, idle. When the inspector leaned against the desk at the front of the room to address her minions, the fat on her bum spread and made unsightly bulges in those dreadful crimplene trousers she'd taken to wearing now the weather was colder. Though Holly had seen her put on a surprising turn of speed occasionally, not even her biggest admirer – the brown-nose Joe Ashworth – would claim she was fit, and the woman's diet would make any doctor weep.

The trouble was, Holly knew that *she* was as wedded to the job as Vera. She could do with making real friends, having more of a social life, but as running was taking up more and more of her time, becoming, she had to admit, a kind of addiction, that wasn't likely to happen.

She started planning a strategy; there was nothing Holly liked better than a strategy. Perhaps she could sign up for evening classes, maybe even join a running club as a way of meeting people outside the job, but then the phone, which she'd strapped to her arm, buzzed. She glanced at it. Joe Ashworth. She didn't *dislike* Joe, but she saw him as competition. She was single, no kids and no commitments, so it should be easier for her to earn promotion. Yet he was a sergeant and she was still a DC. She blamed Vera for that. Joe had always been the boss's favourite.

Holly slowed to a stop and took the call, stretching her calves, trying to steady her breathing.

'We've got a shout. Unexplained death.'

'Where?'

'A place on Holy Island, called the Pilgrims' House. As far as I can tell it's a kind of retreat. I can send you directions from the causeway.'

'Okay,' she said. 'I'll see you there. You'll probably be there before me.' Joe lived in Kimmerston, which was in the north of the county. He was halfway there. Besides, she needed a shower and to change.

Holly had been to Holy Island before, not for work, but as a tourist. Her parents were history nuts and had wanted to see the priory. She took them to the island now, whenever they came to stay. It made a satisfactory day out: sightseeing and lunch. It helped pass the time until, much to Holly's relief, the couple headed back to Manchester and home. She loved her parents – of course she did – but when they were with her, she had to put on a show. They wanted so much to believe that she was happy here, that she'd made friends and loved her job, and she had to play along with their fantasy. She couldn't disappoint them.

She was just leaving the flat when her phone went again.

This time it was Vera. 'Where are you, Hol?' The voice a little too loud, excitable like a child on a sugar rush.

'Sorry, boss, I wasn't home when Joe called. I'm just leaving now.'

'Change of plan. Dr Keating's prioritizing the PM for us. He's doing it late this afternoon in Kimmerston and I'd like you to attend. I don't want to leave here.'

'Fine.' Holly wasn't squeamish. Not usually, though she still occasionally had nightmares about the body they'd found in the forest at Brockburn, the Christmas before.

'Now listen carefully. This is what I want you to ask him. And give me a shout once it's done. We can decide then whether you need to join us here. Have an overnight bag with you just in case.'

The list of instructions was detailed and as soon as the conversation was over, Holly made notes. Vera usually liked to attend the post-mortem herself. This wasn't a time to screw up. Vera was trusting her, and despite herself, that made the DC ridiculously happy.

Holly arrived at Kimmerston before Dr Keating, and went to Bread and Olives to buy a sandwich for lunch. The place was busy and there was a queue, so she didn't have time to take it back to the station and sat instead, wrapped in her coat, on a bench looking out at the river. Keating and the technician were already in the mortuary when she got there, and that made her flustered. She apologized for being late.

'You're perfectly on time, Constable, but it seems that your inspector has a bee in her bonnet about this one. So, let's get started and prove her wrong, shall we? This seems like a classic case of suicide by hanging to me.' He started his introduction, speaking into a Dictaphone. When he came to a pause, she felt able to speak.

'I have a list of questions from Inspector Stanhope.'

'Have you now? And what does she want to know?'

'I'm sorry to interrupt. This must sound impertinent.' Holly's respectable parents were believers, evangelicals, members of their local church, and a doctor came a very close second to the Lord in their hierarchy of reverence. Despite herself, Holly had picked up the same sense of respect.

'Not impertinent at all. I would never say this to her face, of course, but the inspector is a very intelligent woman. She's very often right.'

'She asks if the hyoid bone is broken?'

'Do you know what the hyoid bone is?' Keating sounded genuinely curious, but Holly felt as if this was some sort of test. She wondered if Joe would be this nervous.

'Isn't it the bone at the front of the throat?'

'Exactly. Shaped like a butterfly. Inspector Stanhope's question is apposite. It usually is broken during hanging and strangulation. But not always. No, that is by no means inevitable.'

'And in this case?'

'In this case, it's not broken.' He frowned. 'But I can see no other probable cause of death. I really don't think we can call this as murder just on the fact of the intact hyoid. Not even for Inspector Stanhope.'

Holly felt as she had as a schoolgirl, asking a question in front of the class. 'The inspector wonders if you'd take a swab of the nose.' A pause. 'She told me specifically to ask you.'

He looked at her sharply. 'Did she, indeed? Is that the way her mind's working? I think then perhaps we should indulge her. Just to put her mind at rest, you know.'

He took a swab and inserted it into one nostril. When he brought it out, he held it, towards her. 'What do you see, Constable?'

'It's yellow,' she said. 'Are they yellow fibres?'

'They are indeed.' He handed the swab to the technician, who slipped it into a bag and labelled it. 'I assume we'll find the same result in the other nostril.' He repeated the process, and again held the swab for her to see. 'What does that tell us?'

Holly scrambled to find an answer. Keating waited.

'It tells us that the victim breathed in fibres just before he died,' she said.

'Exactly that. I don't think you visited the locus, so perhaps it was unfair of me to expect you to be more precise than that. There was a yellow cushion in the room where he was found. This tells us, I think, that Mr Kelsall was smothered. The cushion was placed over his face, and held tightly, so when he struggled for breath some of the loosely woven yellow fibres were inhaled. Smothering, too, causes petechial haemorrhaging, and as your boss pointed out to me at the scene, there would still have been ligature marks on his neck if he was strung from the beam soon after death.'

'So, Rick Kelsall *was* murdered.'

'Just so.' Keating gave a lovely smile. 'Your boss was right, and will be, I'm afraid, insufferable. I think perhaps you should go and tell her, so she can be triumphant, and then start to get the investigation moving. I'll complete the post-mortem uninterrupted and will make sure that she gets my report as soon as I can.'

Chapter Ten

JOE DIDN'T RUSH TO DRIVE NORTH. He thought that by the time he arrived the doctor would have decided that this death was suicide. Vera tended to complicate matters, and often the most obvious explanation was the right one. This part of the county had always been special to him, and the trip felt like a journey back in time. It was the place of caravan holidays with his grandfather, an escape from the routine of home. The blackberry week half-term had been one of his favourite times. He remembered Indian summers, the woodland a riot of colour, scavenging the hedgerows and building dens. He thought *his* kids, with their organized after-school activities, the rigid timetable of sports clubs and music lessons, were missing out.

He'd never gone to Holy Island as a lad. His grandfather had been wary, nervous of the tides and of the islanders, the wildfowlers and the fishermen. They might have been an alien race, a left-behind tribe of Vikings. Joe had visited the island once as an adult with Sal and the kids, but they'd moaned because they were stuck there over a tide and there'd been nothing to do. Of course, there *had* been plenty to do, but nothing easy, exciting. No skate park or fairground or swimming pool with slides. When they'd realized that escape was impossible, the children had actually been quite happy, jumping from the dunes and poking in the rock pools. He'd never brought them back though. Sal liked the *idea* of letting the kids run wild, but wasn't so struck by the reality.

He drove carefully across the causeway, hit the edge of the community with its almost suburban houses, and then he was there in the village, this part of the island dominated by the castle. He followed Vera's instructions down a narrow lane until he saw her Land Rover, pulled into the verge. Here, they were too far from the village to hear trippers' voices or the rumble of the shuttle minibuses carrying the elderly and infirm from the car park to the castle. He stood for a moment, taking in the view, listening to the calls of birds he couldn't identify.

Inside, a uniformed officer, a local lad from Berwick, was waiting in the entrance hall. He logged Joe's arrival, obviously excited. Perhaps the thrill was in being close to celebrity, even though the celebrity in question was dead. Or perhaps nothing this interesting had happened since he'd joined the service.

'Dr Keating's already left. The boss is still at the locus. It's that room at the end of the corridor.'

Through an open door in the opposite direction, he saw a comfortable living room, a group of people sitting in easy chairs, a fire. A couple looked up, but perhaps they'd become accustomed to this invasion of outsiders, because they didn't seem very interested and just went back to their reading.

Vera emerged into the passage, before Joe reached Rick Kelsall's bedroom.

'You took your time!' But she didn't seem upset. The words were automatic. Joe could tell she was as excited as the uniformed constable on the door, twitchy like one of the police dogs they sometimes worked with when it had picked up a scent.

'What have we got then?' Joe never minded feeding lines to the boss, acting as her stooge.

'Paul Keating says suicide.'

'What do *you* say?'

'Murder. Without a doubt.' She shot him a little, complicit smile. 'The doc's agreed on an early post-mortem. He'll come round to my way of thinking. In the meantime, we let the other residents think the poor man killed himself.'

She walked ahead of Joe along the corridor to the entrance hall and then up a tight, wooden staircase. 'I've taken this place over for our use. It's one of the unused bedrooms. A bit basic, but it's got a desk and we've brought up a few extra chairs.'

The royal we, Joe thought. It would be the local plod who'd done all the lifting.

Vera was still talking. 'They've even found me a spare coffee machine. A bit ancient, but it seems to work. We should be well fed too. Annie Laidler from Bread and Olives is one of the guests and I'm sure she'll have brought enough to feed an army.'

The room had two single beds, pushed against opposite walls, a desk under a north-facing window, looking out over farmland, towards a pool. There was a radiator, but it gave out little heat.

'It's a bit chilly in here.' Joe shivered to make his point.

Vera sat on one of the beds, her back to the wall, and spread out her legs, the heels of her flat, scuffed shoes on the carpet, toes pointing to the ceiling.

'Aye well, beggars can't be choosers.' She never seemed to

feel the cold. 'Stick on that coffee machine, will you? There's water already in it.'

Joe filled the filter with coffee from a jar and switched on the machine. He knew his place. Besides, he could do with a drink.

'I've had a quick word with the other residents,' Vera said. 'They'd booked the whole place for the weekend. There's one couple – the Hamptons – and three singles, the dead man, Philip Robson, who's a vicar, and Annie Laidler. Ken Hampton has Alzheimer's so he'll need careful handling. They were all at school together. Kimmerston Grammar. It's a kind of reunion. Apparently they meet up October half-term every five years. They were first here for some sort of school field trip fifty years ago. I've had a quick chat to Annie Laidler. According to her, that first weekend was called Only Connect. It must have been important for them still to be *connecting* after all this time.'

Joe thought about that. His best mates were still the people he'd gone to school with. Sal disapproved of some of them, said they were scallies, but she'd never made the mistake of trying to persuade him to keep away. 'I suppose it means they all know each other well. There shouldn't be any problems getting information on the victim.' *Possible victim.*

There was a moment of silence only broken by the coffee dripping into the jug.

'I'm not sure.' Vera was still lying back and she closed her eyes for a moment. 'It's as if they're all kids again. This weekend seems to be more about recreating those early relationships than keeping up with what's going on now. Maybe it seems safer to live in the past. A kind of nostalgia to escape a messy present. And when you're getting on a bit, it's quite nice to pretend that you're young again.'

Joe was surprised. Vera wasn't usually given to profound thought. 'You're thinking that the killer was one of them?'

Vera considered for a moment. 'Could have been an outsider. Rick Kelsall's room was on the ground floor. An old-fashioned sash window, warped a bit so the catch wouldn't fasten properly. It would have been easy enough to push it open from outside, climb in and then close it again afterwards. No sign though. That'll be down to Billy Cartwright and his team, once we've got a response from Doc Keating. His first thought was that it's definitely suicide, so that's how we treat it at the moment. We'll keep everyone away until we hear back from him, preserve the scene as best we can in case there are any finger or footwear prints on the sill. Don't think there'll be much in the garden. There's gravel just underneath the window and besides, the ground was hard with frost.'

Joe thought of the silence that had hit him when he'd first arrived. The only sound the birds, and surely they'd not be calling at night. 'Wouldn't they have heard a car?'

'Maybe, though I've seen all the bottles in the recycling bin. They'd all had a fair bit to drink.'

'How do you think he was killed?'

Vera tapped the side of her nose and looked mysterious. 'Let's wait and see, shall we? Holly is representing me at the post-mortem and she's going to ring as soon as we have an answer.'

Joe felt a brief moment of betrayal. He was Vera's second in command.

The filter machine hissed to a stop. Joe poured out coffee. There was a pile of little cartons of long-life milk in a bowl. It seemed someone had thought of everything. 'I checked Rick Kelsall out online before I set off. There've been rumours recently about his relationships with his female colleagues. Harassment claims. His show was axed.'

'You think one of the women he flirted with killed him for revenge?' Vera rolled her eyes. 'They should have been a woman in the force in the eighties.'

'More than flirting,' Joe said. 'According to an article I read, he was a bit of a bully. All the rumours flying around, his reputation ruined, his show gone, that sounds like a reason for suicide to me.'

'Maybe. Humour me for a while though.' She'd already finished the coffee and passed him her mug for a top-up. 'Let's just suppose it *was* murder. These supposed victims. One of his interns or junior colleagues. Would they really have followed him all the way to Northumberland to kill him? I'd have thought they'd have found themselves a decent lawyer and screwed him for all they could get. Revenge but without the danger of a life sentence.'

Joe didn't have an answer to that. He supposed Vera had a point.

'It's worth following up, though,' Vera conceded. 'That'll be the angle the press will go after, so we need to show we're taking it seriously. Our Superintendent Watkins does get fussed about the media. We'll get Hol onto it when she gets here. They tell me the broadband is good enough here and she's a whizz with her laptop. She'll be able to get us a list of names. Women he treated so badly that they might be tempted to string him up.'

'What do you want from me?' Joe had finished his coffee too and didn't need any more. He was already restless.

'You and I will chat to the Kimmerston Grammar old boys and girls. Let's dig into their secrets. I can't imagine that something which happened fifty years ago would have killed Rick Kelsall now, but as you said before, they know each other well.'

'Are you planning to interview them individually?'

'Not yet. The death is still unexplained at the moment and that gives us a bit of an opportunity. I don't want them clamming up, thinking of themselves as suspects. Though they will be, of course. Much more likely that one of *them* is the killer than that some mysterious stranger turned up in the early hours and climbed in through the window. That's all a bit Enid Blyton and she was out of fashion even when this bunch were growing up. We need to check the tide times first, and see if anyone *could* have made it over in the early hours of the morning. That might clinch it one way or the other. And let's speak to the island guest houses and hotels. It'd be interesting to know if any of Kelsall's harassment victims checked in for a mini-break in the North.' Vera hoisted herself to her feet. Her tone was cheery. 'Come on then, bonny lad. I think there'll be more coffee in the lounge and there was talk of home-made biscuits.'

Chapter Eleven

ANNIE LAIDLER HAD RECOGNIZED THE WOMAN detective as soon as she'd first walked into the Pilgrims' House. She was a regular customer at the deli and you couldn't miss her. It was her size and those awful clothes, as if she didn't give a shit what she looked like, or what people thought of her. That had always made Annie jealous, because after Dan, she still cared too much. Jax knew the woman better; Annie had the idea that there'd been some shared history or that Vera had once done her a favour, because often Jax served her ahead of the queue and slipped something special into the bag, a treat that was never paid for.

Now, the detective stood in the doorway, her bulk blocking the light. The group had been waiting patiently for the first hour or so, but after all this time they were starting to feel cooped up. They'd made plans for a walk and were fidgeting to be allowed out before the light went. It seemed odd to Annie that the others should be worried about something like that when Rick was dead. She could concentrate on nothing else, other than the fact that he was gone, lost to her forever. Like

Freya and Isobel. But they hadn't seen him, hanging, looking so old and so odd. And she'd probably been closer to him than any of the others.

'We were wondering if we could go out.' This was Phil, using his rich, deep vicar's voice, reasonable and conciliatory. 'Of course, it's dreadful that Rick killed himself, but I'm not sure that we can tell you much about it. I hadn't seen him for a couple of months before last night.'

The inspector moved further into the room. A slender, younger, ordinary man was standing behind her. Annie thought he'd always be in Vera's shadow. Literally and figuratively. 'This is Sergeant Ashworth,' Vera said. 'Joe. He's the one who does the real work.'

Although she was a senior detective, Annie thought of the woman as *Vera* because that was what Jax always called her, shouting at her across the crowded shop, her voice joyful as if it had made her morning that the big woman was there.

'The thing is,' Vera went on, 'until we get a final verdict from the pathologist we have to treat the death as unexplained, so I'd like a quick chat with you all. Just going through the motions. I know none of you felt like eating anything earlier, but maybe we could talk now over a late lunch? I don't see why you shouldn't go out after that though.' There was a pause and a wolfish grin. 'As long as you all stick together. We wouldn't want any of you running away.'

Annie supposed that was intended as a joke, but nobody was laughing. They were staring at the woman in silence. This woman was demanding food, but Annie wasn't sure she could eat. Because suicide was bad enough – Rick, who was so alive and confident and full of himself, no longer with them – but now the detective was implying that perhaps there was another explanation for his death. That took her back more than forty years. To another unexplained death, followed by probing questions from insensitive police officers. She wasn't sure she'd be able to bear it all over again.

All the same, the others seemed hungry. Annie had cooked a big pan of soup at home and brought it with her for Saturday lunch, and they ate that with more of Jax's bread. Annie poured a little into her bowl and pretended to eat. They were sitting, with the two police officers, at the long table in the kitchen. It was scrubbed pine, scratched and stained, and had probably been there that first time, when they'd all really got to know each other. A window let in the autumn light, which reflected from the cutlery and lit up their faces, making everyone look flat, a little unreal, actors in an old movie.

Vera ate greedily, but she still managed to ask questions.

'You've known him since he was a bairn, this Rick Kelsall. What was he like?'

Somehow then, magically, the embarrassed silence left the rest of the group and they started to talk. About Rick's energy and his charisma, his ambition to move away from the North to London. About his parents who were a bit posher than theirs. Doctors, living in a big house on the edge of the town. It was all gossip and anecdote, but Vera listened with an intensity that made Annie want to warn her friends. *Take care! She looks like a bag lady, but she's sharp. So sharp.*

'His folk were lefty liberals,' Philip said, almost back to his younger sarky self. 'They could have lived anywhere, one of the smarter parts of the county, but they liked the idea of mixing with the plebs. They liked the fact that Kimmerston Grammar had a good reputation. They could give their son a good education without compromising their principles.'

'That's a bit unkind.' Despite herself, Annie was drawn into the conversation. She'd loved the Kelsall house, with its space. Once it had probably belonged to a pit-owner. It stood on raised ground looking down at the town. After the cramped council house she shared with her parents and siblings, the airiness and the confident clutter took her breath away. There were books in piles in corners and corridors and one room had a grand piano. Rick had been able to play it, without music, just by ear. Tunes she vaguely recognized from the radio. Jazz. Blues. At Christmas, a huge tree had stood in the hallway, reaching right up to the first floor. It had taken a stepladder to decorate it, and they'd all gone to help. His parents had been easy, relaxed and had fed them wine. Her mam and dad had never drunk wine in the house.

'His parents aren't still around though?' Vera had already checked, Annie could tell. This was more about moving the conversation on, filling a slightly awkward gap.

'No, his mum died quite young, when Rick was still at university. Breast cancer, I think. His father was in sheltered housing, still very bright, very independent, until he passed away earlier this year.' Annie looked down the table. 'A couple of us went to his funeral . . .' Her voice tailed off. She was remembering the crowd at the crematorium, friends, colleagues and former patients. There'd been bright sunshine and the people who couldn't fit into the chapel had stood outside, the eulogies broadcast to them by loudspeaker. Rick had spoken of course. It had been before his public fall from grace and the audience had murmured how brave he was, how well he was holding it all together.

'Did Mr Kelsall have any siblings?'

'No,' Philip said. 'Rick was the classic only child.' His voice was sharp, almost bitter. Again, Annie thought the vicar was turning back into the spiky adolescent; thoughts of Christian charity seemed to have left him.

But you were so close. Such very good friends. Why would you bad-mouth him now?

'Meaning?' Vera turned her gaze onto him and waited for an answer.

Annie wanted to warn Philip to choose his words carefully, but just in time he seemed to remember he was a God-botherer. 'Oh, independent, confident, resilient.'

'Spoiled rotten?'

'Well, you know how it is with only kids. That's probably always the way. Inevitable.'

'No.' Vera seemed to be talking to herself and not to them. Her voice was sad. 'It's not inevitable. Not always.'

Soon after, they all headed out. They'd have coffee when they got back, they decided. The weather was too glorious to stay inside. And they wouldn't drive off to the mainland after all. The detective had made it clear that she'd prefer them to stay on the island, and besides the light would soon be fading. They'd walk out to the coast, and then head north past the lough up to Emmanuel Head to watch the long slow rollers break on the beach. They needed fresh air and to stretch their legs. *To remind ourselves that we, at least, are still alive.*

'We'll be searching your rooms.' Vera shouted this after them, when they were already kitted out with coats and boots, setting off down the lane, away from the house. 'You understand, don't you, pets? You don't mind? I can assume you've given permission?'

What could they say at that point? Rick would have stood

up to her and called her out on it, talked about warrants and civil rights, but the rest of them didn't have his courage. They looked at each other and shrugged awkwardly, then set off towards the rocky east coast.

There was a good footpath following the shore, but they saw few other people. Most day trippers stayed to the south of the island. A couple of birders with binoculars strung round their necks were scouring the ditches that ran into the lough, looking for migrants. One elderly woman in shorts and hiking boots overtook them. Their group walked slowly, adjusting their pace to Ken's, and to the pace of the elderly spaniel. Nobody spoke. Rick wouldn't have been so polite. He'd have run on, needing to get rid of his restless energy, and would have stood at the point, watching their approach, mocking them for their slowness.

Annie moved easily. She thought that working in the shop had been good for her – the lifting and reaching had kept her healthy and strong – but she was quite happy to walk in silence too. She wasn't sure what to say to the others, because surely *they* were the most likely suspects if this turned out to be murder. Her friends weren't stupid. They must realize that too.

They came to a stile and a path leading from the main track, across sheep-cropped grass through the dunes to Emmanuel Head. At the marker stone, they stood for a moment, then they climbed a giant hill of sand, and sat at the top, looking north and east. It was very clear and still, the silence broken by the cries of gulls.

'We should come here later,' Philip said. 'Look out for the northern lights. It's clear enough.'

There was no response. Annie knew that after chapel, they'd want to be in by the fire, not trekking all the way out here with the faint hope of a green light in the sky. The lights had only appeared once in the fifty years they'd been coming to the island.

The first time they'd seen Emmanuel Head had been from the sea. Miss Marshall had arranged for them to go kayaking on the Saturday afternoon of Only Connect. A break from all the talking and introspection and something else to push them out of their comfort zone, she'd said. There'd been an activity centre close to the harbour, a single instructor, who lived and operated out of one of the Herring Houses. He'd been very fit, Annie remembered, the subject of much discussion among the other girls. He'd given them a lesson and they'd paddled sedately north round the island. It had been a still day then too, but not so cold, the end of a late Indian summer.

Rick had shown off, of course. He'd paddled ahead of them, then tipped his kayak sideways using the paddle. They'd watched him perform a complete turn underwater, before righting it, dripping wet and grinning. He'd learned water sports with his dad; they were that sort of family. Back at the jetty, the instructor had been furious and had bollocked him in front of the group. Annie could still remember the man's face, as red as the logoed cagoule he was wearing.

If you want to fucking kill yourself, that's down to you, but not while I'm in charge. I've got a business to think about.

Rick hadn't been thrown at all. He hadn't been rude, or stupid, and he'd apologized. Kind of:

'I was taught you had to practise the move, in case you needed to right yourself after an accident. But I'm sorry, I should have let you know what I was planning.'

He'd stood on the jetty. His sopping clothes had made him look even more skinny, more puny, but he hadn't seemed embarrassed or humiliated by the scene. Nothing really, *had* ever got to Rick, which was why Annie now found murder easier to accept than suicide.

'Can the police really be thinking it might not be suicide?' Louisa spoke out loud, but perhaps they'd all been thinking the same thing. Ken hadn't uttered a word since they'd set out and was sitting beside his wife, one hand absently stroking Skip's neck, the other on Lou's leg. It was as if he needed something solid to hang on to, something to stop him sliding down the steep slope of sand. He was staring into the distance. Annie loved the fact that Lou didn't fuss over him, but sometimes she seemed to ignore her husband altogether. He might not have been there.

'I think it's more likely than suicide,' Annie said.

'It seems so melodramatic, so theatrical.' Lou paused. 'But I keep thinking that Rick would have loved the drama. Being absolutely the focus of all this attention.' A pause. 'He always wanted to be the star in the school play, but Philip was so much better and beat him to it.'

Then they all jumped in again, sharing memories, telling the same old stories, because if they were talking about the past, somehow they didn't have to think too much about the present.

Philip was halfway through another old chestnut – Rick and Charlotte, who were already an item then, playing lovers in a Restoration comedy with so much authenticity that the review in the *Kimmerston Gazette* had said it should be X rated – when Annie broke in:

'Oh my God. Charlotte. Someone needs to tell her.' Because Rick's ex-wife Charlotte had come north again, once her modelling career was over, and had reinvented herself as a life coach.

She ran yoga and exercise classes, and her website talked about building confidence and fulfilling one's dreams. She targeted older women, who remembered her as a celebrity, and millennials, who believed that if they wanted something enough they deserved to have it. Charlotte was still glamorous for her age and she was back in Annie's life, to the extent that she shopped at the deli and they met up occasionally for a glass of wine.

'Won't the police have done that?'

'I don't know. He'd had another wife since her, and how would they know?'

'They were in the news all the time when they *were* married.'

Annie couldn't see Vera Stanhope reading the gossip columns or trashy magazines, and the younger detective was too young to have been around when Charlotte and Rick were at their peak of newsworthiness. She got out her phone. She couldn't bear the idea of Charlotte finding out that Rick was dead through the press. When she was drunk – and despite always being in the media talking about well-being and health, Charlotte very often *was* drunk – she told Annie that Rick was the only man she'd really loved. *I'd have him back like a shot, you know. If he asked me.*

Annie looked at her phone. 'No signal. I should have known. It's crap here. We should get back now anyway, shouldn't we? See if there's any news.'

Ken suddenly moved away from Lou. He lay on his side and before his wife could stop him, he was rolling inland down the sandhill, over and over, like a small boy. The movement was completely deliberate. He must have been pondering the possibility while he was clutching on to Lou's leg.

They scrambled to their feet and chased after him, worried about his safety, because previously this weekend the dementia had made him seem clumsy and unbalanced, but really, Annie could see, there was no danger. Ken was having fun. In his head he was young again. He reached the flat sandy grassland before them, sat up and started to laugh, a huge belly laugh that was so contagious they couldn't help joining in. Philip reached down, took his hand and pulled him to his feet.

Once he was upright, Ken seemed to become confused again. He looked around for Louisa, and appeared to have found himself suddenly back in the present. Annie tried to remember if they'd rolled down the dunes like that on their first weekend. She had a vague memory of dizziness, a tangle of bodies, an excuse for illicit, exciting touching as they rolled together. Then landing in a heap, unable to get up because they were laughing so much. But the image was blurred and uncertain. Perhaps Ken's long-term memory was better than hers.

They took another route back: a path across a marshy field, inland of the lough, straight to the house. The light had faded and the sky was shades of pink and grey, and they wanted to be in the chapel just before dusk. There was a strange group superstition about being late for the gathering. Their breath was already clouding in the still air. It would be another cold night.

Chapter Twelve

HOLLY PHONED NOT LONG AFTER THE residents had headed out for their walk. Vera and Joe were in their makeshift office in the bedroom at the top of the stairs. Joe was hunched over a laptop. He wasn't as good as Holly at digging into the mysteries of the Internet, but he was a lot better than Vera.

'Dr Keating says you're right,' Holly said. 'This is definitely murder. Suffocation.'

Vera listened carefully to the details and grinned. Catching her face in the mirror over the dressing table they were now using as a desk, she thought she never looked so happy as at the beginning of a complex case. She could see the years disappearing. But Rick Kelsall had died before his time, and, really, it was no laughing matter. What was wrong with her that she could take so much pleasure in another person's death? Then she thought that the satisfaction she took in a murder investigation wasn't just about her. She was fighting, raging, for the victims who could no longer fight for themselves. This was an excuse, perhaps, but the idea made her feel better about herself.

'You'd best make your way here then,' she said to Holly. 'There's still time before the tide. It's a full murder inquiry now, so we need all hands on deck.'

Still holding the phone, she thought about sending an 'I told you so' text to Paul Keating, but after all there was no need to gloat. It was enough to know she'd been right. It was just as well she *had* been right because she'd already called in the CSIs and she'd just heard from Billy Cartwright that they were on their way. Instead, she clapped Joe on the back and told him to get the coffee machine on again, because it was going to be a long day.

This was now officially a crime scene and Vera should have closed down the whole building and sent everyone else away. She should have done that as soon as she saw the body and suspected murder. But then her witnesses would have scattered all over the country, and she might have lost track of them. Vera was a control freak, and she liked having the suspects close. The last thing she wanted was to involve another police service in a high-profile case, because leaks would be inevitable. She knew she'd keep things tight here. Besides, she'd always thought that rules were there to be stretched – almost to breaking point – and she had the excuse of the tides.

She phoned the superintendent. 'Nothing I can do, sir. I won't be able to get the potential suspects off before high water, and there's no spare accommodation on the island. It's school half-term holiday and the place is heaving.' Watkins, her boss, had grown up in the Welsh Valleys and had little understanding of the sea. He was panicking about the media – the murder of a high-profile journalist was his worst kind of nightmare – and he was more than happy to leave the details to her. Then, he'd be able to blame her if things went wrong.

She and Joe made their plans, their hands wrapped around the mugs of coffee. This was what she loved best. The beginning of an investigation when she could believe that she was the best detective in the world. She'd soon lose that confidence, but now, before the inevitable cock-up, she felt certain, on top of the world.

'Have you checked last night's tide times and the situation with accommodation?'

'Yes.' Joe was sitting in his overcoat. 'No crossing would have been possible between five p.m. and ten-thirty p.m. and then the tide covered the causeway again between six-thirty and eleven this morning.'

Vera thought about that. She'd crossed before eleven, but in the Land Rover, and half an hour earlier, even with the four-wheel drive, it would have been tricky.

'So, if the killer came from outside the island it would have been between ten-thirty in the evening and six-thirty in the morning. Or they'd arrived before high tide during the day, and waited. That doesn't help much with time of death. We already know that Kelsall must have been killed between midnight and early this morning.' Vera paused. 'Any useful information on people staying on the island?'

Joe checked his notes. 'I've only checked the pubs, hotels and B&Bs. It's harder to track down second-home owners and the holiday cottage contacts. Most of the overnight visitors are families. There was one single woman, staying in the Seahorse, but she gave her address as Kimmerston, so I don't think she can be one of Kelsall's victims.'

Vera thought Joe had missed the point. An abuse survivor planning revenge would hardly give her own name and address. 'Is she still here?'

'No. She checked out this morning and left the island very early before the tide.'

'That's a bit odd, don't you think?' Vera said. 'I can't imagine a tourist getting up that early on a Saturday morning to get off the place. Hardly worth coming just for an evening.' She looked out of the window, thoughtful. 'Have you managed to check out the Internet for information about Rick Kelsall and his relationships with his female staff?'

'I've done a bit of digging. He wasn't a very nice man, our victim.'

'In what way?'

'He was forced to resign from his recent post on the weekend politics show, when a young colleague accused him of harassment. That was early this year. More recently all sorts of past incidents have come to light.'

'What sort of incident? Anything that might have led to criminal charges?'

Joe shrugged. 'I'm still trying to get all the details. There's nothing very specific.'

'Maybe he wasn't so different from most men in the media of his generation,' Vera said. 'Entitled. Thinking he was God's gift, even though he was an old git. A bit ridiculous. Suggestive but nothing physical. Let's not judge until we know. Maybe the production company wanted an excuse to get rid, let in a bit of fresh blood. It'd be useful to talk to the woman who made the first complaint, though. If it *was* something serious and it never got to court, that would be more interesting.'

Joe nodded. 'The complainant's identity was never made public but the company will know. I'll track her down.'

'Anything else?'

'He was married twice, and had other live-in lovers. First

wife was called Charlotte, someone he went to school with. She went on to be a model in London, then a small-time actress. A bit of a celebrity at the time apparently. For a year or so they were a golden couple. I found pictures of them and their babies and their beautiful London gaff in *Hello!* magazine. Until Kelsall found himself a younger model and the dream went sour. After they separated, Charlotte moved back north.' Joe paused but Vera could tell there was more to come. Something significant. 'Her maiden name was Thomas, and she took that again when she divorced.'

That brought Vera up sharp. 'One of *the* Thomas clan?'

'Yeah, her dad was Gerald and her uncle was Robbie.'

'One-time heavies, runners of protection rackets and loan scams.' *Who never got caught. Who went on to become respectable businessmen running much of the hospitality industry in Newcastle and on the coast. Apparently reformed. Who reinvented themselves as pillars of society.* Though Vera wasn't sure she'd ever believed in reformation. They'd be very elderly today, though, even if they were still alive. She couldn't imagine them as potential hitmen these days. She looked back to Joe. 'What's the woman, this Charlotte Thomas, up to now?'

He looked up. 'She's got her own business. Calls herself a life coach. Works from a big converted pub in Kimmerston, near the river. You've probably walked past it. I remember the renovation. It's all yoga and meditation, with a bit of confidence-building and business advice thrown in.'

'How's the business doing?'

Joe shrugged. 'Hard to tell. She's got a very flash website. The business is called Only Connect.'

That struck a chord. 'Annie told me that was what that first weekend was called. The weekend that brought them all together? I presume Charlotte was a part of that too.' *And it must have been important to her. Why else would you give your business the same name?*

'I suppose so,' Joe said, but Vera could tell that he couldn't see that the name was significant. How could some school trip of the past be important to a murder in the present?

'We need to inform her of Rick Kelsall's death as soon as possible,' Vera said. 'Have we got a number for her?'

'Yeah, they sent it through from Kimmerston. Want me to do it?'

'Nah, I'll give her a ring. You carry on digging for info on Kelsall.'

Vera went outside to make the call. It was cold, but she needed a blast of fresh air to help her think straight, to clear the fog in her brain. Through one of the upstairs windows, she could see Joe, staring at the computer screen. Her boy. Her favourite. Sometime, she supposed, she'd have to release him and send him out into the world beyond her sphere of influence, but not yet. She'd miss him too much.

She'd dialled and was still thinking of Joe and how she was a selfish cow for keeping him on the team, given that his wife was so ambitious for him, when a woman answered.

'Yes. Charlotte Thomas.'

The voice was classier than Vera had expected. The Thomas family had never been exactly classy, even in their recent, respectable phase.

'This is Inspector Vera Stanhope, Northumbria Police.'

A brief moment of hesitation. The woman would have grown up with unexpected calls from the police, knocks on the door in the middle of the night, but if she'd had any anxiety at all, she covered it well.

'How can I help you, Inspector?' It was really a very lovely voice. Husky, deep.

'I'm afraid I have some bad news about your ex-husband, Richard Kelsall.' Vera stopped for a moment. She hated doing this over the phone. 'He died, either last night or in the early hours of this morning. I wonder if we might talk?'

Now the silence on the other end of the line was deep and dense. Vera waited.

'So, Rick's dead at last?' Her voice was flat.

'You don't sound surprised,' Vera said.

'I suppose I'm not. When I knew him, it was all he thought about. Dying. And living each day to the full, as if it was his last. A strange paradox. He took risks. Almost a game of dare with himself.' A pause. 'I used to joke that he was playing poker with a God he pretended not to believe in.'

Vera didn't know how to answer that or even what it meant, so she said nothing.

'How did he die?' This time, the woman's question was sharp, quite different in tone. 'Some foolish adventure? He could never accept that he'd get old eventually.'

'Where are you?' Vera asked. 'In Kimmerston?'

'No, I've been visiting a friend in the north of the county.'

'I wonder if you could come here then,' Vera said. 'I'm at a place called the Pilgrims' House on Holy Island. I prefer not to talk on the phone. Do you know it? The tide's fine for crossing until this evening and I'll make sure we're finished while it's still safe for you to get home.'

Again, that moment of hesitation. 'Yes,' Charlotte said. 'I know it. I'll come as soon as I can.'

Back in the office, they continued their search on Charlotte Thomas. Vera stood behind Joe, looking over his shoulder.

'Show me that Only Connect website. I've got no idea what a life coach is about.'

He pressed a couple more buttons. 'It says they "help their clients to fulfil their potential emotionally, physically and professionally".'

Vera thought she was none the wiser. She was still pondering the idea of fulfilling her emotional potential, when there was a noise in the road below: the CSIs and Holly arriving almost at the same time. Vera went down to meet them and gave Billy Cartwright a tour of the house.

'Can you get your guys to start in the bedrooms? The residents are out at the moment but they'll be back soon.'

'They're still staying here! Vera, are you mad? This is a murder scene.'

She shrugged. 'Doc Keating called it as suicide until he did the post-mortem and by then it was too late to bring them all back and ship them off the island.'

'You're playing games, Vera.'

But Billy liked playing games himself and he didn't make any more of a fuss. His investigators moved like white-suited bulky ghosts, silently, searching for any minute piece of evidence which might link an individual to the dead man's room. Because, as all rookie cops knew, every contact leaves a trace.

Back in the makeshift office, the conversation about Charlotte Thomas continued, but now there were three of them. 'Life coach!' Vera said. 'What a load of bollocks.'

'Not everyone's as strong as you, boss.'

Vera stared back at Holly. 'Are you saying you'd consult someone like that?'

There was a moment of silence. 'Maybe not, but I wouldn't condemn anyone who found it helpful.'

Vera stood behind Joe, so she could look at the screen, and saw a photo of a woman who'd been Rick Kelsall's first wife. She looked twenty years younger than the friends staying in the Pilgrims' House. In the picture, she was in black leggings and a black T-shirt, and the page was advertising virtual exercise. 'Is that her? It must be an old photo.'

'No,' Holly said. 'It was only taken six months ago.'

'She's worn well.' Vera struggled to keep the envy, the admiration, out of her voice.

'She's probably had work done,' Holly said.

'Ooh, not like you to be bitchy about a sister, Hol.'

They grinned at each other briefly. Sometimes, Vera thought, she could almost believe that Holly had a sense of humour. That they might end up working very well together. That Hol would become an outstanding detective.

The woman arrived in one of those flash cars, usually driven by ageing men during their mid-life crisis. A red convertible, though there wouldn't be many days in Northumberland when it would be comfortable to drive with the roof down. More fashion statement than mode of transport.

She must have left her friend soon after getting the call and looked as if she'd prepared for a photo shoot for *Homes and Gardens* rather than a country stroll with a mate: groomed, and well dressed in an understated, elegant sort of way, in jeans which would never bag at the knee and a tweed jacket. Vera watched from the window in the room they were using as an office, as the woman got out of the car, one gleaming leather boot after the other. Her loose hair could almost have been a natural blonde. The skin on her face was smooth and tight. Holly was standing beside Vera.

'She's definitely had some work done,' Holly said. 'Look at the wrinkles on her neck.'

'Meow.'

They shared another grin.

One of the uniforms showed Charlotte inside. Vera went downstairs and introduced herself. The woman even smelled expensive, of something citrus-fragranced and subtle. They walked upstairs into the makeshift office and Vera offered coffee.

'No,' Charlotte said. 'I never drink the stuff. I can't take caffeine these days. What's going on? I suppose they were all here for one of the reunions.'

'You knew about those?'

'Of course! I was here for the first weekend when we were still at school, but I didn't even stick that out until the end. Not my thing, that forced jollity. I never returned, even when Rick and I were still together. He was always closer to the others than I was. But I knew all about them.' Her back was straight but her age showed in the hands clasped on her lap, freckled with brown spots, white with tension. 'Inspector, what is going on here? There wouldn't be this fuss for a heart attack, or even a car accident.'

'No.' Vera looked at her. 'Nor for suicide, and that was what this was meant to look like.' A pause. 'Your ex-husband was murdered.'

For a moment, there was no response. Not even confusion or surprise. But perhaps the shock was so great that it took the woman a moment to process Vera's words. Then Charlotte began to laugh. It was deep, throaty and very theatrical, and Vera wasn't convinced by it at all.

'So,' Charlotte said. 'He finally provoked someone beyond

reason. I might have killed him myself, but I never had the courage.'

'Why might you have done that, Miss Thomas?'

The woman took a long time to answer. From outside the building came the conversation of the other residents returning from their walk. A snatch of laughter, which seemed to echo Charlotte's. None of them, it seemed, felt the need to put on a show of mourning for the man. Vera wondered if there'd been something about the victim that made his friends reluctant to display a sadness they couldn't quite feel. Would Rick Kelsall have mocked hypocrisy? She felt herself warming to him.

'Because he was the most self-centred bastard in the world and he treated me like shit.' A pause. 'But that didn't stop me adoring him. He made me feel more alive than I've ever been before or since. I can understand why someone would have wanted him dead, but I always had the feeling that one day he'd grow up and come back to me. And now, Inspector, that will never happen.' She stared, dry-eyed, out of the window, seeming not to notice the sound of the front door opening and the chatter of the others as they made their way into the house.

Chapter Thirteen

HOLLY HAD WATCHED THE ENCOUNTER BETWEEN Charlotte and Vera with interest. She'd arrived at this strange house unsure what she'd find. There had only been a short time to catch up with the geography of the building and its surroundings, and get a quick briefing from Joe on the residents, before this woman turned up. It struck Holly that Charlotte Thomas looked like some sort of minor film star, expecting admiration wherever she went.

Charlotte was the older woman but seemed much closer to Holly in age and outlook. Holly thought of herself as a feminist but could see how tempting it would be to have one's skin stretched, and the years erased. It was more about being taken seriously than for reasons of vanity. Holly would never consider plastic surgery to make herself attractive to men, but might if it made her seem stronger, more powerful.

Vera nodded towards the door. The house was small enough for them to hear the conversation of the people in the hall below, the sound of boots being removed and coats being hung up.

'Do you keep in touch with them all?'

'Only Annie,' Charlotte said. 'She lives not far from me. I use her deli.'

'Of course.' Vera got to her feet, suddenly brusque, almost impatient. 'I'd like you to give a statement to my colleague here. I'll see you before you go.' Then she'd left the room. For someone of her build the boss moved remarkably quickly, and Holly didn't really see her disappear.

Holly felt a moment of panic. She was completely ill-prepared. What did Vera expect of her? Here she was, alone with the woman who'd once been married to their victim, unsure whether this should be considered a formal interview or one of Vera's 'chats'. It felt like a kind of test.

To give herself time, she sat at the dressing table turned desk, found the A4 notebook she always carried in her bag, and took up her pen.

'When was the last time you saw Mr Kelsall?' It seemed as good a place as any to start.

Charlotte was sitting on one of the other kitchen chairs in the room and she crossed her legs. There was a moment's silence. She seemed to be weighing up her answer.

'Thursday.'

'This week?' Holly was surprised. She'd thought that estranged couples would keep a distance.

'Yes. Rick was driving up a day early for the reunion and he asked if he could stay.'

'Was that normal?' Holly paused. She didn't want to sound unsophisticated about other people's relationships. It might be perfectly possible for divorced people to maintain a friendship, or even more than that. But in her conversation with Vera, the woman had given no hint that she'd met Kelsall so recently.

'No. Usually his trips north were flying visits. Literally. He'd get off the plane at Newcastle, hire a car and head here to Holy Island and his friends. Always too busy to make a detour to visit me, especially now that our kids have grown up.'

'How old are your children?'

'Oh, positively middle-aged. And ridiculously successful. Sam's a photographer based in Hong Kong and Lily's a lawyer in London. Rick meets her more often. I see pictures on Facebook of drinks outside bars in fashionable parts of London, delicious meals he's obviously paid for.'

'But this time he drove and he came to see you?'

'Yes, I had a phone call from him on Wednesday lunchtime. I'd just finished leading a virtual meditation session. "You around, Lottie?" He always called me that.' Charlotte looked sad and for a moment seemed almost her real age. '"Any chance I could have a bed for the night tomorrow? Before I connect with the others. It'd be good to catch up."'

'And you agreed?' Holly wondered if perhaps, under the gloss and the sophistication, this woman was as lonely as Holly herself. Certainly, she didn't seem to have the same strong friendship group as the people staying at the Pilgrims' House. And what sort of support could her family, with their background of criminality, provide?

'Of course. I always did what he asked. I even agreed to a divorce when he wanted to marry his new delicate flower of a girlfriend, though it was the last thing I wanted.' The woman paused. 'I'd seen the press of course. All the nasty rumours, which I'm sure were at least halfway true. He'd be struggling to see that he'd done anything wrong, and Rick always needed people to love him. I thought he'd be hurting.'

'And was he?'

'He was, a bit, I think. But he was . . . he was putting on a very good show.'

'Could you take me through the evening?'

'He turned up at about six, quite hyper because he'd been sitting in the car for hours. He was always worse than the children about travelling, having to sit still. He stood just inside the door, bouncing on the balls of his feet, fizzing. I could tell he'd be fidgety all evening if he didn't get some exercise, so I suggested we go for a walk. We wandered down to the river at Kimmerston and stopped for a drink on the way home. He seemed a bit calmer by then. It was a lovely evening and we sat outside that new wine bar that opened just before the pandemic, not far from Annie's deli. The whole area has become a bit bougie lately, with little stores and craft workshops. In the summer the place came to life again, even more buzzy than before. People preferring to shop local maybe, aware of food miles, the climate emergency.'

'You didn't call in to see Annie?'

'No.' Charlotte's voice was cool. 'The shop will have been closed, and even after all this time, I wanted him to myself. We had a couple of glasses of wine and we talked. Rick seemed actually quite upbeat, considering the fact that he'd been sacked. He brushed aside the allegations of harassment. He said that the whole scandal had been triggered by an intern he'd tried to be kind to. A dreadful misunderstanding, which had got out of hand. Then, more ambitious little creatures had come out of the woodwork with their twisted stories and their lies, wanting their moment of fame. His colleagues had refused to support him, because they were scared of the management.'

'Is that how you saw it?'

Charlotte shrugged. 'Who knows? Rick could always tell a

good story, put on a brave face. But, yeah, I believed him at the time.'

'He'd been asked to resign,' Holly said. 'He'd lost his income and his reputation. He didn't seem at all upset?' She found that hard to believe. She wouldn't have been able to bear the humiliation.

'It was obviously a shock. He hated the fact that people would see him as a sordid abuser of women, but he seemed confident that he'd be able to restore his reputation in the end. It would never have been about the money. He's always made far more from his lectures and after-dinner speaking than he did from his salary. I'd guess that most of his audience would have been older businessmen who applauded his attitude to women. He validated their own dinosaur views.'

'And did *he* hold those dinosaur views?'

Charlotte took a while to answer. 'He loved women. Not as sexual objects necessarily, though I think the possibility that he might sleep with them was always close to the forefront of his mind. But he saw them as interesting beings to explore; they sparked his curiosity. He had this energy that made him reach out to them physically and emotionally. He wanted their attention. It would have been quite scary for younger women, I think. All the personal questions, the hand on the shoulder, somehow pulling them in, charming them of course, but intimidating them too.' A pause. 'He wasn't just the groper and the lecher the press has made him out to be, but I can see how he could make junior female colleagues uncomfortable, how they might feel he was making demands on them.' She paused. 'Really, Rick should have stuck with me. I understood him, and, actually, I bored him less than the others did. But he had this need for change, for excitement. He always believed that there was something much more interesting just around the corner.'

'Was there one complainant? Someone who prompted the production company to take action at last?'

There was a pause. Charlotte closed her eyes for a moment. Again, Holly thought, she was wondering how much to reveal. This time, it seemed, the woman had decided to keep the information to herself.

'I presume there was, but I can't tell you anything about her, I'm afraid. Rick didn't go into details, and the young woman has a right of privacy, don't you think?'

You know, Holly thought. *Why won't you tell?* She stared at the woman, but Charlotte remained silent. 'What did you do after your drink outside the wine bar?'

'We went back to my house.' Charlotte gave her address in a swanky street close to the river. 'I'd left a casserole in the oven. Veggie, which he turned his nose up at – he was always such a carnivore – but he ate it. We drank too much wine. Rick did that to excess too. Nothing in moderation. That was his motto.'

'Did he give any indication that he was scared, anxious?'

'No. We did what we always did when we got together. We remembered the old times.'

'When you were married?'

'No.' Charlotte smiled. 'There was nothing so good about *those* days. Things were already starting to fall apart. Before that. When we were still at school. He loved talking about those times. His glory days, I suppose, when everyone really did love him.' A pause. 'I'd heard most of the anecdotes before, of course, but he seemed even more fixated on the past than usual. He told me that he was writing a novel. He was very excited about it. The idea had been sparked, he said, by things that had happened when we were all very young. He was looking forward to going back to Holy Island, because that was where it had all started. He was like the old Rick, excited, buzzing, full of ideas. "Just you see, Lottie," he said. "You'll understand everything in a new light."'

'What did he mean?'

Charlotte shrugged. 'I don't know. I was just surprised, I suppose, that he was taking all the bad press so well.'

Holly couldn't see that stories of fifty years ago could have triggered the violent death of an elderly man, but she jotted that down anyway. Just in case. Vera liked the detail of an investigation. It was the boss's strength, but also her weakness. She could dig away at the tiny details, losing sight of the overall picture. The past was her territory. She always said it explained the tensions and stresses of the present. Holly had learned more about Vera's past during the recent Brockburn investigation, and perhaps it had made more sense of the woman.

'He wanted to sleep with me.' Charlotte was talking again. 'At least he said he did. He knew I'd say no. I've got a bit more pride these days. And I'm not sure he'd have asked if he thought I'd say yes.' A pause. 'So, it was just a goodnight kiss in front of the fire. Very chaste. Rather romantic.' She looked up. 'We were in bed by about one. That's quite early for Rick. I suspect he stayed awake for a while checking his phone for the news. He was a news junkie.'

Holly nodded. 'And the next day?'

'I didn't have any work commitments until the afternoon, so we had a late breakfast. Halfway through his phone rang. He seemed pleased to get the call and went into the other room to take it. *Sorry, darling. Confidential.* Turning it into a drama, though it was probably routine.'

Holly wrote that down too. They'd be able to check the identity of the caller.

'Soon after that he said he should head off. There was someone he had to see, before meeting the others here at the Pilgrims' House. Being mysterious all over again, just for show. He asked me if I wanted to join the group for the weekend. I told him I had work to do, and anyway, I'd rather stick pins in my eyes. I'd had quite enough of Rick's reminiscences the night before. So, there was the obligatory farewell kiss and off he went.' Charlotte sat back in the uncomfortable chair.

'You seem very dismissive of Mr Kelsall's nostalgia for your schooldays, yet you named your business after the time you spent here as teenagers, the weekend when you all became close friends.'

Charlotte briefly closed her eyes again. 'Only Connect? There is nothing nostalgic about that, Constable. It is, I suppose, a mission statement for the company. Our whole ethos is about bringing together the mind and the body, connecting our clients with their real ambitions and helping them to realize them in reality.'

A phrase of Vera's came, unbidden, into Holly's head. *What a load of bollocks!* 'You seem very passionate about the business.'

'Oh I am.'

'So, you have no plans to retire?'

Charlotte smiled. 'Absolutely not! I suppose I'm of an age when I should be thinking of retirement, but I can think of nothing worse. I'm terrified of boredom. I need something to get up for every morning. I'm really not a good works and coffee morning sort of woman.' She paused. 'My father was still running his own business into his seventies.'

'You never considered working with your family?'

There was a pause before Charlotte gave a wintry smile. 'I did for a while, when I first came back to the North-East, but it didn't quite work out.'

'Why was that? Perhaps you didn't approve of your father's business practices?'

'I'm not quite sure what you're implying, Constable.' Charlotte's voice was sharp. 'And I can't see how my family's companies can have any relevance at all to my ex-husband's murder.'

'Your father and your uncle had a reputation for violence.' Holly tried to keep her tone even. 'You can understand why I'm exploring the matter. If Mr Kelsall treated you badly, perhaps one of your family members felt he had a score to settle.'

'None of my relatives has ever been convicted of a criminal offence.' The voice was firm. If Charlotte was rattled, she wasn't showing it. 'And while my father might well have wanted to kill Rick when he ditched me for another woman, that was a very long time ago. He considers now that I'm much better off without the man.' She paused. 'Besides, Dad's very elderly, very frail. He moved in with my sister nearly a year ago and he seldom leaves the house.'

'You don't have any idea where Mr Kelsall might have gone yesterday morning?' Because, Holly thought, the woman would have *wanted* to know, even if she couldn't bring herself to ask. Her love for Rick Kelsall was a scab that needed scratching. Though they might have been divorced for years, she still seemed to be jealous, and to want to be a part of his life.

'No.' Charlotte paused. 'It could have had nothing at all to do with the phone call. He might have gone to Kimmerston cemetery. He sometimes did that if he had time when he was home. It had become a morbid kind of sanctuary for him. He said it brought him peace, though I think there was more to it than that. The idea of all those bodies under his feet gave him an odd thrill. I told the inspector. It seemed as if he was obsessed with death.'

Holly didn't know what to say. For an uneasy moment she seemed to have lost her way in the interview. To cover her confusion, she returned to the easy formula.

'What were you doing yesterday night and early this morning?'

Charlotte must have been expecting the question because she gave another little smile. 'You're asking if I have an alibi for the time Rick was killed? I'm afraid I can't help you. I had a number of online meetings in the afternoon and then I went home. I ate the remains of the casserole and I had an early night. I always find Rick's energy exhausting.'

'You didn't make any phone calls or send any emails overnight?'

'To prove that I was at home? Certainly not, Constable. I'm a great believer in proper sleep hygiene. All screens are switched off an hour before bedtime. If you look at the Only Connect website you'll see it's what we tell our clients, and I have to practise what I preach.'

'And early this morning?'

'I went for a run before breakfast. Just as it was getting light. It was rather a beautiful dawn, if a little icy under foot. One of my neighbours might have seen me.'

Now Holly did set down her pen and she got to her feet.

'Thank you, Miss Thomas. We know where to find you if we have more questions.'

Charlotte stood up slowly, making it clear she was in no hurry to leave, that in no sense at all was she running away.

'Was Mr Kelsall visiting any specific grave in the cemetery?' The thought had come into Holly's head very suddenly. Her flat overlooked a big cemetery in Newcastle, but she'd chosen it for the peace and quiet. She couldn't imagine wandering around it to get a thrill from being so close to the dead. 'His mother and father perhaps?'

'No.' Charlotte paused for a moment. 'A friend. Isobel Hall. She died on the island too. At least on her way back from here. I was working in the South, so I only heard about the accident second hand, but the others will be able to give you the details. It happened at the first five-year reunion. She was one of my best friends. It's one of the reasons why I never come back to the Pilgrims' House with the others. It seems in such very poor taste to be celebrating when she's not here.'

Again, Holly was left floundering for something to say. Charlotte walked out through the door and Holly heard her footsteps, firm on the stairs. She wondered if the woman would make some attempt to see the residents, the close friends of her former husband. A gentle buzz of conversation was coming from the common room. But Charlotte left by the front door, and walked straight to her car. Perhaps she was in a hurry, anxious about being stranded on the island as the tide came in. Perhaps, for some reason, she wanted to avoid them.

Chapter Fourteen

IN THE KITCHEN, ANNIE WAS ORGANIZING tea and cakes. She focused on arranging Jax's magnificent baking prettily on the plates, trying to push out of her mind the picture of Rick Kelsall, hanging from a beam in the bedroom at the end of the corridor. The grey, thin hair on his chest, the staring eyes.

The others had come back from their walk with an appetite, and had decided they'd just have time for a late afternoon tea before heading to the chapel. The shock of Rick's death had left them quiet, subdued, but with a need for routine, to do what they'd always done. It provided a reassurance perhaps that life could continue without him.

Annie had once again refused their offers of help. She felt at ease in the kitchen and after the company of the walk, she needed a moment alone. Besides, Philip would take responsibility for supper. Another tradition. She imagined it would be vegetarian, probably shepherd's pie, his usual standby and easy to make in advance. There was a dish, wrapped in foil, in the fridge. Rick would have teased and claimed a desire for steak or a venison stew, though he'd never volunteered to cook. His contribution had always been the cases of wine.

She carried a tray to the common room where the others were waiting. Someone had revived the fire. The curtains were still open, although it would be dark in an hour. This far north, evening descended quickly at this time of year; soon, it would be winter.

Charlotte had gone. She'd done a little wave at Annie through the window before getting into her car, but hadn't joined them. Annie thought of the last time they'd met up. Charlotte had called into the deli just on closing time.

'Come for a drink with me, darling. I'm *so* bored.' The implication was of course that Charlotte would *have* to be bored to want Annie's company.

It had been the summer, and they'd sat in a pub, drinking pints as if they were students again, and ordering, but not eating much of, a dreadful lasagne. As usual, the talk had returned to the past.

Later, after the second pint, Charlotte had moaned about her business, about how difficult it was for people in a parochial place like Kimmerston to open their minds to the changes that a life coach could make. She hadn't asked Annie any questions about her life, but Annie hadn't minded that. It had been quite relaxing to sit there, getting quietly drunk, listening to the murmur of Charlotte's complaints.

Now, in the Pilgrims' House common room, Annie poured tea and handed around mugs and milk. Vera Stanhope and Joe Ashworth appeared at the door. Annie couldn't help smiling. Vera seemed to have an almost spooky ability to tell when food was being served.

'Ooh, is that one of Jax's coffee and walnut slices?' Vera had already taken a piece from the tray and was holding it with a paper napkin, triumphant as if she'd had to fight the others off for it. She stood in front of them, with her bum to the fire, blocking out most of the heat, and set the cake carefully on the mantelpiece.

'We'll need statements from each of you,' she said. 'Best to do it today, while everything's still clear in your mind, and so you can leave in the morning.' She beamed widely and then she had a mouth full of traybake, so the words that followed were only just intelligible. 'So, we'll start as soon as you like in the spare room upstairs. Holly's using it at the moment, but I think she's just finished. Annie, do you want to come first, pet? You can bring your tea.'

'I can't come now,' Annie said. 'It's nearly time for chapel.'

'Chapel?' Vera seemed bewildered and amused at the same time.

'It's a condition of using the Pilgrims' Retreat House. Chapel every evening at dusk. I'm sorry, we can't miss it. It's only twenty minutes.'

'And do you do the whole thing? A service. Prayers and hymns? On your knees and up on your feet? The glorified hokey-cokey?'

'Nothing like that.' Philip broke into the conversation. He too seemed amused. Certainly, he wasn't offended. Perhaps he saw Vera as a possible convert. A challenge at least. 'It's a period of silent meditation. But those of us with faith use it as a chance to pray.'

'Eeh, this case is so complicated, I could do with a period of peaceful contemplation, myself. Is it okay if I join you?'

'Of course, Inspector. You'd be very welcome.'

They got dressed in their outdoor clothes and trooped out

into the chilly evening, walking slowly, two by two, as if they were real pilgrims, or the monks who'd lived on the island centuries before. Philip lit the candles. They sat in silence, but Annie couldn't feel the peace that usually came with the place. She was aware of Vera Stanhope, sitting in the same pew as her, watching them all with her bright, conker-brown eyes.

Later, walking back to the house, in the chill, clear air, which took her breath away, Annie found Vera beside her once again.

'You're all right to give your statement first? We'll go on up, shall we?'

It wasn't really a question and Annie could do nothing but follow in Vera's wake, like a small tug in the shadow of a giant liner.

A woman in her thirties was in the room, tapping on a laptop. She was wearing office clothes and had an expensive haircut, short and a little severe. Practical, Annie supposed, for a police officer.

'This is our Hol,' Vera said. 'She's part of the team.'

The woman looked up, gave Annie a brief nod, then turned her attention to Vera. 'I could do with a word, boss.'

'Why don't you grab yourself a cuppa and some cake if there's any left? I'll just have a chat to Annie here, and then I'm all yours.'

Annie thought the words were tactless, dismissive, and not the way a boss should talk to a younger colleague, but the constable seemed to take it in her stride. She nodded again and left the room. Vera sat heavily on a chair, which had been carried from the kitchen, and gestured for Annie to take the one opposite.

'So,' she said. 'Tell me about all the people here. Why do

you think one of them might have wanted to kill your old friend Rick?'

Annie was lost for words for a moment. Besides the shock generated by the question, she felt this was not the way a police interview should be conducted. Again it seemed that she was being encouraged to respond in a certain way.

'I don't think any one of us would have wanted to kill him! He was a friend.'

'You're telling me that the perpetrator was some random stranger, who drove out to a tidal island in wildest Northumberland in the middle of the night? You don't think that's even more improbable?' Vera gave a little smile and fixed Annie with a stare.

'Rick had enemies,' Annie said at last, 'but that was all to do with his work.'

'Tell me about this bunch, just the same. Your gang from the school. It was a comprehensive by the time I went there, but I believe it was a grammar in your day?'

'Yes.' Annie tried to gather her thoughts, to decide how much should be shared. Vera seemed to squeeze the air from her. She was finding it hard to breathe, as if she was walking into a gale.

'But it's not the usual school reunion. Not everyone's invited. Only some of the people who were here at the Pilgrims' House for that bonding weekend fifty years ago?'

Annie nodded. 'There was this young teacher, straight from college. She taught English and drama and came with all these new ideas about self-expression. How we should all try to understand each other. She was very intense. Charismatic in a vaguely spiritual way. Perhaps everyone was a bit new age then, trying to find themselves, but it was new to us. A kind of revelation. So, she brought a dozen of the new sixth form here, split us up into two groups, asked us to trust each other and to be completely honest. A kind of prolonged encounter session. I think the others thought it was a bit of a joke, but our group took it seriously and became very close.'

Annie looked up at Vera. 'I suppose it was all self-indulgent nonsense, dangerous even, playing with young people's psyches, but it seemed very important to us then. It changed the way we looked at the world and each other.' She paused. It seemed important to explain. 'It was the early seventies. A different time. School was still strict; we were all supposed to conform. And then this teacher came along who encouraged us to be open and honest. Suddenly feelings mattered. That stayed with us.'

'And the name of the teacher?'

'Judy Marshall.'

'Is she still around, do you know?'

Annie nodded. 'Yes, she comes into the deli. She retired a while ago. I'm not sure she'd enjoy the way education has gone now. According to Lou, it's all tests and results.'

'And how many of this gang were there on that first weekend?'

'Rick was there with Charlotte, his girlfriend of the time.'

Vera nodded. 'I've just met her.'

'Philip and Ken.'

'Philip the vicar and Ken is the poor guy with dementia.'

'Yes. Louisa, Ken's wife, was at school with us, but she was younger and wasn't invited to Only Connect.'

'What's the significance of that name?'

'It was Miss Marshall's idea. She taught us A-level English

and it's a quote from a book we were reading for the exams. *Howard's End*. E. M. Forster.'

Vera nodded as if the book were entirely familiar to her. 'Anyone else part of your special gang? Anyone who doesn't come to these reunions?'

'My ex-husband, Daniel. He was there that first time too.' Annie wasn't sure what else to say about Daniel. 'He still lives locally. He joined the family business. He thinks the whole idea of the reunion's daft. He only came back once, to the first reunion, even when we were married.'

'Is he Daniel Laidler?'

'No, I went back to using my maiden name when he left.' Annie paused. 'He's Daniel Rede.'

'And that was it? Just the six of you in your gang?'

Annie was tempted to lie, but Vera's stare seemed to pierce the skin and bone of her skull, enter her brain and read her mind. 'There was another lass, she was in the other group for Only Connect but she hung out with us. Isobel Hall. Issy. She was there for the first reunion. She's dead now though.'

'Oh?' Just a tip of the head, but Vera was demanding an answer.

'A road accident.'

'And when was that?'

'Five years after Only Connect.'

'So, she died at your first reunion?'

This woman was quick, Annie thought. She hoped the others didn't under-estimate her. 'Yes. Well, not quite. Not in the house here. She was on her way home and crashed off the causeway, just before the tide. No other vehicle was involved, according to the police. They think she must have braked suddenly for some reason, and that the road was slippery with seaweed. Her parents were distraught.' Annie paused again and looked at Vera. 'She was Louisa's older sister. Louisa was at that first reunion, because she'd already hooked up to Ken by then, but she wasn't in Isobel's car. Ken had offered to give her a lift home later.'

Annie remembered Isobel's funeral. No dark clothes, her parents had said. It should be a celebration of their beautiful daughter's life. But it had rained and it hadn't properly got light all day, and the bright coats and scarves had been drained of colour. The small church had been full, so the younger mourners had stood outside under the dripping trees to make room for the rest, listening to the service through the open door. Louisa had been inside, of course, the loyal Ken sitting next to her, holding her hand, belting out the hymns with his glorious tenor.

Vera was speaking now, breaking into the memory. 'Nobody would have born a grudge though for Isobel's death, not after all these years. And why would they have blamed Rick Kelsall?'

Again, Annie hesitated. She could shrug and pretend she had no idea what might have led up to Isobel's accident, but again, she thought this woman would find out the truth, and it would be terrible to be caught out in a lie. A sin of omission at least.

'Rick and Isobel had been bickering on and off all weekend. Not all that serious. Kind of jokey remarks, picking at each other. They were very similar really.' Thinking about it now, Annie thought Isobel had been a female version of Rick. No wonder the sparks had flown. She saw that Vera was waiting for her to continue. 'Then that morning there was an enormous row. They were outside the house and I could see there was some sort of confrontation. Suddenly Isobel drove off in a huff. Upset. Too fast, not concentrating and too close to the tide. The rest of us had decided to wait until later in the afternoon once the causeway was clear.' She looked directly at Vera, willing her to understand. 'But we didn't tell anyone about the argument. Not the police or Isobel's parents. It wouldn't have helped. Better for people to think it was just a tragic accident, not that Isobel had flounced off in one of her tempers.'

'Well, it certainly wouldn't have helped your pal Rick.' Vera's words were hard. 'He'd just be starting off on his career. Out of university and with stardom waiting. It might have made things a bit easier for the lass's parents to understand how it happened.'

'Perhaps. We didn't think so at the time. Knowing that she'd died, after a row with a close friend, feeling angry and unloved. That seemed unkind.'

Vera nodded, accepting that the argument might have some validity. 'Maybe. It's always dangerous to play with the truth though. Playing God.'

Annie thought Vera wouldn't mind playing God if she believed she could get away with it.

The detective stared at her. 'Did you know what the row was about?'

Annie shook her head. 'None of us could understand it. Usually, they got on okay. But he could be cruel if he was in one of his moods. They seemed to be getting on okay for most of the weekend. Like I said, there was the occasional sniping, a kind of banter, earlier on, but nothing serious. In a way, it was almost intimate.' Annie paused and then chose her words carefully. 'I wondered if they'd been having some sort of fling, and he ended it on that Sunday morning. He was already engaged to Charlotte by then. Isobel wasn't used to rejection. I can see how she might have kicked off.'

Vera nodded. 'Well, the man seems to have a history of playing with women's affections, though from what I can tell, he's been bullying his most recent victims, harassing rather than rejecting them. You say Louisa was there, that weekend her sister died. Did she know about the row? Her sister storming off in a hurry?'

Again, Annie found her mind tracking back to that first reunion weekend. They'd all graduated and thought themselves so grown-up. On the brink of an adventure. It was the mid-seventies. There'd been a drought all summer and the ground had dried hard as concrete, and even in October they'd been waiting for rain. Rick had already announced his engagement to Charlotte, but she wasn't at the Pilgrims' House. She'd said something urgent had come up. Some audition or casting. Or perhaps that was an excuse and she was at home with her rich scally family. Louisa had been there with Ken. Rick had teased them all weekend. *You two still together. My God, you're positively middle-aged.* And Dan had been resentful and brooding because the weekend hadn't been as much fun as he'd hoped. Or because he was grieving as much as her. She'd only recently come to realize that might have been the case.

'Yes,' Annie said. 'Louisa was there. But she didn't see the argument. She was out for a romantic walk with Ken, and when they came back, they announced that they were engaged. We'd just started celebrating when one of the islanders rushed in to tell us about the accident.' A pause. 'We didn't tell Lou or Ken about the row either. It was bad timing as it was, and we didn't want to make things worse. We kept it as a secret between us. Rick, Philip, Daniel and me.' She hesitated again. 'Daniel wasn't there when they were arguing, but I told him later.'

'And you've kept the secret all this time?'

'Yes!' Again, Annie took time to choose her words carefully. 'We've never talked about it. Not even among ourselves.'

Vera looked at her. 'Well, *you* might not have blabbed, but I don't see how you can vouch for the others.'

'I know them. They wouldn't.' But Annie wasn't really sure about that. There was nothing Rick liked better than telling stories. He'd been doing it the night before he died, entertaining them all with tales of his exploits with Miss Marshall. And Philip might have used Isobel's death in a narrative of his own, to make some sort of point. What was a sermon, after all, if not a story?

'Last night,' the inspector went on, 'Rick wasn't doing the same thing, was he? Teasing, picking on one of you, being cruel as he had been to your friend Isobel all that time ago?'

Annie shook her head. 'No, he didn't treat us like that. Besides, we'd known him too long to be upset by that sort of behaviour. We'd have called him out on it, given as good as we got.'

'But he could still be badly behaved with young lasses, it seems. Apparently, he thought he was a ladies' man. I gather he was a little old-fashioned in his dealings with women. One of those men that think banter is okay even if it's offensive.'

'Not with us.' Annie made sure her voice was firm. 'He's always the perfect gentleman these days. A good friend.'

'And in the past?'

Annie had a memory of Rick at a party, outside in the garden on a summer's night, pushing her against a wall, hands everywhere. But that had been her fault, hadn't it? She'd probably encouraged him to think it was what she'd wanted. And in one sense she *had* wanted it, had been flattered by the attention. Things had seemed very different then.

'Not then either. Not with me.'

Vera shot her a look, sceptical, but then she moved on. 'Let's just speculate for a moment, shall we? Let's say that one of these people staying here killed Rick. Who would be the most likely? Which of them would have the nerve to hold a cushion over his face, squeezing the air from his lungs, listening to him fighting for breath, and then to string him up to make it look like suicide?'

Annie felt sick. She took a deep breath, then, despite herself, she found herself playing along. 'Not Philip,' she said. 'When he was younger, he had a temper and he could be a bit chippy. But not since he was born again and found religion.'

'Now he's all sweetness and light?'

Annie grinned. 'He is rather. It makes you sick.'

'So that leaves Ken and Louisa.' Vera stopped. 'And you!'

'Rick had a thing about Louisa once he and Charlotte split up. This time, it was a bit different from his usual attempts at seduction. He claimed to love her. Ken was always so laid back he was horizontal, but even he got a bit pissed off.' Annie thought this was safe territory, because not even Vera could think that Ken, who could now barely remember his wife's name, would have the ability to have killed Rick.

'Years ago, was that?'

'Well, it started years ago, but I think Rick turned on the routine every time they met. Blatant, not trying to hide it from Ken. It was kind of jokey: *Come on, Lou! Have a bit of excitement for once in your life. Ken's a lovely guy, but a bit boring. A bit safe.*'

'But not really a joke?'

'I don't know. Perhaps a joke in bad taste.'

There was a moment of silence before Vera spoke again. 'It seems to me that you're pointing me in the direction of someone we know was unlikely to be a killer. Who are you protecting, I wonder? One of your friends? Or yourself?'

Chapter Fifteen

PHILIP WAS INTERVIEWED BY THE YOUNG female detective. She seemed tense, not nervous exactly, but focused, determined to get this right. He thought she felt she had something to prove. He found himself trying to put her at her ease – a habit that went with his job – and perhaps because of that, he was less cautious with his answers than he might have been.

They were in a corner of the common room. Louisa and Ken were upstairs, talking with the sergeant.

'A young woman died here during your first reunion,' DC Clarke said. 'Can you tell me what happened?'

'She drove out too close to the tide, and the car was swept from the causeway. A terrible accident. She was just twenty-two.' He paused. 'She was Louisa's older sister.'

'What led up to it?'

Philip couldn't quite understand how this might be relevant, but it was easier to talk about Isobel than to think through the implications of Rick's death.

'There was some sort of argument with Rick. I couldn't

hear what was said. They were out in the lane and I was watching from one of the rooms upstairs.'

'Could you guess what they were fighting about?'

'Isobel was a little spoiled. She was pretty and bright, and her parents doted on her. I sometimes felt sorry for Lou, who seemed always to be in her shadow. Issy had just graduated with a first from university and her dad had bought her a car. She really believed she could have anything she wanted.'

'And what *did* she want?'

'Rick,' Philip said. 'I think she wanted him, that perhaps there had been some sort of fling on the island that weekend. But Rick was engaged to Charlotte, and there were already plans for the very grand wedding. He would have made it clear that anything that had happened between him and Isobel wasn't serious.' He looked up at the detective. 'She just drove off. As if somehow, she could control the tide, as well as the rest of her life.'

'It must have been a terrible shock.'

'It was. In a way I suppose it locked the rest of us together.' For some reason, he wanted this young detective to understand. 'It changed me, certainly. Afterwards, we sat in the chapel and I had a glimpse of something different. Something beyond the everyday. A new way of living. In the tragedy, there was intense joy too.'

'A religious experience?'

'Yes,' he said simply. 'Exactly that. So of course, I regret the tragedy of an early death, but in a strange way I'm grateful for it too.'

'You were all close before that,' the detective said. 'Because of Only Connect, the weekend you spent here?'

Philip nodded. He shut his eyes briefly. 'Very close. Intense,

as only the young can be. We thought we were the first generation to be so open, so honest, though of course our parents
had lived through the war, and they must have formed intense
relationships too. They were close to death every day.' He
looked again at the woman. 'We'd become very selfish. For us,
it was glorious parties, hours discussing music and books, too
much alcohol.' A pause. 'I saw that, in the moment in the
chapel after Isobel's death. I realized there was another way.'

'You remained friends with the others, although they didn't
share your faith.'

Philip laughed. 'Of course! Rick was still as close as a brother.
And I gave up trying to convert him years ago!'

'When did you last see him?'

'A couple of months ago. He'd just been told to resign. He
was very low. He didn't think he'd done anything wrong. *I
wouldn't have upset those girls for the world, Phil.* This weekend,
he seemed much brighter. Optimistic. Happy. He had a new
project. He'd decided to write a novel, and he was full of it.
That's why his suicide came as such a shock.'

'He didn't kill himself,' the detective said. 'It was murder.'
Her voice was cold, flat. She was stating a fact, nothing more.
But Philip felt as if his world was falling apart.

Chapter Sixteen

JOE STOOD OUTSIDE THE PILGRIMS' HOUSE for a moment and looked out at the stars. There was no real front garden, only a strip of grass next to the lane and a white bench leaning against the wall of the house. All the land was at the back. He'd been interviewing Louisa and Ken Hampton, and something about the ill man had moved him almost to tears. Ken had held his wife's hand throughout the conversation, had smiled occasionally, but hadn't spoken. He was still physically big, but now he seemed entirely passive and dependent, a giant, compliant child. Joe had let himself out of the building before Vera could start asking questions about the interview – he wasn't ready yet to replay it for her – but now, standing with his back to the house, the cold air seemed to clear his mind of the discomfort, the upset.

There were no street lights here and they'd shut the curtains in the house, so no light seeped out. Joe didn't have Vera's affection for wild spaces, for the great outdoors, but there *was* something spectacular about this: so many stars and a sense of the darkness stretching for ever, that made him dizzy and a little scared. He'd been brought up as a Methodist and they still took the kids to church when they had a free Sunday, but he wasn't sure his faith was strong enough to cope with this emptiness. The size of it all. His insignificance in comparison.

He heard the door open again and saw Holly standing next to the bench. 'The boss wants us in. A final meeting before calling it a night.' She shivered and he only realized just how cold it was then. It would freeze again in the night, and be another clear day when the sun came up in the morning.

'I just needed a moment,' Joe said, 'after talking to the Hamptons. It must be so hard for them both.'

Holly stood behind him. She was looking up at the stars too. 'It happened to my grandmother,' she said. 'Dementia. It's horribly common, but somehow we never think it'll happen to us.'

'Harder for the relatives maybe, than the sufferer.' But Joe thought that couldn't really be true. He'd rather die than be like Ken Hampton, lost and confused, the object of pity.

Holly touched his arm. She seemed to realize that he was deep in thought. 'We'd better get in. Can't keep madam waiting.' They shared a quick grin and made their way into the house.

Vera was in the bedroom they'd made their base. The filter machine was gurgling, dripping coffee, and now three chairs were placed around the desk. They sat very close to each other, with their knees almost touching. The boss had interviewed Annie Laidler, Joe had spoken to Louisa and Ken as a couple and Holly had taken on the vicar. The friends had had their dinner, and now they were all back together, sitting in the common room, talking quietly. Drinking Rick Kelsall's wine. Joe supposed they'd be sharing the experience of the interviews, checking that their stories matched. He thought suddenly that this investigation, involving a group of elderly people, might turn out to be the weirdest he'd ever been involved with.

'Are you letting them all go in the morning?' Holly was doing the honours with the coffee and set three mugs on the low table. Joe put his hands around his mug, letting the warmth defrost his fingers.

'They shouldn't still be here anyway. Even with Rick Kelsall's room sealed they're contaminating a crime scene. Besides, we can't really keep them.' But Vera sounded reluctant. Joe could tell she would *like* to keep them local. She went on: 'I can't see any of them making a run for it, can you?'

Joe shook his head. 'They've all got too many ties at home.'

'Not just that! They're bright. They were grammar school kids. Nothing would point to guilt like doing a runner.' Vera paused. 'Ken and Louisa live just over the border in Cumbria, so it'd be easy enough to go back to see them if we need to. I wonder if we could persuade the vicar to extend his holiday for a few days, stay in the county. Worth a shot, I think.'

'You really think one of this group killed him?' Joe couldn't see it. They were all so respectable. The only chancer among them had been the victim.

'I don't *think* anything this early in an investigation.' A pause. 'Joe, when you spoke to the Hamptons, did Louisa mention anything about a sister?'

'No.' He was puzzled and couldn't see where this was leading.

'Charlotte talked about a sister who died at the first reunion,' Holly said, 'and I followed it up with the vicar.'

'Annie Laidler gave me the details too. The lass's name was Isobel and she was part of the original Only Connect group. Is it odd, do we think, that Louisa didn't mention the accident?

Her only sister dying too, at one of these navel-gazing gatherings.' Vera paused before answering her own question. 'Maybe not. We shouldn't read too much into it. After all this time, Louisa might not have thought it was relevant. *I'm* interested though, because Annie said the death occurred immediately after Isobel had a row with Rick Kelsall. Let's get more details of the incident, shall we? There must have been an inquest. I can't see Louisa waiting more than forty years to avenge her sister, but we've got bugger all else to go on.'

She stretched her legs and stifled a yawn. 'Anything useful from the vicar, Hol?'

Holly shook her head. 'Not much. Kelsall went to see him soon after he was forced to resign, but claimed there was no truth to the women's allegations.'

'Well, he would,' Vera said. 'It doesn't get us any further forward.' She gave them both a mischievous glance. 'The whole bunch of them could be in it together of course. Like that film. The train stuck in the snow. We'd never find out if they kept to their stories.'

'But why would they? I can't see that any of them has a motive.'

'How would we know? Unless one of them broke ranks and gave us the low-down.'

Holly looked across at her, very serious. 'Do you really think that was how it happened?'

'Nah,' Vera said. 'Not really. But they're close. Mates. They'll be protecting each other. Keeping secrets. Which might or might not be relevant. Anything else from the jolly vicar?'

Holly shook her head. 'A bit more background on the victim. Because they both lived in London, Rick saw him more frequently than the others. Philip was still a good friend and they'd meet for a drink every now and again. And Rick was writing a book. Charlotte mentioned that too.'

Vera nodded. 'That's interesting. Something else to chase up with Rick's former employer.' She looked across at Joe. 'You were researching that earlier. Did you manage to find someone at the production company willing to talk?'

'Sorry,' he said. 'I didn't get anywhere. Most of the staff aren't working this weekend and when I did get a response, nobody was willing to give out personal contact details.'

The women looked at him. Joe thought they were both thinking that Holly would have done better. This was confirmed when Vera spoke again. 'You take that on, will you, Hol? We need the name of the first woman to make the complaint against Rick Kelsall. The one who started the ball rolling, and lost him his job. I know victims of sexual assault have the privilege of anonymity but we really need to speak to her.'

'Sure, boss.' There was a definite edge of triumph in Holly's voice. There were times when Joe felt as he had in the classroom, when all his pals had seemed brighter than he was.

'How did you get on with Louisa and Ken, Joe?'

'Well, it was Louisa who did all the talking. Ken nodded every now and again as if he agreed, but I wasn't sure he understood the questions.'

'Anything useful?'

'Nothing new at all. As you said, the couple live in Cumbria and they drove over, arriving early afternoon on Friday. Rick was already in the house. Louisa said he seemed in very good spirits. She was surprised after all the fuss in the press.'

'When was the last time they'd seen him? Before this weekend.'

Joe thought back to the conversation. The woman, controlled, upright, and the big man with his hand covering hers on the arm of her chair. 'In the summer. They went to London for a few days. Ken had already been diagnosed with dementia, and they wanted to do things like that while they still could. One of their kids lives and works in the City, and they stayed with him. They met Rick for a meal. He was already feeling under pressure at work then, apparently. Louisa said he seemed anxious, but more worried that anything he'd said might have been misinterpreted. *You know I wouldn't want to offend anyone for the world. You understand that, don't you, Lou? Sometimes I get carried away, that's all.*' Joe looked up. 'That almost sounded like an admission to me, though at that point no specific allegations had been made.'

'According to Annie, Rick always had a soft spot for Louisa. He fancied himself in love.' Vera hesitated for a moment. 'Or maybe he just lusted after her. Did that come across?'

Joe shook his head. 'But I don't think she'd have responded. She appears very level-headed.' A pause. 'A bit cold maybe. Former head teacher. Ambitious. She was sent in to run schools in special measures. Now she does some work for Ofsted, assessing other teachers. You could tell she looks after her husband well, but there's not a lot of warmth there.' He paused. 'It all seemed a bit mechanical.'

'Aye well, I suppose the wife knows she's in it for the long haul. You have to keep back a bit in reserve.'

Joe remembered then that Vera's dad had suffered from dementia in the end and she'd moved back home to help care for him until he died. 'Just before they both left,' he said, 'I asked one question to Ken, directed it only to him. Louisa was already halfway out of the room. I asked him what he made of Rick.'

'And?' That was Holly.

Joe could tell Hol was getting impatient now, because he was the one doing most of the talking. He could understand her impatience. He'd been hoping he'd be able to get home tonight. It was the last weekend of half-term and Sal always got a bit scratchy by the end of the school holidays. But they'd missed the tide and they'd have to stay over, and now he wanted to be in his room in the Seahorse before it got any later, so he could say goodnight at least to the older kids. So, he just answered the question, without discussing what he thought about it. 'Ken gave a little chuckle and said Rick was a rascal. Always had been. And he got away with murder because he could charm the teachers. It was as if in his head they were still teenagers.' Joe looked up at them. 'Then Ken said: *But Rick's closer than a brother. I'd do anything for him.*'

Chapter Seventeen

Saturday evening during a reunion was usually a quiet affair. By the last night of the weekend, they were all talked out and starting to be concerned about their livers, so while, of course, they'd still have a drink, it would be more restrained, less of a party. This evening was even quieter than normal. Annie was starting to realize that Rick had been the person who held them together, the lifter of spirits, the joker. He'd been like some sort of happy drug, forcing them to forget their age and leave their inhibitions behind. Without him, they had all become more boring, less entertaining.

With a sudden clarity, she saw that this would be the last time they'd all be together. In five years' time, Ken's illness would have reached a stage where Louisa would prefer not to bring him away. He might even be living in a care home. Although these days people were more reluctant to send their loved ones into care, Annie couldn't imagine Louisa looking after him herself once he became very demanding. Philip would have properly retired. Only Annie would still be working, holding the fort at Bread and Olives while Jax worked her magic in the kitchen. After fifty years, she thought, she might actually lose touch with these people who'd been so close to her. The years, stretching ahead of her, seemed empty, devoid of light or fun.

There was a noise in the hall behind her and she turned to see Vera Stanhope in the doorway.

'That's us off. Done for the night.' The detective sounded cheery, glad to be going, and in that second Annie wished that she could leave too, that she could drive over the causeway to her little terraced house on the edge of Kimmerston. If the prospect of life without her friends had seemed dark and depressing the moment before, that of the evening *with* them felt like an ordeal to be endured rather than enjoyed.

'Don't worry,' Vera went on. 'There'll still be the uniformed officers keeping an eye.'

Outside there was the sound of a car engine starting. 'That's my colleagues. We're staying on the island though. We've missed the tide to get home tonight.' Vera paused. 'What time are you all leaving in the morning?'

'Not early,' Phil said. 'Late morning.'

'I was wondering,' Vera turned to him, 'if it might be possible for you to extend your holiday for a few days. Not here on Holy Island necessarily, but somewhere local. There might be other questions and I can't stand virtual interviews. I'm so crap at the tech. It would stretch the budget to send an officer down to London just for a chat.'

There was a moment of silence and then Philip gave a little laugh. 'No problem, Inspector. That was already part of the plan. It's a long way to come just for the weekend. A friend of mine owns a holiday cottage here on the island and I'll be staying for the rest of the week. I'll let you have the address and you have our phone numbers.'

Annie stared at him, shocked. How odd that Philip hadn't mentioned this before! It seemed as if it had been a deliberate strategy to keep the information to himself. And who was the friend who owned the holiday cottage? Of course, it didn't need to be anybody local. It could be a Londoner who'd bought a place as an escape. Only a southerner would be able to afford island prices these days. But still the secrecy seemed strange. She expected Vera to leave then, but the woman was still standing, looking around the room. She saw the photo that Annie had brought out earlier, and picked it up.

'Is this from the old days?'

'It was taken on that first weekend fifty years ago.'

Vera turned to Annie. 'Eh, pet, I'd know you anywhere. Those cheekbones.' She put the photo on a table and sat down. Annie had hoped the detective was on her way to her car. Vera unnerved her. 'Tell me about the others.'

So, Annie had no choice but to explain. 'That's Isobel, Lou's sister. She's looking lovely here, Louisa.'

'I remember that dress. Laura Ashley. I envied it, but Issy would never let me borrow it.' Louisa looked down and seemed lost in memories.

'The short one's Rick, Charlotte's the glamorous blonde standing next to him. Philip and Ken are the radgies with the flares and the attitude.'

'And who's this good-looking fellow?' Vera pointed to Daniel.

Annie could see that Dan had been very good-looking. She'd been drawn to him by the dark hair, the almost black eyes. Her nana had said, in her most disapproving voice, after meeting him for the first time: 'That lad's got gypsy blood. You want to steer clear of him.' But her nana had been wary of everyone who lived more than twenty miles from

Kimmerston. Annie had been attracted to him just because he looked different, exotic.

'That's my ex,' she said lightly, and then she changed the subject, turning to the others. 'We'll still kick off with our usual walk before we leave, shall we?'

'Another tradition?' Vera smiled.

'One of Rick's ideas,' Annie said. 'A bracing walk to clear the head before the drive home.' She looked round the room. 'We should still do it, shouldn't we? Just to remember him?'

'He used to swim in the lough, so we'd walk there and watch,' Louisa said. 'But I don't think any of us will be doing that tomorrow.'

'He was one of those wild swimmers?' Vera seemed fascinated. 'They get everywhere, these days.'

'Not so fashionable fifty years ago,' Phil said, 'but he swam then too. And on every Sunday morning at a reunion since.'

'Perhaps we *should* swim!' The words were out before Annie had really thought about it: the icy water, the frosty grass on bare feet, while they were getting ready for the plunge. 'A kind of tribute.'

She was half hoping they would all say she was crazy and they couldn't contemplate it, but nobody did. There was a moment of silence. Perhaps nobody wanted to be the first to dismiss the idea.

In the end, Philip spoke, laughing. 'Why not! Rick would love it! All of us, me especially: overweight – monster belly and wrinkled skin – blue with cold, floundering about. He'd be looking at us and mocking.'

'Well, that'll be a sight to be sure,' Vera said. 'I might come and watch. It deserves an audience.'

'For me it'll be a very quick dip,' Annie said, 'and I don't have my bathers with me, so it'll be knickers and a T-shirt.' She was pleased with the plan all the same. Despite the cold and knowing she'd make an absolute fool of herself. And it was awesome that the others had agreed. Better something like this than that they all just slide away without acknowledging Rick's death. She remembered a poem they'd done in English A level with Judy Marshall. T. S. Eliot. Better a bang than a whimper, she thought. Rick's philosophy every time.

'Rick would have gone skinny-dipping.' Louisa's eyes were glinting suddenly with mischief. This was the old Lou. The person who'd attracted Rick, made him jealous when it was Ken who got in first. Not respectable head teacher Lou.

'Is that a challenge?'

'Why not?' Lou looked around the group. 'Why not?'

Chapter Eighteen

WHEN VERA GOT BACK TO THE Seahorse, Joe and Holly were sitting in the lounge bar, with drinks and cutlery in front of them. They were chatting as if they were almost friends. Vera wasn't sure what she made of that. It was good that they had a constructive working relationship, but she wouldn't want them forming some sort of alliance against her.

The lounge had been arranged with tables, like a restaurant, but it still felt like a traditional pub. There was no television. No piped music. A coal fire belted out the heat and covered every undusted surface with a fine coating of soot. The dining tables were a new addition in the lounge. The Seahorse had only just started serving food, an attempt to attract tourists as well as the locals. In theory. In the snug, which had its main door from the street, there was lots of noise. It seemed all the islanders had decamped there.

Vera looked across the hall into the smaller room, at the locals standing at the bar, the elderly men playing dominos, the women at the dartboard, and felt a moment of envy. In the over-heated bar, there was a sense of community which she'd never experienced in her personal life, except perhaps when she went to visit Jack and Joanna. They always managed to make her feel welcome.

'Well,' she said. 'They're planning on going skinny-dipping in the lough in the morning. A kind of tribute to Rick Kelsall. I might go and watch.' A pause. 'I might even join them.'

The look of horror on the young officers' faces made her laugh. 'Ah, I'm only kidding. About me, at least. The world's not ready for that. But really, I thought you youngsters weren't into body-shaming. You should have a word with yourselves.'

A young waitress arrived and Vera ordered pie and chips and a pint. She waited until the lass had disappeared behind the bar before speaking again.

'Did you find out any more about the single woman who was staying on the island on Friday night?'

'Yes.' Holly was drinking white wine and soda, which had never seemed like much of a drink to Vera. Neither one thing nor the other. 'She was staying here. Gave her name as Joanne Haswell, but no ID was required and she paid in cash.'

'So, she hadn't booked in advance?' Vera thought that was very strange. Would you just turn up to a place like Holy Island on spec and risk being stranded with nowhere to stay?

'No.'

'Was that usual?'

'The landlady thought it was a bit weird, but there's not much call for single rooms, apparently, not over half-term at least, so there was no problem finding her a place.'

'Have we got a description?' Vera was running through possibilities. 'Was she a young woman?'

Holly shook her head. 'Middle-aged. The landlady checked

her in and had her down as a teacher making the most of the last weekend of half-term. She didn't remember anything else.'

'Not one of Kelsall's victims seeking revenge then,' Vera said. 'Those were all young lasses, weren't they?'

'I still haven't got any details,' Holly said, 'but that's certainly the impression given in the press.'

Vera took out the photograph she'd taken from Annie Laidler. She wiped the table with a napkin and put it so they could all see. 'This is the Pilgrims' House lot, at that first weekend. Still kids.' She pointed with a stubby finger. 'In the middle is Judy Marshall, the teacher. Let's see if we can track her down. She hardly looks older than they are, so she's probably still alive. Can you recognize the others?'

'That's Annie! She's hardly changed.' Joe shook his head. 'The others? That's obviously the glamorous Charlotte and the short, skinny one is Rick Kelsall.' A pause. 'He'd have been bullied at our school, looking like that.' He pointed to the two lads standing together. 'And they'd have been the ones doing the bullying.'

'Ken and Philip,' Vera said. The lads were staring out at the camera, intense, unsmiling. She stuck out her finger again. 'That's Annie's ex, Daniel. I'll talk to him. He was at the first reunion when this woman died, apparently after having a major row with Rick Kelsall. And this is the deceased: Louisa's big sister, Isobel Hall.' Her finger hovered over the image. 'She's bonny too, isn't she?'

Bonny, she thought, was an understatement. The young woman was wearing a high-waisted floral dress, and she had a black cloak around her shoulders. It looked as if she was an actor in a romantic costume drama, but perhaps the girls did dress like that in the seventies, even when they weren't trying to impress. The breeze had caught her hair and dark curls were blowing away from her face. Vera spoke to the woman in the picture.

'Eh lass, let's find out why you died.'

It was nearly closing time and though the noise in the public bar was as loud as ever, the lounge was empty. Holly and Joe had finished their meals and headed upstairs. To their separate rooms. Vera had a little giggle at the thought that it might be otherwise. She'd slipped in another beer when the pie had arrived and drunk it so quickly that it had gone to her head. A proper pint! It was impossible to imagine Holly and Joe having a wild night together. Joe was too upright and Holly too uptight. But all the same . . . She giggled again.

She climbed the stairs with its threadbare carpet to her room. It was big and draughty, and over the bar. She propped the photo up against the dressing table mirror, and random thoughts drifted in and out of her head, as the sounds of the late drinkers provided a background.

Only Connect. Let's connect those young things to the people they've become and we might get some sort of answer. She was still listening to the laughter below when she fell asleep.

Chapter Nineteen

THE GROUP DECIDED THAT THEY'D GO to the lough early, before Vera Stanhope made it out to the Pilgrims' House to see them. She might insist on coming too and this escapade was mad enough at their age. The last thing they needed was an onlooker. Besides, the swim was for Rick, not a kind of performance for an outsider to gawp at. They took the direct path to the lough across the frozen fields. Not more than half a mile from the house, so they'd be able to hurry back into the warm for breakfast. Annie had been up before the rest of them and had put together flasks of coffee, found an airing cupboard with extra towels.

The sun was up, but very low in the sky, the beams sliced by the trees in the spinney next to the house. The branches were almost completely bare now, black against the light. They'd gained an hour, because the clocks had gone back, so it seemed somehow that they were beyond time. In a different zone altogether. There was a buzz of excitement as they walked. They were giggly as kids, but well wrapped up in heavy coats and hats and gloves, so by the time they arrived at the water,

Annie was roasting. They stood, an awkward little group on the bank, and for a moment she wondered if they'd back out. If someone would say: *Look guys, this is crazy, we don't have to do it*. If that did happen, she'd probably agree and traipse back to the house for sausage sandwiches.

But Philip was already taking his clothes off. Hard to believe now that he was a vicar, that if he weren't taking the week off, he'd be giving a sermon, standing in the pulpit for the first communion service of the day in front of a small gaggle of elderly women. And he didn't just take off his outdoor clothes, but everything!

He had his back to them and was running to the water, and then everyone was following. Louisa, firm-stomached and gym fit. Even Ken. Following Louisa's lead, he'd taken off his clothes and folded them on top of the waterproof coat she'd put on the bank, like an obedient child getting ready for bed.

Hitting the water was intense. It was like being stabbed with needles, and the cold took Annie's breath away, making her feel panicky and anxious. She gave a strangled scream of pain. Philip had already swum to the other bank, a brisk crawl, insulated perhaps by all that fat. Louisa followed him, leaving Ken behind on the bank. Her husband watched her, seeming bewildered, bereft, so Annie thought she should go back and check on him. But then he plunged in too, and was spluttering and laughing. Not hurt by the cold, but joyous, as if he hardly felt it, like a child splashing in a paddling pool on a glorious summer's day.

Suddenly, Annie felt more alive than she had since she was a girl. It was a bit better than any drug she could imagine. A high. It was the cold and being with friends, the strange adventure of it, so outside her daily routine. And this place. The quiet, the trees sculptural and reflected in the water. The memories of all those other times.

They didn't stay in long. Soon they were out and shy again, wrapping themselves in towels, shivering. But still glowing. Louisa seemed quite a different person. Relaxed. Annie realized how uptight the woman had been for the whole weekend.

'Wasn't that fabulous?' she said. 'Why haven't we done it before? Why did we just come and watch when Rick took the plunge?'

'He never asked us to join him,' Louisa said. 'He just wanted an audience.'

They sat huddled in their coats and jerseys, drinking the coffee from Annie's flasks, teeth still chattering, and it was only then that Vera approached them.

'Well!' she said, when she was close enough to speak. 'I didn't know where to look.'

'You were watching?' Louisa seemed amused rather than cross.

'I got here just as you were all getting into the water. I wasn't expecting you to have such an early start, but when nobody was there at the house, I knew where you'd be. Then I thought you wouldn't want me here while you were getting dressed. All that fumbling with underwear. I never liked it, even when my dad took me to the beach up at Newton for a treat.' She paused for a moment and seemed lost in reflection. 'Not that he did very often. Only when he had other reasons for being there, and then it was the ice cream I liked best, not the water.' Another pause and a wide smile. 'But you don't need to worry. I averted my eyes.'

Annie got to her feet then. The arrival of Vera had spoilt the moment, made her relive finding Rick's body again and made his death seem real. For a moment the exhilaration of the icy water had made her forget. She led the others back to the house. Vera walked beside her. 'What's the plan now?'

'Breakfast and then everyone will head home. Except Philip, I suppose, as he's staying on the island for the rest of the week. I'll hang on for a bit to tidy up. We've got the place until midday.'

'That's always your job, is it? Doing the cooking and clearing up the mess?'

'No!' But Annie thought Vera was right and certainly there'd been times when she'd resented it. Not the chores themselves but the assumption that she'd be the last person here, to do the last sweep of the place and return the keys. 'We share the cooking and the others have much further to go than I do. It just makes sense.'

Vera didn't comment, but Annie thought the woman had read her mind and understood. Assumptions would probably have been made about *her* too, throughout her career.

Breakfast would be sausage and bacon sandwiches eaten in the kitchen, wrapped in paper napkins to save dirtying plates again. The meat bought from a local farm shop, naturally. Annie grilled bacon and sliced the remaining deli sourdough bread, while the others started packing. Another of the weekend rituals. Sometimes she wondered if it would be different if she had a partner with her. It felt occasionally that because she was single, she was seen as a lesser being, or at least as if there was nobody else on her side. That she was taken for granted. *Good old Annie, provider of hot drinks, comfort food, and sympathy.* As if she never felt lonely and that, at her age, she didn't have a right to expect more than this. As if they were doing her a favour simply by letting her tag along.

Vera hovered while she prepared breakfast, offering to help, but actually getting in the way. All the time, she was probing Annie with questions about the others, their relationships with Rick, and any problems they might have had with him.

'I can't see,' Vera said, 'how a vicar could be so relaxed with someone like Rick Kelsall. All his women.'

Annie looked up, then realized she was still holding the bread knife, as if it were some sort of weapon, and set it down on the counter.

'Philip has never been judgemental.'

'Hating the sin but not the sinner,' Vera said. 'I've never found it that easy to separate the two.'

Annie was saved from having to answer, because the others trooped in. It was almost as if they'd been waiting until the food was ready. They ate quickly. Most years they lingered, chatting, until the last minute, not wanting the weekend to be over, but today they were eager to go, wary of every word they exchanged with the inspector listening in. The carefree swim seemed from a different time. Vera left the building with the rest of them. She stood for a moment talking to Louisa. Annie wondered what that could be about, but the conversation was soon over.

Vera waved the Hamptons and Philip off, and stood by her battered Land Rover until their cars had disappeared down the lane. Annie saw that Rick's vehicle had already gone. The police must have taken it for some kind of forensic investigation. She was willing Vera to go too, so she could clear the place and get home to grieve in peace, but the woman stood, solid as the rock in the crags above them holding Lindisfarne Castle.

In the end she opened the door of her Land Rover, fished

in the dash and handed Annie a card. 'My numbers. Home and work, and the mobile will get me anytime. At least when I've got reception. It's not brilliant in my cottage. If you think of anything that might help, just give me a shout.'

Vera had slipped the card into Annie's hand in a way that was almost furtive, though there was nobody watching. Annie nodded, and, at last, Vera did climb into her vehicle, started the engine and it drove off, belching fumes and noise.

Chapter Twenty

JOE THOUGHT IT WAS ODD TO drive off the island. It was as if he were shifting from somewhere dreamlike, made up of water and shimmering light, back to the real world, solid and mundane. It wasn't like him to have such fancies, but he thought he could understand why the friends had returned to the Pilgrims' House every five years. It wasn't just about catching up with people they were close to. The place had a certain magic. They'd all grown up to have responsible jobs, and commitments, and things had become a little routine and predictable. The island transported them back to a time when they were young and free, and life was exciting and full of possibilities.

He'd almost arrived home when there was a call from the boss, her voice as loud on the phone as it was in person.

'I was chatting to Louisa before she left. Her mam's still alive. She's ninety and living in her own home. It's an address in Morpeth. She's sharp as a tack apparently.'

Joe could tell what was coming next and tried to pre-empt her. 'Sal needs me back. She's planning a proper Sunday lunch and I promised I'd be there.'

'No rush.' Vera's voice was easy, relaxed. She knew she'd get what she wanted from him. She always did. 'You can go later this afternoon. I'd do it myself but you're so good with old people. A lovely manner. That's what everyone says.' A pause. 'Just talk to her about Isobel. Louisa hasn't been very forthcoming and she said she was in a rush to get home when I tried to talk to her just now. You can understand that, with a husband like Ken. He was fretting when they were setting off, but he provides a convenient excuse. I can't help thinking that Isobel's death is in some way connected to her family. According to Louisa, the lass was her mam's favourite. The apple of her eye. Let's see what she says.'

Joe didn't argue. There was no point. 'It'll have to wait until after lunch.'

'Of course. Whenever suits you best. Give me a shout this evening and tell me what you've got.'

Mrs Barbara Hall lived in a detached bungalow on a quiet street on the edge of the town. The garden was immaculate and a handrail led to the front door. She knew that Joe was coming. She was slender, upright, and looked younger than Joe had been expecting. He thought how sad it was that Louisa's mother was so much more independent than her own husband.

'You're absolutely on time.' There was a hint of a faint Scottish accent in her voice. 'I do value punctuality. The kettle has just boiled. I'll make tea.' She looked at him sharply. 'You do take tea?'

'Certainly.'

'Make yourself at home in the sitting room and I'll bring it through.' She returned with a tray, and a plate of small scones, already buttered and covered with jam.

'The jam is shop bought, I'm afraid. I used to make my own.' A pause. 'Would you pour. I have arthritis in my wrists, and sometimes I'm not so steady.' She looked at him. 'I understand that you're here because of the murder on Holy Island. I've been watching it on the news. I watch far too much television these days. I used to despise it, but it passes the time.'

'The victim, Rick Kelsall, was a friend of your daughters.'

'Of Isobel, my elder daughter. Louisa was younger.'

'You knew him?'

'Oh yes! We knew them all.' Her voice was warm. 'People talk about their schooldays being the happiest time of their lives, but that wasn't true in my case, Sergeant. I grew up during the war, and even afterwards it was a drab time of rationing and restriction. Of boredom. My father had been badly affected by his experiences – he'd been in Burma – and he was constantly angry. My mother couldn't stand up to him and her life was a misery. My happiest time came later, when I was a wife and a mother, watching my girls grow up into strong young women. It was a joy to see them have the happiness at school that I'd missed out on: the friendship, the excitement of new ideas. We had rather a large house then. My husband was an engineer and he had his own business. We were doing very well. We encouraged the girls to bring their friends into our home. I tried not to intrude, but I loved their company.'

'Can you remember the names of Isobel's friends?'

'Oh yes, I can. I remember them all, vividly. There was Annie Laidler. She was the quiet one, shy. It was as if she felt she didn't really have the right to be there. Philip seemed the complete opposite, a bit edgy, arrogant even, but underneath, you could tell he was a very nice boy.' She looked up, suddenly amused. 'He went on to become a priest. In my wildest dreams I would never have predicted that for him. Charlotte Thomas was lovely to look at, but a bit shallow, I always thought. Ken was kind, staid, a bit boring. Daniel had dark, romantic good looks. There was a touch of Heathcliff about him. He wasn't as academic as the others, and that made him something of an outsider, but look what he's gone on to become!'

Joe must have looked confused, because she went on to explain. 'He's Daniel Rede. You must have heard of him! He runs that big holiday park on the bay, very close to the island. And also half the holiday homes in rural Northumberland, if my gossiping neighbours are to be believed. He'll be worth more than the rest of them put together. Certainly, more than Rick, for all that he's become so famous.'

'Rick was a special friend of Isobel's?'

'I think he was. Not a boyfriend, though she had plenty of those too, but the two of them were very close. Rick was an only child and his parents were both doctors, always busy. Rick treated Isobel more like a sister. They confided in each other.' She looked up at Joe and smiled. 'And he was like the son I never had.' There was another pause. 'We gave them a room in the basement. The teenagers played music there, listened to records, ate the suppers I made for them. They drank, I suspect, too much. It was all candles, posters on the walls. And they talked. They never stopped talking. I suppose I was living vicariously, but I loved the fact that those conversations were going on just beneath my feet.'

'You said that Isobel had boyfriends. Did she go out with any of the boys in the group?'

'If she did, Sergeant, she never confided in me.' A pause. 'I did have the sense that she had a serious crush on one of them, but that it was never reciprocated.' There was another moment of silence. 'Or perhaps that the boy was already taken, and she was dreaming of the unattainable. That was probably more likely. Isobel usually told me everything, but she knew I'd disapprove if she tried to break up an established romantic relationship.' Barbara didn't sound disapproving. Joe thought she would have forgiven her elder daughter anything.

Joe considered the information. At the time that the group had first gone to Holy Island, hadn't all the lads been taken? They all had girlfriends. Except Philip. Ken had been going out with Louisa, Rick with Charlotte, and Annie with Daniel. Who was most likely to have caught Isobel's fancy? If there'd been sibling rivalry, perhaps Ken had been the object of the young woman's desire. She certainly wouldn't have admitted to her mother that she lusted after her younger sister's boyfriend! But the argument outside the house before Isobel's accident would suggest it had probably been Rick who'd floated through the lass's dreams at night. Joe decided to move on, or rather to go back to the beginning.

'They went to Holy Island, on some sort of team-building course run by the school.'

'Yes,' Barbara said. 'Only Connect. That was the start of it, the trigger for those intense, very close friendships. Isobel came back changed. Lit-up. It seemed almost as if she'd had an evangelical experience. All that mattered, she said, was honesty. You could forgive anything if you had a true understanding of the other person, if there was a real connection. My husband disapproved. He thought it had been wrong for people with no training in the field to mess with the young people's minds. He still believed that emotions should be tightly restrained.'

'And you? What did you think?'

'I thought it was glorious. It felt as if they were properly alive, vivid, in a way that I never was as a young person.' She paused. 'I envied them. I wished that I'd been there.'

'Was Louisa a part of the group? Was she invited to the gatherings in the basement?'

Barbara Hall frowned. 'Not at first, though she very much wanted to be. She was three years younger, and I suppose she felt left out. She was always competitive, always saw Isobel as some sort of rival, though really there was no need. Louisa was stunning in her own right: bright, beautiful. But perhaps a younger sibling can sometimes feel daunted when the older sister is so successful.'

'She must have joined in when she started going out with Ken?'

'Yes.' The old woman paused. 'I did wonder if that was the only reason that she went out with him. To infiltrate the gang.'

Joe thought infiltrate was a strange word to use. It sounded aggressive, almost as if Louisa was a sort of terrorist. 'She and Ken married, though, so there must have been more to the relationship than that!'

'Yes.' Barbara sighed. 'I suppose there must. I never thought that the marriage would last. I'd have found the man far too boring. And yet here they are. Forty years on. Poor Ken. They've been happy enough, I suppose. Until the illness took hold of him, at least.'

It didn't seem to Joe like much of an endorsement, but he wasn't here to talk about Louisa's relationship with her husband. 'It must have been dreadful when Isobel died.'

She stared at him, clear-eyed now. 'Do you have children, Sergeant?'

'I do.'

'Then perhaps you'll understand. It's the guilt that's so hard. We gave Isobel the car to celebrate her graduation. She'd got a first-class degree and we were very proud of her. Otherwise, she'd have taken a lift home with Louisa and Ken, and she'd have been safe. That haunted my husband until he died.'

'Did you ever find out what caused the accident?'

A silence. 'I suspect Isobel caused it, Sergeant. She was always reckless, a little wild. It was what made her so intriguing. Of course, I *could* blame Louisa and Ken for disappearing onto the island, so that Isobel hung around at the Pilgrims' House until just before the tide. I *could* blame her other friends for not persuading her to wait until the causeway was clear again.' A pause. 'But long ago, I decided that way lay madness. It was easier to accept the guilt myself.'

'I think perhaps her friends did try to persuade her,' Joe said.

When Annie Laidler had seen Rick and Isobel arguing just before the accident, Joe thought it was likely that the man had just been telling Isobel to wait on the island for the tide to go out again. There was possibly nothing sinister in the encounter at all.

'Why are you here, Sergeant?' For the first time since he'd arrived the woman sounded tired. 'All that happened so long ago and I can't believe that my daughter's death can be relevant to your present investigation.'

It seemed to Joe that she was right, and that they were clutching at straws. 'My boss is always keen on the detail,' he said. 'On the background. And we thought it might be upsetting. Another Holy Island death. Even though so many years have passed, it must bring back distressing memories.'

Barbara Hall sat so long in silence, that Joe wondered if she was ill, if she'd had some kind of mini-stroke perhaps. 'Mrs Hall?'

'Then it was very kind of you to visit,' she said at last. 'I've enjoyed telling you about Isobel. She comes alive for me when I talk about her. As she was then of course, not as she would be now. She'd be an old woman too now and I suspect she'd have hated that. I have more lovely memories than bad.' There was another pause, and when she spoke again her voice was bitter. 'I wish my younger daughter had been as thoughtful. She didn't phone to tell me about Rick's murder. *She* didn't realize that all those memories would come back. She let me find out about his death on the television news. I find that hard to understand.'

Chapter Twenty-One

VERA GOT OFF THE ISLAND JUST before the tide. She could feel the tug of the current, swirling around the Land Rover's wheels at the deepest point of the causeway. She could see how Isobel might have misjudged it. A young lass, a bit headstrong, after an argument with a lad, wouldn't want to hang on, waiting in a toxic atmosphere with no escape. She'd be prepared to take a risk. She'd been driving a light little car, with no weight to it, and the power of the water had swept it away. There was probably no more to the accident than that.

Vera was at home when Joe phoned. She was restless, not able to settle to anything, the facts of the case rolling round in her head like breakers on a beach, making no sense.

'Well? What have you got for me?'

She listened as Joe described his conversation with Barbara Hall. 'So, Annie's ex is Daniel Rede, who runs that place on the coast!' Until then, Daniel had been a shadowy figure, on the edge of the group. Because he hadn't been at the Pilgrims' House on the night of Rick's murder, Vera had dismissed him as a possible suspect.

'According to Louisa's mother and I'm sure she'd know.' Joe paused. 'She said that Rede's minted. Worth all the rest of them put together.'

'Well, it's a big place he's got there.'

'I used to go camping with my grandad when I was a lad. It was canny rough then, but now it's all glamping and luxury lodges. They say the restaurant at the top of the old tower is up for a Michelin star!'

'Fancy!' Vera wasn't impressed. She thought that meant you'd come out as hungry as when you went in. 'Did you get anything else useful?'

'It's probably not relevant now, but it sounds as if there was a real rivalry between Isobel and Louisa. And you were right. Isobel *was* the apple of her mother's eye. There still seems to be a tension between Barbara and Louisa. I'm not sure there's very much contact.'

'Any idea why?'

Joe took a moment to answer. 'No. Unless Barbara blames her somehow for still being alive. If one of the daughters was going to die, I get the impression Barbara would much rather it had been Louisa.'

'Oh!' Vera couldn't quite restrain a little gasp of pain. She knew what it was like to be an unwanted child, the unloved survivor. Hector, her father, would have saved his wife over his daughter every time.

She switched off her phone and looked again at the yellowing photograph of the young friends. They were all becoming more alive for her now. Apart from Isobel who was dead. And Daniel, who lived as close to Holy Island as it was possible to get and still be on the mainland. Daniel, who was apparently minted. Vera thought of Annie Laidler, working in the deli from dawn to dusk, living in a little terraced house, and wondered what she made of her former husband's extreme wealth. Vera pulled on her coat and set out again.

Rede's Tower was on the coast to the south of Holy Island. It didn't call itself a holiday park. That would have sounded far too vulgar. The classy sign next to the road said Rede's Tower Lodges, and a drive swept down through managed woodland to the old pele tower, a tall stone building which must have been built as a look-out against raiders from the sea. The tower had been renovated, to provide the hub of the site. Tall windows had been built into the top floor and must provide a magnificent view. The restaurant might be worth visiting, Vera thought, even if the food was shite.

She'd been here once with Hector, keeping watch while he was stealing peregrine chicks. That had been long before the place was tarted up and turned into a playground for the wealthy middle classes. The falcons had bred on the tower's parapet and Hector had risked his life scrambling up the crumbling stonework to reach them. The adventure, the adrenaline rush, had been as important to him as the cash he'd made from the Middle Eastern falconer who'd bought them.

The building was close to the water. The tide was out and there were acres of sand stretching across the bay towards the island. At low tide, it might seem as if it would be possible to paddle across, but Vera knew that gave a false impression. The bay was crossed with deep gullies, invisible from the shore, full even at dead low water.

There *were* still caravans on the site, but they were closer to the main road and hidden from the tower by a belt of pines. The lodges spread across landscaped acres and had the best views of the sea. The geography of the site seemed deliberately to mark class distinctions. Social mobility meant moving from the vans to the wooden lodges, with their hot tubs, firepits and the hammocks strung from the veranda roofs.

Vera parked by the restored pele and went into reception. A young woman in a burgundy uniform sat behind a desk. The walls were thick and it was strangely quiet inside. They'd kept and glazed the slit windows on the lower floors, so there was little natural light.

'If you're here about the cleaner's job, it's the room at the top of the stairs, first door on your right.'

'Ah no, pet, I'm not a cleaner. Not in the way you mean, at least, though I've cleared up a few messes in my time. Detective Inspector Vera Stanhope.'

'Oh God, I'm so sorry! There've been women in all day. We wouldn't usually interview on a Sunday, but we've got lots of people off sick and we're a bit desperate. The place has been booked up for months.'

'Nothing to be sorry about. And nothing wrong with being a cleaner.' Vera leaned against the desk. 'I'd like to talk to Mr Rede. Mr Daniel Rede.'

The woman looked up and her tone changed, became a little less open. 'I'm not sure. He's taken the weekend off and that happens so rarely that I wouldn't want to disturb him. Perhaps I could help you?'

'Sorry, pet. It's not to do with the business. I do need to speak to him.' She paused, then made her voice confidential. 'This is personal. An old friend has died.'

'Oh right.' The woman still sounded doubtful, but more sympathetic. 'I suppose it'll be okay in that case. He and Katherine are at home.'

'He's not here then?'

'They built a house on site. If you follow the track through the nature reserve, past the No Vehicles sign, you'll come to it. I'll give them a ring to let them know you'll be on your way.'

'You do that, pet.'

But Vera was wondering about the nature reserve. As a child, she'd pretended to hate Hector's distorted passion for the natural world, but somehow his knowledge of birds and plants had seeped into her consciousness and hatred had turned to affection. She had binoculars in the Land Rover and thought she might go for a wander, afterwards.

She hadn't been expecting much in the way of a reserve. She'd thought it might be a gesture to the eco-minded, affluent families who'd stay here. But driving past, she saw a substantial pond with a reedbed to one side, surrounded by scrubby bushes and trees. A couple of wooden hides looked out over the water, which reflected the coloured, dying leaves. It was tranquil, but with the turning of the year, a little sad.

The track turned sharply and there, on the edge of the woodland, stood a spectacular house. It was all wood and glass, a part of its landscape, the colour of the trunks of the trees. When the leaves were new and green, it would be completely hidden from the public spaces of the site. A Range Rover was parked outside next to a smaller hatchback, and Vera pulled up beside it. She got out and stood for a moment.

Daniel Rede opened the door almost immediately and knew who she was. As she'd promised, the receptionist had phoned to warn him of her approach.

'Come on through.'

He led her down a passage and into a room that was full of light. It faced east, one wall made of glass, and outside there was nothing to cast a shadow. This room looked out over the bay. The incoming tide was sliding over the sand. There was a view to Holy Island, which seemed so close that she felt she could reach out and touch it. With binoculars it might be possible to make out the Pilgrims' House, though the drive north to the causeway would take at least half an hour. And there *were* binoculars, on a table next to the window. Perhaps the nature reserve had been created through passion, not through affectation or a pretence at a green credential.

This outlook was so different from the part of the house built into the woodland, that the view was a shock. For a moment, Vera could do nothing but stare at it. She had a brief moment of envy. She was happy in Hector's little house in the hills, but this was spectacular. It was like living on a great liner, or in a lighthouse, and she'd never before been indoors but felt so close to the sea.

Vera turned her attention to the room itself. The furniture was sleek and smelled of money. The pale stained floorboards were covered in a long and beautiful rug in primary colours. She hoped she didn't have dog shit on her shoes. Somehow though, the space wasn't intimidating or pretentious. There were books on the shelves, piled on top of each other, the Sunday newspapers lay on a coffee table beside a couple of used mugs. Through an open door, Vera could hear a television and she caught a glimpse of a smaller, darker room. Football. A splash of black and white on the screen. Newcastle United. This place was classy but, still, it was definitely a home.

'It is a bit special, isn't it?' Daniel was standing beside her, looking out at the view. 'I never get tired of it. Different every day.' The accent was local. He glanced back towards the room with the television.

'I'm sorry,' she said. 'I'm making you miss the match.'

He smiled. 'It's nearly over and we'll not make up the difference now. It'd take a miracle. Probably best not watching the final agony.'

'You're a Toon supporter.' It wasn't a question.

'Lifelong. For my sins.'

He was wiry, tough. Not an inch of spare flesh. The dark hair of the photograph had gone, but he still had eyes the colour of coal. 'Sorry, Inspector, take a seat. How can I help you?'

She'd been preparing to dislike him, because Annie was, if not a friend, an acquaintance, and after a divorce it seemed it was impossible not to take sides. But there was something tentative and diffident about him, which she found very appealing.

'What a beautiful place!' She needed time after the shock of the light and the sea to prepare her questions.

'When I first started working here for my grandfather, I lived in a rusty caravan, so yes, this is a little bit different from that. We built here two years ago. Katherine wasn't sure about living on the job, but I talked her round.'

'Katherine's your wife?'

'My partner.' He smiled again. 'I keep asking her to marry me, but she says we're fine as we are.'

'I want to take you back a bit further than two years.'

'You're here about the murder on Holy Island. Rick Kelsall.'

'You'd heard?'

'It was on Radio Newcastle this morning.'

'Annie Laidler didn't tell you?'

He shook his head. 'Annie and I don't communicate much these days. I can't blame her.' He paused. 'Of course. It'll have been one of their daft reunions. It's that weekend. She'll have been there.' Another beat. 'How is she?'

'Shocked,' Vera said. 'She found the body.'

Someone must have scored because there was a distant sound of fans cheering, but he wasn't distracted.

'Poor lass.'

'I'm just looking for a bit of background. You were at school with most of them. Did you keep in touch?'

'Not so much after Annie and I split up. I was the one to leave so you can understand why our friends stuck by her. But, yeah, we keep in touch a bit. We used to meet up for a drink occasionally if the lads were back home visiting relatives. Now, it's the odd Zoom call.'

'You were there for that first weekend fifty years ago. What did they call it? Only Connect?'

He nodded. 'They wouldn't get away with it now. Letting kids stay up all night. Drinking. Smoking.'

'Is that how you remember it?'

'That's how it was! The others might have been taken in by all the fancy ideas, but it was just a glorified party, with the teacher so keen on wanting to appear cool that she turned a blind eye.'

'You were there for the first reunion?'

'Yes. Annie's idea. We were a real item by then. Only just married, but we'd been together since school.'

'What was it like?'

He shrugged. 'More of the same. Drinking. Staying up all night.' He paused. 'Drugs.'

'That was the weekend Isobel Hall died.'

'Yes.' He looked at her. 'I never went back after that.'

'Were you close to Isobel? Is that why you didn't go back?'

He shook his head. 'No, nothing like that. It just wasn't my scene.'

'What do you remember about the afternoon before she drove off? I understand she'd had a row with Rick Kelsall.'

'Oh, Rick had been picking at her all day. I'm not sure exactly what triggered it. Probably the fact that she hadn't been taken in by his charms. He was all extremes. If you couldn't love him, he provoked you to hate him. I didn't care about him enough to do either, which is why he left me alone.'

'You were still married, though you never went to another reunion?'

'Yeah, we struggled on for a few more years.' He seemed about to elaborate on the disintegration of the marriage, but thought better of it. 'I didn't mind Annie meeting up with her old mates, and I always had work as an excuse. I'd inherited this place by then.' He nodded vaguely towards the door through which they'd entered, towards the outside world. 'It wasn't plain sailing and I was working every hour in the day. We came close to losing it. The worst time of my life.' He thought and corrected himself. 'One of them, at least.'

'It was a family business?'

'Yeah, my grandfather had it first.' A pause. 'He'd not recognize the place now.' Vera thought the idea made him sad rather than proud.

'You must have made a fortune from it! Did that make it hard to get on with the others?' Vera was still trying to work out why Rede had never made it back to Holy Island to meet up with his friends. Even if he didn't want to stay all weekend, he was close enough just to pop in for a meal. Maybe to gloat a bit, throw the cash around, prove how well he'd done in the end, even if he'd never been as brainy as them. 'Was there a bit of envy creeping in? I can imagine Rick Kelsall not liking someone else being top dog, at least when it came to money.'

He shook his head and gave a little laugh. 'Nah, nothing like that. As I said, it just wasn't my scene. I'd only scraped into the Grammar at the thirteen-plus and I was never going to make it to university. They were all about words. Ideas. Talk about books and plays and feelings. It left me cold. Maybe they were just showing off how clever they were, but it made me feel that I shouldn't be there.'

She nodded. She'd met people like that. Folk so insecure that they needed to put other people down.

'So, you weren't tempted to go over to meet them all this weekend?'

He gave a little laugh. 'I wasn't invited, Inspector!' A pause. 'And even if I had been, I wouldn't have gone.'

'When was the last time you saw Rick Kelsall?'

'Oh goodness, quite a while ago.' He seemed to be choosing his words carefully. 'He was the one of that gang that I had least in common with. He was so confident. It was like he could get away with anything. He charmed the teachers and he could get good grades without putting in much work. I was a plodder. Everything was so much more of an effort. So, I kept in touch with Ken and Philip more. Katherine has got to know Rick a bit through her work. He interviewed her a couple of times for his show.'

Vera was about to ask for more details about that – who was this Katherine that Rick Kelsall had wanted to interview – when there was the sound of the front door opening.

'That'll be her now,' Rede said. 'She's been out for a walk. She's not really into footie. She'll do anything to avoid it.'

A woman came in and Vera had her second shock of the day. She caught herself staring, open-mouthed, like a character in some kids' cartoon. Because this was Katherine Willmore, Police and Crime Commissioner for North Northumberland. A lawyer turned quasi-politician, voted into post by the community, and essentially Vera's boss. It hadn't for a moment occurred to her that Rede's Katherine might be this woman. Vera forced her mouth shut and stood up. An automatic response, though Willmore, in jeans and a long black jumper, in stockinged feet, looked very different from the woman in the smart suit who appeared in conferences and on the media.

Vera had met her several times but didn't expect to be recognized. Willmore looked at her, however, and smiled.

'Inspector Stanhope? I thought I recognized the Land Rover. It has reached mythical status within the service. Are you here for work? To see me?'

'For work, ma'am. But not to see you.' Vera had never liked the idea of political appointments to oversee the police force, but she had time for Willmore, who was efficient, intelligent. She listened to grass roots police officers and backed them when they needed support, even when the management team seemed oblivious. 'I'm investigating the Rick Kelsall murder.'

'Yes, of course.' Katherine sat on one of the sofas, her legs tucked beneath her. 'Do sit down, Inspector. You might be at work, but I'm very definitely not. So, let's drop the formality, shall we?'

'Your partner was at school with Rick Kelsall and knew the people staying with him in the Pilgrims' House on Friday night. I'm here for a bit of background.'

'Are they all potential suspects?'

'They are. And certainly witnesses. I was hoping for an

outsider's view. But Daniel said that you'd seen Mr Kelsall more recently than he had.'

Katherine looked at her partner, but she'd spent too much time in court for her face to give anything away.

'I was telling the inspector that you'd given him a couple of interviews,' Daniel said.

'I had,' Katherine said. 'I've been trying to change the attitude to domestic abuse throughout my career, and I'll continue putting that at the top of the agenda as PCC. I've become the go-to person on the subject for many members of the press, and I'm happy to oblige. Anything that keeps the subject in the public eye. And in the minds of politicians.' She smiled at Vera. 'But you'll know that, Inspector. You've heard me on my soap box often enough.'

Vera nodded. 'Yet Rick Kelsall has been accused of harassment himself recently.'

'So it seems.' Katherine seemed about to add to the comment, but didn't continue.

'The accusations around his behaviour didn't put you off appearing on his show?' Vera was intrigued. It seemed an odd decision.

'Oh, the last time I appeared with him was almost a year ago, long before his reputation was tarnished by the popular press.'

That seemed a strange way to describe what had happened to Kelsall's career, especially from a person who was known for championing the need for victims of abuse to be heard and believed. Vera thought she'd get Holly to dig up some of those old interviews. She'd be interested to see a recording of any conversations between Kelsall and Willmore.

The PCC must have picked up Vera's confusion because she added: 'Of course, I wouldn't do it now.'

Vera nodded again to show that she understood. 'I think that's all I need to know at the moment. Thanks for your help. I'll let you get back to the match, Mr Rede.'

He smiled sadly. 'They'll have lost, most likely. I always start the season with great hopes, but by this time of year, I'm already disappointed.'

Vera smiled back. It was Katherine who led her back through the house to the door into the woods. 'Of course, do get in touch if we can help in any way.'

Vera stood for a moment in the shade. She was hungry now and decided she wouldn't bother with the walk around the pool. That could wait for another time. She was just about to get into the Land Rover and drive away when she looked up at the house. From an upper window, a woman was staring down at her. It wasn't Katherine Willmore. This woman was younger, hardly more than a girl. She saw Vera looking and the face disappeared. It was as if she'd never been there at all.

Chapter Twenty-Two

ON MONDAY MORNING, ANNIE SET OFF for work early even though she knew she'd be there long before Jax turned up. It had taken her hours to get to sleep and she was awake again before dawn. She'd taken a mug of tea back to bed, but once it was finished, she was restless and had to get up, get out. It was milder, a hint of dampness in the air, a blustery wind from the west. The washing from the weekend was still in the machine, but there was no point hanging it on the line. She could smell that rain was on its way.

In the street the dead leaves on the pavement were already soft, without their icy crunch. She unlocked the door of the deli and went inside, and was immediately wrapped up in the smell of the place, savoury and yeasty, with an undertone of spice. She put on the coffee machine, so that the drinks would be ready when Jax got in.

Annie had hoped that the routine of work would help her to relax, to forget the sight of Rick, hanging like a strange misshapen puppet from the rafter in the grandest of the Pilgrims' House's bedrooms. But she'd been in the shop on the day that he'd died and she wasn't sure she'd be able to relax here again. This place and the details of his death were twisted together, like the puppet's tangled strings.

Jax burst in soon after, big and loud and full of sympathy. 'Oh honey, I heard on the news. I know he was a friend.' But she wanted the story, and Annie had always given Jax what she wanted, so she had to relive that moment again.

'You were the person to find him?' Horror and theatre mixed together and she put her arms around Annie and held on to her, squeezed her so tight that Annie almost stopped breathing. She felt like a small mammal squashed by a boa constrictor, and she had to push Jax away.

The morning passed almost in a daze, a dream. She went through the motions, but was hardly present. It was hard to imagine her life continuing without Rick Kelsall. He'd been there for her for every crisis in her adult life and suddenly she felt very alone.

Daniel appeared suddenly. Annie had her back to the door, stretching to pull a bottle of balsamic vinegar from the shelf behind her, and when she turned around there he was, standing just inside the shop. By now it had started to rain. He was wearing an old Barbour jacket, which could well be the same as the one he'd worn when they were still together. He might be rich now, but he'd never liked shopping. There were raindrops in his hair.

Jax had seen him before she had.

'Why don't you take a break? We won't be busy for the rest of the day. Monday's always quiet.'

It would have taken Annie too much effort to have come up with an excuse, so she fetched her coat from the cupboard in the kitchen and walked with Daniel out into the street. He led her into a coffee shop, which was empty too. There was a hissing coffee machine and condensation was running down the window. It felt as if they were completely alone here, separated from the rest of the world.

'I'm sorry,' Daniel said. 'I know how much he meant to you.'

No. You really don't. You have no idea.

'What do you want, Dan?' Her voice didn't sound angry, though it had upset her, his turning up in the shop. Thrown her and made her confused. It sounded distant and very tired.

He waited before answering because the waitress was heading over to take their order.

'It is still a cappuccino you like?'

She nodded, though these days she usually went for a flat white. Again, she couldn't summon up the effort to explain that she was no longer the person he remembered.

'A woman detective came to the tower yesterday,' he said. 'I couldn't work out why. She didn't really explain. I mean, I knew Rick Kelsall was dead, but why would she want to talk to us?'

'They think he might have been murdered by one of us.' Annie could tell the words were flat, that they showed no emotion. Better that, than that she should break down in front of Dan. She imagined him holding her, stroking her hair, reassuring her that everything would work out. He'd done that when Freya had died, before he'd lost patience with her. 'By one of the group staying at the Pilgrims' House. She seems very thorough. I suppose she was looking for background information from someone who once knew us all well.'

'She believes one of the people at the reunion killed Rick?'

A pause. 'But that's crazy! I never particularly liked them, but they're not killers.'

'Why are you here?'

He shrugged. 'I don't know. An impulse, maybe. I just wanted to check you're okay.' He paused. 'And I suppose out of curiosity, if I'm honest. To know what happened over the weekend.'

'Nothing happened over the weekend. No rows! No dramas!'

'Do the police think they'll be able to sort it out quickly?' He looked up from his coffee. 'The woman who came to the house didn't seem very sharp.'

'Was that Vera Stanhope?'

He nodded. 'Katherine said she's an inspector.'

'I had to tell her about Isobel's accident. She's been digging into all our pasts.'

'What did you tell her?'

'Just that Isobel had a row with Rick and then she drove off the island at high tide and killed herself.'

'She asked me about that too.' Daniel looked up at Annie, and she found herself staring into the dark eyes. 'It was an accident, wasn't it? You're not keeping anything from me?'

'Of course not! What could there possibly be to hide?'

He didn't answer.

Eventually she found the silence intolerable. 'Why are you really here, Dan? What's this all about?'

'I suppose I'm worried that the business might be affected.' He had the grace to sound sheepish. 'The past year has been hard enough, with the weather so unreliable, and the last thing we need is an unsolved murder of a minor celebrity on our doorstep, all over the press, just as we're getting back on our feet . . .' His voice tailed off. 'I'm sorry, that must seem crass.'

Of course, she thought, *the business. That has always been his passion. He cared more about the tower than he did about me.* But somehow, she resented the obsession less than she had in the past. It was good to be with someone who'd known Rick, who had, despite the men's differences, been a good friend.

It had been months since she'd last seen Daniel and that had been at a distance in Kimmerston market. She'd glimpsed him through the crowds. He'd been standing at the cheese stall, laughing with the owner. Easy. Confident. Now, she felt a pull of the old attraction, despite his age, despite the lingering sense of betrayal. His hand was lying on the table next to the folded paper napkin and she was tempted to reach out and touch it.

'Does Katherine know you're here?'

He looked at her and shook his head. 'This is nothing to do with Katherine.' A pause. 'She's always so busy, though of course this will be difficult for her too. If the connection were to get into the press.'

Annie thought there was no connection. Not really. 'Did she send you to talk to me?'

'No!' Daniel sounded genuinely offended. 'No! Of course not.'

The waitress came with the coffees. There was a dusting of chocolate powder on the top of hers. She hated that, the sweet graininess of it, but she sipped it just the same. There was another moment of silence until the woman walked back to the kitchen.

'Vera Stanhope's a clever woman,' Annie said. 'Don't be fooled by her appearance. She'll sort it out quickly. By next season everyone will have forgotten about Rick Kelsall's death, and tourists will be flocking to Rede's Tower, glad of a holiday in your eco paradise.'

He smiled, unoffended by the mocking tone. 'Perhaps. Look, I'm sorry, I probably shouldn't have come.' He'd finished the coffee and stood up, so he was looking down at her. 'Really, I did want to check you're okay.'

'It was kind.' Annie wasn't sure what else to say. She couldn't ask him to sit down again, to be company, to stop her brooding about what had happened at the weekend. 'Keep in touch, yeah?'

'Yeah.' He smiled suddenly, and though his face was older, the smile was just the same as when he'd been a teenager. 'I'd like that.'

Then he disappeared, almost as suddenly as he'd arrived in the shop. Annie could hardly believe that the encounter had taken place. She finished the coffee and walked back to Bread and Olives. Jax was serving a couple of middle-aged tourists. When they left, she put her arm round Annie.

'What did that rat want?'

Jax knew more than anyone else about the background to their marriage and divorce. Once, on the anniversary of Freya's death, Annie had drunk too much and everything had spilled out. The grief and the guilt. Most especially the guilt. They'd been in Jax's home, a flat in a converted warehouse on the edge of the town looking out over the river. It had been late summer, rolling out towards autumn, warm and laid-back. They'd sat on the balcony in the golden light reflected from the water. It should have been a relaxed conversation, funny, entertaining.

'What is it with you and men?' Jax had asked.

For some reason, Annie had ditched her usual answer about loving her own space, not needing a man in her life. She'd started talking and she couldn't stop.

'I was young, still at Newcastle Poly. Not planning to get pregnant. Certainly not, but chaotic, not eating properly, stressing about finals. All that stuff. I always was a bit obsessive. And Dan and I were together, properly together. He was working for his grandfather, but we met up most weekends, and every vacation I went and stayed with him. Then, when I found out I was expecting, there was this excitement, you know, and the sense that everything was right. That being a mother was what I wanted. What I could do. Because I was a *very* mediocre student. Kind of semi-detached, I suppose. I wanted Dan's baby more than anything.' The words had tumbled out. It had been years since she'd talked about it. Perhaps she'd never talked about it. Not properly, except to Rick Kelsall. Her parents had been sorry about Freya of course, but there'd been an element of blame too. Of suspicion. They still hadn't quite been able to accept that Freya's death had been unavoidable. And nor had Annie. Guilt had lingered and tarnished every part of her life.

'Rede's Tower was a very different sort of place then. His parents gave us a caravan on the site to live in. It had a leaky roof when we moved in, but Dan mended the roof and really, I made it very cosy. Not a bad place to bring a baby. It was a little girl. Dan was with me when she was born and he gave her the name. Freya.' Annie had paused. Gulped for breath and gulped the wine, though Jax *never* offered wine that should be swigged.

'And in the delivery room afterwards, he asked me to marry him. There were tears running down his face. He said he wanted us to be a real family. I could see my life stretching ahead of me. I had everything I wanted. A month later we were in the registry office, with our families and our very close friends.' *Rick, Phil, Charlotte, Ken, Lou, Isobel. Everyone in the pub afterwards, getting giggly drunk. Even me, although I was breast-feeding. Then back to the caravan.*

In the apartment with its stylish art and the evening sun pouring through the window, Jax had poured more wine and waited for the rest of the story. Annie had known she couldn't stop there.

'Freya had been with us all day, and seemed happy and well. But she didn't wake up in the night for a feed, and when I got up late, panicked and sick with anxiety she was lying still and cold in her cot. Dead. Cot death. You don't hear so much about it now, but then it was a thing. I was twenty-one, with a new husband and a dead baby.'

'Oh, my love.' Jax had been in tears. 'My poor love.'

A couple of months later it had been the Pilgrims' House reunion. The first time Annie had been away from Rede's Tower since Freya's death, apart from the funeral. She'd been reluctant to go but Rick had persuaded her. He could charm anyone to do what he wanted, but especially Annie. 'Come,' he'd said. 'It'll be good for you to be with friends.'

And for a while, it had been. Dan had been a bit quiet, but he'd wanted to be there. He'd enjoyed being somewhere different, where the atmosphere lifted occasionally and people felt they could laugh. There hadn't been much laughter in the caravan. Everyone had understood when Annie had wanted long walks on her own, or time alone in the chapel. They'd swept Daniel off to the pub, provided him with company when he'd needed it. Then Isobel had crashed her car and there'd been another death. Another funeral.

'Is that why you divorced?' Jax had asked that late summer evening in the airy apartment, as she'd opened another bottle of wine. 'Because you lost Freya?'

Annie had thought about that and tried to explain:

'I guess so, though we were very young. Perhaps it wouldn't have lasted anyway.'

I stuck memories of the baby in a big black box at the back of my head. But sometimes they jumped out, like a jack-in-a-box, and nothing between us was the same again. I couldn't love Dan like I loved Freya, because she would always be perfect. Of course, he resented that. I couldn't blame him.

She hadn't spoken those words though. Jax had reached out for her hand and they'd sat in silence, staring over the water, until the sun had set.

Back in the present, in the shop that had become a second home, Annie leaned into Jax's chest, then pulled herself gently away. 'Dan's not a rat,' she said. 'He came to offer support, to see how I was doing.'

'Just take care,' Jax said. 'He'll be after something. I've never yet met a man who only wanted to offer support.'

Chapter Twenty-Three

THERE WAS A BLUSTERY SHOWER JUST as Vera was running from her car into the police station. The place was an anachronism, Victorian red brick, not fit for purpose, and soon, she knew, the authority would decide to flatten it, move the officers to a new concrete building out of town and sell the site for residential development. Kimmerston was going up in the world and it would make someone a fortune. Vera thought that might be the time she'd start considering retirement. Though she was always moaning about this place, she couldn't imagine being based anywhere else.

She called her core team into her cramped office to plan actions for the day. This wasn't the formal briefing she'd organize for the whole team that evening, but a chance for them to gather their thoughts and think of an immediate way forward. She hung her coat over the radiator to dry and throughout the meeting it steamed, smelling like wet dog, causing a stream of moisture to run down the filthy window like tears down a made-up face.

'Joe, you went to see Isobel and Louisa's mum. Fill us in.'

There weren't enough chairs for him to sit, so he was leaning against the door.

'It seems there's no love lost between Louisa and Barbara, her mother. Louisa only lives just across the border in Cumbria, and Barbara's very elderly now, but there doesn't seem to be much contact.' He frowned. 'It wouldn't hurt her to phone or Facetime once in a while.'

'I'm guessing Louisa's got her hands full with her husband,' Vera said. She thought you could only do *so* much caring, and it was easy for Joe to judge. He talked about his kids a lot, but left most of the hands-on childcare to Sal.

'Maybe, but I think the coolness goes back a lot further than that. There was a good bit of sibling rivalry as the girls were growing up, I'd say. And the mother didn't hide the fact that Isobel was the favourite. If Rick was killed because someone blamed him for Isobel's death, I really don't think that person would have been Louisa. I'm not saying Louisa was glad her sister died, but I don't think she was so moved by the loss that she's brooded over it for all these years and taken revenge.'

'I agree,' Vera said. 'That never made sense to me. Why now? This must have been triggered by something much more recent. But you got some useful info on Annie Laidler's ex from Barbara, and we've been able to follow that up.'

'Yes.' Joe directed his answer to Holly and Charlie. 'Daniel, who was in the Pilgrims' House at the original weekend and the first reunion, turns out to be Daniel Rede, the owner of Rede Tower lodges, that flash holiday place not far from the island.'

'I went to see him yesterday afternoon.' Vera paused and took a deep breath before making the dramatic announcement. 'And who should be in his house but our esteemed PCC, Katherine Willmore.'

'What was she doing there?' Holly seemed almost starstruck. She'd always admired Willmore. Vera had guessed that she liked the style and the politics of the woman: sleek, professional, pragmatic. Now, she thought Hol might see Willmore's involvement in the investigation as a chance to get to know the woman better; Holly might even see the contact as a potential step to promotion.

'She's Daniel Rede's partner.' Vera paused again. 'Which they've been very discreet about. Has been for years apparently, though I've never seen anything about the relationship in the press. I haven't told Watkins yet. This is really going to rattle his cage. A high-profile journo is one thing. The big boss on the edge of the case is another altogether.'

'We have to treat her as any other potential witness, don't we?' Charlie always looked half-asleep, as if he were hardly listening, but often, Vera thought, he was the sharpest member of the team.

'She's not even that though, is she?' Holly was standing up for the woman already, battling on her behalf. 'They might live on the same bit of coast as the locus, but there's no evidence that either she or Daniel were on the island that night. All they can do is provide a bit of background information. I still think that Rick Kelsall's treatment of younger colleagues is more relevant as a motive than something that happened years ago.'

'You're probably right, Hol.' Sometimes, Vera thought, managing the team was like dealing with a bunch of squabbling teens. She might never have been a mother, but she certainly understood the concept of sibling rivalry. 'Have we tracked down the complainant in the harassment case yet?'

Holly shook her head. 'Nothing so far. The production

company have really kept a lid on it and I haven't found anyone in the media who's willing to talk.'

'Well, if anyone can track her down, you're the person to do it.' Vera had learned that, while *she'd* find these snippets of praise patronizing – would make her feel like throwing up in fact – they could motivate her DC. 'And can you front up contact with Rick Kelsall's former colleagues and bosses? I assume he had some sort of business manager or agent. Talk to them as well as the executives at the TV company. Persuade them to give you a bit more than the company line. Rick had talked to Charlotte and to his friends about writing this book, about bringing the past back to life. We really need to find out more about that. If he was planning some major reveal about what happened, we might find that Isobel's death is relevant after all.'

'You think someone killed him to stop the book being written?' Charlie was sceptical.

'Well, it's some sort of motive, and we don't have a lot else to go on so far.'

'What about money?' Joe said. 'According to Barbara Hall, Kelsall wasn't as rich as Daniel Rede, but he won't have been on the breadline. Do we know who benefits financially?'

'Not yet. I'll chase it up today.' Vera was juggling priorities in her mind. She'd need to see Watkins to explain about Katherine Willmore's involvement. That would have to come first. 'Joe and Charlie, you take the local angle. See if you can track down Judy Marshall, the teacher who set up that first weekend in the Pilgrims' House. She wasn't much older than the students, and we know she's still local.'

'You really think we need to go back that far, boss?' Holly was sticking her oar in again. The scrap of praise hadn't kept her content for long. Now she was back challenging Vera's judgement. Poking the bear.

'I wouldn't ask if I didn't think it was important.' But Vera's voice was reasonable, conciliatory. The last thing she'd really want was a 'yes-woman', who couldn't think for herself. 'Rick Kelsall hadn't lived here for years. But this is where he was killed. Why? Something about those early relationships had become toxic, destructive. Let's scroll back and find out where that could have started.'

Watkins had a large office at the top of the building. He was much more comfortable with conference calls and Teams than in-person conversations. He'd been fast-tracked through promotion without much real policing experience, but he was great with budget planning and spreadsheets and he could talk a good game. He'd embraced the new technology, the importance of digital investigation, as a drowning man does a lifebelt. When Vera knocked on his door, he seemed shocked to see a live human, though she'd warned his secretary that she was on her way.

'Vera, how can I help?' He always sounded warm, supportive, though in Vera's experience real support was seldom forthcoming.

'It's the Rick Kelsall murder, sir.'

'It definitely *is* murder, is it?'

'Yes, the post-mortem confirmed that on Saturday.' Vera tried to contain her impatience. The man already knew that. His preferring this to be suicide wouldn't change the facts. 'But we have an additional complication.'

'Tell me.'

'I visited one of Rick Kelsall's friends yesterday afternoon.

There's a possibility that an event in the past played a part in his murder, so we're doing a bit of digging into his history.'

Watkins tried to smile. 'I do know how you enjoy a bit of digging, Vera, but don't get distracted. We're investigators not archaeologists.'

And you're neither. You're a glorified pen-pusher, who wouldn't know a killer if he bit you in the arse. 'It does seem relevant in this case.' A pause. 'Sir.'

'Go on.'

'When I went to the home of a potential witness – a man called Daniel Rede – I met his partner. Katherine Willmore.'

She'd been expecting shock, horror, but the man seemed unsurprised. 'Of course, she's moved in with Daniel now, hasn't she? They've been an item for years, of course. They met when she was still a lawyer. At some charity do.' He looked up, aware of the danger despite the easy words. 'Is Daniel a suspect?'

'Not at this point. I was there for background information.' Vera thought she should have realized that Watkins would know the pair socially. When it came to brown-nosing, he'd put the wiliest politician to shame, and he had an instinct for gossip.

'No reason to overreact then, is there?' Watkins's smile was genuine now. 'The last thing the service locally needs is our PCC all over the media. Another distraction in a high-profile case, I'm sure you'll agree.'

Vera had just sat back at her desk when her phone rang. A call-handler taking initial responses from the public. 'There's a guy on the line who says he's Kelsall's solicitor. Shall I put him through?'

'Please. What's his name?'

'Stanwick. Gordon Stanwick.'

'Isn't he local?' Vera had been expecting someone high-powered from London.

'Yeah. He's from Stanwick and Crosby. They're in Market Street.'

'Tell him I'll come and see him in his office then, would you?' Unlike the boss, Vera thought she preferred face-to-face contact every time. You couldn't read body language on a screen. Or smell fear. 'If it's convenient, I'll be there in half an hour. Any problems, give me a shout.'

It seemed there were no problems, so she grabbed the coat, which was almost dry, and went out into the town.

Vera had come across Gordon Stanwick before, not because he was a criminal lawyer, but because he'd handled Hector's affairs. Hector had left everything to her in his will, which had surprised her. She'd always assumed that her father was closer to his small gang of friends than his daughter, and that they might benefit instead of her. Stanwick was a grey, ageless man, who thrived on detail. There'd been very little money left in Hector's accounts, but she'd been glad of the cottage and the Land Rover. Stanwick had offered her a glass of very good single malt, with the gravity of a priest at communion, when he shared the details of the will with her. 'I always feel that these moments deserve to be marked.'

Now, he was waiting for her in the downstairs lobby. He hadn't changed at all in the intervening years. She'd thought him middle-aged then, but he must have been a young man, playing the role. He led her upstairs.

'I saw about Mr Kelsall's death on the news and thought I should get in touch.'

'I was a little surprised that you were handling his affairs.'

'Well, we looked after his parents,' Stanwick said. It sounded as if he were a care worker rather than a family lawyer. 'A lot of people like the sense of continuity, even when they move away.'

'You prepared Mr Kelsall's will?'

'We did, and I updated it earlier in the year after his father died.'

'That will have been before Rick lost his job with the television company?'

'Indeed, it was. But really his salary was only a minor proportion of his total income. He made far more through his freelance work and he still has a considerable sum to pass on.' He looked at her over his rimless spectacles. 'But I'm sure you're a busy woman, Inspector, and you'd like to know who benefits from his will.'

'Indeed I would, Mr Stanwick.'

He raised his eyebrows at her repeating one of his favourite phrases and then he smiled.

'He has two children from his first marriage and they inherit his London flat, which would, at today's valuation, be worth at least a million pounds.'

'For a flat?'

'I understand that it's a well-appointed flat in a sought-after area. They also inherit the greater proportion of his savings. There are modest legacies of twenty thousand pounds each to Philip Robson and Kenneth Hampton, with thanks for their friendship over many years. The remainder of his wealth, including the value of his parents' house in Kimmerston, is to be split equally between two women: Charlotte Thomas and Annie Laidler.'

It took Vera a while to take in all the information. Twenty thousand pounds didn't seem particularly modest to her, and while passing on the bulk of his wealth to his children seemed normal and appropriate, the substantial sums bequeathed to Charlotte and Annie were astonishing. She knew Rick's parents' house. The doctors had been well known in the town for as long as she could remember, and while it wouldn't fetch anything like London properties, it was substantial, in a good part of town, and would make the women a lot of money.

'Did Mr Kelsall explain that last bequest? To the two women?'

'No. I did ask him about it, but he wasn't forthcoming.'

'Was it a part of the original will, or did he add it while he was updating after his father's death?'

'It was a part of the update. Dr Kelsall remained in the family home until not long before his death, so I suppose it would have seemed more relevant after the funeral.'

'Do Charlotte and Annie know of the provisions of the will?'

'I haven't informed them yet. Of course, Mr Kelsall might have done.'

'He saw both women in the days just before he died,' Vera said, 'so perhaps he did tell them.' She thought that would fit in with what she'd learned of the man. He'd love the role of benefactor. Saviour. He'd want their gratitude, their adoration.

Out in the street, she was already planning her next move. She'd talk again to Annie and Charlotte. Of the two, Annie probably had more need of Kelsall's money, but sometimes appearances were deceptive. Jax had told Vera that Annie had invested in the deli, and besides, Vera found it hard to imagine Annie killing for the prospect of a more comfortable retirement. Charlotte, however, seemed to have a lifestyle which would be expensive to maintain. Vera knew that her prejudices were influencing her judgement here. She liked Annie, but had found Charlotte, with her smooth and glossy exterior, hard to fathom.

She was thinking she might call into Bread and Olives to buy something for her lunch, was drooling at the prospect of one of Jax's sandwiches, when her phone went. Holly. A little breathless.

'Ma'am, I've tracked down the identity of the woman who made the complaint against Kelsall, the first one that went public.'

'And?'

'It was a young intern, who was there on work experience after she graduated.'

'Do we have a name for her?'

A pause. 'Yes. She's called Eliza.' Another pause. 'Eliza Bond.'

'Should that mean something to me?' Because Vera could sense Holly's excitement at the end of the line.

'She took her father's surname,' Holly said, 'and kept it after her parents separated. Her mother's name is Willmore.'

Vera remembered the pale face staring down at her from Rede's astonishing house.

'She's the PCC's daughter?'

'Exactly.'

'Bugger!' Because, although Vera felt a moment of glee when she thought of Watkins's discomfort at hearing this news, there was no doubt that it would make the investigation very much more complicated.

Chapter Twenty-Four

IT WAS CHARLIE WHO TRACKED DOWN Judy Marshall, former teacher, former charismatic changer of young people's lives. She was working in a food bank based in a church hall, just off Kimmerston Front Street. It was only half a mile from the police station, so the detectives decided to walk.

'How did you find her?' Joe realized that Charlie had a network of informal contacts but this was quick work, even for him.

'One of my elderly neighbours is a volunteer there. She's chatty. Lonely, I suppose. I've only got to be in the garden five minutes and she's there, offering cups of coffee and home-made cake.'

'You want to be careful. She might have designs on your body . . . A handsome bloke like you . . .'

Charlie was single now, with a daughter who was a final-year student at Newcastle Uni. He'd been through a patch of loneliness and depression himself, after a messy divorce. There'd been times when Joe would have been more careful, and certainly wouldn't have made bad jokes about a new relationship. But these days, his colleague seemed in a much better place.

Charlie grinned. 'I think I could do better than that, even if I *was* in the market for romance. She's eighty if she's a day.' A pause. 'Does good cake though. I remembered her talking about a Judy who works with her. A woman who used to teach at the Grammar. Apparently, it's *our* Judy and she's in charge at the food bank today.'

A gust of wind blew a scrap of litter along the pavement. Joe picked it up and threw it into a bin. He'd been in the food bank before. He'd taken along a young lass who'd been picked up for shoplifting. She'd had no previous convictions and it'd been baby milk she'd been hiding under the quilt in the pram, not luxury items for her own use. Her man had been made redundant when the firm he worked for went bust. Joe had seen desperation in her face, and shame, and in the end, they'd let her go with a caution. Vera's decision. And it had been Vera who'd sent Joe after the lass.

'Take her to the food bank at St Paul's. Go in with her. She'll be too proud or too embarrassed to go there herself. Make out you're a friend. Last thing she needs is to go in with a cop.'

Joe had felt awkward walking into the building, anxious despite himself, that he'd be seen by someone he knew. Knowing it was ridiculous, but feeling second-hand the stigma of someone who couldn't feed their kids.

The church was old and squat. He and Sal had been married there, and had had their photos taken on the steps outside. His family had been a bit wary at first. They were Methodist not C of E, and were worried they might get things wrong, but the elderly vicar had put them at their ease, and they'd recognized all the hymns. The food bank was in the hall next door, a big barn of a place, built at a time when the congregation had been bigger, when the Sunday School had been thriving.

Judy Marshall was quite clearly the person in charge. She was tall and slender, with white hair, cut short, slightly curly. Her skin was clear and her eyes were very large and very blue. She moved like a dancer and Joe could tell she'd have been stunning to look at as a young woman. She was supervising the filling of the shelves and must have said something amusing, because suddenly the people around her began to laugh.

She walked up to them with a smile of welcome. The hall was high-ceilinged, dusty. She was wearing a long sweater over leggings and ballet pumps, which added to the first impression Joe had of her as someone who could dance. The soft shoes made a sliding sound on the wooden floor. 'How can I help you? Is this your first time?'

'You *are* Judith Marshall.'

'That's me!' The voice was still professionally cheery, but she was curious. 'At least that was my maiden name. It's Judith Sinclair these days. Judy to my friends.' She looked at them. 'Did I teach either of you?'

Joe shook his head, smiling. Her good humour was infectious. 'Any chance of a chat?' He introduced himself and Charlie, and held out his warrant card to convince her.

'Of course.' She called out to a colleague. 'Can you take over for a bit?' She led them down the length of the hall, past makeshift wooden shelves piled with tins and jars, and through a door, which led down a short corridor and into the church itself. There was a smell of wood polish, candle wax and incense. At the centre of the church she stopped, so suddenly that

Charlie nearly walked into her. She turned towards the altar and bowed her head, a gesture of reverence, and stood for a moment before continuing. An automatic response, but one that still seemed deeply felt. She was a believer then, a member of this church. They walked through another door and into the vestry. The vicar's robes were hanging on a coat hanger on a hook on the door. There was an electric kettle on a tray, half a dozen mugs and a jar of instant coffee.

'Can I offer you a drink?' She seemed completely at home. 'This is my sanctuary when things get too much at the food bank. The vicar's very good about letting us use it. We hear such heartbreaking stories and sometimes we need a place of escape.'

Joe shook his head.

'What is this about, Sergeant?'

'One of your former pupils died at the weekend. Rick Kelsall.'

'Yes. I saw the news. I remember him, of course. Not just because he went on to become something of a celebrity. He stood out even then. We all knew he was destined for something special.' She paused. 'It wasn't only that he was academically gifted. He had a confidence, an ambition that set him apart from the other students.'

'Is that why you remember him so well? You must have taught thousands of pupils over your career.'

'One of the reasons. But I was in my first year as a qualified teacher. Very young. Very idealistic. I saw teaching as a vocation. I remember most of that cohort. The ones who came later have become rather a blur.' She paused and stared at him with the startling blue eyes. 'Why are you speaking to me after all this time, though? I haven't seen Rick for years.'

Joe didn't answer directly. 'You were never invited to one of their reunions?'

She paused, playing for time, he thought. Something about this conversation was making her uncomfortable. 'I'm not sure I know what you mean.'

'Rick Kelsall and a group of other students became close friends at a weekend you organized called Only Connect. Now, they come together every five years in the Pilgrims' House on Holy Island. You must remember it, because it was where the first weekend took place. That happened in your first year as a teacher too.' Joe waited for a moment, but she didn't respond. 'It seemed to have made a huge mark on them at the time. One of the parents described the kids as coming back different, lit-up, almost evangelical.'

'They were a very sensitive group. It was a privilege to be there with them. Actually, it was probably the highlight of my teaching career. I never managed to achieve the same response from any other group of students.'

'Yet you didn't go to their first reunion? I'd have thought they would have invited you to join them. As you were so influential.'

'They did invite me to the first reunion,' Judith said.

'But you didn't go?'

She shook her head and seemed to be choosing her words carefully. 'I was a bit naive when I first started teaching. I wasn't much older than the sixth-formers and I was in a strange town, a long way from home. Perhaps I didn't keep sufficiently detached from them. That was probably why I found the weekend so moving, why it was such a success. I was a part of it, as much participant as leader.' She looked up and smiled. 'It changed me as much as it changed the kids. Something very special happened in those quiet evenings in the chapel.' Another pause. 'It was the start of a journey into faith. When we got home, I started to come here, to St Paul's. I met Martin, my husband, here.'

'You're married?'

'I'm widowed. My husband worked as an intensive care nurse throughout his career. The week after he retired, he was killed in a road traffic accident.' She looked up at Joe. 'A truck swerved across the carriageway and into his car. The driver was on his phone and lost concentration.'

There was a moment of silence. Joe couldn't think of anything at all to say. It seemed such a tragedy, such a waste. He couldn't understand how the woman could remain so positive. He was still struggling to find an appropriate response, when Judith continued talking, explaining her relationship with her pupils.

'By the time the first reunion came around, five years after the Only Connect weekend, I was a bit more savvy, and I'd developed more appropriate friendships. By that time, I was going out with Martin. I was flattered to be asked, of course, but I knew it would be a mistake to go.'

'Even though by then you were no longer in a position of responsibility where they were concerned?' Joe wasn't sure he bought this explanation. 'I can see you'd want to keep your distance when you were teaching them, but not when they were adults.'

'As I said, by then I'd moved on. The last thing I wanted was to spend a weekend with a bunch of young people in an uncomfortable house on the island.'

'When was the last time you met Rick Kelsall?'

'Oh gosh, years ago. He was on the other side of Kimmerston Front Street and I went up to him and introduced myself. I was a bit starstruck I suppose – not my style at all – but he was at the height of his fame at that point. He had his wife with him. Charlotte. I taught her too.'

'Did they remember you?'

'They did! It was all rather wonderful. Rick said I'd given him a love of the written word. We chatted for a bit and then they went on their way.'

'They didn't talk about Only Connect? It was so important to them they've been meeting every five years ever since.'

Judith shook her head. 'I don't really think it was *so* important, you know. The Only Connect weekend seemed to have taken on a kind of mythical status within the school, but that group would have become close friends anyway. They were into the same things. Music. Drama. They all took part in the school play that I produced.' She seemed to think carefully before speaking. 'I think it was the island that made it so special, the evenings in the chapel, the sense of history and spirituality. Did you know that one member of the group later became ordained?'

'Philip? He was there this weekend when Rick Kelsall died.'

'Yes, Philip. I *have* kept in touch with him. He's spending this week in my holiday cottage on Holy Island and he's invited me to go and see him. I'm looking forward to it.'

'You own a property on the island?'

She nodded. 'My husband and I bought it years ago. It was our escape from work.'

'Did you spend the whole of your career in Kimmerston Grammar?' Charlie asked. 'You never wanted a change?'

'Well, it became a comp soon after of course, but yes. Martin was a local man. We settled down and had children. Any ambition I once had seemed less important than the family. I suppose I got complacent. I was happy enough as a classroom teacher and I never wanted to go into management. Our sons have grown up and moved away.' She paused. 'It was dreadful when Martin died. Such a shock and we had so many plans, so many adventures left to experience. I struggled at first, but I've got good friends, and the church. I've thrown all my energy into the work here.' She gave a little smile. 'When I meet the folk who use the food bank, I realize I'm so much better off than many people of my age.'

Charlie seemed satisfied by the response. Joe wasn't convinced. He didn't think the woman was lying, but there was something missing, something she wasn't telling them.

'Have you kept in touch with any of the others? Any of Rick's friends, I mean, besides Philip Robson.'

'Not really. I see Annie Laidler in Bread and Olives when I go in. I do see more of Charlotte. I treat myself to a weekly class in her new studio. I've always enjoyed yoga and after Martin died, I found her meditation sessions very helpful. She's rather a good instructor. Much more empathetic than you might expect.' She paused to emphasize her confusion. 'But really, Sergeant, I don't understand this fixation with the past.'

'Rick Kelsall was murdered,' Joe said. 'Somebody put a cushion over his head and held it there until he could no longer breathe.' He looked at her, trying to gauge her reaction. 'And he died at the Pilgrims' House, at one of the reunions when he was with his old school friends. They all have to be considered potential suspects. That's why we're fixated with the past.'

There was another silence. 'I'm sorry,' she said. 'I hadn't realized. Of course, then I can understand the focus on the old friendships.'

'I know it's a long shot,' Joe went on, 'but nothing happened all those years ago, which might have come back to haunt them?'

Judith held his gaze for a moment, before shaking her head.

'After fifty years? Really, Sergeant, I don't think that's very likely, do you? They were kids, interesting, lively kids. I didn't meet anyone there who would possibly have gone on to become a killer.'

Back at the station, Holly was at her desk, speaking on the phone, intense, focused as only she could be. She ended the call and looked up at Joe and Charlie as they walked past.

'I've just arranged calls to someone at the TV production company where Rick worked and with his agent. They won't be free until this afternoon.'

'Giving them time to get their story straight.' Charlie could be a cynical bastard, Joe thought, but this time he was probably right.

'Probably.' Holly gave a quick grin. 'But they wanted to foist me off with a secretary and someone from HR, and at least I've persuaded them to speak to me in person.' A pause. Joe sensed an elation, a moment of triumph. 'But that's not the most important call I made today. I've finally tracked down the complainant in the Rick Kelsall sexual assault case. I told the boss earlier. It was Katherine Willmore's daughter Eliza.'

'Well,' Charlie said. 'The PCC didn't pass on that gem of information when she was talking to our Vera yesterday. I'm not sure how she thought she'd be able to keep it secret.'

'Willmore's got powerful friends,' Holly said. 'She worked in London before she moved here. She'll have contacts in the police and the press. And she knows the law well enough to persuade them of the need to keep the victim's identity secret.'

She tipped her head towards the ceiling. 'The boss is talking to Watkins now.'

'How did you get the info?'

'I was at school with a journo on one of the tabloids.'

'Is that who you were talking to when we came in?'

Holly shook her head. 'No, that was Rick's mobile provider. They'll send through the full list of transactions but I wanted to know if there'd been any significant calls in the days before his death.'

'And?'

'Apart from a couple of texts to his kids, there were only two numbers, both phone calls, both incoming. One was the call he took when he was at Charlotte's on the Friday morning before heading to the island. The other he received late on the evening of his death. That's probably the most important because it might give us a more precise time of death. I'm trying to track it down. I'll let you know as soon as I get it.'

Joe nodded. This was all valuable information and would probably be more use to them than a foray into the past, but he was still thinking of Judith, still trying to reconcile the seventy-year-old woman in the food bank with the idealistic young teacher who'd changed the way a group of teenagers had looked at the world. He thought of the faded photograph, the group of kids squinting into the sun, and the teacher in the centre, who'd looked no older than the rest of them.

Chapter Twenty-Five

WHEN VERA LEFT THE SUPERINTENDENT, she was almost
sorry for the man. She'd asked him if he'd like to talk to
Katherine Willmore about the fact that her daughter had been
the victim of Rick Kelsall's harassment. The *apparent* victim,
because so far there'd been no criminal charge brought. And
with Kelsall dead, there probably wouldn't be. 'It might come
better from a more senior officer.'

'Oh, I don't think that would be at all appropriate.' The
words had come tumbling from Watkins's mouth, a torrent of
panic. 'There'd be a conflict of interest. We meet socially. It
would be much better coming from you.'

They'd looked at each other, both of them knowing that he
was a coward and that this was an excuse.

In her office, Vera phoned Willmore's secretary, a young
man with an impeccable public-school accent.

'I'm afraid Miss Willmore is working from home today. I
could probably set up an appointment for tomorrow morning
in the office. She's got a free slot at eight-fifty.'

'Nah, you're okay, pet.' Attempting the kind of West End

Newcastle Geordie spoken by the older members of the Thomas clan, and just about making it. 'This is personal. I'll catch her later.' She wasn't entirely sure that he'd understood a word she'd said.

Vera had planned to see Charlotte to talk about Rick's will before the bombshell about Katherine Willmore's daughter had hit, but that would have to wait until she'd spoken to the PCC. Vera wandered out into the main office and perched on Holly's desk.

'What do we know about this life coach business of Charlotte's?'

'I haven't gone into it in any detail. Not since that first day on the island. And that was just checking out her website.'

'I'd be interested to know how solvent she is. Since the Thomas family has gone almost legit in their old age, they'll likely have had less coming in, and she's not the celebrity draw that she once was. Rick's left her all that money in his will, and it might be a motive.'

'She hardly looked on the breadline when she turned up to Holy Island.'

'A few smart clothes and a fancy car,' Vera said. 'That could all be show. She might have had the clothes for years. I understand that the classics never go out of fashion.' She'd read that in a magazine in the dentist's waiting room, but she could tell that Holly was impressed.

'I'll see what I can find out.'

'Then I'd like you to go and see her. I want to know if Rick told her he was leaving half his parents' house to her in his will. You built up a good relationship when you spoke to her on the island. Get her to trust you. Encourage a bit of girly gossip about the rest of the group. See what she made of Isobel

Hall. They sound like two of a kind. Charlotte might not have been on the island when the lass drove her car off the causeway, but maybe she had some idea about the background to the accident.'

Holly nodded, pulled out a notebook, and started writing.

Vera continued talking. 'We know Rick stayed with Charlotte the night before he died. What did they talk about? Does she know Katherine Willmore? It's possible after all. They could even be friends. Charlotte was at school with Daniel, and while Katherine might not have needed a life coach, I can see her doing yoga to relax in her spare time. They could mix in the same circles.'

Holly nodded again. She looked earnest, the swotty school-girl trying to gain her teacher's approval. Vera felt a little moment of affection. Of pride.

'I'm going to chat to Katherine Willmore. That's a big coin-cidence, her daughter being the person to make those allegations against Kelsall. Let's see what she has to say for herself. We'll catch up this evening at the briefing.'

'Sure.' At last Holly looked up from the notes. 'Cool.'

This time, when she got to Rede's Lodges, Vera didn't stop at reception in the tower. She hadn't phoned to make an appoint-ment with Willmore. She drove on through the nature reserve. The branches seemed stripped of leaves after the wind over-night and a breeze pushed the water in the nature reserve pool into little waves. The place was quieter than it had been at the weekend. She parked outside the house, camouflaged by trees. There were no other vehicles there, but all the same she rang the bell and waited. No reply. She looked up to the window where she'd seen the pale face the afternoon before. It was still there, peering out. Did the lass spend all her time in her room, staring out at the world? A kind of modern Rapunzel, waiting for someone to rescue her. Vera waved just before the face disappeared from sight, then rang the bell again. She heard faint footsteps inside the house and then the door was opened.

The young woman who stood inside was wearing a shape-less brown woollen dress that reminded Vera of a sock. She still managed to look good in it. Vera thought perhaps the young could look good in anything.

'You must be Eliza. I work with your mother. I was here yesterday.'

'Mother's not at home.'

'It's not really your mam I want to speak to.'

Eliza stood aside and let Vera in. They stood in the hall with its sharp, white walls and pale wood floors. A kind of no-man's-land between the woods and the sea.

'You must know why I'm here, pet.'

Eliza might be in her early twenties, but Vera saw her as a girl, delicate, only half-formed. It was hard to believe that she'd had the courage and confidence to take on Rick Kelsall and a TV production company. Vera couldn't imagine her ever being brash or defiant.

'You had a run-in with Rick Kelsall and now he's dead. You can see why I might want a chat. Nothing formal. Do you want to give your mam a shout? We can wait until she gets back.'

Eliza shook her head. 'No, come on through. I wanted to come down and speak to you yesterday, but I didn't quite have the nerve.'

'Were you listening then? While I was speaking to Daniel?'

'I was on the stairs.' She smiled. 'I couldn't hear much

though, and Mum shooed me back upstairs when she came in.' A pause. 'I'm kind of in hiding. Not from the police. From the press. My mother's got a horror of my name coming out.'

'Daniel,' Vera said. 'He's your step-dad?'

'Kind of. They're not married though.'

'What do you make of him?'

'I like him! He's very different from my dad, but they divorced ages ago. Daniel adores my mother. He makes her very happy.' She considered for a moment. 'I love spending time with them.'

Vera nodded towards the door leading to the long, light living room with its view of the water. 'Shall we find somewhere a bit more comfortable to sit?'

'Oh God, of course. Sorry. I'm all over the place. Everything's just been a bit shit.'

Vera thought it had been more than a bit shit for Rick Kelsall, but she didn't say anything. The view was quite different this afternoon. A grey, stormy sea, lit by occasional blasts of sunlight as the clouds parted.

'How long have you been back? I thought you were living in London.' Vera settled on a very comfortable sofa.

'I was, but Mum thought I'd be better here. She didn't trust me not to blab.'

'About the sexual assault complaint against Rick Kelsall?'

The girl nodded and blushed. 'She drove down and got me. And honestly, it was a relief to get home. I don't think I'm actually a city girl.'

'How long have you been here?'

'Just over a month.'

'Did you have any contact with Kelsall when he was here in Northumberland?'

She looked up at Vera and seemed to shrink inside the loose, woollen dress. '*I* didn't.'

'But Katherine and Daniel did?'

She didn't answer and Vera could hear the stormy waves outside, the sound a background rumble, even through the expensive triple glazing of the enormous windows.

'It was Daniel who got me the internship,' Eliza said at last. 'He'd been to school with Rick and I wanted it so much. An experience like that, it's gold dust if you want to work in the industry.'

'So, Daniel pulled a few strings?' He did it for Katherine, even though he and Rick hadn't been close as boys, and Rick would have loved that, acting the benefactor again, handing out favours, knowing how hard it must have been for Daniel to ask.

She nodded.

'Where did they meet, your parents and Kelsall?'

'Here. He was on his way to Holy Island.'

'On Friday lunchtime?'

She nodded again. 'It was a last-minute thing.' The phone call he'd got when he was at Charlotte's.

'What was the meeting about? To give Kelsall a chance to explain his crass behaviour to you, to apologize? Yet you say you didn't see him.'

'No, I left it all to Daniel and my mother. It was a secret that I was here at all. Nobody else knew. I stayed in my room.' A pause. 'Mum said she might be able to sort out the situation, that if she talked to him, she thought she'd be able to make the mess go away.'

'But, as I understand it, pet, he was the person in the shit. Not you. You were the victim. Nothing to blame yourself for.'

A silence. Eliza was thinking through the answer.

We all turn our lives into stories, Vera thought. We all want to make excuses for the stuff we're ashamed of.

'The whole thing was blown out of proportion,' Eliza said. 'And once it had started, I couldn't find a way to stop it.'

'Was there a sexual assault?'

The direct question seemed to take her by surprise. She stared back, but there was no answer.

Vera went on: 'Did Rick Kelsall touch you in an inappropriate way?'

Still no direct answer. 'He made me feel uncomfortable.' The words were mumbled, half-hearted.

Vera nodded slowly. 'Some men can do that to you, and they mean to do it; they like the power. I can think of a few in my time.' A pause. 'But there was no physical contact? No assault?'

Eliza shook her head.

'So, it was the bullying that upset you and started the whole thing off?'

'He behaved in the same way to all the younger staff.'

'But you were the one to make the complaint?' Vera was struggling to understand how this had become such an enormous story. There must be overbearing boors in many offices throughout the country. Of course, not all the complainants were the daughters of Police and Crime Commissioners, but that didn't explain why two people had been killed.

'I was set up,' Eliza said. The words came out in a rush. 'I've been such a bloody fool.'

Vera was aware that time was passing and that Katherine and Daniel could turn up at any moment, but Eliza was in no state to be hurried. 'Who set you up?'

'There was a runner in the office. Stella. Not much older

than me. Bright. Ambitious. I thought she was my friend. Nobody else took much notice of me. I've always been a bit in my mother's shadow. Stella and I were in the pub after work one night and her boyfriend was there. We were talking about Rick, about what a lech he was, about how he treated the younger women.' She looked up at Vera. 'They were listening to me, laughing at my jokes. Nobody much has ever done that. My mother was the centre of attention wherever we went and I was shy. I didn't mind being overlooked. At university I kept to my own small crowd. But it was quite heady that night in the pub and I'd had a few glasses of wine.' She looked up at Vera. This was confession time. 'I exaggerated a bit to get a reaction. And agreed with Stella when she made him out to be a bit of a monster. To make the story more interesting.'

Vera nodded. She'd known police officers who were more keen on a good story, a story that would lead to a conviction, than the truth.

'Stella's boyfriend was a journalist on a tabloid. Also, it seemed, hugely ambitious. Two days later it was plastered all over the front page. *Rick Kelsall is a sex pest. Pretty young intern tells all.* It was a nightmare. They'd exaggerated even the story I'd given them, and I thought everyone who knew the company would be able to work out who'd told the press. There was nothing concrete. It was all innuendo, but the implication was that I'd been raped.'

'Did you explain to your mother what had really happened?' Vera thought that, despite what she'd said, Eliza had been the victim in the case. She'd been abused twice. She'd been bullied by a powerful man in the public eye, and then she'd been exploited by a journalist for his own ends.

'I phoned her. The press had already contacted her for her

views. She said she'd sue if they made my name public, and she called in every favour she was owed. It was a nightmare for her. If it all came out, she couldn't be seen to support Rick Kelsall over her own daughter. Not in a case like this. Not when her reputation rests on her support for women in cases of abuse.'

Not even if Kelsall had done nothing wrong. Vera thought this gave them the strongest possible motive for murder. She wondered why the man hadn't already gone public to clear his name. Some strange notion of chivalry? Because there was at least some foundation in the allegations, if not in Eliza's case, of some of the other women who had since come forward? Because he enjoyed the notoriety? Or because it made him feel good to do a favour for a powerful woman?

'I suppose it all became a bit of a circus.'

Eliza paused for a moment. 'The press had gone to the company for comment. It was like a snowball rolling down a hill, getting bigger and bigger and completely out of control. I got called in to HR at work. I was really anxious, certain I'd been found out, but instead they were dead sympathetic: "We're so sorry, we'll do anything we can to support you." There was even a promise of a job when the internship ended. I did try to explain but, honestly, they weren't interested. They just wouldn't listen.' Eliza stopped talking and looked up at Vera, willing her to understand.

'What happened then?' Vera was sympathetic, but she needed the whole story.

'I took a couple of weeks' sick leave. I thought the whole thing might just blow over. But then more women started posting stuff online about Rick, and as soon as I went back to work, the management were on my case again, wanting me to make a statement and a formal complaint to the police.'

'Maybe they had their own agenda.' Vera thought management often did.

'I think they'd been looking for an excuse to get shot of Rick. He was under contract at a high salary and his ratings were down.' She looked up at Vera. It was confession time again. 'In the end I stopped protesting. I would have felt such a fool to admit that I'd exaggerated for effect.'

'Aye, and perhaps they wanted to prove to the world that they took allegations of bullying and harassment seriously. It was all about appearance. Nobody was really interested in the facts.' Vera smiled at the girl. 'By then, it must have seemed as if you'd lost control of the whole thing.'

'It was horrible!'

'It must have been quite a relief when Mr Kelsall died. The story would have died with him.'

'No!' Eliza's horror seemed genuine. 'All I felt was guilt. I wanted to apologize, and I knew now that I wouldn't have the chance. The false allegations would be linked to him forever. That Friday when he came for lunch, I was all for coming downstairs and explaining to him what had happened, but my mother said not to. She said she and Daniel would sort it. I could hear them talking in the room below my bedroom, but I didn't do anything to put it right.'

'Do you do everything your mother tells you?' Vera was genuinely curious. She didn't have much knowledge of young people, but she'd disagreed with everything Hector, her father, had stood for, just as a matter of principle. Wasn't it the role of children to rebel against their parents?

'I suppose I do,' Eliza said. 'She has a very strong personality and I'm a bit pathetic. I hate confrontation.'

'Did they sort things out? Katherine, Daniel and Kelsall?'

'I think they must have done. My mother seemed more relaxed that afternoon after he'd gone.'

'Do you know what they'd decided?'

Eliza shook her head. 'Mother said it was best that I didn't know, but that they'd come to an agreement.'

Vera thought that would be a very interesting conversation to have with Katherine Willmore. 'Where are your mother and Daniel? Do you know when they'll be home?'

'Not until late this evening, they said.'

'Ah well, I'll leave you in peace then.' *And after all,* that *interview would be better had formally, in the police station.* 'Can you let me have your mam's mobile number?'

'Sure.'

'You will be okay here on your own until they get back?' Because she still couldn't see Eliza as a fully formed woman. She seemed so innocent, so childlike.

'Of course.' Eliza stood up. 'Thanks,' she said, 'for properly listening.'

'Eh, pet, that's what detectives do. That's what'll help us catch Rick Kelsall's killer.'

Chapter Twenty-Six

HOLLY WENT ONLINE TO RESEARCH THE women she intended speaking to before she made the calls. These were the professionals who'd played a big part in Rick Kelsall's working life. Sally Baker was the executive producer at the television company where Rick Kelsall had been employed for most of his career. There were photographs of her at awards ceremonies, looking glamorous if slightly dishevelled. She was in her late forties. Holly could find no mention of a husband or children, but in the photographs, she was often on the arm of a good-looking man, an actor or another producer. She was a short woman and her head was usually tilted upwards, staring adoringly into her companion's eyes.

The resignation of Rick Kelsall was widely covered, and Sally Baker was quoted in most of the articles. *We will not tolerate this kind of behaviour, even in our most established stars. Rick has recognized that he acted inappropriately and has resigned.*

'Poor Rick,' Baker said, when Holly was put through to her. 'Though really, I think he might have enjoyed all this drama, and being the centre of attention again.'

It seemed an unsympathetic response.

'You don't seem surprised that somebody killed him.' Holly's tone was conversational. She didn't want to sound too disapproving. She needed the woman to talk.

'Honestly? I'm not. He provoked me almost to murder at least once a month.' A pause. 'He was a consummate professional, of course, but he hadn't realized that the business has moved on. We don't have the resources that we had when he started out. He could be rather demanding.'

'So, you weren't sad to let him go?'

'I'm not saying that. I actually liked the man. As a person. To spar with and bounce ideas off. I had the confidence to stand up to him and he knew better than to mess with me, but he was becoming a bit of an embarrassment.' Baker paused. 'A dinosaur.'

'You weren't surprised when Eliza made her allegations?'

'Well, I was rather. She's a timid little thing. I wouldn't have thought she was Rick's type. He was never particularly attracted to the innocent little interns.'

Holly wondered if Sally Baker had been Rick's type. She could imagine the two of them having a fling after a few too many drinks at some wrap party. Then Sally living with the awkwardness of seeing him at work every day, wondering if he was going to make her indiscretion public. Perhaps she'd had her own, very personal, reasons for wanting to get rid of him.

'Yet you believed Eliza?'

There was a moment of silence and Holly wondered if Baker had hung up on her or if the connection had been lost, but after a few seconds the woman responded.

'Of course! We have to, these days. There can be no more

sweeping these things under the carpet and blaming the victim. Really, if there was any sniff of a cover-up, the press would rip us apart.'

So, truth, Holly thought, had nothing to do with it.

The woman was still speaking. 'Then there was Eliza's mother. Of course, we had to take Katherine Willmore into account. She's a very powerful woman, with an axe to grind when it comes to women's issues.' There was another pause. 'Though she was much more concerned about keeping her daughter's name out of the press than pushing for justice. She'd have been perfectly happy, I think, if we'd taken no action at all against Rick.'

'So why *did* you get rid of him?'

Baker took a while to answer. 'We decided that the whole thing was bound to come out in the end and we couldn't be seen to have been complicit.' She paused, then her tone softened, became more confidential, almost conspiratorial. 'And to be honest, Rick didn't present the image that the company needed anymore. He had a loyal following with the oldies, but we're trying to target a younger audience, and Rick Kelsall wasn't the man who would pull in the under-thirties. Or even the under-fifties.'

'So, the allegations came at a very convenient time for you?'

'Well, that is a *little* harsh, but yes, I suppose it's true.'

'When did you last see Rick Kelsall?'

There was another hesitation.

'Actually, it was just the week before he died. We met up in Soho for a few drinks and a bite to eat.' A pause. 'It was in a way a farewell celebration. Just the two of us. Obviously, I couldn't do anything more formal – we could hardly have a jolly leaving bash in the office – but it seemed a bit heartless just to send him on his way after all those years. He'd seen the company through some difficult times. There were periods when his show kept us afloat.'

They'd definitely had a fling.

'How did he seem?'

'Surprisingly buoyant,' Baker said. 'And I don't think it was all bravado. He said he had other fish to fry. He was moving in a new direction. We drank too much champagne, then I staggered home and hadn't heard from him since. It was a shock to see his face all over social media yesterday.'

'He didn't give any details of his new ventures?'

'No,' Baker said. 'It was all very mysterious. But then there was nothing Rick liked better than a good mystery.'

Holly's research into Rick Kelsall's agent had pulled up her website. Cecilia Bertrand ran an agency representing clients who worked mostly in the news media. There was one photograph, showing a tiny, elderly and very elegant woman. Everything about her was beautifully styled and understated. She was sitting in a wood-panelled office, behind a large desk, with a long window behind her. References from other sources described her as 'the queen of broadcasting' and 'deliciously ruthless'.

Cecilia was obviously expecting Holly's Zoom call and she answered immediately. Her voice was beautifully modulated, almost regal, but as the conversation went on Holly discovered that she could swear like a Newcastle United fan on match night.

'How can I help you, Constable? Of course, I'll give you everything you need. Such a fucking tragedy, just as Rick was about to embark on his exciting new project.'

'What exactly was that?'

'He'd turned his hand to writing. A thriller. Of course, every bugger in the media is doing it at the moment, but it seems he was really rather good. Not my field, but my co-agent got him a very good deal with a major publisher on the strength of a synopsis and some early chapters. He promised me he was writing like a demon and he'd have the first draft finished by the end of the year.'

'Had you seen what he'd written so far?'

'I'm afraid not. He was most secretive about the whole thing.'

'So would that have replaced his television income?' This was a completely new world and Holly was struggling to work out the implication of the information.

'Well, he made more from personal appearances and lectures than he did from his salary. These days the Beeb is notoriously mean-spirited when it comes to presenters. But Rick Kelsall was no pauper, Constable. He had a good lifestyle, despite paying off two wives and supporting his kids. And yes, he got a very nice advance from publishers here and in the US. He was using incidents from his personal experience to kickstart the story, and there's nothing the media likes more than revelation about a celebrity's past.'

'Can you give me any detail about the content of the novel? It could be useful in our inquiries.'

'I'm afraid I can't. As I said, he submitted a short synopsis, but that was rather vague. Sketchy even.' A pause then an admission. 'Hardly more than a paragraph, actually.'

Holly wondered how the woman could make any judgement about the quality of Kelsall's writing on the strength of a brief synopsis. And how a publisher might be persuaded to part with an advance. Perhaps celebrity would be enough.

Cecilia seemed to read Holly's mind. 'If Rick was struggling a bit with the *structure* of the writing, the daily grind so to speak, the thought was that a good editor would be able to help.'

Or even write the thing for him . . . 'You must have some idea about the plot.'

'Well of course! It started with a killing on a small island. He was absolutely fired up by the idea, though he's been hugely secretive ever since.' She stopped suddenly. 'Shit, that's all rather prescient, isn't it? As if he were predicting his own death.'

'Could I see what he'd written?'

'Of course! I'll email it across.' Cecilia Bertrand paused for a moment. 'If you find any material on his computer, of course, we'd love to see it. It would be ours under contract. He might even have nearly finished that first draft. My God, the publisher would wet themselves if we could deliver something they can use. They might be able to find some big name willing to complete it. Can you imagine the publicity? It would be a worldwide sensation.'

She closed her eyes, dreaming, it seemed, of posthumous fame and fortune for Rick Kelsall. And fortune for her. All pretended sadness at her client's death had disappeared.

Holly ended the meeting and sat for a moment at her desk. She thought that Vera would be delighted at the information she'd gained. The advances from publishers, which Cecilia had negotiated on her client's behalf, meant that Kelsall's decision to leave a proportion of his estate to Annie Laidler and Charlotte Thomas was even more relevant as a motive. And the fact that his thriller was about a death on an island brought Isobel Hall's car crash back into focus. She was about to call Vera to pass on the information, when her own phone rang. It was the boss, asking if Holly was ready yet to interview Charlotte Thomas. And with a request of her own.

Chapter Twenty-Seven

KATHERINE WILLMORE STILL WASN'T ANSWERING HER phone. The schoolboy secretary told Vera that the Police and Crime Commissioner had given instructions that she wasn't to be disturbed. Vera had left messages asking the woman to call her back urgently, but so far, there'd been no response.

When she returned to Kimmerston from Rede's Tower, it was earlier than Vera had expected. The conversation with Eliza had left her excited. Suddenly she'd been given a new perspective on the case, and her brain was jumping with possibilities. Eliza's exaggeration of her problems as an intern at last provided a concrete motive for Kelsall's death. Katherine Willmore would be vilified by the press if it came to light that her daughter had made a false allegation of rape. Throughout her career, Katherine had insisted that women should be listened to. Her position as PCC would be untenable. And Vera couldn't see why the information *wouldn't* have come to light. Kelsall was hardly a shrinking violet and he would surely have loved the chance to be vindicated, to prove to the world that he'd been forced to resign without reason. Vera wondered why the man hadn't gone public before. Perhaps he was waiting for the optimum time, financially, or perhaps there were other motives for the delay which might explain his murder.

Vera decided that it was time to refocus the investigation. She found it hard to believe that Watkins could be right in any situation, but perhaps she had been wasting time by digging into the past. It was much more likely that this crime was rooted in the present. Perhaps she *did* allow herself to become distracted by history, by the need to understand.

She didn't feel ready to return to the police station, and parked the Land Rover in the town, next to the river. There was a group of children in the play park on the other side of the water. The wind seemed to be making them flighty, unable to settle. They raced and chased and their screams of laughter, and the mothers' chatter, provided a background to her thoughts.

Vera turned her attention to the other possible motive that had come to light during the day: Kelsall's will and the money left to Annie Laidler and Charlotte Thomas. She'd asked Holly to interview the life coach about the legacy, but now she regretted the decision. Charlotte, after all, was at the centre of the investigation, and Vera wanted to be in on the discussion. It wasn't that she didn't trust Hol to do a good job, but she was a control freak. She'd always found it hard to delegate to the team.

'Have you visited the glamorous Charlotte yet, Hol?'

'Sorry, boss, I've been trying to get more of a handle on the state of her business before doing the interview. I've just had two fascinating conversations with Kelsall's agent and his former employer, and that took up a load of time too.'

'Okay, great. You can pass on all *those* details when we meet up.' But Vera's focus was on Rick's ex-wife now. 'What have you got on Charlotte's finances? Any indication, for example, that Gerald or Robbie Thomas invested in her company?'

It was a long shot, because the men were so elderly, but Vera was thinking that a smart yoga studio in Kimmerston might be a good vehicle for the family to launder any profit from organized crime.

'Not yet. I think that's beyond me and we'd need forensic accountants to check on it. But you were right. Charlotte's business is in a pretty ropy state. The inheritance from Kelsall might just keep it afloat. And after the discussion I've just had with his agent, it seems that he had even more to leave than we supposed.'

'How would you feel if I joined you for the chat with Charlotte Thomas? You can carry on being her best buddy and I can ask the awkward questions.'

There was a silence. 'Sure.' Because what else could Holly say after such a request from her boss? Vera couldn't tell whether the younger woman was resentful that her inspector was muscling in, or relieved that she wouldn't have to take full responsibility for the encounter. 'Of course.'

'I've had a most interesting conversation with Eliza and I'll fill everyone in at this evening's briefing. But let's track down Miss Thomas and see what she has to say for herself.'

Holly joined her on the bench looking out over the river. Vera had bought them takeaway coffees. She'd bought sticky buns too but she'd eaten them before Holly had arrived. The wind caught at their hair and their clothes, and snatched away the words as they spoke. The play park on the opposite bank of the river was quiet now.

'What's the deal with Charlotte's business then?' Vera wiped away cappuccino froth from her upper lip.

'She took over a building near here a couple of years ago. It had been a pub, but she had it stripped out and turned into a space for yoga, meditation, Pilates, and somewhere her fitness coaches could do their personal training. All very flash. There are photos on her website.' Holly paused. 'The bar had once belonged to her father, Gerald. He'd let it run down. It must have been losing money over the years, so I suspect he was glad to get shot of it. Although she didn't have to pay for the building, Charlotte still needed a loan for all the work on converting it, and of course it takes time to build a clientele. My guess is she over-extended herself.'

So, Charlotte had *benefited indirectly from the family's criminal activity.* Vera couldn't see, though, how that might be a factor in Kelsall's death.

'Her father and uncle couldn't help her out with the development?'

'I don't think the financial crash was very kind to their businesses either. It's a long time since they were real players. They moved into hospitality when they were too old for organized crime. And they're very elderly now. One's in a care home with dementia and the other's living with his other daughter in Fenham. They're pretty well back where they started, financially and geographically.'

'The big question is whether Rick Kelsall told Charlotte she was a beneficiary in his will when he stayed with her the night before he headed for the island.' Vera got to her feet. 'I imagine that's a bit of information he'd have wanted to pass on in person.' She lobbed her empty coffee cup into the nearest bin. 'Let's go and find out.'

The house was a three-storey Georgian end of terrace in a quiet road set back from the bars and cafes of the town's main street. It ran from the market square to the river.

'She could sell this to prop up the business.' Vera wouldn't fancy living here, surrounded by neighbours, but she thought that lots of people would.

'It's been re-mortgaged,' Holly said. 'Besides, I suppose it suits the image. Her whole business is about helping people to be successful and fulfil their ambitions. It would be hard to convince people to trust her if she were working out of a scuzzy ex-council house on the edge of town.'

'I suppose.'

They'd reached the front door. Vera knocked. No answer.

'Perhaps she's working,' Holly said. 'If she's on a call with a client she probably wouldn't break off to open the door.'

Vera looked through the window and saw a formal dining room. A polished table and six chairs. A sideboard with gleaming glassware. But this was the shop window. It would be interesting to know what was going on further into the house. 'Let's see if there's a way in at the back.' This was what Vera missed, now she had to spend so long at her desk. The prying and nebbing into other folk's business.

There was a narrow road at the side of the house, leading to an alley running behind the terrace. A high brick wall marked the boundary of the houses. Some had garage doors leading into the backyards, but the entrance to Charlotte's was through an arched door. It wasn't bolted and Vera pushed her way in. The yard would be a sun trap in mid-summer. There were terracotta pots with flowering plants and bushes, a set of garden furniture. Nothing fancy, but pleasant. Charlotte wouldn't be ashamed to have her friends here for drinks. A French window led into the house. Vera peered through and saw a comfortable living room, everything well used and a bit shabby. A smaller window to the right looked into the kitchen. No sign of Charlotte. Vera tried to open the French window but it was locked.

'She must have an office upstairs,' Holly said.

'Aye, but she'd have seen us, wouldn't she? Heard us banging around, at least? Surely she'd come down and let us in.' Vera looked up to the windows on the first floor, but the angle was too steep for her to see anything.

'Perhaps we should phone when we get back to the station and make an appointment.'

'Aye, I suppose so.' Vera knew she sounded churlish, and Holly was right. They should have phoned in advance. It wasn't Charlotte Thomas's fault that she wasn't there when they just landed on her doorstep. All the same, Vera couldn't help feeling a sharp, illogical frustration that made her want to blame someone. 'Where's this yoga studio of hers?'

'Not far. At the other end of the street.'

'Let's just check that out then, shall we? While we're here.'

The studio was on a corner site, not very far from the busy main street. There was nothing now of the pub it had once been. Vera could remember it, a dark, cavernous place, with too many television screens showing football or snooker. Slot machines that competed in sound with thudding background music. As Kimmerston had gone upmarket, the place's customer base had shrunk. The people in the new estates went to the sleek wine bars or artisan pubs where earnest bar staff sold craft ale. Not to this place. She tried to recall its name.

'The Greyhound!' Triumphant because it had come to her.

'Sorry?'

'That's what it was called. There used to be fights every Friday night.'

The front had been painted primrose yellow. *Only Connect* was written in grey cursive script along the fascia. There were blinds at the windows, a deeper yellow, all pulled down. Vera supposed you wouldn't want passers-by gawping when you were doing a downward dog or standing on your head. She'd tried yoga once when her doctor told her she should give it a go, that it might help her to relax. She'd found it boring and faintly ridiculous, and she'd been intimidated by the wiry old women who could do things with their bodies that she'd never have thought possible. She'd soon given it up.

There was a bell by the door, a little sign. *Please ring and wait.* Vera pushed it and heard it ring inside. But she didn't wait. Instead, she tried the door. It opened.

She was aware of Holly following, but she gave her full attention to the large open space. The interior of the old pub was transformed. The place was still cavernous, but this was a cathedral to healthy bodies, with white walls, a ballet barre and mirrors along one side. It must have cost a fortune to refurbish. Light filtered through the thin blinds. A lithe and Lycra-clad Charlotte was lying on a yoga mat in the centre of the floor, eyes shut. The high priestess of fitness. An open laptop was on a tall stand, facing her.

'She must use that to record her sessions.' Holly was whispering, assuming that the woman was in deep meditation. 'You can access them for a price through her website if you can't make it here to the studio.'

But Vera had never known anyone lose themselves in a meditation that was this deep. Meditation had caused *her* mind to race and her body to fidget. And her mind was racing now.

She moved quickly towards Charlotte. There was no movement as she approached.

'Boss?' Holly finally suspected that something was wrong.

Vera didn't answer. She was already stooping over Charlotte, feeling for a pulse. She saw the burst blood vessels in the eyes, and at the same time noticed a foam cushion lying on the floor close to the woman's head. It would be used to support the head during some of the more demanding yoga poses. But the killer had found another use for it.

Vera stood up and now she did look back at Holly. 'She was smothered,' she said. 'Just like Rick Kelsall. Can you phone Doc Keating and Billy Cartwright? Let's get the carnival on the road.' A pause. 'You okay to stay here as first officer on the scene?'

Holly nodded.

'I'll go back to the station and let the rest of the team know that we're now working on a double murder. Then I'll go and notify her father of her death. He might be a crooked bastard, but he shouldn't hear from the press.' Vera didn't move towards the door though. She pulled on a pair of gloves. 'I'll do a quick search before I go. Just to see there's no one lurking in the back there somewhere. We could have frightened them off as we came in.' *And to have a bit of a nose, before the crime scene team come and chase me away.*

A door at the back of the studio led to a series of treatment rooms, with couches, sinks and an array of oils and creams on identical yellow shelves. It seemed to Vera again that this must have been a very pricey venture. No wonder the woman had had to re-mortgage her house. Charlotte's optimism that her former glory would bring in the punters had been misplaced. Beyond the treatment rooms, a corridor led to

Charlotte's office – all pale wood and more signature primrose paint. The computer was still switched on. Presumably she'd been working here before recording the yoga class. Vera wondered if there was a facility for the yoga to be live streamed. If so, the session must have been finished before Charlotte had been killed. Otherwise, a group of wealthy, middle-class women, stretching and breathing in their living rooms, would have witnessed a murder, and though Vera had a very low opinion of that particular group, she thought one of them would surely have had the gumption to phone 999.

She was tempted to look at the material on the computer, but the cyber team would find out and she'd have to explain why she was nebbing. There'd be a timer on the laptop which had been filming her yoga session, so it should be possible to pinpoint death with some accuracy. It would be between the last videoed class and Vera and Holly's arrival.

Vera walked back to the main hall. Holly was on her phone, talking, it seemed, to Paul Keating.

'No sign of anyone there,' Vera said. 'No break-in. They must have used the same door as us. Someone in the street might have noticed. Let's get a team out canvassing.'

As she made her way out, Vera looked down at Charlotte Thomas, a woman who'd spent her whole life striving to look young. All that effort, Vera thought. And what good had it done her in the end?

Chapter Twenty-Eight

VERA WALKED FROM THE CRIME SCENE in Kimmerston to the place where she'd left the Land Rover, glad of the few minutes' exercise, the breeze on her face. From there, she drove straight to a Newcastle suburb and the house where Gerald Thomas now lived with his younger daughter. In the spring it would be a leafy street of substantial Victorian terraced houses. Now the trees were bare, but the place was still attractive, welcoming. They weren't far from the Town Moor, the large open space in the city where cattle grazed, and the wide street felt airy, open to the sky. Holly had been wrong; Thomas hadn't quite slipped back to the poverty into which he'd been born.

Vera had expected to hit rush hour traffic, but she'd sailed through the city centre without any hold-up. She squeezed into a parking space just big enough for the Land Rover, and sat for a moment. It was never pleasant to inform a relative of an unexpected death, especially the death of a son or daughter, and she needed some time to prepare herself for the ordeal. Even if the recipient of the news was a man who should be serving a prison sentence.

She rang the bell and heard it resonate inside, then came the sound of footsteps. The door opened to reveal a young woman. A student perhaps. Jeans, sweater and specs. Air pods. She must have been expecting someone else because she looked surprised. She took out the headphones. 'Yes?' Faintly hostile, but then Vera did look like someone collecting for Christian Aid.

'Who are you, pet?' Vera thought it was always best to know who she was dealing with.

'Ellie. Ellie Thomas.'

'I'm looking for Gerald.' Vera hadn't been sure until then that she'd got the right place. The floor in the hall had been stripped and sanded. A bike was leaning against the wall. This could be a shared student house.

'Why do you want Grandad?' Ellie was still wary. Perhaps she'd grown up with strangers looking for her grandfather.

'It's personal, pet. I've got some bad news for him.' A pause. 'For you all.'

'Everyone's in the kitchen. We're just about to eat.'

'I'll come through then, shall I? Is it this way?'

Before Ellie could object, Vera had marched on to the end of the hall, and through another door into a large kitchen. The two rooms at the back of the house must have been knocked through at some point. One of the walls was painted a deep, warm red, on the other, a noticeboard held photos, newspaper cuttings. There was a long table, set for a meal. This felt like a real, multi-generational family home.

An older woman – Charlotte's sister and this young woman's mother perhaps – stood by a stove. She seemed just about to dish up, and turned, a large serving spoon in her hand. At one end of the table sat a very elderly man. At the other end, another man, in late middle age, probably the cook's partner. In the middle a third, in his twenties, her son. The Thomas clan glared at Vera. Gerald stared at her through rheumy eyes and thick glasses but still he recognized her, even after all these years.

'Inspector Stanhope.' The voice was wheezy. It took a lot of effort for him to speak. 'I'm guessing that you are still an inspector? I never thought you'd climb the greasy pole much beyond that rank.'

'Never wanted to, Gerald.' Vera took an empty seat next to him.

'What's this about? Bursting in here without warning. Just as we're about to eat.' His daughter, the woman at the stove, interrupted. Vera could tell that she was spoiling for a fight. She must have been a good bit younger than Charlotte, but she hadn't worn so well, or perhaps she hadn't bothered to have the surgery.

'It's about Charlotte.'

'What about her?' The woman set down the spoon on the kitchen bench. She'd obviously decided that the meal would have to wait.

Vera ignored the question. 'And you are?'

'Amanda. Charlotte's sister.'

'Maybe you'd best sit down, Amanda. I've got some bad news.'

Amanda looked at her father, who gave a little nod, and then she too took her seat at the table.

'Charlotte's dead.' Vera had always thought it best to be blunt when she was giving bad news, so there was nothing to distract the listener, nothing to suggest false hope.

'How?' Gerald almost coughed out the question. She thought

that he'd been expecting it, or something similar. He'd known as soon as she'd appeared at the kitchen door that it would be bad news. Why else would she be there, on her own? Without the support of another officer. The others looked blank, numb.

'It's still down as a suspicious death at the moment,' Vera said, 'but your daughter was murdered. We found her in her yoga studio. The old Greyhound. You'll know the place, Gerald. You used to own it.'

He gave another almost imperceptible nod and Vera continued. 'I'm as sure as I can be that she was smothered.'

'Who killed her?' Gerald demanded, his eyes bright, feverish.

'Eh, pet, we've not reached that stage yet.'

'But you'll have some idea. Her ex was murdered two days ago.' The man was as sharp as he'd always been. 'You're not telling me that was coincidence.' The rest of the family were watching the exchange in silence. Gerald Thomas might be old but he was still very much in charge.

'I've come straight from the crime scene,' Vera said. 'I thought you'd want to know. I've not had time to gather my thoughts yet, never mind form any sort of theory.' She paused. 'When did you last see your daughter?'

He looked at Amanda. 'When was it? In the summer? July?'

'Aye,' Amanda said. 'She deigned us with her presence for an afternoon.'

Vera looked at her. 'So, you didn't see very much of her?'

'No. Not since Dad's business went tits up and he couldn't bail her out anymore.'

'That's not fair!' But Gerald's voice was uncertain.

'She's always been ashamed of us,' Amanda said. 'Even when we were living in Kimmerston and she was at the Grammar, how often did she bring her friends home? You spoiled her like a bloody princess and she treated you like shite.' Years of sibling resentment seemed to be fermenting inside the woman's head and spewing out through her mouth. Maybe, Vera thought, the woman had been waiting for a time when she could say these things to her big sister. She'd planned how to confront her with the injustice, and now she realized that the opportunity had been lost forever.

'Mandy!' Her father seemed on the verge of tears. 'That's enough.'

But it seemed that the woman couldn't stop. 'She didn't even want us at her wedding! They were going to slope off and do it without telling us. Until Rick made her see sense.'

'You got on all right with Rick, then?' Vera thought it was time to stop the outburst. The woman would regret it later, and Vera had to be back in Kimmerston soon, to talk to the team and catch up with the latest information.

'Yes,' Amanda said. 'Rick was okay. He could mix with anyone. No airs and graces with him, when she did allow him the occasional visit. He always took an interest in us all; he was full of questions even as a lad. I wasn't surprised when he turned out to be a journalist.'

'Have you seen *him* recently?'

Amanda shook her head. 'Not for years. Only on the telly. And he's not been on there for a while.'

'Charlotte met Rick while they were both at school,' Vera said. 'They were together at a weekend team-building course on Holy Island. Rick Kelsall was killed when he was attending a reunion of old school friends there. Any reason, do you think, why Charlotte didn't ever join them?'

'She just didn't fancy it,' Gerald said. 'She didn't like it the first time round. It was a cold, miserable place. Shared bathrooms and everyone having to muck in with the cooking and washing-up. She was used to better.'

'You do remember her going then?'

'Yeah,' the man said. 'She phoned me halfway through the first day, asking if I'd pick her up and take her home. It was bloody inconvenient. I had a box booked at St James' Park for the football. I'd invited people I needed to impress.'

'But you went all the same?'

'Of course he did.' Amanda spat out the words. 'She was his golden girl, his little princess.'

'She was miserable.' Gerald glared at her. 'I'd have done the same for you.'

'Like hell you would.'

'Can you think of anyone who might have wished Charlotte harm?' Vera directed the question to the whole table.

In the end, it was Amanda who spoke for them all. 'Nah, she could be a stuck-up bitch, but I can't think of any reason why anyone would want to hurt her.' Round tears, as big and smooth as pearls, had started rolling down her cheeks. The student daughter got to her feet and put her arms around her. 'Not now,' Amanda went on. 'She was a nobody now. A sad, lonely cow. No man in her life and she hardly ever saw her kids.' She looked at Vera, a sudden moment of realization. 'You know what? I felt sorry for her. What harm could she possibly do to anyone?'

When Vera let herself out, nobody seemed to notice.

Chapter Twenty-Nine

VERA GOT BACK TO KIMMERSTON HALF an hour before the evening briefing. When she arrived in the big room, the whole team was waiting for her, sitting in rows. As she stamped to the front, she could feel their eyes on her, waiting for answers. As if she was part matriarch, part guru. Suddenly she felt the weight of responsibility, because at this point, she had nothing definitive to tell them.

Billy Cartwright was there to update them with information from the scene. Paul Keating had already been in touch to confirm the cause of death: 'No chance of finding fibres in her nostrils this time. The pillow was used for yoga. Plastic-covered. But you were right, Vera. As you usually are. She was smothered.' The Belfast voice was dry. 'There's a chance that we'll find some stray DNA, but don't hold your breath.'

It was dark outside. They spoke under the stark light of the neon strip lamps. A summer's haul of dead flies was trapped in the plastic casing. Vera had gone straight to see Watkins on her return from informing the Thomas family of Charlotte's death. It had been a fractious meeting. At first, he'd seemed frozen by panic, incapable of taking in the information that there'd been another murder on his patch. He was aware of his own lack of experience, but didn't have the confidence to trust his team. Vera had spent thirty minutes massaging his ego and reassuring him that all would be resolved. Neither sat well with her, but she was learning some pragmatism as she got older. There was no point, she'd learned, in raging against the inevitable, and incompetent bosses seemed to be as inevitable as death.

Now though, she was still scratchy after the encounter. The superintendent's tension was contagious. She stood at the front of the room, looking at them.

'So,' she said. 'We've got two high-profile victims on our patch and we need a result fast.' A pause. 'Rick Kelsall was murdered on Holy Island and three days later his ex-wife Charlotte Thomas was killed in her fancy yoga studio only half a mile from here. Both were smothered to death, so I think we can safely assume that these incidents are linked, though they were divorced more than twenty years ago. The pair met on Thursday night before Kelsall headed out to the island on Friday.' She paused and turned to the whiteboard behind her.

'At first, we focused on the people staying with Kelsall in the Pilgrims' House: Ken and Louisa Hampton, Philip Robson and Annie Laird. Annie lives in Kimmerston and works in Jax's deli, so she's only a couple of minutes' walk away from the latest crime scene. I want to know if any of the remaining individuals were in Kimmerston this afternoon. That's a priority for tomorrow. More recently, we've been widening our pool of potential suspects, and that brought us to Daniel Rede and Katherine Willmore. You'll all have heard of Willmore.'

There were nods and muttered murmurs of recognition.

'Her daughter Eliza made allegations of sexual harassment, which led to Kelsall losing his job. Eliza had since admitted that the allegations were false. That might have given Eliza, or perhaps even Willmore, a motive for murder. Neither of them would want the lass portrayed as a malicious liar. So, this is sensitive, but we will of course investigate without fear or favour.'

She paused for a moment, and saw that most of them had recognized the reference, and noticed the sly little grins, before continuing. Investigating without fear or favour had become a mantra for the commissioner. She trotted it out at every possible occasion.

Vera went on. 'Holly, you've been talking to the TV company. Can you tell us a bit more about that?'

Holly stood for a moment without speaking. She was always cautious, always determined to use the right words. Vera felt herself becoming impatient, but she held her tongue.

'Sally Baker was Rick's boss,' Holly said at last. 'She was surprised when Eliza made the allegations against him. According to Baker, Rick didn't usually go for innocent young interns. But the management team felt they had to support her. In this climate, they couldn't be seen not to take the allegations seriously.' There was a pause. 'Baker came across as pretty hard-nosed to me. She wasn't bothered about what had really happened, and I don't think she felt any real sympathy for Eliza. It was all about the image of the company, and they weren't too sorry to lose Kelsall, whose ratings were dropping.'

'So, the company had got what it wanted.' Vera looked out over the group. 'I chatted to Eliza this morning. Informally. Kelsall was an insensitive boor, but it doesn't sound as if he'd done anything that might lead to a criminal charge. Eliza got duped by a journo, and that's how the story got splashed all over the tabloids. Honestly, I can't see any reason why she'd want to kill the man – she was mortified by the fact that she'd got him sacked – and she had no motive at all for Charlotte, but let's keep an eye on her.' She turned back to Holly. 'What else have you got from your phone calls to London?'

Holly described her conversation with Cecilia Bertrand.

'Kelsall was writing a novel, a thriller set on an island where a murder takes place. Using his own experience.' Holly paused. 'There wasn't a murder on Holy Island though, was there? Not until *he* died. It all feels a bit weird, a bit creepy. As if Rick Kelsall was predicting his own death in a novel. Or using another, earlier death as a jumping-off point for his story.'

'Would that be a kind of revenge, do we think?' That was Joe getting immediately to the point. He looked over at her. 'It could be a way of getting back at someone who was never charged with a crime.'

'But who Kelsall thought was guilty all the same?' she said. 'Could be.' Then she remembered the words of her neighbour Joanna and repeated them as if she knew exactly what she was talking about. 'But all writers are parasites. They use the information that comes their way to make the story. Perhaps it was a kind of laziness. Perhaps Kelsall used something that had really happened to save him making stuff up. It wasn't necessarily revenge.'

And if that stirred things up, caused trouble for other people, Rick Kelsall wouldn't be the sort to be too concerned. And if he was challenged, he'd say it was all fiction.

'Of course, there *was* an earlier death,' Holly said. 'Isobel

Hall drove her car off the causeway at the Only Connect first reunion. And we're already looking into the circumstances surrounding that incident.'

'Do you think Kelsall was suggesting in his book that Isobel's death was murder rather than an accident?' Joe said.

'We won't know, will we, until we read the thing.' Vera glared, not angry at him, but that the process of getting hold of the novel was going so slowly.

'His agent has only read a sketchy synopsis,' Holly said. 'She's sending that over to me. There's no evidence that very much else exists, though Kelsall had already been paid an advance.'

Vera was thinking she'd need to talk to Joanna about how this publishing business worked. 'That doesn't sound as if that'll tell us much. But there was a laptop in his room. Perhaps his book will be saved on that. I assume the machine will still be with the digital team.'

'Yes,' Holly said, 'but I think they'll be concentrating on communication and social media, rather than saved documents.'

'Give them a ring, Hol. See if they can track it down and email it across to you.'

'Will do.'

Vera turned to Billy Cartwright, the crime scene manager, who was sitting at the back. 'Have you got anything for us? On either locus?'

'Nothing beyond the obvious. Both victims were killed where they were found according to Doc Keating.' He paused for a moment and was uncharacteristically serious. 'We're stretched, Vera. The scene on Holy Island is a bugger to get to and now we've got another right on our doorstep. We can't use the same team on both because of cross contamination. So, don't expect the impossible. Okay?'

Vera nodded to show she understood. She didn't have to like it though. With bloody Watkins breathing down her neck, she needed a quick result.

At home in her cottage in the hills, she was about to put the kettle on, when it occurred to her that Joanna would be back from her bookish weekend away. She pulled on her wellies and walked down the track to the farm. The clouds had cleared and there was light enough from the moon to see where she was going. She tapped on the door of the house and walked into the kitchen without waiting for an answer.

Joanna was standing by the range, stirring a pot of something savoury, which made Vera realize that it was a long time since she'd eaten. The sticky bun by the river was a distant memory. Joanna was tall, stately, with long dark hair, recently streaked with a little grey.

'How did it go?' Vera was genuinely curious.

'Okay. I was a bit nervous. My first time in front of such a big audience. Some of the other writers were okay but there were a couple of pretentious pricks. You didn't miss much.' She turned to face Vera. 'I was just about to open a bottle of wine. Fancy a glass?'

'Eh, pet. I'd love one.'

'I saw on the news about the murder on Holy Island. I assume that's where you've been all weekend?'

'There's been another. Not on the island.' Vera knew it would be all over the late evening's news – there'd been press and cameras outside the studio before she'd left – so no harm in telling her neighbour. 'Just down the road from the police station.' A pause. 'I found the body. Charlotte Thomas. I don't suppose you knew her?'

'The model? My brothers had her posters all over their walls when they were growing up. I suspect she provided their first sexual experience.' Joanna was wielding a corkscrew with the ease of someone for whom it was a daily ritual. 'Supper's a bit late tonight. Jack's been wrestling with the tractor again. Do you want to stay? I don't suppose you've had time to eat. It's nothing special. Mutton stew. And I called into the farm shop for some Northumberland cheese this afternoon.'

'Are you sure?'

Joanna smiled. 'You know me, Vee. No polite gestures. I wouldn't ask if I didn't want you here.' She poured a glass of red and handed it to Vera, who settled herself into the rocker next to the range, a dog at her feet.

She must have been snoozing, because the next thing she knew, Jack was washing his hands at the kitchen sink and the table was laid. A loaf of home-baked bread on the board and bowls for the stew. There was still wine in her glass.

'How's it going, Vee?' Jack was a Scouser. Joanna called him, with love and respect, her bit of rough. He'd been a scally when he was younger, had had his brushes with the police. It still astonished him that there was an officer he could like and welcome into his home.

'She's working on a double murder.' Joanna was ladling stew into the bowls. 'So probably a bit knackered.'

'No more than usual.' Vera thought this was the best meal she'd ever eaten. She turned to Joanna. 'I could use some inside info on the publishing business. Apparently, Kelsall was writing a thriller, and basing it on a death which happened years ago. He could do that?'

'Sure. Lots of writers have used true crimes as a jumping-off point for their novels.'

'That's the point though. There wasn't a crime. Not officially. At the time, it was put down as an accident.'

There was a moment of silence. 'I'm not any sort of expert,' Joanna said, 'but I'd have thought it would be very risky to make an allegation of murder, if the setting or the event were recognizable. Even if it was in a novel, and especially if any of the people involved were still alive.'

Vera nodded. *But the one thing we know about Rick Kelsall is that he did love taking a risk. And he did love making mischief.*

Joanna cleared the bowls and brought out plates and cheese. She poured more wine.

Vera hadn't been sure about this couple when they'd first moved in. Now, she wasn't sure what she'd do without them.

Chapter Thirty

WHEN VERA GOT INTO HER OFFICE early on Tuesday morning there was a voicemail message from Katherine Willmore. Very sharp. Very stern.

'I'm surprised that you thought it necessary to speak to my daughter without having the courtesy to talk to me first. I understand that you'd like to speak to me now. I'm tied up for most of the day, working from home. You can see me here at ten o'clock if it's something so urgent that it can't be done on the phone.'

Well, Vera thought, that's me told. Ma'am.

She was tempted to send Holly and Joe to interview the woman, to put her in her place and show her that she wasn't worth the attentions of a senior officer, but they'd both be too over-awed to ask the hard questions. So she set off up north again, out to the coast.

There was no Range Rover parked outside the house, and no face looking down from an upstairs window. Katherine Willmore let Vera in, and led her, without a word, not to the large sunlit room looking out over the bay, but to an office shaded by trees. This time, she wasn't to be treated as a guest, but as an unwelcome intruder.

Vera thought it was best to go on the attack from the start. 'I came to speak to *you* yesterday. I didn't even know that your daughter was here. You didn't mention that you had a daughter when I was here to see your partner on Sunday, or that she was the complainant in a sexual assault allegation against a murder victim.'

'In a case like that, she has a right to anonymity.'

'But not in *this* case, not in a murder inquiry. And not to an investigating officer. Anyway, from what Eliza told me there was no real case against Rick Kelsall. She made a false allegation, spurred on by an unscrupulous journalist and the company chiefs.'

Silence. Then: 'Not entirely false. It's clear that Kelsall was a bully.'

'Rick Kelsall was here on Friday morning, before he went onto the island. It didn't occur to you to tell me that?' Vera paused. 'Besides anything else, you must have realized that we'd find out. It was foolish. Someone would have seen him! We'll be able to trace his movements from the satnav in his car or his phone.'

'I must admit that my judgement was a little clouded.' The defiance of the voicemail was completely gone now. The woman was pale and scared. 'But Eliza's my only daughter. I was trying to protect her. She's got her life ahead of her. The last thing she needed was some sort of scandal, Rick Kelsall accusing her of lying.'

'Is that what he was threatening? To go public with what had actually happened?'

'No! No, he was actually very decent about it. We'd worked

out a statement, which we could give to the press, saying that Eliza and Rick had both been victims of a hostile tabloid press and a television company who wanted rid of an older presenter for their own ends. We'd agreed to release it at the end of this week. Now of course, the press will still be poking their grubby little fingers into his affairs, sniffing into the reasons that he left his job, trying to make some spurious link between the allegations and his murder.'

Vera wondered about the timing of that. Could it be significant that Kelsall had been killed before the statement had been made public? She didn't see why it should be.

Willmore looked up at her. 'So you see, Inspector, the last thing we wanted was Rick Kelsall dead. A bland statement, leaving Eliza's name out of the copy but giving her side of the story, would have diffused the situation. Rick would have gone in front of the media as a wronged man, saying he completely understood how a young woman had been manipulated by unscrupulous individuals, and the whole affair would have been over. Now, it's likely to linger on.'

'How did Eliza come to be working for him in the first place?'

'Well, that was why the whole thing was so awkward. Kelsall was doing us a favour. Daniel asked him if Eliza could do some work experience there. She's always been fascinated by the news. Not because she wanted to be a politician; she's a shy little thing. But rather presenting it, making it clear for the ordinary reader, listener or viewer, and it's almost impossible to get an internship in the media if you don't have contacts.'

'You didn't have contacts in the field?' Vera sounded deliberately sceptical.

'Well of course, but I couldn't be seen to be lobbying on behalf of my daughter.'

'But you could ask your boyfriend to do it for you?'

Willmore had the grace to blush. She didn't reply.

'Daniel and Rick were still friends?' Vera said. 'That wasn't the impression Daniel gave when we talked.'

'Not friends exactly. But they were acquaintances, and Daniel was willing to ask Rick. For Eliza's sake.'

'Oh no, for your sake, surely.' Because Daniel is besotted, Vera thought. Even I could tell that. 'And Rick agreed?'

'He did. I can show you the email. "Anything to help my old friends in the North. Let's catch up when you're visiting Eliza. I need to pick your brains about a project of my own." Daniel was surprised. I don't think he was expecting such a positive response.'

'Did they meet up?' Vera thought this contradicted everything Daniel had told her about his relationship with the people who'd spent the weekend at the Pilgrims' House. He'd given the impression that they'd had nothing in common, even as teenagers.

'Yes! Rick's company helped Eliza find a room in a shared house in London with some other employees and Daniel drove her down. I was caught up with work here, or I'd have taken her. Daniel booked himself into a hotel and he and Kelsall went out for a meal and a few drinks.'

So, Daniel lied to me. All to protect his lover's daughter.

'What was the project that Rick wanted to discuss?'

Katherine Willmore shrugged. 'Oh, I don't know. I don't think Daniel ever told me. Maybe Rick wanted to move north again. Lots of people seem to be deserting the city at the moment.'

'Maybe.' But Vera thought this might have had more to do with Kelsall's novel. That seemed to have been preoccupying him in the weeks before his death. 'Is Daniel around? I can ask him myself.'

'No,' Katherine said. 'He's out on the road, scouting another development opportunity. We can't fit in more accommodation here at the tower without it feeling overcrowded, so he wants to find new sites. We think the climate emergency will generate a move to holiday at home. Who knows, global warming might even make Northumberland the perfect place for a staycation.'

'Could you ask him to give me a ring. I'd like to speak to him.'

'Of course.' The woman had regained her confidence, her poise.

'Where's Eliza?'

'We sent her to stay with her father. He's a professor in Durham. He's not her favourite person – she took my side in the divorce – but we thought she could do with a change of scene.'

'Where the police couldn't find her?'

Katherine smiled. She'd decided to take Vera's comment as a joke. 'Something like that!' She shifted in her seat and looked at her watch. A sign that she thought the interview was over.

'Did you ever meet Charlotte Thomas? Rick Kelsall's ex-wife.'

There was a brief hesitation. 'Not in person. I'd heard of her, of course. The famous model turned actress. Though I was just too young to be aware of her when she was at the height of her career. I have friends who've become her clients.' A pause. 'I believe that Daniel had some business dealings with her. She was hoping to open a studio here at Rede's Tower. Yoga. Pilates. It might have gone down well with our customers, but I don't think he could get the figures to add up.'

'You were never tempted to consult her?'

'I think I've become sufficiently successful without the help of a life coach, don't you, Inspector?'

Vera nodded to concede the point. 'Mr Kelsall was staying with Charlotte the night before he came here to discuss plans for dealing with the harassment allegations.'

'Was he? I don't think I knew that. Daniel made the arrangements for the meeting.' Willmore gave the impression of being not the least bit interested. 'Is that important? And I'd have thought you'd do better speaking to Charlotte than keeping me from important business.'

'Oh, I would have spoken to her,' Vera said. 'In fact, I tried to speak to her yesterday. But by the time I got to her yoga studio she was dead. Murdered. Smothered like Rick Kelsall.'

Willmore stared at the detective. The colour drained from her face. She seemed incapable of speech. A breeze blew a branch onto the window. The sound as it scratched the glass startled them both.

'You really didn't know?' Vera found that hard to believe. Even if the PCC hadn't heard the news reports, Watkins would have told her. It was her role to know, to keep on top of anything happening in her patch.

'Honestly, Inspector, I didn't. I've had my work phone switched off. There were dozens of messages and I haven't checked them all. I needed some time to think about Kelsall's death, to decide what to do for the best.'

'You got back to me.'

'So I did.' Katherine gave a little smile, but offered no other information.

Vera continued: 'Where were you, ma'am, yesterday? We don't have a precise time of death yet, so I need your movements for the whole day. And it would be helpful if you could confirm where Daniel was, as he's not here to tell me himself. Neither of your cars were here when I was talking to Eliza.'

'I don't know about Daniel. He was out all day. I think there was a meeting in Kimmerston with the council planning officer in the morning. Again, that would be about his ideas for expanding the business, looking at options for further development.'

'And in the afternoon?'

'I'm not Daniel's keeper, Inspector.' Anxiety was making Katherine shrill. 'You could talk to Mel on reception. She keeps his diary.'

Vera nodded. 'Thanks, that's very helpful. I'll talk to her on the way out.' A pause. 'And where were you, ma'am?'

'You're asking me to provide an alibi?' The voice was even tighter, higher.

'A matter of procedure. Following the rules without fear or favour. I'm sure you understand.' Repeating the commissioner's catchphrase.

Katherine took a deep breath and seemed to bring herself back under control. 'Of course, Inspector. You must excuse me. This has all been rather a shock and I haven't been thinking clearly. I was in Kimmerston but only in the morning. I had a meeting with Superintendent Watkins. I'm sure that will be alibi enough.'

'I'm sure it will. And the afternoon? We believe that was when Charlotte Thomas was killed.'

'I was on Holy Island. Nothing to do with work. I had plenty of time owing and I wanted to clear my head. Your turning up on Sunday afternoon with news of Rick Kelsall's death had thrown me rather. I knew I should have told you about Eliza's involvement and I suppose I wanted to work out a game plan. I always think better when I'm walking. It was an impulse.'

'You were on your own?'

'Yes. And I didn't go anywhere near the Pilgrims' House. There was no attempt at all to interfere with the investigation. But I suppose the island was in my head, because of the news.'

'Did anyone see you while you were there?' Vera was keeping an open mind. Walking helped her to think too, though she wasn't sure she'd have gone back to the site of a murder as a civilian, if murder was the subject of her work.

'I had tea in the Old Hall hotel!' The woman sounded relieved. 'It wasn't terribly busy. Half-term was over and the weather wasn't as good as it was over the weekend, so there was a gaggle of journos, but very few tourists. The staff might remember me.'

'How did you pay for your afternoon tea?'

'I'm not sure. With my debit card probably. Don't we all pay with our cards these days? Cash seems almost obsolete.'

'Then we'll be able to check,' Vera said. She smiled and got to her feet. She hoped that they'd hear less of the 'keeping to the rules without fear or favour' mantra, and that Katherine Willmore might be a little less inflexible in the future. 'Please tell Daniel to get in touch with me. We do need to speak to him.'

She drove again past the pool, stopped for a moment and wound down the window to listen to the calls of the waterfowl. In the distance, a woodpecker was drumming.

The same receptionist was at the desk in the tower. She recognized Vera. 'I'm sorry, but Mr Rede is out. I think Katherine is at the house.'

'I know. I saw her. She said you might be able to help me. I need to know where Daniel was yesterday afternoon. Katherine said that you keep his diary.'

'I do.' The woman clicked on her computer. 'He was in Kimmerston from late morning. A planning meeting.'

Vera nodded. That confirmed what Katherine had said. 'And the afternoon?'

'I've got nothing marked in, so I presume he was working here, either on site or in his office at home.'

'Did you see him yesterday at all?' Vera kept her voice conversational, but Mel was a good employee, and was non-committal.

'Honestly? I can't remember. I'm pretty sure he was around later on, but I can't be sure.' Which was no help at all.

Chapter Thirty-One

BACK IN THE POLICE STATION, VERA shouted Joe and Holly into her cramped office to sort out the detailed plans for the day. She'd made coffee for them. *That* didn't happen very often. Outside, it was market day and she could hear the traders shouting jokes to the passing shoppers. Everything seemed vibrant and alive. There was something joyous about the activity, the bustle.

It hit her suddenly that apart from Eliza, all the suspects in this case were ageing. Death was a reality to them in a way that it wasn't for younger people, including Joe, for example, who sat across the desk from her now and was wittering about planning a holiday with his family. She supposed that older people made fewer plans. They had less time to fill, no endless possibilities stretching into the future. Could this be important for the way this case worked out? If so, as an older woman herself, she had no excuse for getting it wrong.

'Chase up the digital team again,' she said. 'I want whatever was on Rick Kelsall's laptop. Most especially a novel about a murder on Holy Island.'

'I've already asked them,' Holly said. 'They say all his files had been deleted. They're struggling to recover them. They'll be able to do it, but possibly not by end of play today.'

'Are they saying the killer could have deleted everything on his laptop?' This was new information. She was about to rage against Holly for not telling her sooner, then realized that would be unfair. She'd only just returned to the station from her jaunt to talk to Willmore.

'I think it's a possibility.'

'Wouldn't they need a passcode?' Vera was getting better at tech, but she was still unsure. 'If they were going in to delete all his files?'

'Perhaps,' Holly said. 'Unless Kelsall was using his laptop when he was killed. Or he'd closed it without turning it off. In that case, you'd just need to click to sign in again.'

'We need to talk again to that group from the Pilgrims' House.' Vera leaned forward across the desk to make her point. 'If Charlotte Thomas's murder isn't some sort of coincidence – and I really can't believe that it is – then we have to consider all those individuals as suspects in the second killing too.'

'You really think one of those people came into Charlotte's yoga studio and smothered her?' Joe obviously found the idea impossible. Did he think all elderly people were benign, harmless? Vera smiled at the notion. Hector, her father, had been cruel into his eighties. And even with the dementia of alcoholism, he'd raged against death, fought it as if he were one of his beloved peregrines ripping into a pigeon with talon and beak. Hector had died just as he'd lived: angry at the world which had deprived him of Vera's mother, the only person he'd ever loved.

'I don't think we can dismiss them,' Vera said. 'It might seem improbable, but surely not as improbable as two random killers targeting victims who knew each other, who'd been to school together and had recently met up.' She paused. 'The killer must have known where Charlotte would be. So, a client perhaps?'

'Judith Marshall had used her yoga classes,' Joe said. 'She described Charlotte as empathetic.'

'The teacher? She'll be worth talking to then. Another link.'

Outside, a busker started singing. Something sweet and lyrical about teenage love.

'Joe, you've already built a relationship with Louisa and Ken Hampton,' Vera went on. 'Go and see them. Louisa's a smart woman and she might be more prepared to talk about the others if you can get them on their own. It was her sister who died at the first reunion, after all. I know the focus has shifted to Eliza Willmore and the harassment allegations, but I still have a feeling that Isobel Hall's death wasn't a straightforward accident. Rick Kelsall's novel makes it more significant, doesn't it?'

'I suppose that makes sense.'

'Find out where they were yesterday afternoon.' Vera paused. 'I can't see Ken having a clue where he'd find Charlotte's yoga studio, let alone knowing how to kill her, but Louisa strikes me as ruthless, organized. We know there was no love lost between her and her sister. I wonder if Isobel's accident was some sort of prank that went wrong. Could Louisa have given her the wrong tide times in the hope that she'd be stranded, embarrassed? She wouldn't want that to come out after all this time.' She grinned. 'Besides, a trip to Cumbria will do you good. It might widen your horizons.'

'Yeah, yeah.'

'I'll have a chat to Annie Laidler. It seems to me that she was closer to Rick Kelsall than anyone.'

'Now that Charlotte's dead,' Holly said, 'will Annie inherit all the money from the sale of the Kelsall house in Kimmerston?'

Vera didn't answer immediately. The busker changed tunes. This was louder, angrier. Some sort of protest song.

'Good point, Hol. I'll have to check with the lawyer.' But Vera couldn't see profit as a motive for Annie. She'd cared for Rick since they'd been teenagers together. Perhaps she'd even been in love with him all that time, despite his decades of chasing other women.

'What about Philip Robson?'

'Ah, the God-bothering Phil, who's still in a holiday cottage on Holy Island. Let me think about him. Perhaps you're right, Hol, and I've dismissed him too easily.'

When Vera got to the deli, she filled a basket with goodies. It was about time she contributed something when she next went to visit Jack and Joanna. The smell in the shop almost made her faint with desire. When she reached the till, Vera asked Jax for Annie. 'Is she on her break?'

'Nah,' Jax said. 'She phoned in sick this morning. Hardly surprising, the shock that she had at the weekend. I wasn't really expecting her in yesterday.'

'But she came into work?'

'Yeah, she wasn't really herself, but she was here.' Jax paused. 'Her ex came to see her, took her out for coffee. To offer his support, he claimed. A bit late for that, I'd have said.'

'What do you mean?'

'It's not really my story to tell. They lost a baby and she still hasn't got over it, even after all these years. I suspect he could have been a tad more sympathetic at the time.' Jax raised her eyebrows, an expression of disapproval. 'No, that's being kind. He could have been a *lot* more sympathetic.'

In the queue behind Vera, the customers were starting to get restive.

'Look,' Jax said. 'Like I said, not my story. You'll need to ask Annie for the details. If you think it's important. But it happened years ago!'

Vera thought that everything important to this case had happened years ago. She asked Jax to remind her of Annie's address, paid for her shopping and left.

Annie lived in a narrow, terraced house. The street had been built on a slope, and there were communal gardens across a paved path, where a mother was playing with a toddler, a little girl pushing a toy pram. Because of the slope, steps led up to the front door. There was a cat sitting on the windowsill in the autumn sunshine. Annie didn't seem surprised to see Vera, had perhaps been waiting for her.

'Jax told you I was on my way?' Because that was what any friend would do.

'She did.' Annie looked as if she hadn't slept for days. 'Come in.' The cat slid in with Vera.

Annie had knocked through the whole of the ground floor into one space, so the sunlight flooded into what must once have been a very dark house. There was art on the walls and shelves full of books.

'Well, this is lovely.' Vera couldn't imagine putting this much effort into somewhere to live. She'd never really bothered about her immediate surroundings, though she'd always needed outside space. A long horizon. A place to breathe.

'It was all rather gloomy when I moved in.' Annie seemed pleased with the response. 'Coffee?'

'No thanks, pet, I'm awash with the stuff. I've just got a few more questions.' She sat on the sofa. There was a small wood burner, lit, giving out enough heat to make the room cosy.

'You'll have heard that Charlotte Thomas was killed yesterday.'

Annie nodded. She sat on the floor close to the stove, with her back to an easy chair. Her normal position in the room.

'Only it seems a coincidence,' Vera said. 'Two Kimmerston Grammar former pupils, murdered within a week of each other. You do understand why I need to speak to you?'

'I suppose so.'

'Give me a clue.' Vera had to make an effort to stay sharp. She liked Annie, and in this comfortable room she felt more like a friend than a police officer. Relaxed, easy. 'Tell me a story which would make sense of it all.'

'I can't!' Annie said. 'Honestly, I've been awake all night, thinking about it.'

'Is there anything to link Charlotte Thomas's death with Rick Kelsall's? Apart from the fact that they were once married. Why would anyone want them both dead now?'

'Really,' Annie said. 'I don't have any idea.'

'Money's always a very potent motive.' Vera shot a glance at Annie, who just looked confused. 'Has Mr Kelsall's solicitor been in touch with you?'

She shook her head.

'Rick left you money in his will. A half share in the proceeds from the sale of his parents' house. The other half was to go to Charlotte. Now that she's dead, I'm presuming you cop for the lot.'

'You really think I'd kill for money?' Annie shook her head in apparent disbelief.

'What will you do with it? Retire?'

'God no! What would I do all day? Jax has dreams for the business. She'd love to open a restaurant. Something relaxed and unpretentious but with brilliant food. Maybe I can make that happen.' The idea seemed to cheer her.

'Did you know that your ex is shacked up with our Police and Crime Commissioner?'

'I'd heard.'

Of course you had. People would have been rushing to tell you.

'Her daughter is the lass Rick was supposed to have abused.'

'He wouldn't have done that.' Her voice was stubborn, immovable.

'Did you know she was the apparent victim? Her name's Eliza. A bonny little thing. Daniel dotes on her apparently.'

A shadow of pain flashed across Annie's face. Vera thought that had been cruel. The woman had lost a daughter.

'No, I didn't know. Rick could be discreet about some things.'

'Rick was at Daniel's place on Friday morning before he went over to the island. Though both Katherine and Daniel lied about that when I first asked about Kelsall. According to the girl's mother, they were putting together a statement to the press, which would have made them both come out of this smelling of roses.' A pause. 'I can't see that happening now.'

'So now everyone will remember Rick as a sexist bully! Because the girl lied to the media.'

Vera supposed that was true. It wasn't much of a legacy. 'Yes, he died before he could put his name to the statement which would have implied both he and Eliza had been victims of the press. It's almost as if someone didn't want him cleared . . .'

She allowed her voice to tail off, hoping that Annie might suggest a possible answer, but the woman remained silent.

'Where were you on Monday?' Vera made no attempt to hide the reason behind the question.

'I was at work.'

'All day?'

'I started at eight and finished at four.'

'We're still trying to trace Charlotte's movements, but we're pretty sure she was killed after four. She was in her yoga studio. It's hardly any distance from the deli.'

'I came straight home after my shift.'

'Can anyone confirm that?'

'No! I live alone. How could they?'

'These are tight little houses. Someone might have heard the cistern fill while you were running a bath, been aware of you moving about.'

'There's a deaf old man on one side and a single mother with a teething baby on the other, so they're hardly likely to have noticed!' Annie was starting to get rattled.

Vera didn't mind that. The woman might lose control and let things slip out.

'Jax said Daniel came to see you yesterday. I visited him on the way back from the island on Sunday. Very flash place he's got at the tower.'

'I wouldn't know.' Annie was spitting out the words now. 'I've never been in the new house. When I lived there, we were in a shitty caravan.'

'But he did come to see you in Kimmerston yesterday. You

and Daniel must still be friendly, if he came all the way from Rede's Tower to offer his support.'

'I doubt if that was the only reason for him turning up in town.'

'Ah yes, he had a planning meeting apparently. We're checking that out too. Did he say where he was going, once he'd left you?'

Annie shook her head. 'We weren't together very long. Just went out for a coffee. It was kind of him, I suppose.'

'No hard feelings then, about the divorce?'

'We married too early,' Annie said. 'That was all. I was infatuated. I adored him. He wasn't quite as smitten. We both worked to make a go at it, but we grew up in different ways.'

'Why the rush to get married?' Vera was interested. That curiosity again, making her pry. 'I know there was a bairn, but even that long ago, marriage wasn't compulsory if you found yourself pregnant.'

'Really, we'd been a couple since school. Settled, I thought. Marriage seemed a logical step.' A pause. 'I thought we'd be together forever.'

'What happened to the baby?'

'You've been speaking to Jax. I'm sure she'll have told you.' The bitterness was back in her voice.

'Nah, pet. She said it was your story to tell.'

'She was called Freya. She died at four months. An unexplained death they called it. Your people came in, not accusing me of murder. Not in so many words. But implying it. Perhaps that's why I understand what Rick was going through. I know what it's like: people talking about you behind your back, believing the rumours. Not that I cared then. I didn't care about anything except losing my baby. And the guilt. I knew I didn't mean to kill her, but I must have done something wrong, mustn't I? Because babies don't just die, do they? You don't just wake up in the morning and find them dead. It had to be my fault.'

'Sometimes.' Vera's voice was gentle, like a whisper. 'Sometimes folk do just die. That's why we call the deaths unexplained. And that's the worst experience ever for the people left behind.'

'They did find a cause. Infant meningitis. Everyone thought that should make me feel better about myself. Honestly, though, it didn't help. Because I should have noticed she was ill. I should have done something. But it was our wedding night. A party. I'd drunk champagne. My mother had offered to take her for the night, but I wanted her to stay with us. If I hadn't done that, she might be alive. She'd be middle-aged. With children of her own. Even grandbairns if she'd been like me and got started early.'

'You know, pet, you can't live like that. The guilt will ruin you.'

'I know,' Annie said. 'It already has.'

There was a moment of silence. Annie opened the stove, using a glove on the hearth so her hand wouldn't burn and she threw in a log.

'Daniel didn't feel the same way?'

'Daniel just thought we should go ahead and have another child. As soon as possible. He never said, but I could tell he thought I was morbid. Self-indulgent. He found my grief boring. He did say that he wanted a life.'

'You never had another baby?'

Annie shook her head. 'I couldn't face it. What if we lost her or him too? Besides, it would have seemed as if we didn't care about Freya. As if a replacement would do just as well.'

Vera thought she could understand Daniel's desire to move on. Annie was still haunted by guilt after more than forty years. She couldn't have been an easy woman to live with. Katherine Willmore, with her ambition and her principles, would have seemed uncomplicated in comparison.

'He knew how close you were to Rick,' Vera said. 'He understood how another apparently unexplained death would affect you. That showed some sensitivity.'

'I know!' Now Annie just seemed exhausted, as if all the emotion had drained away from her. 'He was never insensitive. Not really. He was just able to move on more quickly than I could and I resented it. I was jealous, I think, that he seemed to find it easier to do.'

'He was there at the first reunion, the weekend that Isobel died in the car crash?'

'Yeah, the one and only time!' Annie gave a little smile. 'It was okay though. He really made the effort to get on with people.'

'Has he kept in touch with any of that group? Perhaps some of them were friends in their own right, not just through you?'

Annie shook her head. 'He was always different from the rest of us. Sporty. Practical. More into football than talking.'

'Yet he talked Rick Kelsall into giving his woman's daughter a job.'

'I don't know anything about that. Perhaps he wanted to impress Katherine Willmore that he had friends in high places too.' Annie's voice was hard, bitter.

Vera paused for a moment. After all, perhaps she'd have to trawl back through past relationships, past events. 'How did Daniel end up at the Pilgrims' House in the first place, if it wasn't his thing? That Only Connect weekend was voluntary, wasn't it?'

Annie turned away. Vera thought her cheeks were flushed and not because of the heat. The woman was blushing!

'Because of you! It was his chance of getting off with you!'

'Aye.' Annie turned back, shyly. 'Something like that.'

'Did you know Rick was writing a novel?'

The change in tone seemed to shock Annie and she stared at Vera. 'No.'

'But he was talking about it, that night in the Pilgrims' House. Not long before he died.'

'He was talking a lot,' Annie said. 'He always did when he was drunk. I must have zoned out.'

'He was very excited about it apparently. It's set in Holy Island. Based on real events. I wondered if that could give us some kind of motive for his death. He might be planning to wake dogs that the killer wanted to let lie.'

'I'm sorry.' Annie gave a little shake of her head. 'I don't know what you're talking about.'

Vera couldn't quite accept that Rick wouldn't have confided in Annie about his book. Even if she hadn't listened when he'd talked about it in general terms to the group, he would have discussed it with her. Probably in more detail. Annie had been his admirer and his support since he was a boy. His validation. Surely he'd have wanted to share his excitement with her. But Vera could tell this wasn't the time to push it. Reluctantly, she got up from the comfortable sofa, and stood for a moment in the pleasant sunlit room.

She reached into her bag and took out the photograph of the group taken at the first Only Connect weekend. 'I thought you'd like this back. Thanks for lending it to us.'

Annie took it. 'It seems such a very long time ago.'

'If you think of anything that might help, do get in touch with me. Okay?'

Annie scooped the cat into her arms, cradled it and nodded.

Outside, the toddler was still playing. Vera checked her phone. There was a message from Ashworth to tell her he'd made an appointment to see Louisa and Ken and was heading out now. And giving the Holy Island crossing times for the following day if she wanted to talk to Phil Robson, so she wouldn't have to check for herself. Vera gave a self-satisfied smile as she walked back to the car. She'd trained her boy well.

Chapter Thirty-Two

ANNIE LAIDLER STOOD AT THE BAY window and watched Vera walk away down the alley. There was something comforting about the woman, her bulk and her determination. When the detective reached the road, Annie turned back into the room.

She thought about Rick leaving her all that money, suddenly moved almost to tears. It wasn't the money itself that was so important, though it would certainly take away some of the stress of everyday living. To go to the supermarket without checking the price of every item before buying! To put on the heating in the bedroom before ice started to coat the inside of the window! To think that when she got very old and frail she might afford proper sheltered accommodation, somewhere pleasant with a view and no smell of piss! All that would be wonderful of course. And to help turn Jax's dreams into reality would pay back some of her friend's kindness.

More emotional was the idea that Rick had been thinking about her. Properly considering her needs and comfort. Leaving her money hadn't been one of his fleeting notions or grand gestures. He'd taken time to go to his solicitor and write it into his will. He hadn't even boasted to her and the others what he was doing. It hadn't been about the gratitude and applause. It was almost as if Rick had known that he'd die before her, and had wanted to see her properly provided for.

Annie went to the bedroom and changed for work. After all, she couldn't sit brooding here all day. She and Jax had plans to make.

Chapter Thirty-Three

IT STARTED RAINING AS SOON AS Joe Ashworth hit the Cumbrian border and that fed into all his prejudices. He saw Cumbria as a place of floods, of wild westerlies, of chaos and ignorance. Only the Lake District had a semblance of civilization but that was overrun by tourists from the South, and he distrusted the South even more than the West.

Louisa and Ken lived in a smart new-build on the edge of a village outside Carlisle. It was detached, stone-built, with views to the hills, but an easily managed garden. A sensible place for a couple of retirees. Joe thought of Louisa as a sensible woman.

'You will have heard about Charlotte Thomas's death.' They were sitting in an uncluttered living room, all pastel shades and soft furnishing. Ken's attention came and went. When he'd come into the room, the dog at his heels, Joe had thought he'd been recognized by the man. Now, he wasn't so sure. The rain beat against the window. In the field beyond the garden half a dozen soggy sheep were sheltering behind a drystone wall.

'Yes.' Louisa was dressed as if she were at work, Joe thought.

A skirt and soft wool jersey. Shoes, not slippers. She was carefully made-up. Perhaps she considered this interview as work, at least that she had a role to play, a position to maintain. 'We saw it on the news this morning.'

'Charlotte was the same age as your sister Isobel?'

'Yes, they were in the same year at school as Ken, Phil, Daniel, Annie and Rick.'

'It must have been a terrible shock when Isobel died.'

'Of course. Unthinkable.' Louisa stared out at the rain. 'My parents were never quite the same again. It was as if the sun stopped shining.'

'And you?'

It took Louisa a long time to answer, and when she did speak, there was nothing glib in her words. They were considered. Shockingly honest. 'It was a horrible time. As the second child, I'd rather resented Isobel. She was brighter than me, certainly prettier. Much more confident. She'd gone to a good university and I'd only made it to teacher training college. I'd envied the attention she'd got. When she died, of course, I was stricken with guilt. It was almost as if I'd wished her to die. As if I'd caused it.' She turned to Joe. 'And she was still the centre of attention. She became saintly in my parents' eyes. Even at her funeral, I knew that I'd never be able to live up to her. It's easy to be perfect if you're not still around to make mistakes.'

Joe Ashworth said nothing. He'd learned the power of silence from Vera, and he sensed that Louisa had more to say.

'But of course, she wasn't saintly. None of us are. She was demanding and petulant if she couldn't get her own way. She was more sly than me. She told my parents she was revising at a friend's house when she was in the pub or out with a boy.

I couldn't see the point of lying. Perhaps I should have cultivated the knack.'

'Were there lots of boys in her life?'

'Oh yes, she was a terrible flirt. She thrived on admiration.
And she was very good-looking.'

'I've seen a photo of you all at that first reunion,' Joe said.
'You were stunning, just as pretty as her.'

'Perhaps I was,' Louisa said. 'Though I didn't see it at the
time. And perhaps that's why she couldn't quite like me.'

Joe thought how clear-eyed the woman was. There was no
sentimentality in her vision of the past.

'Why are you asking all these questions, Sergeant? Why the
obsession with the not-so-good old days?'

'Rick Kelsall was planning a novel,' Joe said. 'Set in the past.
A thriller set around a death on Holy Island, and based, apparently, on real events.' A pause. 'It was as if he was predicting
his own murder. Or digging up buried secrets. That's why
we're interested again in Isobel's death. I'm sorry if it seems
callous, insensitive, to take you back to those times.' He paused.
'Did you have any idea why Isobel was in such a rush to get
off the island that day?'

Louisa looked at him. 'It was the sort of woman she was.
Impulsive. If she wasn't happy, she would leave. Nothing would
stop her. Only of course the tide did. Not even Isobel could
stop the water as it flooded the causeway.'

Ken got to his feet and began to wander up and down.
Louisa seemed glad of the interruption. She stood up too and
took his hand.

'Are you bored, love? Why don't I find you a programme
to watch?'

She led him into another room. The dog lumbered after

them. Joe heard the theme music of a popular daytime soap, then a door shutting, as Louisa came back to join him.

'I'm sorry, Sergeant. Ken can get restless.'

'Did you know that Rick was writing a novel? I was thinking he might have consulted you if he intended to use Isobel's death as a jumping-off point.'

She seemed genuinely amused. 'That wasn't Rick's way of working! It would never have occurred to him that it might upset me if he turned Isobel's death into some sort of enter-tainment. Which would also make him a profit.'

'Would it have upset you?'

There was a silence. The rain seemed to be easing a little. 'Probably not! Not after all this time.'

'Do you know a woman called Katherine Willmore?'

Louisa frowned. 'The name's familiar.'

'She's the Police and Crime Commissioner for Northumber-land.'

'Of course. I've heard her talking on the radio.'

'It was her daughter Eliza who'd made the complaints against Rick Kelsall.'

'And lost him his job? I can see that the TV company would have been reluctant to take on Willmore's daughter in a legal wrangle.' Louisa gave a little smile. 'Poor **Rick**. He'd tried it on with the wrong woman this time.'

Joe didn't want to explain that the case was more nuanced than it appeared. Now everyone would assume Kelsall was guilty, just as Louisa had done. He moved on.

'How well did you know Charlotte?'

'Not well at all. She and Isobel were close friends though. Two of a kind. She was very upset when Isobel died.'

'Charlotte wasn't on the island that day?' Joe still couldn't see how Isobel's accident on Holy Island could have anything to do with the recent murders, but Vera would want to know all the details.

'No, I think she'd moved on, made much more exciting friends in those early days. Rick was always loyal to us and rearranged his affairs so he could be there. Charlotte was very different. A weekend with us, certainly with me, wouldn't have appealed.'

Joe thought that sounded as if there was some sort of personal animosity between the women.

'You didn't get on with Charlotte?'

Louisa shrugged. 'We just didn't have very much in common. Her life was full of glamour and excitement. I started teaching and got married to Ken. Worked hard, and later took a degree in education. We had children of our own. We must have seemed very conventional to her. I suspect we would have bored her.'

'So you haven't seen her since you were at school together?'

'We kept in touch for a while.' Louisa still seemed reluctant to give a direct answer. 'I suppose because of our shared connection through Isobel. She and Charlotte really were the very best of friends. Some years it was only Christmas cards. I watched her career from a distance, with, I must admit, a little envy. She must have heard about Ken's illness on the grapevine, because she sent me a note, saying she was thinking about me. That was kind.'

'What about the others at Pilgrims' House this weekend? Philip and Annie. Were you closer to them?'

There was a moment of silence while Louisa chose her words carefully. 'Philip has changed since I knew him as a teenager. He was more challenging in those days. He made me think. I suppose he's happier now, but not so interesting.'

'He never married? Never had a permanent relationship?'
She shook her head. 'Not so far as I know.'

'Not even in those early days, while you were all at school?'

'No. He was always rather a loner.'

'What about you? You were very young when you met Ken.'

She looked up at him, amused. 'What are you asking, Sergeant? If I had an affair?'

Joe thought she might not have been to university, but she was highly intelligent. Before he could answer, she went on:

'Rick was always suggesting a fling. It had become rather a boring standing joke. Now, with Ken as he is, I might have agreed. I miss physical contact, intimacy.'

Joe was shocked, embarrassed, which was probably what she'd intended.

'Can we go back to Charlotte? When did you last see her?'

'I'm not being awkward or obstructive, Sergeant, because I can't be certain that it *was* her. It seems such a strange coincidence.'

'Tell me.' He realized that was classic Vera. After a few drinks, she could get quite lyrical about prising info from suspects. *Witnesses all have stories to share. Give them time and space and they'll tell them. They might not be true stories, but they can still give us a glimpse of the truth.*

'I thought I saw her on Holy Island.'

'She was there, of course,' Joe said. 'We called her on Saturday after Rick Kelsall's body was found.' He remembered the woman, turning up in her ridiculous little car, wearing her smart clothes, confident and polished.

'No, it was the evening before that. The Friday. I went for a walk just before chapel. Philip had already arrived and they said he'd keep an eye on Ken. You see, he's very kind. I don't like to leave Ken on his own now, especially in strange places. He gets confused very easily. It was a treat to go out on my own. I've missed that the most since his illness has progressed: the peace of being alone. It was a beautifully clear afternoon, and I got the last of the sun. I only walked into the village and back. There were lots of people around. Families, enjoying the weather. And I saw Charlotte. At least I thought it was her. She really hasn't changed so much over the years. From a distance at least. She glanced up the street and then disappeared into one of the cottages.'

'You didn't knock?'

Louisa shook her head. 'No, how embarrassing if it had been a complete stranger! And even more embarrassing if it had been Charlotte. What would I say? As I've explained, we were never close friends. We'd both have found the encounter extremely awkward.'

'You say she looked up the street before going into the cottage. Didn't she see *you*?'

'She saw me, Sergeant, but she didn't recognize me. Unlike Charlotte, I've aged considerably since we last met. To her, I would have been just another older woman in anorak and walking boots. The island is full of them.'

'Was she on her own?' Joe thought that this might be some sort of breakthrough. He imagined Vera's pleasure, the excited glint in her eye, when he passed on the information.

'She was when I saw her. But I had the sense that someone had let her in to the cottage. That she'd knocked and then the door had opened, but I didn't see anyone inside.' Louisa paused. 'I must admit that I was rather curious. I walked past and glanced in through the window. But the room next to the street was empty.'

'Can you show me exactly where the cottage was on Google Maps?'

'Oh, I think so. On street view. It had a pale green door.'

Joe started fiddling with his phone, but she had the image on the screen of her iPad before he'd even found the app.

'Here, this is the one.' Joe saw a pretty cottage in the main street. 'If you give me your email address, I'll send it across to you.'

'I have to ask where you were yesterday afternoon.'

'That was when Charlotte died?'

He nodded.

'I was here,' she said. 'I'm always here unless I can get some respite care for Ken, and that's become much more difficult as his condition has progressed. It's a very pleasant prison, but it feels like a prison all the same.'

'Lou!' It was Ken, calling her from the other room. 'Lou, where are you?' It sounded like panic. 'Where are you?'

Chapter Thirty-Four

THE CONVERSATION WITH ANNIE LAIDLER WAS still haunting Vera. She hated the idea of the woman grieving for the baby who'd died more than forty years before. Not just grieving, but blaming herself for it. Rick's murder seemed to have made the sadness more intense, more immediate. It was as if Annie had kept her guilt locked up for all this time, but now the memories were out of the cage.

Her phone rang. Joe. 'Yes? I hope you've got some good news for me, because there's bugger all to smile about here.'

There was a moment's pause. Even mild swearing shocked him. Especially when it came from a middle-aged woman.

'Louisa Hampton thinks she saw Charlotte Thomas on Holy Island the evening Rick Kelsall was killed.'

'And she didn't think to tell us! The victim's ex-wife was wandering round the place on the evening of his death, but she didn't think it was important until after the woman died.'

'She wasn't certain. After all, she'd not seen her for years.' A pause. 'I know the house she went into. Louisa picked it out on Google Maps. She thinks somebody else was inside.'

'Well, that's something, I suppose.' Vera knew she sounded grudging. 'Katherine Willmore claims to have been on the island when Charlotte was killed. She's used afternoon tea in the Old Hall as her alibi. What is it with the place? It's as if the island's some sort of magnet, sucking people in. Some bloody black hole. It has to be the centre of the investigation.' Her mind was chasing through the options. 'Someone will have to go and check. They can talk to Philip Robson at the same time.'

'I can't do it.' Joe's voice was so firm that Vera could tell this was probably non-negotiable. 'It's Sal's birthday, and to get all that done, I'd have to stay over. She's planned a special evening.'

'Eh, pet, I wouldn't want to be the cause of marital dishar-mony. I'll get Hol up there.' She paused for a moment, because sometimes the thought of Holly stealing his thunder made Joe change his mind. Not today though.

There was a moment's hesitation, and the background sound of a truck rumbling past, before he asked: 'Did you get anything useful from Annie Laidler?'

'I'm not sure. Probably not. I'll fill you in on the details when you get back. I take it you *will* be back for the briefing. You're not sloping home straightaway. We're not paying you for part-time work.'

Joe didn't say anything. Vera suspected he *had* been hoping for a sneaky end-of-shift getaway. 'We'll make it an afternoon meeting,' she said brightly, 'so Holly can be there at least at the beginning and still get onto the island while there's some daylight. You'll be home in plenty of time for the candle-lit supper. I'll make sure to speed it through.'

'Thanks.'

Vera could tell he was still grumpy, but she was the boss, and, really, she didn't care.

They were at the briefing in front of the whiteboard, all crammed in to the room. Gurgling radiators and peeling paint providing the backdrop to their deliberations. Billy Cartwright had managed to sit himself next to the prettiest lass in the room, and she seemed to be laughing at his jokes. Vera could never work out how Billy did it. He was no oil painting and weedy with it. Maybe there was something of the Rick Kelsall about him. He had that persistence that came across to younger women as old-fashioned charm. Or flattering adoration.

'So, we've got two murders, connected in the present and the past. The victims, Rick Kelsall and Charlotte Thomas. Formerly school friends, lovers and husband and wife. And Kelsall must still have felt something for the woman, or felt that he owed her, because he'd left her a heap of money in his will. You'll all be aware now of the details surrounding the murders. Two high-profile people, which is seriously giving Mr Watkins the jitters, and because of that, we're under pressure to clear it up quickly. The other complication, of course, is that our respected Police and Crime Commissioner Katherine Willmore . . .'

Someone chortled in the back row, but Vera continued without appearing to notice.

'. . . is also very much involved in the case; her daughter Eliza was Rick Kelsall's intern and ostensibly made allegations of sexual harassment against him, and was the cause of him losing his job. Though according to Katherine, there was no assault, it was all a misunderstanding, and Rick had agreed to put out a statement blaming the press and the TV company for fake news.'

Joe stuck up his hand. It seemed he was still managing to focus on the investigation, despite his plans for a romantic evening with Sal. 'Does that statement exist anywhere? Surely, if Kelsall and Willmore had a meeting they'd have put something in writing?'

'Good point, Joe. We need to know if they *did* cobble together the statement and it's not a fantasy dreamed up after the man died. I'm assuming it'd be child's play for a journo and a lawyer to write something bland to shift the blame from both Kelsall and Eliza. Willmore didn't volunteer it, but then I wasn't bright enough to ask.'

'It might be on Kelsall's laptop,' Holly said.

'So it might. Along with his bloody novel, and that hasn't appeared yet either.' She looked out at the room. 'Before you disappear to wherever you're going, Billy, put a rocket up the bums of your digital team. Tell them they're slowing down the course of this investigation big style.'

Billy looked hurt in a theatrical way and turned to the young PC beside him for support, but Vera saw him tapping away on his iPhone, presumably passing on the gist of her comments.

'I'd really love to know what Charlotte was doing on the island on the Friday night.' Vera was talking to herself now, rather than the team. 'I can't think that it was to meet Kelsall. He'd stayed the night with her on Thursday, so there was no need for another secret assignation. Was there someone else in the group she'd agreed to meet? Another man? A potential lover? It wouldn't be Ken, surely. Or is Philip the vicar hiding something from us?'

There was no reply and Vera continued. 'But why didn't the

woman tell us she'd been on the island when we interviewed her on Saturday afternoon? And if she was there for social reasons, to catch up with a friend, why the secrecy? Why not just bowl up to the Pilgrims' House with a bottle of wine and join in the party? Surely she wouldn't have been there just for a night away on her own, for the peace and the solitude. She could get that at home.'

Vera paused and ran the evening of Kelsall's death in her mind. They'd all been drinking, that was clear, but surely if any individual had slipped out of the house for a meeting with Charlotte, the rest would have noticed the absence. But perhaps not. You could make a plausible excuse. Need for fresh air, to look at the stars, to take the elderly dog for a walk. 'We'll have to talk to them again,' she said. 'Find out if they remember anyone going AWOL at all.' It seemed to her once more that the answer to both murders lay back on the island.

Joe stuck up his hand again. Tentative this time. 'Something did occur to me while I was talking to the couple in Cumbria. We dismiss Ken, because of his dementia, but he wasn't ill that time when they were young, on the island for the first reunion. Nothing to have stopped him then being the cause of Isobel's accident. And Louisa is protective of him. Not exactly affectionate, but I can see her fighting for him. For the reputation he had as a head teacher. A good man. And I'd say she's cold enough to be a killer.'

Vera nodded her agreement. 'We keep an open mind then. We can't rule any of them out.' She turned to Holly. 'So, you're our shining hope for a breakthrough. We need you to find out what Charlotte Thomas was doing on Holy Island, and to check Katherine Willmore's alibi for Monday afternoon.'

She smiled out at her team, but it was all show. The progress on the case felt frustratingly slow. There were times at this point in a case, when it felt as if she was wading through treacle.

Holly was about to answer when her phone buzzed. 'Sorry, boss, it's Kelsall's mobile provider. I've been waiting for them to get back to me.' She listened for a moment, ended the call and looked out at the room. 'Kelsall had a call very early on Saturday morning – just after midnight. I asked them to track down the caller and let me know.'

'And?'

'It came from Judith Sinclair. Whose maiden name was Judith Marshall.'

'The teacher who brought them all together in the first place?'

Holly grinned and nodded.

'That's for me then,' Vera said. 'I'll head out there this evening when I've done here.'

When everyone had left, she went back to her desk and her computer. There was always a backlog of work that had more to do with the management of the team than the work in progress. She was about to leave, when she saw that Rick Kelsall's agent had finally sent through the short synopsis she'd used to entice publishers. Vera looked at it briefly, but couldn't focus and decided that it could wait for tomorrow. It was more important now to talk to Judith Sinclair.

Chapter Thirty-Five

HOLLY FOUND HOLY ISLAND DIFFERENT, QUIETER. The children were back at school and there were always fewer people staying during the week. The place was left to the locals and to older people, who'd retired with proper pensions and who had the freedom to holiday when they liked. The weather had changed. A sea fret had blown in from the east, blocking out the sun.

Holly booked into the Seahorse. She was given the same room as she'd had before. Number five. A double bed squeezed into a single room, with a shower room attached. Black mould crawling up the plastic shower curtain. No sea view. An ill-fitting sash window looked out over the empty street. She wondered about asking if there was anything else available, but she doubted if another room would be much better. Besides, this was cheap and the police service budget was always tight.

Di, the landlady, recognized her, peered at her through her thick spectacles. 'Oh, I thought you'd finished your investigation here on the island.'

'Not quite.' Holly smiled across the reception desk. 'I don't suppose you've had any more thoughts about the single woman who stayed here on Friday night?' It would be another loose end to tie up. Something else to make Vera happy. At least for a moment.

'Yes! I spoke to my staff. One of our barmaids reckons she recognized her as a regular. She'll be working later.'

'Thanks.'

'Would you like dinner?' Di had turned back to hostess mode. 'The kitchen's open until nine.'

'No, not this evening.' The Seahorse served traditional pub food, mostly carbs and all of it fried. Vera's idea of heaven, but not Holly's. She'd brought a picnic to eat in her room.

Before that, she headed out onto the island. She wanted to check out the cottage Charlotte had visited before it was too late for a polite enquiry. The mist was thicker now, and though it wasn't yet dark, everything was shadowy and very still. There were people in the public bar, but from the street she could only hear the buzz of quiet conversation. Occasionally, people emerged from the gloom. A couple of teenagers, very young, shyly holding hands, not expecting anyone to see them. An elderly man with a stick, who used it to push his way into the Seahorse bar. There was a sudden shaft of light on the pavement before the door swung closed behind him.

Holly got out her phone and checked the photo of the cottage, which Joe had sent through. She found it easily enough. A green door leading straight from the pavement. Small, white-washed, in the middle of a terrace. It was quite dark now and the curtains had been drawn. Somebody was in, because there was a chink of light where the curtains didn't quite meet, but the gap was tiny and she couldn't see through it. In the distance she could hear the mewling of a foghorn.

She knocked on the door. Close to the house now, she could tell that there was music playing inside, so indistinct that she could only make out the beat, an accompaniment to the foghorn on the shore. There were footsteps and the door opened. A large man stood inside, silhouetted against the light behind him. It took her a moment to make out who it was and he spoke first.

'Oh, hello.' The man seemed surprised to see her, but not shocked. 'I'm sorry, I don't remember your name. We met at the Pilgrims' House on that terrible day when Rick's body was found.' His voice was rich, welcoming, and it was that which identified him for her. 'Everything about that day is such a blur. Do come in!'

'Mr Robson.' *Should it have been Reverend Robson?* Holly wasn't sure. She introduced herself.

'Philip, please.'

He stepped aside and she walked straight into a warm and comfortable room, with an open fire and a couple of armchairs facing it. On the windowsill a pair of binoculars and an RSPB field guide. The music was unfamiliar. Jazz, coming from a radio. Philip Robson switched it off.

'I'm guessing you have more questions for me about Rick Kelsall. Please do sit down.' He pointed to a chair next to the one where he'd obviously been sitting. There was a book on the arm, opened, page down. Mick Herron's *Slow Horses*. One of Vera's favourites. She'd given a copy to Holly, who'd enjoyed it too.

'How can I help you? It must be urgent for you to have come all this way. Can I get you something? Coffee? Tea?'

Holly shook her head. There was an air of concentration in the small room, a focus she didn't want to break.

'Have you heard that Charlotte Thomas is dead?'

'No!' Philip seemed genuinely astonished. 'I'm still treating the week as a kind of retreat and I've been trying to avoid the news. I have no computer here, no television.' There was a pause as he tried to process the information. 'Poor Charlotte, what a dreadful thing.' He looked at Holly. 'What exactly happened? How did she die?'

'She was murdered. Just like Mr Kelsall.'

A moment of silence.

'None of your friends contacted you?' Holly couldn't quite believe that Annie or Louisa hadn't been in touch with the news. Another violent death within the group. Wouldn't that trigger a frisson of excitement or even of fear? Surely, they'd be wondering if one of them would be the next victim.

'I have no phone reception here, Constable. I thought that was why you turned up unannounced on my doorstep.'

'Have you been here on the island since you left the Pilgrims' House?'

'I have. I've had some wonderful walks. It's been very peaceful. Just what I needed after a busy year. Most of the trippers left on Sunday, so I've almost had the place to myself.' Robson gave a little laugh. 'There's been no more skinny-dipping though.'

Holly ignored the comment. 'You haven't been tempted to go further afield – to catch up with family or friends on the mainland?'

'What is this about, Constable? Are you asking me to provide an alibi? If so, I'll need to know where and when poor Charlotte was killed.'

'She died in her yoga studio in Kimmerston,' Holly said. 'It's impossible to pinpoint a precise time of death, but it was yesterday. Late afternoon or early evening.'

'I haven't driven at all, since I moved my car from outside the Pilgrims' House to the alley at the back of the cottage here, but of course I have no way of proving that.' He paused. 'I have been going to the chapel every evening for six o'clock prayers. Some of the islanders might have noticed the candlelight.'

'Charlotte Thomas was seen coming into this cottage on the Friday night when Rick died,' Holly said. 'That's why I'm here. I hadn't realized it was where you were staying.' *Though I should have checked. That was stupid.*

'She was in this house?'

'Yes. Our witness thinks someone else was already in the cottage to let her in.' Holly looked over at him. 'You weren't here, before chapel on Friday, to check the place out?'

'No! I knew it wouldn't be mine until the Sunday lunchtime. I assumed there'd be other holidaymakers here over the weekend.'

'Wouldn't Charlotte have told you all she was here and come to see you in the Pilgrims' House?' Holly paused. 'You were old friends after all.'

'Charlotte wasn't really one of us.' For the first time Philip seemed uncomfortable. 'She didn't even stay for the first weekend of Only Connect. She got her father to come and get her in his very smart car on the first day.'

'And she wasn't here for your first reunion.' A statement not a question.

'That's right. She said she had better things to do. I think she regretted not being here after Isobel died. They really were very good friends, and it would have been a chance to see her for the last time.'

The fire cracked, sending up sparks. Holly thought this wasn't helping very much. The man seemed to have no knowledge of Charlotte's stay, and hadn't much of an alibi for the day before. Perhaps the owner would be able to tell her more. She'd check that in the morning.

'Can you let me have the contact details for your landlord?'

'Landlady,' Philip said. 'Here's her card.'

Holly took it and glanced at it. Gull Cottage, Holy Island. Then the owner's name.

'Judith Sinclair. She's the teacher who set up Only Connect?'

'Yes.' Philip glanced up at Holly. 'I've kept in touch with her, and we've become quite close over the years. She and her husband belonged to a church in Kimmerston. Judy still does. Her husband inherited some money when his grandparents died and they bought this place. A kind of bolthole, when teaching got a bit stressful. Now she lets it out to supplement her pension.'

'Was Judith here over the weekend?'

'No, at least I don't think so; she would have told me if she was.' The response was easy, just like the rest of the conversation, but Holly sensed a moment of hesitation. 'And I really think she'd have let me know if Charlotte was going to be on the island too.'

'Who let you in to the cottage on Sunday?'

'Nobody! I knew where the keys would be: in an old privy in the backyard.'

'Had the cottage been cleaned since the last tenants?' This was important, Holly thought, though if Charlotte had been here, there would surely be some sign of her presence, a stray fingerprint, whether it had been cleaned or not.

'Oh yes.' Philip was relaxed again. 'Someone had definitely been in to clean. The grate had been swept, the pots and pans in the kitchen all put away. Clean sheets on the bed.'

'When do you leave?' Holly asked.

'Friday. I'm back on duty on Sunday. It's a long drive and there'll be a sermon to prepare.'

She stood up then. She couldn't get through the barrier of his warmth and his politeness. Charlotte had been here – it would be too much of a coincidence otherwise – but Holly was no clearer why or how Philip Robson fitted in to the investigation.

In the Seahorse, the landlady had been looking out for Holly and scurried from the bar to catch her before she headed up to her room. 'If you want to chat to Linz, the barmaid who remembers that single woman who paid by cash, she's on shift now.' Desperate to help, to be able to tell her friends she'd been part of a major police investigation.

Holly had been looking forward to some time to reflect on the conversation in Gull Cottage, before sending a report across to Vera, but if they could dismiss the mystery guest, she could let Vera know about that too.

Linz was waiting in the lounge bar, so Holly found herself sitting on a stool there.

'What's your tipple?' The landlady hovered beside her.

'Well, G&T, but really, I don't need anything yet.'

'Nonsense.' The landlady nodded to Linz and a large gin appeared on the bar. 'It's on the house. Only glad to help.'

Holly insisted on paying, and explained it would be against the rules to accept it for free.

Linz was skinny with sharp features and black hair. She had something of the Goth about her. Panda eyes and a long black skirt. She told Holly that she'd grown up in Ashington, but she loved it here. 'I like it best in the winter,' she said. 'Then it's mostly locals and regulars in the bar – some real characters – and you can have the island to yourself. It's not so good for business though. Di makes most of her money over the summer, when the trippers come.' She nodded towards the landlady, who was standing at the other end of the bar, pretending not to listen.

'So, you recognized the single woman, who paid cash at the last minute?'

'Yep. She's a regular. Joanne Haswell. Her name was in the booking, but Di didn't recognize it. I did as soon as she asked. She works at the Ministry at Benton. She quite often turns up on the offchance, when she knows there'll be time to get off the island if we don't have space. If you're a civil servant, I guess the work's pretty boring and sometimes you want to be impulsive, take a bit of a risk.'

Holly nodded. She finished her drink and was about to head back upstairs, when Linz started talking again.

'I'll tell you who else was here on Friday night.' Linz spoke quickly and her accent – pure Pitmatic – was so thick that Holly struggled to follow. 'Cathy, who works in the kitchen, pointed her out to me. Apparently, she was famous at one time. A bit of a celebrity. I wouldn't have known her of course. Before my time.'

'Who was that?'

'The woman who was murdered in Kimmerston yesterday!' Linz looked across the bar, her black-rimmed eyes almost mischievous. She understood the impression she was making. 'I only just saw it on Facebook before coming down to work. Charlotte Thomas. She was here in the bar sitting over in the window.' She nodded towards a padded bench seat with a table in front of it.

'She wasn't on her own?' Because even now, women didn't go into a bar on their own. Certainly not older women, unless they were waiting for someone and even then, they'd feel uncomfortable.

'Nah, she was with another woman and a guy.'

'Can you describe them?'

Linz screwed up her face to show she was thinking. 'The woman looked even older. But she was bonny with it, like. Good cheekbones. You knaa.'

Holly nodded. Could that be Judith Sinclair? It seemed possible. But the description could also apply to Annie Laidler or Louisa Hampton. 'And the man?'

Linz shook her head. 'Sorry, I didn't really see him at all. He had his back to me all the time and the pub was crazy busy all night. I only had glimpses of the women through the crowded tables and they weren't here for very long.'

'He didn't buy the drinks?' Because that was still usually how it worked, especially for older people. It was the man who went to the bar, even if a woman had slipped him the cash to pay.

'It's all table service,' Linz said. 'Di's trying to take the place upmarket. I didn't take their orders, so I wouldn't know.' A pause. 'I didn't see them leave either. I googled the woman when I took five minutes to go to the loo, and when I got back another group had taken their place.'

'Do you know what time they were here?'

'Mid-evening? Seven? Seven-thirty? Sorry, like I said, the pub was really busy.'

Holly went up to her room, switched on the kettle and made a mug of herbal tea. She never travelled without teabags these days. Orange and cranberry, her favourite flavour. She sent an email to the boss and to Joe, describing her conversation with Robson and the barmaid's description of the people in the Seahorse. She ate the salad she'd made, and then, guiltily, the packet of biscuits that was on the tray next to the kettle.

When she'd finished, it occurred to her that it would be reassuring to have someone else to email or to text. Someone special. She hadn't really had a boyfriend since she'd moved north. Work had always come first. She felt a sudden stab of loneliness, like a physical pain, and thought she couldn't carry on like this.

She checked her emails once more and saw that Cecilia Bertrand had sent through the synopsis of Kelsall's novel. There were still no further details from the digital investigations team. There was hardly more than a paragraph but, perhaps because she was so tired, the words seemed to make little sense. She couldn't see how the story hung together. She forwarded it to Vera and decided she'd look again in the morning. She cleaned her teeth and got into bed, and fell asleep listening to the mournful wail of the foghorn.

Chapter Thirty-Six

HOLLY'S EMAIL ARRIVED, JUST BEFORE VERA set out to see Judith Sinclair. It was another reason to talk to the former teacher. She'd already phoned in advance, playing the role of slightly disorganized older woman.

'You don't mind, do you, pet? I know you've already had a chat with my officers, but I just want to check a couple of their details. It wasn't quite clear from their notes.'

Judith lived in a village just out of the town. It was surrounded by established housing developments, and had become hardly more, these days, than a suburb of Kimmerston. She and her husband had probably bought their home from new, Vera thought. It felt to her as if Judith was rooted in the community. When Vera arrived, she was still in the small front garden, raking leaves from the lawn. It was almost dark and in the other houses lights were being switched on. Vera thought it was a strange kind of obsession to be working at this time of the evening. A need for order, or for activity. She moved easily. This woman was fit. She'd have no difficulty holding a cushion over Rick Kelsall's head. Or even, Vera thought, hoisting him into a makeshift noose.

Charlotte might be more difficult to overpower, but if Holly's information was right, the women knew each other. Judith would be able to approach her without causing suspicion.

'Come in, Inspector. I waited until you arrived before I stopped for tea.'

The kitchen looked out on a garden, which was longer, backing onto a field of sheep, very white in the dusk. Here, there was still a sense of space, of the village it had once been. Judith put on the kettle and made tea in a pot.

'Have you been here long?'

'Since we were first married. When we retired, we thought we might move further out into the country, but we never quite got round to it, and then when Martin died, I was glad to be here, among people I knew well.'

'After all, you had your bolthole in Holy Island if you needed an escape.' Vera heaved herself onto a stool at the breakfast bar. She thought Judith had probably planned to take her into an immaculate lounge, but this seemed less formal. The woman would like to be in control of situations. This might throw her a little.

'Oh, are you comfortable there, Inspector? We could go into the other room.' Frowning. Not answering the question implied in Vera's comment.

'This is perfect.' She sipped the coffee. 'How often do you get up to the cottage?'

'Oh, not as often as I did when Martin was alive. Now it's more useful as an alternative form of income. I suppose I could sell this house and downsize, but I'm happy here. All my memories are in the place. It's good to have the space when my children visit with *their* families.' She smiled. 'I love to travel. The holiday home supports my wanderlust.'

'When were you last at the cottage?'

There was a pause. Vera thought this was a woman who'd feel awkward about lying. Was she trying to find a form of words which would be true, but would also manage to imply that she hadn't been close to the place where a man she'd taught had died? In the end, Judith decided that truth was the best option.

'I was there on Friday. I needed to clean the place for a new tenant. There's a woman who usually cleans for me, but she's away on holiday, so I went up and made a night of it.'

'But you didn't go to the Pilgrims' House? You must have realized all your former students were there.'

'No!' The answer was quick and firm. No need to think about this one, to twist words to form a story, a half-truth. 'I knew they were there of course. I'm friendly with Philip. But no, I didn't meet any of the Pilgrims' House group. Not even him. I left very early on Saturday morning. It was a very swift stay.'

'You were in the pub though, the Seahorse, with a couple. Who were they?'

A silence. A white face. Anger. 'Has somebody been spying on me, Inspector?'

Vera smiled at the thought. 'Of course not! But a man was killed there. We're detectives. Of course we make inquiries.' A pause. 'The barmaid thought that the woman with you was Charlotte Thomas.' Another longer pause. 'You've probably heard that she's dead now too. Of course, it's probably a coincidence, but you were seen within a mile of one victim on the night of his death, and you were with the other just a couple of days before she was killed. You do see that you have questions to answer.'

'You can't possibly suspect me of being a murderer.' Her voice was imperious. It would have quelled the noise in any classroom. 'That's ridiculous. What reason would I have?'

'Why did you meet Charlotte Thomas on Friday evening?' Vera had stood up to plenty of teachers in her time.

'She phoned me before I left here on Friday morning. On my landline. I very nearly didn't answer, because nobody ever uses that these days. Only scammers and cold callers. I suppose I was still in the directory. She said she wanted to catch up, or rather to ask my advice. I told her I was just setting off for the island – hoping to put her off – but she said she'd meet me there.'

'What did she want to discuss with you?'

'I'm afraid I can't tell you, Inspector. It was a confidential conversation.'

'She's dead!' Vera couldn't believe what she was hearing. 'This might help me catch her killer.'

'She might be dead, Inspector, but she has living children. Sometimes a reputation is all that the dead have left to them, and I intend to honour that. We had a drink in the Seahorse. One drink because she was driving back to Kimmerston that night. We talked about old times. She asked for my advice and I gave it. I can't see at all how our conversation might relate to her death.'

'You lied to my officers when they asked you if you'd seen any of your students recently.'

'I did,' Judith said. 'I regretted that. I'm not by nature a liar. But I knew there would be more questions and it was Charlotte's secret to keep and not mine to share.'

'Who was the man with you in the pub?'

'Some local birdwatcher.' Judith was dismissive. 'If you talk to your spies in the pub, they'll tell you he was there when we arrived. We asked if we could share his table. The place was busy. One of the reasons we only had one drink was that we couldn't talk without being overheard. Charlotte had wanted a glass of wine and I had nothing in the cottage to give her, but we didn't stay long.'

The women stared at each other over the granite counter. Vera had the power to intimidate when she needed it, but Judith was steely, unmoved. Vera couldn't help admiring her courage. She gave it one last shot. 'What is this really about? You're either lying to me or to yourself. There's more going on here than a need to preserve a dead woman's reputation. Charlotte Thomas revelled in notoriety. She wouldn't mind the gossip. She'd have enjoyed any press she could get, even after her death.'

Judith shook her head. 'I won't be drawn, Inspector. Would you like another cup of tea? You're very welcome. If not, I think perhaps you'd better leave. I'm sure that you've had a very busy day.'

Vera didn't move. 'Why did you phone Rick Kelsall late on Friday night?'

There was a silence.

'I don't know what on earth you're talking about.'

'We checked the calls made to Mr Kelsall's mobile. The last call he received came from you. Not from your landline, but from your mobile phone.'

Judy Sinclair sat, motionless. 'You must be mistaken.'

'Are you telling me that you didn't make that call?'

Still there was no reply. At last, the woman spoke. Vera couldn't help admiring her poise. 'Are you charging me, Inspector? If so, we should probably complete this conversation somewhere more formal. If not, I believe I'm not obliged to answer your questions.'

'Perhaps somebody else made that call using your phone.'

Judith Sinclair stared at Vera. 'Perhaps they did, Inspector, but I've already explained that this conversation is at an end.'

Vera slid off the stool. Without a word, Judith walked her to the door and saw her into the garden.

Chapter Thirty-Seven

THE NEXT DAY, VERA WOKE EARLY, before it was quite light. On impulse, she decided on a walk before heading for the office. The movement of walking sometimes helped to shuffle facts into place, and made her see things more clearly. She pulled on her boots and the old waxed jacket that had hung behind the door when she was a teenager, and set off. The rising sun shone on the dying bracken on the hill behind the cottage, turning it to bronze. The whole hillside seemed to glow. She'd not go far. Just to the crags, where the peregrines bred most years, and she'd seen her fist ring ouzel. She'd been seven or eight and she'd run back down the hill, full of it.

'A male, Dad. I got the white crescent at the throat.'

He'd hardly looked up from the table where he'd been working on a dead badger, stuffing it for a farmer who hated animals and wanted it as a kind of trophy.

'Oh aye,' he'd said. 'I get the eggs every year for my collection.' She'd not known collecting eggs was illegal then, but she'd known it was wrong, and whenever she'd seen anything special after that, she'd kept the information to herself.

At the top of the hill, she stopped, her back to the rocks and, squinting against the sun, looked east towards the sea. A line of light on the horizon, glimpsed through the gleaming silver blades of the wind turbines in the mid-distance. She didn't mind them, thought they had a beauty of their own. From here, they looked like dandelion clocks, as if a strong enough gust would blow them away. Joanna was a bit of a green activist, and when people moaned about the turbines, she'd come out with the same response. 'Which would you rather? A wind farm or a nuclear power station? Or no heat in the winter?' Vera had started using the same line.

She realized she was dodging the problem of the murders, pushing them to the back of her mind, letting in stray memories, odd encounters. Hector was always there, bullying her from the grave. She couldn't judge Annie for her inability to let go of the past when she allowed Hector to rule her life. She pulled herself to her feet and started down the hill. The sun had risen. This was a new day. Perhaps today, she'd make sense of these murders.

When she arrived at the police station, Vera phoned Holly. There was no reception on her mobile, so Vera tried the landline of the pub. The landlady answered. 'Ooh yes, Inspector, I'll see if I can find her.'

They carried out their conversation with the noise of a hoover in the background.

'I've never met a witness before who just refused to talk,' Vera said. 'I don't mean the scallies who "no comment" in the interview room, but respectable people. Even if they have things to hide, they usually make up some sort of story. They need to justify their actions if only to themselves. But I got nothing out of the woman. No excuses even. She didn't deny making that call to Kelsall, but she simply refused to discuss it.'

'You sound impressed, boss.'

'Aye well, Judith's a worthy opponent. But she'll end up talking. They all do in the end. In the meantime, I want you to check her story. Let's see if you can track down the mysterious birder who was sitting at the women's table in the Seahorse. I'm still not convinced he's the stranger Judith makes him out to be.'

'I've found no evidence that they were together. He didn't buy their drinks. I've checked. Judith bought hers and Charlotte's on her card.'

'That doesn't mean anything. Two independent women, nothing to stop them buying their own drinks.' But Vera was wavering. She could see what Holly was getting at. 'See if you can track him down. He might even be staying at the pub. Did you get any sort of description?'

'No. It was busy and he had his back to the bar.'

'Someone must have seen him!' Vera wished she was there, asking the questions. She was tempted just to drive up and take over.

'I'll ask.' Holly was clearly resentful now. She didn't need Vera's interference, the implication that she couldn't do her own job. 'I'm just on my way to the Old Hall to check Katherine Willmore's alibi for Monday afternoon. I'll come back to the pub at lunchtime when there are more people around.'

'Yeah.' Vera thought that she should apologize, but couldn't quite find the words. 'Just let me know as soon as you get anything.'

'Of course, boss. Of course.'

Vera ranged around the open-plan office looking for Joe

and Charlie, but they weren't there. She phoned the digital investigators, pushing for action on Kelsall's laptop. A grumpy young woman said that all major files in Kelsall's computer had been deleted and would take time to access, but they'd found some notes, which he'd sent as an email to himself and which seemed to relate to the novel. Would Vera like to see it?

'What do you think?' The response sounded too loud and too angry even to her. 'Sorry, pet. Yeah, just send it over.'

The forwarded email came through almost immediately. It was, as the investigator said, just a series of notes. There were clumps of scene-setting and snatches of dialogue. She thought it was like Kelsall's brain. She had the impression of an over-active imagination, a lack of focus. What did they call it in kids? Attention deficit disorder? Kelsall seemed to be jumping from one character to another, without a single storyline. She couldn't see how it could mean anything even to the writer.

One short paragraph made more sense than the others:

Outside. Tide coming in. R tries to tell I that this has to end. He's being responsible for once. It really isn't a good idea. But she refuses to listen. Tells him it's her decision. This is the jumping-off point for the whole plot.

Vera tried to make sense of this. R and I were obviously Rick and Isobel. Annie had said that Rick and Isobel had been rowing before Isobel stormed off in her car. Annie had assumed that they'd had a fling while Charlotte was elsewhere, or that Rick had been flirting and Isobel had rejected his advances. But this read as if something different had been going on. If Rick was ending an affair, it wouldn't be Isobel's decision, as the snippet of text implied. She couldn't force him to stay with her.

She got on the phone to Paul Keating, her impatience growing while his assistant went to find him.

'If there was a car crash, an accident, no suspicious circumstances at the time, would there be a PM? We're talking forty years ago. And would it be able to tell if the woman was pregnant?'

She listened to the answer and switched off her phone.

Chapter Thirty-Eight

THE OLD HALL WAS THE MOST expensive hotel on the island. It was small, beautifully restored to its Elizabethan glory, surrounded by a high stone wall to stop curious tourists from peering inside. The restaurant was much lauded for its traditional British cuisine. Holly thought the place was certainly more Katherine Willmore's style than the Seahorse. She decided that she'd come here for a night when or if she ever got promotion, then wondered who she might invite to celebrate with her. She experienced the same sense of loneliness, of emptiness, as she had the night before, because she couldn't come up with even one name.

There was a small courtyard garden and Holly walked across that and then into the building through an arched door, which looked as if it might be original. Inside, she was met by a smooth young man in a suit, who asked if he might help.

She introduced herself and showed her warrant card. 'Just routine inquiries.'

'About the murder on the island last weekend?' There

was that same salacious curiosity as had been shown by the landlady in the Seahorse. They wanted the killer caught of course, because murder might be bad for business, but it also generated excitement, a vicarious sense of danger. Besides, killers became famous, the stuff of headlines and social media, and these days, everyone wanted to be close to celebrity.

'Among other things.' Holly tried to sound boring. 'Could I look at your guest list for Friday night?' The mysterious birdwatcher seen by Linz and then mentioned by Vera might have been staying at the Old Hall. If they could get contact details, he could be dismissed from the inquiry.

'Of course!' He went behind a desk and opened his computer, clicked on the keyboard. 'I'll print it out for you.'

'Could you email it to me too?' She'd send it on to Joe and the rest of the team. Let them do some of the leg work. She put her card on the desk beside the computer, saw a framed photo there of him with a woman and a baby. He looked too young to have a family and again she had the sense of time slipping by, of middle age approaching, of time leaving her stranded and alone.

'Of course,' he said again. On a shelf below the desk, a printer whirred and he pulled out a copy of the registration page.

'Could you talk me through them? I'm interested in a man on his own. Possibly a birdwatcher.'

'Sure. We have a lot of return guests. Our clients are *very* satisfied by the service we provide.' He was becoming corporate once more. 'Look, the lounge is empty now. Why don't I order us both some coffee and I can talk you through the list there?'

Holly suspected the coffee here would be very good. 'Why not?'

The coffee came in a silver pot with home-made shortbread biscuits. He introduced himself as Jason, one of the assistant managers, and chatted about the hotel until the waitress left them alone. Then he put the sheet of paper on the low table in front of them and talked her through it.

'These three are families. One from Hampshire and two from Manchester. They've never stayed with us before. They booked together. Friends from uni, I think.'

'Could you describe the men?' Holly made neat notes on the paper.

'In their thirties. Obviously minted. I heard them talking over dinner. I think they all work in IT.'

'They had dinner with you on Friday?'

'They ate with us every night, so they could keep checking on their children, who were sleeping in their rooms. We gave the kids afternoon tea.'

Unlikely then, that one of them would have met two older women in the Seahorse.

Jason worked down the list. Most of the guests were elderly: two widows who were friends and came every year, several couples in their seventies, a group of retired academics, who'd first met when they were undergraduates on a field trip on the island.

They aroused Holly's interest briefly. One of them might be the birdwatcher in the pub. 'Did you notice if any of them went out on Friday evening?'

He shook his head. 'They'd hired a room for private dining and we laid on a special dinner. Man, could they drink! I'm sure that none of them left. By the end of the night, they could hardly stagger up to bed.'

Holly finished her coffee and allowed Jason to pour her another cup. She'd get the team in Kimmerston to follow up the details, but it seemed unlikely that the person sitting with Judith and Charlotte in the Seahorse had stayed in the Old Hall. 'I'm also interested in Monday. Not a resident this time but a woman who said she had afternoon tea here.'

'Ah,' he said. 'I wouldn't necessarily have details for those. Most people book, of course. We do get very busy. But we allow walk-ins especially mid-week.'

'This woman says she's a regular. Her name's Katherine Willmore.' Holly realized he might jump to the conclusion that the PCC was some sort of suspect. 'Of course, again this is routine. We have to check even people on the periphery of a case. To follow the rules without fear or favour.'

Jason smiled to show that he understood. 'Of course. She and Daniel are regulars. He runs Rede Tower, so there's a business connection too. We work very closely on promotion.'

'Could you check if Katherine was here on Monday afternoon?' There was, after all, only so much coffee a woman could drink, and Holly wanted to get back to the mainland.

'I wasn't on duty, but I can talk to a colleague who was.'

'If she was here, could you check if she paid by card? That might confirm her account of events and give us a definite timeline to work on.' Holly smiled. 'And I know I can be assured of your discretion. Rumours can start very easily and you wouldn't want a respected public figure to be the subject of gossip or false news.'

'Oh, of course! Katherine and Daniel are valued guests. I

can check the card details first then there'll be no need to include anyone else in the conversation.'

Holly thought of the woman and child in the photograph on his desk. He was smart, this man of theirs. He had the knack of making himself indispensable. He'd go far.

Jason returned very quickly with another printout. 'Yes, Katherine was definitely here on Monday afternoon and she did pay for afternoon tea by card. A Visa debit.'

Holly looked at the receipt and thought that the cost of afternoon tea for one was more than she'd expect to pay for a decent dinner for two. The payment had been made at twelve minutes past four. It was highly unlikely, therefore, that Katherine had made it to Kimmerston in time to smother Charlotte Thomas before she and Vera had found her body in the studio. Not quite impossible, but very unlikely.

She was about to leave, when she had another thought. 'Charlotte Thomas,' she said. 'The woman who was killed in town on Monday. Was she a regular here too?'

Jason got to his feet. 'Not recently,' he said. 'When I first started here, she was in the place all the time. Often with famous friends. But no, I haven't seen her for ages.'

Out in the courtyard, Holly realized that the mist had rolled in again. Perhaps it was something to do with the tide or the time of year. She could hardly make out the wall on the other side of the garden, and the foghorn had started its haunting call once again. Holly had a sudden image of drowning sailors crying for help. And that made her think of Isobel Hall, who'd been younger than she was, in a car tipping off the causeway into the water. It wasn't cold, but she found that she was shivering.

She made her way back to the Seahorse to prepare for

leaving. She still had several hours before the tide would cut off the island from the mainland, but she thought she'd done nearly all she could here. She wanted to talk again to Di and Linz about the man who'd been sitting at the window table in the lounge bar with Charlotte and Judith. Judith had told Vera that he was a stranger, a visiting birdwatcher, and Holly wanted to confirm that it might have been true. Linz was the better witness of the two but she hadn't been serving breakfast. Di had said she'd start her shift at lunchtime so she should be there now.

The dining room was quiet, and Linz was leaning on the public side of the bar, waiting to show guests to their tables. She greeted Holly as an old friend.

'Hiya! You here for lunch?'

'Why not?' She could have something light. A sandwich. She wouldn't have a chance once she got back to the station, and by the time she got home, she wouldn't feel like eating much.

Linz showed her to the table in the window and gave her a laminated menu, freshly wiped with a grubby cloth. 'The crab's good. Local.'

'I'll have that then. A crab sandwich. With a side salad.'

'Good choice.' Linz was just about to walk away, but Holly called her back. 'Last Friday night when the three people were sitting here, are you sure the guy was part of the group? We've spoken to the older woman and she reckons he was nothing to do with them, that he was some visiting birdwatcher, who was just sharing the table with them.'

Linz shrugged. 'I dunno. He could have been, I suppose.'

'You didn't recognize him as a regular?'

'Sorry, as I said, he was just a back, a jacket and grey hair.

I only got a glimpse of those. There were other tables between him and the bar.'

Holly was disappointed. She'd have loved something more to take back to Vera.

Linz spoke again.

'If he's a regular birder, one of the locals would know. A few of them moved here once they retired. They're all friends. I can ask around for you. See if any of them were in Friday night and recognized him.'

'Thanks,' Holly said. 'That'd be great. You've got my number.'

Linz was about to go into the kitchen with the order, when she stopped and turned back. 'I did see that woman again though.'

'Charlotte Thomas? The woman who died?'

'No, not her. The older one with the white hair.'

'When did you see her?' Holly wasn't quite sure how important that would be. They knew already that Judith Sinclair had spent the night in Gull Cottage.

'Later that Friday night. After my shift I went out on the island.' She paused, suddenly a little awkward. 'I've got a bloke who lives here. One of the fishermen. Most nights I stay with him unless I'm on early breakfasts.'

'How late?'

'Eleven? Something like that. We're quite strict about closing the bar at ten-thirty, and then there was a bit of tidying up. It certainly wouldn't have been later than eleven-thirty.'

'Where did you see her?'

'Out to the east of the island.'

So not close to Gull Cottage. 'Could she have been coming back from the Pilgrims' House?'

Linz looked at her, aware of the implications of the question. 'Yeah, she could.'

Holly went outside to phone Vera. She passed on the information. 'I was going to come back to Kimmerston now, but what do you think?'

'Stay,' Vera said. 'You've got a while before the tide. See if anyone else saw Judith Sinclair wandering around the island at night. And if your barmaid can get a fix on that birdwatcher.'

Holly went back inside to finish her lunch.

Chapter Thirty-Nine

PHILIP SLEPT POORLY AFTER THE VISIT from the young detective. He wished he'd gone straight back to London after the reunion weekend. He felt that his orderly world was falling apart. He couldn't see how Charlotte's death could fit into any sort of pattern. He'd understood why Rick had married her – she'd been a trophy, a validation for a small man with an inflated ego – but Philip had assumed that she'd been out of Rick's life for years. Now, it was the chaos that most disturbed him, the unexpected. Rick had lived his life on the edge and really his death had come as no surprise. Rick was never going to leave this world easily, peacefully, without drama. He wouldn't have wanted to. Charlotte's murder, however, had shocked Philip profoundly.

In the early hours, it occurred to him that he could go now. The tide was out so he could pack up the car and he could drive away. Who could stop him? Not Vera Stanhope and her team. Back in the suburban rectory there would be nothing to remind him of his old life, the guilt and the anger. People would be pleased to welcome him home a little earlier than expected. They'd have seen the news and be sympathetic.

Then he remembered that Judith had planned to come to the cottage. She'd phoned while he was still at the Pilgrims' House, asking if she could visit for a night. She'd sounded distressed, but also eager to see him. He'd been flattered by the request and was looking forward to the woman's company. He admired her and she'd been in his mind recently.

Once the decision to stay had been made, Philip fell into an uneasy sleep. He woke to an image, part memory, part dream. They were young, all in the basement of the Halls' house in Kimmerston. Ken was bent over his guitar, and he was singing: James Taylor's 'You've Got A Friend'. Ken had always been musical and in middle age, he'd joined a choir, amateur but celebrated. Philip had gone to watch a performance in Carlisle. Now, he supposed, all that was lost to the man. It had been so much a part of his life and now it was gone.

He must have drifted back to sleep, because when he woke again it was day and a milky light was coming through the window. Philip got up and saw that the light was filtered through mist. There was a loud knocking on the front door. He pulled a sweater over his pyjamas and went to answer.

Judith stood there, looking very small, very anxious. 'Oh,' she said. 'I've woken you after all. I came on early, before the tide, but I've been waiting in the car for a reasonable hour.' She walked into the house. 'Oh Philip, I've been so very foolish.'

She seemed close to tears. He gathered her into his arms and held her tight.

Chapter Forty

JOE WOKE UP THE MORNING AFTER Sal's birthday feeling old. He'd never had a hangover when he was younger. He and Sal must have polished off a bottle of fizzy wine each to celebrate, because there were two empties in the recycling bin in the kitchen. He didn't drink much these days, especially on a school night, and now it showed. Sal seemed okay. She was singing along to Radio Two and getting the kids ready for school, eating toast thick with marmalade, and emptying the washing machine all at the same time. Crumbs had sprayed all over her top. She realized and wiped them off with a cloth, then folded the clothes ready for the line. Multitasking. Something he'd never quite got the hang of. He made himself tea and didn't bother with the toast she'd left for him.

Vera was already in the office, though he'd got in early. She called him into her room. The radiator had decided to work again, and it was as steamy as a sauna in there. Outside it had started to drizzle again and she'd hung her damp coat on the back of a chair.

'Sal enjoy her birthday?' Vera's voice was bright. 'Good night?'

'Yeah!' As he said it, he knew it was true. He'd got all that he'd ever wanted with Sal and the kids, a kind of contentment, and it *had* been a good night. He was about to explain about the cake that Jess had made for her mam, and the presents Sal had got, but Vera had already shifted her attention back to work. Whenever she asked about the family, it was just going through the motions. She had no real interest. But then, he thought, he wasn't much interested in other people's kids either.

'I want you to do a bit of digging around Annie Laidler and Daniel Rede,' Vera said. 'Their baby died when it was just a few months old. Cot death, they thought at first, but the parents came under suspicion too. Poor Annie's still haunted by it. They were living in a caravan up at Rede's Tower when the bairn died and it must have seemed a bit of an unconventional lifestyle at the time. They were very young. Our lot were involved anyway, stomping in with their big boots, just at the time when everything was most raw. The death was viewed as unexplained until it turned out in the end that the poor little scrap had been suffering from infantile meningitis. But it happened around the time there was that second death. Louisa's sister Isobel driving off the Holy Island causeway in a temper, too close to the tide. That was unexplained too. Both incidents would have happened forty-five years ago, but there's a bloke who was a young officer then who's still alive and up for a bit of a chat about the olden days.' A pause. 'I remember him from my cadet days. Not a cheery soul, but a good policeman. Solid.'

'There'll be files.' Joe thought an in-person interview was a lot of effort for two accidental deaths.

'Of course there'll be files. They might even have been computerized and easy to access, though I very much doubt it. But files don't tell us what was really going on in a cop's head when they were interviewing the witnesses. And I've never yet met a cop who hasn't got a long memory.' Vera stopped up sharp. 'There'd have been post-mortems in both cases. And those records *would* be more detailed. It occurred to me that Isobel might have been pregnant and Doc Keating says you'd be able to tell, even if she was only a few weeks. She looked up at Joe. 'I'll follow that up later. I'm seeing Judith Sinclair first, to find out why she's pissing us about. I want you to chat to the police officer who was involved in the Isobel Hall accident. Make him very happy by asking his advice. Buy him a pint at lunchtime. Or a pie. Or both. Let's find out what was going on all those years ago.'

Joe nodded. When the boss had a bee in her bonnet, it was best to humour her.

'He lives on the coast. Before you meet him, call in at Rede's Tower and see if our friend Daniel is there. Hol's tracking down Katherine's alibi on Holy Island, but we still don't know where her bloke was on Monday afternoon. I've left messages for him but he's not called me back. I'd like to know what's going on with him. Everyone says he's a very busy chap, but it's starting to look suspicious to me. And if not that, then bloody rude.'

Joe was glad of an excuse to go back to Rede's Tower. It was a trip into nostalgia. As he'd explained to Holly, he'd spent weeks of his childhood summers there. His grandfather had owned an old caravan, very close to the shore. There'd been no fancy facilities in those days. No facilities at all, except one outside tap for drinking water and a concrete block with two stinking toilets and a shower that rarely worked. But to Joe, it had been paradise. Freedom. In his memory the days had been endlessly sunny. He'd gone crabbing with his grandad and disappeared for hours with the other feral lads on the site, playing on the beach or in the scrubby piece of woodland just inland.

There *had* been rain but only at night. He remembered the sound of rain on the metal roof of the caravan, the sense that this was his den, safe, warm, protective. Now, he had a shed at the bottom of the garden and when it was raining, he went there to bring the memory back. Sal thought he was doing useful tasks – sharpening tools or tidying the shelves – but very little got done because he sat on a broken garden chair, his eyes shut, remembering the past as the rain rattled the corrugated iron roof.

When the kids had come along, he'd wanted to get a caravan at Rede's. 'It'd be great for weekends away. They'd love it!' But Sal had put her foot down. The nearest she was prepared to get to camping was a lodge at Center Parcs.

There was a lay-by just before the turn-off to the holiday park, and Joe stopped there, to allow a few more minutes of childhood memory, but nothing was at all as he recalled it. A mist had rolled in from the shore and made everything shadowy, shifting. Occasionally it cleared and Joe saw the shape of wooden cabins where once his grandfather's caravan had stood with a few others, forming a circle, like a wagon train in an old-fashioned Western.

Now, in the spinney, they'd built an elaborate children's adventure playground. One of the structures rose above the layer of mist, and reminded Joe of a scaffold with its gibbet. His imagination was running wild. It was drinking too much the night before and not enough sleep, or a weird kind of prejudice. Because it wasn't as he'd remembered, he was determined to dislike the place.

The pele tower itself had been derelict when they'd stayed on the site, and now the stone had been cleaned and repointed and the slate roof replaced. Proper windows put in. He thought he might persuade Sal to consider a weekend here now, but he wouldn't suggest it. It wouldn't be the same.

He drove on and pulled in to the visitors' car park. He sat for a moment to get a sense of the place. There was a new stone building attached to the tower, glass fronted. A cafe and restaurant. All very tasteful. Joe got out of the car and made his way to find Daniel Rede.

Once she realized that Joe wasn't a guest checking in, the receptionist thought he must be a salesman and tried to put him off. 'I don't think Mr Rede is on site today. I'm sure I can find someone else to help you.'

He showed her his warrant card. 'I won't take up a lot of his time, but it is rather urgent.'

'As I said . . .' But before she could insist that Daniel wasn't there, a man walked in through a door behind her.

'Don't worry, Jan. I'm back on site. I'm very happy to help the officer.'

Joe wasn't sure what he'd been expecting. Some kind of businessman perhaps, but not this. Daniel Rede was wearing a checked shirt and jeans and looked more like a retired farmer than the head of a multimillion leisure company. 'I know Inspector Stanhope has been trying to get hold of me. I'm sorry. We seem to keep missing each other. It's been a busy week. How can I help you?'

'Just a few more questions,' Joe said. 'You'll have seen there's been another death.'

'Of course! Charlotte. Kelsall's first wife. Another dreadful tragedy. And quite unnerving actually. Do you mind if we walk while we talk? There's been a complaint about the hot tub attached to one of our superior lodges. The filtration system wasn't working properly. The customers are regulars and I want to check it's properly fixed.'

'Fine.' Joe followed him out of the building. 'You're still very hands-on then?'

'It's the only way, a place like this.' He turned to Joe, gave a quick grin. 'We charge a fortune – you wouldn't believe what people will pay for a sea view, fresh air straight from Scandinavia with a bit of luxury thrown in. But the punters are demanding. They expect personal service. I like to keep on top of the detail, and as your boss is aware, I've not been on site much in the last few days.'

Joe thought there was more to Rede's focus on the everyday detail of the operation than a desire to give good customer service. The man seemed restless, unsettled. He was probably one of those practical men who were better at making and mending than sitting and staring at a screen. And perhaps he was jittery because murder was bad for business. 'I stayed here as a kid,' Joe said. It seemed a way in to break the ice. 'It's a bit different now.'

'I started working here as soon as I left school,' Daniel said. 'My grandfather ran the place then and it was mostly people from the region who came to stay. Newcastle families wanting to escape the smoke and soot of the city. Pitmen needing a bit of fresh air in their lungs. But everything changed. People wanted more from a holiday. We were having to compete with package tours to Spain. We couldn't give them guaranteed sun, but we could provide the other things they got abroad: a bar, entertainment in the evening, play spaces for the kids. Then staycations got a bit more fashionable and we decided to move upmarket. Now we get regulars who come from London for a couple of short breaks a year.'

'I can see that makes business sense . . .'

'But you miss the old days?'

'Aye.' Joe laughed. 'Maybe.'

'Sometimes,' Daniel said, 'I do too.'

They'd arrived at the row of wooden lodges closest to the water. These were as different from Joe's grandfather's caravan as it was possible to be.

'Each site is different.' Rede seemed to have forgotten his nostalgia for the past. Now, he could have been selling the place to a potential visitor. 'And each has its own outdoor space. If you live in the city, you don't want to be overlooked by your neighbour. We planted the hedges. Sea buckthorn. Authentic. We know they'll want outdoor facilities so we've added a firepit, a covered balcony in case the weather's bad, like today.' He sounded as proud as the new father he'd once been. 'The hot tubs are all wood burners. With all this managed woodland, we're not short of logs, and we make sure they're properly dried before we hand them over. Let me just check this has been properly fixed by the maintenance guy, then I'm all yours.'

Joe walked on a few yards to the bank of pebbles that separated the beach from the development. He looked back at the lodge, which could have accommodated a family of eight in comfort. His father would have made a comment about the injustice of it: these palaces for the rich to holiday while the poor lived in modern slums or were homeless. The mist cleared for a moment and he could see the shadow of Holy Island on the horizon, suddenly very large, very close.

Daniel Rede joined him, looking out over the water. 'All

sorted,' he said. 'I knew it would be – we've got a great team – but I still feel the need to check. Katherine says I should delegate more, but in the end, I'm responsible. It's my name on the place.'

'You're not tempted to sell up, retire?'

'Nah! What would I do all day? My life would seem pointless.'

Joe thought of the other people who'd been at the Pilgrims' House on the night of Rick Kelsall's death. Annie was still working, but perhaps she needed the income. Louisa and Ken had retired and Philip was talking about giving up the priesthood soon. They all seemed content. But he wasn't here to discuss the possibility of ageing well.

'We're just checking people's movements for Monday afternoon. That was when Charlotte Thomas died.' Joe paused. 'We know you were in Kimmerston in the morning.'

Daniel didn't seem to resent the question. 'That's right. A planning meeting first thing, then I called in on Annie. She and Rick had always been close. I don't think there was ever anything romantic between them, but they were very good friends. I just wanted to check that she was okay.'

'And later?'

'I was out recceing potential sites along the coast. As I said, we want to expand the business.' He paused. 'I didn't meet anyone until early evening. That was when I called in on a farmer near Amble, but I didn't think we'd get planning permission for a development of the scale that we'd need to be viable, so we didn't chat for very long. I can give you his details. In the afternoon, I was looking at a caravan site near Whitley Bay. Whitley's going up in the world these days. All artisan bakers and indie shops. It might suit us very well. But that was a covert operation. I didn't want the owner to know I was interested.' He stopped. 'I know you have to ask, but really I didn't know Charlotte very well. I certainly had no reason to want her dead.'

'You were at school with her though?'

'Even then, we didn't really know each other. I didn't start at the Grammar until I was thirteen and we didn't come from the same sort of background. Like I said, my grandad ran this place then, and you'll know what it was like. Run-down. A bit of a shambles. There was no money in it until I took it on. The other Grammar school lads treated me like some sort of gypsy.'

'You haven't seen Charlotte more recently?'

'Once or twice.' A pause. 'She wanted to set up a well-being centre here on site. A kind of glorified spa. We had a couple of meetings.'

'You didn't take her up on the suggestion?'

'Nah. It was a bit awkward because Katherine liked her, but I couldn't see it making us much profit once she'd taken a cut. She wanted us to fund the initial set-up. I thought we'd be better keeping it in-house. It sounds harsh, but Charlotte Thomas wouldn't have been the draw she might once have been. Our target demographic is people in their thirties and early forties. They would never have heard of her.'

Later, Joe found himself sitting in a pub in an ex-mining community by the coast, buying a pint for a former sergeant, who'd been based in Northumberland for the whole of his career. The man was called Pete Allen, and as Vera had said, he had a memory that went back years. By the time Joe got there, it was lunchtime and the place was empty apart from a few other men of Allen's generation. Regulars, who nodded gravely to each new customer as they walked through the door. They were coming together for company, and to help the day slide on.

Allen had a grey moustache, which dipped into the beer, grey hair, grey eyes. A sadness, which he wore like his grey overcoat. His missus had left him years before. He'd told Joe that even before they'd met. When Joe had phoned to make the appointment, he'd asked Allen if he'd be free for a pie and a pint or if he'd need to be home for his midday meal. 'I'm always free.' Allen's voice had been flat, uncomplaining.

Joe got more details in the pub. The wife had run away with an insurance broker from Bellingham, apparently. She'd claimed it was Pete's fault, the shifts, never knowing when he'd be home. 'But it wasn't that,' Allen said. 'I bored her. She was a lively thing. I knew from the start that it wouldn't last.'

That gave Joe a jolt. Sometimes Sal said *he* was boring, staid, old before his time. It always came across as a joke, but there was a moment of fear. Might she be attracted by someone more exciting, more reckless?

Gentle, misty rain ran down the dirty windows, which wouldn't have let in much light, even on a sunny day. Everything in the place was covered with a sticky, brown varnish, the colour of toffee: the wood panels on the walls, the bar, the settles where the old men sat sharing a desultory conversation.

'Aye,' Allen said. 'I remember that year. Two deaths within months of each other and the same people involved. It would stick in your mind.' He looked up. 'What's your interest then?' For the first time showing a spark of curiosity

'Two more deaths with the same people involved.' Joe paused. 'But this time murder.'

'That man from the telly on Holy Island? And the woman who'd been some sort of model and actress in the seventies and eighties?'

Joe nodded.

'They'd be the sort who'd end up fighting their way out of the jungle on a reality show. I can't abide folk who think they're celebrities.' There was a long silence. 'But I suppose we can't go round killing them.' Another pause. 'More's the pity.' For the first time, he gave a little smile.

'It's the same group of people,' Joe said. 'The same witnesses and suspects, as the deaths you were looking into of the bairn and the young student. My boss thinks it's a weird coincidence.'

'I suppose it is.'

'Tell me what you remember,' Joe said. 'While you're sorting things out in your head, I'll get you another pint.'

'Eh, bonny lad, I've not finished this one yet.'

'All the same, I won't want to interrupt once you get started.'

Allen nodded to show that made sense, and watched Joe go up to the bar.

'The baby dying,' Allen said, once Joe had settled down again, his orange juice untouched on the table in front of him, 'that was just sad. But we had to investigate. A young couple, living as they did, in a caravan up at Rede's Tower. Suspicion was that the poor little lass might have been shaken to death by one of the parents. They were all cramped into such a small space and they might have been desperate. I've never had a bairn, but you could see how you might be driven to it, if it was the sort that cried all night. And you had a bit of a temper.'

'Did Rede have a temper?'

'We asked around but found no evidence of that. A nice enough chap, everyone said. Laid-back. Supportive of his woman. I'm not sure he ever wanted the child – a young man, it'd surely cramp his style and Daniel Rede was ambitious for his business even then – but he went along with it for her sake.' Allen paused. 'I don't think he grieved the loss in the way that the lass did, but that didn't mean he'd commit murder to get his freedom back.'

Joe nodded to show he understood what Allen was saying. He sipped his orange juice, thought that this liquid had never been anywhere near an orange, and he waited for the man to continue.

'I was pleased when the doctors said it was meningitis. Natural causes. Without that, the pair would have been under a cloud all their lives. Rumours that they were child-killers. People don't forget.'

'I'm sure there were still rumours,' Joe said. 'Sometimes folk prefer the drama to the fact.'

'That's true too.'

They sat for a moment, the silence broken by a sudden heavier shower of rain clattering against the window and the muted conversation of the men on the other side of the room.

'Then there they were,' Allen said, 'three months later, on Holy Island and another death. A car crashing off the causeway into the sea and a young woman drowned. I knew them at once. You wouldn't miss them. Annie Rede she still was then, and such a pretty thing even though she was so skinny. She'd lost weight. I suppose it was the grief.'

Joe could hear the sympathy in his voice and thought the man had had a bit of a crush on Annie Laidler. Perhaps that was why the facts of these cases were so strong in Allen's mind. 'That was put down as an accident,' Joe said. 'Is that how you saw it?'

Pete Allen took a while to answer. 'It was an odd one,' he said at last. 'It's not unusual for cars to get stranded on the causeway. Trippers misread the tide tables at each end of the road, or think they've got a car that's big enough and fast enough to outrun the tide. Each year people get caught out. But they don't die. There are towers along the road. You see that you're not going to make it and you leave the car and climb the tower until the water goes down again. You get a bit wet and the car is ruined, but you're okay. Even if it's a high spring tide and in bad weather.' He paused. 'And the water was well up by the time Isobel Hall left the island. Anyone with any sense would see that they wouldn't make it across. It was pure recklessness.'

'You pushed for a post-mortem?'

'Aye, the boss did. We just wanted to be sure, you know, because something jarred. No real suspicion of foul play, but we wanted an explanation.'

'Had she been drinking?'

'Well, that was our thought too. There was a bit of alcohol in her blood, but that could have been left over from the night before. They'd all been boozing then, apparently. Not enough to cloud her judgement though. Not according to the doc.' Allen paused. 'I did wonder about suicide.'

'You think she drove into the water deliberately? Not a nice way to go.'

'She wouldn't know that though, would she?' Allen looked up from his beer and stared at Joe with his sad, grey eyes. 'She was young. Hardly more than a bairn herself.'

'The same age as Annie Laidler. I suppose they were friends?' Joe didn't let on about Only Connect, the fact that they were there for its five-year anniversary.

'There was a group of them, all staying in the Pilgrims' House.' Allen looked up sharply. 'That was where the TV journalist was found dead.'

Joe nodded.

'Unlucky sort of place then,' Allen went on. 'A strange coincidence. Maybe that's the reason they're planning to close the retreat.'

'It's being closed for the season?'

'Not for the season. Forever. I saw it in the local paper. The nuns are selling it off. I suppose they'll turn it into some sort of private self-catering or guest house. It'd need someone with money to take it on. Places on Holy Island sell for a fortune.'

Joe wondered if that was significant, but couldn't see how it might be. He'd pass on the information to Vera and let her decide. 'What conclusion did you come to in the end about Isobel Hall's death?'

Allen shrugged. 'It went down as accidental, but it didn't sit quite right with me. To be honest, it's one of those ones that stick with you. The cases that you wake up wondering about.'

'You'd have checked the car?'

'Yes, nothing wrong with the vehicle. Nothing they could find, at least, after hours in the water, being battered by the current.' He looked at Joe over his beer. 'You're thinking one of them might have tampered with it?'

'It must have occurred to you too.'

'Something was going on there. They came across as bright young things with their lives ahead of them. But they were a weird bunch. Arrogant. Secretive. I couldn't take to them. Except Annie Laidler. She was different.'

Oh yes, Joe thought. You definitely took to her.

'You say they did a post-mortem on the lass in the car,' Joe said. 'My boss wondered if she might have been pregnant.'

'Is that what she told her boyfriend? Wanting to hang on to him?'

Joe shook his head. 'We don't know anything for certain. Just a line of inquiry.' Then he had a thought. 'Did she have a boyfriend? One of the group staying at the Pilgrims' House? Rick Kelsall playing away while his woman was at work in London?'

'It seems she was the kind to play those sorts of games.' Allen drained the last of the beer from his second pint. 'But they all closed ranks and if she was having a fling, nobody admitted it. And no, she wasn't pregnant. I'd have remembered that. Two babies, it'd have stuck in my mind. Another coincidence. Besides, like I said, this case is not one I've ever forgotten.'

Outside on the pavement, after the gloom of the pub, it was a shock to see how light it was, to realize that it was still early afternoon. Joe had parked by the scruffy little harbour and sat there to phone Vera.

'So, Isobel wasn't pregnant,' she said. 'Another fine theory out of the water. I've heard back from Hol. Katherine Willmore's alibi for Monday checks out. Did you manage to get hold of Daniel Rede?'

'Aye.' Joe replayed the conversation. 'He had no concrete alibi between seeing Annie Laidler late morning and meeting a farmer in Amble early evening. It would have been tight but he could have killed her. We could look at CCTV in Whitley to rule him out.'

'I'll get Charlie onto it.' Vera sounded preoccupied. 'Get back here, Joe. This case is doing my head in. All these respectable elderly people making out that they're innocent. I need a younger mind to make some sense of it.'

Chapter Forty-One

IN HER OFFICE, VERA WAS WAITING impatiently for Joe to return. Restless and needing something to focus on, she looked again at the synopsis Kelsall's agent had sent through. She'd skimmed it when Holly had first shared it, and had thought it was too vague to be important. Having read Kelsall's notes now she thought it might be more relevant.

The novel was titled 'Stranded'. She'd expected something with a little more detail, but the piece was scarcely more than a few lines long. It read more like a blurb on the back of a jacket, something to tease the readers and hook them in. Perhaps Kelsall's name and notoriety had been enough to sell the project to a publisher. Perhaps it was a giant scam to get a huge advance and he'd never have got round to completing it.

The man could write though, she'd give him that. The synopsis certainly made her want to find out more. And not just because she thought the finished work might contain a clue to the double murder.

A group of twenty-somethings find themselves stranded on Holy Island, in North Northumberland. The place carries with it an atmosphere of spirituality, almost of the supernatural. After all, this is where Christianity first arrived in England, and the centuries of worship and prayer seem trapped in the landscape itself. There's been a tension between the friends throughout the weekend. They've obviously known each other for years and are very close, but something has happened to fracture the friendships. As the story progresses, the reader discovers that secrets of the past have come back to haunt them. An autumn fog blurs the boundary between the land and the sea, and in this strange marginal world there's a tragedy. A young woman dies. It seems, at first, that this was an accident, but an accident would surely be too convenient . . .

The theme of the novel is hypocrisy, and it explores the lengths some people will take to hide the sins of the past.

The last sentence struck a chord. Surely this was the theme of the investigation too. These respectable older people – a priest and a couple of teachers – might all have their own reasons for hiding the sins of the past. The others on the periphery of the case were pillars of the community too: the Police and Crime Commissioner, a prominent businessman and an elderly churchgoer famous for her good works. Even Annie had a certain position within the town. The least respectable members of the group – Rick Kelsall and Charlotte Thomas – were already dead.

Her phone rang. It was Holly with news that Judith Sinclair had been seen wandering round the island, on the evening of Kelsall's death. Through her open door, Vera saw that Charlie was back in the office. She stood up and shouted him in.

'I need all you can get on Judith Sinclair. Seems there's a chance she was close to the Pilgrims' House after all on the night Kelsall died. Despite her denying any contact. And she was part of the group from the beginning. She started the whole thing off.'

Charlie nodded. Vera knew he was the best person in the team to get what they needed. He knew this town. Elderly women and young tearaways both confided in him. He could listen. There was something unthreatening and sympathetic about him. He was a universal favourite uncle.

He'd slid out of her office before she realized he was gone.

Still restless, she got her coat and car keys. Judith Sinclair had been pissing her about with her moral high-handedness and refusal to speak. Now it was time for her to talk. She drove out to the tidy street where Judith had lived since she'd first been married. This time it was a neighbour in his garden, pruning back shrubs before the winter. He straightened when he heard the latch on Judith's gate.

'You won't find Mrs Sinclair in,' he said. He had a pleasant voice. Vera wondered briefly if he and Judith had been more than friends, then saw a wife peering through immaculately white nets. *How bored she must be!* Vera thought. *If she's got nothing better to do than vicarious gardening.*

'Any idea how long she'll be?' Because he would know. Nothing would be hidden in this suburban paradise. Except, perhaps, murder.

'There's a friend staying in her cottage on Holy Island. She's gone to see him. She must have left canny early. Her car was gone when I woke up.'

Vera swore in her head, but smiled at the neighbour. This wasn't his fault. 'Of course. Thanks.'

When she got back to the station, Joe had returned and was at his desk.

'Any news from Hol?'

He shook his head.

'Judith Sinclair is there, apparently. On Holy Island. She's staying the night with Philip Robson in Gull Cottage.'

Joe seemed not to think this important. 'Yeah, she told us that she was going to see them at some point during their stay.'

'She was out on the island the night Kelsall was murdered.'

'You can't really think she's our killer?' Joe looked at Vera as if she was crazy.

'I think she knows more than she's letting on.' Vera hit the buttons on her phone. 'No response from Holly.' Reception on the island was notoriously patchy, but Vera felt irrationally resentful at the lack of an answer. She left a message. 'Holly, just to let you know Judith Sinclair's up on the island. Call me back as soon as you get this!'

It was still only late afternoon, but the whole police station was dark. No sun and no light. Vera padded through the main office, unable to settle. Joe was trying to feed back his interviews with Daniel Rede and Pete Allen but she was finding it almost impossible to focus.

'Who has most to gain from these people's deaths?' The words came out as a cry, stopping Joe in mid-flow.

'Annie Laidler if we're talking about money,' Joe said. He was always down to earth. Always prosaic. Vera knew he kept her grounded. 'Eliza Bond if we're talking reputation, and by extension Katherine and Daniel who might want to protect her. We've only got their word that Rick Kelsall was prepared to be gracious about the false accusations she'd made against him. He might have been planning something dramatic as an act of revenge on the lass for losing him his job. Katherine would hate that, wouldn't she? Her daughter being one of those women she claims don't exist. The women who cry rape.'

'I don't think this is about money.' Again, Vera found it impossible to keep still. She was pacing once more, knowing it was irritating Joe as well as ratchetting up the tension in the room, but not being able to help herself. She remembered the paragraph Kelsall had put together to sell his book to a publisher. 'This is about hiding the sins of the past.' She punched Holly's number into her phone. Again, it rang through to voicemail.

'She's probably driving back.'

'She'd answer though, wouldn't she?' Vera snapped. 'She's got hands free. What's she playing at?'

Charlie came in, so quietly and unobtrusively, that for a moment neither of them registered his presence.

'What have you got for me, Charlie?' Vera came finally to rest in front of his desk.

'I've been chatting to one of Judith's former colleagues. He started teaching in the Grammar at the same time as her. Apparently, she was quite wild in her early days. Not above fraternizing with the students. Drinking. Going to their parties.' A pause. 'There was talk of relationships.'

'You mean sex, Charlie? Is that what you're saying?'

'There were rumours.'

'She'd be scared, wouldn't she, if that came out in Kelsall's book? A respectable woman of God with a history of debauching young lads.'

'More likely the other way round,' Charlie muttered. 'From what I could gather.'

Vera ignored the comment. 'Was Kelsall one of her conquests?'

'According to the chap I spoke to. But again, he stressed they were staffroom rumours. Apparently, one of the senior teachers had a word with her. Told her to be more careful.'

Which was why, Vera thought, Judith didn't take up the young people's invitation to join them at the first reunion.

'Then she got religion,' Charlie said, 'and she went the other way. Strait-laced and upright. Spiritual.'

'We're going to the island!' She thought she'd been bubbling up to this all day, like a pan simmering on the hob, and finally coming to the boil. Now the action seemed inevitable. 'I don't like the fact that Holly's not communicating with us, we know that at least two of our suspects are there, with others not far away. That's where it started and that's where it'll end.' She was aware that the dramatic voice, the impulsive decision, didn't suit her. Her colleagues were staring as if they hardly recognized her.

'H'away then,' she said, changing tone. 'Get your coats. Charlie, take your own car. Joe, you're with me.' A pause. 'You'd better tell Sal it's likely to be an all-nighter. If we get a move on, we'll just get there before the tide, but there's no way we'll get back.'

Chapter Forty-Two

HOLLY HAD PACKED HER BAG AND put it in her car, ready to head off back to the mainland when the text came through. A number she didn't recognize. She'd given her contact details to Linz, in fact to everyone she'd met on the island since her arrival, so that didn't provide any information about who might be ringing.

Understand you're looking for the birder who was in the Seahorse on Friday night. Might be able to help. Just heading out to do a migration census in the area around the lough. Could see you there in half an hour? Phone reception impossible there so will have to meet in person.

There was nothing to identify the sender. Was the assumption that Holly had been told to expect the communication? Perhaps Linz had put the word out on the island, had asked anyone who might be able to help to get in touch with Holly direct. The text didn't give a clue as to gender, but Holly assumed it was a man. She tried to phone the number, but it didn't even go to voicemail, just cut off. Crappy reception, she supposed. She checked the time. The lough was just beyond the Pilgrims' House, so she should be able to drive most of the way and park there. There was still more than an hour before she'd need to leave for the mainland. She went back into the Seahorse and paid her bill. Di was there, behind the desk in reception.

'All done then?' Curiosity oozing out of every pore.

'For now.'

Holly got into her car and drove not towards the causeway, but down the main street of the village and into the centre of the island. The fog had lifted during the middle of the day, but was thicker again now. She almost missed the narrow turning towards the Pilgrims' House. When she pulled up outside, there was another vehicle parked there. She wondered if this belonged to the birdwatcher who was offering information. She sat in her car for a moment and tried to phone Vera to let her know what was happening, but she couldn't get through.

Outside the air was damp and chill. She couldn't imagine how anyone would be able to see a bird in these conditions. This felt like a pointless game of hide and seek and she had the same tension as she'd felt when she'd been a child, searching for hidden classmates, anxious that they might suddenly jump out to frighten her.

She climbed a stile and walked east towards the lough. She could hear the calls of wading birds, and then heard voices. She didn't see the group until she almost stumbled on them. Four people of indeterminate gender, dressed in wax jackets and wellingtons, crouched over a ditch. A fine net had been placed across it, only visible because of the drops of moisture caught on the mesh. They seemed to be extricating a bird from it. She waited, watching, before speaking. It seemed a delicate operation, and the bird was so frail that she was anxious an interruption might damage it.

'I'm DC Clarke. Did one of you ask to speak to me?'

They looked blank.

'The message said you were doing a migration census and asked me to meet you here.'

'This isn't a census.' The youngest of the group straightened and gave a joyous laugh. 'This is a bloody rarity. A paddyfield warbler. A new bird for me. A lifer.'

'What are you going to do with it?' She was distracted momentarily by his enthusiasm.

'We're going to ring it, take a few photos to convince the world that it is what we claim it to be, and then we'll release it.'

'Were any of you in the Seahorse on Friday night?'

'No, when we're on the island we use the Anchor.' An older man who could have been the young speaker's father. 'But we weren't here on Friday. It gets busy at weekends and it was clear. You need a bit of cloud and murk for a good fall of migrants.'

Holly thought this was ridiculous. Could the presence of these men be a coincidence, with the person she was supposed to meet waiting for her somewhere closer to the lough? She looked at her phone. Still no reception. But she did see the time. If she didn't get to the mainland soon, she'd miss the tide and be stuck here for another night. She couldn't bear the thought of returning to the Seahorse, to the noisy bar and the depressing room. She turned and followed the path back to the stile and the road.

All the way back to the lane she had the same sense that she was in the middle of an elaborate game of hide and seek.

This time though, she thought, she was the hider. Somewhere in the gloom, the seeker was following. She caught the sound of long grass moving and once, she believed she heard the squelch of a boot in wet mud. But when she stopped to listen, there was nothing. Her imagination and the fog playing tricks with her. The noises could be anything: cattle in an adjoining field, the birdwatchers bringing their trophy bird to be ringed. The text message could have been a hoax, sent by a local who enjoyed taunting the police. Or from a genuine member of the public who was still waiting for her in the marsh. Well, she thought, let them wait. As soon as she got back to Kimmerston, she'd trace the number and speak to them.

When she was on the lane and she could see the grey silhouette of the Pilgrims' House, her heart rate slowed. She pictured herself at home in her clean, white flat, running a bath, pouring herself a glass of wine. There'd be the evening briefing first, but she had plenty to report back. She didn't imagine that Joe would have discovered as much.

She'd reached the car, when she saw there was a light in the chapel. The flicker of candlelight. It wasn't dusk, just the gloom of late afternoon, but perhaps it was Robson, observing the ritual of peace and prayer. She was about to drive off, but curiosity got the better of her. Curiosity and the possibility of another snippet of information to pass on to Vera. Again, she wondered why Vera's approval was so important to her, why she felt this need to please.

Holly pushed open the chapel door. Inside, everything was quiet. Nobody was sitting on the pews in silent meditation. It occurred to her that she should blow out the candles, because they might be a fire risk. Then there was a footstep behind her. She heard that, and then there was nothing.

Chapter Forty-Three

THEY JUST CROSSED THE CAUSEWAY BEFORE the tide came in. Everything was grey and shadowy in the sea fret, so it felt like a drive into the unknown. The unfamiliar. Nothing looked quite the same. Charlie had gone ahead of them in his faster car. Vera had sent him first, knowing that the more robust Land Rover would fare better than his old vehicle. All the same, seawater tugged at their wheels as they drove along the road towards the island.

They'd still heard nothing from Holly and Vera was scared for her. She felt as if she was drowning, that she couldn't breathe, couldn't think. It was anxiety filling her mind, but also, mostly, it was guilt. For having sent Holly to the island alone; for all the barbed comments and criticisms during the course of the young woman's career. For the sins of omission, the times when Holly had done brilliant work and Vera had refused to recognize it.

She'd told Charlie to go to the Seahorse, to book their rooms and find out when Holly had left. It was possible that she'd still be there; she might even be interviewing a suspect in the lounge, having left them a message at the police station. But Vera didn't believe that. Holly was punctilious and she'd have made every effort to be back for the briefing. Or at least to have contacted Vera and Joe direct.

They parked outside Gull Cottage. Vera recognized Judith Sinclair's car, a small and sensible hatchback, pulled tight into the pavement. She was out of the Land Rover and banging on the door before Joe could join her. Philip Robson opened it.

'Inspector, come in.'

The fire was lit and the warmth of the room hit her and made her feel slightly giddy. Joe followed her into the room. Judith Sinclair sat by the fire, shocked it seemed by the violence of the knocking. She was drinking tea. Robson's hair looked slightly damp, and he was using the wide wooden windowsill as a seat. He had the air of someone who has just come in from the cold, red-faced. The news was on the radio. Something gloomy to match the weather.

'Have you seen DC Clarke? Holly.'

'I saw her yesterday.' Philip reached out and switched off the radio. 'I answered all her questions then.'

'And *you* spoke to me yesterday, Inspector.' Judith Sinclair's voice was precise. Disapproving. 'I have nothing to add.'

'Well, I have something to add to you.' A pause. 'Are you willing to talk in front of your friend? Or would you prefer to speak somewhere a little more private?'

There was a hesitation. Judith would have liked to say that she didn't have anything to hide, but perhaps she wasn't sure that was true. Philip saved her from further awkwardness. He stood up and gathered the empty cups. 'You stay in here. I should be making a start on supper anyway.'

Vera took a seat, leaving the windowsill to Joe. 'You haven't seen my colleague?'

'I haven't. I arrived early this morning and I've been here ever since.'

'And your friend?'

'Philip was out a while ago. He said he needed a walk. Fresh air. He's not long come back.'

'We've been talking to some of your former colleagues,' Vera said. 'Apparently you were quite wild when you started teaching. You went to students' parties, drinking. There were rumours of relationships.'

'I was young, Inspector. And things were very different in those days. It wasn't unknown for teachers to have relationships with their students. Not quite such a crime. Though most of the wayward teachers were male. Of course.' A pause. 'I should have explained when you came to my house this morning.'

'Why the sudden change in attitude?' Vera was always suspicious when a witness suddenly became reasonable.

'Philip reminded me that these things seldom stay hidden, and he seemed to think you would be discreet.'

'Only if what you have to say has nothing to do with murder.'

'I went to the Pilgrims' House on Friday night.' Judith paused. 'As I told you yesterday I was here to change the sheets and clean before Philip moved in on Sunday. I have a standing invitation to the reunions and I thought it would be fun to turn up and surprise everyone.'

'Did you drive?' Nobody had heard a car.

'No. I decided to walk. It was a beautiful evening, cold but very clear. There was a moon. I didn't even need a torch.'

'You didn't go in?'

'No, when I got there, I felt a little nervous and hesitated a while before I opened the door. I was standing just outside the common room window and I could hear Rick Kelsall talking. Boasting. Recounting his exploits.' There was another hesitation. 'He was never a brilliant actor, but he always had a voice which would carry. "I once slept with Miss Marshall." Those were the words I heard. And the laughter. And the others egging him on to tell the rest of the story. I didn't know what to do. It was a ridiculous situation. There I was, eaves-dropping, carrying a couple of bottles of prosecco to share with the group, but I couldn't go and join them.'

'Had you slept with him?'

There was a little nod. 'Once. At a student party. I'm sure you can understand how I felt. My past coming back to haunt me in such a cruel way.'

Vera thought she could. 'Embarrassing. What did you do then?'

'I walked back here.'

'You didn't wait until they'd all gone to bed, go into his room and confront Rick Kelsall?'

'No! That would have been shameful. How could I face him after those things he'd said?'

'Perhaps you waited until he was asleep. Easy enough then to hold a cushion over his face until he stopped breathing. The only way to ensure your reputation. To be certain he didn't write that scene into his book. The general reader wouldn't recognize you, but your former students and colleagues would.'

'No!' Her face was white, drained of all colour. 'I swear I didn't kill him. I couldn't commit murder.'

'But you did phone him? We have a record of the call.'

'Yes, I phoned him. I had to know if he planned to use the incident in his novel. That was what he was talking about in the common room. How he was writing a thriller, which would expose everyone's secrets.' She paused. 'He answered the phone, but he didn't even seem to know who I was and what I was talking about. He was drunk, barely conscious.'

'Where does Charlotte Thomas come into the tale?'

'I'm sorry?'

'She was seen coming into your cottage earlier that day. Late afternoon, and then you were together in the Seahorse in the evening. You've already admitted that.' Vera paused. She wanted to shake the woman. To force the information from her. 'You've told me this much. I need the rest.'

'Charlotte had met Rick on Thursday night. I'd done yoga classes with her, so we were acquaintances, and she called me at home on Friday morning. She'd been upset by something Rick had told her, she said. She needed my advice. Could she come and see me? I was just about to set out for Holy Island and the cottage. I told her if the matter was that important, she could come and meet me here.'

'Was it that urgent?' Vera was growing increasingly impatient. There was still no news of Holly and this was wasting time.

'It was Rick's book again.' In the kitchen there was the sound of pans, of a table being laid. 'I assume that you've researched Charlotte's background. I hadn't realized that her family had such an unsavoury past.'

'A criminal past,' Vera said.

'That would feature in Rick Kelsall's novel too, apparently. Charlotte was distraught. She'd been a wealthy young woman. Her children hadn't realized how much of her wealth had come from the proceeds of crime. She didn't want them to know. She wondered if there was a way we could get together – all of us who'd been in the Pilgrims' House for Only Connect

– and persuade him to let the past go. To write real fiction, not a kind of sensationalized reality. All of us had secrets of a kind. Kelsall seemed to be using them to mock us all. Making mischief.'

Vera remembered the conversation with the Thomas family in Fenham. Charlotte had clearly been trying to keep her distance for decades. The last thing she'd want, as she was trying to establish her shiny new business, would be for their past to be rehashed. 'What reason would Kelsall have for mischief making?'

Judith didn't answer immediately. 'I think he was bored, Inspector. As a teenager, he couldn't bear to be bored. Recently, he'd been attracting less attention. Perhaps he wanted to feel powerful again, alive, even if that meant being the object of people's fear and hostility.'

'An odd way to go about feeling alive.' But, Vera thought, perhaps that was why Hector had been so irascible, had drunk so much when he got older. In his belligerent moods and bad temper, at least he got a reaction. It was a kind of living. 'What advice did you give to Charlotte?'

'I agreed that the two of us, at least, could make a joint approach to Rick. Charlotte gave me his mobile number, in case I wanted to talk to him, and we planned to meet up later this week to plan tactics. But then, of course, he died.'

He was killed, which is rather different. Someone taking matters into their own hands perhaps. Someone not prepared to wait.

'Who was the man in the pub with you?'

'Really, it was nobody we knew. As I told you, it was just a random birdwatcher. The place was busy and we shared our table with him. There was no more to it than that.'

This time Vera felt inclined to believe her.

Chapter Forty-Four

THEY FOUND CHARLIE IN THE SEAHORSE, talking to the landlady and a barmaid with a white face and black eyes. The bar was open but quiet. They were sitting in the lounge around the table where Vera had eaten breakfast with Holly and Joe only three days before.

'Your colleague definitely checked out,' Di said. 'I took the payment myself. And her car's not there.'

'She was here for lunch.' That was the Goth. 'She was asking about a birdwatcher, a guy who was in the bar on Friday night, with Charlotte Thomas and an older woman. I'd thought the three of them were part of the same group, and she was asking if I could have been wrong. He might just have been sharing their table.' She looked up at them. Vera could tell that she wanted to help. 'I'm sorry. I didn't see him. Not properly. Only his back.'

'But you do table service,' Joe said. He was being very stiff, very formal, trying to hide his fears and control his panic. Vera had seen him act that way before when he was scared of losing it. He and Holly had grown closer during the case. This wasn't just about a colleague in danger. It was personal. 'You must have seen him while you were taking the order.'

Linz looked between the detectives and her boss. 'But it's only table service for food and that group weren't eating.' A pause. She seemed almost close to tears. 'I wish I could help, but honestly, I can't remember anything about him.'

'That's okay, pet. Not your fault at all.' Vera could see how everyone had assumed that the strange man sitting with Judith and Charlotte had been known to them. It seemed even more likely now that Judith had been telling the truth.

'I told Holly I'd put the word out. Ask if any of the regulars or the locals knew who he might be.' The barmaid's voice was eager now. 'And I did!'

'Did any of them get back to you?'

'No, but then they wouldn't. I gave them Holly's mobile number and told them to contact her direct.'

'Could you ask again?' Vera said. 'See if anyone has been in contact with her. She's missing and we're starting to get anxious.'

'Sure.' Linz was on her phone already. 'Sure.'

'Holly was in the Old Hall this morning.' Di, the landlady, leaned across the table. 'I saw her go in at around coffee time.'

Vera nodded. She knew about that visit. Holly had been there to ask about Katherine Willmore's alibi and it had checked out. If the DC had picked up anything else that was useful there, surely she'd have passed on that information to Vera too. But perhaps something had come to Holly later. A little niggle. An itch. It happened to Vera sometimes during the course of an investigation. And perhaps Holly had gone back to scratch. It was what *she* would have done and she'd trained all her staff well.

'I'll just wander along to the hotel,' she said, 'just in case something occurred to her and she went back.' Not believing that it would help, but needing to move again. Not bearing just to sit here, doing nothing. 'Joe, you wait here in case she comes back or we get more information. Charlie, you drive around the island. Everywhere. Farm tracks and lanes, private drives. We're looking for Holly's car.' She hesitated, felt in her pocket and held out her keys. 'Take the Land Rover. That'll get you down some of the rougher paths.'

Charlie stared at her, astonished by the honour. Nobody was allowed to drive the boss's vehicle. But he said nothing and he took the keys.

Out in the road, the light had seeped away to nothing. The mist held in the orange glow of the street lamps. Vera had been to the Old Hall once before. She'd been invited to dinner by her smart relative, Elizabeth, as a thank you for finding a killer. She hadn't really wanted to go, but had accepted the invitation, only because she'd known that Elizabeth had been hoping she'd refuse. Let the old woman pay for a decent meal and endure her company for one evening! Elizabeth had booked to stay the night there. Vera had driven home. One way of making sure she wouldn't drink too much. She hadn't wanted Elizabeth thinking she was like Hector, and besides, drink made her argumentative.

She'd decided that there was no point in arguing with an old woman who was seeing her world change and become almost unrecognizable. In the end, it had been a pleasant enough occasion. Elizabeth was used to being courteous to her tenants, and had treated Vera as if she were a farm worker, competent and necessary but not socially her equal. Vera had held her tongue and, when she got home, she'd poured herself a large whisky. She'd drunk a grateful toast to Hector for escaping his family and for making his own way in the world. It was one of the few times she'd ever felt grateful to him.

The Old Hall was busier than she'd been expecting. The lobby opened into the bar, where couples were taking pre-dinner drinks. Everybody was dressed up, very smart in a glitzy, celebratory way, and she was out of place, in her grubby jacket, her mud-spattered boots. She had, in the past, been mistaken for a bag lady. And more recently at Rede's Tower as a cleaner. A young man in a suit approached her, all smiles. Perhaps he thought she was a rich, eccentric, potential guest.

'Can I help you, madam?'

Discreetly, she showed him her warrant card. People were already staring, and she didn't need any more of an audience.

'Please, come into the office.'

He led her away from public view.

'My colleague was here this morning.'

'Ah yes, I was on duty and I spoke to her myself. She asked about one of our regulars.'

'Katherine Willmore?'

'Yes, I was able to tell her that Ms Willmore was here. I found a copy of her credit card receipt.' He smiled. Someone else, Vera thought, needing to be praised just for doing his job.

'You haven't seen DC Clarke since then?'

'No, and I've been at the front desk for most of the day.' The smile crawled over his face again. 'She asked about another potential guest. A single man. A birdwatcher. I'm afraid I wasn't able to help with that inquiry.'

'We're a little anxious about my officer,' Vera said. 'We've lost contact with her. Probably nothing. Signal problems or a mislaid phone. There's nothing else you can tell me?'

She sensed a moment of hesitation, but when she looked at his face, the smile was back in place.

'I'm sorry, Inspector, I wish I could help. It's a horrible evening for anyone to get lost.'

She nodded and went outside. In the car park, she took out her torch, and checked all the vehicles, but Holly's car wasn't there and she didn't recognize any of the other registration plates as belonging to witnesses in the case. She made her way back to the Seahorse. But now, she had her own itch, her own need to explore it, to scratch.

In the Seahorse, the lounge was filling up and Linz, Joe and Di had moved to the landlady's private sitting room on the first floor. It looked out over a courtyard at the back, where empty bottles and kegs were stacked. Inside, heavy red velvet curtains had been drawn against the gloom. A Calor gas heater had just been lit. It gave off little heat as yet, but a considerable smell of fumes. The room had been furnished with cast-off furniture from the bar and one low sofa, with a red velvet throw tucked over it. The effect was that of a junk shop crossed with a traditional curry house and Victorian brothel. Vera found it very comforting.

When Vera was shown in by another member of staff, Linz was talking on the phone. She seemed excited and was talking very fast. Then she listened. 'When was that? Did you see where she went?' She switched off her phone and faced the room. 'That was Tom Cadwallender, one of the local ringers. Nobody he knows had contacted your mate, but they did see her earlier. There was a rarity in a ditch by the lough and they were trying to catch it.'

Vera nodded. 'In a small mist net?'

'Yeah!' Linz eyed the inspector with increased respect. 'She seemed to think one of them had asked her to meet him. She'd had a text apparently saying he'd be there, but it hadn't come from one of them.'

'No name, I suppose?'

Linz shook her head.

Of course not. It would be a trap. Like the mist net catching the bird.

'Did they see anyone else?'

'Nah,' Linz said. 'One of them thought they heard someone, banging around in the fog, but it could have been anything.'

'The nearest place to park for the lough is the Pilgrims' House.'

'Charlie phoned earlier, boss.' Joe, still at his most formal, still anxious. 'He checked for Holly's car there. No sign of it.'

'We'll check ourselves, shall we? Let's walk, so we don't miss anything. Holly's car might not be there, but we might find Holly.'

Chapter Forty-Five

JOE HATED THIS. BEING OUT IN the dark and no street lights at all once they got beyond the boundary of the village. Worrying about Holly, because Holly didn't get herself into dangerous situations. She was sensible and followed the rules, not like the boss. And although she was younger and fitter than the boss, he sensed that she wasn't so resilient, so cunning or so brave.

They walked in silence. Vera seemed to be thinking. He hoped she'd pull some solution out of the bag at the last minute, like some overweight female magician. She often did. But Joe thought this scenario was unlikely to be so easily resolved. It didn't feel like any sort of magical illusion, and anyway, occasionally tricks went wrong; surely people could drown in tanks of water or get sawn in half or stabbed when knives were thrown.

They walked at the same pace, one each side of the road. There were no other cars out tonight. It was late now, and sensible people were eating their supper or watching television. The tide must be nearing its height because in the distance he could hear the scrape and suck of shingle on the shore. Every so often, there came the howl of the foghorn. Each time, the sound shocked him.

They shone their torches into the side of the road and into the rough grazing beyond the hedges and the stone walls. Nothing but motionless sheep, blurred by the mist, staring back with yellow eyes, dazed by torchlight. Once, he was startled by a wispy figure, standing quite still in a field. It was a scarecrow, wearing a coat like Vera's.

When they got to the Pilgrims' House, there were no cars parked outside. There was still a strip of blue and white tape strung across the width of the building, telling everyone to keep out. Vera was crouching, looking at tyre marks.

'More than one car has been parked here, but they could have belonged to those birding friends of Linz's.' She ducked under the tape and tried the front door. It was locked and she walked on until she was standing next to the window, right at the end of the house. 'Get in there, Joe. It leads to Rick Kelsall's room. If the killer opened it, you should be able to manage it.' A pause. 'And if he was smothered by someone already in the house, this is your chance to show me how clever you are. Otherwise, just break it.'

At first, he thought he would have to break the glass, but the original sash window was only just held by the catch inside and when he jiggled it, he could lift the pane. He climbed into the room, where once Kelsall's body had been hanging from a beam. 'No lights,' Vera said. 'We don't want the world knowing we're here. Just open the door and let me in.'

The place was silent, and already felt damp, colder than it had been outside. He let Vera through the front door and they went round all the rooms, shining light into every corner.

'No sign that anyone's been here since the forensic team left,' she said. There was fingerprint dust everywhere, congealing in the damp air.

He went back into Kelsall's room, shut the window and slid the catch across again, and they went outside, pulling the door behind them to lock it.

He thought they'd head back then, to the warm red room above the bar in the Seahorse, but Vera was already on her way to the chapel. This door opened immediately. She stood on the threshold and shone her torch ahead of her.

'Someone's been in here. Mucky footwear prints on the floor.'

'That could have been from days ago. Philip Robson using it for his dusk meditation.'

'Aye, maybe.' She didn't sound convinced. 'There's that smell of candlewax too. Strong. I'd say the candles have been lit very recently.'

They walked in, avoiding the footprints. Vera walked up to the altar and shone a light on the candlesticks. 'Look, they've been left to burn right down. Philip strikes me as a careful man. He'd have blown them out.'

'So, you think Holly lit them for some reason?'

'Nah!' Vera was dismissive. 'This was another trap. They were lit to lure her in. She met the birders on the marsh and then she'd have come back to her car to drive off the island. But if there was candlelight in the chapel, she'd have gone inside, wouldn't she? She'd want to investigate.'

She walked back towards the door, shining her torch under each of the pews. Nothing. The place was as bare and austere as it had always been. Then she stopped so suddenly that Joe, following behind her, always a few steps in her wake, the Prince

Consort to her Queen, almost bumped into her. She crouched again, moving easily in spite of the weight she carried. He saw a stain on the flagstone.

'Blood,' she said.

'It could be anything.'

She didn't answer, but continued outside, leaving him to follow.

Back at the Seahorse, they saw the Land Rover parked outside and found Charlie in Di's sitting room, drinking tea. It was much warmer now, the heater giving a steady glow. Linz was serving in the bar downstairs, but the landlady was in the room too. There was the smell of bacon frying. 'I thought you might be hungry.'

'She was there.' For once, Vera didn't seem distracted by the thought of food, though Joe saw that she ate the sandwich in a couple of bites when it was presented. 'In the Pilgrims' House chapel. No sign of her car, Charlie?'

'Honestly, boss, I've been all over the island. Up to the castle and along the track as far north as I could go. I looked in the Herring House courtyard. The hotel car parks. That house on the Snook. Everywhere I can think of.'

'Still, it must be somewhere.' Anxiety was making Vera snappy and irrational. 'It can't have disappeared into thin air.'

Joe tried to focus on practicalities. The thought of Holly, being held somewhere against her will, made his brain turn to water and that would help nobody. He remembered their drive over the causeway, the water splashing against the Land Rover as Vera drove too fast ahead of the tide. 'They couldn't have taken her off the island? Just before we came on or just after?'

'After would be a stretch,' Vera said, 'especially in Holly's car. You'd get so far, but I doubt you'd make it all the way across.'

'Isn't that what happened to Isobel Hall?'

Vera looked at him, held his eyes. 'You're thinking history repeating itself?'

'I don't know. Just thinking aloud.'

'This fog,' she went on, 'nobody would see to call the alarm. If she was unconscious, you'd just leave her in her car, halfway across and wait for the tide to take her. The authorities might put that down as an accident. Any head wound could be a result of the car being swept away.'

By the time she'd finished speaking, they had their coats back on and they were halfway down the narrow stairs. Joe was praying to the God of his grandfather that he was wrong, that they'd find Holly's car hidden in the acres of dune near the causeway, that his imagination was running wild. All three of them crammed into the Land Rover's bench seat. They drove past the Lindisfarne Hotel, where a solitary smoker stood in the doorway, his back to the light, and the row of bungalows. It seemed to Joe that there was a bit of a breeze and that the mist was lifting a little. But that could be wishful thinking, or his imagination playing tricks again.

Vera drove too fast and almost slid where driven sand had made the road slippery. She only came to a stop when the water was lapping the wheels.

'It must be high water,' she said. 'Soon it'll be on its way out.' She was out of the vehicle, shining her torch into the darkness, but all it hit was a grey bank of fog. 'We need the lifeboat!' She was panicking now and Vera never panicked. 'Charlie, get on to them.'

'No evidence she's out there, boss.'

'And no evidence that she's not. Do it!'

Charlie was on his phone, muttering a message they couldn't hear because he was still in the Land Rover. He raised his voice. 'The nearest lifeboat is Seahouses. They're shouting them now.'

'Surely some bugger on this island has a boat!'

'I'm talking to the coastguard.'

Joe was standing beside his boss, peering into the gloom. Vera was right about the tide. The water was sliding away from them. Again, he thought he felt a breeze on his face. Looking up, there was one star, which disappeared almost as soon as he glimpsed it. The mist might be clearing above them, but over the water it seemed to be as thick as ever. The light of their torches bounced back at them. Vera got back into the Land Rover and put the headlights on full beam. And that was when he saw it. The fog thinned briefly and the image was sharp and clear, held for only seconds in the beam. A car, a hundred yards away from them and no longer on the causeway. It had rolled onto its side, so swamped with water that only a few inches of the door panel and the wing mirror showed. If Holly had been in there, she'd had no chance of survival.

He'd shouted to Vera, but she'd already seen it. 'Charlie, tell the coastguard that we need that boat now! And an ambulance on standby at the mainland end of the causeway.'

Joe marvelled at his boss's ability to act. He was frozen in grief. There was nothing he could do. Even if he swam to the car, it would be too late to save Holly, and besides, his boots seemed rooted to the concrete. He was overcome with a dreadful lethargy and his only thought was that Holly wouldn't have responded like this. She wouldn't have been as pathetic as him if *he* were in trouble. Holly would have known the right thing to do. He climbed in beside Vera, opened the window.

She switched on the Land Rover engine and backed up a little. Joe had no idea what plan she might have in mind. They were in no danger now the tide was on its way out. But there was a dip in the road and by reversing a few yards, the front of the vehicle was tilting up slightly. Again, Joe felt wind on his face. Definitely not his imagination this time and looking up there was a scattering of stars. With her headlights still on full beam, Vera turned the steering wheel a touch to the right. The beam moved above the water, until it hit what she was looking for. Still shadowy, a wooden tower, with a ladder to reach it. One of the refuges for trapped drivers and walkers. The closest tower to the island.

'There's something there.' Vera was talking very quietly to herself.

Joe could see it too, but thought it wasn't Holly. This was a pile of rubbish, seaweed and discarded plastic left by an abnormally high tide. The water was ebbing away from them quickly now.

'Any news on the lifeboat, Charlie?' The boss, calm. Icy.

'They've launched. On their way from Seahouses. But the locals are scrambling too.'

'That might be too long. I'll drive in as far as I can get with the Land Rover. Then it's down to you, Joe.'

'You think that's her?'

'I'm willing to take a chance on it.' A moment's pause. 'Are you?'

'Of course.' Though he wasn't sure. The fog had thickened again and the water would be freezing. He wasn't a strong swimmer and had nightmares about drowning. About cold saltwater covering his head and the tide pulling him under. But he knew that Holly would do the same for him, and really there was no question.

Vera drove the Land Rover forward at walking speed until the sea reached the top of the wheel arch. 'I'll have to stop now, or you'll not get the door open.'

'Where's the tower?' Panic was overwhelming him, just like the water of his dreams.

'Ahead and to your left. Look, I could go.'

'No!' That would be shameful. This was a fool's errand. But he couldn't let Vera show him up. He'd be ridiculed for the rest of his career. He thought Charlie had had more sense than to volunteer, but the man turned to him, apologetic.

'I'm sorry. I can't swim.' The words a cry. He would rather be out in the water, than sitting here, helpless.

Joe put a hand on Charlie's arm, then he pushed the door open and slid out. He stumbled immediately on the uneven surface beneath his feet, and tripped forwards so the water reached his chest. The cold seeped through his clothes and took his breath away. He pushed against the weight of it, staying on the causeway, following the beam of the headlight. It shone a path through the mist.

He only saw the refuge when Vera shifted the car slightly so the light pointed to the left and he could see the base of the tower again. Steps leading up, like the structure in the Rede's Tower adventure playground. It looked close enough to touch, but when he moved towards it, suddenly, he was out of his depth, weighed down by his jacket and boots. He'd stepped off the causeway without realizing. The water covered his face and he panicked. This would be the end then. No glory, no saving of a colleague, but another officer's life wasted.

Then his thoughts cleared like the fog and he lunged forward and grabbed on to one of the underwater rungs of the ladder, and pulled himself clear of the tide. He stood there for a moment, spluttering, gripping the slippery wood, his life depending on holding tight. Then he began to climb, every step an effort because of the weight of his waterlogged clothing.

As he reached the platform, he was above the level of the headlights' beam, but the mist was definitely clearing and the darkness wasn't quite so dense. He felt for the shape they'd seen from the shore. Wet cloth. Nothing moving. He heaved himself onto the platform and took his torch from his jacket pocket. It was still working. The first thing he saw was Holly's face. White. No sign of life. He wrapped himself around her. He was cold, but not as cold as she was and if she was close to death, he didn't want her dying alone, with no human contact.

Then suddenly he heard the call of wading birds, frightened from their roost by the sound of an engine and more lights, and the fat inflatable rib circling the tower and a man in a yellow oilskin climbing the ladder as easily as if it were an obstacle in a kids' playground. His own voice demanding to know if his friend was alive.

Chapter Forty-Six

VERA WATCHED THE SCENE FROM THE vehicle, wishing she was there, sitting with Holly at the top of the tower, holding her, trying to breathe some warmth and some life back into her body. Holly had saved Vera's life once. Vera wondered briefly if that was why she was feeling so wretched. Because, above anything she hated a sense of obligation, of a kindness done that might have to be repaid. Or perhaps, it was a kind of arrogance. If anyone could keep Holly alive, it was Joe, but she'd never really trusted her team to do the important things without her. It was about time she learned that lesson and gave her team some freedom to act alone.

The mist was shifting now, patchy, so her view of the tower was dream-like, unreliable. There was no communication with Joe. She didn't know what he'd found there. Perhaps she'd imagined the shape as a body, and she'd set off this whole drama with no cause. Then the coastguard's inflatable arrived, scaring the roosting birds with its noise and capturing the tower with flashlights, so the platform looked like a stage, a scene in a bit of performance art. Joanna had taken her once to a place in Newcastle, an avant-garde theatre, hoping to broaden her mind, but Vera had just been confused. Her thoughts now were swirling like the mist, unfocused. Charlie was still beside her, muttering under his breath, his own kind of prayer or incantation. It could have been an odd musical accompaniment to the unfolding performance. Then the boat was off again, heading to the mainland, and the platform was empty.

By now, the tide was ebbing fast. It was impossible to judge the depth of the water on the causeway in the dark, but Vera was willing to take a chance. Anything was better than this ignorance. She drove on slowly, heading for the opposite shore and the flashing lights of the waiting ambulance. Then the water level dropped and she could move more quickly. The crew in their thigh waders had already lifted Holly ashore and she was in the ambulance. The door was open and a paramedic was leaning over her. Joe was standing on dry land, wrapped in a foil blanket, shivering. Vera jumped from the Land Rover. With surprise she noticed that there were no creaking joints, no pain in her knees. She supposed that adrenaline would do that to you. Fear would take you away from the mundane trials of the present.

'Well?' The question directed to Joe and to the boat crew. 'Is she alive?'

'Just,' he said.

'You should come too, mate!' The paramedic. 'Get checked over.'

'No.' He looked at Vera. 'I've got work to do.'

'Where are you taking her?' Vera was at her most imperious.

'The emergency and trauma hospital just outside Kimmerston.' He looked at her. 'They won't let you question her tonight.'

'I'll have one of my team there, keeping an eye on her. Let them know.' Vera stared at him. 'Tell them this was an assault dressed up as an accident. Attempted murder. Not some daft young woman taking a chance with the tide.' For some reason it mattered to her that the medical team shouldn't think that of Holly. There was nothing irresponsible about her officer.

He nodded.

She saw that Charlie was already back on his phone arranging for someone to be waiting at the hospital for Holly.

The ambulance was off then, blue lights flashing. They heard the siren when it hit the main road. Vera thanked the coastguard crew, but they were awkward. They didn't need her kind words and just wanted to get home and warm. The three detectives were left standing there.

'We need to get you out of those wet clothes,' she said to Joe. 'Or you'll catch your death. And I need a drink.'

She turned the Land Rover round and they drove back to the Seahorse. There were still stragglers in the bar but Di was waiting for them in her snug red lounge. She found clothes for Joe. 'I'll stick yours in the washer and put them to dry. They'll be ready for you in the morning. My Trev died three years ago, but I can't quite bear to give away his things.' Trev had been considerably larger than Joe, and the sergeant sat in an enormous tracksuit, his feet in a pair of sheepskin slippers. Vera allowed herself a brief grin, but made no comment.

Di disappeared for a moment and returned with a bottle of whisky and three glasses. She was still curious, but sensed their anxiety and understood that they needed to be alone. 'I'm off to my bed. My turn to do the early breakfasts. Just shut the door behind you when you head off yourselves.'

Vera could have kissed her. 'Thanks. You're a life-saver.'

She poured the whisky and they sat for a moment in silence.
'All being well, we'll talk to Hol in the morning.' Vera was
holding her glass with two hands. 'No guarantee she knew who
knocked her out though. I'd guess she was hit from behind in
the chapel, and she only gained consciousness briefly when
the water got into the car. Most people wouldn't have been
able to get out and find the refuge. It was a mixture of luck
and courage.'

Charlie's phone rang. There was a brief conversation, unen-
lightening to Vera and Joe.

'That was the guy at the hospital. They're giving her a brain
scan and keeping her sedated until they know the results. She
was hypothermic. Any later and the cold would certainly have
killed her.'

'She'll be all right though? She will pull through?'

Charlie shrugged. 'You know what doctors are like. They've
not really told him anything.' A pause. 'Still critical they say.
Life-threatening injuries.'

A silence. Vera couldn't allow herself to think about that.
Holly was tough, a fighter. 'Let's make plans then. We'll get a
bit of sleep then head off before the next tide.'

'You don't think the killer's still here?'

Vera shook her head. 'I don't think so. They'll have left just
before the water took Holly's car off the causeway, and headed
away to set up an alibi for themselves. No evidence of contact
then. They knew we were here and wouldn't want to be on
the island when we heard about the *accident*.' She waved her
fingers in the air to indicate quotation marks.

'What about the vicar?'

Vera reconsidered. It was too easy to dismiss Philip. He
might seem settled and content, but he had a reputation to

lose too. His identity was bound up with the notion that he was a *good* man.

'You're right of course. The killer could have come back to the island to hide in plain sight, instead of making a run for the mainland. Charlie, you stay here, go and talk to him.' She thought Philip would underestimate Charlie. They'd think he was plodding, unimaginative. 'Check the tread on his car tyres. See if there's sand there and if it matches the marks we found outside the Pilgrims' House.'

'You have an idea who it is, don't you?' The question came from Joe, who knew her too well.

'Nothing certain.' She shot him a quick grin. 'And I've often been wrong.' But an idea was starting to form, like shapes emerging in a landscape when the fog starts to clear. Vera remembered the notion that had come to her walking away from the Old Hall Hotel earlier, the itch that had to be scratched. 'We should know by the end of tomorrow, though.' She looked at the clock on the mantelpiece. 'By the end of today.'

She was waiting outside Bread and Olives when it opened. Jax and Annie were inside, deep in conversation, and Jax didn't see her until she unlocked the door.

'I was hoping for a word with Annie.' Vera was hit as usual by the distinctive, delicious smell of the place.

'Okay.' Jax sounded a little dubious. Wary on behalf of her colleague. 'She's not been well. This business has really upset her.'

'Of course,' Vera said. 'It would.'

'Go into the garden. We won't get busy for an hour.'

They'd turned the yard behind the shop into an outside

social space. It was hardly a garden, though they'd planted up a few pots. There was an assortment of tables and chairs: wrought iron, plastic, wood. They still served breakfast and lunch here at weekends. Annie looked tired, almost frail. Vera tried to imagine her hitting Holly hard enough to cause possible brain damage. She'd have had to be desperate.

Jax made them coffee and served it in large mugs, hot milk in a jug on the side, then retreated into the shop. Vera could see her watching them from inside, tense and anxious. She nodded towards the window. 'She's a good friend.'

'She is,' Annie said. 'The best.'

'First off, where were you yesterday evening?'

'At home.'

'On your own?'

'I'm usually on my own, Inspector.' There were dark rings around her eyes.

'Do you get lonely?' Vera wondered where the question had come from.

There was a silence. 'When Daniel and I first separated I loved the time to myself. As I've got older, I've found it more difficult. People surrounded by families. Children and grand-children.' A pause. 'I get very jealous. I have friends of course.'

Vera nodded. She had Joanna. And her colleagues at work. Joe and Charlie. Holly. Who was still sedated, still unconscious. Still a weight on Vera's conscience.

'You have Jax,' Vera said. 'You had Rick Kelsall.'

Annie looked up at her. 'He was my best friend. I miss him so much.'

'I want to take you back forty-five years.' They were sitting on the wrought-iron garden chairs, a table between them. 'The day Isobel Hall died. You said there was a row between her and Rick just before she set off too close to the tide. It would help me to know exactly what it was about. You must have been curious. You must have asked him.'

Annie shut her eyes. Vera thought the woman was back there, outside the Pilgrims' House, still in pain because her baby had died only months before. It seemed cruel to make her relive that weekend, but Vera had to know.

'I did ask him,' Annie said. 'After she'd driven off in such a hurry, but before we heard her car had crashed. "What is it with you two?" He said Isobel was a flirt and a tease. Impossible. He was trying to laugh it off, but I could tell he was angry, irritated.'

'You assumed something had gone on between them over the weekend? Even though he was already engaged to Charlotte? And then Isobel had wanted more? Some sort of commitment?'

'Maybe, though that wasn't really her style either. But he had that sort of charisma that led to his women making demands.'

'You never made demands on him.' It wasn't a question.

Annie smiled. 'That's why we got on so well.'

There was a moment of silence. A murmur of conversation in the shop behind them.

'One of my officers was attacked on Holy Island last night,' Vera said. 'If there's anything else you can tell me, even if it's just a suspicion, a little niggle, it might help us find out who killed Rick.'

And Charlotte, though you've never cared for her.

For a minute Vera expected Annie to speak, that there might be a revelation, even some sort of confession, but she just shook her head. 'I should go back to work. It's getting busy.' Vera followed her into the shop and then out into the street.

Outside on the pavement, there was a queue of people waiting to go into the deli. Vera heard Annie shout in the next customer. She sounded friendly and professional, but Vera thought she could hear a shake in her voice, which was almost like the start of a sob, and that was a kind of confession in itself.

Vera had left her car at the police station and started the walk back. She knew she should arrange a meeting with Watkins, feed back the latest information on Holly, ask permission for the next move. But the thought of crawling to Watkins and begging him to let her take the next step horrified her. She knew now. No proof, but she knew. The killer was panicking – the attack on Holly had been planned at the last minute and irrational. People under pressure didn't think straight and Vera was good at getting suspects to make mistakes.

She was walking away when Charlie phoned. 'I checked out Gull Cottage.'

'Yes?' She'd almost forgotten he was going to see Philip Robson.

'They've gone. Him and Judith. Cleared out. When they didn't answer the door, I found the key where you said it would be, in the old outside lav. All their stuff has gone, their cars too.' He paused. 'It might not mean anything.'

'No,' she said. 'It might not.'

There's only one way to find out.

Instead of going into the station and to her stuffy office, she climbed into her Land Rover. She'd have to do this solo. The others had too much to lose. She fumbled for her phone, which was at the bottom of her bag, and made a phone call. No answer, but she wasn't expecting one. Katherine Willmore was a busy woman, who always let her secretary take her calls, and it was too early for him to be in the office yet. Vera left a message. 'This is urgent. Please make sure Miss Willmore gets it immediately, wherever she is.' She looked at her watch, then she made one more call and drove north.

Chapter Forty-Seven

IT WAS CLEAR AND SUNNY, MUCH as it had been when she'd first arrived at the Pilgrims' House five days before. Dead leaves underfoot. Quiet and still. Because the door was shut, she wasn't sure whether the man had done as she'd asked and come to meet her. As she approached there was the familiar smell of creosote. All bird hides smelled the same and it was the scent of her childhood, trailing after Hector, being told to sit still, while he recced the sites of nests he could rob. She opened the door and saw that the place was empty, except for one figure, back on. The flap overlooking the lake was open and sunlight flooded in from the east. You'd see practically nothing on the lake with the sun in your eyes, but that wasn't why he was here in the Rede's Tower nature reserve. He wasn't birdwatching today.

'Daniel,' she said. 'Good of you to meet me.'

'Why here?' He turned towards her. 'We could have talked in the house if you needed to see me. It'd be more comfortable there. I'd even make you a coffee.'

'Ah,' she said. 'Neutral territory. I wasn't sure whether Eliza would be back. We wouldn't want her earwigging.' A pause. 'Or Katherine.'

Because Katherine's the unknown quantity here. Who knows how she'll react? And what Watkins will make of it.

Vera squinted into the sun, saw the silhouettes of mallard and tufted duck on the water. 'We don't want to involve her unless we have to. Besides, I'm at home in a place like this. My father was a birdwatcher. Of a kind.'

'How can I help you, Inspector?'

'I spoke to Annie this morning. I caught her at the deli, just as it was opening.'

'Oh? How's she doing?'

'She's sad. Maybe a bit lonely. She's lost a good friend.'

'I'm sorry,' he said. 'I'm still very fond of her.'

'But Katherine? She's the love of your life these days?'

'You know, I might sound like a soppy git, but really, she's the best thing that ever happened to me. I adore her.' He turned towards Vera and gave her an open smile, wide and lovely. She could see how Katherine might have fallen for him.

'Is that what all this is about? Are you protecting Katherine here?'

'I don't know what you mean.'

'Then let me explain. Tell you the story that Rick Kelsall was going to tell in his novel. Though I don't think it was so much a novel as a piece of mischief. I'm not even sure that he'd written much more than a synopsis and a few notes. Planning it was enough, a way of bringing the past back to life. Making the man feel alive and young again. Replacing the attention that he had when he was on the telly every week. Stirring things up.'

'Aye well,' Daniel said. 'He was always good at doing that. Not so good at putting things back together again.'

'He had a row with Isobel Hall just before she drove off the causeway and died. Everyone blamed him for that. There was always a lingering sense that he'd caused the accident, by treating her badly. He didn't enjoy being cast as the villain in the piece.' Vera leaned forward, her elbows on the shelf where the birders rested their telescopes, the smell of stagnant water and rich vegetation seeping into the hide. 'He wanted to set matters straight and tell his own side of the tale after all this time.'

'I wouldn't know,' Daniel said.

Vera ignored that and continued. 'It was a terrible time for you, that first reunion on the island. You were only there for Annie. You'd lost your baby a few months earlier and Annie was severely depressed, wrapped up in her grief.'

'Aye.' Daniel spoke slowly, reliving the pain. 'She couldn't let it go. Every thought was a torment, about what we might have done, what we should have done. The possibilities going round and round in her head like a whirlpool, but knowing that nothing would change the outcome. It was as if she was drowning in the guilt.'

Oh, Vera thought, I know exactly how that feels.

Rede was still talking. 'It was a kind of madness.' He looked up at Vera. 'I think she's a bit mad now, after all this time, though she hides it very well.'

'You're still very fond of her.'

'Of course.'

'Still protective?'

He turned his attention back to the pond. 'I don't know where you're going with this.'

'I'm exploring all the possibilities. I like Annie, but liking someone doesn't stop me thinking they might have done something criminal.' A pause. 'Wicked.'

'Now you're being crazy! Annie wouldn't hurt a fly. She certainly wouldn't kill Rick Kelsall.'

'Maybe not, but humour me, will you? Let's go back to that weekend. The first reunion. The end of a long, hot summer, apparently. Even here in the North. You'd lost your baby. Everyone's nerves would be frayed. You were all just in your twenties by then, but not quite ready to be adults. Not quite grown up. Except for Annie, who'd had to grow up very quickly.'

He stared out at the water in silence. A pair of mallard flew off, all noise and splash.

'You must have felt trapped,' Vera went on. 'You didn't want to be there with the people you didn't have much in common with. You'd only agreed to come along to support Annie, to stop her doing something silly.' A pause. 'She'd talked about suicide? Maybe made a few tentative tries at it.'

Daniel nodded. She could just see his profile. 'I saw marks on her wrists. She wouldn't talk to me! I think she'd had a sort of breakdown. But she refused to see a doctor. She kept saying that she was okay. That it was normal to be sad when you've lost a baby.'

'But this was more than sadness, wasn't it, pet? This was depression. Deep and dangerous. And you were young too. It was a stressful time for you. We didn't understand mental illness then. Not as we do now. Maybe you saw the weekend as some sort of escape. A way of sharing the burden at least. There'd be other people around to help look after her.'

'Yes!' He was grateful that she understood.

'You were hoping for a breakthrough in her mood, but some time to yourself too. Company. Even a bit of fun.'

'That makes me sound heartless.' Daniel shot her a glance. 'But you're right. I loved Annie, but she was dragging me down with her. I tried to help her, but it seemed there was nothing I could do.'

'Eh, pet, I'm not judging. Sometimes we do what we have to, just to survive.'

'Aye well. That was what it felt like. Like I was swamped by responsibility, that if I didn't get a break, I'd go mad myself.'

'And then along swanned Isobel,' Vera said. 'Full of light and energy. Just graduated and full of confidence. She'd always fancied you. Her mam told my sergeant, there was someone special in her life, but that he was already taken. I think that was you. So, there she was. Flirting and giving you the sort of attention you'd not had since the baby died. Seeming sympathetic, but really hoping to get her man at last. The man of her dreams. Who could resist that?' Vera paused. 'I'm guessing that you two had a bit of a fling that weekend. Sex in the sand dunes? Sneaking off together while Annie was still grieving and guilty.'

He smiled sadly. 'Something like that. It seems a bit pathetic now, but at the time it felt . . .' He struggled to find the words. '. . . just what I needed.'

'A kind of tonic?'

'Like you said: an escape. And Isobel made me laugh. We both knew it wasn't serious.'

'Well, not serious for you perhaps. Serious enough for Isobel, who'd always needed what she couldn't have.' Vera looked across at him again, but he was still staring out of the slit window of the hide. 'Did Annie work out what you were up to? All the sudden disappearances? Never being there for her?'

'No!' he said. 'She was still lost in that world of her own.'

Vera nodded. 'You're saying she was too depressed to notice you carrying on under her nose? Too depressed to see the betrayal, to want some sort of revenge?'

'Yes!' His voice was loud now. 'And we were discreet. Honestly, we didn't want to hurt her. She couldn't have known.'

'Not that discreet,' Vera shot back. 'While Annie might just have been too wrapped up in her own memories to realize what you were doing, the others noticed.'

'No,' Daniel said. 'You've got this all wrong.'

'Or perhaps not all the others.' Vera continued speaking as if there'd been no interruption. 'Just Rick Kelsall, who was Annie's special friend. Who loved her like a brother and understood her better than anyone in the world.'

Silence.

'Rick didn't blame you,' Vera went on. 'He knew what you'd gone through. He blamed Isobel. Arrogant, entitled Isobel, who'd decided to seduce you, to get the man she'd always wanted. That was what the row was about.' A pause. 'Did Annie hear them arguing?'

'I think she must have done,' Daniel said at last. 'She'd been to the village and appeared in the middle of it.'

'So, she *did* know that you and Isobel had had a fling?'

'Maybe. At that point she might have guessed from the words flying between Isobel and Kelsall. But she never mentioned it.'

'It was something else that festered between you for the rest of your marriage. Something else for her to chase round and round in her head when she was lying awake at night.'

Now he did turn to her. 'I did try to make a go of that marriage, you know. I wasn't some kind of unfeeling monster. I did my best to mend it. We went to counselling and I was as kind as I could be. I stayed as long as I could. But in the end, the only sane thing was to walk away.'

'To focus on your work.' *That's always been my answer.*

He nodded again. 'Yes, until Katherine came along and I fell for her. Head over heels. Then work didn't seem quite so important.'

'Was it Annie, who sent Isobel off to her death? Is that what you've all been hiding all these years?'

He took a moment to respond. 'She might have said something. Some recrimination or challenge. But I never saw it as Annie's fault. It was Isobel's decision to rush away like that. It was an accident.'

'Aye,' Vera said, 'and it was in Isobel's nature to make the grand gesture. Maybe she imagined herself stranded on one of the refuge towers waiting to be rescued. By a knight in shining armour. *Her* knight.'

'Maybe.'

'Do you think Annie killed Rick Kelsall? Because he was planning to bring the whole thing out in the open after all these years? To bring back all those dreadful memories.' Now, Vera thought, they were getting to the heart of the matter.

'The way he's always behaved, he had no right to make any kind of fuss.'

This, Vera thought, was no kind of answer.

'But he was Annie's friend,' she said. 'He thought the world of her. I'm not sure he'd have done anything now to hurt her.'

'Rick Kelsall was a selfish man.' Daniel turned towards Vera in his effort to make her understand. 'He was totally absorbed in his own desires. He'd sacrifice anyone, even Annie, to pull himself back into the limelight.'

'But he wasn't planning to sacrifice Annie.' Vera kept her voice very low. 'Was he, pet? He had someone very different in mind as villain of his piece.'

'I don't know what you mean.' With these words, Daniel seemed to lose the veneer of sophistication he'd developed during his life with Katherine. He turned back into a churlish teenager. The secondary modern kid, who'd scraped a place in the Grammar at the last chance. Still the chippy outsider, who'd never quite fitted in.

'Oh, I think you do. In his book, Rick never intended to blame Annie for Isobel's death. It was a much more interesting target. Rich businessman married to the Police and Crime Commissioner, famous for her moral stance on all issues.' A pause. 'Annie would never have killed Rick Kelsall.'

'What are you saying?' The words came out as a growl.

'Let me explain, if you don't quite understand.' Now Vera could have been Judith Sinclair, a teacher standing in front of her classroom. 'Though I think you know perfectly well what I'm saying. We'll go back a few months. Back to the early summer. People were listening to a young Swedish lass and deciding it wasn't cool to be flying to exotic places. They'd holiday in Britain instead. You'd long divorced from Annie, and taken up with Katherine. You'd built this business up into the success it is now, and people were flocking to the seaside for a change of scene. Everything rosy. Perfect. No longer any reason for you to prove yourself. You could finally believe you were as good as the rest of the world.'

Vera paused for a moment and shot a glance at Daniel. He was staring out at the reserve. Still and silent and as hard as granite.

'There were obviously no hard feelings between you and Kelsall,' Vera went on, 'because he took on your stepdaughter as an intern. Only then Eliza made some foolish allegations, exaggerating his behaviour, and he lost his job. And he felt the need to fight back. To re-establish himself in the eyes of his public. And to get his own back for his misfortune, like some pathetic schoolboy scrapping in the playground, after some-one's called him a rude name. That's how we come to be here, exploring the past and the reasons for two people's deaths.'

'It wasn't my fault Kelsall lost his job.' Daniel spat out the words. 'That was down to him. His responsibility. His inap-propriate behaviour. And he had the nerve to preach to me about something that happened forty-five years ago.'

'Yes,' Vera said, staying almost calm. 'I can see that must have rankled. None of us likes a hypocrite.' She took a breath. 'When did Kelsall come to see you to let you know what he was planning? To tell you he was writing a fictionalized version of an event that happened all that time ago. Something suffi-ciently close to the truth that the people involved and their friends and family would understand, and not look at you in quite the same way again. Something that might sour your relationship with the love of your life.'

'He came here to the house to talk to Katherine about the statement they'd make jointly about Eliza's allegations. The way she'd been manipulated by the press.'

'You saw him then? Is that when he threatened to expose you?'

'He tracked me down after that meeting. I was here on site. He called into reception on his way out, and they pointed him in my direction. It was one of those glorious days that we had last week. We walked on the beach. *He* talked. Kelsall always very much liked the sound of his own voice. He was playing with me. Mocking the business in that sarky way that some people do. Calling it a holiday camp, as if it was fucking Butlins. He said he wasn't entirely sure he would agree to the statement about Eliza, and whatever happened things wouldn't be the same for us. Not once his book came out. People might not be so keen to stay in our *holiday camp* once they knew the sort of man I was. A man who'd driven one young woman to consider suicide and another to her death. He might have the reputation of being a bastard to women, but he'd never had that effect on them. He'd never driven them to kill themselves.' Daniel paused for breath. 'His tone was jokey but it was a very real threat.'

'You had a lot to lose,' Vera said. 'Katherine. This place. Your perfect life.'

'Everything I've worked for!' It came out as a scream. His control was unravelling at last. Vera could see now that she'd get a confession from him.

'So, that night you drove onto Holy Island.'

He stared at her, with his mouth clamped shut.

'And you killed Rick Kelsall.'

Still, he didn't answer.

'You can tell me!' Vera forced herself to smile. 'We're on our own here and I'm not recording the conversation. I wouldn't know how. I just want to understand for my own satisfaction.' A beat. 'And besides, I think you want to tell me. You want someone to know the truth. You're not some kind of monster.'

Daniel was still staring over the water. The sun had shifted a bit, had moved behind a clump of trees, so the view was clearer; he wasn't looking into the light. 'I didn't go there to kill him. I wanted to talk to him, just to sort things out between us. To persuade him.'

'But you *did* kill him, didn't you, Daniel?'

'I had a key to the Pilgrims' House,' Daniel said. 'I'm planning to buy it. I've told you we wanted to expand the business and I already have interests on the island.'

'The Old Hall Hotel.' Vera didn't want to stop his flow, but that was part of the story too. 'You hold a share in that.'

He nodded.

'I knew where Kelsall slept.' His voice was bitter. 'Always the best room in the place. I went in and he was asleep. Looking so pathetic. His mouth open, stinking of booze. Snoring.'

'So, you held a cushion on his face and you killed him. Then you strung him up to make it look like suicide.'

'Lying there. So weak. It was as if he was inviting me to do it.' Daniel paused. 'I was home before Katherine woke up. It's not very far around the bay.' He turned to face Vera. 'She knew nothing about this. I did it for her. Think of the embarrassment if the whole thing came out. If Kelsall backed down on his agreement to tell the truth about Eliza's allegations.'

'And the fact that you had a sexual romp with a young woman just weeks after your baby had died. In front of your wife.'

'I didn't do it for me!' He sounded as if he almost believed it. 'It was for Katherine and Eliza. And for everyone who works here.'

'What about Charlotte?' Vera asked. 'How does she fit into all this?'

'That was bad luck. She'd been on the island that afternoon.'

'She was there with Judith Sinclair. They had a drink together in the Seahorse.' Vera looked up at him. 'Were you there with them?'

'No!' He seemed genuinely confused.

So, that had been a stray birder just as Judith had claimed, but he'd played his part in the story all the same. He'd had a walk-on part in the drama.

'So, tell me, Daniel, why did Charlotte have to die?'

'She was driving off the island as I was driving on that Friday night. The night Kelsall died. She recognized me. Waved.'

'And later, she tried her hand at a bit of blackmail.'

We know she was hard-up and she'd been brought up to make the most out of any situation. Her family had been in the business of extortion too.

'Yes, by then the whole thing was running out of control. I didn't know how to stop it.' He was close to tears. Vera could almost feel sorry for him. If it weren't for two people dead. And Holly lying barely alive in the hospital in Kimmerston.

'And my officer?' Her voice sharp now. Icy. 'What happened there? I know that was no accident. She wasn't a woman to take risks.'

'She was in the Old Hall, asking questions about me and Katherine.'

'Not about you. About a single birdwatcher. The man sitting in the pub. Some stranger we thought might be involved.'

'I thought she was looking for me. I always carry binoculars when I'm out and about. A habit. I don't feel dressed without them.'

Vera nodded. Hector had been just the same. He was never without them, even on a trip to the shop in Kirkhill, even drinking tea on the bench outside the cottage.

'And Jason at the hotel phoned you to tell you the police were making enquiries.'

'He thought I'd want to know. He's a good lad. I told you

I have a stake in the hotel. I've been grooming him to be manager.'

'So, you set a trap for her. The barmaid at the Seahorse was asking people to contact the officer if they were the person she was looking for. You'll know all the locals if you've got interests in the island and you'll have heard about the request on the grapevine. You sent her a text, asking her to meet you.'

Daniel said nothing, so Vera continued. 'You followed her from the lough back to her car. You'd lit the candles in the chapel hoping that she'd go in to investigate, and of course she did. She wouldn't miss something like that. She's one of my best officers. Then you hit her. So hard that she was unconscious, that she's still in hospital with possible brain damage. You put her in her own car and drove her off the island. Halfway across the causeway, just as the tide was coming in, you got out and lifted her into the driver's seat. You left her there. The fog was so thick that nobody saw the car. You waded back to the island. I suspect that you had your grand four-by-four waiting, hidden in the dunes. You must have driven off to the mainland just before the island was cut off by the sea.'

'I saw your Land Rover arriving,' Daniel said. 'Just before I put her car on the causeway.'

So, if we'd been half an hour later, we might have seen Holly's car. We could have rescued her, saved her the cold wait on the tower before she lapsed back into unconsciousness.'

Vera felt like weeping, but this wasn't a time for self-pity. 'Then you went home. Another alibi established. I presume it was Isobel's death that gave you the idea. It was like rewriting history.'

'You have no evidence,' he said. His mood had changed

again. Now he was the ruthless businessman, crushing his rivals, fighting for his empire. 'No proof at all.'

He turned towards her and for the first time in the encounter, Vera felt real fear. After all, Rede had been prepared to throw suspicion on Annie Laidler, a woman he'd once cared for. He'd tried to kill Holly Clarke. What arrogance had led Vera to believe that she could persuade the man to confess, to be led quietly away to the police station? If any of her officers had been so foolish, she'd have thought them unfit for the job.

'People know where I am,' she said.

But she could tell that he wasn't listening. Daniel Rede was beyond reason and logic. He believed he'd achieved the perfect life as he approached old age – a beautiful, intelligent woman, a daughter to replace the one he'd lost, wealth and position to give him the confidence he'd lacked as a teenager – and now he saw it all slipping away from him. She could see now that he would fight to protect it, even if the fight was irrational and pointless.

He moved slowly and deliberately. She supposed she could run, but although he was older, he was fitter than she was. He'd catch her. And even now, as he took the binoculars from his neck, and leaned across to put the strap around hers, she thought there was something undignified in running. There were worse places to die than here, with the smell of warm creosote and vegetation, to the soundtrack of bird calls. He pulled the leather tight. She tried to get her fingers underneath it to pull the strap away, but everything seemed to be in slow motion and she was too late. The breath was being squeezed from her and she was light-headed, dreamy. There was no pain now. Out of the hide window, she saw a buzzard, sailing high over the trees and she was there with it, looking down on the woodland and the lake and the sea beyond. At a landscape that was as close to home as it was possible to be. In the distance, from her vantage point in the sky, she fancied she could glimpse the hills, the wind turbines like dandelion clocks, the crags where she'd seen her first ring ouzel.

There was a sudden noise, which shattered the peace and fractured the dream. It was a human voice, screaming, horrified. It seemed to come from a long way off, but it got closer, more discordant. Vera found herself back on earth, in the hide, in pain, struggling to breathe.

'Let her go!' A woman was shouting. The tone was shrill and unpleasant to the ear, but it was effective. The strap loosened. Daniel's face was still so close to Vera's that she could smell him. Aftershave, attractive and rather heady. His breath with a hint of coffee. The woman's voice again, each syllable given equal weight. 'Let her go!'

This time, Rede did as he was ordered. Vera felt the drag of the binoculars on her neck, as he released the tension on the strap. The skin hurt where the leather had cut into it. She breathed deeply, felt her lungs fill.

The door was pushed open and Daniel was gone. He barrelled past Katherine Willmore and they heard his running footsteps on the boardwalk, disappearing further into the reserve. Katherine came further into the hide. She lifted the binoculars from Vera's neck and set them on the wooden shelf. Vera raised her head and saw that the PCC was crying. She was dressed for a meeting, and the tears ran through her mascara and made black trails down her face. Vera wanted to warn her of the mess on her face, because surely the press would soon get wind of the story and the woman wouldn't want to be seen like that. But she could hardly speak. There was just a croak like a raven.

'I very nearly didn't come.' Katherine collapsed onto the bench, her back to the window, her legs facing the door. 'My secretary passed on your message, but I thought it was ridiculous.'

'Did you . . . ?' That was all Vera could manage.

'I listened,' Katherine said. 'Just as you told me to. I heard it all.' The tears hadn't stopped. They rolled down her cheeks. Vera found herself fascinated and tried to remember the last time *she'd* cried. Hector's funeral? Nah, she hadn't thought him worth her tears. Unless it was for a sad life, wasted.

'I'll contact Superintendent Watkins.' Katherine took a spotless handkerchief from the pocket of her jacket, wiped her face. 'Tell him we need Daniel to be found, arrested.'

'Did you suspect?' Vera had found her voice at last.

There was no reply.

Vera had wanted to drive straight back to Kimmerston to coordinate the search for Rede, but Katherine wouldn't hear of it, of her driving alone, so they were sitting together in the perfect house with its view of the sea, drinking perfect coffee. Distant. Civilized. Vera had refused the ambulance, the doctor.

'Eh, pet, some people would pay for that kind of experience. What do they call it? Auto-erotic.' Knowing it was the last sort of thing the PCC would want to hear, but feeling sorry for the woman, needing awkwardly to lighten the mood.

Was it shame that had driven Daniel to kill to maintain the illusion of perfection? Or a genuine desire to protect Katherine and her daughter from hurt? Vera could have forgiven him that, could have forgiven him even the deaths of Rick Kelsall and Charlotte Thomas, but not the attack on Holly. *Her* officer. That was unforgivable.

Katherine got to her feet and walked to her office. She left the door open and Vera could hear her talking on the phone, maintaining the professional voice even while she continued to weep, silently. Vera wondered if that was a genuine reaction to the fact that her man was a killer, or because her own professional standing had been compromised. Certainly, she'd take a huge hit in the press. Any good work she'd done in the past would be ridiculed. She'd be forced to resign. Was that the cause of her tears? Perhaps, Vera thought, she was getting cynical in her old age. It was possible that Katherine would support Daniel through the trial and visit him in prison, bring him back here and look after him when he was released as a very elderly man. But she couldn't really see it.

She dozed. It was the warmth of the sun shining through the glass and the shock. Hardly sleeping the night before. The satisfaction of a case brought successfully to a conclusion.

She woke when Katherine came back into the room. She was no longer crying but her face was drawn, serious.

'They've found him?'

'Yes. He was in his car in a lay-by on the A1. He just seemed to be waiting for them to get him. He didn't put up any sort of fight.'

Vera nodded. It was a bit of an anticlimax maybe. Rick Kelsall would have injected a bit more drama if he'd been telling the story. But it was a satisfactory conclusion.

'Your team has been trying to get in touch with you.'

'Oh aye? Wondering why I've gone AWOL?' *Why I didn't take them into my confidence.*

'It's your DC. Holly Clarke.'

Vera brightened. 'She's come round? They've started to question her?'

A silence. 'Her head wound was too severe,' Katherine said. Her voice was very gentle. 'Nobody can understand how she had the strength to swim out of the car and drag herself onto the tower.' A pause. 'She died in the night.'

That was when everything went silent and the light seemed to leave the room.

Chapter Forty-Eight

HOLLY'S FUNERAL WAS IN KIMMERSTON, in the church where Joe and Charlie had first talked to Judith Sinclair. Vera had expected her parents to take their daughter's body home, but they'd said Holly would want to be remembered here, where she'd been so happy, so satisfied at work.

'She was always rather a restless child,' Raymond Clarke said. 'A little apart. Rather driven. Other people never quite lived up to her expectations. She found her true home in the police service.' He was a thin, quiet man, with Holly's face and Holly's reticence. The mother was larger, more outgoing. She hugged Vera when they first met, then immediately apologized, for being so forward.

'I'm so sorry, Inspector. I don't know what came over me. But my daughter admired you so much.'

Vera had been expecting anger from the parents, a desire for vengeance, directed not perhaps at Daniel Rede, but at the Kimmerston team and Vera in particular. It would have been much easier to accept than their forgiveness. They were Christians and had made, Vera could tell, a conscious decision to forgive her, to be kind. Somehow, their strength and under-standing made her own guilt harder to bear.

The couple were staying in Holly's flat, but they came first to the police station and that was where the meeting had taken place. They'd wanted, they said, to see where Holly had worked, where she'd been so content. Vera could hardly say that content-ment hadn't been the most obvious trait in their daughter's character.

The mother, Joan, sat in Holly's chair in the open-plan office. 'It isn't quite as I imagined,' she said. 'I was expecting more noise, more bustle.'

Vera didn't know how to say that usually it would have been busier, but that the team were grieving. 'We're all feeling very quiet,' she said in the end. 'Very sad.'

Joan looked up and apparently on impulse, she invited Vera for supper. 'Come to the flat tomorrow.' It would be the evening before the funeral. Vera could hardly refuse. She felt she was responsible for their daughter's death and she would have given them anything they asked.

'Could I bring my sergeant? Joe Ashworth. Holly worked most closely with him.' Vera didn't think she could survive an evening alone with this gentle couple, who were struggling so hard to be generous in their grief. Rage against the injus-tice of a daughter lost would have been very much easier to bear.

'Oh, of course, Holly spoke of him all the time.'

In the end, they survived the occasion better than Vera could have imagined. She wished she'd met Holly's parents earlier. It might have helped her understand her officer better. They were earnest and principled. Holly had inherited that from them, but rebelled against their gentleness in her ambition and her desire for justice at any cost. And for success. Hers had been a black and white world. Theirs was a muted shade of grey.

The four of them sat round the pale wood table, eating a simple meal. There was wine, a good red, of which Joanna would have approved. Vera and Joe said very little. They listened to the parents remembering their daughter. By the end they were all weeping quietly but without embarrassment. Vera was weeping because now she understood the woman better than she had done when she was alive. She blamed herself for that. Her stubbornness. Her hard certainties.

The funeral service was quiet. Most of the people in the pews were colleagues. Philip Robson must have driven back from London to be there. He was sitting with Judith Sinclair, and Annie joined them just before the service started. Some of the Clarkes' relatives had travelled up for the occasion. Katherine Willmore was in a pew at the back. Unobtrusive and alone. Vera thought that had taken courage. The county knew now that the Police and Crime Commissioner's partner was a killer. The police officers in the church would recognize her. The hymns were traditional. Everything was very civilized, very polite, very reasonable.

Outside it had started to rain, a November drizzle, boring like the service. Vera suddenly wanted to shout out loud, to howl at the grey, overcast sky, to let the world know that Holly Clarke had *not* gone gentle into that dark night. She'd been fierce and strong and brave and she'd fought to the end.

But in the end, she had no right to express her opinion. Not here and now, though she might when she got drunk later with Joe. So, she went up to Raymond and Joan, hugged them first, and thanked them again. She offered them all the support the service could give. Then she got into her Land Rover and drove back to her cottage in the hills to grieve in her own way. There, she could howl to her heart's content.

David Hirst

ANN CLEEVES is the multimillion-copy bestselling author behind three hit television series—*Shetland,* starring Douglas Henshall; *Vera,* starring Academy Award nominee Brenda Blethyn; and *The Long Call,* starring Ben Aldridge—all of which are watched and loved in the United States. All three are available on BritBox.

The first Shetland novel, *Raven Black,* won the Crime Writers' Association Gold Dagger for best crime novel, and Ann was awarded the CWA Diamond Dagger in 2017. She was awarded the OBE in 2022 for services to reading and libraries. Ann lives in the United Kingdom.

READ ALL OF
ANN CLEEVES

THE TWO RIVERS
SERIES

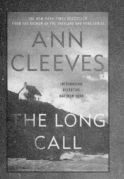

The Heron's Cry

The Raging Storm
ON SALE 9/5/23

THE SHETLAND
SERIES

White Nights

Red Bones

Blue Lightning

Dead Water

Thin Air

Cold Earth

Wild Fire

THE VERA STANHOPE
SERIES

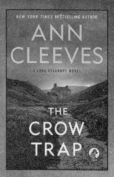

Telling Tales

Hidden Depths

Silent Voices

The Glass Room

Harbour Street

The Moth Catcher

The Seagull

The Darkest Evening

The Rising Tide

AVAILABLE WHEREVER
BOOKS ARE SOLD

 MINOTAUR BOOKS